IMMIGRANT EXPERIENCES IN NORTH AMERICA

Immigrant Experiences in North America

Understanding Settlement and Integration

Edited by
Harald Bauder and John Shields

Canadian Scholars' Press
Toronto

Immigrant Experiences in North America: Understanding Settlement and Integration
edited by Harald Bauder and John Shields

First published in 2015 by
Canadian Scholars' Press Inc.
425 Adelaide Street West, Suite 200
Toronto, Ontario
M5V 3C1

www.cspi.org

Canadian Scholars' Press Inc. gratefully acknowledges financial support for our publishing activities from the Government of Canada through the Canada Book Fund (CBF).

Library and Archives Canada Cataloguing in Publication

Immigrant experiences in North America : understanding settlement and integration / edited by Harald Bauder and John Shields.

Includes bibliographical references. Issued in print and electronic formats. ISBN 978-1-55130-714-5 (pbk.). --ISBN 978-1-55130-715-2 (pdf).-- ISBN 978-1-55130-716-9 (epub)

1. Canada--Emigration and immigration. 2. United States--Emigration and immigration. 3. Canada--Emigration and immigration--Government policy. 4. United States--Emigration and immigration--Government policy. 5. Canada--Emigration and immigration--Economic aspects. 6. United States--Emigration and immigration--Economic aspects. 7. Immigrants--Canada--Social conditions. 8. Immigrants--United States--Social conditions. 9. Social integration--Canada. 10. Social integration--United States. I. Shields, John, 1954-, editor II. Bauder, Harald, 1969-, editor

JV7220.I4376 2015   325.71   C2014-907380-1   C2014-907381-X

Cover and text design: Peggy Issenman, Peggy & Co. Design

Printed and bound in Canada by Webcom

MIX
Paper from
responsible sources
FSC® C004071

Contents

Preface

Immigration, settlement, and integration are defining issues of our times; they drive demographic change, propel economic development, transform cities and towns, shape political debates, and challenge established national identities. Prior to the publication of *Immigrant Experiences in North America*, Canada and the US lacked a strong common textbook that addresses immigration, settlement, and integration issues in a thorough and interdisciplinary manner. This book fills that gap. It provides a comprehensive introduction to these issues in the North American context, spanning both US and Canadian experiences and highlighting national, regional, and urban similarities and differences.

A team consisting of American and Canadian expert researchers and educators contributed the individual chapters of the book. A particular opportunity presented itself through the remarkable range and quality of research and teaching expertise on immigration, settlement, and integration bundled at Ryerson University, which is located in downtown Toronto, one of the epicentres of immigration, settlement, and integration in North America. In terms of research, many of the contributors to this book are affiliated with the Ryerson Centre of Immigration and Settlement (RCIS). The RCIS website (www.ryerson.ca/rcis) describes the centre as

> a leader in the transdisciplinary exploration of international migration, integration, and diaspora and refugee studies. In addition to supporting research in these areas, the Centre's mission includes mentoring students and consolidating Ryerson's reputation as the pre-eminent site of knowledge development and exchange with governments, community organizations, and other academics. The overall goal of the RCIS is to advance policy-related research and scholarship in the areas of immigration and settlement studies, both nationally and internationally.

In addition to being experts at the cutting-edge of their fields of research, the contributors also tend to be outstanding teachers and experienced educators. Many contributors are teaching at Ryerson University in the renowned Graduate Program in Immigration and Settlement Studies (ISS), which was launched in 2004 as "Canada's first graduate program devoted to advanced study of immigration policy, services and experience" (www.ryerson.ca/graduate/programs/immigration), and a PhD program in Policy Studies with a specialization in Immigration, Settlement, and Diaspora Policies. To provide a comprehensive North American and well-rounded interdisciplinary perspective, leading scholars from universities in the US and other parts of Canada joined our team.

Together, we—the editors and contributors—hope that this book will not only fill a gap in the North American educational market and help enlighten students about important topics related to immigration, settlement, and integration, but that it will also frame the field in respect to post-secondary education and raise critical awareness of what we believe are defining issues of our times.

Harald Bauder and John Shields
Toronto, June 2014

Acknowledgements

At Canadian Scholars' Press, we thank Lily Bergh, Andrea Gill, and Emma Johnson, and former commissioning editors Daniella Balabuk and James MacNevin. John Shields thanks Massey College at the University of Toronto where he resided as the Ryerson Fellow (2013–14) during the formative stage in the writing of this book.

How to Use This Book

This book is designed as a text for mid- and upper-level undergraduate courses at American and Canadian universities and colleges with a thematic focus on immigration, settlement, and integration. Accordingly, the chapters are written in accessible language, introduce key concepts, include images and graphics, and contain illustrative case examples.

The 16 chapters that follow after the Introduction each cover a separate theme related to the topic of immigration, settlement, and integration. By covering a wide range of themes, the reader will gain a comprehensive understanding of the topic in a North American context. Rather than presenting new empirical findings in very specialized niche areas of research, the chapters provide summaries of existing research and outline key trends, facts, and arguments that have been presented in the scholarly literature on a particular theme.

We deliberately did not organize the chapters into subthemes. Although we arranged the chapters in a way that they can be read sequentially, we do not intend to prescribe an order in which the material must necessarily be covered. Rather, we encourage readers to explore the chapters in the order of their preferences and interests, and offer instructors the possibility to arrange the chapter sequence to fit their course outlines.

The chapters follow a similar format, which provides a certain degree of consistency throughout the text. Each chapter includes key concepts that appear **bold** in the text and are included in a combined glossary in the back of the book. In addition, each chapter contains case examples (text boxes), and some chapters include photos, graphics, or maps that illustrate the subject matter. Furthermore, the chapter authors have made recommendations of a small number of key readings as a point of entry into further study for those readers who are particularly interested in a chapter's theme. These key readings are listed at the end of each chapter, followed by the list of references. Finally, an index will help readers to find the location of key concepts and important ideas, people, and places that are covered in the text.

Overall, this book is an introduction to immigration, settlement, and integration across North America. It is not strictly a comparative text between the US and Canadian immigrant experience. This experience, however, is situated in particular national, regional, and urban contexts. Thus, it is especially important to pay close attention to national laws, policies, and political traditions that shape the immigrant experience. Chapter 1 by Robert Vineberg sets the stage by offering a historical perspective of immigration in North American, which is followed by two chapters by Philip Kretsedemas (Chapter 2) and Myer Siemiatycki (Chapter 3) exploring US and Canadian policy contexts. The latter two chapters, however, do not necessarily present a direct comparison of the policy environment in both countries, but rather cover different terrain of the policy landscape in the US and Canada and thereby give the reader a comprehensive view of how national policies and politics frame immigration, settlement, and integration.

Given the research interests and location of the chapter contributors, many empirical case studies and illustrative material are taken from the context of Toronto. Toronto is next to New York and Los Angeles as a major immigrant gateway to North America. Many of the immigrant experience, settlement patterns, and integration trends that can be observed in Toronto also occur in other parts of North America. Of course, the Toronto experience cannot be generalized in all cases, which is why *Immigrant Experiences in North America* contains ample illustrative material and empirical examples from other North American cities and regions.

The book presents a multidisciplinary perspective. Its contributors represent, for example, the disciplines of commerce, education, geography, journalism, psychology, policy studies, political science, sociology, and urban and regional planning. This multidisciplinary perspective is reflected in the different scholarly approaches, uses of language, and methods that each chapter assumes. For example, in a medical context, authors may use the term *sex* as a biological category, while a feminist-inspired perspective would use *gender* to signify that distinctions between men and women are social constructions. Both terms are used in this book. In terms of methods, geographers, for example, often present maps as a tool to illustrate their theories and models, while those in other disciplines may rely more heavily on narratives or other ways of presenting data.

The authors also assume a variety of political and ideological positions. Some chapters focus more on representing facts and interpret these facts in a sober and objective manner. However, as advanced students of the philosophy of science know, what appears as "objective" fact may at some level be highly subjective. For example, although statistics often measure differences between, say, black and white populations in a seemingly objective way, the "fact" that the population is divided into black and white is a social construction related to processes of colonialization. Some authors therefore dig deeper into the power dynamics that structure the immigration, settlement, and integration experience, and assume a politicized position. We believe that it is important for our audience—especially undergraduate students—to be exposed to and engage these various disciplinary traditions and scholarly positions. Given the complexity of the subject matter, only a well-rounded perspective can equip our society's future leaders with the knowledge and tools to make the right decisions on matters of immigration, settlement, and integration.

Immigrant Experiences in North America, of course, also has its limitations. The theme of citizenship, for example, is not covered in a separate chapter. In fact, we believe that the sheer volume of literature on citizenship—which has exploded in the last two decades—could not be sufficiently treated in this text and would require a separate text (or undergraduate course). Nevertheless, we briefly discuss citizenship in the Introduction to help the reader situate this concept in the wider subject matter of this book. In addition, we do not explicitly cover refugees as a separate theme but rather discuss refugee issues in a wider migration and settlement context. Obviously, we had to make tough decisions about which materials to include and exclude from this text, but we believe that the current selection represents the best possible solution.

Contributors

Mehrunnisa Ahmad Ali's research focuses on immigrant children, youth, and families, and the preparation of service providers to work with them. She is currently director of Ryerson University's graduate program in Early Childhood Studies. She enjoys learning and teaching about how knowledge is constructed, spread, and used for instrumental purposes.

Maria Adamuti-Trache is Associate Professor at the University of Texas at Arlington, department of Educational Leadership and Policy Studies. She obtained a doctoral degree in higher education from the University of British Columbia. Her main research interests are in the areas of immigration, higher education, and K–16 STEM education.

Tariq Amin-Khan is Associate Professor in the Department of Politics and Public Administration and in the Program of Immigration and Settlement Studies at Ryerson University, Toronto. His research is on the post-colonial state, the security state, issues of globalization and international development, multiculturalism and diaspora identities, and nationalism in post-colonial societies. His most recent book is *The Post-Colonial State in the Era of Capitalist Globalization: Historical, Political and Theoretical Approaches to Site Formation* (Routledge).

Morton Beiser is Professor of Distinction in the Department of Psychology, Ryerson University, Scientist, Li Ka Shing Knowledge Institute at St. Michael's Hospital, Professor Emeritus of Cultural Pluralism and Health, University of Toronto, and Founding Director and Senior Scientist, Ontario Metropolis Centre of Excellence for Research on Immigration and Settlement (CERIS). He has authored more than 185 scientific publications and 3 books and has been the principal investigator for immigrant and refugee health research projects with funding totaling almost 20 million dollars. He chaired a federal task force on mental health issues affecting immigrants and refugees in Canada and was chair of Citizenship and Immigration Canada's Medical Advisory Committee. Dr. Beiser is a member of the Order of Canada.

Raymond M. Garrison is a Senior Supervisor at the Institute for Social Research at York University. He has a keen interest in social issues and their broader societal and policy implications, including immigrant settlement experiences.

Sutama Ghosh is Associate Professor in the Department of Geography at Ryerson University. Her research interests include migration and settlement experiences of newcomers in Canadian cities. In 2007, Sutama's doctoral research won the Housing Studies Achievement Award from the Canada Mortgage and Housing Corporation.

Charity-Ann Hannan is a PhD candidate in Policy Studies at Ryerson University and a graduate of Ryerson University's MA program in Immigration and Settlement Studies. Her research interests include employment equity legislation in Canada and critical perspectives of race, class, ethnicity, and diversity.

Tony Hernandez is the Eaton Chair in Retailing and Director of the Centre for the Study of Commercial Activity at Ryerson University. As a Professor within the Department of Geography, his teaching and research focuses on demographic change and tracking the evolution of the consumer service landscape across Canada.

Philip Kretsedemas is Associate Professor of Sociology at the University of Massachusetts Boston. His research examines the dynamics of migrant racialization and the regulation of migrant flows by the state. He is the author of *The Immigration Crucible* (Columbia University Press, 2012) and *Migrants and Race in the US* (Routledge, 2013).

Mustafa Koc is Professor of Sociology at Ryerson University. His research involves food security, immigration, and globalization. His publications include *For Hunger-Proof Cities, Interdisciplinary Perspectives in Food Studies*, and *Critical Perspectives in Food Studies*.

April Lindgren is Associate Professor at Ryerson University's School of Journalism, and Director of the Ryerson Journalism Research Centre. Her research explores the role of local news in cities. Prof. Lindgren, who worked for more than 25 years as a journalist, has degrees from Carleton University and the Graduate School of International Studies in Geneva, Switzerland.

Lichun Willa Liu is a post-doctoral fellow at the Prentice Institute for Global Population and Economy at University of Lethbridge. Her research interests are focused on transnational migrations and work, aging, and health, and healthcare.

Leslie Nichols has a PhD from the Policy Studies program at Ryerson University. She has a MA in Work and Society from McMaster University and a BA (Honours) with distinction in Women and Gender Studies and Historical Studies from the University of Toronto.

Michael Samers is Associate Professor of Geography at the University of Kentucky. He has previously taught at the Universities of Liverpool and Nottingham. His research interests include the political economy of migration and immigration, labour markets, and alternative forms of economic development. He is the author of *Migration* (Routledge, 2010).

Nandita Sharma is Associate Professor of Sociology at the University of Hawaii at Manoa. Her research interests address themes of human migration, migrant labour, national state power, ideologies of racism and nationalism, processes of identification and self-understanding, and social movements for justice.

Myer Siemiatycki is Professor of Politics and Public Administration at Ryerson University, where he holds the Jack Layton Chair. He is the founding, past director of Ryerson's graduate program in Immigration and Settlement Studies. His research has explored immigrant political participation, state immigration policy, and political transnationalism in Canada.

Mitchell Snider is a PhD candidate at the University of Kentucky. His MA thesis explored masculinity and transnational identities among Latino horse-farm workers outside Lexington, Kentucky. His research interests include immigrant motilities, gender, identity, transnationalism, and Latino immigrant lives in the United States.

Kristen Soo is a recent graduate of the MA Immigration and Settlement Studies program at Ryerson University. Her MA major research paper focused on food security among newcomers in Canada.

Vappu Tyyskä is Professor of Sociology at Ryerson University where she is the Program Director of the MA in Immigration and Settlement Studies. Her research deals with immigrant women, families, and youth, including projects on immigrant women's English language proficiency; and intergenerational relations and family violence in immigrant communities.

Lu Wang is Associate Professor in the Department of Geography at Ryerson University. Her research interests include health geography, immigration, transnationalism, and economic geography. Her methodological interests include spatial analysis, statistical modeling, and mixed-method approach. She has published articles in journals such as *The Professional Geographer, Social Science and Medicine, Health and Place, Environment and Planning A, GeoJournal,* and *Journal of International Migration and Integration.*

Shuguang Wang is Professor and former and interim Chair of the Department of Geography at Ryerson University. His teaching and research focuses on retail location analysis, the urban geography of retailing, the ethnic economy, Chinese immigrants in Canada, and the economic geography of China.

Robert Vineberg has 35 years of experience in the Canadian federal public service, of which 28 were with the immigration program, serving abroad, in policy positions at national headquarters in Ottawa, and most recently, as Director General of Citizenship and Immigration Canada's Prairies and Northern Territories Region. He retired from the public service in 2008 and is currently a Senior Fellow with the Canada West Foundation. His publications include *Responding to Immigrants' Settlement Needs: The Canadian Experience* (Springer, 2012), which he authored, and *Integration and Inclusion of Newcomers and Minorities Across Canada* (McGill-Queen's University Press, 2011), which he co-edited.

Zhixi Cecilia Zhuang is Assistant Professor in the School of Urban and Regional Planning at Ryerson University. Her current research focuses on emerging suburban ethnic retail landscapes and aims to explore place-making practices in these ethnic retail neighbourhoods and their implications for municipal planning.

The Editors

Harald Bauder is the Academic Director of the Ryerson Centre for Immigration and Settlement (RCIS) and Professor in Geography and in the Graduate Program in Immigration and Settlement Studies (ISS) at Ryerson University. His books include *Immigration Dialectic: Imagining Community, Economy, and Nation* (University of Toronto Press, 2011), *Labor Movement: How Migration Regulates Labor Markets* (Oxford University Press, 2006), and *Work on the West Side: Urban Neighborhoods and the Cultural Exclusion of Youths* (Lexington Books, 2002), and he edited the volumes *Immigration and Settlement: Challenges, Experiences, and Opportunities* (Canadian Scholars' Press, 2012) and co-edited *Critical Geographies: A Collection of Readings* (with Salvatore Engel-di Mauro, Praxis e-Press, 2008).

John Shields is Professor of Politics and Public Administration at Ryerson University. He is Senior Scholar and past Director of the Ontario Metropolis Centre of Excellence for Research on Immigration and Settlement (CERIS), and the former managing editor of the *Journal of International Migration and Integration*. He is also a Ryerson Fellow at Massey College, University of Toronto (2013–14). His immigration-based research has focused on settlement services, labour market integration, and knowledge mobilization/knowledge transfer and evidence-informed policy.

UNDERSTANDING IMMIGRATION, SETTLEMENT, AND INTEGRATION IN NORTH AMERICA

JOHN SHIELDS AND HARALD BAUDER

Introduction

North America has been a major attraction for immigrants to work and settle. As **settler societies** that were founded by large scale **immigration** and permanent **settlement**, the United States of America and Canada have considerable common experiences with immigration, settlement, and **integration**. This book explores these experiences but also highlights some of the differences between the two national contexts. Examining immigration, settlement, and integration in North America and drawing on both US and Canadian experiences enriches our understanding of immigration in each country and allows us to view the immigration phenomenon in a more holistic way.

To begin, it is important to set immigration in its larger context. Migration on a global scale has been expanding rapidly with the advance of globalization, more than doubling between 1970 and 2005 from 82 million to some 200 million (Betts 2011:1). It was during the second half of the 1980s that global migration rates began to increase significantly. In addition, the migrant flows to developed countries became far more diverse during this period. As of 2010, an estimated 213 million people, about 3% of the global population, resided outside of their country of birth (Coe, Kelly, and Yeung 2013:177).

Migration is clearly a global phenomenon. Yet it is still viewed predominantly through national lenses, especially in the North American context. The assumption that nation-states are the natural framework for understanding global migration and other phenomena is called **methodological nationalism** (Wimmer and Glick Schiller 2002). In this chapter—as well as in this entire book—we are trying to mitigate the fallacy of methodological nationalism by exploring the North American context, mostly as an immigrant destination. At the same time, we recognize that the US and Canada are important nation-states that shape the immigration, settlement, and integration experience through national laws and policies. Therefore, it is also important to examine national differences and similarities between the US and Canada.

Demographic Impacts

North America has been an important migrant destination for centuries. In terms of sheer numbers, the US has received on average the largest annual number of permanent settlers of any country (Duncan 2012:136). Although Canada has a much smaller population than the US, in more recent decades it has actually outpaced the US in terms of the proportion of immigrants it annually admits, relative to the country's size. Historically, the US—more so than Canada—has long been a beacon attracting immigrants because it is seen as a land of endless opportunity and wealth, and one that has opened its doors to immigrants to settle its vast territories and provide the workforce for its rapidly expanding economy. In the late nineteenth and early twentieth century, Canada was often viewed as a stopover for many newcomers looking to move on to the US as their ultimate destination. In the latter part of the twentieth century Canada became more open in its global outlook and developed more modern and welcoming immigration policies. Today, the US and Canada are both attractive settlement endpoints in their own right (Lightman and Bejan 2013).

Immigration is dramatically reshaping the North American landscape. The US and Canada, in contrast to most highly industrialized societies, have an expanding population because of factors related to immigration. In the US, Latino/Hispanic groups are driving population growth, both because they are the largest groups immigrating to the US and because the birth rates among Latinos and Hispanics living in the US are higher than that of other groups (Passel and Cohn 2008; Reuters 2008).

The foreign-born population of the US is projected to increase from 12% of the population in 2005 to an estimated 19% in 2050 (El Nasser 2008). The ethnic and racial composition of US society between 2005 and 2050 will also dramatically shift. The European-origin, or "white," population—excluding those of Hispanic origin[1]—will decline from 67% of the population to 47%, the Hispanic population will jump from

14 to 29%, the Asian population will also increase from 5 to 9%, and the African American population will hold steady at around 13% (El Nasser 2008). These shifts are already being felt among the youngest generation: over half the children under the age of one belong to minority groups (Morello and Mellnik 2012) and by 2050 it is estimated that 62% of the broader child population in the US will be of non-European origin, up from 44% in the mid-2000s (U.S. Census Bureau News 2008).

In the context of ethnic and racial shifts, it is important to view categories, such as Hispanics, African Americans, or Asians, critically. Although these categories are often taken for granted, they are the result of practices of **racialization**, whereby the European origin group is usually an unmarked category that is depicted as the unmentioned "norm" (see Chapter 8 by Nandita Sharma).

The geographical distribution of where immigrants settle is highly uneven across the US. Recent US immigration has been concentrated in six states—California, New York, Florida, Texas, Illinois, and New Jersey (Legrain 2006:51). In addition, immigration tends to be urban bound (see Chapter 16 by Sutama Ghosh and Raymond M. Garrison for a discussion of the patterns of immigrant settlement in gateway cities in North America). While at the beginning of the twentieth century "whites" dominated the population of large cities in the US, by 2000 this group had become a minority population in fully 35 of America's 50 biggest urban centres (Asthana 2006). Despite the urban **concentration** of immigrant settlement, there has been a parallel trend toward settlement in mid-size and smaller cities and towns, where labour markets are less saturated and living costs are lower. This **deflection of immigrants** away from traditional gateway cities can be observed, for example, in Los Angeles where rents are high and strict city ordinances have increasingly made jobs and homeownership inaccessible for poor immigrants (Light 2008).

Similar demographic trends to the US are anticipated in Canada. By 2031 the population born outside the country is projected to increase from some 20% in 2011 to between 25 and 28%. The effects of immigration are transforming the ethnic and racial composition of Canada. The **visible minority** population—which is Canada's official terminology to identify **racialized**, nonwhite persons—could jump from 16% of the population in 2006 to between 29 and 32% in 2031. The largest visible minority group is, and will continue to be, of South Asian origin, followed by those of Chinese origin. Unlike in the United States, where the "black" population consists mostly of the American-born descendants of slaves, Canada's "black" population has grown in recent decades as a result of migration from the Caribbean and Africa. This population is projected to double by 2031. The Filipino-origin population could also double in size over this time period, and the Arab and West Asian–origin population may triple in numbers (Statistics Canada 2011).

As in the US, the foreign-born population is not evenly distributed across Canada.

In 2006 about 28% of Ontario and British Columbia's total populations consisted of foreign-born residents, while Alberta's, Manitoba's, and Quebec's foreign-born populations ranged between 12 and 17%, with other provinces having much smaller shares (Statistics Canada 2008). In terms of where most newcomers settle, Ontario leads the way with 40% of all arriving permanent residents in 2011(although its share has been declining over the years), followed by Quebec (20.8%), British Columbia (14.0%), and Alberta (12.4%) (Welcome BC n.d.).

Contemporary immigration to Canada is also very much an urban affair with most newcomers settling in large urban metropolitan areas, and in particular the Montreal, Toronto, and Vancouver regions. Immigration is changing the face of Canadian cities. "The vast majority (96%) of Canadians belonging to a visible minority group will likely live [in 2031] in one of the 33 census metropolitan areas, and visible minority groups could comprise 63% of the population of Toronto, 59% of Vancouver and 31% of Montréal" (Statistics Canada 2011). Nevertheless, the deflection of immigrants to smaller cities and less populous provinces can also be observed in Canada and has been encouraged by federal immigration and settlement policies.

Managing Immigration, Settlement, and Integration

Especially in the contemporary period, **immigration** is structured and guided by laws and policies enacted and enforced by nation-states. Robert Vineberg (Chapter 1), Philip Kretsedemas (Chapter 2), and Myer Siemiatycki (Chapter 3) offer an examination of US and Canadian immigration policy. At its core, **immigration policy** is concerned with determining "who gets in and how many are permitted." In this way, immigration is inherently discriminatory as it favours some and denies entry to many others. Moreover, national immigration policies are the result of political processes that seek to balance economic interests and other needs and desires of a country, as well as domestic political realities (Duncan 2012). Hence, immigration policy is driven by larger structural forces in society as well as national interest groups and political actors.

US and Canadian immigration policies operate based on different policy structures. The US has a highly decentralized political structure with many political actors and a formal division of powers and checks and balances between Congress and the president. While this makes policy in the US relatively stable, important reforms of US immigration policy have also been delayed. Canada's parliamentary system, by contrast, centralizes power in the hands of the political executive. This concentration provides considerable power and flexibility for the federal government of the day to reform immigration policy. In fact the current federal government has brought forth a broad agenda of immigration changes (see Chapter 3 by Myer Siemiatycki) without the ability of the legislature to modify or block these changes (Alboim and Cohl 2012; Boyd 2014).

Policies also regulate the immigrant experience after newcomers have arrived. During their period of **settlement** there are, for example, programs designed to assist immigrants to adapt to their new land, measures to provide newcomers with access to rights and services, and symbolic messages regarding immigrants that governments project. Both concrete supports and government messaging are important in setting forth what Jeffrey Reitz (1998) has called "the warmth of the welcome" that newcomers encounter. The concepts of the **"melting pot"** and **"multiculturalism"** described in Case Example 1 illustrates how interlocking concrete policies and symbolisms create this warmth of welcome in different ways for immigrants in the US and Canada.

From a policy perspective, the settlement period is supposed to initiate the process of integration into the social fabric of the destination country. Researchers often measure integration in terms of a general convergence between native-born and immigrant **labour market outcomes** and life chances. The concept of "integration," however, is contested. Measuring it solely in economic terms is very limited. In addition to economic participation, some people argue that the concepts entails that immigrants 1) identify with the receiving country rather than anchoring their identity in the country of origin; 2) participate with the institutions of broader society; 3) learn the official or dominant language(s) and communicate on an ongoing basis with it; and 4) build friendships and networks that extend beyond one's ethno-specific group (Tolley 2011). This immigrant integration process can extend into second and even third generations (Richmond and Shields 2005). Critics argue that the integration concept implies that there is a cohesive national body into which an immigrant can integrate, but it is difficult or impossible to define what the characteristics of this national body are. A more fundamental critique of the concept suggests that immigration policies have already selected who will be new members of society, and these new members have a democratic right to participate in society, independent of others identifying them as integrated or not.

That immigrants and their descendants integrate into society is a common expectation throughout North American society. In fact, settler societies define their national identities through immigration—without immigration, the US or Canada as settler nations would be inconceivable (Bauder 2011; Honig 2003). There are important differences, however, in the manner in which immigrant integration takes place in contemporary Canada and the US. Our case example suggests that there may be different approaches associated with multiculturalism in Canada and the American melting pot idea. Correspondingly, there have been different policy approaches toward settlement and integration.

The contemporary Canadian integration narrative speaks to a commitment to a "two-way street" approach, recognizing that newcomers need to accept responsibility for adjusting to their new society but that Canada also has an obligation to help newcomers in this process and to recognize and respect differences as embraced in multicultural policies. Both immigrants and Canadian society are changed in the process (Tolley 2011). As part of this commitment, the Canadian government provides financial support for a wide range of settlement and integration programs, including language training, job search and other labour market help, newcomer orientation workshops, and housing assistance. These programs are typically delivered by nonprofit agencies located close to the communities they serve (Richmond and Shields 2005). Community-based organizations providing services to immigrants also play an important role in giving newcomers a voice with policymakers and with society more generally (Evans and Shields 2014). In addition to settlement and integration assistance, the government assumes a strong role in promoting the rights of ethno-racial groups (Shields 2004).[2]

In contrast to Canada's top-down approach, the dominant American approach to settlement has favoured bottom-up action by individuals and civil society. Equity is addressed on a more individual rather than societal level. In addition, courts—rather than a proactive state as in Canada—enforce equality. This bottom-up approach also informs the laissez-faire attitude toward immigrant integration in the US. Immigrants become part of American society through individual hard work and with the assistance of family, friends, and sometimes voluntary and faith-based organizations. "Much like the 'invisible hand' of laissez-faire capitalism, which produces a self-regulated market based on the individual actions of many people, the predominant approach to social cohesion and societal attachment, as it relates to immigration, rests on the invisible hand of individual integration and assimilation" (Bloemraad and de Graauw 2012:36).

A number of the chapters in this volume (see, in particular, Chapter 3 by Myer Siemiatycki, Chapter 4 by Tariq Amin-Khan, and Chapter 8 by Nandita Sharma) identify **neoliberalism** as a powerful force that continues to shape contemporary immigration and settlement policy in North America and beyond. The authors of individual chapters will explain in greater detail how neoliberalism impacted their particular areas of examination. Generally, neoliberalism took the place of Keynesianism as the dominant public policy paradigm in the 1980s. **Public policy paradigms** are the intellectual frameworks—the key ideas especially related to the "proper" role of the state within society and economy—through which policymakers and other key opinion makers in society make sense of their world and that are used to guide their policy actions (Bradford 2000). US president Ronald Reagan and United Kingdom prime minister Margaret Thatcher are seen as the leading political figures in the vanguard of the neoliberal policy shift in the Anglo-American world. Essentially, neoliberalism supports policies that promote a "free market" through market liberalization, privatization, and deregulation, and that foster "globalization" through the free flow of goods and capital, but not the free movement of workers and people across borders. The promotion of market-based solutions to economic and social problems implies that most policy problems have arisen because of "government failure," and that state intervention would result in more problems rather than solutions (Burke, Mooers, and Shields 2000). Hence, according to neoliberals, the role of government and the size of the state need to shrink (Shields and Evans 1998). This is not to say, however, that there is no role for the state or that the state should be weak. In fact, neoliberals argue that the state under Keynesianism—which favoured the broad use of an activist state—actually weakened the power and effectiveness of government because it fragmented the state's energies. Under neoliberalism the state becomes stronger because it focuses on its more limited but core functions. Thus, a very strong neoliberal state enhances the role of government as the enforcer of a law-and-order agenda and commander of a strong military to combat domestic and foreign threats (Shields 1990).

Neoliberalism has taken special aim at rolling back and hollowing out the social protections that were part of the social and labour policies of the Keynesian welfare state. It also rejects the high taxes needed to support these policies (Shields 2004). Hence, under neoliberalism we have witnessed the expansion of wealth and income inequality (Piketty 2014). In terms of immigration policy, this has generally meant a shift to a greater emphasis on the short-term economic benefits of immigration over other considerations, the "tightening of border controls and crack down on undocumented migrants," and, in Canada, cutting back government funds to settlement supports (Dobrowlsky 2013:197–198). The restructuring of immigration policy along more neoliberal lines is evident in recent changes to Canadian immigration under the Harper administration. It is also visible in the border control measures taken by the US government, especially since September 11, 2001.

Irrespective of the approach and public policy paradigm to settlement and immigration pursued by the US and Canada, North America is becoming ever more diverse. This is reflected in the changing ethno-racial makeup of our workplaces, residential neighbourhoods (see Chapter 16 by Sutama Ghosh and Raymond M. Garrison), and retail shopping areas (see Chapter 9 by Cecilia Zhuang, Tony Hernandez, and Shuguang Wang); the kinds of food consumed (see Chapter 12 by Mustafa Koc, Kristen Soo, and Willa Lichun Liu); and the rise of an **ethnic media** (see Chapter 15 by April Lindgren). It is also manifest in differential outcomes for immigrants versus the native-born in areas such as health (see Chapter 13 by Morton Beiser and Chapter 14 by Lu Wang), education (see Chapter 11 by Mehrunnisa Ahmad Ali),

Case Example 1: American Melting Pot versus Canadian Mutliculturalism

American immigration has symbolically been guided by the concept of *e pluribus unum* (one out of many) (Margai and Frazier 2010:2), which links to the idea of an American melting pot. This is often juxtaposed with the modern Canadian motto that Canada is a "community of communities," a notion that effectively captures the multicultural idea. While the abstract concepts of a melting pot and multiculturalism oversimplify the lived experiences of immigrants, they are firmly entrenched in the way people think about the different approaches to absorbing newcomers in American and Canadian societies.

The idea of the melting pot suggests that newcomers are transformed by their encounter with America and reinvented in an American mould—in essence, "Americanized" (Thernstrom 2004; Jacoby 2004). Becoming Americanized entails accepting "the nation's democratic principles [and institutions], respect for individualism and hard work and willingness to learn English" (Salins 2004:102). Appreciation for the separation of church and state made Americans broadly tolerant of religious and other culturally centred differences newcomers might bring with them. Moreover, American popular culture, especially with the advent of mass communication in the twentieth century, has been a powerful force for newcomer **assimilation** (Gans 2004:34). While including immigrants, the melting pot idea excluded African Americans and Indigenous populations from the national imagination.

The melting pot appeals to the notion of the "American creed." This notion stretches back to the founding of the American republic and the notion of equality and free-dom for all, along with the ability to pursue the American dream. While not always the reality, especially given the history of slavery in the US, it has been the national aspiration. "The American creed remains a cornerstone of America's sense of com-mon purpose," its notion of social cohesion (Bloemraad and de Graauw 2012:36).

The Canadian experience differs from that of the US. Canada is historically a bi-national country, cofounded by French and English peoples. Furthermore, Canadian national identity was forged not out of revolution, as in the US, but out of a rejection of revolution and a resistance to the US (McBride and Shields 1997). Canada's road to full nationhood was slow, with full independence from Great Britain coming only after World War I. A pan-Canadian **nationalism** and Canadian identity—at least within English-speaking Canada—was only firmly established in the latter part of the twentieth century. Newcomers to Canada were said to be part of a mosaic (rather than a melting pot) where immigrants were encouraged to celebrate their ethnic heritage and the notion of hyphenated identities like *Italian-Canadian* or *Indo-Canadian* were considered to be an integral part of the richly textured fabric of the country. The Canadian government embraced the notion of the mosaic in its pronouncement of multiculturalism as official policy in 1971. The existing English-French duality, which marked the birth of the country, served as a foundation for its expansion into multiculturalism. "The expectation that multiculturalism, as a philosophy and a policy, helps build Canadian society is now one of the major tenets in contemporary political thought across the country" and it became "enshrined in the Canadian constitution" through its Charter of Rights and Freedoms in 1982 (Reitz 2009:6).

Multiculturalism is generally seen as an alternative to assimilationist approaches to immigration settlement. William Kymlicka, a leading multicultural theorist, contends that multiculturalism policy in Canada has been a success in promoting successful immigrant integration and has unified the Canadian population as measured, for example, by the frequency of inter-ethnic marriages and high rates of elected members with immigrant backgrounds in government bodies compared to the US (Reitz 2009; Kymlicka and Walker 2012). The Canadian federal department of government responsible for immigration, Citizenship and Immigration Canada (CIC), puts the debate over multiculturalism in the following terms:

> Supporters argue that multiculturalism assists in the integration of immigrants and minorities, removing barriers to their participation in Canadian life and making them feel more welcome in Canadian society, leading to a stronger sense of belonging and pride in Canada. Critics argue that multiculturalism promotes ghettoization and balkanization, encouraging members of ethnic groups to look inward, and emphasizing the difference between groups rather than their shared rights or identities as Canadian citizens." (CIC 2010:7)

and **food security** (see Chapter 12 by Mustafa Koc, Kristen Soo, and Willa Lichun Liu). Problems related to the social inclusion of immigrants are a major problem in North America (Shields 2004).

Very importantly, in both Canada and the US, the economic performance of immigrants has been a key aspect of successful integration. In recent decades, however, there have been considerable difficulties for many newcomers in obtaining stable employment commensurate with their skills and education. We now turn to the economic role of immigration in North America.

Economy and Immigration

The economies of most developed nations—not just settler societies like the US and Canada—have grown "structurally" dependent on immigration (Cohen 1987). In fact, immigration is a tool to regulate national economies by attracting a desired labour force (Bauder 2006). Immigrants are especially seen as being important for 1) managing the demographic trend of an aging native-born workforce; 2) meeting current and future labour market needs of the economy; 3) improving national competitiveness through **human capital** enhancement; and 4) contributing to the tax base of society (Fargues, Papademetriou, Salinari, and Sumption 2011). As Natasha Duncan observes,

> Industrial states are becoming more reliant on immigrants to power growth and compensate for their decreasing and aging populations, at least in the short term. States that have been resistant to immigration ... have come to recognize its significance for their economies, societies, and even welfare systems as the benefits of high-skilled migrants include filling skills gaps, knowledge spillovers, and larger contributions to the host state's pension programs. (Duncan 2012:147)

A problem for most of the developed countries of the Global North is that their populations are getting older on average and proportionately fewer workers are paying into social security coffers to support a growing number of retirees. Some countries are also facing population decline, raising the question of whether economic growth can be sustained with a declining workforce. In this context, immigration is seen "as a palliative in slowing population decline and subsequently labor shortages" (Duncan 2012:40).

Moreover, immigration of highly skilled workers is seen as an easy and relatively fast solution to addressing skill shortages. At the global scale and especially to the developed countries, the flow of highly skilled migrants, although still a distinct minority among the total stock of migrants, has become more sizable. For example, between 1990 and 2000, some 7 million highly skilled workers migrated, with 5 million of them leaving the Global South and moving to the Global North. While this "race to the top" opens up opportunities for some of the well-educated from the Global South to enhance their living standards (Duncan 2012:22–23), it also produces a **brain drain** from the developing world whereby developing societies lose their "investments" into educating these migrants. Moreover, it may result in a **brain waste** if the immigrants cannot apply the skills and education they acquired abroad after they immigrate and settle in their new country. Chapter 6 by Michael Samers and Mitchell Snider further examines the structural forces that produce these negative labour market outcomes for immigrants. As well, Chapter 7 by Mari Adamuti-Trache looks specifically at **highly educated immigrants** who have immigrated to North America and considers the extent of their success in integrating into the domestic workforce.

Despite the problematic nature of the South-North migration of the highly skilled, North American policymakers see highly skilled immigrants as desirable on a number of grounds. In addition to enhancing the human capital of the national workforce, skilled immigrants are perceived to be "less threatening" to social order than unskilled immigrants are, more adaptive to their new society, more likely to possess or acquire the necessary language skills, and less likely to rely on public resources (Duncan 2012:9). As a consequence, immigration policy in North America (as well as developed countries in other world regions) is being reshaped to encourage skilled migration.

On the flip side, immigration works as a regulatory economic tool by keeping undesirable workers out or by imposing restrictive conditions on workers. For example, immigrants are often deskilled and become exploitable through mechanisms such as the denial of citizenship and status, stereotypes associated with ethnic origin or accents, discrimination based on skin colour, or the nonrecognition of foreign credentials. As exploitable workers, migrants and immigrants often contribute a disproportionate share to the economic well-being of a country relative to the rights and entitlements they possess. In other words, to national economies "migrants and immigrants are valuable because they are vulnerable" (Bauder 2006:22).

In this respect, unskilled migrant labourers face considerable barriers to permanent residency and ultimately citizenship in North America. Although North America was once very open to unskilled labour recruitment, today it has carefully controlled borders and imposes strict criteria for permanent settlement. The increasing use of **temporary foreign workers** who are admitted under short-term visas demonstrates the adaptive capacities of the US and Canada to squeeze economic value out of migrant labour (see Chapter 8 by Nandita Sharma). Unskilled or deskilled labour, largely from the Global South, is being widely used to do many undesirable jobs for low wages, but the US and Canadian governments have no long-term obligation to offer these workers citizenship. Aside from temporary worker programs, there is widespread use by employers throughout North America of **illegalized immigrants** (Bauder 2013), who are an extremely exploitable form of labour, living under constant threat of detention and deportation (see Chapter 5 by Charity Hannan). In this context, the denial of citizenship rests at the core of temporary foreign workers' and illegalized immigrants' vulnerability and exploitability. Citizenship is the topic to which we turn next.

Citizenship

Although none of the chapters in this book focuses explicitly on citizenship (which is beyond the scope of this book), this topic relates in many ways to immigration, settlement, and integration. In terms of immigration, citizens tend to have the right to leave and enter the country. Immigration rules only apply to noncitizens. The US and Canada grant citizenship based on the principle of *jus soli* (law of the soil). According to this principle, persons born on US or Canadian soil generally possess citizenship of the respective country. Other countries, such as Germany, have historically favoured the principle of *jus sanguinis* (law of the blood), according to which citizenship is passed on from one generation to the next, independent of where a person is born. Both the US and Canada also grant citizenship to persons born abroad, provided that they are the children of citizens who can demonstrate a close connection to the country (such as being born there).

A third citizenship principle is **jus domicile (law of residence)**. Scholars have recently argued that this citizenship principle deserves serious attention (Bauder 2014), especially as large numbers of illegalized immigrants are de facto residents in a country or a city but are denied access to rights, basic government services, and fair treatment in the labour market. If the domicile principle were followed, these immigrants would qualify for status and citizenship. In a way, **naturalization**—that is the acquisition of citizenship by immigrants—already implements the domicile principle for "legal" immigration.

Citizenship also relates to the integration of immigrants. In fact, integration is sometimes measured by the rate of naturalization among newcomers. The 2006 Canadian census, for example, found that 85.1% of foreign-born residents had become Canadian citizens. The naturalization rate in Canada is much higher than in the US where the rate has been about 40% (Tolley 2011:14). In the 1970s the naturalization rates in Canada and the US were about the same, resting in the percentange range of the high 60s, but moved in very different directions starting in the 1980s (Picot and Hou 2011). In the last few years, Canada has tightened citizenship acquisition rules, resulting in some decline in naturalization rates (Winter 2014).

The relatively low naturalization rate in the US is significant because citizenship is more than a legal status in the US, but is also "a notion of membership and common purpose" (Bloemraad and de Graauw 2012:37). In light of the socially entrenched idea of the melting pot, the inability or unwillingness of many migrants to become citizens is problematic for their acceptance and inclusion in American society. Nevertheless, the US figures also illustrate that settlement in a new country does not necessarily require taking up citizenship of that country.

Public Debate

Immigration has been a hotly debated topic. Although the US and Canada are both settler societies that would not exist without massive immigration, public support for immigration cannot be taken for granted, and varies across North America. Compared to other Western nations, "Canadians are more likely to say that immigration is beneficial, less likely to believe that immigrants are prone to crime, and more likely to support multiculturalism and to view it as a source of pride" (CIC 2010:7) and the vast majority of Canadians support multiculturalism and immigration as an important marker of Canadian identity (CIC 2010:8). By contrast, Americans have been more divided over the immigration issue. While a majority continues to be broadly supportive of immigration in general, they do not want see an increase in immigration numbers, favour tighter border controls, and remain divided over what to do about illegalized immigrants residing in the US (Jones 2012).

The main political division in the US is largely between conservatives attempting to cling to a more traditional notion of Anglo-American society, coupled with beliefs in a small government, and liberals supporting a more open society and a substantial role for government. The election of Barack Obama and the conservative reaction represented by the Tea Party is one manifestation of this division. Ethnic minority voters—many of them immigrants themselves or second generation (i.e. the children of immigrants)—were key to the Democrats' presidential victories in 2008 and 2012. Furthermore, the demographic trend toward growing Latino and other newcomer populations threatens conservative political currents. The reaction to this immigration threat has been prominently articulated by Samuel P. Huntington (2005), who writes about a domestic clash of cultures between English-speaking Anglo Protestant Americans and Spanish-speaking Catholic Latino immigrant populations who allegedly threaten to turn America into a bilingual and bicultural country with values that run against American core beliefs. In essence, Huntington suggests that

America is being turned into an "alien nation" from within (Legrain 2006:11, 243, xi). The Latino challenge, according to this position, is accented by the threat posed by Muslim newcomers and their suspected illiberal value system (Legrain 2006:xi) (see Chapter 4 by Tariq Amin-Khan).

Immigration and its relationship to social welfare is another important and contested political issue. A common argument is that high levels of immigration and diversity erode support for social programs because the nonmigrant population sees immigrants and ethnic minority groups as a burden and wishes to exclude them from social benefits provided through taxes raised by the state. In fact, Robert Putnam uses US data to argue that racial and ethnic diversity is highly correlated with the decline of interpersonal trust in society (Putnam 2006). Trust is what creates the bonds necessary for social solidarity upon which the modern welfare state rests. In the US there is a long-established and widespread perception that blacks and Latinos are heavy users of welfare support because they lack sufficient work ethic (Lewis 1969; Wilson 1987).

The Canadian case, however, is different. The fact that Canada is ethnically highly diverse with high rates of immigration has not negatively affected public support for Canadian social welfare programs. The view that immigrants are heavy users and abusers of welfare supports is not as widespread in Canada as in the US. Interestingly, those Canadians with the strongest sense of nationalism are also the strongest supporters of immigration and see multiculturalism and diversity as a core defining feature of Canada. This pattern of public support of immigration seems to be an anomaly not only in North America, but among Western democracies (Banting, Soroka, and Koning 2013).

Conclusion

Immigration, settlement, and integration represent an ever-changing terrain. For example, the question of "who gets in" has shifted dramatically in North America over time. In the nineteenth century, newcomers of all skill levels were welcome and needed to populate the frontier and labour in the factories and workshops. Lazarus's poem in Case Example 2 speaks to the particular democratic impulse in America in terms of welcoming all classes of newcomers. Of course, this did not extend to notions of racial equality, as the dark history of slavery attests to. In addition, as the movie *Gangs of New York* testifies, in the nineteenth and early twentieth centuries, there were considerable ethnic conflicts as well as nativist sentiments among elements of the American population against newcomer groups such as the Irish and Italians.

In the early part of the twentieth century, "open door" immigration policies were increasingly challenged—although racial exclusion had always been practised. The US took an early lead in more closely monitoring the doorway when it introduced systematic immigration selection criteria in 1917, requiring all newcomers to pass a literacy test. In 1967, Canada became a leading innovator by introducing a **points system** for selecting immigrants based on human capital criteria of education, language, occupation, skills, and age. This system is centred on a human capital model that emphasizes adaptability to a flexible labour market (see Chapter 3 by Myer Symiatycki and Chapter 6 by Michael Samers and Mitchell Snider). The adoption of the points system enabled Canada to move to a less racially discriminatory system of selection while adjusting to a modern economy by focusing on skills-based immigrant recruitment. It also allowed for the targeting of French-speaking immigrants, which helped overcome French-Canadian political opposition in the province of Quebec to increased immigration levels.

Canada, moreover, introduced three distinct broad classes of immigration: the economic class (which includes the points system), the family class (designed to facilitate family reunification), and refugees (to meet Canada's international humanitarian obligations). This mixed system of immigrant recruitment has provided the Canadian government with a tool to meet its immigration objectives. Correspondingly, preference has been given in the last decade to economic class immigrants.

In the US, immigrant admissions are based on a quota system that gives preference to family reunification considerations. In fact, family reunification makes up between two-thirds and three-quarters of all newcomers annually. While there have been calls for the US to reform its immigration recruitment system along the Canada points system (Borjas 2000), entrenched interests in the American Congress and public support for family reunification have prevented such changes. Nevertheless, the US has circumvented political opposition to economically driven immigration by turning to the less contentious use of skilled temporary foreign workers and subsequently enabling these workers to apply for permanent residency status (Boyd 2014; Chapter 2 by Philip Kretsedemas). Despite important differences between US and Canadian immigration approaches, there is a certain convergence of policy direction and immigration trends in both countries. Canada, for example, now makes extensive use of temporary foreign workers to fill labour market needs, and has undertaken steps to provide some of these workers with pathways toward permanent citizenship, thereby emulating US policies.

The US and Canada also have in common that immigration is increasingly becoming feminized. The term **feminization of migration** describes how migration has shifted along the gender dimension, with women migrants becoming increasingly numerous and assuming increasingly important economic roles. "Women have become immigration subjects in their own right, rather than being considered

Case Example 2: Give Me Your Tired, Your Poor ...

Emma Lazarus's poem "The New Colossus," which is prominently displayed in the pedestal of the Statue of Liberty, is revealing of earlier periods of immigration to North America (even though many immigrants were rejected based on criteria such as poor health):

> Give me your tired, your poor,
> Your huddled masses yearning to breathe free,
> The wretched refuse of your teeming shore.
> Send these, the homeless, tempest-tost to me,
> I lift my lamp beside the golden door!

Source: The Statue of Liberty and Ellis Island Website. www.statueofliberty.org

the accompanying 'luggage' of male 'breadwinners' who have migrated for work and have then brought over their spouse and children" (Triandafyllidou, Gropas, and Vogel 2007:6). The trend toward the feminization of migration relates to the increasing demand for migrant labour in household and caregiving roles, such as child-minding and housecleaning, that have traditionally been performed by women. In addition, labour markets in North America and elsewhere have opened up skilled occupations, especially nursing, to women, although other professional areas have also become attractive possibilities for women migrants. The topic of immigrant women is becoming a prominent issue of immigration debate in North America, as Leslie Nichols and Vappu Tyyskä elaborate on in Chapter 10.

By adopting a more North American approach to viewing immigration, American and Canadian students and researchers can gain new vantage points from which to view and consider their own policies and practices in the immigration, settlement, and integration field. Both national contexts enable learning from each other's policy successes and failures. For example, Canada would benefit from observing the pitfalls of excessive use of low-skilled temporary foreign workers with no path to citizenship. Significant numbers of these workers, who have recently been recruited in Canada (see Chapter 3 by Myer Siemiatycki and Chapter 5 by Charity Hannan), will inevitably form a population of illegalized residents who have overstayed their short-term visas and contracts, as the American experience with large numbers of low-skilled nonstatus workers living in the shadows of US society shows. In turn, American readers may benefit from learning about Canada's long history of providing an immigrant-integration model that places access to citizenship at the centre and provides corresponding government supports for integration. In America, family re-unification still lies at the focal point of permanent settler recruitment, while Canada is currently making it harder for immigrants to reunite with their families. Canadian policymakers would be wise to remember that immigrant families are critical for the successful integration of newcomers over the longer term. To be sure, there is no one best approach to successful immigration, settlement, and integration. Cross-national learning is therefore highly valuable for better grasping the implications of various policy measures. At the same time, the US and Canada share a history and geography that provides a crucial context for gaining a comprehensive understanding of the range and the nuances of immigration, settlement, and integration experiences.

Notes

1. Hispanics have in some circles come to be "redefined as a quasi-race in the US" (Gans 2004:35).
2. Federal settlement and integration services are restricted to permanent residents. The vulnerable and rapidly growing number of temporary workers (see Chapter 8 by Nandita Sharma) are excluded from these services (Lightman and Bejan 2013:M-54).

Questions for Critical Thought

1. Explain what some of the advantages are to taking a North American rather than a country-specific approach to studying immigration and settlement.
2. Recognizing that the US and Canada are important nation-states with national laws and policies, is there a common immigration, settlement, and integration experience in North America? What are the characteristics of this common experience?
3. What, in your view, are the most important things, both positive and negative, that Canada and the United States can learn from each other in the area of immigration and settlement? After you finish reading the book, you may come back to this question and reflect on how your answer to this question has changed.

Key Readings

Boyd, M. (2014) Recruiting High Skill Labour in North America: Policies, Outcomes and Futures. *International Migration* 52(3): 40–54.

Castles, S., H. de Haas, and M.J. Miller (2013) *The Age of Migration: International Population Movements in the Modern World*, 5th ed. New York: Guilford.

Samers, M. (2010) *Migration*. London: Routledge.

Media Links

Migrant Integration Policy Index (MIPEX):

www.mipex.eu

This index is a fully interactive tool and reference guide to assess, compare, and improve immigrant integration policy. There are many features on the website, including country profiles and the ability to construct comparisons between countries like Canada and the US.

Immigration: Stories of Yesterday and Today (US):

teacher.scholastic.com/activities/immigration/index.htm

This interactive website has a wealth of information and interactive features including graphs, photos, and immigrant interviews, as well as an interactive tour of Ellis Island, which was the prime gateway into the US for some 12 million immigrants between 1892 and 1924.

Pew Research—Hispanic Trends Project

www.pewhispanic.org

This project by the non-partisan Pew Research Center chronicles the impact of Latinos in the US. The website contains numerous reports, interactive material, and other resources.

Ryerson Centre for Immigration and Settlement (RCIS):

www.ryerson.ca/rcis/index.html

The RCIS is a major research centre located at Ryerson University in Toronto, and focusing on immigration and settlement research. The website has numerous features including academic working papers and research briefs.

Rethinking Immigration—An Interactive *Globe and Mail* website:
www.theglobeandmail.com/news/national/time-to-lead/
rethinking-immigration-the-case-for-the-400000-solution/article4217388/
This interactive website, created by one of Canada's leading national newspapers, explores numerous facets of immigration policy and experiences today. It includes in-depth analysis, charts, video clips, and much more.

Implementing Immigration Policy: Provinces and States in Comparative Perspective:
www.youtube.com/watch?v=XykQVeJGbok
A one-hour video by Dr. Richard Vengroff, a Fulbright research chair at Carleton University in Ottawa, Ontario, Canada, and professor at Kennesaw State University in Atlanta, Georgia, US. The lecture compares contemporary Canada-US immigration policy with a focus on the subnational level. There is also a link to the PowerPoint slides for this lecture:
www.schoolofpublicpolicy.sk.ca/_documents/_outreach_event_announcements/
Presentations/2013.03.06%20-%20Richard%20Vengroff%20Lecture.pdf

References

Alboim, N. and K. Cohl (2012) *Shaping the Future: Canada's Rapidly Changing Immigration Policies.* Toronto: Maytree Foundation. maytree.com/wp-content/uploads/2012/10/shaping-the-future.pdf?utm_source=mailoutinteractive&utm_medium=email&utm_campaign=New+Maytree+Report+on+Recent+Immigration+Changes

Asthana, Anushka (2006) The Changing Face of Western Cities. *Washington Post,* 21 August. www.washingtonpost.com/wp-dyn/content/article/2006/08/20/AR2006082000629.html

Banting, Keith, Stuart Soroka, and Edward Koning (2013) Multicultural Diversity and Redistribution. In Keith Banting and John Myles (eds.) *Inequality and the Fading of Redistributive Politics*, pp. 165–186. Vancouver: UBC Press.

Barone, Michael (2004) New Americans After September 11. In Tamar Jacoby (ed.) *Reinventing the Melting Pot: The New Immigrants and What It Means to Be American*, pp. 261–269. New York: Basic Books.

Bauder, Harald (2014) Domicile Citizenship, Human Mobility and Territoriality. *Progress in Human Geography* 38(1):91–106.

Bauder, Harald (2013) Why We Should Use the Term Illegalized Immigrant. *RCIS Research Brief* 2013/1. www.ryerson.ca/rcis/publications/index.html

Bauder, Harald (2011) *Immigration Dialectic: Imagining Community, Economy, and Nation.* Toronto: University of Toronto Press.

Bauder, Harald (2006) *Labor Movement: How Migration Regulates Labor Markets.* New York: Oxford University Press.

Betts, Alexander (2011) Introduction: Global Migration Governance. In Alexander Betts
(ed.) *Global Migration Governance*, pp. 1–33. Oxford: Oxford University Press.

Bloemraad, Irene and Els de Graauw (2012) Diversity and Laissez-Faire Integration in
the United States. In Paul Spoonley and Erin Tolley (eds.) *Diverse Nations, Diverse
Responses: Approaches to Social Cohesion in Immigrant Societies*, pp. 35–57.
Montreal: McGill-Queen's University Press.

Borjas, George (2000) The Case for Choosing More Skilled Immigrants. *American
Enterprise* 11(8): 30–31.

Boyd, Monica (2014) Recruiting High Skill Labour in North America: Policies, Outcomes
and Futures. *International Migration*, 52(3): 40–54.

Bradford, Neil. (2000) The Policy Influence of Economic Ideas: Interests, Institutions
an Innovation in Canada. In Mike Burke, Colin Mooers, and John Shields (eds.)
Restructuring and Resistance: Canadian Public Policy in an Age of Global Capitalism,
pp. 50–79. Halifax: Fernwood Publishing.

Burke, Mike, Colin Mooers, and John Shields (eds.) (2000) Critical Perspectives on
Canadian Public Policy. In Mike Burke, Colin Mooers, and John Shields (eds.)
Restructuring and Resistance: Canadian Public Policy in an Age of Global Capitalism,
pp. 11–23. Halifax: Fernwood Publishing.

Chappell, Rosalie (2014) *Social Welfare in Canadian Society*. 5th ed. Toronto: Nelson.

Citizenship and Immigration Canada (CIC) (2010) *The Current State of Multiculturalism in
Canada and Research Themes on Canadian Multiculturalism 2008–2010*.
Ottawa: Minister of Public Workers and Government Services Canada.

Coe, Neil M., Philip F. Kelly, and Henry W.C. Yeung (2013) *Economic Geography:
A Contemporary Introduction*. 2nd ed. Hoboken, NJ: Wiley.

Cohen, Robin (1987) *The New Helots: Migrants in the International Division of Labour*.
Aldershot, UK: Avebury.

Dobrowolsky, Alexandra (2013) Nuancing Neoliberalism: Lessons Learned from a Failed
Immigration Experiment. *Journal of Migration and Integration* 14:197–218.

Duncan, Natasha T. (2012) *Immigration Policymaking in the Global Era*. New York:
Palgrave Macmillan.

El Nasser, Haya (2008) U.S. Hispanic Population to Triple by 2050. *USA TODAY*, 2
December. usatoday30.usatoday.com/news/nation/2008-02-11-population-study_N.htm

Evans, Bryan and John Shields (2014) "Nonprofit Engagement with Provincial Policy
Officials: The Case of Canadian Immigrant Settlement Services and NGO Policy
Voice." *Policy and Society* 33(2):117–127.

Fargues, P., D.G. Papademetriou, G. Salinari, and M. Sumption (2011) Shared Challenges
and Opportunities for EU and US Immigration Policymakers.
www.migrationpolicy.org/pubs/US-EUimmigrationsystems-finalreport.pdf

Gans, Herbert J. (2004) The American Kaleidoscope, Then and Now. In Tamar Jacoby (ed.) *Reinventing the Melting Pot: The New Immigrants and What It Means to Be American*, pp. 33–45. New York: Basic Books.

Griffith, Andrew (2013) *Policy Arrogance or Innocent Bias: Resetting Citizenship and Multiculturalism*. Toronto: Anar Press.

Honig, Bonnie (2003) *Democracy and the Foreigner*. Princeton, NJ: Princeton University Press.

Huntington, Samuel P. (2005) *Who Are We? The Challenges to America's National Identity*. New York: Simon & Schuster.

Jacoby, Tamar (2004) Defining Assimilation for the 21st Century. In Tamar Jacoby (ed.) *Reinventing the Melting Pot: The New Immigrants and What It Means to Be American*, pp. 3–16. New York: Basic Books.

Jones, Jeffrey M. (2012) Americans More Positive about Immigration. *GALLUP Politics*, 16 June. www.gallup.com/poll/155210/Americans-Positive-Immigration.aspx

Kymlicka, Will and Kathryn Walker (eds.) (2012) *Rooted Cosmopolitanism: Canada and the World*. Vancouver: UBC Press.

Legrain, Philippe (2006) *Immigrants: Your Country Needs Them*. Princeton, NJ: Princeton University Press.

Lewis, Oscar (1969) Culture of Poverty. In Daniel P. Moynihan (ed.), *On Understanding Poverty: Perspectives from the Social Sciences*, pp. 187–220. New York: Basic Books.

Light, Ivan (2008) *Deflecting Immigration: Networks, Markets, and Regulation in Los Angeles*. New York: Russel Sage.

Lightman, Naomi and Raluca Bejan (2013) Down but Not Out—A Comment on the 15th Canadian National Metropolis Conference 'Building an Integrated Society'. *Transnational Social Review—A Social Work Journal* 3(4):M-52–M-57.

Margai, Florence M. and John W. Frazier (2010) Multiculturalism and Multicultural Education in the United States: The Contributory Role of Geography. In John W. Frazier and Florence M. Margai (eds.) *Multicultural Geographies: The Changing Racial/Ethnic Patterns of the United States*, pp. 1–10. Albany, NY: SUNY Press.

McBride, Stephen and John Shields (1997) *Dismantling a Nation: The Transition to Corporate Rule in Canada*. 2nd ed. Halifax: Fernwood Publishing.

Morello, Carol and Ted Mellnik (2012) Census: Minority Babies Are Now Majority in United States. *Washington Post*, 17 May. www.washingtonpost.com/local/census-minority-babies-are-now-majority-in-united-states/2012/05/16/gIQA1WY8UU_story.html

Passel, Jeffrey S. and D'Vera Cohn (2008) US Population Projections: 2005–2050. *PewResearch: Hispanic Trends Project*, 11 February. www.pewhispanic.org/2008/02/11/us-population-projections-2005-2050/

Picot, Garnett and Feng Hou (2011) Divergent Trends in Citizenship Rates among Immigrants in Canada and the United States. *Analytical Studies Branch Research Paper Series*, Catalogue no. 11F0019M—No. 338. Ottawa: Statistics Canada. www.statcan.gc.ca/pub/11f0019m/11f0019m2011338-eng.pdf

Piketty, Thomas (2014) *Capital in the Twenty-first Century*. Cambridge, MA: Harvard University Press.

Putnam, Robert (2006) E Pluribus Unum: Diversity and Community in the Twenty-First Century—The 2006 Johan Skytte Prize Lecture. *Scandinavian Political Studies* 30(2):137–174.

Reitz, Jeffrey G. (2009) Assessing Multiculturalism as a Behavioural Theory. In Jeffrey G. Reitz, Raymond Breton, Karen Kisiel Dion, and Kenneth L. Dion (eds.) *Multiculturalism as Social Cohesion: Potentials and Challenges of Diversity*, pp. 1–47. Milton Keynes, UK: Springer.

Reitz, J.G. (1998) *Warmth of the Welcome: The Social Causes of Economic Success for Immigrants in Different Nations and Cities*. Boulder, CO: Westview Press.

Reuters (2008) Whites to Become Minority in U.S. by 2050. *Reuters*, 12 February. www.reuters.com/article/2008/02/12/us-usa-population-immigration-idUSN1110177520080212

Richmond, Ted and John Shields (2005) NGO-Government Relations and Immigrant Services: Contradictions and Challenges. *Journal of International Migration and Integration* 6(3–4):513–526.

Salins, Peter D. (2004) The Assimilation Contract: Endangered but Still Holding. In Tamar Jacoby (ed.) *Reinventing the Melting Pot: The New Immigrants and What It Means to Be American*, pp. 99–109. New York: Basic Books.

Shields, John (2004) No Safe Haven: Work, Welfare, and the Growth of Immigrant Exclusion. In Philip Kretsedemas and Ana Aparicio (eds.) *Immigrants, Welfare Reform, and the Poverty of Policy*, pp. 35–60. Westport, CT: Praeger.

Shields, John (1990) Democracy Versus Leviathan: The State, Democracy and Neo-Conservatism. *Journal of History and Politics* 9:153–174.

Shields, John and Bryan Evans (1998) *Shrinking the State: Globalization and the "Reform" of Public Administration*. Halifax: Fernwood Publishing.

Statistics Canada (2008) Canadian Demographics at a Glance, 25 January. www.statcan.gc.ca/pub/91-003-x/2007001/4129908-eng.htm

Statistics Canada (2011) Ethnic Diversity and Immigration, 30 September. www.statcan.gc.ca/pub/11-402-x/2011000/chap/imm/imm-eng.htm

The Statue of Liberty and Ellis Island Website (n.d.) libertystatepark.com/emma.htm

Thernstrom, Stephan (2004) Rediscovering the Melting Pot—Still Going Strong. In Tamar Jacoby (ed.) *Reinventing the Melting Pot: The New Immigrants and What It Means to Be American*, pp. 47–59. New York: Basic Books.

Tolley, Erin (2011) Introduction: Who Invited Them to the Party? Federal-Municipal Relations in Immigrant Settlement Policy. In Erin Tolley and Robert Young (eds.) *Immigrant Settlement Policy in Canadian Municipalities*, pp. 3–48. Montreal: McGill-Queen's University Press.

Triandafyllidou, Anna, Ruby Gropas, and Dita Vogel (2007) Introduction. In Anna Triandafyllidou and Ruby Gropas (eds.) *European Immigration: A Source Book*, pp. 1–17. Farnham, UK: Ashgate.

U.S. Census Bureau News (2008) An Older and More Diverse Nation by Midcentury. Washington, DC: U.S. Department of Commerce. web.archive.org/web/20080822044429/http://www.census.gov/Press-Release/www/releases/archives/population/012496.html

Valpy, Michael (2013) Q&A with EKOS Research President Frank Graves. *Toronto Star*, 7 December.

Welcome BC. (n.d.) Immigrants to Canada by Province of Destination. Victoria: Government of British Columbia. www.welcomebc.ca/welcome_bc/media/Media-Gallery/docs/immigration/PR-tables-for-CIC-print-edition.pdf

Wilson, William Julius (1987) *The Truly Disadvantaged: The Inner City, the Underclass, and Public Policy*. Chicago: University of Chicago Press.

Wimmer, Andreas and Nina Glick Schiller (2002) Methodological Nationalism and Beyond: Nation-State Building, Migration and the Social Sciences. *Global Networks* 2(4):301–334.

Winter, Elke (2014) Becoming Canadian: Making Sense of Recent Changes to Citizenship Rules. *IRPP Study* 44, January.

Chapter 1

TWO CENTURIES OF IMMIGRATION TO NORTH AMERICA

ROBERT VINEBERG

Introduction

From the first days of European colonization in the New World, **immigration** from Europe to the Americas was a phenomenon that transcended national boundaries, both in Europe and in the New World. Originally the motivation was solely on the part of the colonizers and the colonists seeking a new life, and perhaps fortune as well, in the New World. Only when the European **colonies** in the New World grew large enough to create their own nation-states or, as occurred in North America, colonial provinces with representative governments, did these political units start promoting immigration, usually from their traditional homelands first and then from other European countries as well. In most cases, immigration to the Western Hemisphere from the rest of the world was severely limited until at least the 1960s.

In North America, both the United States and Canada have long traditions of being immigrant-receiving countries and both have promoted immigration for the last two centuries. Immigration to North America is really a single phenomenon, but both Americans and Canadians have tended to study immigration to their respective countries in isolation. This is unfortunate because the public, lawmakers, and policymakers in both countries have much to learn from each other.

This chapter will demonstrate the strong similarities in the immigration traditions of both countries over the past two centuries and will also illustrate the many differences in approach that have taken place over time, due both to geography and economy and to political decisions taken. In doing so, it also examines and compares the broad patterns of immigration to both Canada and the US and between the two countries.

This chapter begins with a brief examination of the constitutional basis for immigration management in both countries. It then examines the major nineteenth century migrant movements to both countries, followed by the boom and bust period of the early twentieth century, and concludes with a look at the more recent **immigrant** policies and movements, from the end of the Second World War to the present.

Image 1.1
Immigrants Just Arrived from Foreign Countries—Immigration Building, Ellis Island, New York Harbor, 1904

Source: Library of Congress, Prints and Photographs Division [LC-USZ62-15539].

Immigration and the Canadian and American Constitutions

Both Canada and the United States are federal states and, by virtue of being federal states, the question of which level of government is vested with the power to regulate immigration must be addressed. Managing immigration in the first years of the United States remained important to each state, while the federal government also viewed immigration as important to the nation as a whole. As a result, the Constitution of the United States was somewhat ambiguous in dividing authority with respect to immigration. Article 1, Section 8 of the American Constitution enumerated the powers of Congress, including that of naturalization. In Article 1, Section 9, "Limits of Congress," it was stipulated, *inter alia*, that the "Migration or Importation[1] of such Persons as any of the States now existing shall think proper to admit, shall not be prohibited by the Congress prior to the Year one thousand eight hundred and eight, but a tax or duty may be imposed on such Importation, not exceeding ten dollars for each Person." Finally, Article 1, Section 10 enumerated the powers prohibited of states, including the conduct of foreign relations (United States Constitution 1787). In 1889, linking immigration to the conduct of foreign relations, the United States Supreme Court "articulated the plenary power doctrine on immigration. According to that doctrine, the regulation of immigration and immigrants falls under the exclusive and unreviewable purview of the federal government" (Filindra and Kovács 2011:1, 2). The US federal government has long considered immigration and immigration enforcement to be its own area of authority but recent court decisions, federal legislation, and interpretations by the Department of Justice have opened the door, somewhat, to state participation (Wishnie 2002:287–288).

In Canada, the Constitution Act—originally known as the British North America Act—(Constitution Act 1867) is more explicit with respect to immigration. Federal powers, enumerated in section 91, include naturalization and control of aliens (ss. 91(25)). However, Canada in 1867 was a vast, underpopulated country whose major industry was agriculture. The former British North American colonies had extensive experience in administration of both agriculture and immigration and felt strongly that they needed to remain involved, while acknowledging the paramount interest of the new federal government. Therefore, section 95 of the Constitution Act (1867) accorded concurrent jurisdiction only in these two areas but stipulated that in the case of conflicting legislation the federal legislation would prevail. Immigration did not include immigration enforcement (i.e. control of aliens). This was deemed to be in the exclusive federal jurisdiction (ss. 91(25)), but all other aspects dealing with bringing in immigrants, such as selection and **settlement**, were within the concurrent jurisdiction.

In Canada in the early years following federation, the provinces continued to be active in immigration, but interest waned during the First World War, recovered somewhat in the 1920s, and then disappeared during the Great Depression. Following the Second World War, for many years the Canadian provinces pretty well left immigration to be managed by the federal government. However, beginning in the 1970s, the province of Quebec, followed by other provinces, insisted on being able to select immigrants for its needs and not just on a national basis, so the Canadian government entered into a series of agreements with most provinces and territories to allow for provincial participation in immigrant selection (Vineberg 2011). By contrast, for more than a century the American government has not permitted states to be involved in selection of immigrants.

It should be noted that in Canada enforcement is legislated federally but which level of government handles immigration enforcement is not an issue given that section 92(14) of the Constitution Act (1867) assigns responsibility for the administration of justice to the provinces, regardless of whether the statute is federal or provincial. While the national police force (the Royal Canadian Mounted Police) and federal immigration enforcement officers of the Canada Border Services Agency take the lead in most cases, local police have full authority under the constitution to enforce the provisions of the Immigration and Refugee Protection Act (2001).

Nineteenth Century Immigration Movements

While migration to North America began in the late sixteenth and early seventeenth century, the volume of immigrants in any given year was relatively small. Migration from Europe to North America only gained in popularity after the end of the Napoleonic Wars. From the beginning of the French Revolution in 1789 until Napoleon's final defeat at Waterloo in 1815, Europe was embroiled in conflict. That conflict and the blockade of the continent by the British Royal Navy also led to the War of 1812 in North America, as the blockade hindered the free passage of American vessels to Europe. The continual wars placed a great strain on military manpower and no European nation wished to see its potential soldiers emigrate to North America or anywhere else.

The end of the Napoleonic Wars opened the way to large-scale emigration from Europe as the military imperative no longer applied and the withdrawal of military spending from European economies set off a continent-wide economic recession that resulted in surplus labourers, many of whom were willing to seek opportunities in the New World (Kelley and Trebilcock 2010:45). Nevertheless, the numbers that travelled to North America remained limited. The voyage was long, expensive, and perilous.

Many of the emigrants leaving the United Kingdom in the early 1800s were Scots, and a Committee of the British House of Commons was struck to look into issues affecting Scotland, including emigration. It observed "[t]hat Persons emigrating from different Parts of the United Kingdom, have in various Instances, suffered great Distress and Hardship, on account of the crowded State of the Vessels, the want of a sufficient stock of Provisions, Water, and other Necessaries for the Voyage, and in various other Respects." Therefore, the committee recommended "[t]hat, it is expedient to regulate Vessels carrying Passengers from the United Kingdom to His Majesty's Plantations and Settlements abroad, or to Foreign Parts, with respect to the Number of Passengers which they shall be allowed to take on board, in proportion to the Tonnage of such Vessels, as well as with respect to the Provision of proper Necessaries for the Voyage" (Committee on the Survey of the Coasts, &c. of Scotland 1803:4, 5).

In response to the report, the first Passenger Act (43 Geo III, Cap.56) was passed by the Imperial Parliament in 1803 (Kelley and Trebilcock 2010:44). Of course the provisions in the law raised the costs of ocean travel and actually served to discourage emigration, as the British wished to do at the time. The United States passed similar legislation in 1819. In the United States, the Act for Regulating Passenger-Ships and Vessel (3 Stat. 488)[2] is also known as "**steerage** legislation" (Hutchinson 1981:21).

In the nineteenth century the US drew immigrants from all over Europe while Canada, until the 1890s, only sought immigrants from the UK. Nevertheless, the US numbers were relatively small compared to later years, mostly due to the high costs of travel and the risks involved in the days of sail. Once steamships entered the North Atlantic passenger business, reliability increased and costs decreased, leading to more migration. It was only in 1842 that the United States recorded over 100,000 immigrant arrivals but by the early 1850s, 300,000 to 400,000 were arriving each year. During the Civil War years, American immigration dropped to less than 100,000 annually but rebounded after the war, reaching a high of almost 800,000 in 1882 (see Table 1.1). Following the Civil War, the US pace of industrialization increased and more people moved to the western territories. Immigrants, particularly those fleeing the Irish potato famine, saw the US as a land of opportunity. By contrast, the provinces of British North America were a collection of small agrarian colonies, as yet without a western frontier. So the number of immigrants to Canada was tiny. In 1867, the year of Canadian Confederation, only 10,666 immigrants arrived in the new country. In 1870, Canada purchased its Northwest Territories (what is now Manitoba, Saskatchewan, Alberta, and the three northern territories) from the Hudson's Bay Company and Canada gained its own western frontier. The boom years in the early 1880s brought the nineteenth century peak of 133,000 immigrants in 1883 but for most years the numbers were much lower (see Table 1.2.). Furthermore, many Canadians left to go to the United States, so **net immigration** was much lower. It has been estimated that

Table 1.1
Persons Obtaining Legal Permanent Resident Status in the United Sates, Fiscal Years 1820–2012

Year	Number	Year	Number	Year	Number	Year	Number
1820	8,385	1870	387,203	1920	430,001	1970	373,326
1821	9,127	1871	321,350	1921	805,228	1971	370,478
1822	6,911	1872	404,806	1922	309,556	1972	384,685
1823	6,354	1873	459,803	1923	522,919	1973	398,515
1824	7,912	1874	313,339	1924	706,896	1974	393,919
1825	10,199	1875	227,498	1925	294,314	1975	385,378
1826	10,837	1876	169,986	1926	304,488	1976[1]	499,093
1827	18,875	1877	141,857	1927	335,175	1977	458,755
1828	27,382	1878	138,469	1928	307,255	1978	589,810
1829	22,520	1879	177,826	1929	279,678	1979	394,244
1830	23,322	1880	457,257	1930	241,700	1980	524,295
1831	22,633	1881	669,431	1931	97,139	1981	595,014
1832	60,482	1882	788,992	1932	35,576	1982	533,624
1833	58,640	1883	603,322	1933	23,068	1983	550,052
1834	65,365	1884	518,592	1934	29,470	1984	541,811
1835	45,374	1885	395,346	1935	34,956	1985	568,149
1836	76,242	1886	334,203	1936	36,329	1986	600,027
1837	79,340	1887	490,109	1937	50,244	1987	599,889
1838	38,914	1888	546,889	1938	67,895	1988	641,346
1839	68,069	1889	444,427	1939	82,998	1989	1,090,172
1840	84,066	1890	455,302	1940	70,756	1990	1,535,872
1841	80,289	1891	560,319	1941	51,776	1991	1,826,595
1842	104,565	1892	579,663	1942	28,781	1992	973,445
1843	52,496	1893	439,730	1943	23,725	1993	903,916
1844	78,615	1894	285,631	1944	28,551	1994	803,993
1845	114,371	1895	258,536	1945	38,119	1995	720,177
1846	154,416	1896	343,267	1946	108,721	1996	915,560
1847	234,968	1897	230,832	1947	147,292	1997	797,847
1848	226,527	1898	229,299	1948	170,570	1998	653,206
1849	297,024	1899	311,715	1949	188,317	1999	644,787
1850	369,980	1900	448,572	1950	249,187	2000	841,002
1851	379,466	1901	487,918	1951	205,717	2001	1,058,902
1852	371,603	1902	648,743	1952	265,520	2002	1,059,356
1853	368,645	1903	857,046	1953	170,434	2003	703,542
1854	427,833	1904	812,870	1954	208,177	2004	957,883
1855	200,877	1905	1,026,499	1955	237,790	2005	1,122,257
1856	200,436	1906	1,100,735	1956	321,625	2006	1,266,129
1857	251,306	1907	1,285,349	1957	326,867	2007	1,052,415
1858	123,126	1908	782,870	1958	253,265	2008	1,107,126
1859	121,282	1909	751,786	1959	260,686	2009	1,130,818
1860	153,640	1910	1,041,570	1960	265,398	2010	1,042,625
1861	91,918	1911	878,587	1961	271,344	2011	1,062,040
1862	91,985	1912	838,172	1962	283,763	2012	1,031,631
1863	176,282	1913	1,197,892	1963	306,260		
1864	193,418	1914	1,218,480	1964	292,248		
1865	248,120	1915	326,700	1965	296,697		
1866	318,568	1916	298,826	1966	323,040		
1867	315,722	1917	295,403	1967	361,972		
1868	138,840	1918	110,618	1968	454,448		
1869	352,768	1919	141,132	1969	358,579		

* Includes the 15 months from July 1, 1975, to September 30, 1976, because the end date of fiscal years was changed from June 30 to September 30.

Source: U.S. Department of Homeland Security, 2012.

Table 1.2
Canada: Permanent Residents, 1860–2012

Year	1860	1861	1862	1863	1864	1865	1866	1867	1868	1869
Number	6,276	13,539	18,294	21,000	24,779	18,958	11,427	10,666	12,765	18,630
% of Population	0.2	0.4	0.6	0.6	0.7	0.6	0.3	0.3	0.4	0.5
Year	1870	1871	1872	1873	1874	1875	1876	1877	1878	1879
Number	24,706	27,773	36,578	50,050	39,373	27,382	25,633	27,082	29,807	40,492
% of Population	0.7	0.8	1.0	1.3	1.0	0.7	0.6	0.7	0.7	1.0
Year	1880	1881	1882	1883	1884	1885	1886	1887	1888	1889
Number	38,505	47,991	112,458	133,624	103,824	76,169	69,152	84,526	88,766	91,600
% of Population	0.9	1.1	2.6	3.0	2.3	1.7	1.5	1.8	1.9	1.9
Year	1890	1891	1892	1893	1894	1895	1896	1897	1898	1899
Number	75,067	82,165	30,996	29,633	20,829	18,790	16,035	21,716	31,900	44,543
% of Population	1.6	1.7	0.6	0.6	0.4	0.4	0.3	0.4	0.6	0.9
Year	1900	1901	1902	1903	1904	1905	1906	1907	1908	1909
Number	41,681	55,747	89,102	138,660	131,252	141,465	211,653	272,409	143,326	173,694
% of Population	0.8	1.0	1.6	2.5	2.3	2.4	3.5	4.2	2.2	2.6
Year	1910	1911	1912	1913	1914	1915	1916	1917	1918	1919
Number	286,839	331,288	375,756	400,870	150,484	33,665	55,914	72,910	41,845	107,698
% of Population	4.1	4.6	5.1	5.3	1.9	0.4	0.7	0.9	5.0	1.3
Year	1920	1921	1922	1923	1924	1925	1926	1927	1928	1929
Number	138,824	91,728	64,224	133,729	124,164	84,907	135,982	158,886	166,783	164,993
% of Population	1.6	1.0	0.7	1.5	1.4	9.0	1.4	1.6	1.7	1.6
Year	1930	1931	1932	1933	1934	1935	1936	1937	1938	1939
Number	104,806	27,530	20,591	14,382	12,476	11,277	11,643	15,101	17,244	16,994
% of Population	1.0	0.3	0.2	0.1	0.1	0.1	0.1	0.1	0.2	0.2
Year	1940	1941	1942	1943	1944	1945	1946	1947	1948	1949
Number	11,324	9,329	7,576	8,504	12,801	22,722	71,719	64,127	125,414	95,217
% of Population	0.1	0.1	0.1	0.1	0.1	0.2	0.6	0.5	1.0	0.7
Year	1950	1951	1952	1953	1954	1955	1956	1957	1958	1959
Number	73,912	194,391	164,498	168,868	154,227	109,946	164,857	282,164	124,851	106,928
% of Population	0.5	1.4	1.1	1.1	1.0	0.7	1.0	1.7	0.7	0.6
Year	1960	1961	1962	1963	1964	1965	1966	1967	1968	1969
Number	104,111	71,698	74,856	93,151	112,606	146,758	194,743	222,876	183,974	164,531
% of Population	0.6	0.4	0.4	0.5	0.6	0.7	1.0	1.1	0.9	0.8
Year	1970	1971	1972	1973	1974	1975	1976	1977	1978	1979
Number	147,713	121,900	122,006	184,200	218,465	187,881	149,429	114,914	86,313	112,093
% of Population	0.7	0.6	0.6	0.8	1.0	0.8	0.6	0.5	0.4	0.5
Year	1980	1981	1982	1983	1984	1985	1986	1987	1988	1989
Number	143,137	128,641	121,175	89,186	88,272	84,347	99,355	152,079	161,586	191,550
% of Population	0.6	0.5	0.5	0.4	0.3	0.3	0.4	0.6	0.6	0.7

Year	1990	1991	1992	1993	1994	1995	1996	1997	1998	1999
Number	216,451	232,809	254,793	256,641	224,385	212,866	226,071	216,035	174,195	189,950
% of Population	0.8	0.8	0.9	0.9	0.8	0.7	0.8	0.7	0.6	0.6
Year	2000	2001	2002	2003	2004	2005	2006	2007	2008	2009
Number	227,455	250,637	229,048	221,349	235,823	262,242	251,640	236,753	247,246	252,174
% of Population	0.7	0.8	0.7	0.7	0.7	0.8	0.8	0.7	0.7	0.7
Year	2010	2011	2012							
Number	280,691	248,748	257,515							
% of Population	0.8	0.7	0.7							

Source: Citizenship and Immigration Canada, Facts and Figures (2011, 2012).

over the quarter century from 1870 to 1895, while 1,400,000 immigrants entered Canada, 1,900,000 left, mostly for the United States[3] (Keenleyside 1948:224). Why? There were several reasons. Prior to 1885 and the completion of the Canadian Pacific Railway, access to the Canadian West was extremely difficult compared to the American Midwest, which was accessible both by railway and by water via the Great Lakes. The American climate was warmer, and while free land was still available in the United States most immigrants chose the US over Canada.[4] The US was also much more industrialized than Canada, and American industry sought workers, mostly from Southern Europe, and Italy in particular, but also from Canada, especially from the province of Quebec and the Maritime provinces, to work in the mills of New England. Meanwhile, Canadians saw the burgeoning American cities as corrupt and crime-ridden and wanted to discourage immigration to Canadian cities. As a result, the Government of Canada sought **agriculturalists** to settle in the vast but largely unpopulated Canadian West and did nothing to encourage immigration to its cities.

In the 1890s, Canada's competitive position vis-à-vis the US began to change for a number of reasons. The arrival of the Canadian Pacific Railway in the Canadian West meant that immigrants could travel directly to the Canadian Prairies without having to detour through the US and being enticed to stay. Canadian scientists also successfully developed new strains of wheat that required shorter growing times, making farming north of the forty-ninth parallel more practical. Finally, the free land in the US was largely gone by 1890. American historians often refer to the "closing of the frontier" in 1890. This is the time that immigration to Canada finally began to catch the imagination of Europeans and Americans.

Canadians and Americans tend to study their histories, including immigration histories, in isolation. The unique perspective of this book is that studying both together results in a much clearer understanding of both histories. In an early attempt to look at immigration to both countries as one movement, Paul Sharp wrote that "The mass migration into the Canadian West was the last advance in the long march that had begun on the Atlantic seaboard [of the United States]" (Sharp 1950:287). While the price of land was soaring in the American West, 160 free acres were still available in Canada for farmers, and neighbouring land could be bought for about one-tenth of the price south of the border. Suddenly the Canadian West was more attractive than the American West. But someone had to get the word out.

In 1896 the Conservative Party, which had governed Canada continuously since Confederation in 1867, except for a single five-year period, was defeated by Wilfrid Laurier's Liberal Party. Laurier knew that the key to Canadian prosperity was to get large numbers of people to settle in Western Canada and for that task he appointed the Member of Parliament from Brandon, Manitoba, Clifford Sifton, as his Minister of the Interior. Sifton, born in Ontario, moved west to Manitoba as a young man and made a fortune, mostly in newspapers. His experience as a newspaper man and, later, as a minister in the Manitoba provincial government, prepared him well for his new job. In 1899 he told the Canadian House of Commons, "[i]n my judgement, the immigration work has to be carried on in the same manner as the sale of any commodity; just as soon as you stop advertising and missionary work, the movement is going to stop" (House of Commons Debates 1899:columns 8654–8655). He spent millions on advertising "The Last Best West" in Europe and in the United States. In Europe, he changed the previous policy of seeking only British immigrants and started promoting Canada as a destination for other Europeans, provided they lived in Northern or Central Europe. This change was controversial. Many objected to people who were apparently so different coming into Canada. Working with inner-city immigrants in Winnipeg early in the twentieth century, J.S. Woodsworth wrote

> English and Russians, French and Germans, Austrians and Italians,
> Japanese and Hindus—a mixed multitude, they are being dumped
> into Canada by a kind of endless chain. They sort themselves
> out after a fashion, and each seeks to find a corner somewhere.
> But how shall we weld this heterogeneous mass into one people?
> (Woodsworth 1909:203)

Sifton did not advertise in Southern Europe, as there was a feeling in Canada that the United States was being harmed by massive immigration from countries such as Italy and Greece (see Case Example 1).

In the United States, Sifton sought not only Americans but also the second- and third-generation Canadians who had moved to the US earlier in the century. He invested heavily in expanding facilities to help immigrants settle successfully in Canada, in contrast to the American approach of largely leaving immigrants to their own devices. Across Canada, but particularly in the West, Sifton expanded the

Case Example 1: Skim Milk versus Cream

In 1911 the *New York Times* published a series of long articles on immigration to Canada. One article, entitled "Bruce Walker, Autocrat of Canada's Immigrants," argues that Canada's immigration system is selecting better immigrants than that of the US because Canada "gets the Cream of Immigration and we [the US] get the Skim Milk." Bruce Walker was the Commissioner of Immigration in Winnipeg, Manitoba. Under the Superintendent of Immigration in Ottawa, there were two Commissioners of Immigration: one in London, England, managing overseas operations and another in Winnipeg managing the settlement of Western Canada. The article described Walker as an autocrat because of the wide powers accorded to him under Canada's immigration legislation, long before today's system of appeals was introduced. The *Times* wrote that,

> Among the men in charge of the work of settling the far corners of the earth there is perhaps none wielding power equal to that of this man. When Canada decided to pick her settlers, choosing only those who would make her a homogeneous nation, and letting only the chosen in, she selected her ablest men to carry out her immigration policy and she gave them a free hand.

Walker is quoted as saying,

> We seek our settlers only in the northern half of the continent of Europe and in the United States. We want first of all the British, second Americans, then people of a few other nations of Northern Europe. On the other hand we deliberately discourage any attempts to bring in emigrants from Southern Europe and we carry on no propaganda there.[5] They are unsuited to our climatic conditions and are out of harmony with the traditions [of Canada].

> We want farmers and farm workers-people who will go out to the land and help make it productive; not people who will mass together in the cities.... thus we are happily immune from the disadvantages of your mixed immigration and their serious disadvantages in over-crowded slums, thronged labor markets, and unassimilated population. (*New York Times* 1911)

The article was eloquent praise of Canada's immigration policies but was the *Times* not, perhaps, using the story about Canada to argue for the imposition of stronger controls on the American immigration system?

system of "immigration halls" to provide temporary shelter for immigrants on arrival and en route to their destinations. Originally called "immigration sheds," the more impressive term *immigration hall* was adopted later and became the common usage by the 1890s. By 1911, there were more than 50 immigration halls in Canada, mostly in the Prairie provinces. The immigration hall became the tangible symbol of Canada's commitment to its immigrants in the late nineteenth and early twentieth centuries. The concept of truly providing for the immigrant rather than just "getting them out of the way" was a key element in the government's thinking (Vineberg 2012:69–71).

The closing years of the nineteenth century saw huge changes in North America due to immigration, moreso in the US but increasingly so in Canada. However, the period also witnessed a racist reaction to non-European immigration. In both the United States and Canada there was a huge shortage of manpower to build the transcontinental railways and other infrastructure. Employers met the demand by importing foreign labour from Asia, mostly from China. The Chinese came with hopes of earning enough money to return home and live comfortably there but the salaries were low and the work was back-breaking. Most could not afford to go home or to send for their families. Meanwhile, resentment and attitudes of superiority fuelled anti-Chinese movements in both countries. The United States moved first, passing legislation in 1882 (22 Stat. 58) to exclude Chinese workers from immigrating (Hutchinson 1981:430). Canada followed in 1885, passing a Chinese Immigration Act that imposed a $50 **head tax** on all Chinese immigrants (Chinese Immigration Act 1885). Why did this happen when it did? The railroads had largely been built by this time and railroad companies were no longer lobbying governments to allow Chinese immigration to continue, so governments gave in to the anti-Chinese public opinion on their west coasts. The US government renewed its Chinese exclusion legislation several times over the next half century, while Canada increased its head tax, to $100 in 1900 and then to $500 in 1903, and in 1923 excluded Chinese immigration almost entirely (An Act Respecting Chinese Immigration 1923). Both countries also imposed restrictions on Japanese and South Asian immigrants.

The Early Twentieth Century

The North American economies were strong as the twentieth century dawned and both the US and Canada were increasingly seen as the Promised Land. In 1905, both countries surpassed all previous immigration records: the US admitted more than 1 million immigrants and Canada admitted more than 200,000 immigrants. Patterns of immigration to North America, which in many years of the nineteenth century had favoured the US by a factor of ten to one or more, were changing.

Image 1.2
The Registry Room, Ellis Island, circa 1907–1912

Source: U.S. National Parks Service.

Canadian promotion of immigration and the lure of free land caused Canadian immigration numbers to swell to more than 400,000 in 1913, while immigration to the US stayed within the range of 800,000 to 1,300,000 from 1903 to 1914. So, with immigration numbers to Canada equalling fully one-third of immigration numbers to the US, Canada was becoming an increasingly attractive destination. And if we look at immigration in proportion to population, Canada, with a population of under 8,000,000 in 1913, received more than 5% of its population while the much larger US, with a population of 97,000,000 in the same year, received only a little over 1% of its population (see Table 1.3). Again, throughout this period Canada focused on attracting agriculturalists from Northern and Central Europe and discouraged the immigration of others, including those from Southern Europe, which remained a major source for the US. In addition, Canada became increasingly more attractive to Americans and Europeans who had originally immigrated to the United States. From 1890 to 1914, perhaps 1.25 million people emigrated from the US to Canada (Sharp 1950:286). During the two decades from 1896 to 1914, over 3,000,000 came to Canada while only 1,300,000 left (Keenleyside 1948:225). Net migration was strongly positive for the first time in Canada's history.

Table 1.3

Canadian and US Immigration Compared 1867–1914

	CANADA			US		
Year	Population	Immigration	Percentage of Population	Population	Immigration	Percentage of Population
1867	3,463,000	10,666	0.3	37,375,703	315,722	0.8
1868	3,511,000	12,765	0.4	38,213,216	138,840	0.4
1869	3,565,000	18,630	0.5	39,050,729	352,768	0.9
1870	3,625,000	24,706	0.7	39,904,598	387,203	1.0
1871	3,689,000	27,773	0.8	40,938,327	31,350	0.1
1872	3,754,000	36,578	1.0	41,972,060	404,806	1.0
1873	3,826,000	50,050	1.3	43,005,794	459,803	1.1
1874	3,895,000	39,373	1.0	44,039,527	313,339	0.7
1875	3,954,000	27,382	0.7	45,073,260	227,498	0.5
1876	4,009,000	25,633	0.6	46,106,994	169,986	0.4
1877	4,064,000	27,082	0.7	47,140,727	141,857	0.3
1878	4,120,000	29,807	0.7	48,174,461	138,469	0.3
1879	4,185,000	40,492	1.0	49,208,194	177,826	0.4
1880	4,255,000	38,505	0.9	50,262,382	457,257	0.9
1881	4,325,000	47,991	1.1	51,541,575	669,431	1.3
1882	4,375,000	112,458	2.6	52,820,768	788,992	1.5
1883	4,430,000	133,624	3.0	54,099,961	603,322	1.1
1884	4,487,000	103,824	2.3	55,379,154	518,592	0.9
1885	4,537,000	76,169	1.7	56,658,347	395,346	0.7
1886	4,580,000	69,152	1.5	57,937,540	334,203	0.6
1887	4,626,000	84,526	1.8	59,216,733	490,109	0.8
1888	4,678,000	88,766	1.9	60,495,927	546,889	0.9
1889	4,729,000	91,600	1.9	61,775,121	444,427	0.7
1890	4,779,000	75,067	1.6	63,056,438	455,302	0.7
1891	4,833,000	82,165	1.7	64,361,124	560,319	0.9
1892	4,883,000	30,996	0.6	65,665,810	579,663	0.9
1893	4,931,000	29,633	0.6	66,970,496	439,730	0.7
1894	4,979,000	20,829	0.4	68,275,182	285,631	0.4
1895	5,026,000	18,790	0.4	69,579,868	258,536	0.4
1896	5,074,000	16,835	0.3	70,884,554	343,267	0.5
1897	5,122,000	21,716	0.4	72,189,240	230,832	0.3
1898	5,175,000	31,900	0.6	73,498,926	229,299	0.3
1899	5,235,000	44,543	0.9	74,798,612	311,715	0.4
1900	5,301,000	41,681	0.8	76,094,134	448,572	0.6
1901	5,371,000	55,747	1.0	77,585,128	487,918	0.6
1902	5,494,000	89,102	1.6	79,160,196	648,743	0.8
1903	5,651,000	138,660	2.5	80,632,152	857,046	1.1
1904	5,827,000	131,252	2.3	82,164,974	812,870	1.0
1905	6,002,000	141,465	2.4	83,819,666	1,026,499	1.2
1906	6,097,000	211,653	3.5	85,436,556	1,100,735	1.3
1907	6,411,000	272,409	4.2	87,000,271	1,285,349	1.5
1908	6,625,000	143,326	2.2	88,708,976	782,870	0.9
1909	6,800,000	173,694	2.6	90,491,525	751,786	0.8
1910	6,988,000	286,839	4.1	95,406,536	1,041,570	1.1
1911	7,207,000	331,288	4.6	93,867,814	878,587	0.9
1912	7,389,000	375,756	5.1	95,331,300	838,172	0.9
1913	7,632,000	400,870	5.3	97,226,814	1,197,892	1.2
1914	7,879,000	150,484	1.9	99,117,567	1,218,480	1.2

Image 1.3
Immigrants Arriving at Quebec City, Circa 1925

Source: Library and Archives Canada, C-019935.

Table 1.3 Sources:

United States:
Population: Bureau of the Census (1949) Historical Statistics of the United States, 1789–1945, Series B31–39, p. 26. Washington, DC: U.S. Government Printing Office.
Immigration: 2009 Yearbook of Immigration Statistics (2010), p. 5. Washington, DC: U.S. Department of Homeland Security

Canada:
Population: Estimated Population of Canada 1605 to Present. Ottawa: Statistics Canada.
www.statcan.gc.ca/pub/98-187-x/4151287-eng.htm
Immigration: Immigration Facts and Figures 2009. Ottawa: CIC.
www.cic.gc.ca/english/resources/statistics/facts2009/permanent/index.asp#permanent

The growth in migration reversed itself for both countries with the advent of the First World War. While Canada went to war in 1914, the US only declared war on Germany in 1917; throughout this period, however, the North Atlantic was no longer a safe place for passenger ships and immigration to both countries tumbled. Immigration across the Atlantic did not to return to higher levels until the 1920s, but even then annual numbers were about half of what each country had been receiving in the decade prior to the war. Why did the levels of immigration not return to the pre-war levels? The reason is that both countries decided it was in their interest to end the period of so-called open immigration that preceded the war. The nature of the labour markets in both countries changed dramatically as a result of the war. With very large numbers of men fighting in Europe, industry had turned to women to fill the jobs left vacant by servicemen and to fill new jobs in factories churning out weapons and ammunition for the war effort. At the end of the war, the returning servicemen represented a labour surplus that had to be absorbed into the economy. Both countries felt that their **absorptive capacity** for immigrants was lower than it had been before the war. Therefore, both countries imposed restrictions on immigration but in very different ways.

Canada chose to develop a preference system in which immigrants faced varying degrees of difficulty in being admitted to Canada. The most favoured were British subjects from the United Kingdom, Newfoundland (which did not join Canada until 1949), Ireland, Australia, New Zealand, and South Africa, and American citizens, all of whom were eligible to enter Canada provided they could support themselves until employment was found. Agriculturalists and domestic servants benefited from a travel subsidy from the UK amounting to a 90 percent discount on the sea/rail fare from Liverpool to Winnipeg. The second preference applied to citizens of Northern Europe and Scandinavia, who could enter freely on the same basis as British and Americans, although there was no travel subsidy available. The third preference applied to citizens of Central and Southern European countries, who could only enter Canada if they were agricultural workers, domestic servants, or close relatives of Canadian residents. Any other workers required a special permit issued by the minister of immigration. The fourth preference group comprised the rest of the world, and admission was limited to those whose potential employer or relative in Canada could obtain a ministerial permit (Kelley and Trebilcock 2010:192).

The US opted for a quota system that applied to European immigration. Immigration from the Western Hemisphere was outside the quota and immigration from the rest of the world was essentially excluded. The American quota system introduced "the new and foreign principle of offering preferential treatment to immigrants from Northern and Western Europe as against those from Southern and Eastern Europe" (Bernard 1950:341). The legislation was carefully contrived to

Case Example 2: Unintended Consequences of Mean-Spirited Legislation

The quota legislation introduced in the US in the 1920s was designed to inhibit immigration from Italy and other Southern European countries. However, it also had the unintended result of industries in the American north recruiting African Americans from the south to replace the diminishing supply of Italians. These African Americans left farm work in the south for factory work in the north, creating a shortage in farm labour throughout the south. But as the Western Hemisphere was exempted from the quota, Southern American farmers, in turn, recruited Mexicans, Puerto Ricans, and other Latin American workers to replace the black workers. So two major features of the modern American demographic emerged: large urban black populations in the north and large Hispanic populations in the south came about largely in response to Congress's efforts to reduce Italian immigration! As a side effect, more Canadians also were able to immigrate to the US in the 1920s. In general, American companies paid more than Canadian companies at the time and, therefore, throughout the 1920s, Canada experienced the loss of trained industrial workers, particularly from Quebec, to the United States (Bernard 1950:31, 47).

appear objective but it was not. The quota system was to be based on the proportion of various nationalities in the US population as reported in the 1910 American census. The figure of 3% of the total of each nationality present at the time of the 1910 census was chosen as the annual quota. This effectively froze immigration trends at the point they were a decade earlier. The first quota act (42 Stat. 5) was enacted in 1921 and it allowed for annual immigration from Europe of about 385,000, although only 42,657 could be from Italy. This did not satisfy Congress and a second quota act (43 Stat. 153) was passed in 1924. It reduced the overall allocation from 385,000 to 165,000, based on 2% of individual populations present at the time of the 1890 census, when proportions of Southern European immigrants were lower still. The impact on Italians was even more draconian. The Italian quota dropped to a mere 3,845 per year (Hutchinson 1981:469–470; Bernard 1950:23–26). The legislation had significant unintended consequences for American demographics and for Canada as well (see Case Example 2). It would be four decades before Canada and the US eliminated discrimination on the basis of national origin from their immigration policies.

Later in the decade, the economies of both countries recovered and until 1929, relatively large numbers of people immigrated to both the US and Canada as the economic boom continued. American immigration was up to about 300,000 per year,

Image 1.4
Dutch Immigrants at Quebec City with Their Luggage, 1947.

Source: National Film Board of Canada. Photothèque / Library and Archives Canada, PA-129829.

including both those covered by the quota and those from the Western Hemisphere, who were not covered by the quota. Canada's preference system still allowed more than half that number of immigrants to come to the less-populous country. But everything changed with the stock market crash in October 1929. As the world slid into the Great Depression, both Canada and the US rolled up their welcome mats. In September 1930, a **Presidential Instruction** directed American consular officials to rigidly apply the provisions preventing the admission of any person likely to become a public charge. This provision could be applied to any person, including those from the

Western Hemisphere, so it was very effective (Bernard 1950:33) and immigration fell from 272,000 in 1930 to less than 36,000 in 1932. In Canada, the government issued an **Order in Council** on March 21, 1931, effectively prohibiting all immigration except from the most preferred group noted earlier, who had sufficient means to support themselves, and the wives (but not husbands) and children under 18 of a sponsoring Canadian resident (Order in Council 1931). Immigration to Canada dropped from 105,000 in 1930 to less than 21,000 in 1932. In both countries, numbers remained low throughout the Depression and the Second World War **(see Tables 1.1 and 1.2).**

The provisions restricting immigration throughout this period were also used by both countries to justify the refusal to admit refugees, particularly Jews fleeing Nazi Germany, reflecting, once again, the strong discriminatory practices inherent in North American immigration policies of this period that would result in tragic consequences (Bernard 1950:33; Kelley and Trebilcock 2010:256–261).

Postwar to Present

As the Second World War approached its end, both countries eliminated their prohibitions on Chinese immigration. China was an allied partner in the war against Japan and it seemed inappropriate to bar all immigration from China. The US moved before Canada, repealing its Chinese exclusion laws on December 17, 1943 (57 Stat. 600) (Hutchinson 1981:432). It took Canada until May 14, 1947, to repeal its Chinese Immigration Act (An Act to Amend the Immigration Act 1947). The repeal of the prohibitions did not, however, lead to open immigration for Chinese and other Asian and African nationalities. Both countries imposed tiny quotas for immigration from these countries, apart from allowing spouses and children to be sponsored. Both countries also opened their doors to comparatively more refugees by the end of the war.

Nevertheless, neither Canada nor the US was ready to adopt nondiscriminatory immigration policies. In 1947, the Canadian prime minister, William Lyon Mackenzie King, stated in Parliament that "[t]he people of Canada do not wish to make a fundamental alteration in the character of their population through mass immigration" (Hawkins 1988:93). In the same year, the US Immigration and Naturalization Service stated, "In its broader sense the National Origins Plan [Quota System] was intended to preserve the racial composition of the United States" (Bernard 1950:51). It was not until the 1960s that various factors—the Civil Rights movement in the United States and concern in Canada and other Commonwealth countries over South African apartheid, as well as international pressure within the United Nations for all countries to respect spirit of the Universal Declaration of Human Rights (United Nations

1948:Article 2)—drove both countries to implement changes in their immigration policies. In this case, Canada acted three years ahead of the United States, passing an Order in Council early in 1962 (PC 1962-0082) allowing all persons, regardless of **race** or nationality, to apply to immigrate (Hawkins 1988:125). There was one exception in that extended family members (including fiancés, unmarried brothers and sisters, and minor orphan nephews and nieces) from Europe, the Western Hemisphere, Israel, Lebanon, and Egypt were able to be sponsored by Canadian residents, while immigrants from elsewhere in the world were not permitted to do so. This anomaly was done away with in 1967.

In 1965, the US Congress approved major amendments to the Immigration and Nationality Act (79 Stat. 911) that eliminated the quota system based on national origins but imposed a general quota on the Western Hemisphere as well as other countries (Hutchinson 1981:377). One of the results was that Canada fell under the new Western Hemisphere quota and, consequently, fewer Canadians could immigrate to the US. Whereas in the 1960s, 433,000 Canadians immigrated to the United States, only 179,000 emigrated in the following decade (United States 2012:8). A further factor was the Vietnam War. The draft discouraged young Canadians from wanting to live in the US and encouraged many Americans to move to Canada. Immigration from the US to Canada increased from 17,514 in 1966 to 26,541 in 1974 (Department of Manpower and Immigration 1967/1975:Table 3).

Although both countries adopted nondiscriminatory systems in the 1960s, resulting in tremendous diversification of immigration, the approach to selection of immigrants differed. The US adopted a system of preferences, within an overall quota, that favoured immigrants with relatives in the United States and allocated only a relatively small percentage to skilled workers. By contrast, Canada, while allowing Canadian residents to sponsor close family members, placed greater emphasis on selecting skilled workers to enhance the Canadian labour market. This system was formalized in 1967 by the introduction of a **points system** to select skilled workers in a more objective fashion (Order in Council 1967). The admission criteria allocated a total of 100 points based on the applicant's education, personal qualities, skill level, age, and knowledge of English or French, as well as the demand for their occupation, the labour demand in the area of the country to which they were destined, the presence of a relative in Canada, and whether they had arranged employment. The pass level was 50 points. The points system has been changed a number of times over the years but it remains the key selection tool for Canada. The current points system assesses applicants on English and/or French skills, education, experience, age, adaptability, and arranged employment in Canada. The pass requirement is now 67 points (CIC 2013).

Another area where Canadian policy differs fundamentally from the US is that of provincial involvement in immigrant selection in Canada. Out of linguistic and demographic concerns, the province of Quebec pursued a series of federal-provincial agreements resulting, in 1991, with full authority over the selection of economic immigrants destined for Quebec. Later in the 1990s other provinces, particularly in Western Canada, sought a more limited participation in selection processes. The result was the development of the Provincial Nominee Program, which permits provinces to select predetermined numbers of immigrants to meet the unique needs of the various provincial and territorial labour markets (Vineberg 2011:30, 31, 36–38). Canada has also been more active than the US in funding and implementing orientation, employment assistance, and language training programs to assist immigrant settlement. In general such programs are funded, where they exist in the US, at the state or local level or by charitable organizations rather than by the federal government. By contrast, Canada's federal government now spends in the range of one billion dollars annually on such programs.[6] While these programs are funded by the Canadian government, they are primarily delivered through nonprofit community based organizations, constituting a distinctive approach to assisting newcomers in the **integration** process (Richmond and Shields 2005).

Finally, it needs to be noted that the **immigration policy** environment in the US differs from that of Canada due to the more significant numbers of undocumented immigrants, mostly from Mexico. Canada has the advantage that its only land border is with the United States and, therefore, there are fewer opportunities for large numbers of irregular or undocumented immigrants to reach Canada. The challenge of dealing with the millions of undocumented immigrants has stymied American lawmakers for decades.

Canada's immigration legislation is more flexible than that of the US because the selection system is defined by regulation and the government can amend the regulations by Order in Council rather than having to introduce new legislation into Parliament. The US legislation has not been changed fundamentally since 1965 because, despite many attempts, there has been no agreement in both houses of Congress as to what new immigration legislation should look like. Several attempts at new legislation have failed due to an inability to obtain the bipartisan support usually necessary to pass such legislation in the US.

There is much more that could be said about recent developments in both countries. That has been left for the subsequent chapters in this book to address.

Conclusion

This chapter began with a brief examination of the constitutional basis for immigration management in both countries. It then looked at the major nineteenth century migrant movements to both countries, the boom and bust period of the early twentieth century, and the more recent immigration policies and movements from the end of the Second World War to the present.

As we have seen, for most of the last two centuries the vast majority of immigrants to North America has been attracted to the United States. Immigration to Canada was but a small tributary to the great trans-Atlantic flow of humanity from Europe to the United States. British North America was a collection of small agrarian colonies without a western frontier, while the United States was both rapidly expanding westward and growing its industrial base. After Confederation in 1867, Canada acquired its western territories but the Canadian West remained unattractive until settlers could travel directly there by rail. In the early twentieth century, Canada became an increasingly more desirable destination, although large-scale immigration to both countries was cut off by the First World War. After the war immigration resumed, but both countries introduced restrictions on immigration so that the numbers did not match prewar figures. With the Great Depression of the 1930s both countries essentially closed their doors to immigration, not to open them again until after the Second World War. Since then both Canada and the US have eliminated immigration restrictions based on race and nationality. During this period Canada has increasingly focused on attracting economic immigrants, while the US has chosen to favour the immigration of family members. The Government of Canada has also shared the responsibility for selection of immigrants with its provincial governments and invested heavily in programs to accelerate the integration of immigrants into Canadian society. The US, by contrast, has followed a more hands-off approach to immigrant settlement support.

It should be clear to the reader that, throughout their history, both Canada and the US have been immigrant-receiving countries and they are both likely to remain major immigrant-receiving nations for the foreseeable future. The ability to attract intelligent and hardworking people from around the world has benefited both countries enormously and the two heterogeneous societies in North America are among the very few in the world where anyone from any background can, with relative ease, attain full citizenship and be considered a citizen by the general population, regardless of their accent or skin colour.

Nevertheless, as the rates of population growth among most developed countries continue to fall, more nations—even those who have never in the past considered themselves to be immigrant-receiving nations—are now seeking skilled immigrants.

The competition from other immigrant-receiving countries may become a major influence upon future policy decisions in both the US and Canada.

Notes

1. The use of the word *importation* refers to slaves. Slaves, as chattel, could not "migrate" to the United States.

2. In British and Canadian parliaments, laws were referenced by the year of the reign of the monarch and each law in that year is given a "chapter" number. Thus 43 Geo III, Cap.56 means that the Passenger Act was passed in the forty-third year of the reign of King George III (1803) and it was the fifty-sixth law enacted in that year by the British Parliament. Today, Canadian laws refer to the year of passage but still refer to the chapter number. Hence, the current immigration legislation, the Immigration and Refugee Protection Act is known as S.C. 2001, c.27, meaning "Statutes of Canada, 2001, Chapter 27, or the twenty-seventh law enacted in 2001." In the United States, laws refer to the Congress that enacted them and the order in which they were enacted. Thus the American passenger legislation, 3 Stat. 488, was passed by the Third Congress and was the four hundred eighty-eighth law enacted by that Congress. However, since 1926 laws are arranged in the United States Code, which sorts laws into various "titles" and "sections." Hence the current American immigration and nationality legislation is found in Title 8, in various sections from 117 to 1613. For example, the worldwide level of immigration provisions are known as 8 USC Sec. 1151.

3. Neither the US nor Canada imposed immigration controls on their common border until 1908. Therefore, data on migration in both directions across the Canada-US border prior to 1908 is extremely unreliable.

4. It is likely that a large proportion of those moving from Canada to the United States prior to the First World War were persons who had immigrated to Canada, always with the intention of moving on to the US.

5. The word *propaganda* had no negative connotations prior to its appropriation by the Nazi regime in the 1930s. It simply meant "promotion and advertising."

6. Readers who may be interested in the history of Canadian settlement services for immigrants can refer to Vineberg (2012).

Questions for Critical Thought

1. Identify the major similarities in migration patterns to the United States and to Canada.

2. What are the major differences in migration patterns to the United States and to Canada?

3. Discuss the major reasons for migration from Canada to the United States in the nineteenth century.

4. Identify the areas of discrimination in pre-1960s Canadian and American immigration policy.

5. What are the major differences in current immigration policy in Canada and the United States?

Key Readings

Citizenship and Immigration Canada (CIC) (2013) *Facts and Figures, 2012*. Ottawa: Citizenship and Immigration Canada, Research and Evaluation Branch. www.cic.gc.ca/english/resources/statistics/menu-fact.asp (Accessed April 30, 2014)

Harvard University Library Open Collections Program (n.d.) Aspiration, Acculturation and Impact: Immigration to the United States, 1789–1930. ocp.hul.harvard.edu/immigration/index.html (Accessed July 7, 2013)

Library and Archives Canada (n.d.) Moving Here, Staying Here: The Canadian Immigrant Experience. www.collectionscanada.gc.ca/immigrants/021017-1000-e.html

United States Department of Homeland Security (2013) *2012 Yearbook of Immigration Statistics*. Washington, DC: US Department of Homeland Security, Office of Immigration Statistics. www.dhs.gov/yearbook-immigration-statistics (Accessed April 30, 2014)

Media Links

The Canadian Museum of Immigration at Pier 21:
www.pier21.ca/home
Canada's national museum of immigration is located at Pier 21 in Halifax, where more than
a million immigrants arrived between 1928 and 1971. Its website hosts a growing number
of historical documents and oral histories relating to Canadian immigration.

Ellis Island—National Park Service:
www.nps.gov/elis/index.htm
Ellis Island was the main US port of entry for immigrants from 1898 until 1924. Its website
has historical documents and photos and multimedia relating to immigration to the US.

U.S. Immigration Before 1965—History.com:
www.history.com/topics/u-s-immigration-before-1965
This History.com website has a summary of the history of US immigration and several
videos relating to the history of immigration to the US.

Crossroads of Culture—The Canadian Museum of History:
www.historymuseum.ca/cmc/exhibitions/tresors/immigration/index_e.shtml
This Canadian Museum of History website contains links to immigration-related artifacts,
photos, and documents in its collection.

References

An Act Respecting Chinese Immigration (1923) 13–14 George V, Chap. 38.
An Act to Amend the Immigration Act and to Repeal the Chinese Immigration Act (1947)
11 George VI Chap. 19. www.cic.gc.ca/english/multiculturalism/asian/60act.asp
(Accessed July 10, 2013)
Bernard, William S. (1950) *American Immigration Policy—A Reappraisal.* Port
Washington, NY: Kennikat Press (republished 1969).
Chinese Immigration Act (1885) 48–49 Vict. Chap. 71.
Citizenship and Immigration Canada (CIC) (2012) *Facts and Figures, 2011.* Ottawa:
Citizenship and Immigration Canada, Research and Evaluation Branch.
www.cic.gc.ca/english/resources/statistics/menu-fact.asp (Accessed July 7, 2013)
Citizenship and Immigration Canada (CIC) (2013) Six Selection Factors—Federal Skilled
Workers, 3 May. www.cic.gc.ca/english/immigrate/skilled/apply-factors.asp
(Accessed July 13, 2013)

Constitution Act (1867). laws.justice.gc.ca/eng/Const/Const_index.html
(Accessed July 3, 2013)

Department of Manpower and Immigration (1967/1975) Immigration Statistics 1966, 1974.
Ottawa: Queen's Printer for Canada. epe.lac-bac.gc.ca/100/202/301/immigration_
statistics-ef/index.html (Accessed July 13, 2013)

Filindra, A. and M. Kovács (2011) Analysing US State Legislative Resolutions on
Immigrants and Immigration: The Role of Immigration Federalism.
International Migration 59(4):33–50. doi: 10.1111/j.1468–2435.2010.00658.x

Great Britain, Committee on the Survey of the Coasts, &c. of Scotland (1803)
First Report-Emigration, House of Commons, Reports, Vol. IV, Paper No. 80. London:
House of Commons.

Hawkins, Freda (1988) *Canada and Immigration—Public Policy and Public Concern*
2nd ed. Montreal: McGill-Queen's University Press.

House of Commons Debates (1899) July 27.

Hutchinson, E.P. (1981) *Legislative History of American Immigration Policy 1798–1965.*
Philadelphia: University of Pennsylvania Press.

Immigration and Refugee Protection Act (2001) (S.C. 2001, c.27). laws-lois.justice.gc.ca/
eng/acts/I-2.5/index.html (Accessed July 3, 2013)

Keenleyside, Hugh L. (1948) Canadian Immigration Policy. *International Journal*
3(3):222–238.

Kelley, Ninette and Michael Trebilcock (2010) *The Making of the Mosaic: A History of
Canadian Immigration Policy*. Toronto: University of Toronto Press.

New York Times (1911) Bruce Walker, Autocrat of Canada's Immigrants, 15 October.

Order in Council (1931) PC 1931-0695, March 21, 1931.

Order in Council (1967) PC 1967-1616, August 16, 1967.

Richmond, Ted and John Shields (2005) NGO-Government Relations and Immigrant
Services: Contradictions and Challenges. *Journal of International Migration and
Integration* 6(3/4):513–526.

Sharp, Paul F. (1950) When Our West Moved North. *American Historical Review*
55(2):286–300.

United Nations (1948) *Universal Declaration of Human Rights.*
www.un.org/en/documents/udhr/index.shtml (Accessed July 10, 2013)

United States Constitution (1787) www.usconstitution.net (Accessed July 3, 2013)

United States Department of Homeland Security (2012) *2011 Yearbook of Immigration
Statistics.* Washington, DC: US Department of Homeland Security, Office of
Immigration Statistics. www.dhs.gov/yearbook-immigration-statistics
(Accessed July 7, 2013)

Vineberg, Robert (2011) History of Federal–Provincial Relations in Canadian Immigration and Integration. In John Biles, Meyer Burstien, James Frideres, Erin Tolley, and Robert Vineberg (eds.) *Integration and Inclusion of Minorities across Canada*, pp. 17–43. Montreal: McGill-Queen's University Press.

Vineberg, Robert (2012) *Responding to Immigrants' Settlement Needs: The Canadian Experience*. Dordrecht, Netherlands: Springer.

Wishnie, Michael J. (2002) Introduction: Immigration and Federalism. *NYU Annual Survey of American Law* 58(3):283–293.

Woodsworth, J.S. (1909) *Strangers Within Our Gates, or Coming Canadians*. 2nd ed. Toronto: Methodist Mission Rooms.

Chapter 2

THE TRANSFORMATION OF US IMMIGRATION POLICY

PHILIP KRETSEDEMAS

Introduction

The United States has been a centre point for international and global migration for more than three centuries. In the eighteenth and nineteenth centuries it was the primary destination for all European migrant flows (Hatton and Williamson 2008:12–16) and since the late twentieth century it has become the primary destination for all global migrant flows (Migration Policy Institute 2013). Since the late 1980s, US migration flows have undergone a new period of expansion, rivalling the **immigration** boom that ended in the 1920s. In absolute numbers, more migrants are entering the US today than at any other time in US history, although the proportionate size of the US foreign-born population is slightly smaller today than it was a century ago (Kandel 2011:2, US DHS 2013a).

This new era of US migration contains elements of continuity and change. The imperatives of economic growth and family reunification are prominent features of federal **immigration policy**, as they have been for the better part of the twentieth century. Meanwhile, the national origin of US migrants has become more diverse, and European nationals have become a relatively small minority of the cohort of permanent settlers. During this same period US migration flows became increasingly intracontinental, with the majority of new migrants hailing from Mexico, Central America, and South America (US DHS 2013b), and these intracontinental flows have contributed to the expansion of the unauthorized migrant population.

Notably, the growth of this population occurred during the same time that US–Latin American trade relations were being liberalized and free market reforms were being implemented across the Americas (Pastor and Wise 1994). This also happens to be the same period when the US began to make new investments in border security and **interior enforcement** (Cornelius 2001). Hence, economic liberalization, the expansion of migrant flows, and the intensification of immigration enforcement have all occurred in tandem with each other.

This combination of restrictive and open qualities is one of the defining features of US migration policy in the present day. The rest of the chapter examines this relationship in more depth. It describes how the open and closed features of US migration policy are reflected in the composition of US migration flows, the dynamics of migrant recruitment, and the priorities for immigration enforcement. The chapter closes by discussing patterns of social and economic **integration** that have taken shape in this new era of US migration.

Putting Immigration Policy in Context

The process whereby immigration levels expand alongside efforts to control immigration is not unique to the United States. James Hollifield (2004) has described this situation as a **liberal paradox** that is shared by many Western industrial nations. The egalitarian norms and open economies of these nations lead their policies to tilt toward an **open borders** approach to immigrant recruitment. But other factors that are integral to the workings of liberal-democratic societies can lead their immigration policies to become increasingly selective and concerned with security. Public opinion in the US, for example, has historically supported a more conservative approach toward immigrant recruitment than has the opinion of federal policymakers (Brader, Valentino, and Suhay 2008). This body of opinion can exert itself on federal policymakers through the relatively open political process that is afforded to citizens in liberal-democratic societies. Meanwhile, free market advocates who favour an open borders approach to immigration tend to support restrictive measures for other reasons. In this case, restrictive policies are used as a filter—selecting more productive migrants and screening out "undesirables," and not to effect an overall reduction in immigration levels.

The practical result is that restrictive immigration policies can be shaped by an unstable confluence of interests, some opposing the expansion of migration flows and others supporting a more controlled expansion of these same flows. As Daniel Tichenor (2002) has explained, there are several distinct ideological perspectives that have shaped US immigration policy over the past two centuries, and these perspectives can align in different ways depending on the political context. Constituencies that support the legalization of unauthorized migrants for humanitarian reasons may still oppose the overarching policy agenda of free market advocates who view legalization as a more efficient way of securing the labour of a low-wage workforce. Meanwhile, constituencies that support controls on immigration for the sake of protecting the economic interests of native-born workers may still oppose restrictions on migrant rights and object to constituencies that want to restrict migrants for cultural and racial reasons.

It is also important to keep in mind that migration trends are not strictly de-termined by federal policy or public opinion. For example, the changing demo-graphics of US migration flows are often attributed to the 1965 Immigration Act, which eliminated national origin restrictions favouring Europeans. But as Massey and Pren (2001) have explained, the 1965 Immigration Act also included Western Hemisphere quotas that effectively reduced options for legal migration from Latin America. The intensification of **border enforcement** from the 1970s onward may have inadvertently contributed to the growth of the Latino population by giving unauthorized migrants added incentive to settle permanently in the US, so as to avoid frequent border crossings. Hence, Massey and Pren conclude that the growth of Latino migration, from the 1970s onward, occurred despite the efforts of the 1965 Immigration Act, and not because of it.

The decline in European migration from the mid-twentieth century onward has also been shaped by a number of macrosocietal transformations that lie beyond the influence of US immigration policy. The reorganization of the global economy from the 1970s onward, the collapse of the Soviet Union, and expansion of global markets from the late 1980s onward all had a major impact on the dynamics of global migration. One practical consequence is that many European nations that were known for exporting emigrant labour to other nations—such as Ireland, Italy, Greece, and Portugal—were converted into nations of immigration as they began receiving migrant labour from post-Soviet Russia and the Global South (Cornelius and Tsuda 2004). Meanwhile, over the course of the twentieth century the average education and income level of the native populations of these nations increased significantly, and the average birth rate declined (Lesthaeghe 2010). As a result, the pool of "surplus" Europeans available to migrate to the US began to dry up, and European nations became more reliant on migrant workers to provide the mostly low-wage services needed by a more affluent and aging population.

The Expansion of the Nonimmigrant Flow

The change in the national origins of US migrants is one of the more obvious trans-formations that has occurred over the past half century, but it is not necessarily the most important one. A transformation of equal, if not greater, significance is the growing number of migrants admitted with a temporary legal status. This transform-ation has become a defining feature of present day migration trends, and it offers some compelling insights into the open and closed qualities of US migration policy that were described above.

At the beginning of the twentieth century, the flow of noncitizen visitors to the US was a fraction of the immigration flow. By the end of the twentieth century, this relationship was flipped on its head. The annual flow of permanent settlers to the US is now exceeded by a flow of **nonimmigrants**, at a rate of 30 to 1 if counting only air and sea entries—the difference is much larger when land-border entries from Canada and Mexico are included (US DHS 2013c). This unprecedented flow of nonimmigrants has been shaped by a variety of conditions that are tied to the workings of the global economy, including relatively cheap means of international transport and communication, an expanding sphere of global trade, the emergence of new coordinating centres for this process of economic growth that are still located in the advanced industrialized world, and the globalization of professional and low-skilled labour markets (Hatton and Williamson 2008:203–224; Kretsedemas 2012b).

It also bears noting that European migration to the US decreased only among the annual pool of permanent settlers. During the same period of time when European migrants were decreasing among the pool of permanent settlers, the number of Europeans admitted with a temporary legal status increased dramatically, growing more than 30 times in size, from less than 500,000 per year in the early 1960s to more than 15 million per year by the 2000s (US DHS 1997:104–107; 2013d). This transformation is not unique to the European migration flow. Nationals from all regions of the world are entering the US today in record numbers. The vast majority of these people enter as visitors with a temporary legal status who are officially classified as "nonimmigrants."

The growth of the nonimmigrant flow provides a good example of the econom-ic priorities that have been guiding US migration policy from the 1980s onward. Migrants have increasingly been selected on the basis of their economic utility, and this selection process has gravitated, markedly, toward the recruitment of temporary migrants. A good example is recruitment trends for temporary workers. Throughout the 1980s and 1990s, the number of migrants recruited as temporary workers climbed steadily (see Figure 2.1). Since 1998, the temporary worker flow has consistently out-paced the growth of the permanent settler population, and by 2012 this flow was

Figure 2.1

Temporary Workers and Permanent Settlers: Selected Years, 1981–2012*

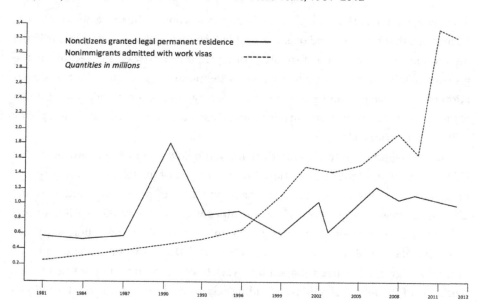

* Nonimmigrant data includes persons admitted with work visas along with spouses and dependants who were admitted through the legal status of the work visa holder. Data does not include migrants admitted with student/exchange visas (S and J visas).

Sources: US DHS 2013a; 2013c; 2010; 2005.

almost three times the size of the growth of the permanent resident population.

Another important development is the blurring of the lines between the **immigrant** population and the nonimmigrant flow. Between 1989 and 1992 more than 2 million noncitizens—most of whom were Mexican unauthorized migrants—were granted permanent settler status by the pathways to legalization created by the **1986 Immigration Reform and Control Act (IRCA)** (Villar 1999). This marked the first time in US history when the majority of people who were granted permanent resident status in a given year came from a population that was already living and working on US soil. In the late 1990s this trend persisted, but for a different reason. From this time onward, new arrivals were gradually eclipsed by people adjusting to permanent residence from a nonimmigrant status (see Figure 2.2). This transformation was not punctuated by the same dramatic surge in adjustments that characterized the IRCA legalization process. It has unfolded more incrementally and unevenly, but it has also been sustained for a much longer period of time. The vast majority of noncitizens who were legalized under IRCA did so within a four-year period. In contrast, the more recent process—where adjustments to permanent residence have

Figure 2.2
Pathways to Permanent Residence: New Arrivals and Adjustments from Nonimmigrant
Status, Selected Years, 1988–2012

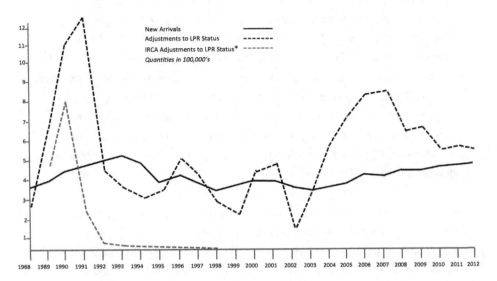

* IRCA adjustments to Lawful Permanent Resident status are also included within quantities for all adjustments to LPR status
(black dashed line).

Sources: US DHS (2013c, 2004).

overtaken new arrivals—has been sustained for well over 15 years. And whereas the IRCA legalization program was of limited duration, the more recent growth of the **adjustee population** has been facilitated by multifarious routes to permanent residence that have become an accepted and permanent feature of US visa policy. As a result, the nonimmigrant flow has become the driving force behind the growth of the traditional immigrant (permanent settler) population.

The majority of people who are granted permanent resident status in the US today are not new arrivals but nonimmigrant residents who typically have to wait for a period of 5 years, 10 years, or more before their application for permanent residence is approved. And in addition to the hundreds of thousands of nonimmigrants who adjust to immigrant status each year there is a population, easily four or five times larger, of immigrant hopefuls who are waiting for their applications to be approved.

The nonimmigrant flow is also stratified by skill level. For example, most Asian nationals attain permanent resident status in the US through family sponsorship. However, the ability of Asian migrants to apply for permanent resident status for spouses, children, and other family members is heavily conditioned by their

Case Example 1: The "Anchor Baby" Discourse

In the **public sphere**, economic complaints about immigrants can become intertwined with racial and gender stereotypes of immigrants. The stigma of welfare dependency, for example, has historically focused on the "poor choices" of poor, **racialized** women (Roberts 1997). Concerns about immigrant "overuse" of hospital emergency room services have similarly focused on the pregnancies of unauthorized Latinas (Chavez 2008:73–96). One of the more recent examples of these concerns is the discourse on "anchor babies" (Ignatow and Williams 2011). According to the **anchor baby discourse**, undocumented immigrant women deliberately give birth to children on US soil, with the expectation that their household will benefit from the citizenship status of the infant child.

Research on these "mixed status" households has found a very different trend, however. US citizen children in these households are more likely to experience socioeconomic barriers—such as higher rates of poverty and limited access to health services—which are indirectly shaped by the noncitizen and undocumented status of other household members (Van Hook, Glick, and Bean 1999). Meanwhile, other researchers have explained that the factors driving unauthorized migration have more to do with labour market dynamics than the attraction of social welfare services, especially considering that unauthorized migration continued to boom after the federal government reduced welfare entitlements for both citizens and noncitizens (Hanson 2007, 2008; Massey and Pren 2001). In this regard, the anchor baby discourse can be faulted for providing an oversimplified explanation of the factors shaping immigrant fertility that reinforces stereotypes of low income minority populations. Ironically, the anchor baby discourse also stigmatizes the same proclivity toward family formation that has been shown to have positive effects by research on immigrant families (Abraído-Lanza, Dohrenwend, Ng-Mak, and Turner 1999; Bersani and Doherty 2013; Oropesa and Landale 2004). This research, consistent with the **Latino paradox** thesis, has shown that family formation and the maintenance of family ties correlate with higher rates of mental well-being and law abiding behaviour, though these family ties tend to erode over time, as immigrants are exposed to stressors that weaken their social connections.

income and education. The US visa system is skewed toward recruiting these sorts of professional-class migrants, as the vast majority of visas are used to recruit skilled migrants with college-level education or higher (Rosenzweig 2006). And these high-skilled visa holders are afforded more options for adjustment and family sponsorship than low-skilled migrant workers.

In contrast, Latino migrants, and Mexican nationals in particular, are concentrated in the pool of lower-skilled migrant workers. It is also notable that unauthorized migration is the primary way that low-skilled migrant workers enter the US, and that Latin American nationals account for approximately 75% of this undocumented migrant population (Hoefer, Rytina, and Baker 2012:4–5).

There are visas available for the recruitment of low-wage migrant workers, primarily the H2 visa. However, the number of migrants recruited with these visas is very small compared to the annual growth of the unauthorized migrant population. Furthermore, these work visas for low-skilled migrants do not offer a route to permanent resident status (Kretsedemas 2012a:22–28). And although the US government has periodically tried to legalize portions of the undocumented workforce, its immigration spending and policy priorities have been mainly focused on enforcement and border control. Hence, professional-class migrants are recruited in a way that affords them an easier, but not guaranteed, route to permanent resident status. The recruitment of low-skilled migrants, by comparison, restricts options for **settlement** and family reunification. The practical result of these recruitment strategies can be seen in settlement trends for Latino and Asian migrants. In recent years, more than 40% of all people who have been granted legal permanent resident status in the US have been Asian nationals, compared to only 28.8% for Latin American nationals.

These trends are striking, especially if one considers that the US Latino population is more than three times the size of the US Asian population. One might expect that Latino migrants would have a "home field advantage" compared to Asian migrants, given the geographic proximity of the US and Latin America and the richly developed transborder social networks of Latino migrant populations. But it would appear that this "advantage" has been realized mainly in the overconcentration of Latinos in the low-skill work visa population and the unauthorized migrant population, as noted earlier. Meanwhile, Asian nationals are disproportionately concentrated in the pool of professional-class visa holders, most of whom are admitted to the US with the right to apply for legal permanent residence. These trends underscore the point that options for family sponsorship are not strictly determined by the size of a migrant's US-based family networks. Skill level also matters.

This disparate treatment of high- and low-skilled migrants has intensified a trend that can be traced to the 1965 Immigration Act (Massey and Pren 2001). Restricted options for permanent settlement have not necessarily deterred low-skilled migrants

Table 2.1

Work Visas and Attainment of Permanent Resident Status for Asian and Latino Migrants, 2010–2012

	Proportion of US Population (2010)	Settler Population Granted Permanent Resident Status (2010–2012)	Professional-Class Work Visas* (2010–2012)	Work Visas for Low-Skilled Labour** (2010–2012)
Asian	5.6%	40.3%	33.9%	1%
Latino	16.3%	28.8%	17%	90.1%

* Using statistics for H1, O, P, and L visas.

** Using statistics for H2 visas.

Sources: Hoeffel, Rastogi, Kim, and Shahid (2012); Humes, Jones, and Ramirez, (2011); US DHS (2013b, 2013f, 2012b, 2011).

from entering the US; they have just created a situation where these migrants are entering with a less secure legal status and, quite often, with no legal status whatsoever. This situation has been used by immigration control advocates to draw attention to the problem of the US's broken borders and by immigration reform advocates to draw attention to the problem of the US's broken immigration system. But it is also consistent with strategies for recruiting low-wage migrant labour that can be traced to the early twentieth century (Kretsedemas 2012a:47–50). Whether they are admitted legally as guest workers or informally as undocumented workers, low-wage migrants have historically been recruited under the assumption that they will not become permanent settlers. In practice, however, this is not always the case. Moreover, the economic forces that draw these migrants into the US tend to clash with other economic and political dynamics that inhibit their long-term integration. These tensions are explored further in the next section.

Immigrants and Welfare Policy

In the US, public opinion on immigrants and the economy can get pulled in contrary directions. Immigrants are often depicted by pundits, policymakers, and the mainstream media as "hard workers" who are good for the economy (Strauss 2012). But immigrants have also been widely criticized for adding to the fiscal burden of middle-income tax payers (Calavita 1996). This criticism is generally directed at low-skilled immigrants, who are blamed for costing the public tax base more than they contribute in tax payments. Academic research has shown that there are parts of the country and ethnic networks in which immigrant welfare use exceeds the national average and that these rates of service use can vary widely between federal and local services or between welfare cash payments and other kinds of public assistance, including publicly funded health services and public education (Borjas 1999). But there is also evidence that many low-income migrant groups use fewer public services than native-borns of a similar socioeconomic status, and that these reduced rates of service access have been conditioned, in part, by worries about their legal status (Van Hook and Bean 2009). It also bears noting that the fiscal cost of migrant populations is just a particular example of the fiscal cost posed by the entire low income population. For example, the rising fiscal costs facing US metropolitan areas are being driven by poverty rates that are rising among both migrants and natives (Joassart-Marcelli, Musso, and Wolch 2005). When viewed in this light, the rising fiscal cost of the immigrant population, and of the US poor more generally, can be understood as a byproduct of widening patterns of income **stratification** in the US.

Nevertheless, the public discourse on the "tax burden" posed by the poor in the US has mainly focused on immigrants, and US policymakers have attempted to respond to these immigration-specific complaints. From the 1990s onward, federal and local governments enacted a number of policies that were geared toward reducing the public costs incurred by immigrant populations. The **1996 Welfare Reform Act (PROWRA)** was a major turning point that introduced unprecedented restrictions on federal-level social services for immigrants (Kretsedemas and Aparicio 2004). These immigrant-specific restrictions were introduced by the Clinton administration in response to a growing climate of anti-immigrant sentiment spurred on by concerns about immigrant welfare use and the rapid growth of the immigrant population, especially the unauthorized (Singer 2004). Notably, the Clinton administration implemented these welfare restrictions during the same time that it was facilitating the continued expansion of US migration flows (Fuchs 1993), expanding the powers of US immigration enforcement by way of the **1996 Immigration Reform Act** and the Antiterrorism and Effective Death Penalty Act (Kurzban 2008), and advancing a program of free-market reforms at the national and global level (Skonieczny 2001). This platform provides an excellent example of the open and restrictive features of US immigration policy that were described at the beginning of the chapter. The migration priorities of the US executive office from the Reagan-Bush era to the present have been very similar: expanding migration flows while increasing enforcement and restricting migrant rights (Kretsedemas 2012a:62–72; Tichenor 2002).

The Clinton administration did use its executive powers, however, to exempt some categories of immigrants from the five-year ban on welfare use that was introduced by the 1996 Welfare Reform Act (Singer 2004). State and local governments were also permitted to use their social service programs—which were partly funded by federal monies—to assist high-need immigrant groups that were barred by the

Case Example 2: Migrants and Human Rights

From the late 1980s onward, there has been a broad-based shift in US law toward restricting migrant rights and cultivating a more selective system of migrant recruitment. During this same period, however, there have been efforts to strengthen migrant rights that draw on precedents and declarations in the realm of international law. One of the central goals of this movement has been to advance a discourse on inalienable rights to which all people are entitled and which are not tied to national membership.

The 1948 Universal Declaration of Human Rights (UDHR) has figured prominently in this new transnational discourse on migrant rights. The UDHR has been especially influential in the realm of refugee law (Goodwin-Gill 1989). In recent decades, however, it has begun to have more influence on rights discourse for labour migrants, and has been used by advocates seeking to defend migrants in the US court system (ACLU Human Rights Program 2014). Notably, human rights discourse has also increasingly surfaced as a consideration in US Supreme Court deliberations on migration issues (Dauvergne 2012). These examples illustrate how human rights discourse can be used to inform and supplement the rights afforded to migrants under national law. There are also more ambitious efforts to advance a system of rights that is largely independent of national law (Soysal 1998). In this case, human rights can be understood as the forerunner to a paradigm of global citizenship that may be recognized by national governments, but which is fashioned by international courts and transnational governing bodies.

federal restrictions. But in the years that followed, the federal government continued to reduce its grant support for state and local governments, which intensified the fiscal crisis many states were dealing with as a result of state and local tax cuts that had been enacted during the robust economic growth of the late 1990s (Lav and Oliff 2008; Singer 2004). These developments intensified a complex of tensions that had been building for some time. Although the public costs of immigration are disproportionately shouldered by local governments, immigration policy decisions are primarily determined by the federal government. Furthermore, the economic benefits of immigration, being largely privatized, do not address the fiscal strain facing state and local governments.

Immigration Enforcement

Perhaps the single most important transformation in immigration enforcement over the past three decades has been the changing relationship between border enforcement and interior enforcement. The border patrol has been historically responsible for the vast majority of apprehensions and removals of noncitizens. Most of these noncitizens have been apprehended at or near the US border and charged with entering the US without authorization.

Whereas border enforcement is carried out primarily by the US border control, interior enforcement is carried out by US Immigration Customs and Enforcement and, more recently, by other federal agencies like the FBI and the US Marshals Service. Unlike border enforcement, interior enforcement usually targets immigrants who have been living in the US for some time, many of whom entered legally, but whose legal status expired for some reason, or who became eligible for deportation due to a criminal conviction.

There are also some important differences in the way that border and interior enforcement trends have varied over time. Border enforcement apprehensions have fluctuated widely over the past two decades, reaching a high of 1.6 million in 2000, dropping by half a few years later, and dipping even further in recent years (see Figure 2.3). But from the 1990s to the present, the number of noncitizens who have been deported by interior enforcement has grown in a steady linear fashion, increasing by over 1,000%, from approximately 33,000 deportations in 1991 to almost 400,000 deportations by 2011 (see Figure 2.3). Some demographers have explained that the decline in unauthorized entries since 2008 has a lot to do with the decline in border apprehensions from this point onward, which indicates that the recessionary economy had more to do with the decline in unauthorized migration than border enforcement itself (Passel, Cohn, and Gonzalez-Barrera 2013). Notably, the recession did not have the same effect on the interior enforcement deportation caseload.

These statistics demonstrate that the federal government's investments in immigration enforcement have had their most pronounced impact on its interior enforcement capacities. It so happens that spending on border enforcement reached record levels in the late 1990s and 2000s (Meissner, Kerwin, Chishti, and Bergeron 2013). Even so, border patrol apprehensions still seem to be more sensitive to fluctuations in the size of the unauthorized migrant population, as well as moral panics over unauthorized migration (see Welch 2002). The expansion of interior enforcement, on the other hand, has been more continual and systematic. It does not appear to be an adaptive response to changing migration levels, but rather an attempt to proactively regulate the migration flow that is focused on monitoring and apprehending migrants after they have entered the US. It also sets the stage for

Case Example 3: Changing Paradigms of Immigration Enforcement: From Unauthorized Border Crossers to "Visa Over-Stayers"

Over the past two decades, interior enforcement actions have gradually eclipsed those of the border enforcement. These enforcement trends can be read in light of the changing composition of the unauthorized migrant population. Border enforcement primarily targets the unauthorized land-border entrant. But the growth of the nonimmigrant flow draws attention to another kind of unauthorized migrant: the **visa over-stayer**, who enters with a temporary legal status and can "lose" this status for a variety of reasons. In the mid-2000s, in the middle of the last great unauthorized migration boom, it was estimated that visa over-stayers were responsible for between 25 and 40% of the annual growth of the unauthorized migrant population (Passel, 2007).

Most of these unauthorized migrants enter the US by air. The federal government has estimated that between 2 and 3% of all noncitizens who enter the US this way over-stay their visas, amounting to between 100,000 and 200,000 persons per year (GAO 1995, 2008: 2). This kind of unauthorized migration is the inevitable result of a policy that allows tens of millions of noncitizens to enter the US as economic guests and is reliant on a complex system of incentives and disincentives to encourage these migrants to leave once their legal status has expired. As a result, the labour market regulation priorities that have historically informed US immigration enforcement (Calavita 2010[1992]) have been joined by a new focus on policing the migrant flow for "criminal aliens" and security threats (Welch 2002).

a relatively new set of enforcement priorities.

Immigration control advocates have historically lobbied for an immigration enforcement agenda that is geared toward restricting migration levels. The attrition-enforcement proposals of the present day are a good example of this approach (Krikorian 2005). The general aim of these proposals is to use get-tough enforcement practices and immigration laws to encourage unauthorized migrants to self-deport. There is little macro-level evidence, however, that immigration enforcement has been used to restrict the growth of the entire migration flow. When enforcement is used as part of a broader immigration control strategy, it has usually targeted particular segments of the migrant population who are often racialized in the popular imagination, such as Chinese nationals in the early twentieth century or

Figure 2.3
Border and Interior Enforcement Actions, 1991–2011

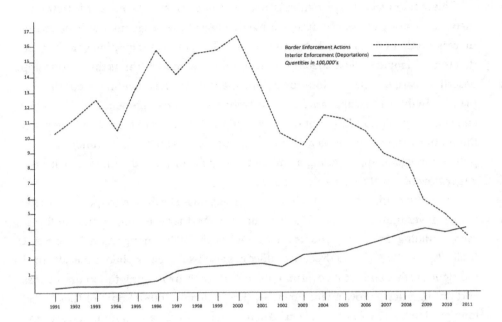

Source: US DHS (2012c).

Arab-Muslim nationals after September 11, 2001 (Hing 2004:28–50; Sheikh 2008). The Mexican unauthorized migrant flow has been the main target for this kind of enforcement, throughout the twentieth century and into the present day. There is evidence, however, that efforts to control the size of this population have been shaped by labour market concerns and not a "classic" restrictionist agenda.

Researchers have shown that border patrol apprehensions of Mexican migrants tend to relax during periods of high market demand for migrant labour and intensify when there is a perceived oversupply of migrant labour. Kitty Calavita (2010) has used this labour market model of immigration enforcement to explain how US immigration enforcement regulated Bracero workers from the 1940s through the 1960s. Calavita's argument has been corroborated by research on the intensification of immigration enforcement in the early 1990s, which increased employer control over unauthorized migrants without effectively restricting unauthorized migration and also afforded employers a new legal loophole for employing unauthorized migrants (Wishnie 2007). Gordon Hanson (2008) has used a similar argument to make sense of immigrant (un)employment and deportation levels in the recession era (2007–2012). Hanson has explained that unauthorized Latino migrants are used as the "shock absorbers" for the US economy—being absorbed into fast growing but unstable labour markets during periods of peak growth and downsized in times of economic decline.

This labour market explanation is most pertinent to the role that border enforcement has historically played in regulating the flow of low-wage migrant labour. But there is another relationship between migration levels and immigration enforcement that is not adequately described by this labour market model. This is the relationship described earlier in which interior enforcement intensifies in a linear, continuous manner. In this case, it appears that immigration enforcement is being used to police an expanding migrant flow, not to restrict migrant flows or to respond to temporal fluctuations in labour market demand. Immigration enforcement functions as a policing mechanism, targeting a small minority of "unwanted" migrants within a larger flow of mostly "desirable" migrants.

The reach of this policing strategy has been expanded by the new opportunities the federal government has created for local police to partner with immigration enforcement, building on the precedents established by the 1996 Immigration Reform Act (Idilbi 2007–2008). The US Executive Office has also issued legal opinions that affirmed the right of state and local governments to craft their own immigration ordinances and immigration enforcement practices (Kretsedemas 2008). Some of these local immigration laws have been challenged in the federal courts, and in some cases, by the federal government itself. A good example is Arizona's Senate Bill 1070, which gave local police broad leeway to question anyone they suspected of being undocumented, and was subsequently challenged by the US Department of Justice (NCSL 2011). The Supreme Court decision in this case struck down most of the enforcement practices that were authorized by this state law. But it left intact the language that authorized local police to screen the legal status of "suspected illegals" which, ironically, had been one of the most controversial features of the law. This Supreme Court decision did not overturn the existing legal precedent that has established unauthorized presence as a civil violation, for the purpose of state and local law enforcement (NCSL 2012). But it has strengthened the legal precedent that allows local police to actively screen people for legal status, and once identified, legal status identifiers can be transferred to federal enforcement, who may choose to criminally prosecute them.

These sorts of federal-local partnerships demonstrate how interior enforcement is being used as an integrated method for apprehending a wide variety of criminal and noncriminal immigration violators. And if deportation rates continue to climb, as they have for the past two decades, it is quite possible that interior enforcement will overtake the border patrol as the primary way that unauthorized migrants are apprehended and removed from the US.

Divergent Patterns of Integration

The open and closed qualities of US migration policy are also reflected in patterns of **integration** for US immigrants. As Fix and Capps (2005) have observed, the US's open policy on migrant recruitment is at odds with the sparse resources it devotes to immigrant incorporation. This apparent lack of support for immigrant integration services may appear to conflict with the popular image of the US as an assimilationist **melting pot**. However, it is worth noting that there is a history of assimilationist discourse in the US that intersects with both liberal and conservative ideas about small government, personal responsibility, and laissez-faire market economics (Salins 1997). From this perspective, sparse government support for immigrant integration is not antithetical to **assimilation**; it is a strategy for encouraging the self-reliant behaviours that are idealized by this discourse on assimilation. These priorities carry important implications for the way that US policymakers and scholars have dealt with the matter of immigrant culture.

It is widely observed that the US has been generally receptive to the religious cultures of immigrants, whereas European nations have tended to construct immigrant religious culture as an obstacle to integration (Alba and Foner 2008). There are many reasons why this is so, but some cultural factors worth noting are the virtues of productivity and self-reliance that have historically defined US assimilationist discourse and that have also been closely tied to popular ideas about religious morality (Zolberg 2008). When viewed through the lens of these values, immigrant religious culture becomes a conduit for assimilation by stressing the cultivation of moral qualities that promote economic self-sufficiency and law abiding behaviour. **Ethnic pluralist theory** in the US has advanced a secularized version of this same argument, explaining how immigrant ethnicity can be understood as a cultural and sociopolitical resource that, among other things, reduces immigrant reliance on entitlement programs (Glazer and Moynihan 1970; Omi and Winant 1994:14–23). By mobilizing as an ethnic group, immigrants cultivate their own **social capital** and other resources that enable them to "pick themselves up by their own bootstraps" and find their own place in the political and economic structures of the wider society. The end result is that US national identity can embrace an assimilationist worldview that is heavily mediated by a belief in personal freedom and an open market economic philosophy that allows for a high degree of racial and ethnic diversity at the local level.

Nevertheless, it is ironic that **naturalization** rates for US migrants are lower than they are for migrants in Canada, where the federal government has embraced a discourse on **multiculturalism**. This difference cannot be explained just by the way that both societies have symbolically defined the nation, but also by their fiscal support for immigrant integration and the legal and political apparatus they have created to mediate the naturalization process. As Irene Bloemraad (2006) has explained, the Canadian system has placed more emphasis on incorporation and settlement, whereas the US system has been more concerned with the selective screening of applicants.

Meanwhile, the expanded nonimmigrant flow has complicated the very idea of long-term settlement. The integration process becomes more ambiguous when it can no longer be assumed that migrants are entering the US with the intent to settle, and when permanent settlement is the serendipitous outcome of decisions made while hopping between various temporary visas. Furthermore, as discussed earlier, patterns of migrant recruitment have become more stratified over the last few decades, with the informalized recruitment of low-skilled migrants and selective recruitment of professional class migrants increasing in tandem with each other. The practical result is that there is no longer one predominant pattern of immigrant integration that is geared toward cultural assimilation and upward mobility. Instead pathways to immigrant integration have become more varied and unequal. The remainder of this chapter describes several of these patterns.

Divergent Patterns of Economic Integration

In the mid-twentieth century, immigrants typically earned less than native-born citizens when they first entered the US, but closed this wage gap within the space of 15 years (Chiswick 1978). However, from the 1990s onward, immigrants have had less success in closing this wage gap. One reason for this disparity is that the educational achievement of the native-born population has been increasing at a faster pace than immigrant education (Card 2005). Another contributing factor is the increasingly stratified wage structure of US labour markets from the 1980s onward (Butcher and Dinardo 2002–2003); notably, migrant workers are disproportionately concentrated in the bottom end of these labour markets.

In many US urban centres, including Chicago, Los Angeles, New York, and Miami, the majority of low-wage workers are now noncitizens (Bernhardt et al. 2009). Within the low-wage employment sector, income disparities and vulnerability to illegal workplace practices, especially **wage theft**, vary by legal status and involve distinctions between naturalized citizens and noncitizens and between noncitizens with and without legal status. There is also evidence that the citizen-noncitizen pay gap becomes much bigger if length of residence in the US is taken into account. Latino noncitizens who recently migrated (less than a year in the US) can earn as much as 60% less than equally skilled white or black native-born workers (Catanzarite 2000). This gap closes considerably for Latino noncitizens who have lived in the US for five years or more, though it tends to be larger for Latinos who are employed in ethnically segmented employment sectors—jobs like meatpacking or garment manufacturing, which recruit heavily from the Latino migrant population.

It is worth noting that these disparities are not exclusive to low-wage migrant labour. Highly skilled noncitizens who recently migrated to the US typically earn less than similarly qualified native-born, and these disparities can be amplified and extended by the strategies used to recruit work visa holders (Luthra 2009). Payal Bannerjee (2010) has also shown that there can be significant income disparities among these migrants, varying by the type of visa that was used to recruit them into US labour markets. So, whether one is looking at distinctions between native and noncitizen workers, between legal and unauthorized low-wage Latino labour, or between more and less secure temporary visa categories among high-skilled Asian labour, it is possible to trace a similar relationship between insecure legal status and exposure to precarities that result in decreased earnings and increased vulnerability to layoffs.

There is little argument, however, that these inequalities are most severe for lower-skilled migrant workers and their families. For example, 2011 marked the first year in which the majority of all poor children in the US were nonwhite, most of them being the children of Latino migrants (Lopez and Velazsco 2011). This surge in the number of poor Latino children was a direct result of the 2007–2009 recession, underscoring the fact that low-wage migrant populations are especially vulnerable to downswings in the economy. Unfortunately, this relationship between blocked mobility and second-generation migrant youth is nothing new. The recent statistics on Latino child poverty have just put an exclamation point on a social condition that had been documented by researchers many years prior to the onset of the recession.

Integration, Blocked Mobility, and Immigrant Youth

Despite widening economic disparities, most migrant youth are acculturating to the US at a rate that is on par with earlier cohorts of European migrants, and this includes appreciably high rates of English language fluency (Kasinitz et al. 2009: 25–64). But there are also **concentrations** of migrant youth for whom language fluency, poverty, and social marginality are closely correlated and, notably, most of these youth come from low-income Latino immigrant households. Latino youth are highly segregated in the public school system, educated in largely ethnically homogenous schools (Frankenberg and Orfield 2012). They are also more likely to drop out of high school than youth from other racial-ethnic groups, though these dropout rates have experienced a recent decline (Fry and Taylor 2013). All of these problems are more acutely experienced by youth with limited English proficiency (LEP) (Ruiz-de-Velasco and Fix 2000).

There is also a very strong correlation between LEP issues and recency of migration. Foreign-born Latino youth with immigrant parents are much more likely to have limited proficiency than native-born Latinos (Rumbaut and Komaie 2010). It is also notable that LEP rates are most concentrated in the lower-income Mexican and Central American population, which makes up a disproportionate share of the unauthorized migrant population. Furthermore, Latino youth who migrate to the US as "older children" are more likely to experience English fluency difficulties than youth who enter the US at a younger age (Capps 2005). Other studies, however, have shown that there are benefits to migrating at a later age.

Research on what has come to be known as the Latino paradox has shown that Latino migrants, regardless of income and education, have significantly lower rates of physical and mental illness than US natives (Abraido-Lanza et al. 1999). This positive effect tends to fade with time, however, and after 15 or more years of living in the US, the health of most Latino immigrants is very similar to US natives of the same socioeconomic status. Chapter 13 by Morton Beiser and Chapter 14 by Lu Wang will discuss immigrant health and mental health in greater detail. Furthermore, Latino youth who enter the US at an early age are more at risk for developing poor health, compared to those who entered later (Lara, Gamboa, Kahramanian, Morales, and Bautista 2005). A similar trend has been observed of Latino incarceration rates. The incarceration rate of new Latino migrants is significantly lower than that of the native population (Rumbaut and Ewing 2007). However, incarceration rates of Latino youth increase in tandem with length of time in the US, to the point where the incarceration rates of US-born Latinos exceed the national average.

It is important to emphasize, however, that these patterns of downward mobility and poor health are not equally experienced by all Latino youth. The children of unauthorized migrants are at a much higher risk than other Latino youth of falling at the bottom end of this class divide. Among Asian migrant populations refugee status has played a similar role, as an index of inequality, with the children of refugees having much higher incarceration rates, school dropout rates, unemployment, and limited English fluency rates than children of other Asian migrants (Rumbaut 2008). The children of African and Caribbean asylum seekers have struggled with similar issues, as illustrated by the adjustment problems faced by Haitian refugee youth in the 1980s and 1990s (Stepick 1998). Even so, the children of black migrants have more typically been cast in the role of **model minorities** (Rong and Brown 2002). This is partly because the recruitment process for black migrants is more selective and more restrictive (Bashi 2004) than it is for other racial-ethnic groups. African migrants, for example, enter the US with higher rates of educational achievement than most other migrant groups (Dodoo 1997).

However, one of the main reasons why black migrant youth are often viewed as model minorities is because their educational achievement and incarceration rates, among other things, are being compared to those of the native-born black population. Mary Waters (1994), for example, observed that the identity choices of black migrant youth can have a significant effect on the way they integrate into the US: as members of an upwardly mobile ethnic group or as downwardly mobile members of an oppressed racial minority. This research has led many immigration scholars to look more closely at the relationship between migrant identity and the dynamics of integration.

Perspectives on Integration and Identity

Classic, straight-line **assimilation theory** presumed that most migrants assimilate into the culture and social networks of the majority population (Warner and Srole 1945). Later versions of assimilation theory described a more varied process. A good example is Milton Gordon's (1964) theory, which described seven dimensions of assimilation that were not necessarily achieved, or achieved in equal measure, by all migrant groups. Gordon's theory also paid attention to the receptivity of the majority culture, observing that migrant pathways to assimilation could be blocked by the prejudice and discrimination of the mainstream society.

This line of argument complements some of the observations made by ethnic pluralist theory, which insisted that there could be group-specific pathways to integration (Fuchs 1990; Glazer and Moynihan 1970). According to pluralists, the retention of cultural identity actually helped migrants to integrate into the civic and socioeconomic life of the US. This argument dovetailed with versions of liberal pluralist theory that were being used to describe the organizational structure of US society (Dahl 2005). These theories depicted the US political system as being generally fluid and open to new coalitions and interest groups. So although there may be elite concentrations of power at any given point in time, these concentrations are not fixed and they do not completely block the mobility of new contenders. In a similar vein, ethnic pluralist theory described the US as a society that is open to new cultures and that has a civic culture strengthened by the interaction among diverse cultures, rather than assimilation to a single cultural norm, but with the caveat that these diverse cultures respect the values and political norms of a liberal-democratic society.

Nevertheless, there are important differences in the way that assimilation and pluralist theory dealt with the matter of difference. Pluralist theory tends to describe cultural difference in an affirmative way, observing that migrants can pursue different pathways to integration and retain their identities while remaining more or less equal to the mainstream society. In contrast, when assimilation theory has paid attention to differences, this is usually to draw attention to the problem of inequality, explaining why some groups are unable to integrate as well as others.

Segmented assimilation theory provides a good example of this line of argument. Segmented assimilation theory was first proposed in the early 1990s in an attempt to explain the patterns of stratification that have been described throughout this chapter (Portes and Zhou 1993). Whereas traditional assimilation theory viewed downward mobility as an anomalous outcome, segmented assimilation posited that downward mobility was becoming the "new normal" for many migrants and their offspring. Immigration scholars explained how this kind of economic integration was being shaped by structural changes in US labour markets, demographic changes in migrant flows, and patterns of migrant recruitment (Waldinger and Feliciano 2004). However, researchers also paid attention to cultural factors and, more specifically, to the racial and ethnic identities of new migrants. This is the same body of research described earlier that examined the identity choices of black migrant youth (Waters 1994).

Researchers found that migrant youth who identified ethnically as Caribbean, African, or West Indian seemed to be less affected by the stereotypes and discriminatory treatment that inhibited the achievement of native-born blacks (Deaux, Bikmen, Gilkes, Ventuneac, Joseph, Payne, and Steele 2007). In contrast, migrant youth who took on the same oppositional identities as native-born blacks were more likely to exhibit behaviours and attitudes that correlated with downward mobility.

Some of the conclusions drawn from this research have been criticized for overgeneralizing the social meaning of black identity. For example, researchers have observed that there is a history of critical-oppositional racial identity politics among the black middle class of the US that has been shaped by an experience of upwardly mobility (Neckerman, Carter, and Lee 1999). There is also evidence that a similar dynamic has influenced the identity politics of many Latino professionals. For example, some researchers have found that educated, middle-class Latinos are more likely to identify as racial minorities than lower-income Latinos, and this is especially the case for Latinos employed in the public sector (Itzigsohn and Dore-Cabral 2000).

Meanwhile, Asian migrants and Asian Americans have had to contend with racial stereotypes that focus on their relatively privileged class status. Asian migrants can be positively stereotyped as model minorities. But they can also be targeted precisely because they are viewed as "alien elites" (Newman 1993:149–170; Yung, Chang, and Lai 2006:345–354). As a result, the consciousness that many Asian migrants and Asian Americans have of their racialized foreignness is not necessarily softened by their middle-class status and, in many ways, it is made all the more conspicuous by this relatively privileged status.

These immigrant minorities are also embedded in transnational social networks that have been shaped by the contemporary dynamics of immigration. Hence, their orientation to life in the US is also being shaped by the cultural, economic, and political ties they maintain with their homeland and diaspora communities in other nations. Furthermore, because most of these migrants enter the US with a temporary legal status, they may not view permanent settlement as the natural endpoint of the migration process. The intensification of immigration enforcement and the lengthy and selective nature of the naturalization process can also send discouraging signals that underscore the importance of maintaining close ties with one's co-ethnics and fellow nationals. Research on transnational migrant communities has begun to explore these kinds of identities that have been adopted by noncitizens who are living in the US, but that are embedded in a transnational network of cultural and economic flows (Bashi 2007; Smith 2005).

This research provides yet another example of how varied the process of integration has become. Skilled migrants who are structurally integrated into professional employment sectors can still live in private cultural worlds that are not only "different" from the US mainstream culture, but are not primarily oriented toward the public life of the US. For other migrants, cultural assimilation can increase the risk of social and economic marginality, a situation that can also be understood as a downwardly mobile form of economic integration. However, there are many low-skilled migrants who are neither culturally nor structurally integrated into the US mainstream society—the non-English speaking, low-skilled, unauthorized migrant worker being a primary case in point. But migrants can also experience a kind of upward mobility that leads them to become more integrated within the public life and political culture of the US, while retaining their inherited cultural identities and establishing social ties with native co-ethnics and other minorities.

Conclusion

This chapter began by observing that US migration policy has historically been shaped by a combination of open and closed qualities and went on to describe how these qualities are reflected in the migration trends of the present day. One of the primary ways that US migration policy continues to be "open" is in the avenues it provides for migrant recruitment.

The portion of the US migrant flow that has experienced the most growth over the past few decades has been people admitted with a temporary legal status. But this open policy toward migrant recruitment has been combined with new restrictions on migrant rights and greater selectivity in the issuance of permanent legal status. As a result, more noncitizens have been allowed to enter the US, but in such a way that they are easier to remove. US immigration enforcement has adapted to this situation. Enforcement levels, which tend to rise and fall with fluctuations in labour market demand for migrant workers, have historically been dominated by border patrol. But over the last three decades, interior enforcement has eclipsed the border patrol and it has produced a deportation caseload that is increasing in a steady linear fashion, irrespective of changes in the broader economic climate. In this era, immigration enforcement is no longer being used just to keep "unwanted" migrants from entering the US, but to remove migrants who act "imprudently" after entering the US (Inda 2006).

This situation has been shaped by concerns about improving migrant selectivity and productivity that are a longstanding feature of US immigration policy. Currently, however, these policy priorities have produced a migrant population that is stratified by legal status in new and unprecedented ways. Socioeconomic distinctions between high- and low-skilled migrants are reinforced by legal status distinctions, and legal status distinctions between unauthorized and legal migrants and between different kinds of legal migrants reinforce gender and racial-ethnic disparities. Meanwhile, the national origins and social networks of the migrant population have become increasingly diverse and transnational. These changes have produced many varied pathways to integration.

In decades past, migration scholars theorized that there could be different group-specific pathways to integration for migrants of different nationalities. Today, however, it has become increasingly apparent that pathways to integration can vary widely within the same migrant group. These pathways vary, most obviously, by legal and socioeconomic status. But they can also be highly individualized, being shaped by identity choices and peer group socialization patterns that vary among migrants who have the same legal status and live in the same neighbourhoods. This growing complexity challenges migration scholars to develop new and better explanations of the dynamics of US migration and of the meaning of integration.

Questions for Critical Thought

1. What is the "liberal paradox" that has historically characterized US migration policy? How should US policymakers resolve or manage this paradox?

2. Why is assimilation a problem for some immigrants? What can these immigrants do to avoid the negative outcomes of assimilation or "Americanization"?

3. Why has immigration enforcement expanded alongside the growth of both legal and unauthorized US migration flows? Is this trend indicative of the failure of the federal government to control immigration, or has it been shaped by other priorities besides immigration control?

4.   What factors have shaped the recent expansion of local immigration laws? What impact are these laws likely to have on the cultural and socioeconomic integration of new migrants?
5.   Are human rights a viable alternative to rights based on national membership?

Key Readings

Bashi, Vilna (2007) *Survival of the Knitted: Immigrant Social Networks in a Stratified World*. Stanford, CA: Stanford University Press.

Catanzarite, Lisa (2000) Brown-Collar Jobs: Occupational Segregation and Earnings of Recent-Immigrant Latinos. *Sociological Perspectives* 43(1):45–75.

Kretsedemas, Philip (2012) *The Immigration Crucible: Transforming Race, Nation and the Limits of the Law*. New York: Columbia University Press.

Massey, Douglas and Karen Pren (2001) Unintended Consequences of US Immigration Policy: Explaining the Post-1965 Surge from Latin America. *Population and Development Review* 38(1):1–29.

Waldinger, Roger and Cynthia Feliciano (2004) Will the New Second Generation Experience 'Downward Assimilation'? Segmented Assimilation Re-assessed. *Ethnic and Racial Studies* 27(3):376–402.

Media Links

The Hispanic Trends Project (Pew Hispanic Center):
www.pewhispanic.org
An overview of demographic statistics, integration, and labour market and migration trends for Hispanic/Latino migrants in the US, and links to timely policy and population reports.

State Laws Related to Immigration and Immigrants (National Conference of State Legislatures):
www.ncsl.org/research/immigration/state-laws-related-to-immigration-and-immigrants.aspx
A comprehensive summary of state and local immigration laws enacted throughout the US, updated three times a year.

The US Immigration Policy Page (Migration Policy Institute):
www.migrationpolicy.org/regions/united-states
Links to statistics on US immigration and a wide range of timely policy reports.

We Are America (Center for Community Change):
weareamericastories.org/stories
A menu of immigrant stories (written text, audiovisual, and photo essays) that document migration experiences and struggles faced after arriving, with a focus on policy reform.

Yearbook of Immigration Statistics (US Department of Homeland Security):
www.dhs.gov/yearbook-immigration-statistics
A comprehensive overview of federal data on migration, including annual admittances by legal status, nationality, and gender; enforcement actions; naturalization rates; and special reports on unauthorized migration.

References

Abraído-Lanza, A., B. Dohrenwend, D. Ng-Mak, and J. Turner (1999) The Latino Mortality Paradox: A Test of the 'Salmon Bias' and Healthy Migrant Hypotheses. *American Journal of Public Health* 89(10):1543–1548.

ACLU Human Rights Program (2014) Immigrant Rights Page. www.aclu.org/human-rights/immigrants-rights (Accessed May 14, 2014)

Alba, Richard and Nancy Foner (2008) Immigrant Religion in the US and Western Europe: Bridge or Barrier to Inclusion? *International Migration Review* 42(2):360–392.

Banerjee, Payal (2010) Transnational Subcontracting, Indian IT Workers, and the U.S. Visa System. *Women's Studies Quarterly* 38(1/2):89–110.

Bashi, Vilna (2007) *Survival of the Knitted: Immigrant Social Networks in a Stratified World*. Stanford, CA: Stanford University Press.

Bashi, Vilna (2004) Globalized Anti-Blackness: Transnationalizing Western Immigration Law, Policy, and Practice. *Ethnic and Racial Studies* 27(4):584–606.

Bernhardt, Annette, Ruth Milkman, Nik Theodore, Douglas Heckathorn, Mirabai Auer, James DeFilippis, Ana Luz González, Victor Narro, Jason Perelshteyn, Diana Polson, and Michael Spiller (2009) *Broken Laws, Unprotected Workers: Violations of Employment and Labor Laws in America's Cities*. New York: National Employment Law Project. nelp.3cdn.net/59719b5a36109ab7d8_5xm6bc9ap.pdf (Accessed October 17, 2013)

Bersani, Bianca and Elaine Doherty (2013) When the Ties That Bind Unwind: Examining the Enduring and Situational Processes of Change Behind the Marriage Effect. *Criminology* 51:399–433.

Bloemraad, Irene (2006) Becoming a Citizen in the United States and Canada: Structured Mobilization and Immigrant Political Incorporation. *Social Forces* 85(2):667–695.

Borjas, George (1999) Immigration and Welfare Magnets. *Journal of Labor Economics* 17(4):607–637.

Brader, Ted, Nicholas Valentino, and Elizabeth Suhay (2008) What Triggers Public Opposition to Immigration? Anxiety, Group Cues, and Immigration Threat. *American Journal of Political Science* 52(4):959–978.

Butcher, Kirstin and John Dinardo (2002–2003) Immigrant and Native-Born Wage Distributions: Evidence from United States Censuses. *Industrial and Labor Relations Review* 56(1):97–141.

Calavita, Kitty (2010 [1992]) *Inside the State: The Bracero Program, Immigration, and the INS.* New Orleans: Quid Pro.

Calavita, Kitty (1996) The New Politics of Immigration: "Balanced-Budget Conservatism" and the Symbolism of Proposition 187. *Social Problems* 43(3):284–305.

Card, David (2005) Is the New Immigration Really so Bad? *The Economic Journal* 115(507):300–323.

Capps, Randolph (2005) *The New Demography of America's Schools Immigration and the No Child Left Behind Act.* Washington, DC: Urban Institute. www.urban.org/publications/311230.html (Accessed October 17, 2013)

Catanzarite, Lisa (2000) Brown-Collar Jobs: Occupational Segregation and Earnings of Recent-Immigrant Latinos. *Sociological Perspectives* 43(1):45–75.

Chavez, Leo (2008) *The Latino Threat: Constructing Immigrants, Citizens, and the Nation* 2nd ed. Stanford, CA: Stanford University Press.

Chiswick, Barry (1978) The Effect of Americanization on the Earnings of Foreign-Born Men. *Journal of Political Economy* 86(5):897–921.

Cornelius, Wayne (2001) Death at the Border: Efficacy and Unintended Consequences of US Immigration Control Policy. *Population and Development Review* 27(4):661–685.

Cornelius, Wayne and Takeyuki Tsuda (2004) Controlling Immigration: The Limits of Government Intervention. In Wayne Cornelius, Takeyuki Tsuda, Phillip Martin, and James Hollifield (eds.) *Controlling Immigration: A Global Perspective.* 2nd ed., pp. 3–50. Stanford, CA: Stanford University Press.

Dahl, Robert (2005 [1974]) *Who Governs?: Democracy and Power in an American City.* New Haven, CT: Yale University Press.

Dauvergne, Catherine (2012) International Human Rights in Canadian Immigration Law: The Case of the Immigration and Refugee Board of Canada. *Indiana Journal of Global Legal Studies* 19(1):305–326.

Deaux, Kay, Nida Bikmen, Alwyn Gilkes, Ana Ventuneac, Yvanne Joseph, Yasser Payne, and Claude Steele (2007) Becoming American: Stereotype Threat Effects in Afro-Caribbean Immigrant Groups. *Social Psychology Quarterly* 70(4):384–404.

Dodoo, Francis (1997) Assimilation Differences among Africans in America. *Social Forces* 76(2):527–546.

Fix, Michael and Randy Capps (2005) *Immigrant Children, Urban Schools, and the No Child Left Behind Act*. Washington, DC: Migration Policy Institute. www. migrationinformation.org/usfocus/display.cfm?ID=347 (Accessed October 18, 2013)

Foner, Nancy and Richard Alba (2008) Immigrant Religion in the U.S. and Western Europe: Bridge or Barrier to Inclusion? *International Migration Review* 42(2):360–392.

Frankenberg, Erica and Gary Orfield (eds.) (2012) *The Resegregation of Suburban Schools: A Hidden Crisis in American Education*. Los Angeles: The Civil Rights Project.

Fuchs, Lawrence (1993) An Agenda for Tomorrow: Immigration Policy and Ethnic Policies. *Annals of the American Academy of Political and Social Science* 530:171–186.

Fuchs, Lawrence (1990) *The American Kaleidoscope: Race, Ethnicity, and the Civic Culture*. Middletown, CT: Wesleyan University Press.

Fry, Richard and Paul Taylor (2013) *Hispanic High School Graduates Pass Whites in Rate of College Enrollment: High School Drop-out Rate at Record Low*. Washington: Pew Research Center. www.pewhispanic.org/2013/05/09/iii-young-hispanics-dropping-out-of-high-school (Accessed October 17, 2013)

Government Accountability Office (GAO) (2008) *Visa Waiver Program: Actions Are Needed to Improve Management of the Expansion Process, and to Assess and Mitigate Program Risks*. Washington, DC: GAO.

Government Accountability Office (GAO) (1995) *Illegal Immigration: INS Overstay Estimation Methods Need Improvement*. Washington, DC: GAO.

Glazer, Nathan and Daniel Patrick Moynihan (1970) *Beyond the Melting Pot*. 2nd ed. Cambridge, MA: MIT Press.

Goodwin-Gill, Guy (1989) International Law and Human Rights: Trends Concerning International Migrants and Refugees. *International Migration Review* 23(3):526–546.

Gordon, Milton (1964) *Assimilation in American Life*. New York: Oxford University Press.

Hanson, Gordon (2008) *Labor Markets in the US and Latin America*. Washington, DC: Brookings Institution.

Hanson, Gordon (2007) *The Economic Logic of Illegal Immigration*. New York: Council on Foreign Relations.

Hatton, Timothy and Jeffrey Williamson (2008) *Global Migration and the World Economy: Two Centuries of Policy and Performance*. Cambridge, MA: MIT Press.

Hing, Bill (2004) *Defining America through Immigration Policy*. Philadelphia: Temple University Press.

Hollifield, James (2004) The Emerging Migration State. *International Migration Review* 38(3):885–912.

Hoefer, Michael, Nancy Rytina, and Bryan Baker (2012) *Estimates of the Unauthorized Immigrant Population Residing in the United States: January 2011*. Washington, DC: US DHS. www.dhs.gov/xlibrary/assets/statistics/publications/ois_ill_pe_2011.pdf (Accessed October 12, 2013)

Hoeffel, Elizabeth, Sonya Rastogi, Myoung Kim, and Hasan Shahid (2012) *The Asian Population 2010: Census Briefs*. Washington, DC: US Census Bureau. www.census.gov/prod/cen2010/briefs/c2010br-11.pdf (Accessed October 29, 2013)

Humes, Karen, Nicholas Jones, and Roberto Ramirez (2011) *Overview of Race and Hispanic Origin: Census Briefs 2010*. Washington, DC: US Census Bureau. www.census.gov/prod/cen2010/briefs/c2010br-02.pdf (Accessed October 29, 2013)

Idilbi, Jason (2007–2008) Local Enforcement of Federal Immigration Law: Should North Carolina Communities Implement 287(g) Authority. *North Carolina Law Review* 86:1710–1751.

Ignatow, Gabe and Alexander Williams (2011) New Media and the "Anchor Baby" Boom. *Journal of Computer-Mediated Communication* 17(1):60–76.

Inda, Jonathan (2006) *Targeting Immigrants: Government, Technology, and Ethics*. Oxford: Blackwell.

Itzigsohn, Jose and Carlos Dore-Cabral (2000) Competing Identities? Race, Ethnicity and Panethnicity among Dominicans in the US. *Sociological Forum* 15(2):225–247.

Joassart-Marcelli, Pascale, Juliet Musso, and Jennifer Wolch (2005) Fiscal Consequences of Concentrated Poverty in a Metropolitan Region. *Annals of the Association of American Geographers* 95(2):336–356.

Kandel, William (2011) *The U.S. Foreign-Born Population: Trends and Selected Characteristics*. Washington, DC: Congressional Research Service. www.fas.org/sgp/crs/misc/R41592.pdf (Accessed October 11, 2013)

Kasinitz, Philip, John Mollenkopf, Mary Waters, and Jennifer Holdaway (2009) *Inheriting the City: The Children of Immigrants Come of Age*. New York: Russell Sage Foundation.

Kretsedemas, Philip (2012a) *The Immigration Crucible: Transforming Race, Nation and the Limits of the Law*. New York: Columbia University Press.

Kretsedemas, Philip (2012b) The Limits of Control: Neoliberal Priorities and the US Nonimmigrant Flow. *International Migration* 50(s1):e1–18.

Kretsedemas, Philip (2008) Immigration Enforcement and the Complication of National Sovereignty: Understanding Local Enforcement as an Exercise in Neoliberal Governance. *American Quarterly* 60(3):553–573.

Kretsedemas, Philip and Ana Aparicio (eds.) (2004) *Immigrants, Welfare Reform and the Poverty of Policy*. Westport, CT: Greenwood-Praeger.

Krikorian, Mark (2005) *Downsizing Illegal Immigration: A Strategy of Attrition through Enforcement*. Washington, DC: Center for Immigration Studies. www.cis.org/ReducingIllegalImmigration-Attrition-Enforcement (Accessed October 15, 2013)

Kurzban, Ira (2008) Democracy and Immigration. In David Brotherton and Philip Kretsedemas (eds.) *Keeping out the Other: A Critical Introduction to Immigration Enforcement Today*, pp. 63–80. New York: Columbia University Press.

Lara, Marielena, Cristina Gamboa, M. Iya Kahramanian, Leo Morales, and David Hayes Bautista (2005) Acculturation and Latino Health in the United States: A Review of the Literature and Its Sociopolitical Context. *Annual Review of Public Health* 26:367–397.

Lav, Iris and Phil Oliff (2008) Federal Grants to States and Localities Cut Deeply in Fiscal Year 2009 Federal Budget. Center on Budget and Policy Priorities. www.cbpp.org/cms/?fa=view&id=1145 (Accessed October 13, 2013)

Lesthaeghe, Ron (2010) The Unfolding Story of the Second Demographic Transition. *Population and Development Review* 36(2):211–251.

Lopez, Mark and Gabriel Velazsco (2011) *Childhood Poverty among Hispanics Sets Records, Leads the Nation.* Washington, DC: Pew Hispanic Center. www.pewhispanic.org/2011/09/28/childhood-poverty-among-hispanics-sets-record-leads-nation (Accessed October 17, 2013)

Luthra, Renee (2009) Temporary Immigrants in a High-Skilled Labour Market: A Study of H-1Bs. *Journal of Ethnic and Migration Studies* 35(2):227–250.

Meissner, Doris, Donald Kerwin, Muzzafar Chishti, and Claire Bergeron (2013) *Immigration Enforcement in the United States: The Rise of a Formidable Machinery.* Washington, DC: Migration Policy Institute. www.migrationpolicy.org/pubs/enforcementpillars.pdf (Accessed October 15, 2013)

MPI (Migration Policy Institute) (2013) Estimates of the Net Number of Migrants, Select Countries, by Five Year Intervals. MPI Data Hub. www.migrationinformation.org/datahub/charts/5.1.shtml (Accessed October 11, 2013)

Massey, Douglas and Karen Pren (2001) Unintended Consequences of US Immigration Policy: Explaining the Post-1965 Surge from Latin America. *Population and Development Review* 38(1):1–29.

National Conference of State Legislatures (NCSL) (2012) *Supreme Court Rules on Arizona's Immigration Enforcement Law.* Denver: NCSL. www.ncsl.org/issues-research/immig/us-supreme-court-rules-on-arizona-immigration-laws.aspx (Accessed October 15, 2013)

NCSL (2011) *Arizona's Immigration Enforcement Laws.* Denver: NCSL, 2011. www.ncsl.org/issues-research/immig/analysis-of-arizonas-immigration-law.aspx (Accessed October 15, 2013)

Neckerman, Katherine, P. Carter, and J. Lee (1999) Segmented Assimilation and Minority Cultures of Mobility. *Ethnic and Racial Studies* 22:945–965.

Newman, Katherine (1993) *Declining Fortunes: The Withering of the American Dream.* New York: Basic Books.

Omi, Michael and Howard Winant (1994) *Racial Formation in the United States: From the 1960s to the 1990s.* New York: Routledge.

Oropesa, R.S. and Nancy Landale (2004) The Future of Marriage and Hispanics. *Journal of Marriage and Family* 66(4):901–920.

Passel, Jeffrey (2007) *Unauthorized Migrants in the United States: Estimates, Methods, and Characteristics.* Paris, France: Organisation for Economic Co-operation and Development. www.oecd.org/migration/mig/39264671.pdf (Accessed October 15, 2013)

Passel, Jeffrey, D'Vera Cohn, and Ana Gonzalez-Barrera (2013) *Population Decline of Unauthorized Immigrants Stalls, May Have Reversed.* Washington, DC: Pew Research Center. www.pewhispanic.org/2013/09/23/population-decline-of-unauthorized-immigrants-stalls-may-have-reversed (Accessed October 15, 2013)

Pastor, Manuel and Carol Wise (1994) The Origins and Sustainability of Mexico's Free Trade Policy. *International Organization* 48(3):459–489.

Portes Alejandro and Zhou Min (1993) The New Second Generation: Segmented Assimilation and Its Variants. *Annals of the American Academy of Political and Social Sciences* 530:74–96.

Roberts, Dorothy (1997) *Killing the Black Body: Race, Reproduction, and the Meaning of Liberty.* New York: Pantheon Books.

Rong, Xue Lan and Frank Brown (2002) Socialization, Culture, and Identities of Black Immigrant Children: What Educators Need to Know and Do. *Education and Urban Society* 34(2):247–273.

Rosenzweig, Mark (2006) Global Wage Differences and International Student Flows. *Brookings Trade Forum* 57–86.

Ruiz-de-Velasco, Jorge and Michael Fix (2000) *Overlooked and Underserved: Immigrant Students in US Secondary Schools.* Washington, DC: Urban Institute. www.urban.org/UploadedPDF/overlooked.pdf (Accessed October 17, 2013)

Rumbaut, Rubén (2008) The Coming of the Second Generation: Immigration and Ethnic Mobility in Southern California. *The Annals of the American Academy of Political and Social Science* 620(1):196–236.

Rumbaut, Rubén and Walter Ewing (2007) *The Myth of Immigrant Criminality and the Paradox of Assimilation.* New York: Social Science Research Council. borderbattles. ssrc.org/Rumbault_Ewing/printable.html (Accessed October 18, 2013)

Rumbaut, Rubén and Golnaz Komaie (2010) Immigration and Adult Transitions. *The Future of Children* 20(1):43–66.

Salins, Peter (1997) *Assimilation American Style.* New York: Basic Books.

Sheikh, Irum (2008) Racializing, Criminalizing and Silencing 9/11 Deportees. In David Brotherton and Philip Kretsedemas (eds.) *Keeping Out the Other: A Critical Introduction to Immigration Enforcement Today*, pp. 81–107. New York: Columbia University Press.

Singer, Audrey (2004) Welfare Reform and Immigrants: A Policy Review. In Philip Kretsedemas and Ana Aparicio (eds.) *Immigrants, Welfare Reform and the Poverty of Policy*, pp. 21–34. Westport, CT: Greenwood-Praeger.

Skonieczny, Amy (2001) Constructing NAFTA: Myth, Representation, and the Discursive Construction of U.S. Foreign Policy. *International Studies Quarterly* 45(3):433–454.

Smith, Robert (2005) *Mexican New York: Transnational Lives of New Immigrants.* Berkeley, CA: University of California Press.

Soysal, Yasmin (1998) Toward a Postnational Model of Citizenship. In Gershon Shafir (ed.) *The Citizenship Debates*, pp. 189–220. Minneapolis: University of Minnesota Press.

Stepick, Alex (1998) *Pride against Prejudice: Haitian Immigrants in the United States.* New York: Allyn & Bacon.

Strauss, Claudia (2012) *Making Sense of Public Opinion: American Discourses about Immigration and Social Programs.* Cambridge: Cambridge University Press.

Tichenor, Daniel (2002) *Dividing Lines: The Politics of Immigration Control in America.* Princeton, NJ: Princeton University Press.

US Department of Homeland Security (US DHS) (2013a) Table 1: Persons Obtaining Legal Permanent Resident Status: Fiscal Years 1820 to 2012. *Yearbook of Immigration Statistics, 2012.* Washington, DC: US DHS. www.dhs.gov/yearbook-immigration-statistics-2012-legal-permanent-residents (Accessed October 11, 2013)

US DHS (2013b) Table 2: Persons Obtaining Legal Permanent Resident Status by Region and Selected Country of Last Residence: Fiscal Years 1820 to 2012. *Yearbook of Immigration Statistics, 2012.* Washington, DC: US DHS. www.dhs.gov/yearbook-immigration-statistics-2012-legal-permanent-residents (Accessed October 11, 2013)

US DHS (2013c) Table 6: Persons Obtaining Legal Permanent Resident Status by Type and Major Class of Admission: Fiscal Years 2003 to 2012. *Yearbook of Immigration Statistics, 2012.* Washington, DC: US DHS. www.dhs.gov/yearbook-immigration-statistics-2012-legal-permanent-residents (Accessed October 11, 2013)

US DHS (2013d) Table 25: Nonimmigrant Admissions by Class of Admission: Fiscal Years 2003 to 2012. *Yearbook of Immigration Statistics, 2012.* Washington, DC: US DHS. www.dhs.gov/yearbook-immigration-statistics-2012-nonimmigrant-admissions (Accessed October 11, 2013)

US DHS (2013e) Table 26: Nonimmigrant Admissions (I-94 Only) by Region and Country of Citizenship: Fiscal Years 2003 to 2012. *Yearbook of Immigration Statistics, 2012.* Washington, DC: US DHS. www.dhs.gov/yearbook-immigration-statistics-2012-nonimmigrant-admissions (Accessed October 11, 2013)

US DHS (2013f) Table 32: Nonimmigrant Temporary Worker Admissions (I-94 Only) by Region and Country of Citizenship: Fiscal Year 2012. *Yearbook of Immigration Statistics, 2012.* Washington, DC: US DHS. www.dhs.gov/yearbook-immigration-statistics-2010-1 (Accessed October 29, 2013)

US DHS (2012a) Table 9: Persons Obtaining Legal Permanent Resident Status by Broad Class of Admission and Selected Demographic Characteristics: Fiscal Year 2011. *Yearbook of Immigration Statistics, 2011*. Washington, DC: US DHS. www.dhs.gov/yearbook-immigration-statistics-2011-1 (Accessed October 17, 2013)

US DHS (2012b) Table 32: Nonimmigrant Temporary Worker Admissions (I-94 Only) by Region and Country of Citizenship: Fiscal Year 2011. *Yearbook of Immigration Statistics, 2011*. Washington, DC: US DHS. www.dhs.gov/yearbook-immigration-statistics-2011-2 (Accessed October 29, 2013)

US DHS (2012c) Table 39: Aliens Removed or Returned: Fiscal Years 1892 to 2011. *Yearbook of Immigration Statistics, 2011*. Washington, DC: US DHS. www.dhs.gov/yearbook-immigration-statistics-2011-3 (Accessed October 17, 2013)

US DHS (2011) Table 32: Nonimmigrant Temporary Worker Admissions (I-94 Only) by Region and Country of Citizenship: Fiscal Year 2010. *Yearbook of Immigration Statistics, 2010*. Washington, DC: US DHS. www.dhs.gov/yearbook-immigration-statistics-2010-1 (Accessed October 29, 2013)

US DHS (2010) Table 25: Nonimmigrant Admissions by Class of Admission: Fiscal Years 2000 to 2009. *Yearbook of Immigration Statistics, 2009*. Washington, DC: US DHS. www.dhs.gov/yearbook-immigration-statistics-2009-1 (Accessed October 24, 2013)

US DHS (2005) Table 24: Nonimmigrants Admitted by Class of Admission: Selected Fiscal Years 1981-2004. *Yearbook of Immigration Statistics, 2004*. Washington, DC: US DHS. www.dhs.gov/yearbook-immigration-statistics-2004-1 (Accessed October 24, 2013)

US DHS (2004) Table 4: Immigrants Admitted by Type and Selected Class of Admission: Fiscal Years 1986–2003. *Yearbook of Immigration Statistics, 2003*. Washington, DC: US DHS. www.dhs.gov/yearbook-immigration-statistics-2003-0 (Accessed October 24, 2013)

US DHS (2000) Table 4: Immigrants Admitted by Type and Selected Class of Admission: Fiscal Years 1986–99. *Fiscal Year 1999 Statistical Yearbook*. Washington, DC: US DHS. www.dhs.gov/fiscal-year-1999-statistical-yearbook-0 (Accessed October 12, 2013)

US DHS (1997) *1996 Statistical Yearbook*. Washington, DC: US DHS. www.dhs.gov/archives (Accessed October 11, 2013)

Van Hook, Jennifer and Frank Bean (2009) Explaining Mexican-Immigrant Welfare Behaviors: The Importance of Employment-Related Cultural Repertoires. *American Sociological Review* 74(3):423–444.

Van Hook, Jennifer, Jennifer Glick, and Frank Bean (1999) Public Assistance Receipt among Immigrant and Natives: How the Unit of Analysis Effects Research Findings. *Demography* 36:111–120.

Villar, Maria de Lourdes (1999) The Amnesty Reveals Intra-Ethnic Divisions among Mexicans in Chicago. *Urban Anthropology and Studies of Cultural Systems and World Economic Development* 28(1):37–64.

Waldinger, Roger and Cynthia Feliciano (2004) Will the New Second Generation Experience "Downward Assimilation"? Segmented Assimilation Re-assessed. *Ethnic and Racial Studies* 27(3):376–402.

Warner, Lloyd and Srole Leo (1945) *The Social Systems of American Ethnic Groups.* New Haven, CT: Yale University Press.

Waters, Mary (1994) Ethnic and Racial Identities of Second-Generation Black Immigrants in New York City. *International Migration Review* 28(4):795–820.

Welch, Michael (2002) *Detained: Immigration Laws and the Expanding INS Jail Complex.* Philadelphia: Temple University Press.

Wishnie, Michael (2007) Prohibiting the Employment of Unauthorized Immigrants: The Experiment Fails. *University of Chicago Legal Forum*, 193–217.

Yung, Judy, Gordon Chang, and Mark Lai (2006) *Chinese American Voices: From the Gold Rush to the Present.* Berkeley, CA: University of California Press.

Zolberg, Aristide (2008) *A Nation by Design: Immigration Policy in the Fashioning of America.* Cambridge, MA: Harvard University Press.

Chapter 3

Continuity and Change in Canadian Immigration Policy

Myer Siemiatycki

Introduction

Canada is often described, with good reason, as a country of immigrants (Triadafilopoulos 2012:2; Andrew, Biles, Burstein, Esses, and Tolley 2012:1; Rodriguez-Garcia 2012:7; Bloemraad 2011:1135; Simmons 2010:2). The 2011 Canadian census revealed that immigrants made up 20.6% of Canada's total population of 33.4 million. This confirms Canada's place as a world-leading immigrant-receiving country. By comparison, at roughly the same time, immigrants accounted for 12.9% of the United States's population, and 3% of the world's total population (Statistics Canada 2013a). So while the United States has a greater total number of immigrants than Canada, the immigration rate is considerably higher in Canada. Measured as a percentage of total population, Canada is more of an immigration country than the United States.

Canada's population has grown through successive waves of migration. Consequently, **immigration policy** has long been an important governmental responsibility in Canada. Immigration policy can be defined as the government's approach to the entry of foreign-born persons into Canada as permanent or temporary residents. More specifically, this entails addressing two fundamental issues related to migration: selection and **integration**. Selection involves determining how many immigrants should be admitted and what the entry criteria should be. Integration addresses the role and place of immigrants in the new country they have moved to.

Both the selection and integration dimensions of immigration policy in Canada have experienced dramatic change over time—this is a major theme of this chapter. At the same time, several constants have endured. Immigration policy has always been strongly shaped by the government's perception of Canada's national self-interest. In Canada, as in other countries, immigration policy is less motivated by general ethical or humanitarian principles than by pragmatic assessment of the receiving country's own population needs (whether economic, cultural, or demographic). This means immigrants have typically been regarded instrumentally as foreign human objects welcomed or shunned depending on whether they are deemed to be of benefit to Canada. The result has not always been an exercise in fairness or generosity on Canada's part.

This chapter progresses from past to present as follows: An opening historical section identifies key aspects of past Canadian immigration policy. Successive sections then examine the distinct approach to **immigrant** selection and integration that developed in Canada during the later decades of the twentieth century. A final section analyzes recent changes in immigration policy that suggest a new Canadian approach to international migration. An implicit message of this chapter, therefore, is that policy is not eternally fixed. It can and does change. It is up to Canadians to decide what immigration policies are worthy of a great country.

Immigration Policy in Historical Perspective

Canada is a relatively young country. It was established in 1867, when several British **colonies** located north of the United States joined together as a new country. Today Canada is widely regarded as a welcoming destination of global migration. However, this was not always the case. "In fact," a leading text on Canadian immigration selection declares, "for most of its history, Canada's immigration practices have been racist and exclusionary" (Kelley and Trebilcock 2010:466). A full inventory of examples is not possible in this chapter. However, it is important to recognize how explicitly and extensively discrimination characterized Canadian immigration policy during Canada's first century as a country, from 1867 to 1967.

For most of this period, Canada selected its immigrants based on country of origin preferences which were only eliminated in 1962. Until then, Canada divided potential immigrants into two categories: preferred and undesirable, based largely on their country of origin and **race**. At the top of the preferred list were British immigrants; also desirable were immigrants from Western and Northern Europe. However, the further removed potential immigrants were from the ideal white, Christian, and preferably British, prototype, the more barriers Canada erected to their migration.

Case Example 1: Who Were Canada's First Immigrants?

According to archeologists, human history in the territorial space of Canada dates back at least 13,000 years (Kelley and Trebilcock 2010). So who were the first immigrants to Canada?

Significantly, Aboriginal people—ancestors of the first humans in Canada—do not self-identify as the descendants of immigrants. Rather, they regard themselves as First Nations, present in this land since creation. Accordingly, this is how an explanatory text in the display of the First Nations Hall exhibit in the Canadian Museum of Civilization describes Aboriginal origins in Canada: "We are not the first immigrants; we are the native inhabitants of the land. We have been here since before the world took its present form." This view is reflected in a Mi'kmaq folktale in which a man declares, "I have lived here since the world began. I have my grandmother, she was here when the world was made …" (Ray 1996:vii).

Importantly then, not all Canadians insert themselves into the national narrative of Canada as a country of immigrants. Canada's 1.4 million Aboriginal people do not regard themselves as descendants of immigrants, and their interface with the Government of Canada is through the Department of Aboriginal Affairs, not the Department of Citizenship and Immigration.

Canada's first migrants were seasonal, temporary workers. They voyaged from Europe to fish the rich waters off the Atlantic coast. Traces of this fishing migration date back a thousand years to the eleventh century and are most notably commemorated at the UNESCO World Heritage L'Anse aux Meadows National Historic Site at the northeastern tip of Newfoundland (Parks Canada 2013). This is the earliest known European site of **settlement** in North America, where Norse fishing crews established temporary summer residency. Interestingly, we will see later in this chapter that temporary labour migration to Canada is once again experiencing a huge revival today.

Essentially, nonwhites and non-Christians were regarded as un-Canadian and stark immigration policy measures were adopted to keep their numbers in the country low.

For several decades from the late nineteenth through the early twentieth century Canada imposed a **head tax** on any immigrants arriving from China. People of no other country faced such a surcharge for admission to Canada. In 1923 this was replaced by an outright ban on immigration from China, staying in effect until 1947 (Li 1998). To prevent South Asian migration, the government passed a law early in the twentieth century, called the Continuous Journey Regulation, specifying that migrants wishing to enter Canada would have to make their voyage in a direct, nonstop boat trip from their country of birth. Canada adopted this measure after assuring that there were no direct ocean voyages from South Asia to Canada (Johnson 1970). On the eve of the Second World War, Canada refused entry to many desperate European Jews seeking a haven from Nazi persecution. Asked how many Jewish refugees Canada should accept, a senior Immigration Department official infamously replied "None is too many" (Abella and Troper 1982). After the war, Canada deported four thousand Canadians of Japanese ancestry in the belief that Japanese Canadians could not be loyal to Canada. During the war, Japanese Canadians had been interned, put to forced labour, and had their homes and property confiscated. In more recent decades, Canadian governments have issued apologies for each of these past immigration policies, now deemed morally unjust and indefensible. Will future Canadian governments have to issue apologies for any of today's immigration policies? Readers may reflect on this question as they read on.

Before examining today's policies, however, let us briefly review the historical pattern of immigrant admissions to Canada. Figure 3.1 charts annual immigrant admissions to Canada over more than 150 years, from 1860 to 2012. The term **immigrant** has very specific definition in Canada, referring officially to "someone who was born outside of Canada and has been granted the right to live permanently in the country." Immigrants, therefore, are foreign-born persons accorded permanent resident status in Canada. This means that other foreign-born persons in Canada are not counted as immigrants—for instance those admitted as temporary residents or those persons identified in Canada as nonstatus, being in noncompliance with government residency regulations for foreign-born persons. In the US, this latter group is typically referred to as undocumented migrants. It is therefore important to recognize that, in Canada, the count of immigrants does not include all foreign-born residents.

Figure 3.1 reveals the rollercoaster ride that has characterized immigrant admission for much of Canada's history. Rocketing peaks and plummeting troughs have followed each other in seemingly recurring cycles until the relatively stable pattern of the past 20 years. For most of its history, Canada had a **"tap-on, tap-off"** approach to immigrant admission.

When newcomers were needed to fill labour needs, the door swung open wide; when the economy and labour market experienced a downturn, the door swung shut. In this fashion, immigration policy resembled a company's human resources practices: when business was good, the company recruited more workers (and

Figure 3.1
Annual Immigrant Admissions in Canada, 1860–2012

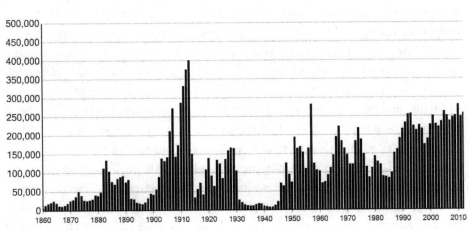

Source: CIC, Facts and Figures (2012). Ottawa: Citizenship and Immigration Canada.

government admitted more immigrants); when business declined, the company stopped hiring and laid off workers (government dramatically reduced the inflow of immigrants and stepped up deportation of previously admitted immigrants).

Immigrant numbers were relatively low from 1860 to 1900 for two reasons. These were generally adverse economic times in Canada, except for the 1880s when construction of the transcontinental Canadian Pacific Railway stimulated economic growth. But perhaps more significantly, these were years when the United States continued to attract most immigrants, with prime farmland still available for distribution. By 1900, Canada could aggressively promote itself in Britain and Europe as the "Last Best West", with millions of prairie acres still available after US farmland had all been claimed. Unprecedented numbers of immigrants were admitted to farm the prairie West and labour in urban factories.

As Figure 3.1 shows, the years 1912 and 1913 were the greatest years of immigration ever, with annual arrivals accounting for more than 5% of the country's existing population. In recent decades, immigration intake has accounted for a far lower share of existing population—typically hovering at 0.7% of population. Canada has never come close to matching either the numbers or rate of immigrant entry of these early years of the twentieth century. Immigration then dropped dramatically through the First World War, recovered during the "Roaring Twenties" of economic growth, but then experienced protracted decline during the economic depression of the 1930s and Second World War. From the late 1940s to 1990 sharp increases and declines continued to mirror the country's economic circumstances.

Since the 1990s the tap-on, tap-off approach has been replaced by a relatively stable admission of between 225,000 and 250,000 newcomers per year. The rollercoaster has given way to a "steady sailing" approach, in response to serious demographic challenges now facing Canada. Like many advanced Western countries, Canada's birth rate has been below its population replacement rate for several decades now. This means the number of births in Canada is less than the combined number of those who die each year, or leave the country to live abroad. In 2005, for instance, Canada had a birth rate of 1.6 (the number of births for each woman in her lifetime), but requires a 2.1 birth rate just to keep population numbers constant going forward (Simmons 2010:233).

This poses serious challenges and choices for Canada. Without high levels of immigration, the country's total population would decline and be increasingly composed of the elderly. This is the scenario playing out in countries like Japan and Russia that have opted not to increase immigration to compensate for declining domestic fertility rates, and are consequently "currently moving into a fairly steep trajectory of negative population growth and aging" (Simmons 2010:238). By contrast, for the past two decades Canada has kept immigration intake stable and relatively high in order to assure ongoing population growth and the intake of employment-ready migrants to replace retiring, aging Canadians. Significantly, the 2011 census demonstrated that Canada led all G8 countries (US, UK, Russia, Japan, Germany, France, Italy, and Canada) in population growth from 2001 to 2011 (Statistics Canada 2012). Once again, immigration is being called upon to solve a domestic Canadian problem. Let us look more closely now at key dimensions of Canadian immigration policy.

Globalizing Immigration to Canada

Much of Canada's current approach to immigration selection was put in place during the 1960s. We look now at how those policy changes transformed Canadian immigration and Canadian society. Later in the chapter we assess how current policy changes are again fundamentally redesigning immigration to Canada.

As we have seen, for much of its history, Canada regarded migrants beyond Europe as undesirable and severely restricted their entry. By 1961, for instance, only 3% of all immigrants in Canada came from Asia; fully 90% came from Britain and other parts of Europe (Statistics Canada 1997). However, changes to Canadian immigration selection policy in the 1960s would truly globalize migration to this country.

In 1962, for the first time, race and nationality (country of origin) were eliminated as criteria for immigrant admission to Canada; instead immigrant selection would largely be based on **human capital** considerations—the likelihood that an individual could positively contribute to Canada's economic prospects. Selection was no longer based on where a person came from, but what they could bring and contribute to Canada. People from Asia, Africa, the Caribbean, and Central and South America who had long been excluded were about to enter in large numbers. Why did such a fundamental change in policy happen?

Immigration scholars have identified various drivers of this policy change, some principled and some pragmatic (Triadafilopoulos 2012; Kelley and Trebilcock 2010; Troper 1993). One dynamic certainly was the growing adoption of anti-racist, pro-human rights values among Canadians by the 1960s. The world had learned the dangers of **racism** from the Holocaust, and soon after the Second World War the United Nations proclaimed the Universal Declaration of Human Rights (written by a Canadian, McGill University law professor John Humphreys). Additionally, through the 1950s and 1960s, Canada and other Western countries were routinely portraying themselves as bastions of freedom and liberty in their "Cold War" with the Communist world. This became difficult to reconcile with ongoing discriminatory immigrant selection policies. For the first time, then, a rights-based dimension and discourse took hold in Canadian immigration policy. This illustrates that values and morality can at times play a key role in shaping immigration policy.

But less altruistic forces were also at play, since by the 1960s discriminatory immigration selection practices no longer served the country's own demographic and economic needs. These were the more pragmatic, self-interested motivations for policy change. By the early 1960s, migration from Britain and Europe was significantly diminishing as those countries stabilized and economically recovered from the destruction of the Second World War. Canada would have to look further afield for the immigrants it required. Additionally, discriminatory immigration policies had become a barrier to Canadian trade with many parts of the world. Countries in Asia, Africa, and the Caribbean that Canada excluded from immigration had now transitioned from European colonies to independent countries. Canada was in an awkward position, seeking trade and economic ties with these countries while treating their citizens as unfit for entry into Canada. Discriminatory immigration selection based on race or country of origin no longer fit either Canadian values or national self-interest.

In 1967 Canada unveiled a comprehensive new approach to immigrant selection that is still largely operational today, based on three distinct streams or classes of immigrant entrants: economic, family, and refugee. Economic class immigrants (sometimes also referred to as independent class immigrants) were selected for their capacity to advance the country's economic performance based on an assessment of their individual human capital attributes. This was calculated based a **points system** assessment of factors such as age, education, training, occupational experience, knowledge of English or French, and prior offer of employment in Canada. In order to be admitted to Canada, applicants needed to accumulate sufficient points for approval. The second category of immigrant admissions is the family class. This allows immigrants to sponsor family reunification of their spouse, parents, and nonadult children, based on the belief that uniting families on Canadian soil promotes newcomer integration to their new country. Refugees make up the final Canadian category. As a signatory to the United Nations High Commissioner for Refugees, Canada is obligated to provide asylum to persons with a "well-founded fear" of persecution in their homeland.

For close to 50 years, then, there have been three immigration pathways into Canada: the economic, family, and refugee classes of selection. The most powerful consequence has been the globalization of Canada's population. This is reflected in Figure 3.2, which tracks the parts of the world where immigrants to Canada have come from since the current three-path immigrant admission system was established in the late 1960s. The transition from the earliest bar on the left to the most recent on the right is extraordinary. It reveals a virtual reversal of roles for Europe and Asia as source continents of migration to Canada. Indeed, the top three source countries of immigrants to Canada from 2006 to 2011 were Asian, with the Philippines leading, followed by China and India. Additionally, Figure 3.2 captures the declining significance of migration from the United States, along with the increased flow from Africa, the Caribbean, and Central and South America (Statistics Canada 2013a). The composition of Canada's immigrant population is thus radically different from the profile in the United States, with its predominant flow from Latin America.

This globalization of migration into Canada has transformed the country into a diverse, multiracial society in a remarkably short period of time. Strikingly, almost 8 of every 10 immigrants (78%) who arrived in Canada from 2006 to 2011 were nonwhite. In 2011 almost one in five people in Canada (19.1%) were nonwhite, up sharply from a rate of just 5% in 1981, when the Canadian census first tracked the country's racial composition (Statistics Canada 2013a).

Canada has its own distinct official terminology for racial discourse. In Canada, the term **visible minority** refers to "persons, other than Aboriginal persons, who are non-Caucasian in race or non-white in colour" (Statistics Canada 2013a:14). The Canadian census asks respondents if they belong to one of 10 identified visible minority groups. The three largest groups recorded in 2011 were South Asians, Chinese, and blacks.

Immigrants and visible minorities are not randomly or evenly distributed across Canada. They are concentrated in a few provinces and in Canada's largest cities. In 2011, an astonishing 94.8% of all immigrants in Canada lived in 4 of Canada's 10 provinces: Ontario (53.3%), British Columbia (17.6%), Quebec (14.4%), and Alberta (9.5%). Almost two-thirds of all immigrants lived in the three largest census metropolitan

Figure 3.2

Region of Birth of Immigrants by Period of Immigration, Canada, 2011

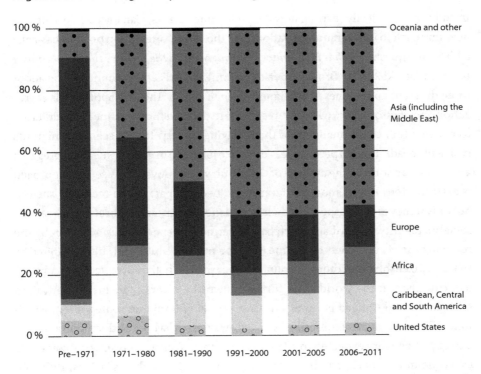

* "Oceania and other" includes immigrants born in Oceania, in Canada, in Saint Pierre and Miquelon, and responses not included elsewhere, such as "born at sea."

Source: Statistics Canada, National Household Survey (2011).

areas: Toronto (37.4% of all immigrants in Canada), Vancouver (13.5%), and Montreal (12.5%). At the municipal government scale, there are sizable cities and towns in Canada where the term *visible minority* has lost its literal meaning because nonwhites are now a majority of the population. For instance in the Vancouver area, visible minorities outnumber whites in the suburban municipalities of Richmond (70.4% of population), Burnaby (59.5%), Surrey (52.6%), and the City of Vancouver itself (51.8%). In the Toronto area, suburban municipalities also lead the way in visible minority population **concentration**: Markham (72.3% of population), Brampton (66.4%), Mississauga (53.7%), and the City of Toronto (49.1%). Immigration has dramatically transformed Canada's urban and suburban landscapes (Statistics Canada 2013a).

Immigrant Integration Policies

In addition to radically revising how it selected immigrants, Canada also developed a new approach to immigrant integration after the 1960s. Integration policies basically address the question *What is the place of immigrants in the country they have moved to?* (Siemiatycki 2012a). Broadly speaking, immigrant-receiving countries can adopt three different approaches to foreigners in their midst. The first approach is segregation and ghettoization, whereby migrants are deemed too fundamentally different to become full, equal members of the receiving society. In this scenario migrants typically are admitted to perform less desirable jobs, live in geographically segregated areas, and cannot become citizens of the country they moved to. A second approach is **assimilation.** In this model, migrants can become part of the receiving society, but only if they give up aspects of their homeland identity and embrace the receiving society's identity. A third approach can be termed *diversity inclusion*, whereby the receiving society stretches to redefine itself as a mix of peoples and cultures united by shared citizenship in a common country. Over the last half of the twentieth century, few countries in the world went further down the diversity inclusion path than Canada. Indeed Canada became a distinct model of immigrant integration, which John Biles and associates describe as "a 'two-way street,' where both immigrants and current citizens are expected to adapt to each other, to ensure positive outcomes for everyone in the social, cultural, economic, and political spheres" (Biles, Burstein, and Frideres 2008:4).

In many respects, this was an unexpected path for Canada to take. For much of its earlier history, Canada's approach to integration combined elements of segregation and assimilation. The few nonwhites admitted before the 1960s were typically ghettoized both residentially and occupationally, and in the case of Asians were long denied voting rights. All others in Canada were expected to embrace British loyalty and values. To Canada's credit, when it opened its immigration selection to the world in the 1960s, it found a way to embrace migrants from the world over as Canadians. This section briefly identifies the elements of Canada's approach to diversity inclusion.

1. Multiculturalism

In 1971 Canada became the first country in the world to officially espouse **multiculturalism.** Its significance has been less any tangible provision of rights or resources to ethno-cultural minorities (few are specified) than a redefinition of what it means to be Canadian (Siemiatycki 2012a). Perhaps the boldest assertion in its founding declaration by former prime minister Pierre Trudeau was his claim that in Canada "there is no official culture, nor does any ethnic group take precedence over any other. No citizen or group of citizens is other than Canadian, and all should be treated fairly" (Trudeau 1971). Significantly, Prime Minister Trudeau identified the goals of multiculturalism to be the fullest participation of immigrants and minorities in all facets of Canadian life.

Multiculturalism redefined what it meant to be Canadian. "Adopting multiculturalism," Will Kymlicka (1998:57) has written, "is a way for Canadians to say that never again will we view Canada as a 'white' country ... never again will we view Canada as a 'British' country." As a result, Irene Bloemraad (2006:153) has noted, multiculturalism "makes room for others." And it does so on a basis of diversity inclusion, by simultaneously validating immigrants' retention of ancestral culture along with their active engagement with and commitment to Canada. Interestingly, polling indicates extremely high levels of public support for multiculturalism across all sections of Canadian society. In 2003, 85% of Canadians surveyed agreed that multiculturalism was important to Canadian identity; and 81% believed it has made a positive contribution to Canadian society (Adams 2007).

2. Citizenship

Citizenship establishes membership in a political community. Some countries never allow immigrants to become citizens of the country they have moved to. At the other end of the continuum is Canada, with one of the world's most permissive approaches to immigrant citizenship. After spending three years in Canada, immigrants admitted to Canada as permanent residents are eligible to apply for citizenship, in a process known as **naturalization**. Also significant, since 1977 Canada has accepted dual citizenship, so immigrants may retain their homeland citizenship when they become Canadian citizens.

Interestingly, Canada has the highest rate in the world of immigrants becoming citizens. The 2011 census revealed that 85.6% of all immigrants who had fulfilled their three-year residency period in Canada had become citizens (Statistics Canada 2013b). Irene Bloemraad, in her book *Becoming a Citizen* (2006), explains why immigrants in Canada take up citizenship at a far higher rate than immigrants in the US become American citizens. Her explanation is that immigrants form a stronger attachment to Canada as a result of more welcoming government policies such as multiculturalism, newcomer settlement programs, and a host of government-provided public services including healthcare and education.

Indeed, Canadian governments fund and oversee delivery of a wide array of newcomer and public services available to immigrants. During their first three years of residency, immigrants are eligible for free language classes and settlement assistance regarding employment, housing, and general orientation. Additionally, immigrants benefit along with the native-born population from the existence of a range of inclusive public institutions providing (often free) access to a wide range of public services such as hospitals, public schools, and libraries. All these services and shared public institutions promote feelings of attachment and belonging among immigrants in Canada (Siemiatycki 2012a).

3. Provincial and Municipal Integration Policies

As noted earlier, immigrant settlement in Canada is particularly concentrated in some provinces, and in the country's largest cities. Not surprisingly then, provincial and municipal governments have also adopted a host of measures to promote immigrant integration. The Province of Ontario and City of Toronto may be cited as examples. In 2007, Ontario became the first jurisdiction in Canada to establish rules for how self-regulating professional bodies assess accreditation applications from immigrants with foreign education and work experience. This arose from concerns that inconsistency and unaccountability in how professional bodies adjudicated foreign credential applications was adversely impacting immigrants. The Fair Access to Regulated Professions Act requires Ontario's 34 self-regulating professions to be fair, timely, and transparent in assessing credentials for professional membership. The act further established an Office of the Fairness Commissioner to oversee the compliance of professional associations.

For its part, the City of Toronto has adopted a host of measures to promote immigrant integration—some symbolic and some very tangible. Half the population of Canada's largest city are immigrants. Accordingly, the city's official motto declares "Diversity our Strength." More tangibly, Toronto's policy initiatives include the Toronto Newcomer Strategy, an Immigration and Settlement Policy Framework, and an Action Plan for the Elimination of Racism and Discrimination. All include tangible guidelines and commitments to advance the well-being of immigrants. Recognizing that Toronto is home to the largest number of nonstatus foreigners in all of Canada, the city has also reached out to this vulnerable population by officially declaring itself a "sanctuary city" in which municipal services would be available to all residents without regard to their formal immigration status. The Canadian experience shows that all levels of government have a role to play in promoting the integration of immigrants and foreign migrants (Siemiatycki 2012b).

Until recently, Canada was frequently cited not only as a leading immigrant-receiving country, but also as a world leader in immigrant integration. Indeed, this

Case Study 2: Cities as Leaders in Immigrant Inclusion and Democracy

In both Canada and the United States, cities have taken a lead role in championing immigrant integration. This reflects the demographic reality that immigrants overwhelmingly settle in cities, where they contribute their labour to the local economy, pay municipal taxes, and rely on municipal services. In cities, the foreign-born are more likely to be treated as neighbours than as strangers or statistics.

Cities across North America have adopted a variety of measures to support their most vulnerable foreign-born. In 2013, Toronto joined 36 US cities (including New York City, Los Angeles, and Chicago) in declaring itself a "sanctuary city" that would provide municipal services to all residents regardless of their national immigration status (Keung 2013a). The foreigners regarded by national governments as illegal are thus treated by cities as equal members of the community.

Additionally, Toronto, like some US cities, supports extending municipal voting rights to noncitizen urban residents. At present in Canada and the United States, voting rights require national citizenship. To vote in a Canadian national, provincial, or municipal election, a person must be a citizen of Canada. The same principle applies to persons wanting to vote in US national, state, or municipal elections.

Today, many residents of American and Canadian cities are not citizens of the country they live in—either ineligible for citizenship or not yet having been naturalized. This applies to approximately one in three residents of Los Angeles and one in seven residents of Toronto (Hayduk 2004:504; Siemiatycki 2009:76). This situation results in large numbers of urban residents unable to vote in city council or school board elections. In 2013, Toronto City Council called on the Province of Ontario to change municipal election rules so that noncitizen permanent residents could vote in Toronto elections. If approved by the provincial government, Toronto would become the largest city in North America with noncitizen residents voting for all municipal officials including the mayor, city councillors, and school board representatives. At present five smaller municipalities in Maryland and two in Massachusetts permit full nonresident local voting rights, while Chicago allows noncitizens a vote in school board elections. Municipalities have become the new frontier for extending democracy and voting rights in this age of migration.

was the verdict of a pioneering study by James Lynch and Rita Simon that analyzed immigrant integration in eight different countries—Australia, Canada, France, Germany, Great Britain, Japan, and the United States. "In every respect," Lynch and Simon (2003:259) concluded, "immigrants in Canada appear to be integrated both culturally and structurally into Canadian society." To be sure, all was not perfect in Canada's immigration record. Economically, immigrants faced stubbornly high rates of unemployment and **underemployment**; politically, they were significantly underrepresented in elected positions of government; and socially, racism and discrimination remained realities of everyday life (Siemiatycki 2012a).

Yet, by the start of the twenty-first century, many observers believed that Canadian immigration policy provided the best formula for immigration success. The Canadian model combined mass immigration based on multiple intake selection streams (economic, family, and refugee classes) with integration measures designed to make newcomers full and equal members of Canadian society through citizenship and multiculturalism policies, along with government-provided newcomer and public services.

Over the past decade Canada has experienced dramatic changes in immigration policy. Observers question whether these new directions will strengthen or undermine the country's immigration success record. We examine these recent policy changes next.

Immigration Policy for Neoliberal Times

Governments do not make immigration policies in a vacuum. Decisions regarding foreign-born entry into Canada are made in the context of influencing factors such as interest group lobbying, public opinion, economic conditions, demographic dynamics, and the government's own political values and goals. Recent years have seen considerable changes to immigrant selection in Canada. Indeed, the authors of the most comprehensive review of the subject begin their study by declaring, "The pace and scope of change in Canada's immigration policies in recent years can leave one breathless" (Alboim and Cohl 2012:1).

Indeed, the Conservative government of Prime Minister Stephen Harper has been especially active in revising Canadian immigration policies, particularly in regards to newcomer selection. The overall thrust has been to better align immigration policy with the goals of the political philosophy of recent decades identified as **neoliberalism**. This is an outlook that regards government's primary role as promoting business profitability and wealth accumulation by enacting policies most in keeping with "free market" business principles. It generally translates into policies designed to lower labour costs and reduce the size of government and its regulation of business activity, which is believed best left to private sector market forces. As we will see, recent Canadian governments have seized on immigration policy as a means of promoting corporate profitability and reducing federal government expenses. The remainder of this section identifies five important new trends in immigrant selection policy.

1. Increased Emphasis on Economic Class Immigrants

There has been a marked shift in the share of annual immigrants selected in each of the three classes of admission. Over the past 20 years we have experienced a massive increase in admissions of economic class immigrants, and sharp decline in family and refugee admissions. Thus, in 1992 the largest class of immigrants admitted were in the family class (39.7%), followed by economic class (37.6%), refugees (20.5%), and 2.2% admitted on other criteria. Figures for 2012 reveal a dramatically different pattern of immigrant selection with 62.4% admitted in the economic class, 25.2% in the family class, 9% admitted as refugees and 3.5% admitted on other criteria (Citizenship and Immigration Canada 2012).

Clearly, Canada is increasingly selecting immigrants based on a singular criteria of maximizing economic benefits to this country. This raises a number of potential concerns. First, it is an approach that fosters a **brain drain** from other (often poorer) countries by selecting their best educated persons for migration to Canada, after their homeland has financed their education. Canadian immigration policy now typically cherry-picks the educated and economic elite of other countries for admission to Canada. Provocatively, this human capital emphasis has led Luis Aguiar (2006:206) to characterize Canada's approach as "social eugenics," still based on assumptions of desirable and undesirable immigrants, with social status (education, occupation, income) now replacing race and nationality as key selection criteria.

2. Reduced Family Class and Refugee Class Admissions

As economic class entrants have increased as share of total immigrants admitted to Canada, family class and refugee admissions have dropped sharply. Family reunification now takes considerably longer and the government has especially signalled its reluctance to admit parents and grandparents of immigrants (typically in their senior years) as immigrants themselves. This is because they are generally beyond their employment years, and are deemed of little economic benefit. Furthermore, the government wishes to avoid incurring the cost of health services that older immigrants would be eligible for as permanent residents. Instead, the government has introduced longer term visitor visas for immigrants' parents and grandparents, with the sponsoring immigrant in Canada responsible for covering any healthcare costs that arise. However, early rollout of the program has generated considerable frustration over a high rate of visa application rejections, despite immigrants in Canada having spent considerable sums to purchase health insurance and return airfare for visiting parents and grandparents (Keung 2012).

The sharp decline in refugee admissions suggests that Canada is not the generous, humanitarian country our politicians often proclaim it to be. Indeed, a recent report by Harvard University legal scholars concludes that Canada has become unwelcoming to asylum seekers. Based on a review of recent changes to refugee selection, they conclude that, "Canada is systematically closing its borders to asylum seekers and failing in its refugee protection obligations under domestic and international law" (Arbel and Brenner 2013:1). Through a host of recent measures, Canada has dramatically and by design reduced both the number of asylum seekers able to claim refugee status in Canada as well as the number admitted. Policy impediments include 1) the Canada-US Safe Third Country Agreement, preventing asylum seekers entering Canada via the US; 2) the Multiple Borders Strategy, enabling Canadian officials abroad to bar asylum seekers from travel to Canada; 3) establishing a more demanding refugee claim process for asylum seekers from Designated Countries of Origin deemed to be safe homelands (including Hungary, despite its record of anti-Roma persecution); 4) establishing a category of "irregular arrivals" typically reaching our shores unannounced by boat, who will face mandatory detention on arrival, less access to due process, and longer wait times for permanent residency even if determined to be bona fide refugees; 5) imposition of visa requirements for countries with large refugee flows to restrict access to Canada; 6) reduction of private refugee sponsorship by individual Canadians or Canadian organizations (typically faith communities); and 7) widespread elimination of federal government healthcare coverage for most refugees and refugee claimants (Arbel and Brenner 2013; Alboim and Cohl 2012).

The adoption of so many measures designed to reduce refugee admissions can be connected to neoliberal government preferences. Through a neoliberal lens, refugees are seen as taking a newcomer place that should go to someone selected to advance Canada's economic performance. Moreover, refugees are regarded as expensive newcomers requiring government staff to adjudicate their claims while they are eligible for healthcare and other social service supports. And finally, at a purely political level, the current government believes it can gain public support by characterizing asylum seekers as "bogus refugees" taking advantage of Canadian generosity.

The measures, identified above, adopted to reduce refugee claims in Canada have proven exceptionally effective. Applications have plunged from 25,088 in 2011 to

7,378 in the first 9 months of 2013 (Keung 2013b). Fewer of the world's endangered people are getting access to applying for asylum in Canada. Some have suggested that recent policies on refugees harken back to darker periods of past policies. Thus, Philip Berger of the group Canadian Doctors for Refugee Care has declared, "This government has been the most hostile and vicious to refugees since the Second World War" (Keung 2013c).

3. Increased Reliance on Temporary Foreign Workers

Perhaps the most radical recent development in Canadian immigration policy has been the country's dramatic expansion of temporary labour migration. As previously noted, immigrants are admitted to Canada as permanent residents, able to stay in the country as long as they wish, and eligible to become Canadian citizens after three years of residency. In this fashion Canada has in the past regarded immigration as more than simply an exercise in meeting economic or demographic needs. It has also been a nation-building initiative of "importing" new and future generations of Canadians.

By contrast, **temporary foreign workers** are admitted at the request of employers to fill labour shortages, under work visas typically ranging from two to four years. Most are limited to employment in the occupation (and in some cases with the specific employer) they were granted entry for, and the vast majority are ineligible to apply for Canadian citizenship,

The past decade has seen a sharp rise in temporary foreign workers in Canada. The annual number admitted doubled from 2003 to 2012, climbing from 102,932 to 213,573. Over the same period, the total number of temporary foreign workers in the country actually tripled from 109,667 to 338,221. The stock of temporary foreign workers in the country soared because the Canadian government extended their visa stay period from two years to a maximum of four years (Citizenship and Immigration Canada 2012). Temporary foreign workers are admitted across the full range of labour market needs. Some are highly educated specialists in their fields (e.g. computer technology, management, engineering) and others take up jobs regarded as low skill and low status (as live-in caregivers, agricultural labourers, and industrial and service sector workers).

Significantly, the 213,573 temporary foreign workers admitted in 2012 considerably exceed the 160,819 immigrants admitted that same year under the economic class. This suggests that Canada is increasingly looking to meet its labour market needs through temporary migration, which requires foreign workers to leave by the "best before date" stamped on their entry visa. This is a dramatic departure from previous policy that regarded migration as strengthening both Canada's economy and its nation-building efforts, as immigrants typically migrated with their immediate family who were all eligible for Canadian citizenship. By contrast, temporary foreign workers arrive without any family and, with few exceptions, are ineligible to stay in Canada permanently or become citizens.

Temporary labour migration is classic neoliberal policy. Employers and government like it because it creates an exploitable workforce that will never have voting rights. Indeed, shortly after its election in 2006, the Conservative government of Prime Minister Stephen Harper declared its strategic economic goal to "gain global competitive advantage" by "creating the world's most flexible workforce" (Department of Finance Canada 2006:6). In this context, "flexibility" means the employers' ability to hire and fire employees as they wish, at wages and working conditions they set unilaterally. Temporary foreign workers were a key element of this strategy, as they are imported for specific jobs and will typically accept whatever wages and working conditions are offered because to complain is to risk being fired and therefore deported, since their stay in Canada is employment related. Additionally, they are generally excluded from protective labour benefits such as employment insurance or health and safety legislation (Kelley and Trebilcock 2010). Nor are they eligible for government-funded immigration settlement programs, creating another incentive for government to favour temporary foreign worker migration over immigrant permanent residents. Rather than raising wages to attract job applicants within Canada, many employers look on **temporary foreign workers** as a supply of cheap labour recruited for them by the federal government. As early as 2007, one of the world's leading publications, *The Economist*, published an article titled "Not Such a Warm Welcome: The Temporary Foreign Workers Pouring into Canada are Often Exploited" (*The Economist* 2007). Temporary labour migration is a recipe for creating an **underclass** of workers in Canada to boost employer profits and limit wages and worker benefits. Critics have called on the government to scale back temporary migration and admit required foreign workers as immigrants with permanent residency and pathways to citizenship (Alboim and Cohl 2012; Siemiatycki 2010).

4. Both Strengthening and Weakening Federal Government Control of Selection

Recent years have seen significant and paradoxical changes in the federal government's control over immigration policy. Simultaneously, the federal government has yielded powers in some areas while tightening its control in others. This section explores both patterns and their significance.

The federal government has put some of its traditional powers over immigration policy in other hands. Immigrant selection is a good example. Long the exclusive domain of federal decision-making, important responsibilities have now been devolved to provincial governments, and nongovernmental actors such as employers, universities, and colleges (Flynn and Bauder 2013).

Quebec was the first province to assert an interest in immigrant selection, flowing from its desire to attract French-speaking immigrants. Since the late 1970s, Quebec has exercised complete control over the selection of economic class immigrants into the province, placing particular emphasis on French-speaking applicants. As a result, the demographics of Quebec's immigrant community are considerably different than other provinces, with significant representation from former colonies of France in Africa, Asia, and the Caribbean. In 1996, the federal government introduced the Provincial Nominee Program (PNP) whereby provinces could select some economic class immigrants to reflect regional labour market needs. Another motivation was to promote a broader diffusion of immigrants across the country, beyond the limited provincial areas of concentration noted earlier. The number of PNP entrants has soared from less than 500 in 1996 to 41,000 in 2012 (Citizenship and Immigration Canada 2012). Employer demand is a key factor in determining the selection of PNP entrants, as it is for temporary foreign workers. And in recent years, the federal government has opened immigrant pathways to international students at Canadian universities. The cumulative effect has been transferring the selection of significant numbers of immigrants from the federal government to the provinces, employers, and post-secondary institutions. Undoubtedly part of the motivation, in keeping with neoliberal inclinations, has been to offload some administrative costs of immigrant selection (staff, office space, and technology) to others.

At the same time, under Prime Minister Harper, the federal government has centralized its capacity for unilateral control of immigration policy still within its jurisdiction. Increasing discretion and authority has been exercised by the immigration minister, enacting important new policies through unilaterally declared Ministerial Instructions. Over the past five years, such decisions have included limiting economic class admissions to occupations identified by the minister; imposing a moratorium on family class sponsorship of parents and grandparents; and cancelling the backlog of 300,000 previously submitted immigration applications. According to Naomi Alboim and Karen Cohl (2012:67), this has resulted in a "weakening of the democratic process" of immigration policymaking as the public and even parliament are frozen out of discussion and input. So while a great deal has clearly changed in immigration selection over the past decade, few of the new policies or approaches have been open to public consultation or debate.

5. Modifying the Terms of Integration

Alongside significant changes to immigrant selection, recent years have seen a turn away from inclusive citizenship, multiculturalism, and newcomer and public services. A brief list of examples would include the following. By dramatically expanding temporary labour migration, Canada sends a signal that it does not want all newcomers to be citizens. Instead, many are wanted only as a short-term supply of lower-cost labour. Additionally, for immigrants eligible to naturalize, the federal government has recently raised the passing grade required on the citizenship test and heightened the language proficiency requirements, resulting in higher failure rates for immigrants seeking to become Canadian citizens. In a single year, from 2011 to 2012, the pass rate on Canada's citizenship exam fell from 83% to 72.5%. Critics contend the government has made citizenship acquisition unnecessarily difficult (Keung 2014; Beiser and Bauder 2014).[1]

Many immigrants and minorities also believe Canada has lessened its embrace of multiculturalism in recent years. A variety of state security measures (as discussed in detail in Chapter 4 by Tariq Amin-Khan), restrictions on religious practice, and pressures to adopt a narrowly defined set of presumed Canadian values all combine to create a more assimilationist or even segregated climate of integration today (Siemiatycki 2012a; Kelley and Trebilcock 2010). Additionally, in its drive to cut government spending, the federal government has reduced funding for newcomer services in some provinces, has eliminated healthcare coverage for many refugees, as we have seen, and has reduced access to programs such as employment insurance or assistance to unemployed Canadians, including immigrants.

Conclusion

The Canadian experience shows that countries can dramatically change their immigration policies over time. For its first century as a country, from the 1860s to the 1960s, Canada's immigration policies combined racism and discrimination to exclude and marginalize most of the world's population. Canada regarded itself as a white, Christian, European country and its immigration policy was designed to replicate and reinforce this self-definition.

Beginning in the 1960s and extending through the rest of the twentieth century, Canada took a new approach to immigrant selection and integration based on greater openness and inclusion. Immigrants were now selected based not on their identity but on their human capital, family ties, or humanitarian claims. Once admitted, their integration would be shaped by a series of diversity- and equity-enhancing measures related to multiculturalism, citizenship, human rights, and newcomer services. Canada came to be regarded as a country that had found the formula for making immigration a success for both newcomers and the host society.

Since the year 2000, immigration policy has again taken a new direction. More than ever, Canada looks to immigration to deliver immediate, short-term economic benefits. This has resulted in dramatic increases in temporary labour migration, with foreigners imported for a few years for specific jobs and then required to leave the country. Among permanent immigrants it has meant admitting far more under the economic class, and fewer under the family and refugee classes. Additionally, the government has adopted various measures to cut its costs administering and supporting immigration.

Until recently, Canada provided immigrants a warm welcome to a cold country. Today, the chill is extending to the country's treatment of newcomers and minorities. The Canadian experience suggests that immigration policies work best when they value newcomers as full and equal members of a diverse society.

Notes

1. Of course, native-born Canadians automatically acquire citizenship without being required to write the test.

Questions for Critical Thought

1. In what ways has Canadian immigration policy changed over time?
2. What factors have influenced Canada's immigration policy over time?
3. What aspect of Canadian immigration policy past and present do you most strongly support and oppose? Why?
4. If you could introduce a single new component of Canadian immigration policy, what would it be?
5. What similarities and differences stand out between American and Canadian immigration policy?

Key Readings

Alboim, N. and K. Cohl (2012) *Shaping the Future: Canada's Rapidly Changing Immigration Policies*. Toronto: Maytree Foundation.

Bloemraad, I. (2006) *Becoming a Citizen: Incorporating Immigrants and Refugees in the United States and Canada*. Berkeley, CA: University of California Press.

Kelley, N. and M. Trebilcock (2010) *The Making of the Mosaic* (2nd ed.). Toronto: University of Toronto Press.

Rodriguez-Garcia, D. (ed.) (2012) *Managing Immigration and Diversity in Canada*. Montreal: McGill-Queen's University Press.

Simmons, A. (2010) *Immigration and Canada: Global and Transnational Perspectives*. Toronto: Canadian Scholars' Press.

Media Links

Citizenship and Immigration Canada, Government of Canada:
www.cic.gc.ca
This is the official immigration website of the Government of Canada.

CERIS: Bridging Migration Research, Policy, and Practice:
www.ceris.metropolis.net/?page_id=5170
The site of an immigration research centre based in Canada's leading immigrant receiving province, Ontario.

No One Is Illegal:
toronto.nooneisillegal.org
An advocacy organization promoting immigrant rights.

Canadian Council for Refugees
ccrweb.ca
This is a research, advocacy, and support organization committed to the rights and protection of refugees and other vulnerable migrants in Canada.

Continuous Journey: A Film by Ali Kazimi:

Part 1: www.youtube.com/watch?v=On_EDTjSW0Q

Part 2: www.youtube.com/watch?v=3gyhoyH9wN0

Part 3: www.youtube.com/watch?v=76ns6SRaDUU

Part 4: www.youtube.com/watch?v=U18EKG8AAeI

This film explores Canada's refusal to allow a boat carrying hundreds of East Indian immigrants to land in the country in 1914.

References

Abella, I. and H. Troper (1982) *None Is Too Many: Canada and the Jews of Europe, 1933–1948*. Toronto: Lester & Orpen Dennys.

Adams, M. (2007) *Unlikely Utopia: The Surprising Triumph of Canadian Pluralism*. Toronto: Viking Press.

Aguiar, L. (2006) The New "In-Between" Peoples: Southern-European Transnationalism (2006). In V. Satzewich and L. Wong (eds.) *Transnational Identities and Practices in Canada*, pp. 202–215. Vancouver: UBC Press.

Alboim, N. and K. Cohl (2012) *Shaping the Future: Canada's Rapidly Changing Immigration Policies*. Toronto: Maytree Foundation.

Andrew, C., J. Biles, M. Burstein, V. Esses, and E. Tolley (eds.) (2012) *Immigration, Integration, and Inclusion in Ontario Cities*. Montreal: McGill-Queen's University Press.

Arbel, E. and A. Brenner (2013) *Bordering on Failure: Canada-US Border Policy and the Politics of Refugee Exclusion*. Cambridge, MA: Harvard Immigration and Refugee Law Clinical Program, Harvard Law School.

Beiser, M. and H. Bauder (2014) Canada's Immigration System Undergoing Quiet, Ugly Revolution. *Toronto Star*, 12 May, A7.

Biles, J., M. Burstein, and J. Frideres (2008) Introduction. In J. Biles, M. Burstein, and J. Frideres (eds.) *Immigration and Integration in Canada in the Twenty-first Century*, pp. 3–18. Montreal: McGill-Queen's University Press.

Bloemraad, I. (2006) *Becoming a Citizen: Incorporating Immigrants and Refugees in the United States and Canada*. Berkeley, CA: University of California Press. www.civilization.ca/cmc/exhibitions/aborig/fp/fpz2f_1e.shtml (Accessed December 27, 2013)

Bloemraad, I. (2011) "Two Peas in a Pod," "Apples and Oranges," and Other Food Metaphors: Comparing Canada and the United States. *American Behavioral Scientist* 56(9):1131–1159.

Citizenship and Immigration Canada (2012) Facts and Figures 2012—Immigration Overview: Permanent and Temporary Residents. Ottawa: Government of Canada.

Department of Finance Canada (2006) Advantage Canada: Building a Strong Economy for
  Canada. Ottawa: Government of Canada.

The Economist (2007) The Temporary Workers Pouring into Canada Are Often Exploited.
  22 November. www.economist.com/node/10177080 (Accessed December 11, 2013)

Flynn, E. and H. Bauder (2013) *The Private Sector, Institutions of Higher Education, and
  Immigrant Settlement in Canada*. RCIS Working Paper 2013/9, 21 pp.
  www.ryerson.ca/rcis/publications/index.html (Accessed December 27, 2013).

Hayduk, R. (2004) Democracy for All: Restoring Immigrant Voting Rights in the US.
  New Political Science 26(4):499–523.

Johnson, H. (1970) *The Voyage of the "Komagata Maru": The Sikh Challenge to Canada's
  Colour Bar*. Delhi, India: Oxford University Press.

Kelley, N. and M. Trebilcock (2012) *The Making of the Mosaic*. 2nd ed. Toronto: University
  of Toronto Press.

Keung, N. (2012) Super Visa Applications for Visitors to Canada Are Often Rejected. *Toronto
  Star*, 14 March. www.thestar.com/news/canada/2012/03/14/super_visa_applications_
  for_visitors_to_canada_are_often_rejected.html (Accessed December 11, 2013).

Keung, N. (2013a) Toronto Declared 'Sanctuary City' to Non-status Migrants.
  Toronto Star, 21 February. www.thestar.com/news/gta/2013/02/21/cisanctuarycity21.
  html (Accessed December 28, 2013)

Keung, N. (2013b) Asylum Claims Plummet under Rigid Rules. *Toronto Star*,
  15 December, A9.

Keung, N. (2013c) Ontario Reinstates Health Care for Refugees. *Toronto Star*,
  10 December, A6.

Keung, N. (2014) Longtime Residents Likely to Struggle on Citizenship Exam. *Toronto Star*,
  12 May, A13.

Kymlicka, W. (1998) *Finding Our Way: Rethinking Ethnocultural Relations in Canada*.
  Don Mills, ON: Oxford University Press.

Li, P. (1998) *Chinese in Canada*. 2nd ed. Toronto: Oxford University Press.

Lynch, J. and R. Simon (2003) *Immigration the World Over: Statutes, Policies, and Practices*.
  Lanham, MD: Rowman & Littlefield.

Parks Canada. (2013) L'Anse aux Meadows National Historical Site.
  www.pc.gc.ca/lhn-nhs/nl/meadows/index.aspx (Accessed December 27, 2013)

Ray, A. (1996) *I Have Lived Here Since the World Began*. Toronto: Key Porter Books.

Rodriguez-Garcia, D. (ed.) (2012) *Managing Immigration and Diversity in Canada*.
  Montreal: McGill-Queen's University Press.

Siemiatycki, M. (2009) Urban Citizenship for Immigrant Cities. *Plan Canada*
  January-February:75–78.

Siemiatycki, M. (2010) Marginalizing Migrants: Canada's Rising Reliance on Temporary
  Foreign Workers. *Canadian Issues* Spring 2010:60–63.

Siemiatycki, M. (2012a) The Place of Immigrants: Citizenship, Settlement and Socio-cultural Integration in Canada. In D. Rodriguez-Garcia (ed.) *Managing Immigration and Diversity in Canada*, pp. 223–247. Montreal: McGill-Queen's University Press.

Siemiatycki, M. (2012b) Toronto: Integration in a City of Immigrants. In C. Andrew, J. Biles, M. Burstein, V. Esses, and E. Tolley (eds.) *Immigration, Integration, and Inclusion in Ontario Cities*, pp. 23–48. Montreal: McGill-Queen's University Press.

Statistics Canada (1997) *The Daily*, 4 November. Ottawa: Government of Canada.

Statistics Canada (2012) *The Canadian Population in 2011: Population Counts and Growth*. Ottawa: Government of Canada.

Statistics Canada (2013a) *Immigration and Ethnocultural Diversity in Canada*. Ottawa: Government of Canada.

Statistics Canada (2013b) Obtaining Canadian Citizenship. Catalogue no. 99-010-X2011003.

Sunahara, A. (1981) *The Uprooting of Japanese Canadians during the Second World War*. Toronto: James Lorimer & Company.

Triadafilopoulos, T. (2012) *Becoming Multicultural: Immigration and the Politics of Membership in Canada and Germany*. Vancouver: UBC Press.

Troper, H. (1993) Canada's Immigration Policy since 1945. *International Journal* 48(2):55–81.

Trudeau, P. (1971) Speech in Parliament, 8 October.

Chapter 4

SECURITY AND ITS IMPACT ON MIGRANTS AND REFUGEES

TARIQ AMIN-KHAN

Introduction

Security, fear, and overarching concerns about terrorism have followed us into the second decade of the twenty-first century. The "war on terror" has linked migration to terrorism by raising red flags of suspicion about migrants' origins, especially if they are from Muslim-majority states. Georgios Karyotis (2011:13) writes,

> Immigrants and asylum seekers are often seen as a threat to public order and stability. They are also often believed to be "plotting" to exploit national welfare provisions and available economic opportunities at the expense of citizens. Above all, they are seen as a threat to the identity of [Western] societies.

Other scholars have also argued about the perceived threat to security of Western state and society from migration in all of its different forms, and the response has been to "fortress" Europe and North America (see Bourbeau 2011; Lazaridis 2011). Western governments, instead of relying on a range of political options, decided to follow the lead of their respective security agencies and have imputed a causal link between migration and security, and migration and terrorism. Then there is the issue of fear that is intimately linked to (in)security. This has largely to do with the fear of the different **other**, that is, a culturally and phenotypically different individual or group considered to be separate and apart from the dominant mainstream Western community, culture, or religion. The *other* happens to be **racialized** individuals or groups. They are either part of the historically oppressed communities, the Indigenous and black peoples in Canada and the US, or are those from Africa, Asia, and Latin America, collectively known as the Global South. The latter enter the domain of security when they land in Canada and the US. This link between migration and security, which has also been termed the **migration-security nexus**, is the concern of this chapter.

Undoubtedly, national security is one of the responsibilities of the state. However, when security becomes an overarching concern of state policy—where surveillance and security trump democratic rights—then such a preoccupation with security can violate the rights of the more vulnerable sections of society and erode democracy. This chapter will critically examine the story of migrants and asylum seekers in the contemporary period of hyper-security. Of concern is the notion of securitization, and Canada's and the US's security and migration policies. **Securitization** is a process whereby those who fit a certain identity-based profile—of the "terrorist" *other* or of someone viewed as liable to indulge in criminal activity to harm state and society—are targeted, treated suspiciously, and/or subjected to **racism** and harm from ordinary members of mainstream Western society, media, and security forces. Another view, with a different emphasis, sees securitization as a process

> through which elites, with "the most effective means of public persuasion and the best resources for suppressing or marginalizing alternative opinions" succeed in defining an issue as an existential threat to fundamental values of society and the state. (Karyotis 2011:14)[1]

Other scholars place emphasis on "securitizing agents" by focusing on the role of politicians, bureaucrats, and media in promoting fear of the *other* and exacerbating the process of securitization (Bourbeau 2011).[2] Ordinary mainstream citizens as well as security personnel in Canada and the US can even treat immigrants and refugees in a manner that may be disrespectful, as well as emotionally and physically harmful, with minimal repercussion (see American Civil Liberties Union 2001 [June 28]; Human Rights Watch 2013; Usova 2013; Amin-Khan 2012a). Therefore, this chapter will analyze how migrants and refugees have become a security concern in North America.

In critically examining immigration and refugee policy in Canada and the US, one notices an increasing convergence in the policies and laws of these two states: they are becoming a common mechanism to criminalize, label as "undesirable" or treat as "security threats" those fleeing persecution or economic deprivation when they reach North America. By examining some aspects of Canada's Immigration and Refugee Protection Act (IRPA) and the US's Patriot Act, the objective is to show that these laws not only securitize and criminalize migrants and refugees; these legislations "represent an arrogation by the Executive of *exceptional* power" (Friedland and Friedland 2006:66). This appropriation of exceptional power may be disturbing in the current conjuncture, but such a move is not unprecedented in the history of liberal Western democracies. Speaking of history, the chapter will also examine the triggers of the present securitization process: Were the events of September 11, 2001, responsible or was this process well underway even earlier? The simple answer is the latter. But the explanation is more involved and compels us to briefly examine the final decade of the Cold War and its end in 1989. The post-1989 period is the general timeframe during which the phenomenon of **globalization** emerged and became part of the lexicon.

The Neoliberal Turn and Its Impetus for the Movement of People

Globalization is both an ideological outlook and a descriptor for rapid technological developments that have contributed, as David Harvey argues, to the "compression of time and space" since 1989. This is felt by the dizzying pace of communication and advances in information technology, while the volume and mobility of financial capital has been truly unprecedented. Equally, *globalization* as a descriptive term signifies the rapid movement of industrial production from Western states to the Global South to take advantage of the abysmally low wages paid to workers. Many also see globalization as making the world more cosmopolitan, marked by worldwide interconnectedness and interdependency (Held, McGrew, Glodblatt, and Perraton 1999; Brown and Held 2010; van Hooft and Vandekerckhove 2010; Ziemer and Roberts 2013). However, very few notice that much of Africa and parts of Asia have been bypassed by globalization and excluded from this interconnectedness and interdependency. This view of interconnectedness also has very little empathy for those living in urban centres of the Global South that are bursting at their seams as displaced people from rural areas gravitate to the cities in desperation to find work.

In contrast to a descriptive understanding, globalization becomes contested when viewed as ideology. As a concept, **ideology** privileges distinctive economic, political, and social ideas and values in order to shape belief and influence outcomes. **Globalization as ideology** is meant to push for the supremacy of the market to achieve unbridled mobility of financial and industrial capital around the globe. As an ideology, globalization comes to be closely associated with the phenomenon of neoliberalism, addressed in more detail below, where there is almost exclusive reliance on the market, while simultaneously, extensive restrictions are placed on government intervention in economic and social affairs, with the purpose of achieving the most favourable economic outcomes for business. This emphasis on the market serves to ideologically reorient the role of the state, from its traditional function of strengthening the public domain for society's uplift to dismantling the public sector in the interest of corporations. As ideology of the market's supremacy, globalization enables the removal of most controls on the unchecked movement of capital, while the movement of workers, as migrants, has been tightly regulated by the Western state.

By briefly examining the historical and still unfolding elements of the current globalization era, we will learn that 1) many countries of the Global South were restructured along the lines of **neoliberalism**, beginning in the 1980s, to facilitate the globalization process; 2) globalization simultaneously created tremendous wealth and poverty (often in different spheres of the globe) with more people in the Global South becoming displaced and precipitously poor, and thus desperate to migrate in search of livelihood; and 3) one significant consequence of neoliberalism and globalization has been the rise of securitization and the targeting of migrants and refugees in Western states. The state in both the West and the Global South, as scholars have argued, has been central in realizing the project of globalization and neoliberalism (Varadarajan 2004; Amin-Khan 2012b). Further, "one cannot make sense of national security policies [framed by the state] without treating processes of neoliberalism as the inescapable grounds for such practices" (Varadarajan 2004:321). This is because the rise of neoliberalism has produced dislocation and uncertainty in the Global South that has compelled people to migrate both within and outside the Third World. The influx of migrants and refugees into Western states has produced anxiety and insecurity in these societies, and this in turn has unleashed the process of securitization and the formation of the security state—with the events of September 11 further intensifying the process. In order to explicate the important link between neoliberalism and securitization, the next few pages of this section are devoted to first understanding the emergence of the project of globalization and neoliberalism, and then how this project is linked to the securitization of migrants to Western states, while subsequent sections address how this coupling of security and migration has unfolded and expanded in Canada and the US.

The term **neoliberalism** marks a return to the idea of the self-regulating "free" market. This is meant to replace the concept of a more regulated market that was introduced after the Great Depression of the 1930s. The need for greater regulation was to avoid a repeat of the calamitous social upheavals that were the result of steep economic decline—a precise consequence of the failure of the self-regulating market, and resulting in very high unemployment. During the 1920s, the self-regulating market actually failed to keep a check on the speculative tendency of powerful corporate investors and investment bankers, among other lapses, and this led to greater regulation of the economy. The regulatory framework, introduced during the 1930s, continued until the 1970s when a series of recessions hit Western economies. This prompted a move for market deregulation and the promotion of the self-regulating market idea. It was meant to signal that the market failures of the 1970s recessions were largely the result of overregulation and government or political failure (Stilwell 2006: 203–204). These advocates of the market, essentially orthodox or neoclassical economists, desired a broader return to orthodox or neoclassical economic thought to ensure the notion of the market's dominance. They pursued the economic ideas of Alfred Marshall, Fredrick Hayek, and economists associated with the University of Chicago who began reformulating the eighteenth- and nineteenth-century classical economic thought of Adam Smith and David Ricardo, among others (see Dowd 2004; Stilwell 2006). Beginning in the 1970s, these neoclassical or orthodox economists became very influential in gradually shaping the economic and social policy of key Western states toward greater market orientation. Neoclassical thought emphasized the supremacy of the market and rejected public (i.e. state) ownership of enterprises, advocating for their privatization, while lobbying strongly for deregulation—a move that was part of a broader strategy of minimal government intervention in economic and social affairs. The objective of neoclassical economists in the name of efficiency, economic growth, and less financial waste has been to route all economic and most social activities and decisions through the market and the private sector. In its current variant, this neoclassical thought, identified as neoliberalism, has developed in tandem as globalization's ideological impulse.

Neoliberalism as a phenomenon of market liberalization, privatization, and deregulation makes the claim that "a largely unregulated capitalist system (a 'free market economy') ... achieves optimum economic performance with respect to efficiency, economic growth, technical progress, and distributional justice" (Kotz 2002:64) More important, neoliberalism has actively strived for the privatization of the public sphere and has successfully achieved this objective. Today, much of the economic activity of public enterprises such as railways, airlines, utilities, and road building and infrastructure projects that were once part of the **public sphere** have been privatized and ownership transferred to private corporations. However, since its emergence in 1983, the effects of neoliberalism in the name of efficiency, economic growth, cost saving, and less government have been most damaging for labour and the poor, whose wages and living conditions have severely eroded (Hart-Landsberg 2006; Kotz 2002). In the process, the rich have become wealthier, resulting in a glaring wealth divide between the well-heeled and the destitute: in the US, the wealth of the richest 1% has increased eightfold between 1979 and 2007 (Lezner 2012). In Canada, the wealth increase has been less dramatic than in the US, but the trend also points upwards (CBC News 2011).

As for workers and the poor in the Global South, the impact of neoliberal policies has been most severe, with ever larger numbers in their ranks slipping deeper into poverty. Martin Hart-Landsberg's study of neoliberalism concludes that "the post-1980 neoliberal era has been marked by slower growth, greater trade imbalances, and deteriorating social conditions" for much of the Global South (2006:9). Before the term *neoliberalism* became popular, similar market-oriented policies had been imposed since the mid-1970s—as conditions on loans, initially termed "condition-alities"—on Third World states by the International Monetary Fund (IMF) and the World Bank. Conditionalities, later renamed structural adjustment programs (SAPs), forced Third World governments to restructure economic and social policy by liberalizing trade, promoting deregulation, and devaluing currency, while removing food subsidies and other social support from the poorest sections of society. These structural changes and the mechanization of agriculture displaced large numbers of people from rural areas and the displaced drifted to the cities in search of work. Unable to find work in the ballooning urban centres, the situation of the displaced was made worse by the extremely limited social support that was available due to IMF-imposed SAPs and the neglect from the ruling elite in the Global South—resulting in the large majority becoming unemployed or underemployed.

Because this captive unemployed labour force was desperately seeking work, real wages saw considerable decline in much of Asia, Africa, and Latin America. The declining wages did not keep pace with the high inflation at the time or the steep devaluations of most Third World states' currencies. The multinational corporations, ever eager to take advantage of lower wages, started to become footloose—willing to roam and move from one country to another at short notice to exploit this captive force of the unemployed. The condition of the poor was further aggravated when governments in the Global South agreed to set up export processing zones (EPZs) in order to attract multinational companies. EPZs have been enclaves where labour laws are deregulated or suspended, privatization is promoted, imports are not taxed, and wages are significantly lowered, while the workday is drastically extended (Amin-Khan 2012b; Wells 2007). In this environment the notion of sweatshop work, which started to unfold with the spread of EPZs, became much more prevalent in many Third World countries. EPZs, or *maquiladoras* in the North and Latin American context, now represent vast islands of industrial production where the country's labour laws are effectively suspended, workplace safety is largely abandoned, and collective bargaining is actively suppressed. Thus, it is no surprise that in the contemporary globalization era, media stories abound about a garment factory's collapse in Dacca, Bangladesh, and factory fires in Karachi and Manila that kill hundreds of workers.[3]

Given the precariousness of work under neoliberalism, the displacement of people from rural regions, and the high rates of unemployment in the urban areas of the Global South, the displaced have been forced to migrate to improve their chances of survival. However, not all of those displaced by neoliberal policies of globalization have moved to Western states. Large numbers of the displaced move within the same state from one region to another, such as from rural to urban areas (termed internal migration). There is also movement across states within the Global South (called South-South migration), which is almost of the same level as the movement from the Global South to the North. The UN Population Division's data reveals that the stock of South-South migrants at the end of 2010 was 73 million or 34% of the different forms of migration, which was almost equal to the South-North stock of migrants in 2010 at 74 million or 35% of total migrants (United Nations 2012). However, there is even movement from North to North and, to a much lesser extent, from North to South. In 2013, the number of international migrants worldwide reached 232 million, from 154 million in 1990—the year marking the beginning of the globalization phenomenon—however, of the total international migrants, 59% or 136 million lived in the North (United Nations 2013).

The case of refugees and asylum seekers, in contrast, is quite different from that of migrants fleeing their neoliberal policy-driven displacement. The refugees from the South, uprooted by wars, authoritarian rule, political conflicts, and persecution based on ethnicity, religion, and culture largely end up moving to other states within the same region. In other words, it is a form of South-South migration. But the accompanying circumstances for the refugees are most oppressive and fraught with hardships: they are forced to live in tents or temporary shelter and with very little means of earning a livelihood. Given the current nature of conflict in Africa, the Middle East, and West Asia, the UN Refugee Agency (UNHCR) estimates 55% of refugees come from 5 countries affected by war: Afghanistan, Somalia, Iraq, Syria, and Sudan (UNHCR 2013a). "More people are refugees or internally displaced than at any time since 1994 [the time of the Rwandan genocide] ... [and] as of the end of 2012, more than 45.2 million people were in situations of displacement compared to 42.5 million at the end of 2011" (UNHCR 2013b). Countries of the Global South host more than 80% of the world's forcibly displaced people as of 2012, compared to 70% a decade back. Pakistan hosts the most refugees in the world—1.6 million people from Afghanistan—followed by Iran (868,200), Germany (589,700), and Kenya (565,000) (UNHCR 2013a).

Coupling Migration with National Security

This section and the next two sections compare and contrast the treatment of migrants and refugees in Canada and the US: how they are profiled and how new immigration and anti-terrorism laws impact them adversely. These sections will offer organic comparisons between the two states, instead of mechanically separating the processes of securitization in Canada and the US. This is done in order to highlight how the securitization process has been a mutually reinforcing trajectory followed by both of these states to successively intensify the targeting and criminalizing of refugees and migrants.

With the onset of globalization, the accompanying dislocation and rising poverty due to neoliberal policies, and the increasing un- and **underemployment** in the Global South since the 1980s, it is not surprising to witness the worldwide movement of displaced people. However, just as the population movement from the Global South began to increase, there was also a coordinated clampdown on the entry of migrants into Western states. Such a step, as mentioned earlier, reveals the contradictions of globalization: while borders have disappeared for the free movement of capital, stiffer and stronger borders have become barriers against the movement of people. The pretext for such moves, in the Canadian context, has been the protection of the economy, an argument "which has long informed Canadian immigration policy" (Gunn, 2013, p. 4).[4] In contrast, during the period of neoliberal restructuring, the US has seen an increase in the new **immigrant** population alongside a rise of anti-immigrant policy activism from mainstream community groups in more than 130 cities across the country (Varsanyi 2011). As of 2010, more than a decade and a half since the North American Free Trade Agreement (NAFTA) among US, Canada, and Mexico became operational, in the state of Arizona there has been a rise of

> two parastatal [auxilliary state] elements associated with Arizona's enforcement apparatus: private prisons and vigilante groups. In the late 1990s, the Immigration and Naturalization Service threw the almost dead private prison industry a bone, offering it contracts to imprison undocumented immigrants. Within a decade, as migration boomed, armed vigilante groups like Ranch Rescue, the American Border Patrol, and the Minutemen, some associated with national white supremacist groups, began forming in southern Arizona and patrolling the desert for supposedly dangerous immigrants. (Miller 2010:4)

Case Example 1: Securitization Timeline: US Immigration Laws

1986, November 6—Immigration Reform and Control Act (IRCA): This was the Reagan administration's attempt to overhaul immigration laws, tighten border controls, and increase **border enforcement**.

1994, October 1—Operation Gatekeeper: Introduced by the Clinton administration to control "illegal" migrants at Mexico's border crossings, and authorized $50 billion to build a 14-mile security fence along the border. Critics considered this move to be the border's "militarization."

1996, August 22—Personal Responsibility and Work Opportunity Reconciliation Act and the Welfare Reform Act: These laws restricted eligibility of "legal immigrants" to access welfare provisions (economic security), while the Welfare Reform Act denied them federal entitlement programs.

2001, October 26—Patriot Act: Anti-terrorism legislation, but with a focus on the securitization of migrants and refugees. Overnight, it increased funding for immigration, border, and security personnel, and for the widespread deployment of monitoring technology at immigration checkpoints

2002, November 25—Homeland Security Act: Significant to securitization, this law transferred the responsibilities of the Immigration and Naturalization Service (INS) from the Justice Department to the Department of Homeland Security (DHS), and the agency was renamed United States Citizenship and Immigration Services (USCIS). The immigrant enforcement and service functions are now under the Border and Transportation Security directorate and USCIS, respectively.

2005, December 16—Border Protection, Antiterrorism, and Illegal Immigration Control Act: This would-be act's intention was to criminalize the assistance of undocumented migrants, among other measures. However, the bill did not become law as it only passed the House of Representatives and was defeated in the Senate.

2006, October 26—Secure Fence Act: Authorized the construction of a 700-mile fence at the US-Mexico border.

2009, December 15/2013, September—Comprehensive Immigration Reform for America's Security and Prosperity: The original bill lapsed in committee; it was reintroduced as an immigration reform bill in September 2013 (Pop Vox 2013).

Source: Russell Sage Foundation (n.d.).

In the US, the rise of often-racist vigilante groups and for-profit prisons has accompanied an overzealousness on the part of some law enforcement officials, such as the 2006 action of Arizona's Maricopa County sheriff Joseph Arpaio. He assembled a 250-strong posse to round up undocumented migrants whom he charged with criminal conspiracy, held in a tent city that he established for 2,000 prisoners, and forced male prisoners to wear pink underwear (Miller 2010:4). Whatever fear or economic insecurity of Western states may have triggered the tightening of borders, the response of state functionaries and ordinary citizens has been less than dignified toward migrants and refugees as their humiliating treatment became normalized and more cavalier. Consequently, it did not take long for Western states in North America, Europe, and Australia to universalize this attitude toward immigrants and asylum seekers from the Global South and to treat them as potential threats to national security.

In Canada, just as the Cold War ended in 1989, immigration laws were revised through Bills C-55 and C-84, which introduced restrictive changes to immigration law and to the powers of the Immigration and Refugee Board (IRB). The refugee determination system was further restricted through Bill C-86 in 1992. "The provision 'danger to the public' enters the Immigration Act with Bill C-44 in 1995, by which a person loses the right to appeal the removal order if the Minister of Citizenship and Immigration" deems such a person as a danger to society (Bourbeau 2011:20). So, by the time the IRPA was enacted in 2002, it reinforced the oppressive use of security certificates, and "expanded the inadmissibility categories to permit refusal of entry on the grounds of security" (Bourbeau 2011:20). Although security certificates were used at the height of the Cold War in 1971 to deal with espionage initiated by visitors to Canada, largely from the former Soviet Union and the Eastern Bloc states, this detention mechanism was formalized in 1991 and made part of IRPA in 2002. However, the troubling element of security certificates has to do with the fact that the person charged is not entitled to know why and on what grounds they have been arrested: only a special advocate appointed by the court is made privy to the information against the accused. This advocate determines to what extent the evidence and/or charges against a security certificate detainee can be shared with the defence counsel. "The security certificate process within the *Immigration and Refugee Protection Act* is not a criminal proceeding, but an immigration proceeding" (Public Safety Canada n.d.). In essence, this means that select criminal laws have been integrated into IRPA with a diminishing need to rely on the Criminal Code for criminal convictions. This change is part of other developments, including the introduction of the Anti-Terrorism Act, steadily underway since the events of September 11, 2001, that have restructured the Canadian state as a *security state*.

Across the border, the notion of national security became a well-entrenched structural reality of the US state much earlier, with the passage of the National Security Act (NSA) in 1947. This act was the impetus for the Cold War, and it also gave birth to the Central Intelligence Agency (CIA). Since the passage of the NSA, national security interests have driven the US's Cold War policy vis-á-vis the Soviet Union and its actions against left-wing governments in the Third World. Migrants from the Global South were not a serious concern until the 1980s. At the time when the ideas of neoliberalism were being introduced, the Reagan administration instituted the Immigration Reform and Control Act (IRCA) of 1986 to broadly reform US immigration laws and to also tighten border controls through increased border enforcement. A more comprehensive securitization of immigration laws began in 1994 (see Case Example 1) when the Clinton administration launched Operation Gatekeeper to control irregular migration across the Mexican border between San Diego and Tijuana, known as a corridor for unauthorized border crossings. Hints about monitoring of migrants and international students became apparent with the September 1996 passage of the Illegal Immigration Reform and Immigrant Responsibility Act. This act, among other moves, required academic institutions to collect information on the status and nationality of foreign students for the Immigration and Naturalization Service (INS) in order to monitor students and those considered security risks. On grounds of economic security, the Welfare Reform Act of 1996 made many legal immigrants ineligible for federal entitlement programs. After the attacks of September 11, 2001, the Patriot Act was hurriedly enacted in October 2001. It introduced many changes to criminal and immigration laws, and broadened the scope of immigrants considered ineligible to enter the US. It also increased funding and personnel for improved monitoring technology at immigration control points. More significant changes affecting landed immigrants, undocumented migrants and refugees, and even US citizens were made with the passage of the Homeland Security Act in 2002.[5]

Why Are Migrants and Refugees Criminalized and Securitized?

The previous section showed how the link between security and migration was established in Canada and the US well before the events of September 11, 2001. François Crépeau and his associates point out how criminality becomes linked to immigration—impacting the rights of migrants—while concluding that the events of September 11 have furthered the securitization of migration:

> The rights of foreigners in host countries have deteriorated due to the connection made between immigration and criminality. Restrictions imposed upon irregular migrants' basic political and civil rights have been accompanied by major obstacles to their access to economic and social rights, including the right to health. The events of 9/11 further contributed to this trend.... Recent policy developments and ongoing international cooperation implementing systematic interception and interdiction mechanisms have led to the securitization of migration. (Crépeau, Nakache, and Atak 2007:311)

The already precarious situation of refugees in Canada became even more so with the arrival by sea of 76 and 492 Tamil asylum seekers, in 2009 and 2010 respectively, fleeing war and persecution in Sri Lanka. The arrival of these asylum seekers was the trigger for the Canadian government of Prime Minister Harper to reintroduce modified versions of earlier proposed "anti-smuggling" legislations in the form of Bill C-31 in January 2012 (see Case Example 2). It was passed as the Protecting Canada's Immigration System Act in June 2012. The act criminalizes groups of asylum seekers and treats them as part of human smuggling operations, while Citizenship and Immigration Canada (CIC) justifies this move, using the instrument of fear to claim that "the Government is ensuring the safety and security of our streets and communities" (CIC 2013).

Thus, each arriving member of an asylum seekers' group is treated as an "irregular arrival" and is subject to detention for up to one year or until his or her asylum application is granted or denied (CIC 2013). Even those who genuinely assist asylum seekers on humanitarian grounds, without any expectation of financial gain, would be treated as human smugglers and subject to imprisonment. Further, children 16 and older can be imprisoned. The Harper government does not hide its disdain of asylum seekers by openly claiming on the CIC website that "the Government is also reducing the attraction of coming to Canada by way of detaining participants in a designated irregular arrival" (CIC 2013). The Act also goes beyond asylum seekers and treats visitors on valid visas from certain designated countries, such as many

Case Example 2: Criminalization of Asylum Seekers

Tamil asylum seekers who could muster $20,000 to $35,000 to pay smugglers in East Asia (Gunn 2013) decided to leave Sri Lanka to escape the military's wrath after the defeat of the national struggle for a Tamil homeland. They arrived on Canada's west coast from ports in Thailand and Malaysia on two rickety cargo vessels: the first batch of 76 refugees on October 17, 2009, and 492 more on August 13, 2010.

The arrival of the first boatload provided the Harper government the pretext to further criminalize immigration laws. This led to the introduction of Bills C-4 (anti-smuggling bill) and C-11 (refugee reform bill). The latter was passed in 2010, but its implementation was delayed. The modified Bill C-31 (incorporating significant elements of Bills C-4 and C-11) passed in June 2012 as the Protecting Canada's Immigration System Act with further securitized provisions, such as obtaining biometric information of visitors and temporary workers on valid visas from select, largely Muslim-majority, states. This law, however, particularly impacts asylum seekers. Even those who support refugees on humanitarian grounds risk being charged as "smugglers." A refugee applicant and "smuggler" could each potentially stay incarcerated for up to one year or until the decision of their case. The law, in contravention of the rights of a child, can imprison 16- and 17-year-old child refugees.

The coverage of the Tamil refugees in the media has also been most troubling. An audit of the media representation and coverage of the Tamils arriving on boats suggests that newspaper reports placed undue emphasis on issues of "criminality and terrorism, and constructed the refugees as risk" to Canada's national security (Bradmore and Bauder 2011:637). The authors of the media audit also found that "Canadian newsprint relied heavily on terms of 'illegality' to describe the Tamil refugees, which worked to legitimize their detention and established the necessary political environment in which the federal government could quickly usher in Bill C-11 during the summer of 2010" (638).

Muslim-majority states, as potential national security risks—singling them out for greater scrutiny and requiring them to provide biometric information. Of concern is that biometric data of this cluster of people—temporary visitors to Canada, students, and work permit holders from the designated countries—in all likelihood will be held indefinitely in a permanent database.

These changes in immigration and other attendant laws in Canada and the US are in stark contrast to how refugees and asylum seekers were treated prior to the 1980s. Through much of the Cold War era (1949 to 1989), refugees, especially from Eastern Europe, were encouraged to seek refuge and were well received in Europe and North America. No distinction was made between "legal" and "illegal" asylum seekers. Even people fleeing persecution, wars, and natural calamities in the Global South during the 1980s were grudgingly accepted by Western states. So what has changed to make Western states treat migrants and refugees from the Global South as a security concern?

Part of the answer, as outlined in earlier sections, has to do with the rise of neoliberalism and globalization and the sheer numbers of displaced people from the Global South trying to migrate to better their survival odds. However, as deterrence is usually the objective of security-focused policy, it can be said that the harsh criminalization of refugees is meant to discourage would-be migrants and asylum seekers. But the reality is that if deterrence is the underlying objective, it is clearly not working. Therefore, it would make sense to pause and take stock: If the problem of the influx of migrants to Western states is due to neoliberal and globalization policies, would it not be appropriate to reverse or dismantle these policies? Would it also not be sensible for Third World states to address social and economic dislocations and have meaningful strategies to alleviate poverty—instead of being wedded to IMF's neoliberal restructuring?

Although these are sensible questions, there is much at stake here for powerful corporations and the wealthy in allowing the state, both in the North and the South, to play a more interventionist role by enlarging social investments in the public sphere, while those in power in the Global South are more committed to following IMF's dictates than to taking steps to genuinely reduce poverty. As the experience of the last three decades has shown, it is simpler for Western states, with the active support of mainstream anti-immigrant groups, to successively strengthen the border and tighten immigration laws in the name of security than to undertake the more difficult task of reining in neoliberalism or addressing poverty in the Global South. The reason leaders of Western states do not or cannot stand up to the wealthy and large corporations is because they too are wedded to the ideology of the market's dominance. It would be an anathema for Western politicians, lobby groups, and corporations that promote the privatization of the public domain on the basis of "efficiency" and "cutting waste" to even contemplate reversing the policies of neoliberalism in the absence of effective opposition to neoliberalism. As documented earlier, the wealth gap between the rich and poor in the last 30 years has grown much wider in favour of the former, while market-orientation of policy, the ideological underpinning of neoliberalism, has benefited corporations as well as the rich. So, for the politicians and bureaucrats in power in the era of neoliberalism and securitization, it is much simpler to enact policy (with the accompanying laws) in the name of security than to backtrack on the ideology of neoliberalism.

The other part of the explanation of why immigrants and refugees are criminalized has to do with issues of identity and **race**. By now, it should be reasonably apparent that for more than two decades since the **migration-security nexus** has been operational, Western states have *not* faced significant consequences for their differential treatment of the racialized, or for the criminalization of refugees and migrants. It is, therefore, no surprise that these states collectively and individually have remained unreflective on how their respective migration and anti-terrorism policies criminalize and dehumanize immigrants, refugees, and **racialized** people generally. Further, Western states—whether they are governed by conservatives, such Stephen Harper in Canada and those heading most European states, or liberals and social democrats like Barack Obama and François Hollande of France—just do not want to veer away from the neoliberal framework because the underlying policies sustain them in power. More to the point, from the perspective of Western states, because neoliberalism-induced dislocations largely affect racialized people from the Global South and the poor and racialized in the North, there is little incentive for these states and their leadership to address the problem of human displacement. The mainstream popular public sentiment about immigrants, especially in the US and to a large extent in Canada, neatly aligns with the harsh attitude of police and security personnel toward migrants and refugees resulting in the latter being targeted as potential criminals or security risks. This happens as the process of **racialization** of the **other** becomes deeply entrenched in society.

Who becomes this *other* has varied over the history of European colonialism and slavery in the Americas, Africa, and Asia. People of continental Europe and those who settled in the Americas, North America in particular, have developed a *sense of self* as accomplished, modern, rational, and enlightened individuals (Said 1995). This sense of self was, and continues to be, contrasted with the *inferiorness* that is ascribed to the *other* from Africa, Asia, and Latin America (see Fanon 1968). The latter have also been considered irrational, traditional, and culturally unsophisticated and thus worthy of being debased and demonized (Said 1995). This peculiar process of identity formation of the dominant and subordinate groups creates the notion of the *self* and the *other*. "Self and *other*, in other words, are always related in identity formation" (Kinnvall 2002:83). Further, since September 11, and because of the threat of terrorism from militant Islamists, migrants and refugees from Muslim-majority states have been targeted and made vulnerable (Amin-Khan 2012a). If one couples the view of self with its self-perception as the injured party—perceived as such by the leadership in Canada and the US since the September 11 attacks—it makes for a potent mix that leaves very little room for empathy toward those deemed as the potentially harmful *other*. Consequently, the criminalization and securitization of migrants and refugees continues as the justification of protecting national security—specifically against those who are perceived to have entered the country "illegally" to inflict harm on the dominant community. Therefore, it is no surprise that migration has been "increasingly linked to criminality, socio-economic problems, cultural deprivation, and lately to terrorism" (Toğral 2011:224).

New Immigration and Anti-Terrorism Laws and the Future of Liberal Democracy

Given the links constructed between migration and criminality, and migration and national security, the post–September 11 environment provided fertile ground for *security* to become a sturdy anvil to shape new immigration policies and anti-terrorism laws in Canada and the US. The Uniting and Strengthening America by Providing Appropriate Tools Required to Intercept and Obstruct Terrorism Act (USA PATRIOT Act, henceforth the Patriot Act) was passed almost immediately in October 2001 giving US law enforcement and security personnel far-reaching extraordinary powers. Soon thereafter, the Homeland Security Act was passed, which paved the way for the establishment of the US Department of Homeland Security (DHS). The formation of the DHS enabled the functions of Immigration and Naturalization Service (INS) to be transferred from the Justice Department to the DHS. This effectively embedded security as the central instrument of **immigration policy**, as many migrants from Muslim-majority states were openly profiled and targeted as possible "terrorists" (ACLU 2009; Usova 2013). Based on this securitization framework, changes were also instituted at the DHS: "the Directorate of Border and Transportation Security and the US Citizenship and Immigration Services took on immigrant enforcement and immigrant service functions, respectively" (Russell Sage Foundation n.d.).

In Canada, just as in other Western states, securitization started to shape immigration policy from the 1990s. As outlined earlier, in 1991 Canada first ratified the notion of the security certificate, which was made part of IRPA when it was enacted as law in 2002—ostensibly to "address the growing global terrorism" (Friedland and Friedland 2006:60). The aim of these certificates is to rapidly deport or indefinitely detain those permanent residents, asylum seekers, and foreign nationals who are deemed to be "supporters of terrorism" or a threat to Canada's national security. The security certificate provision was folded into IRPA when it was first tabled as Bill C-31 on June 6, 2000, but this bill lapsed in October 2000 as an election was called. Upon coming to power, the new government quickly reintroduced IRPA as Bill C-11 on February 21, 2001, and made an important change to the modality of issuing security certificates for permanent residents (noncitizen landed immigrants). The earlier Bill C-31 made a distinction between "permanent residents" (PRs) and "foreign nationals" and the immigration minister could not merely use her or his discretion to issue a certificate in the case of PRs: "the report [against a PR] is referred to the Security Intelligence Review Committee, which investigates the grounds upon which it is based, and then reports its findings to the Governor in Council. The latter then directs the Minister to issue a certificate" (Sinha, Young, and Law and Government Division 2001). Bill C-11 (2001) removed this important oversight for PRs. Thus, the IRPA's security certificate provisos (clauses 77 to 82) not only curtail another level of executive oversight, they even restrict judicial review. Until more recently, proceedings under the IRPA did not allow disclosure of evidence to the accused, that is, until the provision was challenged by Adil Charkaoui and others detained on security certificates (see Supreme Court of Canada 2007). Only after Charkaoui and others' constitutional challenge of security certificates was there some disclosure of evidence through the appointment of a special advocate. So while the Supreme Court's judgment in Charkaoui's case introduced a semblance of due process, it also gave constitutional validity to security certificates. The Supreme Court of Canada did not even ask for a clear definition of *national security*, about which IRPA is completely silent, so that there could be a check on the executive's overreach. This may well be a deliberate omission so as to enable the executive to frame the notion of national security in the broadest possible manner. The removal of oversight and the arrogation of power by the executive branch is a disturbing change underway in Canada. This change signals a "shift in the terrain of the legal landscape ... which enshrine into law exceptional measures ... [that] could be clearly recognized as departures from the rule of law to the rule of sovereign force" (Friedland and Friedland 2006:56, 58).[6]

If the appropriation of exceptional powers by the executive branch of the Canadian state is a concern, what is happening across the border in the US is seriously alarming: the arrogation of exceptional powers by the executive branch of the US government, as widely reported in the media, to indefinitely detain "suspects," authorize torture of "terrorists" through "extraordinary renditions" in secret camps scattered around the world, not to mention Guantanamo Bay (Friedland and Friedland 2006:58). The widely publicized recent disclosures reveal that surveillance by the National Security Agency (NSA) both within the US and abroad has simply been breathtaking in terms of the sheer volume of data that has been collected. Even before September 11, the American Civil Liberties Union (ACLU) took a position against the harsh anti-immigrant legislation that President Clinton signed into law in 1996, according to which a person considered to be in the US "illegally" could be detained indefinitely. On this issue, the ACLU and other immigrants' rights advocates brought a case against the US government and "argued that the 1996 law does not, in fact, give the INS such powers." Their argument was belatedly accepted in the US Supreme Court's June 2001 decision (ACLU 2001). However, for the ACLU this was an ironic win because not long after the decision was handed down, the events of September 11 triggered the quick framing of the Patriot Act, which not only reinstated the indefinite detention clause, but rather broadened it to seriously harm the rights of racialized citizens or permanent residents, specifically Muslims. Nancy Chang, writing about the Patriot Act soon after it became law, says,

> USA *Patriot Act* nevertheless stands out as radical in its design. To an unprecedented degree, the Act sacrifices our freedoms in the name of national security and … [consolidates] vast new powers in the executive branch of government. Under the Act, the executive's ability to conduct surveillance and gather intelligence is enhanced, prosecutors have a set of new tools to work with, including new crimes … and the INS has gained the authority to detain immigrants suspected of terrorism for lengthy, or even indefinite, periods of time. And at the very same time that the Act inflates the powers of the executive, it insulates the exercise of these powers from any meaningful judicial and congressional oversight. (Chang 2001)

The Patriot Act is anti-terrorism legislation, but its overarching concern is with migrants and refugees in, and foreign nationals of interest to, the US. Paradoxically, under section 102 of the Act, subsections a(1) and a(2), respectively, acknowledge that "Arab Americans, Muslim Americans, and Americans from South Asia play a vital role in our Nation," and condemn the "acts of violence that have been taken against Arab and Muslim Americans since the September 11, 2001." The fact that a new law has to specifically acknowledge groups of people from particular regions or religions, both for their service to the US and for the harm perpetrated on them by mainstream Americans, is quite revealing. It shows that these targeted groups in particular, and migrants and refugees more generally, are vulnerable and under serious threat in the US. Nonetheless, many of the controversial provisions of the Patriot Act give extraordinary powers to the US executive branch, while also amending many of the sections of the Immigration and Nationality Act to adversely impact these vulnerable groups. To show how insidious the notion of security has become, two of the more controversial provisions of the act are briefly discussed.

Section 411 of the Patriot Act significantly expands the class of immigrants for removal on suspicion of terrorism, while Section 412 gives tremendous power to the Attorney General and the Secretary of State to issue certificates and detain immigrants or foreign nationals, respectively. "Upon no more than the Attorney General's unreviewed certification that he has 'reasonable grounds to believe' that a non-citizen is engaged in terrorist activities or other activities that threaten the national security, a non-citizen can be detained for as long as seven days without being charged with either a criminal or immigration violation" (Chang, 2001). Further, once charged, if the accused cannot be deported, they can be held indefinitely, with reviews of detention every six months. It is indeed remarkable that the certification process and terms of detention in the US, both without much oversight, are so similar with Canada's security certificate regime. The one difference is that the evidence against the detained person on a US certificate is not disclosed *at all*. The concern with these unreviewable powers of the executive, as the ACLU has taken great pains to report, document, and challenge, is the manifold potential for abuse (ACLU 2009).

Similarly, the monitoring of "foreign students" under section 416 of the Patriot Act has taken on Orwellian dimensions. It is well known that international students and their activities are closely monitored by security and law enforcement organizations, but what is confounding is that their academic pursuits—such as what books they borrow from their university or college libraries—are also equally closely monitored:

> Indeed the Academic Council of the University of California became so incensed with infringements upon the rights of their foreign students, that they unanimously adopted a resolution regarding the foreign student monitoring sections of the USA Patriot Act in 2004. The Academic Council denounced areas of the USA Patriot Act which called for the secret monitoring of email activities and internet communication of their students, the infringement of the right to privacy ... which is manifested in the law enforcement's expanded access to medical, financial, and academic records of foreign students. (Lake 2013)

The University of California libraries also posted warning signs that informed "foreign students" that their records of books and other materials borrowed "may be obtained by federal agents" under the Patriot Act, and that the law prohibits librarians from informing the affected students if federal agents have indeed obtained their records (cited in Lake 2013).

Conclusion

Canada and the United States are said to be founded on the ideals of justice, liberty, and the rule of law for *all* of their residents. Immigrants to the two states have genuinely contributed to the development and prosperity of their respective societies. However, racism, inequality, and lower tolerance of difference have remained, to varying degrees, in Canada and the US. These inequities and ill treatments divide the respective societies along race and class lines, with gender oppression and privilege becoming more complex within and across race and class divides. The pursuit of the "war on terror" has securitized the state and shaped new domestic anti-terrorism and immigration laws. Also enlarged is the racial fracture as is the intensified targeting of the *other* in society by zealous security agencies, politicians and the media. If security is prioritized over liberty, as Mark Neocleous (2008:20, ch.1) points out, then liberalism functions "less as a philosophy of liberty and more as a *technique of security.*" The exceptional powers these security-infused new laws bestow upon the state's executive branch do not just dehumanize the *other*; they corrode the very ideals that are supposed to be the foundation of liberal societies. These new laws carve a trajectory of simmering authoritarianism, denial of due process, and the divisive politics of "us and them."

Notes

1.   Karyotis has relied on van Dijk (1993) for this definition.
2.   Bourbeau describes politicians and bureaucrats as "securitizing agents" and they can be identified in the US as the President, Secretary of Homeland Security, Secretary of Defense, Secretary of State, and directors of the FBI and the CIA; in Canada, they are the Prime Minister, Ministers of Foreign Affairs and Citizenship and Immigration, and the RCMP. I have discussed in another article the role of the media, not specifically in the context of the migration-security nexus, rather in perpetuating securitization and the strengthening of the security state broadly in Canada, Europe, and the US (Amin-Khan 2012a).
3.   For further understanding of the spread of EPZs and emergence of the new international division of labour, since the 1970s, as forerunners to the rise of neoliberalism and globalization, see Amin-Khan (2012b); for an understanding of the increasing strength of multinational corporations through the North American Free Trade Agreement (NAFTA) and the work of the World Trade Organization (WTO), see Hart-Landsberg (2006).

4. In support of this claim, Gunn has relied on Trebilcock and Kelley (2010) and Bauder (2006).

5. Much of the information on the timeline of changes to US immigration law is based on the Russell Sage Foundation (n.d.) with some information from the Migration Policy Institute (2013).

6. Canada's Anti-Terrorism Act is another example of how the executive appropriates exceptional powers that seriously impact people's lives (Pue 2004). This kind of exceptionalism is emulated by the mainstream media and crosses the line of journalistic ethics when columnists become unreflective as they stereotype particular racialized groups using prejudicial language, such as labelling the entire Muslim youth the "jihad generation," based on the arrest of the "Toronto 18" on terrorism-related charges (Amin-Khan 2012a). There is also an insightful media audit of newspaper stories related to the Toronto 18 (Miller and Sack 2010).

Questions for Critical Thought

1. How have globalization and neoliberalism become an impetus for the targeting and criminalizing of refugees and migrants to Western states?

2. What kind of extraordinary power does Section 412 of the Patriot Act provide to the US Attorney General and the Secretary of State, and what is its impact on migrants and foreign nationals in the US?

3. How are refugees and those facilitating "irregular" means of their arrival in Canada adversely impacted by the June 2013 passage of the Protecting Canada's Immigration System Act?

4. When the executive branch in Canada and the US arrogates exceptional powers of detention and surveillance, what is the impact on the privacy and civil liberties of not just ordinary Americans and Canadians but of refugees and migrants? Does the acquisition of such exceptional powers aid or erode democracy?

Key Readings

Crépeau, François, Delphine Nakache, and Idil Atak (2007) International Migration: Security Concerns and Human Rights Standards. *Transcultural Psychiatry* 44(3):311–337.

Hart-Landsberg, Marin (2006) Neoliberalism: Myths and Reality. *Monthly Review* 57(11): 3–18. www.monthly review.org/0406hart-landsberg.htm (Accessed August 9, 2013).

Karyotis, Georgios (2011) The Fallacy of Securitizing Migration: Elite Rationality and Unintended Consequences. In Gabriella Lazaridis (ed.) *Security, Insecurity and Migration in Europe*, pp. 13–30. Farnham, UK: Ashgate.

Kelley, Ninette and Michael Trebilcock (2010) *The Making of the Mosaic: A History of Canadian Immigration Policy*. Toronto: University of Toronto Press.

Toğral, Burcu (2011) Convergence of Securitization of Migration and "New Racism" in Europe: Rise of Culturalism and Disappearance of Politics. In Gabriella Lazaridis (ed.) *Security, Insecurity and Migration in Europe*, pp. 219–238. Farnham, UK: Ashgate.

Media Links

Patriot Act: Reclaiming Patriotism, A Call to Reconsider the Patriot Act:
www.aclu.org/sites/default/files/pdfs/safefree/patriot_report_20090310.pdf
A report on the Patriot Act by the American Civil Liberties Union (ACLU).

Displacement: The 21st Century Challenge:
unhcr.org/globaltrendsjune2013/UNHCR%20GLOBAL%20TRENDS%202012_V08_web.pdf
A UNHCR report on Global Trends 2012 on refugees, asylum seekers, and trafficked people.

Moving Towards a Police State:
therealnews.com/t2/index.php?option=com_content&task=view&id=31&Itemid=74&jumival=11589
An online video in which Michael Ratner of the Center for Constitutional Rights recalls how the post–September 11 environment led to the consolidation of sweeping arbitrary powers within the executive branch of US government, and led to the framing of new laws, including the Patriot Act, that he says now suppress civil rights and significantly curtail rights to privacy.

Hundreds in DC Protest Against the Surveillance State:
therealnews.com/t2/index.php?option=com_content&task=view&id=31&Itemid=74&jumival=10927
A video clip of social activists' statements during an October 2013 protest in Washington, DC.

References

American Civil Liberties Union (ACLU) (2001) In Second Victory for Immigrants' Rights, High Court Says INS Cannot Indefinitely Jail Immigrants. www.aclu.org/immigrants-rights/second-victory-immigrants-rights-high-court-says-ins-cannot-indefinitely-jail-immi (Accessed November 15, 2013)

American Civil Liberties Union (ACLU) (2009) *Reclaiming Patriotism: A Call to Reconsider the Patriot Act*. New York: ACLU.

Amin-Khan, Tariq (2012a) New Orientalism, Securitisation and the Western Media's Incendiary Racism. *Third World Quarterly* 33(9):1595–1610.

Amin-Khan, Tariq (2012b) The Post-Colonial State: Historical Antecedents and Contemporary Impositions. In T. Amin-Khan (ed.), *The Post-Colonial State in the Era of Capitalist Globalization: Historical, Political and Theoretical Approaches to State Formation*, pp. 50–86. New York: Routledge.

Babacan, Hurriyet and Narayan Gopalkrishnan (eds.) (2007) *Racisms in the New World Order: Realities of Culture, Colour and Identity*. New Castle, IN: Cambridge Scholars Publishing.

Bauder, Harald (2006) *Labour Movement: How Migration Regulates Labour Markets*. Oxford: Oxford University Press.

Bourbeau, Philippe (2011) *The Securitization of Migration: A Study of Movement and Order*. Abingdon, UK: Routledge.

Bradmore, Ashley and Harald Bauder (2011) Mystery Ships and Risky Boat People: Tamil Refugee Migration in the Newsprint Media. *Canadian Journal of Communications* 37:637–661.

Brown, Garrett and David Held (eds.) (2010) *The Cosmopolitanism Reader*. Cambridge: Polity Press.

CBC News (2011) Wealth Gap Widens to 30-Year High. *CBC News*, 5 December. www.cbc.ca/news/business/wealth-gap-widens-to-30-year-high-1.1094074 (Accessed December 11, 2013)

Citizenship and Immigration Canada (2013) Protecting Canada's Immigration System Act. Citizenship and Immigration Canada. www.cic.gc.ca/english/refugees/reform.asp (Accessed November 11, 2013).

Chang, Nancy (2001) The USA Patriot Act: What's So Patriotic about Trampling on the Bill of Rights? *Third World Traveler* Winter 2001. www.thirdworldtraveler.com/Civil_Liberties/USA_Patriot_Act_BillRights.html (Accessed November 23, 2013)

Crépeau, François, Delphine Nakache, and Idil Atak (2007) International Migration: Security Concerns and Human Rights Standards. *Transcultural Psychiatry* 44(3):311–337.

Dowd, Douglas (2004) *Capitalism and Its Economics: A Critical History.* London: Pluto Press.

Fanon, Frantz (1968) *The Wretched of the Earth.* New York: Grove Press.

Friedland, A. and Eli Friedland (2006) The Silent Jurists, The Quiet Citizen: An Interrogation of the Post-9/11 Security Measures. *Radical Society* 32(4):56–66.

Gunn, Rosalind (2013) "Controlling Outcomes: Exploring Human Smuggling in the Neoliberal Era." Major Research Paper in partial fulfillment for the MA degree, Immigration and Settlement Studies, Ryerson University: 1–58.

Hart-Landsberg, Martin (2006) Neoliberalism: Myths and Reality. *Monthly Review* 57(11):3–18. www.monthly review.org/0406hart-landsberg.htm (Accessed August 9, 2013).

Harvey, David (1989) *The Condition of Postmodernity: An Enquiry into the Origins of Cultural Change.* Cambridge: Blackwell.

Held, David, Anthony McGrew, David Glodblatt, and Jonathan Perraton (1999) *Global Transformations: Politics, Economics and Culture.* Oxford: Polity Press.

Human Rights Watch (May 2013) Turning Migrants into Criminals: The Harmful Impact of US Border Prosecutions. www.hrw.org/sites/default/files/reports/us0513_ForUpload_2.pdf (Accessed June 14, 2014)

Karyotis, Georgios (2011) The Fallacy of Securitizing Migration: Elite Rationality and Unintended Consequences. In Gabriella Lazaridis (ed.) *Security, Insecurity and Migration in Europe*, pp. 13–30. Farnham, UK: Ashgate.

Kelley, Ninette and Michael Trebilcock (2010) *The Making of the Mosaic: A History of Canadian Immigration Policy.* Toronto: University of Toronto Press.

Kinnvall, Catarina (2002) Nationalism, Religion and the Search for Chosen Traumas: Comparing Sikh and Hindu Identity Constructions. *Ethnicities* 2(1):78–106.

Kotz, D.M. (2002) Globalization and Neoliberalism. *Rethinking Marxism* 14(2):64–79.

Lake, George (2013) The USA Patriot Act and Justice. *International Political Review* February 20. www.theinternationalpoliticalreview.com/the-usa-patriot-act-and-justice (Accessed November 22, 2013)

Lazaridis, Gabriella (ed.) (2011) *Security, Insecurity and Migration in Europe.* Farnham, UK: Ashgate.

Lezner, Robert (2012) The Top 1% Saw Their Incomes Rise 8 Times, 1979–2007. *Forbes*, 22 April. www.forbes.com/sites/robertlenzner/2012/04/22/the-top-1-saw-their-incomes-rise-8-times1979-2007 (Accessed December 11, 2013)

Migration Policy Institute (2013) Timeline: Major US Immigration Laws, 1790 to Present. *Migration Policy Institute.* www.migrationpolicy.org/pubs/CIRtimeline-MajorLaws.pdf (Accessed December 22, 2013)

Miller, John and C. Sack (2010) The Toronto-18 Terror Case: Trial by Media? How Newspaper Opinion Framed Canada's Biggest Terrorism Case. *Journal of Diversity in Organizations, Communities and Nations* 10(1):279–295.

Miller, Todd (2010) Arizona, the Anti-Immigrant Laboratory. *NACLA Report on the Americas* 43(4):3–4.

Neocleous, Mark (2008) *Critique of Security*. Edinburgh: Edinburgh University Press.

Petley, Julian and Robin Richardson (eds.) (2011) *Pointing the Finger: Islam and Muslims in the British Media*. Oxford: One World Publications.

Pop Vox (2013) What's Your Position on the Comprehensive Immigration Reform for America's Security and Prosperity (CIR ASAP) Act? *Pop Vox*. www.popvox.com/bills/us/113/hr3163 (Accessed December 22, 2013)

Public Safety Canada (n.d.) Security Certificates. *Public Safety Canada*. www.publicsafety.gc.ca/cnt/ntnl-scrt/cntr-trrrsm/scrt-crtfcts-eng.aspx (Accessed November 9, 2013)

Pue, W. Wesley (2004) Will Our Anti-Terrorism Act Lead Us Down the Road to Tyranny? *CAUT/ACPPU Bulletin* 51(10). www.cautbulletin.ca/staging/en_article.asp?ArticleID=1245 (Accessed December 11, 2013)

Russell Sage Foundation (n.d.) Interactive Timeline: US Immigration Reform. www.russellsage.org/interactive-timeline-us-immigration-reform (Accessed December 20, 2013)

Said, Edward (1995) *Orientalism*. London: Penguin Books.

Sinha, Jay, Margaret Young, and Law and Government Division, Canada (2001) Bill C-11: Immigration and Refugee Protection Act. www.publications.gc.ca/collections/Collection-R/LoPBdP/LS/371/c11-e.htm (Accessed November 22, 2013)

Stilwell, Frank (2006) *Political Economy: The Contest of Economic Ideas*. Victoria, Australia: Oxford University Press.

Supreme Court of Canada (2007) *Adil Charkaoui v. Canada (Minister of Citizenship and Immigration)*. scc-csc.lexum.com/decisia-scc-csc/scc-csc/scc-csc/en/item/2345/index.do (Accessed November 22, 2013)

Toğral, Burcu (2011) Convergence of Securitization of Migration and "New Racism" in Europe: Rise of Culturalism and Disappearance of Politics. In Gabriella Lazaridis (ed.) *Security, Insecurity and Migration in Europe*, pp. 219–238. Farnham, UK: Ashgate.

UNHCR (2013a) *UNHCR Global Trends 2012: Displacement, the New 21st Century Challenge*. Available at: www.unhcr.org/51bacb0f9.html (Accessed September 27, 2013)

UNHCR (2013b) New UNHCR Report Says Global Forced Displacement at 18-Year High. *UNHCR: The UN Refugee Agency*. www.unhcr.org/51c071816.html (Accessed September 27, 2013)

United Nations (2012) Migrants by Origin and Destination: The Role of South-South Migration. *Population Facts (UN Population Division)* 2012(3). www.un.org/en/development/desa/population/publications/pdf/popfacts/popfacts_2012-3_South-South_migration.pdf (Accessed September 27, 2013)

United Nations (2013) The Number of International Migrants Worldwide Reaches 232 Million. *Population Facts (UN Population Division)* 2013(2). www.un.org/en/development/desa/population/publications/pdf/popfacts/popfacts_2013-2.pdf (Accessed September 27, 2013)

Usova, Georgeanne (2013) Taking Candy from a Border Agent. American Civil Liberties Union (ACLU). www.aclu.org/blog/immigrants-rights/taking-candy-border-agent (Accessed November 15, 2013)

van Dijk, T. (1993) *Elite Discourse and Racism.* New Bury Park, UK: Sage.

van Hooft, Stan and Wim Vandekerckhove (eds.) (2010) *Questioning Cosmopolitanism.* New York: Springer.

Varadarajan, V. (2004) Constructivism, Identity and Neoliberal (In)security. *Review of International Studies* 30:319–341.

Varsanyi, Monica (2011) Neoliberalism and Nativism: Local Anti-Immigrant Policy Activism and an Emerging Politics of Scale. *International Journal of Urban and Regional Research* 35(2):295–311.

Wells, Don (2007) Too Weak for the Job: Corporate Codes of Conduct, Non-Governmental Organizations and the Regulation of International Labour Standards. *Global Social Policy* 7(1):51–74.

Ziemer, Ulrike and Roberts, Sean (eds.) (2013) *East European Diasporas, Migration and Cosmopolitanism.* Abingdon, UK: Routledge.

Chapter 5

ILLEGALIZED MIGRANTS[1]

CHARITY-ANN HANNAN

Introduction

Immigration policies in Canada and the US are designed to enable the legal entry of selected immigrants. People who are not selected to immigrate but enter the country nevertheless typically find themselves in situations where they are denied many of the rights that citizens and other immigrants take for granted. Politicians and the media sometimes refer to these migrants as *illegal*. This term, however, is problematic because only an activity, not a person, can be illegal. Alternative terms that are less problematic and that are commonly used include *undocumented, unauthorized, clandestine, alien,* or *irregular migrants*. More recently, the term **illegalized migrant** has gained popularity. Not to be confused with *criminal migrants, asylum seekers,* or *refugees,*[2] this term draws attention to the state policies that render migrants illegal (Bauder 2013).

Migrants can become illegalized through several channels. For example, they could cross the border while circumventing the required inspection; they could enter a country with fraudulent documentation; they could arrive legally on a tourist, student, or worker visa but stay in the country beyond the visa's expiry date; or they could cross the border as a refugee but stay in the country after their refugee claim was rejected (Goldring and Landolt 2011, 2012; Wasem 2010). Many migrants also become illegalized because of backlogs in the processing of their immigration or refugee papers (Bidone-Kramer 2011). In the US, most illegalized migrants are illegalized when they cross the border from Mexico without the required documentation (e.g. work, student, or tourist permits). Conversely, in Canada most migrants are illegalized when they stay in the country beyond the expiry date of their tourist, student, or work permit. In both countries, once illegalized these migrants are subject to incarceration and deportation if they are caught by police or reported to immigration officials (Goldring, Berinstein, and Berhard 2009; Hanson 2013).

Despite these risks, illegalized migrants continue to remain in Canada and the US to improve their economic conditions or to be with family members. In fact, many employers value illegalized migrants as a disciplined and flexible workforce. Once illegalized, these migrants constitute a vulnerable group, easily exploitable by employers. While often benefiting employers, however, the migrants themselves are excluded from the receipt of government services enjoyed by other workers (Hanson 2013). Unless the native-born population becomes threatened and begins lobbying their politicians for change, illegalized migrants in many cases tend to be tacitly accepted by the government as they provide cheap labour in occupations that native-born workers are reluctant to enter into.

The population of illegalized migrants in Canada and the US has fluctuated over the years, but has increased steadily between the late 1980s and 2007. It is estimated that 3.2 million illegalized migrants resided in the US in 1986. This number decreased to 1.9 million by 1988, after many had become legalized through the Immigration Reform and Control Act (IRCA). By 2007, however, the number of illegalized migrants in the US had escalated to an estimated 11.8 to 12.5 million, after which it declined slightly to 11.1 million by 2010 as a result of the recession, when numerous illegalized migrants returned to their home countries (Passel and Cohn 2010).

Compared to the US, few attempts have been made to estimate the number of illegalized migrants residing in Canada. Of the attempts that have been made, findings show that significantly fewer illegalized migrants reside in Canada than in the US. However, with the growth of Canada's **Temporary Foreign Worker** (TFW) Program these numbers are likely to increase because TFWs may overstay their temporary work visas (Hennebry 2010; Sharma 2006). In 1986, for example, an estimated 36,000 illegalized migrants resided in Canada (Jimenez 2003). A decade later, the number of illegalized migrants was estimated to range between 80,000 and 500,000 people, or between 0.2% and 1.5% of Canada's total population (Linklater 2008; Statistics Canada 2008).

A Brief History of Illegalization

It is possible, in the North American context, to distinguish between four phases of migrant illegalization. These phases are marked by different immigration policies that affected migrants' legal status. In the simplest terms, the Canadian and American states (and former British and American **Colonies**) each passed legislation during these phases that identified specific criteria that people must meet to be allowed into the country. The criteria have changed throughout the four phases and have consisted of a migrant's occupation, health/mental status, criminal history, gender, **race**, country of origin, skills, and whether the country's annual quotas had been met. People who entered the country without meeting the legal criteria of the day were not provided with the documentation (e.g. British subject status, citizenship, permanent residency) entitling them to enter and stay in the country legally, thus rendering them illegalized. With striking similarities between Canadian and American immigration policies and the outcomes of illegalization, capitalist structures and practices, race-based ideology, and the growth of national security have influenced immigration policies in both countries, especially with respect to illegalizing migrants (Avery 1995; Ettinger 2009; Ngai 2005).

The 1860s and 1870s: Selective "Open Door" Immigration Policies

American and Canadian immigration policies were not formalized until the late 1800s, even though nonindigenous people from Europe and other parts of the world had been settling in the regions since the 1600s. The countries' first immigration acts were heavily influenced by the interests of employers and, with the goal of economic expansion, took a selective "open door" approach to immigration. This approach resulted in very few restrictions on people who could enter the country (Avery 1995). The US 1864 Immigration Act (also known as the Act to Encourage Immigration) even appointed immigration officials whose duties included protecting "immigrants from imposition and fraud."

Canada's 1869 Immigration Act established a basic framework for **immigration policy** and prohibited the importation of criminals into the country (Makarenko 2010). More restrictive policies were introduced with amendments to Canada's 1869 Immigration Act and the passing of the 1875 Immigration Act (also known as the Page Act) in the US. The Page Act codified the concept of illegal immigrants for the first time and prohibited the entry of unfree and involuntary labourers from China, Japan, and other "Oriental" countries. It also outlawed the importation of women for the purposes of prostitution, **coolie labour**, and persons convicted of felonious crimes in their country of origin. The act further outlined the penalties, including fines and imprisonment, for violating these laws (Avery 1995; Ettinger 2009).

At the time, employers argued that they needed immigrants to do the jobs that native-born workers would not do. In Canada for example, "immigration recruitment produced a continuous supply of cheap labour that permitted the business community to resist trade union demands for higher wages, better working conditions, and union recognition" (Avery 1995:12). Worker associations and labour leagues on the west coast of North America subsequently began to push for the mutual protection of domestic workers against the influx of Chinese and lobbied for restrictions on immigration in the late nineteenth century (Avery 1995; Ettinger 2009; Reksten 1991). This push and the following policy changes set the stage for the widespread illegalization of migrants in the years to come.

The 1880s to 1950s: Racist Immigration Policies

Unlike the first phase, in which immigration policy was shaped by employers' interests, in the second phase immigration policy was influenced to a greater degree by the interests of the native-born population who supported a restrictive approach to immigration, especially of **racialized** groups (Avery 1995). Correspondingly, the policies of this phase largely targeted the entry of paupers and Chinese nationals. However, Chinese migrants in particular were able to exploit legal loopholes, invent family relationships saying they were in somebody else's family, and forge documents, leading to the **paper sons** phenomenon in both Canada and the US (Avery 1995; Ettinger 2009). Although earlier immigration acts made reference to the concept of "illegal immigrants," Patrick Ettinger (2009) argues that this particular phase marks the "production of the illegal alien as a new legal and political subject" (Ettinger 2009:5).

In the US, the first piece of explicitly racist restrictive legislation was the 1882 Immigration Act (or Chinese Exclusion Act). This act effectively barred Chinese nationals from entering the US, rendering all Chinese immigrants "illegal" after they crossed the border (Cacho 2012). Furthermore, the act "provided for the deportation of any Chinese person unlawfully within the United States and excluded Chinese residents from American citizenship." (Ettinger 2009:30). The 1924 Immigration Act (or National Origins Act) established immigration quotas and "a global racial and national hierarchy" that favoured immigrants from some countries over immigrants from other countries. Excluded were mostly nonwhites including Chinese, Japanese, Indian, and other Asian nationals on the grounds that they were racially ineligible for naturalized citizenship (Ngai 2005:3). While Mexican immigration was not assigned a numerical quota, it was restricted through limited visa availability. Mexicans continued to cross the border without proper documentation, however, becoming the largest group of illegalized immigrants—or "illegal aliens" using the terminology of the time—by the late 1920s (Ngai 2005; Thangasamy 2010).

During the late 1880s, Canada also passed a number of restrictive immigration policies. The 1885 Chinese Immigration Act refrained from formally denying Chinese nationals entry into the country. However, it controlled immigration by requiring them to pay a $50 entrance fee. This fee was raised to $500 by 1903 (Avery 1995). With mounting pressure from the Canadian-born population, the provincial government of British Columbia pressured the Canadian government to ban Chinese nationals from entering the country legally. In 1923, the Canadian government acceded to this pressure and passed the 1923 Immigration Act (or Chinese Exclusion Act), which effectively restricted Chinese nationals from immigrating to Canada. The 1952 Immigration Act continued to be restrictive and enabled the exclusion of immigrants based on "nationality, citizenship, ethnic group, occupation, class or geographical area of origin" (Avery 1995:173).

The 1960s and 1970s: Skill-Based Immigration Policies

In the 1960s, immigration policies shifted from explicitly race-based to skill-based criteria. The US amended its 1952 Immigration Act in 1965, which eliminated race-based selection criteria. The act conceded that "no person shall receive any preference or priority or be discriminated against in the issuance of an **immigrant** visa because of his race, sex, nationality, place of birth, or place of residence" (Immigration Act 1952). The amendment replaced the quota system based on national origin and permitted the immigration of persons who had relatives living in the US, who were members of the professions, who would substantially benefit the national economy because of their exceptional ability in the sciences or arts, who were capable of performing specific skilled or unskilled labour (although not of a temporary or seasonal nature), or who had fled from persecution based on race, religion, or political opinion (Immigration Act 1952). However, only a maximum of 170,000 people per year were allowed entry. Thus, migrants continued to enter the country without legal permission (Orrenius and Zavodny 2012).

Canada made similar amendments to its 1956 Immigration Act in 1967, shifting selection from an emphasis on race to skills. Applicants were given points according to specific criteria, including knowledge of English or French, arranged employment in Canada, level of education and training, employment experience, and whether they had relatives living in Canada. Applicants who met a minimum number of points (which the government can adjust according to its immigration targets) were admitted to enter Canada as immigrants. Influenced by the 1967 amendments, the 1976 Immigration Act created several categories (or "classes") through which immigrants could enter Canada: the family class, including immediate family and dependants; refugees; and a combined third category of independent and assisted family, who would be subject in varying degrees to the **points system** (Avery 1995:190; Immigration Act 1976–1977).

Case Example 1: Regularization in Canada

Illegalized immigrants are framed as a "problem" because they pose a threat to the integrity of the Canadian State (Robinson 1983), constitute violations of human rights and social justice principles, and allegedly adversely affect the labour market. To address this problem, the Canadian government implemented regularization campaigns to encourage illegalized migrants to apply for permanent residence. Between 1960 and 2002, several programs were administered including the 1960–1972 Chinese Adjustment Statement Program, the 1973 Adjustment of Status Program, a 1983–1985 Case-by-Case Adjustment Initiative, a 1994–1998 Deferred Removal Orders Class Regularization Program, and two regularization programs for illegalized migrants residing in Quebec: one for Haitians in 1981 and one for Algerians in 2002. Today, the only option for illegalized migrants to legalize their status in Canada is through an application for humanitarian and compassionate consideration. The success rate, however, is extremely low, with only 2.5 to 5% of applications being approved (Liu 2010).

Canada's first regularization program had two main objectives: to curtail illegal entry of Chinese into the country and to provide legal status to thousands of Chinese migrants who challenged the restrictive immigration laws that the Canadian government legislated the 1880s and 1950s (Kelly and Trebilcock 2010). By 1946, approximately 11,000 of 23,000 Chinese migrants had entered the country illegally to reunite with family members already living in Canada or to search for economic opportunity (Avery 1995:213). Restrictive measures to curb the clandestine immigration industry were short-lived because they violated individuals' human rights. As an alternative measure, the Canadian government adjusted the status of approximately 12,000 Chinese migrants who met the eligibility criteria between 1960 and 1972 (Hawkins 1988). The following excerpt from a report by Status Campaign in Toronto (Khandor, McDonald, Nyers, and Wright 2004:22), however, illustrates that the adjustment program was not successful for everybody:

> Mr. Wong was a man who had gone to an immigration office during the time of this program. There he made a statement and been given a piece of paper. He believed that he was a permanent resident for many years. In 1998, he found out that he was not when he tried to apply for his Old Age Security pension. At this time he had become too old to work and had become homeless because he had no money. An immigration lawyer in Toronto helped him apply for permanent resident status but his applications were refused. In the end he died of a heart attack in 2002 having lived here for almost 50 years without status.

The replacement of race-based with skill-based immigrant selection criteria gave the impression of a more fair and equitable immigration system. However, the implementation of Canada's Non-Immigrant Employment Authorization Program (NIEAP) in 1973 (now called the TFW Program) challenged the notion that migrants should settle permanently in Canada. If TFWs stay past their visa or permit's expiration date, they become illegalized migrants (Hennebry 2010). To address the problem of illegalization, the Canadian government implemented a series of regularization programs, which legalized the status of migrants if they met certain criteria (see Case Example 1).

The 1980s to Present: Skill-Based Immigration Policies

From the 1980s to the present, Canada has continued skill-based immigration and TFW policies, while the US focused on border security policies. A major restrictive immigration policy passed in the US was the **1986 Immigration and Reform and Control Act (IRCA)**. One of the main goals of IRCA was to reverse the illegalization of migrants (see Case Example 2). However, the act also involved fines for employers who hired illegalized migrant workers. This aspect of the act resulted in worse employment outcomes and experiences for illegalized immigrants whose status was not regularized. The act also increased support for **border enforcement**, seeking to curb the illegal entry of migrants. Furthermore, IRCA banned newly legalized migrants from receiving social assistance for five years. The 1996 Illegal Immigration Reform and Immigrant Responsibility Act (IIRIRA) then terminated the provisions under previous legislation that had allowed illegalized migrants to legalize their status even if they lived in the US for a significant period of time, cut off their social welfare benefits, and increased funding for enforcement of immigration laws at the US-Mexico border as well as within the US. In response to such restrictive legislation, state governments and cities began to mitigate the problems illegalized migrants were facing by issuing driver's licences as formal identification documents and by providing **higher education**, and medical care to expectant mothers (Thangasamy 2010:4–5).

In contrast to US legislation that aimed to legalize migrants and curb migrants from illegal border crossings, Canada's policies since the 1980s have created more occasions for migrants to become illegalized. The 2002 Immigration and Refugee Protection Act (IRPA) retained the points system but toughened eligibility requirements for refugees, skilled immigrants, and business immigrants. Amendments to IRPA in 2008 further restricted immigration eligibility and imposed moratoriums on immigrant investors and entrepreneurs, and the sponsorship of parents and grandparents. The Canadian government further denied many requests for humanitarian and

Image 5.1
Immigration Protests, Chicago, 2006

An estimated 100,000 people—mostly immigrants—protested against the controversial "Sensenbrenner" Bill H.R.-4437, which would have criminalized millions of illegalized immigrants and people who provide humanitarian assistance to these immigrants. H.R.-4437 did not become law.

Source: Photograph by Harald Bauder.

compassionate consideration made from outside Canada (Alboim and Kohl 2012). Moreover, the 2002 Canada-US Safe Third Country Agreement prevented refugees who entered Canada via the US to make a claim in Canada and amendments to the Refugee System (Bill C-11) in 2010 limit refugee claims to countries on designated list (Alboim and Kohl 2012).

While Canadian immigration policy became more restrictive, the number of TFWs increased from 89,000 in 2000 to slightly more than 300,000 in 2010 (Foster 2012). Today, low-skilled TFWs are limited to working a maximum of four years before they are forced to return to their country of origin. When the first four-year period ends, on April 1, 2015, Canada is expected to see a surge in the number of illegalized migrants. High-skilled TFWs, in turn, are eligible to apply for permanent residence under the new Canadian Experience Class (Alboim and Kohl 2012).

Case Example 2: Regularization in the US

Numerous regularization programs have been implemented in the US. Examples of these programs are the 1966 Cuban Adjustment Act, the 1986 Immigration Reform and Control Act (IRCA), the 1997 Nicaraguan Adjustment and Central American Relief Act (NACARA), the 1998 Haitian Refugee Fairness Act, and multiple registry programs over the years. According to the Migration Policy Institute, a Washington, DC–based think tank, US legalization programs can be grouped into three overlapping categories: 1) programs that target populations of humanitarian, equitable, or economic interest (e.g. asylum seekers, select groups of workers); 2) programs that cover a large percentage of illegalized persons; and 3) registry programs (Kerwin 2010).

Similar to Canada's 1960 Chinese Adjustment Statement Program, IRCA had the two main objectives of curbing the volume of illegal migration to the US and reducing the number of illegalized migrants living in the country. IRCA legalized approximately 2.7 million people (Orrenius and Zavodny 2012), reducing the number of illegalized migrants in the country to approximately 1.9 million in 1988 (Wasem 2010). By 2011 however, this number had jumped to 11.1 million. At the time of writing, the US is in the midst of debating whether or not to implement another legalization program. While it is clear that IRCA failed to curb the illegal entry of migrants, it is less obvious what the effect of the legislation was on illegalized migrants as a whole. The following excerpt illustrates the adverse effects that IRCA had on the labour market experiences and outcomes of migrants who remained illegalized after IRCA:

> The US General Accounting Office … found "a serious pattern of discrimination" against Hispanics after IRCA's passage in 1986. Likewise, [research by] Donato & Massey … found that the economic penalties accruing to illegal status increased significantly after IRCA was implemented. In the post-IRCA period, undocumented Mexican migrants earned substantially lower wages than legal immigrants from the same communities. Rather than curtailing the hiring of undocumented migrants, employers seem to have adjusted to the increased risks posed by IRCA by reducing the wages of undocumented workers. (Donato, Durand, and Massey 1992:94)

Illegalized Immigrants in the Labour Market

Different theories exist that explain the labour market situation of workers. **Neoclassical labour market theory** suggests that the labour market is regulated through the interaction between the persons available for work (supply) and the number of jobs available (demand), and that supply and demand determine wage rates (Gunderson 1980; Phillips 2012). This theory also argues that variations among workers' wages and work experiences arise from differences in **human capital** (e.g. skills, experience, and formal education). Rational workers will weigh the anticipated improvement in employment outcomes and experiences against the cost and effort necessary to improve their human capital. Studies that have examined the link between migration and **labour market outcomes** over the last three decades found only limited evidence in support of neoclassical labour market theory.

When trying to understand the different employment outcomes and experiences between immigrants and native-borns, and among immigrants themselves, a compelling explanation is provided by **segmented labour market theory**, which suggests that the labour market is divided into primary and secondary segments. Jobs in the primary segment provide high wages, good working conditions, employment stability, advancement opportunities, equity, and due process in the administration of work rules. Jobs in the secondary segment tend to offer low wages, few benefits, poor working conditions, high labour turnover, and little chance of advancement (Doeringer and Piore 1975). In this scenario, the competitive forces that operate in a neoclassical labour market have only a restricted influence on determining the wages and employment of employees. Empirical research related to migrant labour market outcomes tends to support segmented labour market theory. Migrants are often allocated to the secondary labour market segment, where they serve as a "reserve army" of labour, absorbing fluctuations in labour demand and securing stable employment for a workforce of nonmigrants (Piore 1979). More specifically, exclusionary legal practices often erode rights, labour standards, and social entitlements among migrants and subsequently result in growing socioeconomic disparity within the entire workforce (Bauder 2006).

Labour market growth is important to capitalist societies, and to estimate labour market strength researchers typically assess a variety of indicators. These include earnings, occupational characteristics, and employment rates, while accounting for the personal factors such as age, education, gender, and ethno-racial identity. In the context of the illegalized migrant workforce, reliable data is difficult to obtain since most illegalized immigrants are not documented in government databases. Nevertheless, over the last three decades some studies have focused on the effects of the lack of legal status on migrants' labour market outcomes and experiences. The following discussion is based on this research.

Earnings

Neoclassical labour market theory predicts that individuals with similar levels of human capital should yield similar earnings. Indeed, US-based studies using data collected in the early 1980s, prior to the implementation of the Immigration Control and Reform Act (IRCA), show no significant gap between the earnings of legal migrants and illegalized migrants (Grasmuck 1984; Massey 1987). Conversely, studies that analyzed data collected after IRCA was implemented found that illegalized migrants earned significantly less than legal migrants despite similarities in human capital (Davila and Pagan 1997; Mehta, Theodore, Mora, and Wade 2002; Phillips and Massey 1999; Rivera-Batiz 1999; Youn, Woods, Zhou, and Hardigree 2010), indicating that lack of legal status has become an important factor in explaining low earnings over the last three decades.

Other research analyzed the 1989–1992 Legalized Population Survey (LPS), a random sample of 6,193 illegalized immigrants who were residing in the United States in 1987–1988 when they sought legal permanent residence through IRCA (Rivera-Batiz 1999). This research found the average hourly wage of Mexican illegalized migrants to be 58.2% less than that of legal migrants. An analysis of 1,653 illegalized and legal migrants working in the Chicago metro area also yielded similar findings: while illegalized migrant men earned 22% less than legal migrant men, illegalized migrant women earned 36% less than legal migrant men (Mehta et al. 2002). An examination of data from the Mexican Migration Project, which contains information from 7,143 households in Mexico and 456 households in the US, also showed that illegalized migrants earn 22% less than legal migrants (Phillips and Massey 1999). Another analysis of the US restaurant industry found illegalized migrants to receive 92 cents per hour less than legal migrants (Youn et al. 2010).

Gender plays an important role with respect to the earnings of illegalized immigrants. Compared to illegalized migrant women, illegalized migrant men reported higher earnings (Cobb-Clark and Koussoudji 1999; Mehta et al. 2002; Rivera-Batiz 1999). Human capital also has a measurable impact when comparing illegalized migrants with each other (as opposed to comparing them with workers with status or citizenship). Illegalized migrants with English fluency earned more than those without English fluency (Chiswick and Miller 1999; Mehta et al. 2002; Phillips and Massey 1999). In addition, illegalized migrants employed in the manufacturing industry earned more than those who worked in the service and agricultural industries (Mehta et al. 2002). Furthermore, illegalized migrants with access to **social capital**, including friends and/or relatives with connections to labour market opportunities, earned more than illegalized immigrants without access to a similar social network (Aguilera and Massey 2003; Amuedo-Dorantes and Mundra 2007).

Industrial and Occupational Crowding

As with earnings, neoclassical labour market theory suggests that individuals with similar levels of human capital will experience similar occupational mobility. Despite similar levels of human capital, however, illegalized migrants are less likely than legal migrants to be employed in higher paying occupations and industries. In addition, any upward mobility that illegalized migrants experience tends to be limited to "traditional" migrant occupations including but not limited to farm workers, food counter occupations, gardeners, janitors, machine operators, construction labourers, other labourers, and cooks. They are also mostly limited to working in the agricultural, construction, manufacturing, and service industries (Davila and Pagan 1997; Kossoudji and Cobb-Clark 1996, 2000; Powers and Seltzer 1998; Powers, Seltzer, and Shi 1998). Although illegalized migrants have recently been found in high-skill occupations, little is known about their labour market outcomes (Kaushal 2006; Lofstrom, Hill, and Hayes 2010, 2012).

While a considerable number of illegalized migrants were employed in the higher paying manufacturing sector prior to the implementation of IRCA, after IRCA a larger share was working in the lower paying agricultural sector (Davila and Pagan 1997). After IRCA, illegalized immigrants' occupational mobility also became more restricted. When illegalized migrants experience upward or downward mobility, these shifts typically take place within clustered traditional migrant occupations (Kossoudji and Cobb-Clark 1996, 2000). This phenomenon is known as **occupational churning** and represents the workers' attempts to make the most of their opportunities within a well-defined and, in the case of illegalized migrants, often informal labour market (Kossoudji and Cobb-Clark 1996). In other studies, illegalized migrants' occupational mobility was found to be restricted to the secondary segment of the labour market (Powers 1998; Powers and Seltzer 1998).

As with earnings, some illegalized migrants have advantages over others. Compared to illegalized women, who are often locked into domestic-labour jobs with little prospects for career mobility, male illegalized migrants move within a broader range of occupations over time (Powers et al. 1998). In addition, Latino men with strong English skills often experience upward mobility (Kossoudji and Cobb-Clark 1996).

Benefits to Employers

Employers receive a variety of benefits from employing illegalized migrants. One of the most important benefits resides in the controllability of illegalized workers

(Grasmuck 1984; Rivera-Batiz 1999; Champlin and Hake 2006). During phases of rapid industrial transformation, many employers prefer to hire illegalized workers over citizens, legal migrants, or even TFWs because their lack of legal protection prevents them from unionizing and their vulnerability precludes them from protesting against wage erosion (Morales 1983–1984). Employers' threats to report illegalized migrants to immigration authorities, which may result in deportation, can effectively bond these workers to employers, forcing them to work in low-paying occupations and accept inequitable remuneration for their work, which native-born workers would not accept (Donato et al. 1992; Gomberg-Munoz and Nussbaum-Barberena 2011; Kossoudji and Cobb-Clark 1996). While studies have yet to identify the precise effect of the illegalized workforce on the profits of employers, researchers have provided ample evidence that employers generally benefit from hiring illegalized immigrants who can be denied rights and fair wages and by offloading responsibilities for health and other service provisions to these workers.

Conclusion

The above discussion of how Canadian and American immigration policies illegalize migrants illustrates that "illegal alienage is not a natural or fixed condition but the product of positive law" (Ngai 2005:6). The discussion also examined the consequences of the lack of status on migrants' labour market outcomes. In this context, some researchers have argued that illegalized migrants have become a super-exploited class (Gomberg-Munoz and Nussbaum-Barberena 2011). There is some US-based evidence that suggests that illegalized migrants were not as exploited in the early 1980s, prior to IRCA, as they are today. This indicates that recent policy developments have worsened the economic situation of illegalized immigrants in the US.

In Canada, the lack of empirical evidence does not support such a claim. Nevertheless, immigration policies have become more restrictive and TFW programs have been on the rise. These policy developments suggest that illegalized migration will become a more widespread phenomenon and the economic future of this illegalized population is unlikely to be bright.

Notes

1. The ideas for this chapter emerged from a fellowship position that was supported by the Ryerson Centre for Immigration and Settlement (RCIS), the Ministry of Citizenship & Immigration (MCI), and Ryerson University's Policy Studies PhD Program in 2012. The fellowship enabled me to analyze the global English-language literature on the effects of undocumented immigrants on the labour market, resulting in a RCIS Working Paper in 2013: www.ryerson.ca/content/dam/rcis/documents/ RCIS_WP_Hannan_No_2013_1.pdf

2. The distinction between *illegalized migrant* and *criminal migrant* is important to recognize. Kim and Garcia (2011:57) for example, have argued that *illegal alien* is not synonymous with *criminal alien*. According to the Immigration and Nationality Act (INA), "certain conduct may either disqualify an alien from entering the United Sates ("inadmissability") or provide grounds for his or her removal/deportation. Prominently included in this conduct is criminal activity. "Criminal activity" comprises acts violative of federal, state, or, in many cases, foreign criminal law. It does not cover violations of the INA that are not crimes—most notably, being in the US without legal permission." It is also important to distinguish between *illegalized migrants*, *asylum seekers*, and *refugees*. Although the media often portrays asylum seekers as "illegal" migrants, they are in most cases people who have legitimately applied for asylum under the 1951 Refugee Convention on the Status of Refugees because they are fearful of facing persecution in their countries of origin.

Questions for Critical Thought

1. Why have particular migrants, or groups of migrants, been prohibited from entering Canada and the US during different periods, and what does the shifting nature of immigration policies indicate about these prohibitions?

2. Do you think that any changes should be made to the status of illegalized migrants who are currently residing in the US and Canada (e.g. should they be "regularized")? If yes, what changes should be made, and what would be the implications of these changes? If not, why should no changes be made and what are the implications of not making any changes?

3. Should actions be taken to prevent the illegalization of migrants? If yes, what actions should be taken and by whom? If no, why not?

Key Readings

Avery, D.H. (1995) *Reluctant Host: Canada's Response to Immigrant Workers, 1896–1994.* Toronto: McClelland & Stewart.

Donato, K.M., J. Durand, and D.S. Massey (1992) Changing Conditions in the US Labor Market: Effects of the Immigration Reform and Control Act of 1986. *Population Research and Policy Review* 11:93–115

Ettinger, P. (2009) *Imaginary Lines: Border Enforcement and the Origins of Undocumented Migration, 1882–1930.* Austin, TX: University of Texas Press.

Ngai, M.M. (2005). *Impossible Subjects: Illegal Aliens and the Making of Modern America.* Princeton, NJ: Princeton University Press.

U.S. Immigration Legislation Online (2007) library.uwb.edu/guides/usimmigration/ USimmigrationlegislation.html (Accessed November 5, 2013)

Media Links

America Seen through the Eyes of an Illegal Immigrant:
www.youtube.com/watch?v=v_UTYLWfqWs
This video documents the daily experiences of illegalized migrants who are living and/or working in the US.

This (Illegal) American Life:
topdocumentaryfilms.com/this-illegal-american-life
A documentary that shows interviews with an illegalized migrant student who is attending the University of California, Los Angeles (UCLA) in the hopes of legitimizing her status and improving her chances in the US labour market, and an illegalized migrant who came to the US to work because there were no employment opportunities in his hometown in Mexico.

Documentary Exposes the Reality of Illegal Immigration:
video.foxnews.com/v/2374622081001/documentary-exposes-the-reality-of-illegal-immigration-/#sp=show-clips
This video shows Fox News in the US interviewing Dennis Michael Lynch about his documentary on the (alleged) negative impacts of illegal immigration.

Reality Show Filmed Immigration Raids, B.C. Advocates Say:
www.cbc.ca/news/canada/british-columbia/reality-show-filmed-immigration-raids-b-c-advocates-say-1.1313895
Two videos show activists protesting the filming of raids by employees of the Canadian Border Services Agency (CBSA) on illegalized migrants in Canada, for a television reality show titled *Border Security: Canada's Front Line*.

Tories Defend Border Security TV Show:
www.theglobeandmail.com/news/news-video/video-tories-defend-reality-tv-show-about-canadian-border-security/article9923706/
This video shows Canada's Public Safety Minister, Vic Toews, defending his position to support the filming of the arrest of illegalized migrants by Canadian Border Service Agents for a reality TV show titled *Border Security: Canada's Front Line*.

References

Aguilera, M.B. and D.S. Massey (2003) Social Capital and the Wages of Mexican Migrants: New Hypotheses Tests. *Social Forces* 82(2):671–701.

Alboim, N. and K. Cohl (2012) Shaping the Future: Canada's Rapidly Changing Immigration Policies. Toronto: Maytree. www.maytree.com/wp-content/uploads/2012/10/shaping-the-future.pdf (Accessed October 20, 2013)

Amuedo-Dorantes, C. and K. Mundra (2007) Social Networks and Their Impact on the Earnings of Mexican Migrants. *Demography* 44(4):849–863.

Avery, D.H. (1995) Reluctant Host: Canada's Response to Immigrant Workers, 1896–1994. Toronto: McClelland & Stewart.

Bauder, H. (2006) *Labor Movement: How Migration Regulates Labor Markets*. New York: Oxford University Press.

Bauder, H. (2013) Why We Should Use the Term Illegalized Immigrant. RCIS Research Brief 2013/1. www.ryerson.ca/content/dam/rcis/documents/RCIS_RB_Bauder_No_2013_1.pdf (Accessed September 14, 2013)

Bidone-Kramer, C. (2011) Non-Status Workers and the Official Discourse in Canada: A Case of Convenience. Unpublished Master's Major Research Paper, Ryerson University, Toronto.

Cacho, L.M. (2012) *Social Death: Racialized Rightlessness and the Criminalization of the Unprotected*. New York: NYU Press.

Champlin, D. and E. Hake (2006) Immigration as Industrial Strategy in American Meatpacking. *Review of Political Economy* 18(1):49–69.

Chiswick, B.R. and P.W. Miller (1999) Language Skills and Earnings among Legalized Aliens. *Journal of Population Economics* 12:63–89.

Cobb-Clark, D. and S.A. Kossoudji (1999) Did Legalization Matter for Women? Amnesty and the Wage Determinants of Formerly Unauthorized Latina Workers. *Gender Issues* 17(4):3–14.

Davila, A. and J. Pagan (1997) The Effect of Selective INS Monitoring Strategies on the Industrial Employment Choice and Earnings of Recent Immigrants. *Economic Inquiry* 35:138–150.

Doeringer, P. and M. Piore (1975) Unemployment and the "Dual" Labor Market. *Public Interest* 38: 67–79.

Donato, K.M., Durand, J., and Massey, D.S. (1992) Changing Conditions in the US Labor Market: Effects of the Immigration Reform and Control Act of 1986. *Population Research and Policy Review* 11:93–115.

Ettinger, P. (2009) *Imaginary Lines: Border Enforcement and the Origins of Undocumented Migration, 1882–1930.* Austin, TX: University of Texas Press.

Foster, J. (2012) Making Temporary Permanent: The Silent Transformation of the Temporary Foreign Worker Program. *Just Labour: A Canadian Journal of Work and Society* 19:22–46.

Goldring, L., C. Berinstein, and J.K. Berhard (2009) Institutionalizing Precarious Migratory Status in Canada. *Citizenship Studies* 13(3):239–265.

Goldring, L. and P. Landolt (2011) Caught in the Work-Citizenship Matrix: The Lasting Effects of Precarious Legal Status on Work for Toronto Immigrants. *Globalizations* 8(3):325–341.

Goldring, L. and P. Landolt (2012) The Impact of Precarious Legal Status on Immigrants' Economic Outcomes. IRPP. http://irpp.org/2012/ll/29/the-impact-of-precarious-legal-status-on-immigrants-economic-outcomes (Accessed October 20, 2013)

Gomberg-Munoz, R. and L. Nussbaum-Barberena (2011) Is Immigration Policy Labor Policy? Immigration Enforcement, Undocumented Workers, and the State. *Human Organization* 70(4):366–375.

Grasmuck, S. (1984) Immigration, Ethnic Stratification, and Native Working Class Discipline: Comparisons of Documented and Undocumented Dominicans. *International Migration Review* 18(3):692–713.

Gunderson, M. (1980) *Labour Market Economics: Theory, Evidence and Policy in Canada.* Toronto: McGraw-Hill Ryerson.

Hanson, G.H. (2013) The Economics of Illegal Immigration in the United States: Policy Implications. In M. Fix, G. Papademetriou, and M. Sumption (eds.) *Immigrants in a Changing Labor Market*, pp. 53–68. Washington, DC: Migration Policy Institute.

Hawkins, F. (1988) *Canada and Immigration: Public Policy and Public Concern.* Montreal: McGill-Queen's University Press.

Hennebry, J. (2010) Private Interests in Canada's Immigration System. Presented at the workshop on "Global Picture Local Snapshots." Permanently Temporary: Temporary Foreign Workers and Canada's Changing Attitude to Citizenship and Immigration Symposium. Social Planning Toronto, OCASI, CERIS. www.ceris.metropolis.net/Virtual%20Library/other/PermanentlyTemporary.pdf (Accessed October 20, 2013)

Immigration Act (1864) Sess. I, Chap. 246. library.uwb.edu/guides/usimmigration/13%20stat%20385.pdf

Immigration Act (1875) Sess. II, Chap. 141. library.uwb.edu/guides/usimmigration/18%20stat%20477.pdf

Immigration Act (1976–1977) c. 52, s. 1. www.refworld.org/docid/3ae6b5c60.html

Immigration Act (1882) Sess. I, Chap. 126. library.uwb.edu/guides/usimmigration/22%20stat%2058.pdf

Immigration Act (1952) H.R. 13342; Pub.L. 414 library.uwb.edu/guides/usimmigration/66%20stat%20163.pdf

Immigration Act (1986) S. 1200; Pub.L. 99–603 http://library.uwb.edu/guides/usimmigration/100%20stat%203359.pdf

Immigration and Refugee Protection Act (2001) c. 27.

Jimenez, M. (2003) 200,000 Illegal Immigrants Toiling in Canada's Underground Economy. *Globe and Mail*, 27 October, A1.

Kaushal, N. (2006) Amnesty Programs and the Labor Market Outcomes of Undocumented Workers. *Journal of Human Resources* XLI:631–647.

Kelly, N. and M. Trebilcock (2010) *The Making of the Mosaic: A History of Canadian Immigration Policy*. Toronto: University of Toronto Press.

Kerwin, D.M. (2010) More than IRCA: US Legalization Programs and the Current Policy Debate. Migration Policy Institute. www.migrationpolicy.org/pubs/legalization-historical.pdf (Accessed October 20, 2013)

Khandor, E., J. McDonald, P. Nyers, and C. Wright (2004) The Regularization of Non-Status Immigrants in Canada, 1960–2004. accessalliance.ca/sites/accessalliance/files/documents/3.5.1%20&%206-%20Regularization%20Report.pdf (Accessed October 10, 2013)

Kim, Y. and M.J. Garcia (2011) Immigration Consequences of Criminal Activity. In M.A. Yates (ed.) *Immigrants and Illegal Aliens: Removal, Deterrence and Detention Issues*, pp. 57–75. New York: Nova Science Publishers.

Kossoudji, S. and D.A. Cobb-Clark (1996) Finding Good Opportunities Within Unauthorized Markets: U.S. Occupational Mobility for Male Latino Workers. *International Migration Review* 30(4):901–924.

Koussoudji, S.A. and D.A. Cobb-Clark (2000) IRCA's Impact on the Occupational Concentration and Mobility of Newly-Legalized Mexican Men. *Journal of Population Economics* 13:81–98.

Linklater, L. (2008) Director General, Immigration Branch, Department of Citizenship and Immigration, Committee Evidence, Meeting No. 13, February 25, 2008 15:50.

Liu, D.X.E. (2010) Regularization of the Undocumented in Canada: Lessons from Europe and the United States. Unpublished Master's Major Research Paper, Ryerson University, Toronto.

Lofstrom, M., L. Hill, and J. Hayes (2010) Did Employer Sanctions Lose Their Bite? Labor Market Effects of Immigrant Legalization. Public Policy Institute of California. http://ftp.iza.org/dp4972.pdf (Accessed November 5, 2013).

Lofstrom, M., L. Hill, and J. Hayes (2012) Wage and Mobility Effects of Legalization: Evidence from the New Immigrant Survey. *Journal of Regional Science* 53(1): 171–197.

Makarenko, J. (2010) Immigration Policy in Canada: History, Administration and Debates. www.mapleleafweb.com/features/immigration-policy-canada-history-administration-and-debates (Accessed October 20, 2013).

Massey, D.S. (1987) Do Undocumented Migrants Earn Lower Wages than Legal Immigrants? New Evidence from Mexico. *International Migration Review* 21(2):236–274.

Massey, D.S. and C. Capoferro (2004) Measuring Undocumented Migration. *International Migration Review* 38(3):1075–1102.

Mehta, C., N. Theodore, I. Mora, and J. Wade (2002) Chicago's Undocumented Immigrants: An Analysis of Wages, Working Conditions, and Economic Contributions. UIC Centre for Urban Economic Development. www.williamperezphd.com/articles/mehta-theodore-mora-wade-2002.pdf (Accessed August 20, 2013)

Morales, R. (1983–1984) Transitional Labor: Undocumented Workers in the Los Angeles Automobile Industry. *International Migration Review* 17(4):570–596.

Ngai, M.M. (2005) *Impossible Subjects: Illegal Aliens and the Making of Modern America.* Princeton, NJ: Princeton University Press.

Orrenius, P.M. and M. Zavodny (2012) The Economic Consequences of Amnesty for Unauthorized Immigrants. *Cato Journal* 32(1):85–106.

Passel, J.S. and D. Cohn (2011) Unauthorized Immigrant Population: National and State Trends. Pew Hispanic Center. www.pewhispanic.org/files/reports/133.pdf (Accessed November 5, 2013)

Phillips, P. (2012) Labour Market. *The Canadian Encyclopedia.* www.thecanadianencyclopedia.com/articles/labour-market (Accessed October 20, 2013)

Phillips, J.A. and D.S. Massey (1999) The New Labor Market: Immigrants and Wages after IRCA. *Demography* 36(2):233–246.

Piore, M.J. (1979) *Birds of Passage: Migrant Labor and Industrial Societies.* New York: Cambridge University Press.

Powers, M.G. and W. Seltzer (1998) Occupational Status and Mobility Among Undocumented Immigrants by Gender. *International Migration Review* 32(1):21–55.

Powers, M.G., W. Seltzer, and J. Shi (1998) Gender Differences in the Occupational Status of Undocumented Immigrants in the United States: Experience Before and After Legalization. *International Migration Review* 32(4):1015–1046.

Reksten, T. (1991) *The Dunsmuir Saga.* Vancouver: Douglas & McIntyre.

Rivera-Batiz, F. (1999) Undocumented Workers in the Labour Market: An Analysis of the Earnings of Legal and Illegal Mexican Immigrants in the United States. *Journal of Population Economics* 12:91–116.

Robinson, W.G. (1983) Illegal Immigrants in Canada. Minister of Supply and Services Canada.

Sharma, N. (2006) *Home Economics: Nationalism and the Making of "Migrant Workers" in Canada.* Toronto: University of Toronto Press.

Statistics Canada (2008) Canada's Population Estimates. www.statcan.gc.ca/daily-quotidien/080929/dq080929b-eng.htm (Accessed October 20, 2013)

Thangasamy, A. (2010) *State Policies for Undocumented Immigrants: Policy-Making and Outcomes in the U.S., 1998–2005.* El Paso, TX: LFB Scholarly Publishing.

Wasem, R.E. (2010) Unauthorized Aliens Residing in the United States: Estimates since 1986. In O.C. Anderson (ed.) *Illegal Immigration: Causes, Methods and Effects*, pp. 106–119. New York: Nova Science Publishers.

Youn, H., R. Woods, X. Zhou, and C. Hardigree (2010) The Restaurant Industry and Illegal Immigrants: An Oklahoma Case Study. *Journal of Human Resources in Hospitality & Tourism* 9(3):256–269.

Chapter 6

Finding Work: The Experience of Immigrants in North America

Michael Samers and Mitchell Snider

Introduction

Every day in Canada and the United States, citizens and noncitizens alike encounter and depend on immigrants. If we use public transport, buy a sandwich, eat fruits or vegetables, or work in a classroom, a library, or an office that is regularly cleaned, then we rely on immigrants to perform tasks that citizens will often no longer undertake. Thus immigrants or migrant workers are integral parts of our economies. However, there are substantial differences between the experience, reception, and nationalities of immigrants in the United States and Canada, as well as those states' economic activities, **immigration** policies, and the nature of their welfare systems. Are there differences then in immigrants' abilities to find and experiences while finding employment as well as the types of employment that are available to immigrants?

By attempting to answer these questions, we are in effect asking something about the **labour market incorporation** of immigrants. In the simplest of terms, "labour market incorporation" refers to whether or not immigrants find employment and what jobs they will eventually perform in American or Canadian labour markets (in other words, the job market). If we deepen our analysis a bit more, we can ask why immigrants from a specific country might be concentrated in certain kinds of jobs. Why do they receive the wages they do? What employment conditions do they face in each country and what possibilities of promotion do they have?

This chapter is concerned with precisely how immigrants are incorporated into labour markets in North America. While we prefer to use the term *labour market incorporation,* some books or articles also use the term **labour market outcomes**. We are not against the term *outcomes* (and in fact we use it in this chapter from time to time), so long as there is a consideration for how those outcomes come about. Another important feature of this chapter is that we will mainly focus on those immigrants working for a wage at the bottom of the income scale, while leaving a more thorough discussion of salaried, high-income immigrants, entrepreneurs, and other professionals to other chapters in this book, especially the next chapter by Maria Adamuti-Trache. Let us turn now to answering these questions by investigating different theories of labour market incorporation.

Theories of the Incorporation of Immigrants in Labour Markets

There are a number of different perspectives on the labour market incorporation of immigrants. We are going to explore five of these: 1) **human capital** theory and its variations; 2) the dual labour market approach; 3) the labour market segmentation approach (especially studies from the 1970s to the 1990s); 4) the cultural capital/cultural judgment approach; and 5) the migrant network approach. Again, these theories or approaches are preoccupied with the lower end of employment, which includes both documented and undocumented immigrants.

Human Capital Theory and Its Variants

Human capital theory (HCT) finds its origins in the work of the economist Gary Becker (1964). Becker argued that the education, skill level, and other capacities of an individual (what he called their human capital), combined with their aspirations and choices in terms of earnings, status, and job conditions, strongly shape their labour market outcomes. For Becker, these outcomes can be measured in terms of the wages and salaries of migrants, in other words the price of their labour. For many researchers, or at least economists of immigration and labour markets, this is not especially controversial. Most of us would probably expect our educational qualifications and other skills and abilities to have at least *some* effect on the kinds of jobs and income we can obtain, and we can imagine that this might be the case for immigrants as well. No doubt there is *some* evidence to suggest that this is indeed the case. Yet the actual labour market outcomes of migrants seem to throw into question this simple and seemingly commonsense relationship (e.g. Frank 2011; Buzdugan and Halli 2009). In fact, over the last decade in a North American context, analyses based on HCT have become increasingly sophisticated by bringing in variables other than human capital ones, to understand how the labour market outcomes for immigrants are created. These variables include:

- changes over time in one's education, skills, and so forth;
- age;
- gender;
- levels of parental education;
- generational differences (e.g. whether one is a first- or second-generation **immigrant**);
- religious affiliation,
- ethnic and national background or "cultural differences";
- the number of immigrants in a particular group;
- the presence of **ethnic enclaves** (a geographical concept that involves the local
- proximity of entrepreneurs and their co-ethnic employees; see also Chapter 16 by Sutama Ghosh and Raymond M.Garrison); and
- **social capital** (i.e. the resources generated by networks or contacts with other immigrants or citizens in the country of destination (see also, for example, Chapter 11 by Mehruuisa Ahmad Ali and Chapter 13 by Morton Beiser).

When human capital is analyzed with these other variables, they are found to have impacts in terms of whether immigrants participate in the job market, whether they are unemployed, and the wages they earn. When the actual jobs and wages of migrants are different from what one might expect from their human capital (while controlling for other variables) this is referred to as an "ethnic penalty" or "immigrant wage penalty." In other words, this suggests some level of discrimination likely based on the nationality of the immigrant, the colour of his or her skin, other attributes (e.g. language ability), or all of these combined (Reyneri and Fullin 2011). Such discrimination is not only relevant to supposedly "low-skilled" immigrants, but also to highly qualified immigrants, asylum seekers, and refugees (such as doctors or computer engineers) who may end up performing menial jobs as well (e.g. Akresh 2006 in the US; and Buzdugan and Hallie 2009; Creese and Wiebe 2012 in Canada). However, it is not *just* discrimination that matters but also the choice of employers, governments, and professional organizations to not formally recognize or accept foreign credentials, depending on the sector or type of job involved. The result for immigrants is often referred to as socio-professional downgrading (Reyneri 2001), occupational downgrading (e.g. Zuberi and Ptashnick 2012), or the **devaluation of immigrant labour** (Bauder 2006). (See Case Example 1.)

Case Example 1: The Devaluation of Immigrant Labour and Working Experiences in Vancouver, BC, Canada

As in all Canadian cites, immigrants in Vancouver often arrive with a range of skills and professional qualifications. And yet, as Dan Zuberi and Melita Ptashnick (2012) show in interviews they undertook with hundreds of immigrants, many end up working in low-wage hotel and hospital jobs. On one hand, their respondents acknowledged that many of the problems they encountered were due to their weak English skills. However, they also stated that they were pleased to be employed and gained some self-worth from being employed. Some even seemed to feel superior to those who were unemployed or on benefits. On the other hand, they complained of a "decline in occupational prestige," a lack of respect, and the feeling that their non-immigrant Canadian employers (especially the managers) felt that they were "stupid." As one person describes it,

> ... they treat us as if we're stupid. And we're not stupid, I mean, a lot of people are doctors and nurses and they're doing like houseman job, or something, but they're not stupid, but they treat us like we're dumb. And that really bugs us a lot....

> We want to be treated like a human being. And that's got to do with respect, you know, we feel like we're not respected, you know, enough. (75)

Another respondent who worked as a hospital catering associate claimed that

> I finished university in the Philippines ... Bachelor's in Science in Business Management ... I finished also medical technology in the Philippines and then I went to work in Libya as lab tech, but when I came to Canada, they didn't recognize my experience ... all in all about ten years.... [Now, my job is] to assemble ... prepare, and deliver the food. That is breakfast, lunch, and dinner. (78)

The above two anecdotes are only some of the life narratives that Zuberi and Ptashnick discuss. In short, the evidence is clear of significant occupational downgrading or the devaluation of immigrant labour in Vancouver and, by extension, many other cities in North America.

Source: Zuberi and Ptashnick (2012).

Thus, over the last decade HCT analyses have been increasingly combined with the variables discussed above. Further, they also consider how different welfare, immigration, and labour market policies affect immigrants' outcomes in labour markets. In that sense, many studies look like a hybrid of HCT and what is called labour market segmentation (we will discuss this further in the next section). The basic goal of these hybrid studies is to evaluate the relationship between what labour market outcomes *might be predicted* by immigrants' human capital and the *actual* outcomes that occur because of discrimination based on one's nationality, ethnic background, gender, or some combination of these and other attributes.

Some economic and urban geographers (Mattingly 1999; Wright and Ellis 2000; Ellis, Wright, and Parks 2007) also use an HCT approach, but they investigate its *subnational* implications through studies on the relationship between employment niching (why immigrants concentrate in particular industries), housing and residential location data, and human and social capital. The goal in these studies is to determine how these other variables affect immigrants' labour market outcomes both within and between cities and metropolitan areas. In perhaps the most sophisticated of these studies, Mark Ellis, Richard Wright, and Virginia Parks (2007) find that—in most cases—"the residential location of immigrants shapes the concentration of immigrants in certain kinds of jobs. In their words, the spatial accessibility of jobs matters as much as the social access to jobs" (Samers 2010:126). The benefit of this research is that it moves away from only using national-level data in the analysis of labour market outcomes. This provides a more detailed and complex understanding of the considerably variable characteristics of regional and urban labour markets within and between Canada and the United States.

While studies that use an HCT approach are extremely diverse, they do have some overall limitations. First, the simplest of HCT-based analyses rely on problematic assumptions such as holding language skills constant or holding citizenship constant. After all, immigrants' language skills can change over time, as can their citizenship status. Second and relatedly, HCT-based studies are not very useful for showing the impact of changing immigration policies on the labour market incorporation of immigrants. Third, HCT tends to prioritize nationality (often as a measure of one's ethnicity) as a variable to be analyzed, as if nationality or ethnicity (rather than gender, for example) might be important for one's labour market incorporation (Hanson and Pratt 1991). A fourth problem is that HCT is poor at *directly* measuring discrimination. This is mainly because HCT studies typically rely on the quantitative analysis of labour market outcomes. Finally, many HCT analyses use only national rather than subnational data. This is unfortunate as employment opportunities and experiences often vary enormously from region to region within Canada and the United States.

Dual Labour Market Hypothesis

In his well-received book *Birds of Passage*, Michael Piore (1979) describes a dual labour market that consists of two sectors: a primary sector (which contains relatively high-paying, stable jobs with pleasant working conditions and considerable possibility for promotion) and a secondary sector (which contains relatively low-wage jobs that are unstable, involve poorer working conditions, and suffer from "promotion blockages"). Immigrants, Piore argues, are concentrated in secondary jobs based on the recruiting strategy of employers who view immigrants as more accepting of low-wage jobs. The focus is on the *demand* characteristics of labour markets—the industrial structure of the advanced economies and their supposed dualistic labour markets.

While Piore's analysis may be elegant and convincing, it does not necessarily reflect labour markets in twenty-first century Canada and the United States. First, jobs in North America do not simply fall into such a neat dichotomy, even if it appears that extremely low-wage jobs (such as in agriculture, cleaning, construction, domestic work, or restaurants) performed by legal or undocumented immigrants are starkly different from many middle class or high-income jobs. Second, Piore's emphasis on labour *demand* (or what labour market economists call the "demand side") neglects the supply side, that is the availability, characteristics, and practices of workers. Nevertheless, a key insight of Piore that may now seem obvious to many observers is that immigrants were willing to accept the jobs that native-born workers were unwilling to accept. This in turn gave rise to a debate about whether immigrants are a "substitute" for native-born workers—whether they were taking the jobs of citizens—or a complement who performed jobs that no one else wanted to do, therefore providing a valuable service to countries such as the US. Piore argues that they act as a complement. At any rate, Piore himself neglected the importance of **immigration policy**. Third, many of the industrial jobs taken by immigrants between the 1950s and the 1970s were in fact quite stable, if certainly low-paid (Samers 1999). Fourth, Piore said nothing about **informal employment**, highly paid immigrants, or entrepreneurship for that matter. Lastly, he used a rather simple notion of citizenship (one is either a citizen or not, and he assumed this did not change over time). Overall, the dual labour market hypothesis could be considered as a very basic explanation of how workers are placed into certain jobs. Fortunately, a more refined version of labour market incorporation was created around the same time.

Labour Market Segmentation Approach

The labour market segmentation approach (LMSA) stems from the work of radical labor market economists such as David M. Gordon, Richard C. Edwards, and Michael Reich (1982). However, other academics—such as economic or urban sociologists using both quantitative and qualitative evidence—also became involved in this research tradition. **Segmented labour market theory** suggests that employers have created different segments, or divisions within American labour markets. For these authors, each segment has its own rules of operation with respect to pay, working conditions, promotion, and institutions. Instead of just two job sectors then, they emphasize employers' segmentation of workers into a range of job categories that could be specific to a firm or an organization (such as a hospital). LMSA represents an immediate critique of HCT, and is deeply concerned with discriminatory behaviour that *leads to* labour market outcomes. Some studies combine HCT and an LMSA although LMSA tends to rely on *direct* evidence of discrimination in the workplace. That is, researchers actually speak to workers about the problems of finding work or getting promoted rather than relying on statistical data on outcomes.

This segmentation is argued to occur with little regard for the human capital of immigrants. Rather, employers hire and promote workers on other bases such as nationality, gender/sex, or skin colour. For example, employers use prejudicial stereotypes about the characteristics of particular immigrant nationalities ("they're lazy" or alternatively "they work very hard") to gauge the suitability of migrants for particular jobs, rather than migrants' skills and other attributes. What is noteworthy about these early studies of LMSA is that, like the dual labour market, they focused mainly on labour demand—how the demand by employers for certain kinds of jobs and workers led to specific forms of segmentation (e.g. Gordon, Edwards, and Reich 1982). Yet much has changed in labour markets since these studies emerged and it is worth mentioning several changes since, let us say, the early 1980s. First, there has been a massive loss of manufacturing jobs, especially in the Northeast and Midwestern US, as well as parts of Eastern Canada, so that manufacturing jobs only represent somewhere between 20 and 23% of all jobs in Canada and the US, respectively. This suggests that the potential job sites for immigrants have changed, and immigrants are as likely to find themselves in service employment as in manufacturing jobs (which in general have higher skill demands than 30 years ago). In fact, there has been a corresponding rise in service-oriented employment, and service employment now constitutes about 77% of all employment in Canada and about 80% in the United States (World Bank 2012).

Second, economic liberalization has had important impacts on the labour market. Subcontracting (i.e. a process by which larger employers rely on generally smaller suppliers to undertake parts of the production process of any good or service) has greatly increased. Subcontracted suppliers try to reduce costs by paying the lowest wages possible, sometimes relying on undocumented immigrants who can easily be hired and fired, and be hired only part-time or on a temporary basis (Kalleberg 2009). Employers' apparent need for flexibility includes the ability to move people around different work positions at will in the service sector. This kind of job flexibility is accompanied not only by growing part-time and temporary employment but also increasingly the lack of (extended) healthcare and retirement benefits. All of this might seem to deny the significance of segmentation. After all, if employers require flexibility, then the maintenance of rigid segments whereby immigrants or other workers are unable to move would not be desirable.

Third, some authors argue that informal employment has increased in North America since the 1970s (e.g. Schneider, Buehn, and Montenegro 2010), reflecting another significant change in labour market demand. Informal employment (where one is paid as if in a conventional job) is work that is either not registered or it is hidden from the state and/or labour, tax, or social security/insurance authorities (e.g. Kalleberg 2009; Marcelli, Williams, and Joassart 2010). For example, in the US it is common for immigrants to wait outside hardware stores or other locations to be picked up by small construction companies, landscaping firms, or simply other individuals looking to hire immigrants temporarily and "off the books." Many immigrants supplement informal employment with household or community work in exchange for services. For example, they might paint your house if you repair their car; money will not be exchanged. In addition, some jobs contain both formal and informal moments. It is better, therefore, to speak of the "informalization" (Sassen 1998) of immigrant employment rather than making a stark distinction between informal and formal work. Although most informal employment and work is performed by citizens rather than by immigrants, undocumented immigrants who work informally are extremely vulnerable and often cannot obtain the correct papers to work in more formal jobs. Informal employment is also highly gendered, since informal work often exists in the form of domestic work (that is, work as nannies, cleaning persons, child-minders, and the like) which women often perform. Many domestic workers—from Filipino women who clean homes in Los Angeles or Vancouver to Caribbean child-minders in New York City—are indeed undocumented, have little or no rights under national immigration and employment laws, work extremely long hours for very low pay, and are subject to the whims of their employers (e.g. Parreñas 2001; Pratt 1999). Chapter 8 by Nandita Sharma discusses some of the underlying causes and consequences of illegalization and the denial of rights in greater detail.

A related issue is the growth of **immigrant entrepreneurship** (immigrants owning businesses that—if large enough—may hire other immigrants and often cater to an immigrant public, though not exclusively). As self-employed owners of a small grocery store, a bakery, perhaps a halal butcher, and so forth, immigrants often make very low earnings and do not receive many employment and health benefits. Entrepreneurship is very pervasive among *some* immigrant nationalities and such businesses can also operate informally insofar as the owner may pay the workers—often immigrants of the same or a different nationality—"under the table," labour regulations might be violated, or the owner may not declare their revenue to tax authorities. Finally, *diversity* has become the watchword of many employers over the last two decades or so. This may seem surprising since we might imagine that racism and discrimination are important processes in labour markets, and they are. Nonetheless, there is an advantage to diversity for employers (as we will discuss further below). Likewise, problems of segmentation may be less about traditional "white on black" **racism** and reflect, rather, cultural judgments (see below) or other forms of racism and discrimination among a range of groups. For example, in Dayton, Ohio, the number of Turkish and other entrepreneurs from the Middle East has increased substantially over the last decade, but some African American leaders worry about whether African Americans (who constitute some 43% of the city's residents) are being hired by Turkish and other immigrant entrepreneurs in this languishing city with high unemployment (*New York Times* 2013). Nonetheless, there is also some evidence to suggest that in the United States, for example, white citizens "hoard" jobs through networks with other white citizens and exclude Mexicans and other immigrants from relatively high-paying jobs that come with healthcare and other benefits (Waldinger and Luthra 2010).

Above we have sketched changes in labour market *demand*. However, insofar as most LMSA studies focus on labour market demand, they tend to neglect what social scientists call **social reproduction** (i.e. how workers' lives are made possible or "reproduced" through sufficient housing, welfare payments, childcare, mutual aid, and so on). Moreover, many LMSA studies have left out immigration policies, labour market policies, welfare policies, and so forth, which partly create the necessary life conditions that permit people to work. Policies regarding residence visas, housing permits, welfare rights, and work visas also affect how many hours a person needs to work to secure their standard of living (e.g. if they have access to welfare or free medical care). Similarly, the right to public housing, the recognition of immigrants' credentials, or the right to work for unlimited hours all have a potentially strong influence on how immigrants interact with and enter into a segmented labour market (e.g. Preibisch 2012; Rajkumar, Berkowitz, Vosko, Preston, and Latham 2012). Further, policies exist in different international, national, and subnational jurisdictions and have different effects depending on the sector or industry involved, the nationality of immigrants, their gender, and whether they entered Canada or the US as asylum seekers, undocumented immigrants, family members, highly skilled migrants, or another category. For example, at the *international* scale, the North American Free Trade Agreement (NAFTA) enables the free movement of specific categories mainly of skilled workers, such as nurses, between Canada, Mexico, and the US (Gabriel 2008). As Chapter 8 by Nandita Sharma shows, the *national* level of government is perhaps most significant in that Canadian and American government policies and laws dictate who can work, when, where, and for how long, depending on what papers an immigrant is given. To provide an example at the national level of government, following the events of Tiananmen Square in Beijing in 1989 when the Chinese government cracked down on pro-Democracy demonstrators, the American government reacted by halting all deportations of Chinese immigrants from the United States and granted the majority of Chinese residents in the US the right to work. Likewise, the 1992 Chinese Student Protection Act gave most Chinese students the right to permanent resident status. This secure status likely had positive effects on the earnings and income of relatively skilled Chinese migrants (Orrenius, Zavodny, and Kerr 2012). Alongside international and national policies are *subnational* policies (for example, those of provincial and territorial governments in Canada or state governments in the US, as well as of municipalities), which sometimes reflect national policies but also might diverge from them.

For example, in the US, restrictive state policies by individual states such as Arizona or towns such as Hazleton, Pennsylvania, have made life extremely precarious for undocumented immigrants. In Hazleton the mayor of the city succeeded in passing some of the strictest anti-illegal immigration legislation in 2006, including a municipal ordinance that fined landlords who knowingly rented to "illegal" immigrants, suspended the business license of any employer for five years who hired an "illegal" immigrant, and made English the official language, without the possibility of officially translating government documents into Spanish. While the ordinance quickly gathered national media attention, by 2013 the courts of the state of Pennsylvania had ruled the ordinance unconstitutional, and the federal courts refused any appeal (see, e.g. *Washington Post*, "Pa. City Puts Illegal Immigrants on Notice," August 22, 2006, and *Huffington Post*, "Hazleton, Pennsylvania's Immigrant Laws Ban Reaffirmed by Court," July 26, 2013).

A New Version of Labour Market Segmentation Theory: A Cultural Capital/Cultural Judgments Approach

Building on the sociologist Pierre Bourdieu's notion of cultural capital, Harald Bauder (2006) suggests that the cultural judgments of employers (based on an immigrant's accent, dress, bodily behaviour, foreign origin of credentials, etc.) are significant in producing certain kinds of labour market outcomes for immigrants. In other words, if immigrants do not have what employers see as the appropriate cultural capital, employers may not hire them, or may not promote them for advanced positions. In this way, segmentation entails more than just ethnic or racial stereotyping; employers are searching for a specific set of traits for a particular job or set of tasks. In short, to meet the expectations of employers, immigrants have to "dress right," speak with the "right accent," and "know the rules." If they do not, then their human capital will count for little. Nonetheless, as Bauder points out, the cultural capital of immigrants might work in one setting but not in another. For example, he shows that in Vancouver, Canada, where many taxi drivers are turban-wearing Sikh men, the turban becomes a symbol of reliability and integrity, rather than cultural "otherness." Passengers are thus potentially assured by a driver who wears a turban. As Bauder (himself an immigrant to Canada from southern Germany) writes, half-jokingly,

> To use a hypothetical example, if ethnic networks channeled large numbers of traditional, lederhosen-wearing southern German men in to the pizza-delivery business, then wearing lederhosen might become a legitimate practice in this occupation. If this group dominates the occupation, lederhosen may even become a trademark of the occupation which customers learn to expect from the delivery personnel. What this silly example illustrates is that the concentration of an immigrant group in a given occupation affects the corporeal conventions that dominate in that occupation. (Bauder 2006:46)

Thus, in many instances, a diverse workforce or alternatively a workforce involving a specific nationality (for instance, those who are of Mexican origin or Lebanese origin) can be an advantage for employers, especially where the customers for any particular business, product, or service may not necessarily be stereotypical "white" Canadians or Americans (Waldinger and Lichter 2003). For example, in a hospital, government office, or a business where the clientele is Spanish-speaking, hiring workers who also speak Spanish may be beneficial for the government or employers. This pattern of hiring need not relate only to the nationality of customers or clients in a particular neighbourhood or city, especially given how cross-country Internet purchases and other services mean customers and businesses may be spread out geographically.

The cultural capital/cultural judgment approach and these further reflections on diversity remain an important addition to studies on how immigrants secure employment, what jobs they eventually hold, and what opportunities they have for advancement. Although Bauder, for example, explores at length issues of immigration policy and citizenship, if we take his and other similar discussions *as an approach* then, strictly speaking, such studies do not account for the effects of immigration policy and citizenship status, at least not directly. Furthermore, Bauder's approach, as with the others mentioned above, tends to neglect the agency of immigrants themselves, and it is for this reason that we turn to the last of the approaches that we will discuss in this chapter.

Migrant, Immigrant, or Social Network Approach

In the migrant, immigrant, or social network approach, the emphasis falls not on employers but on the practices of immigrants and particularly the social networks of co-nationals (individuals of the same nationality or national origin) or co-ethnics (immigrants of the same ethnicity) involved in finding jobs and providing for other resources, such as housing and legal assistance (e.g. Boyd 1989). In other words, these social networks can contribute to various forms of social capital and an "economy of favors" (Ledeneva 1998) in which immigrants exchange favours with fellow immigrants. Co-national or co-ethnic networks are often referred to as bonding social capital. These can be distinguished from so-called bridging social capital, that is, establishing contacts outside the immigrant's national or ethnic group and—especially in the context of immigration—with citizens (Putnam 2000; Lancee 2010). In both cases, some of these networks (or ties) may be "strong," and some may be "weak." Sometimes, weak ties may in fact be more effective for obtaining necessary resources (e.g. jobs, housing) than strong ties (which can in fact make it more difficult to find a good job) and it is crucial to recognize that not all co-ethnic or co-national networks are strong; they are also often divided by "class," gender, and other social differences. The evidence in a North American context is mixed on the significance of strong co-national or co-ethnic ties (i.e. bonding social capital) for finding jobs, and especially securing higher incomes. For example, Ryan Allen (2009) finds that in Portland, Maine, over time bonding capital hurts the earnings of refugee women.

If immigrants come to be the most numerous workers in any given workplace or even in a certain industry, they might end up excluding other immigrant groups from taking these same jobs (Waldinger and Lichter 2003). This can in turn lead to **employment (or ethnic) niches** and/or "ethnic economies." The former describes "... economic sectors ... where group members are disproportionately represented in the labour force, either in public sector jobs or in private businesses that are typically owned by and managed by whites or members of another ethnic group" (Logan, Alba, and Stults 2003:346). Here, we can easily turn to the example of Vietnamese nail salons. During the course of the 1990s, Vietnamese **immigrant women** developed

Case Example 2: Mexican- and Central American–Origin Immigrants in the Horse Industry around Lexington, Kentucky

In the US state of Kentucky, the number of Latino immigrants (that is immigrants who generally migrated from Mexico and Central America) increased by 300% from 1990 to 2006. They now constitute a large "minority" in a state that is better known for its history of out-migration during most of the twentieth century (Shultz 2008). The Lexington metropolitan area (surrounded by the Bluegrass region) in particular is attractive for immigrants, and unemployment has remained relatively low (except for the first couple of years after the 2008 economic and financial crisis). At the same time, housing—especially in small towns that surround the city—is relatively cheap. The region is arguably "the capital" of the American horse industry, and as such, the Bluegrass region has become the site of an important ethnic niche economy—the thoroughbred horse industry. Formerly an enclave dominated mostly by Irish immigrants, this economy has become dominated by Latino workers. Somewhat differently than the Vietnamese nail salons, the horse farms are generally owned by wealthy white Americans or foreigners, and the industry neither was started nor is controlled by Latino workers. Why are Latinos concentrated in this sector?

Employment in the horse industry includes "on the farm" jobs such as horse breeding and foaling, training, service industry jobs in the local racing tracks, and even jockeying horses. In the past, most of the workers on the horse farms, and particularly the foaling farms—where horses are born or "foaled"—were Irish immigrants who had moved to Lexington during the twentieth century to work in the industry, but have since either found other jobs in the Bluegrass region or elsewhere in the United States, or have returned to Ireland. With the growth of Latino migration to the region, and with the encouragement of employers, Latino workers have now replaced most of the Irish workers on the foaling farms. These farms are, by necessity, located several miles outside the city of Lexington and other nearby towns. The men (though sometimes women) working on the horse farms in Kentucky often live on-site, but others commute from poorer, now predominantly Latino neighbourhoods in the city or satellite towns of Lexington that include Versailles, Paris, and Winchester.

Many of the men who work on these farms are undocumented and thus are employed in "informalized" work. Mexican men in particular (especially those coming from rural areas) often have previous experience with farm work and have some skills that are necessary (or at least useful) for this work. They also tend to use connections (or networks) with family members already on the farm to secure a job. However, their prior experience with farm work, combined with the social networks used to find work and employers' preferences, have favoured younger workers in their twenties and reproduced a strong gendered division of labour that has excluded most Latina women. Indeed, very few women are to be found in foaling work on the horse farms.

At the same time, Latino men have exerted some control over the daily workings of the farms, or at least over the workers, since some farm managers are of immigrant origin: men, middle-aged, bilingual, and also naturalized as American citizens. Though the men may have not purposefully set out to accomplish this, work on the foaling farms has become an ethnic niche for Mexicans and some other Spanish-speaking immigrants.

and now dominate a certain standardized "industry" of nail care (what Eckstein and Nguyen 2011, call "McNails") that has come to be demanded across the ethnic and socioeconomic spectrum in North American society and beyond. Vietnamese women have accomplished this through using both formal and informal Vietnamese networks that led to their domination of the industry and by preventing other non-Vietnamese women from entering the sector or being employed. Similarly, ethnic economies (Bonacich and Modell 1980) refer to entrepreneurs and their co-ethnic employees. Such economies may be spread out across countries, regions, or cities but the relationship between owners, workers, and customers has an ethnic dimension (Light, Sabagh, Bozorgmehr, and Der-Martirosian 1994).

Yet even if immigrants numerically dominate specific workplaces or sectors, their ability to shape their labour market outcomes are limited, since labour market demands, immigration and other policies, their human capital, and discriminatory and other cultural judgments also bear on their fortunes. In fact, above we have stressed how networks help *immigrants* in finding work, but we know very little about how *employers*—especially those of low-wage, informal, and/or undocumented workers—use social networks to secure both a loyal and pliant labour force. Such networks should not be overlooked, since it may be difficult for employers to find reliable workers and the networks that immigrants have assist employers in reducing the time and costs of finding workers. At the same time, immigrants who are already in a workplace may encourage (or even force) the friends or relatives they have recruited to be more loyal and more willing to endure considerably lower wages and poorer employment conditions. All of these processes are likely to benefit the employers of immigrants (see Case Examples 2 and 3). Finally, we must mention the role

Case Example 3: Immigrants from the Middle East Working in a Meatpacking Plant in Brooks, AB, Canada

By the 1990s, a meatpacking plant in the town of Brooks, in southeastern Alberta, began to have trouble finding local workers. The plant initially turned to Canadian citizens from the Atlantic provinces, especially Newfoundland, in the wake of the collapse of the cod fishing industry. After a few years, however, Newfoundlanders would leave the plant and either return to the East or find other jobs in the local economy. Desperate for workers willing to accept the low wages they paid and the tough working conditions, in 1998 the plant turned to recruiting immigrant labour and working with local immigration aid services. Recruiting videos were translated into Arabic and presented to immigrants at the Catholic Immigration Society in Calgary. The plant helped workers with their immigration papers, which mostly involved issues of family reunification. By 2000, immigrant employees of the plant were being paid a $1,000 bonus for referring other friends and family members who worked at the plant for a certain minimum period of time, and this appeared to be common practice in the industry. For Michael Broadway (2007), this stimulated "chain migration" (MacDonald and MacDonald 1964) and the establishment of immigrant enclaves in towns with meatpacking plants, including Brooks. By 2006, immigrants and refugees had grown to approximately 60% of the plant's labour force, and even higher among line workers. In fact, most of the immigrants in Brooks (some 90%) were actually refugees from countries such as Afghanistan, Ethiopia, Pakistan, Sudan, and Somalia. A few more came from Burundi, the Democratic Republic of Congo, Liberia, Sierra Leone, and Tanzania. Yet most had moved to Brooks from elsewhere in Canada in order to find work and join friends and family. In 2005, line workers, most of whom were from Africa, petitioned to become unionized workers and began a strike. However, most of the nonline, clerical, and other employees were white Canadians and crossed the picket line (because they opposed the strike). Violent confrontations took place between employees, line workers, and the police, and several strikers were arrested. The clerical employees took their grievances to Alberta's Labour Relations Board to ban the union. The strike continued for three weeks, but it resulted in a deterioration of relations within the plant and led to a change in the company's recruitment policy. The result: the company, with the aid of a provincial labour recruitment program, brought in 250 temporary workers from China, the Philippines, El Salvador, and Ukraine to work on the lines. What is fascinating about Broadway's study is that very similar processes occurred in a plant he observed in the state of Kansas.

Source: Broadway (2007).

of so-called labour market intermediaries such as recruitment agencies and other institutions and individuals involved in smuggling or trafficking for the purposes of work, often sex/sexual work. We can distinguish between smuggling, which involves bringing someone illegally across an international border, and trafficking, which involves smuggling for the purposes of work. In both sexual and nonsexual trafficking, a migrant is often (but not always) tricked, coerced, or forced through debt and/ or violence to work under substandard and downright horrible conditions. Since their passports are often illegally retained by their employers or the intermediaries who brought them, they remain undocumented and in a semi-permanent state of vulnerability and bondage (Kyle and Kowslowski 2001; Salt and Stein 1997).

Conclusion

For immigrants, paid work is a vital part of daily survival in Canada and the US, as it is elsewhere. In the absence of such work, immigrants must rely on the generosity of friends or relatives—providing goods or doing services for others in exchange for other goods or services—or for some immigrants, eke out a living on welfare benefits. This chapter has focused on how immigrants, and particularly those who are disadvantaged, are incorporated into North American labour markets. Not all immigrants are disadvantaged, however, including those from poorer countries. Many in Canada and the US are highly skilled, relatively highly paid, and are involved in all kinds of economic activities, from engineering and finance to medicine and nursing (Chapter 7). At the same time, it is also true that many highly skilled migrants quickly become low-income earners, often concentrating in very different sectors and occupations from their pre-migration employment. In this chapter we offered an explanation of this **concentration**, their low wages, and their lack of socioeconomic mobility.

We examined a number of different approaches and provided some examples of research findings across and within Canada and the US. At the same time, we noted some of the strengths and weaknesses or limitations of each of these approaches. Beginning with the human capital perspective, we saw that human capital matters for those who are explicitly recruited into highly paid administrative or executive employment, but for many immigrants who come to Canada or the US either as family members, through temporary employment schemes, through asylum, or as undocumented immigrants, their skills and qualifications seem to matter relatively little. Indeed, this has been described, for example, as occupational downgrading or the devaluation of immigrant labour.

Beyond human capital theory, we discussed the notion of a dual labour market and then its more sophisticated version, labour market segmentation, noting especially that attention should be paid to international, national, regional, and local policies to understand how immigrants are segmented into particular jobs. These might include immigration policies related to **naturalization**, work and residence permits, and welfare and housing policies, among others. At the same time, they intersect with the changing nature of labour demand as well as issues of social reproduction (childcare, housing, the use of welfare payments, and so forth). Together, they create immigrants who are more vulnerable to poorer working conditions, long hours, and lower pay than native-born Canadians or Americans.

The last of the theories we looked at concerned migrant or immigrant networks. We showed that immigrants used these networks to find employment, as well as for securing financial assistance, housing, and matters of health. Some research shows that such networks based on ethnic ties or ties with other people from the same country can have positive effects on both finding work and the wages one earns. Ironically, these migrant networks also help employers to find loyal and thus rather compliant workers through an "economy of favours." Nonetheless, some evidence shows that bonding capital may eventually lead to lower incomes over time, at least compared to the incomes immigrants might have if they had more networks with citizens. In any case, given the diversity of immigrant origins, their destinations, the characteristics of immigrants, the labour markets of different countries and regions, and the range of national and subnational institutions and policies, drawing neat and quick conclusions about how immigrants find work and their socioeconomic mobility is a tricky, if not impossible, business. Nevertheless, together these different approaches allow us to better understand how migrants find employment and their fortunes. And yet, as North American society evolves and the nature of immigration changes, perhaps there will be a need to either modify existing approaches or develop entirely new approaches to the ways in which immigrants find work and their experience with it.

Questions for Critical Throught

1. Though human capital theory is useful, why is it insufficient to understand the incorporation of migrants in labour markets?
2. How is labour market segmentation theory an advancement of the dual labour market hypothesis?
3. How can we explain why many highly skilled migrants become low-income earners?
4. Why are studies that only analyze immigration laws and policies inadequate when used to explain immigrants' incorporation into labour markets?
5. Why do social networks matter for labour market incorporation, from both the employer's and the immigrant's perspective?

Key Readings

Bauder, H. (2006) *Labor Movement: How Migration Regulates Labor Markets.*
New York: Oxford University Press.

Samers, M. (2010) *Migration.* London: Routledge

Waldinger, R. and M. Lichter (2003) *How the Other Half Works: Immigration and the Social Organization of Labour.* Berkeley, CA: University of California Press.

Media Links

An Immigrant Class—Oral Histories from Chicago's Newest Immigrants:
www.animmigrantclass.com/excerpts.html
Twenty first-person histories and photographs by recent newcomers to Chicago, from across the globe, documenting their experience of migrating to the United States.

Building New Skills: Immigration and Workforce Development in Canada:
www.migrationpolicy.org/research/building-new-skills-immigration-and-workforce-development-canada
This is a link to a report by Karen Myers and Natalie Conte on immigration, skills, and the Canadian labour market. The report is published by the Migration Policy Institute (MPI). Access to the larger and very rich MPI website is available from this link.

Cesar Chavez and Immigration Reform:
www.dissentmagazine.org/blog/cesar-chavez-and-immigration-reform
An article by Nicolaus Mills about the prominent Mexican-American migrant workers' rights activist Cesar Chavez and American immigration reform. The article was published online on June 28, 2013, in *Dissent Magazine.*

Canada Needs More Immigrant Future Citizens, Fewer Guest Workers:
www.theglobeandmail.com/globe-debate/editorials/canada-needs-more-citizens-fewer-guest-workers/article17968803
An editorial from leading Canadian national newspaper, the *Globe and Mail*, on April 14, 2014, critiquing the direction of current Canadian immigration policy focused on bringing very large numbers of temporary foreign workers to Canada. There are other links to related stories in the newspaper as well.

Women Fight for Immigration Reform in Guest Worker Programs:
http://politicsofpoverty.oxfamamerica.org/2013/10/women-fight-for-immigration-reform-in-guest-worker-programs
An article by Mary Babic published online on October 17, 2013, on the website Oxfam America. In this piece, three guest workers in the US tell their experiences with unscrupulous overseas recruiters.

References

Akresh, I.R. (2006) Occupational Mobility among Legal Immigrants to the United States. *International Migration Review* 40(4):854–884.

Allen, R. (2009) Benefit or Burden? Social Capital, Gender, and the Economic Adaptation of Refugees. *International Migration Review*, 43(2):332–336

Bauder, H. (2006) *Labor Movement: How Migration Regulates Labor Markets*. New York: Oxford University Press.

Becker, G. (1964) *Human Capital*. New York: National Bureau of Economic Research/ Columbia University Press.

Bonacich, E. and J. Modell (1980) *The Economic Basis of Ethnic Solidarity: Small Business in the Japanese American Community*. Berkeley, CA: University of California Press.

Boyd, M. (1989) Family and Personal Networks in International Migration: Recent Developments and New Agendas. *International Migration Review* 23(3):638–670.

Broadway, M. (2007) Meatpacking and the Transformation of Rural Communities: A Comparison of Brooks, Alberta, and Garden City, Kansas. *Rural Sociology* 72(4):560–582.

Buzdugan, R. and S.S. Halli (2009) Labor Market Experiences of Canadian Immigrants with Focus on Foreign Education and Experience. *International Migration Review* 43(2): 366–386.

Creese, G. and B. Wiebe (2012) Survival Employment: Gender and Deskilling among African Immigrants in Canada. *International Migration* 50(5):56–76.

De Graaf, N.D. and H.D. Flap (1988) With a Little Help from My Friends: Social Resources as an Explanation of Occupational Status and Income in West Germany, the Netherlands, and the United States. *Social Forces* 67(2):452–472.

Eckstein, S. and T.N. Nguyen (2011) The Making and Transnationalization of an Ethnic Niche: Vietnamese Manicurists. *International Migration Review* 45(3):639–674.

Ellis, M., R. Wright, and V. Parks (2007) Geography and the Immigrant Division of Labour. *Economic Geography* 83(3):255–281.

Frank, K. (2011) Does Occupational Status Matter? Examining Immigrants' Employment in Their Intended Occupations. *Canadian Studies in Population* 38(1–2):115–134.

Gabriel, C. (2008) A Healthy Trade? NAFTA, Labour Mobility, and Canadian Nurses. In C. Gabriel and H. Pellerin (eds.) *Governing International Labour Migration*. London: Routledge.

Hanson, S. and G. Pratt (1991) Time, Space, and the Occupational Segregation of Women—A Critique of Human Capital Theory. *Geoforum* 22(2):149–157.

Gordon, D., M.C. Edwards, and M. Reich (1982) *Segmented Work, Divided Workers*. Cambridge: Cambridge University Press.

Kalleberg, A. (2009) Precarious Work, Insecure Workers: Employment Relations in Transition. *American Sociological Review* 74(1):1–22.

Kyle, D. and R. Koslowski (eds.) (2001) *Global Human Smuggling*. Baltimore, MD: Johns Hopkins University Press.

Lancee, B. (2010) The Economic Returns of Immigrants' Bonding and Bridging Social Capital. The Case of the Netherlands. *International Migration Review* 44(1):202–226.

Ledeneva, A. (1998) *Russia's Economy of Favours: Blat, Networking and Informal Exchange*. Cambridge: Cambridge University Press.

Light, I., G. Sabagh, M. Bozorgmehr, and C. Der-Martirosian (1994) Beyond the Ethnic Enclave Economy. *Social Problems* 41(1):65–80.

Logan, J.R., R.D. Alba, and B.J. Stults (2003) Enclaves and Entrepreneurs: Assessing the Payoff for Immigrants and Minorities. *International Migration Review* 37(2):344–388.

Marcelli, E., C. Williams, and P. Joassart (2010) *Informal Work in Developed Nations*. London: Routledge.

Mattingly, D. (1999) Job Search, Social Networks, and Local Labour Market Dynamics: The Case of Paid Household Work in San Diego, California. *Urban Geography* 20:46–74.

MacDonald, J.S. and L.D. MacDonald (1964) Chain Migration, Ethnic Neighborhood Formation, and Social Networks. *The Milbank Memorial Fund Quarterly* 42(1):82–97.

New York Times (2013) Ailing Midwestern Cities Extend a Welcoming Hand to Immigrants, 6 October.

Orrenius, P., M. Zavodny, and E. Kerr (2012) Chinese Immigrants in the US Labor Market: Effects of Post-Tiananmen Immigration Policy. *International Migration Review* 46(2):456–482.

Parreñas, R.S. (2001) *Servants of Globalization: Women, Migration, and Domestic Work*. Stanford, CA: Stanford University Press.

Piore, M. (1979) *Birds of Passage*. Cambridge, MA: MIT Press.

Pratt, G. (1999) From Registered Nurse to Registered Nanny: Discursive Geographies of Filipina Domestic Workers in Vancouver, BC. *Economic Geography* 75(3):215–236.

Preibisch, K. (2012) Migrant Workers and Changing Work-place Regimes in Contemporary Agricultural Production in Canada. *International Journal of Sociology of Agriculture and Food* 19(1):62–82.

Putnam, R.D. (2000) *Bowling Alone: The Collapse and Revival of American Community.* New York: Simon & Schuster.

Rajkumar, D., L. Berkowitz, L.F. Vosko, V. Preston, and R. Latham (2012) At the Temporary-Permanent Divide: How Canada Produces Temporariness and Makes Citizens through Its Security, Work, and Settlement Policies. *Citizenship Studies* 16(3–4):483–510.

Reyneri, E. (2001) *Migrants' Involvement in the Underground Economy in the Mediterranean Countries of the European Union.* ILO—International Migration Working Paper no. 41.

Reyneri, E. and G. Fullin (2011) Labour Market Penalties of New Immigrants in New and Old Receiving West European Countries. *International Migration* 49(1):31–57.

Salt, J. and J. Stein (1997) Migration as a Business: The Case of Trafficking. *International Migration* 35(4):467–494.

Samers, M. (1999) "Globalization", Migration, and the Geo-political Economy of Migration of the "Spatial Vent." *Review of International Political Economy* 6(2):166–199.

Samers, M. (2010) *Migration.* London: Routledge.

Sassen, S. (1998) *Globalization and Its Discontents.* New York: New Press.

Schneider, F., A. Buehn, and C.E. Montenegro (2010) *Shadow Economies All over the World: New Estimates for 162 Countries from 1999 to 2007.* The World Bank Development Research Group Poverty and Inequality Team & Europe and Central Asia Region, Human Development Economics Unit, Policy Research Working Paper 5356 July.

Shultz, B.J. (2008) Inside the Gilded Cage: The Lives of Latino Immigrant Males in Rural Kentucky. *Southeastern Geographer* 48(2):201–218.

Waldinger, R. and M. Lichter (2003) *How the Other Half Works: Immigration and the Social Organization of Labor.* Berkeley, CA: University of California Press.

Waldinger, R. and R.R. Luthra (2010) Into the Mainstream? Labor Market Outcomes of Mexican-origin Workers. *International Migration Review* 44(4):830–868.

Wright, R. and M. Ellis (2000) The Ethnic and Gender Division of Labour Compared among Immigrants to Los Angeles. *International Journal of Urban and Regional Research* 24(3):583–600.

World Bank (2012) World Bank Statistics, 2008–2012. data.worldbank.org/topic/gender (Accessed October 30, 2013)

Zuberi, D. and M. Ptashnick (2012) In Search of a Better Life: The Experiences of Working Poor Immigrants in Vancouver, Canada. *International Migration* 50(1):60–93.

Chapter 7

Experiences of Highly Educated Immigrants

Maria Adamuti-Trache

Introduction

The past two decades have been characterized by extensive movement of skilled workers to migrant-receiving countries such as Canada and the United States. Many of these individuals are **highly educated immigrants** who arrive in North America with university degrees obtained elsewhere. Nevertheless, research, media, and anecdotal evidence suggest that these **immigrants** experience significant barriers to social and economic **integration**. First, this chapter provides an overview of the global context of labour migration and the immigration policies that favour the recruitment of highly skilled workers, and briefly contrasts Canadian and US immigration policies by presenting recent trends in immigration. Second, since the conditions under which highly educated immigrants settle in the new country matter, the chapter will then focus on Canada's immigrants by introducing research and data that describe whether and how these immigrants advance their careers in their newly adopted country. The chapter provides statistics on immigrant employment and earnings as a basis for discussion of **underemployment**, **occupational mismatch**, and devaluation of pre-migration **human capital** in Canada. The chapter concludes with evidence that higher-education policies that are favourable to nontraditional and adult students are likely to create a viable path toward economic and social integration for highly educated immigrants.

Globalization and Immigration

Many argue that the intense increase in worldwide migration at the turn of the millennium is the result of globalization processes that extend economic, social, political, and cultural practices across frontiers, regions, and continents. As described by Suárez-Orozco (2001), global markets are evading national borders and the production of goods and services have become completely internationalized. New information and communication technologies allow people to connect rapidly around the world, freeing them from "the tyranny of space and time" (348). Finally, globalization generates new patterns of large-scale immigration that is transforming both receiving and sending countries. Because of intense worldwide migration, some 214 million people currently live outside their country of birth; the International Organization for Migration (2010) estimates that the figure could increase to 405 million by 2050.

The website of the International Organization for Migration displays amazing patterns of migration between countries, showing millions of immigrants being pulled from developing regions into wealthier parts of the world.[1] Canada and the United States are among the top five immigrant-receiving countries. The inflow of permanent migrants in 2006, for example, was about 1.3 million in the United States and 250,000 in Canada, representing about 0.4% and 0.8% of their populations (Kelley 2009). Why do people migrate? Kelley's (2009) study provides a simple explanation of migration using the words of an Uzbek migrant to Russia: "If things were better there, I wouldn't be here" (36). People have multiple reasons to immigrate, but most common is their response to economic necessity and the prospects of finding decent jobs and building a better life in a new country.

Nevertheless, the immigrant population is quite heterogeneous with respect to educational background. Statistics show that immigrants to Canada and the United States are in general more educated than the native-born population. According to the 2010 US census, the percentage of adults 25 years and older with a bachelor's degree or higher was 30.1% for the native-born population as compared to 35.1% for naturalized US citizens (i.e. foreign-born individuals who acquired citizenship). For the same age group, the percentage of population with less than a high school diploma was 9.6% for the native-born population as compared to 18.9% for naturalized US citizens.[2] Canadian data from the 2011 National Household Survey show similar patterns. About 20.3% of the Canadian-born population 25 years and older had a bachelor's degree or higher, as compared to 31.1% of the foreign-born population. For the same age group, the percentage of population with less than a high school diploma was 17.4% for the Canadian-born and 17.1% for immigrants.[3] These statistics show that the **immigrant** population is polarized in terms of levels of education, but there is a clear tendency for both countries to receive more highly educated than poorly educated immigrants.

Brain Gain and Immigration Policy

Several perspectives can provide an appreciation of the current trends of large flows of highly educated immigrants to North America. First, the **brain drain** and **brain gain** perspective is useful to understanding the circulation of human capital among countries. The brain drain from the poorer to the richer countries is caused by higher demand for skills and knowledge in more technologically advanced economies. Developed countries are interested in attracting the most talented workers in the world in order to stimulate creativity in workplaces by encouraging competition and to compensate for insufficient domestic human capital to support economic growth. Meanwhile, highly educated immigrants possess human capital and are interested in using it in the global labour market in order to improve their occupational chances and obtain better returns on prior investments in education. Docquier and Marfouk (2006) present data on international migration among OECD countries, looking for winners and losers in the race for brain gain. Certainly, all countries lose and gain skilled workers due to global migration. The net brain gain (i.e. the difference between the numbers of highly educated people who arrive and those who leave the country), as a percentage of all working-age residents (who are actively contributing to the labour market), provides an indication of successful recruitment and retention of skilled workers. The authors found that in the year 2000 Australia and Canada were the top winners, with net brain gain ratios of over 10%, meaning that, due to international mobility, these countries gained more than 1 skilled worker for every 10 workers in the native population. The net brain gain ratio was around 5% for the United States, followed by Switzerland and New Zealand. By contrast, countries like Ireland, Greece, Mexico, and Portugal experienced a net brain loss.

A second perspective in interpreting the current immigration trends in the receiving countries is to examine their immigration policies. The brain gain is not a random phenomenon. Rather, it is the result of selective federal government immigration policies targeting skilled applicants. The notion of "Canadian exceptionalism" (Bloemraad 2012) is partly associated with Canada's immigration **points system**, which admits people with skills that are thought to contribute to the economy. Economic immigrants, who represent more than half of the new permanent residents arriving to Canada, are selected based on their potential to join the labour force by assessing their level of education, official language skills, work experience, and adaptability traits.[4] In addition, the number of undocumented immigrants seems to be relatively low (i.e. illegal immigrants do not come in large waves to Canada), which preserves the selectivity of the immigration process. However, Bloemraad contends that Canada's unique immigration experience is only partially the result of economic selection and geography; it is also shaped by principles of diversity, **multiculturalism**, and tolerance that are crucial to Canadian identity. According to Bloemraad, a key aspect of the Canadian model is the view that immigration contributes to nation-building, a view that is embraced by two-thirds of Canadians. "The Canadian immigration-as-nation-building paradigm is rooted in a particular set of policies and institutions: it is about permanent settlement and integration into a diverse citizenry, where legal systems, public policy, and political structures encourage engagement and membership" (Bloemraad 2012:7).

On the contrary, the composition of the immigrant population of the United States is rather different, with over 11 million unauthorized immigrants estimated in 2011, representing more than a quarter of the total US immigrant population. While US immigration policy is quite selective in terms of granting legal permanent residence, asylum, or even authorized temporary statuses for long-term residence and work, achieving comprehensive immigration reform is tougher in the United States and the American public remains divided over this issue. Another major concern in the United States is the apparent shortage of highly skilled workers in science and engineering, which has prompted possible changes in the immigration policy.

The top immigrant-receiving countries have quite similar opportunities to recruit highly educated immigrants from the global market. However, specific immigration policies may result in uneven conditions for the social and economic integration of newcomers in Canada and the United States. For instance, the majority of highly educated people entering the United States have specific temporary work visas offered by employers. They could apply for lawful permanent residence ("green cards") if they wanted to stay in the United States and could maintain certain types of employment. Meanwhile, highly educated immigrants to Canada admitted under the Federal Skilled Workers program rarely have any prior employment arrangements. As permanent residents ("landed immigrants"), they have the same rights as Canadian citizens, can take any available job, can be unemployed looking for a job, or can be outside the labour force. They do not have to leave Canada if they do not find continuous employment. However, many go through quite traumatic experiences during the job search process when they start to realize that Canadian employers systemically fail to appropriately recognize their pre-migration human capital.[5]

Case Example 1: Diverging Policy Directions in Canada and the US

This is an excerpt from an article published by the American Association for the Advancement of Science (Benderly 2013). The article compares current immigration policies in Canada and the United States and discusses policy changes driven by the barriers facing highly educated immigrants in Canada. Anticipated changes in Canada's decades-old points system may follow the model of the skilled-worker systems in Australia and New Zealand that match applicants' skills against skilled occupations where there is a genuine shortage of workers. While Canada may slightly change direction regarding high-skilled immigration, the apparent workforce shortages in science, technology, engineering, and mathematics (STEM) occupations in the United States have generated calls for changes to high-skill STEM immigration policies. American experts argue that opening the gates to immigration without regard for domestic demand will damage the career prospects of STEM workers in the United States, as has already happened to many highly educated immigrants to Canada.

> During the years of discussion and debate leading to the current drive to reform the U.S. immigration system, the experience of Canada has been held up as a model, especially in regard to its policies concerning high-skilled immigrants. For nearly 5 decades, Canada has admitted immigrants based on a points system—the world's first—that gives the advantage to people with such characteristics as **higher education** and professional skills. With enough points, individuals can legally move to the country whether [or not] they have a promise of work.

> The United States, on the other hand, has generally tied skilled immigration to specific promises of employment. Many U.S. politicians have argued for introducing something like the Canadian system in the United States in order to meet a mythical shortage of technical skills. The "Gang of Eight" immigration bill now under consideration in the Senate moves in the direction of eliminating employment requirements for many immigrants who hold graduate degrees in STEM (science, technology, engineering, and mathematics) fields.

> Canada, however, is now moving in the opposite direction, toward high-skilled immigration based on employment, according to the news magazine *Maclean's*.

Source: Benderly 2013.

Characteristics of Immigrants to Canada

Which characteristics of immigrants to Canada may either favour or hinder their labour market integration? First, most internationally educated immigrants to Canada are university-educated, which should be an advantage in an innovative and knowledge-based economy. The 2006 census indicates the presence of 1.4 million internationally educated immigrants in the core working-age group (individuals aged 25 to 64 with post-secondary education), of which 70% have university degrees (Plante 2010). The share of university-educated immigrants is about 78% and 82% among recent (1996–2001 arrivals) and very recent (2001–2006 arrivals) immigrants, respectively.[6]

A second characteristic of the new waves of immigrants is their diverse ethnolinguistic background, which could prove beneficial to employers wanting to be competitive in the global market. Between 1996 and 2006, the numbers of educated immigrants from China, South Korea, the former Soviet Union, Eastern Europe, Iran, and Pakistan more than doubled compared to the number of immigrants coming from the same parts of the world before 1995 (Plante 2010). Conversely, over this period there is a clear decline in the numbers of educated immigrants from the United Kingdom, the United States, Hong Kong, and some Central and Western European countries. This dramatic shift in the sources of immigration to Canada plays a major role in changing the dynamics of immigrants' economic outcomes. Canadian employers have shown reservations about hiring immigrants educated in nontraditional source countries, which results in significant economic hardship for this newer group of immigrants who experience a gradual devaluation of their human capital.

Third, not all immigrants receive their university education in their countries of birth, which means that many experience global mobility prior to immigrating to Canada. For instance, Plante (2010) suggests that significant numbers of internationally educated immigrants come to Canada after receiving their highest degrees in the United States, the United Kingdom, or France. Of the 103,700 Canadian immigrants educated in the US and the 119,400 educated in the UK, only 48,100 and 90,300, respectively, were born in these countries. Similar trends are noticeable for France: data indicate that of the 36,200 Canadian immigrants who were educated in France, only 25,800 were born there. Receiving education in an anglophone or francophone country prior to immigrating to Canada, where English and French are the two official languages, should be an asset for newcomers. Furthermore, only 18% and 3% of the internationally educated immigrants reported English and French, respectively, as their mother tongue. The large majority reported a different language learned in childhood, but very few (about 4% among the very recent immigrants and 1%

among established immigrants) reported not being able to conduct a conversation in either official language. This is not surprising because foreign-language instruction is a component of a well-rounded education in many countries, particularly for a highly educated person. However, good conversational skills are not sufficient to find meaningful employment, particularly in knowledge occupations, and even the highly educated immigrants need to enhance their language proficiency and often pursue specialized language training.

Finally, many highly educated immigrants have expertise in occupations that are crucial in a technologically advanced society. When comparing the programs of study reported in 2006 by internationally educated immigrants and Canadian-born individuals aged 25 to 64, Plante (2010) noticed similarities and differences. The most common program of study for both immigrants and nonmigrants is business and related fields (20%). Proportions ranging between 10% and 13% differentiate only slightly the immigrants and the Canadian-born in health related fields. However, engineering programs were significantly less popular among Canadian-born (3%) and Canadian-educated immigrants (7%), as compared to internationally educated immigrants (16%). In particular, about 21% of immigrants who arrived between 1996 and 2006 reported engineering as their program of study. Some discrepancy is also noted in fields related to computer and information sciences, which are the choice of about 3% of Canadian-born workers as compared to 7% of Canadian-educated immigrants and 6% of internationally educated immigrants. The distribution of immigrants across programs of study is not surprising considering the shortage of scientists and engineers in Canada and the attempt by the federal government to recruit skilled immigrants with qualifications and experience in information technology, science, engineering, and healthcare. The problem is that strict licensing requirements and a lack of familiarity with the Canadian business context and culture undermine foreign-trained immigrants' access to these professions, compared to their Canadian-born and Canadian-trained counterparts (Boyd and Schellenberg 2007; Girard and Bauder 2007).

Labour Market Outcomes

Highly educated immigrants who arrived in Canada within the past two decades have an apparent human capital advantage that should make them competitive and thus produce positive **labour market outcomes**. Most of those who held university degrees at arrival have expertise in fields in which there is a shortage of qualified workers such as science, engineering, and healthcare. Even if the number of newcomers working in professional occupations in natural and applied sciences has decreased significantly between 2003 and 2012 (from 26,000 to 10,000), these individuals still represent about one-third of immigrants with professional occupations (Citizenship and Immigration Canada 2012). Meanwhile, there has been an increase in the number of immigrant professionals in healthcare (from 2,100 to 8,100), and social sciences and education occupations (from 4,000 to 8,600), which may reflect slight changes in immigration policies targeting specific immigrant skills. The majority of recent highly educated immigrants are coming from nontraditional source regions such as Eastern Europe, Asia, and Africa, and most of them obtained university degrees in their countries of origin. Canadian employers are less familiar with the quality of these qualifications, generally place little value on foreign work experience, and are more interested in hiring workers who have close knowledge of Canadian labour market contexts. This results in relatively poor economic outcomes and a gradual devaluation of immigrant human capital. Former Canadian immigration minister Jason Kenney declared in an interview that the declining economic welfare of immigrants is a "huge problem" and "it's impossible to calculate the opportunity cost of productivity, the cost to our economy, represented by the unemployment and underemployment of immigrants" (McMahon 2012).

This section provides statistics on immigrant employment and earnings as a basis for discussion of underemployment, occupational mismatch, and devaluation of pre-migration human capital. Employment status is a basic indicator of workforce integration. There is a tremendous amount of data and research showing that immigrants who arrived in the last two decades experienced a slow integration in the labour force. Picot and Sweetman (2011) used recent data (2006–2010) from Statistics Canada's Labour Force Survey to obtain employment rates for university-educated immigrants by their period of landing. These rates increase from 68.5% among very recent immigrants (less than 5 years since arrival) to 79.2% among recent immigrants (6 to 10 years since arrival), and continue to slowly increase to 84.8% among long-term immigrants (16 to 20 years since arrival) without reaching the employment rate of 85.5% among Canadian-born workers. The first five years in Canada seem to be the most difficult in securing employment. Highly educated immigrant women have significantly lower employment rates compared to both immigrant males and Canadian-born women. Employment deprivation during the first five years after arrival, with less than 60% of highly educated immigrant women being employed, is an important sign of deskilling, a process that may gradually lead to human capital devaluation.

Assuming that highly educated immigrants are able to find employment, how much do they earn and how large are the earnings gaps between immigrants and Canadian-born workers? Picot and Sweetman (2011) note, "More recent entering cohorts of immigrants to Canada are having greater relative unemployment difficulties than their earlier entering counterparts, despite their higher educational levels and the fact that more of them are in the skilled economic class. The decline is much less evident when measured by employment rates, but ... it is particularly evident in the earnings of employed immigrants. Immigrants to Canada are finding employment, but their jobs are paying less than previously" (14). The study shows the decline in the earnings of recent cohorts of immigrants, measured by the increasing earnings gap between full-time, full-year immigrant and Canadian-born workers. Data also show that for immigrants who arrived after 1990, the major improvement in earnings appears during the first five years in Canada. Another Canadian study found that the average weekly wage ratios are as low as 0.58 for men and 0.64 for women when comparing highly educated immigrants who arrived between 2001 and 2005 and their Canadian-born counterparts (Bonikovska, Hou, and Picot 2011). An earlier immigrant cohort that arrived between 1996 and 2000 experienced a slightly higher earnings ratio of 0.70 for both men and women during their first five years in Canada. Interestingly, over the past 40 years, the ratios of wages earned by highly educated immigrants to the United States and their native-born counterparts never fell below 0.80 regardless of cohort, time since arrival, and gender.

Poor earnings among highly educated immigrants are attributed to under-employment, a common situation among high-skilled immigrant workers who are assigned to low-paying jobs for which they are overqualified and where their skills are underutilized (Gilmore 2009). In 2008, over 60% of highly educated immigrant workers, compared with 41% of their Canadian-born counterparts, worked in jobs that did not require their levels of education. Underemployment affected two-thirds of very recent immigrants who landed within the previous five years. From the immigrant perspective, being underemployed is associated with earnings that are inconsistent with pre-migration qualifications, a loss of occupational status, and a gradual devaluation of their human capital.

Many highly educated immigrants end up working in occupations with little connection to the field of study of their university degree or their previous oc-cupation and area of expertise. This occupational mismatch leads to a gradual disengagement from their previous occupation and professional community, isolating the highly educated immigrants and aggravating the deskilling process. This is particularly true of knowledge occupations with high rates of scientific discovery and in which companies have to respond quickly to innovation. In such cases, workers need to constantly upgrade their knowledge and skills, which makes career interruptions and changes quite problematic. If immigrants cannot practise in their occupations when entering the host-country labour market, they become less competitive over time. Zietsma (2010) examined the occupational attainment of highly educated immigrants trained to work in regulated occupations such as engineering, medicine, nursing, teaching, and law. In order to practise these occupations in Canada, immigrants need to have their foreign credentials recognized and go through an accreditation process required by professional associations prior to finding a job within that regulated occupation. Among those employed in 2006, 62% of the Canadian-born and only 24% of foreign-educated immigrants were working in the regulated profession for which they trained.

Occupational mismatch is a serious concern among highly educated immigrants to Canada, most of whom are economic immigrants and thus specifically targeted to address shortages in particular occupations. The selection of immigrants through a points system is based on the assumption that the criteria employed in the process are meaningful and will correctly predict the employability of new immigrants in the Canadian labour market. For instance, in 2006, 52% of highly educated immigrants who studied outside Canada were trained to be engineers. Of this particular group, only 19% matched their training and occupation after arrival (Zietsma 2010). Boyd and Schellenberg (2007) found that, in 2001, only 26% of foreign-trained engineers, compared with 41% of Canadian-born engineers, held jobs in engineering occupations, while more than half of them worked in technical occupations or jobs unrelated to engineering. If Canada is indeed experiencing a shortage of engineers, then the recruitment of immigrant engineers who subsequently become taxi drivers after arrival cannot resolve the workforce shortages in the engineering field.

Canadian Higher Education

Researchers and policymakers observed possible hindrances to the smooth transition of highly educated immigrants into the Canadian workforce. Knowledge of the receiving country's language is one of the most important determinants of labour market adjustment among new immigrants (e.g. Chiswick 2008). This creates a disadvantage for the new waves of immigrants to Canada who mostly originate from non-English or non-French-speaking countries and may have practised their profession in another language. In addition, since recent immigrants come from developing countries, there is a perception among employers that both pre-migration qualifications and pre-migration work experience are questionable. As a result, employers treat immigrants like new labour market entrants (Picot and Sweetman 2011) who have additional disadvantages: they may not speak the language well and/ or may lack knowledge of the North American culture. Recent immigrants know that the hardest test after arrival is to find a first meaningful job, because the lack of Canadian work experience is a persistent excuse for not being hired. Accepting any job offer or even volunteering is usually the advice given to newcomers to help them

Case Example 2: Who Drives Taxis?

A government report recently confirmed the urban myth that overqualified immigrants are indeed taxi drivers. Using 2006 census data, the report "Who Drives a Taxi in Canada?" shows the composition of taxi drivers by highest level of education. Of the 255 cab drivers who earned a PhD or have a medical degree, 200 are immigrants (Xu 2012). Overall about 5% of Canadian-born taxi drivers, as compared to 20% of all immigrant taxi drivers, have university degrees. The graph below shows that about 40% of very recent immigrants (who landed between 2001 and 2006), 31% of recent immigrants (who landed between 1996 and 2001), and 14% of established immigrants (who arrived before 1996) are highly educated. The report also shows that one of every three taxi drivers is born in India or Pakistan and most post-secondary educated immigrant taxi drivers have backgrounds in business, engineering, or architecture.

Figure 7.1
Taxi Drivers by Highest Level of Education

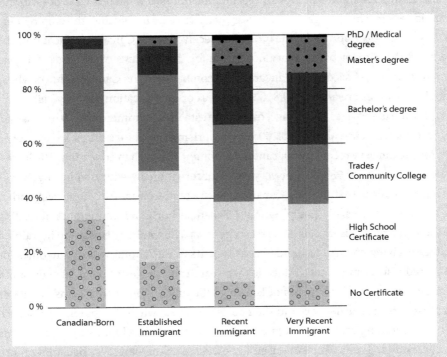

Source: Statistics Canada, Census of Population 2006.

enter the labour force, build a social network, and improve language skills. Although valuable, this advice is particularly faulty in the case of highly educated immigrants for whom "work" has the broader meaning of building a long-term career in the occupation for which they are passionate. These individuals need a more strategic action plan because their time is precious and making the right choice matters in reaching professionals goals.

What other options are available to highly educated immigrants who want to have a successful and meaningful career? A growing body of research shows that Canadian-educated immigrants are better integrated into the labour market compared to those who rely only on their foreign education. Using 2006 census data, Plante (2010) compares employment and earnings of Canadian-born and immigrants aged 25 to 64 who completed post-secondary education.[6] For instance, Canadian-educated individuals who were not attending school in 2006 had comparable employment rates irrespective of immigrant status. Employment rates were 83% for Canadian-born and established immigrants, 84% for recent immigrants, and 80% for very recent immigrants. However, discrepancies exist among internationally educated workers, with employment rates of 83% for Canadian-born (who studied abroad), 77% for established immigrants, 79% for recent immigrants, and 71% for very recent immigrants. It is interesting to observe that among very recent immigrants (with less than five years in Canada), the employment rate is drastically improved if the individual received some Canadian education (71% versus 80%). Similar patterns are noticeable for the earnings of full-time, full-year workers with post-secondary education. As compared to the Canadian-born, whose median earnings are about $49,800 (regardless of their location of study), all immigrant cohorts earn less on average, except the established immigrants with Canadian education, who earn about $50,700. Not surprisingly, earnings ratios are improved for recent and very recent immigrants who obtained Canadian education. The lowest median earnings of $33,700 for very recent internationally educated immigrants is about two-thirds that of their Canadian-born counterparts. Although many other factors affect the earnings gap between Canadian-born and immigrants, including real and perceived discrimination, research shows that obtaining education or training in the receiving country has undeniable benefits to the labour market outcomes for highly educated immigrants. Educational research also suggests that higher education experience has "wider benefits of learning" (Schuller, Bynner, and Feinstein 2004) because it helps learners expand their social network, which is a potential resource for job-searching and creates opportunities for career development. Whether this is due to immigrants acquiring useful knowledge or the employer becoming more confident in hiring an immigrant who is educated in Canada, the reality is that highly educated immigrants gain some leverage to negotiate their credentials after completing education and training in the host country.

Is the investment in higher education an option for highly educated immigrants? Canada has a complex higher education system that falls under the responsibility of the provinces and territories. Students are trained in various academic and vocational specializations in public and private degree-granting institutions that vary from province to province, and include universities, university colleges, community colleges, institutes of technology, and specialized institutes. Compared to the United States, Canada has a more affordable higher education system. The demographic of Canadian higher education institutions is changing through increased enrollment of **nontraditional students** who invest in further education and training. Nontraditional students are particularly remarkable because a vast majority consists of adult workers engaged in lifelong learning. Universities and colleges in Canada and the United States have encouraged their presence on campuses by adjusting instruction to accommodate their needs (e.g. part-time programs, evening classes, online courses, student services). This environment should be welcoming to adult immigrants, particularly the highly educated, if they wanted to pursue further education. However, if further education is indeed a viable path toward the economic and social integration of highly educated immigrants, specific higher education policies should target this group and customized programs should address their needs. For instance, Boyd and Schellenberg (2007) observed that foreign-trained engineers appear to be slightly more educated than Canadian-born engineers. Targeted programs developed by higher education institutions should build on this foundation and help foreign-trained engineers to acquire the knowledge and skills that are specific to new technologies or different managerial contexts.

A final question is whether highly educated immigrants are seeking further education after arrival and what choices they make regarding this. Research based on data from the Longitudinal Survey of Immigrants to Canada (LSIC) shows that almost half of very recent highly educated immigrants in the sample pursued post-secondary education within four years of arrival.

Highly educated immigrants to Canada correctly perceive that moving to a new country may involve major changes in their professional lives and most are ready to engage in further education. This adjustment strategy is not surprising for individuals who possess human capital and feel drawn toward growing their asset. Recent changes in immigration policies emphasize once more that Canada places a priority on recruiting and developing human capital. First, the federal government decided in 2008 to ease immigration rules for international students by creating a Canadian Experience Class immigration stream that would make work experience and/or education in Canada the key criterion for vetting applicants. The new immigrant class follows the human capital model of the Canadian immigration policy by recruiting skilled immigrants in addition to those admitted under the Federal Skilled Worker

Case Example 3: Longitudinal Survey of Immigrants to Canada

The Longitudinal Survey of Immigrants to Canada (LSIC) was conducted by Statistics Canada and Citizenship and Immigration Canada under the Policy Research Initiative, and followed a representative sample of new immigrants and refugees who landed from abroad between October 2000 and September 2001 over the four years after their arrival. Researchers and policymakers have employed LSIC data to better understand various aspects of the lives of new immigrants and their families. This data set is appropriate to study the labour market experiences of highly educated immigrants and their involvement with Canadian post-secondary education. For instance, a sample of 3,000 highly educated immigrants aged 25 to 49 showed that 46% pursued formal post-secondary education within 4 years of arrival. Seventeen percent of immigrants pursued university education (in the same or a different field of study as their pre-migration highest degree) while 29% of immigrants attended community colleges and other non-university institutions. Especially those attending non-university institutions experienced problems in having their pre-migration work experience accepted by employers. The most likely to attend non-university institutions were immigrant engineers. The most likely to pursue university education in Canada were immigrants who reported good language skills.

Source: Adamuti-Trache (2011).

program. Second, the expanded Provincial Nominee Program empowers employers to recruit skilled professionals such as engineers, accountants, and professors coming from the United States and Mexico to overcome specific regional labour force needs. As pointed out by Picot and Sweetman (2011), "The new approach gives employers (by extending job offers and arranging temporary work permits) and post-secondary institutions (by screening and admitting students) a greater role in the selection process" (4). Nevertheless, the message is clear: Canadian immigration policy aims to increase the stock of human capital, but there is a preference for skills acquired and/or tested within the Canadian or North American context. Since federal skilled workers are still a dominant group among the current and future highly educated immigrants to Canada, a "get Canadian education" strategy could be beneficial in the long term.

Conclusion

This chapter provides evidence that the apparent mismatch between the qualifications and skills of highly educated immigrants and their labour market performance is a concern that highlights a tension between the intent and outcomes of Canadian immigration policy. Similar problems are anticipated in the United States in response to the current effort by the federal government to facilitate the retention of talented people in science, technology, engineering, and mathematics (STEM) occupations. If the recruitment of highly skilled STEM immigrants and the retention of foreign students who graduate in STEM fields from American universities do not receive employers' support, highly skilled immigrants will not have fair access to jobs that fully utilize their qualifications and skills. In both countries, highly educated immigrants clearly rely on the willingness of North American employers to appreciate credentials and work experience partially acquired abroad. As suggested by Canadian data, when employers fail to recognize the value of foreign human capital, many highly educated immigrants engage in higher education to obtain domestic human capital (i.e. specific skills, new credentials) that will potentially improve their chances of competing in the labour market. Canadian data show that about half of the highly educated immigrants who arrived in the past decade pursued higher education after arrival.

Nevertheless, immigrants' decision to invest in further education is often a personal strategy that receives little or no formal institutional support, and highly educated immigrants take the risk of obtaining minimal returns on education. An important aspect of making the pursuit of higher education in the new country a successful strategy is to encourage employers and post-secondary institutions to think about the investment in education made by highly educated immigrants more as a societal—rather than an individual—matter. Obtaining additional qualifications and continuing to work in the same underpaid job that does not utilize one's knowledge, skills, and abilities is abusive not just to the individual but to the whole notion of human capital investment. Referring to Canada, Reitz (2005) comments that "the sustainability of the immigration program in the evolving global labour market is in question" and suggests there is a need to develop "adequate institutional means to facilitate the effective utilization of immigrant skills" (13). Government, businesses, and higher education institutions should partner in finding better ways to ensure growth of both domestic and foreign human capital. If obtaining some kind of education and training in the new country is imperative for highly educated immigrants to enter the workforce and properly utilize their skills, this strategy should be better institutionalized by immigrant-receiving countries to ensure the **"brain waste"** is stopped.

Notes

1. The International Organization for Migration hosts an interactive app tracking migrants around the world. The dynamic graphics are based on World Bank data from 2010. www.iom.int/cms/en/sites/iom/home/about-migration/world-migration.html

2. The United States Census Bureau provides data from the 2010 Current Population Survey that can be used to examine the educational attainment of the US population by citizenship status. Table 1.5: www.census.gov/population/foreign/data/cps2010.html

3. Statistics Canada's website provides access to data from the 2011 National Household Survey used to create a series of tables with information on highest certificate, diploma, or degree by immigrant status and other characteristics. Topic: Education and Labour, Catalogue Number: 99-012-X2011042: www12.statcan.gc.ca/nhs-enm/2011/dp-pd/dt-td/index-eng.cfm

4. Citizenship and Immigration Canada's website contains information on selection criteria for the Federal Skilled Workers category and the immigration points system: www.cic.gc.ca/english/immigrate/skilled/apply-factors.asp

5. A recent *Maclean's* article (www2.macleans.ca/2013/04/24/land-of-misfortune) titled "Why the World's Best and Brightest Struggle to Find Jobs in Canada? Why Do Skilled Immigrants Often Fare Worse Here than in the U.S. and U.K.?" examines the pros and cons of immigration outcomes for highly educated immigrants to Canada and the United States.

6. Although this report does not examine separately the highly educated immigrants, one can extrapolate findings to this group, which is especially dominant among recent and very recent immigrants.

Questions for Critical Thought

1. Discuss the concepts of brain gain, brain drain, and reverse brain drain from various perspectives such as economic, political, social, and cultural viewpoints. Reflect on the fairness of these processes and identify positive and negative aspects associated with each of them.

2. Although Canadian immigration policy favours the recruitment of highly educated individuals, these immigrants experience serious employment barriers after arrival. Reflect on possible changes in the immigration policy and/or labour market policies that may improve this situation.

3. This chapter provides evidence that many highly educated immigrants pursue post-secondary education after arrival to Canada. Reflect on positive and negative aspects of this strategy from the perspective of the individual and the host society. Do you think this action would increase or decrease the return on investment in education for highly educated immigrants?

Key Readings

Chiswick, B.R. (2005) *High Skilled Immigration in the International Arena.* IZA Discussion Papers, No. 1782. hdl.handle.net/10419/33657 (Accessed August 23, 2013)

Organisation for Economic Co-Operation and Development (2002) *International Mobility of the Highly Skilled.* Policy Brief. Paris, France: OECD.

Triadafilopoulos, T. (ed.) (2013) *Wanted and Welcome? Policies for Highly Skilled Immigrants in Comparative Perspective.* New York: Springer.

Media Links

America's Brain Drain:

www.cbsnews.com/videos/americas-brain-drain

This video, by CBS News on January 30, 2011, presents issues related to America's brain drain with focus on reverse brain drain.

Canadian Immigration: Finding Work:

www.youtube.com/watch?v=DxE0l1MCuUk

Canadian immigrants who applied for immigration as skilled workers discuss their challenges in finding work in this clip of TVO's *The Agenda with Steve Paikin*, January 24, 2011.

Ontario Bridge Training:

www.ontarioimmigration.ca/en/working/OI_BRIDGE.html

Ontario bridge training programs help internationally trained individuals (with post-secondary education) integrate quickly into the labour market.

IMPRINT:

www.imprintproject.org/webinars-trainings/webinars/#alternativecareers

IMPRINT is a coalition of organizations active in the United States in the emerging field of immigrant professional integration. On their website, you can find a series of webinars that took place between November 2012 and March 2014 that discuss this topic.

References

Adamuti-Trache, M. (2011) First 4 Years in Canada: Post-Secondary Education Pathways of Highly Educated Immigrants. *Journal of International Migration and Integration* 12(1):61–82.

Benderly, B.L. (2013) Canada to Scrap Points System for High-Skilled Immigration. *Career Magazine*. Washington, DC: American Association for the Advancement of Science. sciencecareers.sciencemag.org/career_magazine/previous_issues/articles/2013_04_26/caredit.a1300086 (Accessed August 23, 2013)

Bloemraad, I. (2012) *Understanding "Canadian Exceptionalism" in Immigration and Pluralism Policy*. Washington, DC: Migration Policy Institute.

Bonikovska, A., F. Hou, and G. Picot (2011) Do Highly Educated Immigrants Perform Differently in the Canadian and U.S. Labour Markets? Catalogue no. 11F0019M-No. 329. Ottawa: Statistics Canada.

Boyd, M. and G. Schellenberg (2007) Re-accreditation and the Occupations of Immigrant Doctors and Engineers. *Canadian Social Trends* (Fall):2–10.

Chiswick, B.R. (2008) The Economics of Language. Discussion Paper no. 3568. Bonn, Germany: IZA. http://ftp.iza.org/dp3568.pdf (Accessed August 23, 2013)

Citizenship and Immigration Canada (2012) Facts and Figures 2012. Ottawa: CIC. www.cic.gc.ca/english/resources/statistics/menu-fact.asp (Accessed August 23, 2013)

Docquier, F. and A. Marfouk (2006) International Migration by Education Attainment, 1990–2000. In C. Özden and M. Schiff (eds.) *International Migration, Remittances & the Brain Drain*, pp. 151–199. Washington, DC: The World Bank.

Gilmore, J. (2009) *The 2008 Canadian Immigrant Labour Market: Analysis of Quality of Employment*. Catalogue no. 71–606-X. Ottawa: Statistics Canada.

Girard, E. and H. Bauder (2007) Assimilation and Exclusion of Foreign Trained Engineers in Canada: Inside a Canadian Professional Regulatory Organization. *Antipode* 39(1):35–53.

International Organization for Migration (2010) *World Migration Report 2010. The Future of Migration: Building Capacities for Change*. Geneva, Switzerland: IOM. publications. iom.int/bookstore/free/WMR_2010_ENGLISH.pdf (Accessed August 23, 2013)

Kelley, B. (2009) *International Migration. The Human Face of Globalisation*. Paris: OECD.

McMahon, T. (2012) Why the World's Best and Brightest Struggle to Find Jobs in Canada? Why Do Skilled Immigrants Often Fare Worse Here than in the U.S. and U.K.? *Maclean's*, 24 April. www2.macleans.ca/2013/04/24/land-of-misfortune (Accessed August 23, 2013)

Picot, G. and A. Sweetman (2011) *Canadian Immigration Policy and Immigrant Economic Outcomes: Why the Differences in Outcomes between Sweden and Canada?* Policy Paper no. 25. Bonn, Germany: IZA. http://ftp.iza.org/pp25.pdf (Accessed August 23, 2013)

Plante, J. (2010) *Characteristics and Labour Market Outcomes of Internationally-educated Immigrants*. Catalogue no. 81-595-M—No. 084. Ottawa: Statistics Canada.

Reitz, J.G. (2005) Tapping Immigrants' Skills: New Directions for Canadian Immigration Policy in the Knowledge Economy. *IRPP Choices* 11(1):1–18.

Schuller, T., J. Bynner, and L. Feinstein (2004) *Capitals and Capabilities*. London: Centre for Research on the Wider Benefits of Learning.

Suárez-Orozco, M.M. (2001) Globalization, Immigration and Education: The Research Agenda. *Harvard Educational Review* 71(3):345–365.

Xu, L. (2012) *Who Drives a Taxi in Canada?* Ottawa: Citizenship and Immigration Canada.

Zietsma, D. (2010) Immigrants Working in Regulated Occupations. *Perspectives* February, 13–28. Catalogue no. 75-001-X. Ottawa: Statistics Canada.

Chapter 8

Immigration Status and the Legalization of Inequality

Nandita Sharma

Introduction

State **immigration policy** often does more than simply regulate the movement of people into the country. It also profoundly shapes how one experiences life within the country. **Immigration** policy establishes the criteria by which people either will or will not be accepted as migrants to enter the country. However, through the allocation of different **immigration statuses** to people, it also affects the kind of rights and entitlements migrants will or will not have access to. The state category that persons migrating to the country are placed in determines the level of wages employers will pay, the kinds of working conditions, protections, and social services migrants will have a right to (or not), and even whether they will be free to move within the country or free to change employers or, even more basically, be free to not work if they choose. Along with the legal distinction made between citizens and noncitizens, whether one is placed in the category "permanent resident," "foreign worker," or "illegal" will affect one's social, political, economic, and legal position. This chapter uses the case of Canada to illustrate how immigration status affects migrants.

The Canadian Context

Undergirding the differential allocation of rights and entitlements in Canada are the ways in which immigration policy informs ideas of national belonging. Whether one is given official state permission to enter or not, whether one is given a status that corresponds with access to rights and entitlements or not is shaped by which **racialized**, gendered, sexualized, and classed bodies are seen to "belong" in Canada or not. Importantly, however, those who are deemed to not belong are not always excluded from the territory of Canada but are instead subordinated within Canadian society. Immigration policy, then, both reflects and organizes the differential allocation of power in the country and in the world.

There weren't always regulations and restrictions on people moving to Canada or the US (or anywhere else on the planet). In Canada, the first immigration regulations and restrictions were enacted in the late nineteenth and early twentieth centuries. The first was the infamous 1885 Chinese Immigration Act that restricted the entry of most people from China by imposing a **head tax** on their admittance. This was followed in short order with the 1908 Continuous Journey regulation, which attempted to prevent the free mobility of fellow imperial subjects from British India; the 1908 "gentlemen's agreement" between Canada and Imperial Japan, which restricted immigration from Japan to only 400 persons per year (reduced to 150 by 1928); the exclusion of black farmers from Oklahoma in 1910; and the 1923 Chinese Immigration Act, which excluded all Chinese persons from coming to Canada.

During this time, however, not all persons' mobility was restricted. Each of these regulations and restrictions was implemented at a time when Canada continued to admit hundreds of thousands of persons, almost all of whom came from Europe. In particular, Section 38 of the Canadian Immigration Act of 1910 gave the Canadian government the power to prohibit the entry "of immigrants belonging to any race deemed unsuited to the climate or requirements of Canada." People from "warm countries," including those in Southern Europe and throughout Asia, Africa, and Latin America, were deemed to be either less suited or simply unsuited for immigration to Canada, which apparently was considered a cold country. At the same time, a category of "preferred" migrants was established consisting of those persons from Britain, Western Europe, and the United States who were positively racialized as white and, even more preferentially, as Anglo-Saxon and Christian.

From the start, then, Canadian immigration policy has been racist. It (falsely) assumed that there were indeed different "**races**" of people, assumed that these races were hierarchically arranged with some superior to others, and assumed that only those deemed to be a member of a "superior race" should have greater freedoms to migrate to Canada. This was compounded by discriminatory citizenship laws, which in Canada denied **naturalization** to negatively racialized migrants until after the Second World War. Without access to citizenship, negatively racialized immigrants were denied access to education and to high-status and better-waged employment. Together, then, immigration and citizenship policies determined which persons within Canada would have greater freedoms, rights, and entitlements.

Racist decisions on whom to admit and whom to reject were also highly gendered, classed, and sexualized. Women were viewed merely as reproducers (of people, of "culture," etc.) and, as such, in service of the project of "nation" building. Not suiting the Canadian nation-building project—a project based on a settler society imagined as white and Christian—non-European women were particularly subject to immigration restrictions in Canada. In contrast, the mobility of women from Europe was encouraged although their freedoms were confined within normative ideas of proper female behaviour. It was expected that women from Europe ought to come accompanied by their husbands or quickly marry men racialized as white upon their arrival. Moreover, immigration officers were granted wide discretionary powers when deciding to admit or deny a person's entry on the basis of whether they deemed a person "moral" or "immoral." Consequently, women and men viewed as "deviant" because of their enactment of supposedly improper gender or sexual roles were refused entry. This was institutionalized in the 1952 Immigration Act when homosexuality was identified as a ground of exclusion.

From the start, then, decisions made by the Canadian state were not about regulating the movement of all persons. Instead, immigration policy helped to construct a racist, sexist, and heterosexist hierarchy in Canada by determining whom it would admit and whom it would not. In the process, normative ideas of what it meant to be a Canadian man or woman were established. Canadianness came to be defined against nonwhite persons and against practices considered by state policy (and individual state officials) to be deviant.

Immigration policy was not only a major element of how the Canadian state constructed highly discriminatory ideas of what constituted Canadianness, but was also very much about making the space occupied by Canada part of a highly competitive global system of capitalist investment, production, and profit. Therefore, the differences organized by regulations and restrictions on immigration were never meant only as a way to prevent the movement of those who had been cast as undesirable. Instead, many persons deemed to be undesirable lived and worked in Canada but in highly subordinated conditions. Theorists Gilles Deleuze and Félix Guattari (1987) have termed the process by which hierarchies within nation-states are constructed **differential inclusion**.

The process of differential inclusion was highly profitable for both the state and capitalists. Restrictions on the freedoms and rights of persons deemed undesirable and/or immoral worked to lessen the claims such persons could make on the state and worked to lessen the wages employers could pay them. Moreover, the ability of persons deemed undesirable to effectively resist their subordination was severely weakened by the support given to such discriminatory policies by those considered (and considering themselves) "Canadian." Paradoxically, and predictably, such support contributed to the competitive advantage of employers hiring "undesirable" persons.

In 1967 racist criteria for admittance to Canada, wherein certain people from Europe were "preferred," was finally eliminated and a **points system** put in its place. The points system was largely meant to address the needs of employers as there was a significant labour market shortage of workers in Canada throughout the post–World War II period caused by the postwar economic boom. At this time, drawing preferred immigrants from traditional European source countries became more difficult because of Europe's own need of labour for postwar reconstruction. Moreover, by the mid-1960s most of the former **colonies** of various European empires had their independence acknowledged. As such, there was strong diplomatic pressure to remove explicitly racist references in immigration (and other areas of) law. Both of these developments led to the Canadian state turning to previously "nonpreferred" immigrants to replace the diminished flow of immigrants from Europe.

What was not eliminated, however, was the process of differential inclusion. Not only were the overtly discriminatory provisions of immigration law kept in place for homosexuals (until 1978) and for same-sex spousal sponsorship applications (until 2002), the discretionary power to exclude "immoral" persons was also kept in place. Moreover, starting in 1973, Canada expanded its **temporary foreign workers** programs through its Non-Immigrant Employment Authorization Program (NIEAP). By classifying certain people migrating to Canada as **nonimmigrants**, the state was able to deny temporary foreign workers the same rights and entitlements available to immigrants (which, legally, only refers to those granted a status of permanent resident). Central to the legal subordination of temporary foreign workers in Canada was the legal denial of freedom to them. Those categorized as temporary foreign workers did not have the right, as free persons do, to choose their employer. Instead, they were legally tied to a single employer, occupation, and, consequently, a single geographic site. Moreover, since their legal residence in Canada hinged on their working for this specified employer, their becoming unemployed became a ground for their deportation. Those classified as temporary foreign workers were, hence, effectively rendered unfree in Canada and made to work in unfree employment relations as a condition of their entry and continued stay in the country.

Under Section 6 of the Charter of Rights and Freedoms (henceforth, the Charter) the Canadian state is not permitted to render Canadian citizens or permanent residents as unfree. Thus, the terms and conditions of Canada's temporary foreign workers programs would be unconstitutional were they applied to such categories of persons. However, conditions of unfreedom are not considered unconstitutional for those given the status of nonimmigrant or temporary foreign worker. Through the simple act of placing a person in the category of temporary foreign worker rather than under the immigration status of permanent resident, the state thus ensures that some persons living and working in Canada can be legally denied rights and freedoms.

While this may seem too obvious, it is useful to remember that it is the Canadian state that makes temporary foreign workers so vulnerable. That is, temporary foreign workers exist within a state bureaucratic classification scheme designed to hold people in a particular relationship of exploitation and social/political subordination in the country. Indeed, the category of temporary foreign worker was created precisely to produce this subordination and continues to be used in ever-expanded form to ensure this outcome.

The remainder of this chapter will outline the changes brought in by Canada's 1973 Non-Immigrant Employment Authorization Program (NIEAP). Further, it will discuss the dominant (and dominating) ideas of nationalized, racialized, gendered, and sexualized belonging that give such programs their legitimacy. Then it will describe the ways that Canada's temporary foreign workers programs reshape the labour force made available to capitalist investors and employers. Lastly, and importantly, it examines what people are doing to end the subordination of those legally made unfree in Canada.

Canada's Temporary Foreign Workers Programs

Since 1973, the Canadian state has considerably expanded both the scope and the scale of its **temporary foreign workers** programs. The most striking change that this led to is the shift in the (im)migration status that people migrating to Canada are given. Since the expansion of these programs, fewer and fewer people are being admitted to Canada as immigrants (those with the status—and rights—of permanent residents) while more and more persons are admitted as temporary foreign workers with the legal status of "nonimmigrant worker."

This shift was rapidly entrenched in the Canadian immigration regime. As early as 1976, of all persons migrating to Canada with a stated intention to work in the paid labour force (including those in the independent class, the family class, the refugee class, and the nonimmigrant class of temporary foreign workers), the majority, or 53% (69,368 persons), were given the status of temporary foreign worker. That same year, only 47% (61,461 persons) were admitted as immigrants with the right of permanent residency. Over time, the number and proportion of all persons admitted to Canada

Case Example 1: Temporary Foreign Workers in the United States

Most people legally (im)migrating to the US arrive not as immigrants (i.e. with permanent resident status and rights) but as nonimmigrant "guest workers," primarily with one of three kinds of H visas: H-1B, H-2A, or H-2B. Since the H visa system began in 1986, there has been a significant shift in the status given to persons granted official permission to enter the United States to work. In 2009, about 48% of all persons admitted to the US were given the status of "foreign worker" (including family sponsorees, immigrants selected for employment purposes, investors, refugees and asylees, and others, plus all those on various H visas) (Homeland Security 2012). The importance of an **unfree labour** force of guest workers is clearer when we compare the number of people issued employment-based green cards (144,034) with the numbers admitted as H-visa workers (545,549). We see that in 2009, 74% of all persons receiving official permission to enter the US labour market were admitted with H visas while only 26% were granted the rights of permanent residency.

as either temporary foreign workers or permanent residents have fluctuated but a clear trend has emerged. Almost without exception, the majority of persons being recruited to Canada in any given year are temporary foreign workers. For example, in 2011, 55% (300,111) of all those migrating to Canada were categorized as temporary foreign workers while only 45% (248,748) were given the right of permanent residency (CIC 2012:4–5).

This shift is even more noticeable when we compare only those categorized as temporary foreign workers with those permanent residents designated as economic immigrants (i.e. skilled workers, business immigrants or provincial and territorial nominees, along with those who have successfully converted their temporary live-in caregiver status to permanent resident). In 2011, out of a total of 380,121 temporary foreign workers and economic immigrants, only 21% (80,010) were granted the right of permanent residency while 79% (300,111) were made to labour in Canada as temporary foreign workers (CIC 2012:4–6). Even more specifically, when we compare the number of persons admitted as temporary foreign workers with only that part of the economic **immigrant** group that was specifically admitted as immigrant workers (i.e. excluding business immigrants, who totalled 11,641 persons), we see that in 2011, the number (68,369) and proportion (13%) of persons granted permanent residency rights shrinks considerably while the proportion of temporary foreign workers increases to a whopping 87% (CIC 2012:6). These figures show us that Canada's immigration system has decidedly moved away from admitting people as permanent residents (i.e. immigrants) to admitting people as temporary foreign workers who mostly labour under conditions of unfreedom. Canadian immigration policies since the mid-1970s, thus, have been geared toward providing a permanently temporary workforce to employers.

Categorizing people as temporary foreign workers has two main—and related— advantages for the state and for employers. First, those so categorized are denied the ability to claim a large number of state-granted rights and entitlements that citizens and permanent residents possess. For instance, the vast majority of temporary foreign workers cannot claim employment insurance or provincial welfare assistance, even though they contribute to these programs either directly through income taxes and payroll deductions or indirectly through the general goods and services taxes paid at the time of purchases. Unlike citizens and permanent residents, those categorized as temporary foreign workers cannot rely on social welfare benefits but instead must continue to work. History has shown that the availability of such social welfare benefits has been enormously effective in raising the wages and living standards of persons with access to them. Prohibitions on temporary foreign workers accessing most social welfare programs thereby contribute to the relative cheapness of the wages they are paid and to the vulnerabilities they face when challenging their discrimination.

Secondly, and as mentioned above, temporary foreign workers are legally denied the protection of freedom that is granted to citizens and permanent residents. If persons categorized as temporary foreign workers are dissatisfied with a particular job or occupation or geographical location—for example, if the wages they are paid are poor and there are better jobs elsewhere, if their working conditions or housing conditions are experienced as unacceptable, if an employer is not fulfilling his or her part of the labour contract, or even if the employer is being abusive—the employees cannot, for the most part, leave their employment and seek alternative employment without the express written permission of an immigration officer. If they are not granted such permission, most temporary foreign workers are subject to deportation. Thus, if they violate any terms of their contracts, not only do temporary foreign workers lose their jobs, they also lose their legal standing in Canada.

Unfree temporary foreign workers work throughout the labour market in Canada and in a wide range of occupational sectors. Temporary foreign workers work in both (relatively) low-cost, low-skilled as well as (relatively) high-cost, high-skilled jobs. Some work as live-in caregivers, agricultural workers, and restaurant workers, and some work as software engineers and doctors. However, there are important gendered and racialized differentiations among those who fill such occupations. Overall, men are highly overrepresented in professional occupations while women are concentrated and overrepresented in the service occupations—particularly personal service occupations, such as domestic work. This, of course, is not atypical of the distribution of women and men within the broader Canadian labour market. Thus, it seems that the temporary foreign workers programs reflect and further entrench the gendered division of labour already in operation in Canada. Likewise, this labour recruitment system operates in a racialized manner. Consistently, the vast majority of workers in (relatively) high-skilled occupations arrive from other "rich world" countries, while people from the "majority world" predominate within certain of the lowest-paying occupations with the poorest documented working conditions, such as agricultural or domestic work. Canada's temporary foreign workers regime, therefore, essentially reflects—and further exacerbates—the racialized and gendered labour market already existing in Canada.

Aside from being tied to their employer, many temporary foreign workers, including those regulated by Canada's Live-in Caregiver Program (LCP), the Seasonal Agricultural Worker Program (SAWP), and the even more restrictive Pilot Project for Occupations Requiring Lower Levels of Formal Training program, introduced in 2002, find themselves facing further restrictions on their freedom and mobility within Canada. At the time of writing, the LCP, for example, legally required temporary foreign workers (who are mostly nonwhite women) to live in the same residence as their employers. There have there been numerous and well-documented cases of physical, emotional, and sexual abuse arising from precisely this condition. Persons regulated by the SAWP often have curfews imposed upon them, are prohibited from receiving visitors of the opposite sex, and may be fired if they become pregnant (Preibisch 2010). It is important to recall that such stipulations would constitute a clear violation of Section 6 of the Charter if applied to persons with the legal status of citizen and permanent resident.

In the case of those employed through the Pilot Project for Occupations Requiring Lower Levels of Formal Training program, the Canadian state has written itself out of its responsibility to intervene in the conditions of work for those recruited through it. This leaves these workers with no official recourse if their employer reneges on his or her part of the contract. Moreover, the standard contract that is drawn up (by employers, with the assistance the International Organization for Migration) and which potential recruits must sign, contains terms for employment that, again, would be considered unconstitutional were they imposed on citizens or permanent residents. For the duration of their employment, workers are told that they should "avoid" joining any group or association, not show any signs of what the employer considers "disrespect," and not have sexual relations. The contract even contains a clause regarding the length of the person's hair (Flecker 2014). In short, Canada's temporary foreign workers programs empower employers and the state in relation to the temporary foreign workers by creating extra conditions of control against workers' rights and freedoms, controls that are unavailable to the state or employers in their efforts to control citizens and permanent residents.

Understanding that people are made into temporary foreign workers by the Canadian state is a necessary corrective to the two dominant narratives that try to justify their differential treatment. The first narrative represents temporary foreign workers as people who are naturally inclined toward jobs and working conditions seen as undesirable by Canadians. The following 1973 quotation by Member of Parliament H.W. Danforth (Kent-Essex), in which he tries to encourage the House of Commons to continue making temporary foreign workers available to agricultural employers, is a good example of such a tactic:

> The attitude of this government has been that if you do not want to
> work, you should not have to do so. I raise this matter because the PM
> [Prime Minister Trudeau] reaffirmed the position of the government
> that a Canadian should not have to work if he does not want to. Mr.
> Chairman, many people do not like to work in agriculture. They do not
> like the monotony, the conditions and the fact that you work some-
> times in heat and sometimes in cold. That is all right; they do not like
> it and they should not be forced to work at it. We all agree with that....
> How [then] do they [employers] obtain labour? Many of them have
> encouraged offshore labour over the years which comes from three
> sources, the Caribbean, Portugal and Mexico. We need this labour
> ... and these people are used to working in the heat. They are used
> to working in agriculture, and they are satisfied with the pay scale ...
> Everybody is satisfied: the workers are satisfied, the primary producers
> are satisfied and the consumers of Canada are satisfied because we are
> getting the crops harvested. (House of Commons Debates 1973:5836)

To legitimize the fact that "offshore workers" (i.e. temporary foreign workers) can be made to work under conditions considered unacceptable by Canadians, Mr. Danforth relies on ideologies of **racism** and **nationalism** to argue that certain, largely nonwhite, foreigners are a wholly different type of people—the type who are satisfied with what Canadians reject. This works to position them as "naturally" inferior to Canadians (which, along with being a legal category, is also often a racialized one).

The second dominant narrative justifying the making of people into temporary foreign workers insists that regardless of how difficult or even dangerous their work is or how little they are paid for it, temporary foreign workers are lucky to live and work in Canada. Even, or perhaps especially, when they are doing jobs that Canadians do not want, comparisons are often made between the relative poverty or the lower earning power in the places where temporary foreign workers hold nationality. In such arguments, as Sedef Arat-Koç (1992) puts it, "immigration ceases to be viewed as a labour recruitment mechanism and becomes a system of 'charity.'"

Both of these legitimization tactics help to construct a kind of "common sense" surrounding the exploitation of temporary foreign workers by rendering as unpolitical the very real differences legislated between them and citizens and permanent residents who have the right to refuse work they find unsatisfactory and to choose both their occupation and their employer.

Interestingly, rendering the difference of citizenship and (im)migration status unpolitical does not mean denying that these differences exist: quite the opposite. We can see this in the following 1971 statement by then–prime minister Pierre Trudeau who, when responding to a question about whether his government would consider imposing conditions of unfreedom on unemployed Canadians, stated, "No ... the government will not commandeer the work force. The whole political philosophy of the government is based on freedom of choice for citizens to work where they want" (House of Commons Debates 1971:4508).

This statement highlights what is, ultimately, the crux of the issue. Trudeau acknowledged that the Canadian state will not—indeed cannot—make those categorized as its citizens work under unfree conditions. This is because within a liberal-democratic nationalist framework, citizens are supposed to be free. However, within this same liberal-democratic framework, it is legally possible and socially permissible to exploit people as unfree labour in Canada with no "freedom of choice ... to work where they want" if and only if they are categorized as temporary foreign workers. With this category in place, a system of unfree labour in the liberal-democratic state of Canada is able to proceed. With the organization of national difference through state categories, the Canadian national state can simultaneously be a liberal democracy and an authoritarian state. How one experiences the Canadian state depends on one's citizenship and (im)migration status.

National Sovereignty and Global Capitalism

Today, although this has not always been the case, there is an internationally recognized right of national states to determine the membership of their societies. Since Canada, the US, and many other states do not deny those born in their territories citizenship status, a main mechanism to shape the citizenry is through immigration and naturalization policies. It is the legitimacy that ideas of national sovereignty hold in today's world that makes it possible to set the legal ground for the creation of a hierarchy of rights and entitlements within each individual nation-state.

This organized inequality is deemed universally legitimate in part because of the enormous influence that ideas of nation-ness have on our feelings. Nationalism profoundly shapes who we think we are, with whom we feel connected and, re-sultantly, against whom we define our "**imagined community**" (Anderson 1991). Just as importantly, nationalism allows for the historically novel—and thoroughly ideological—idea that those who make up the nation are equal and that the only legitimate basis of inequality is that between nationals and foreigners. Not only does this conceal the very real inequalities that exist within the category of citizen and deny the existence of the many similarities that exist between people across national divides, nationalism also provides those recognized as citizens with a sense of right-eous power over those persons deemed to be foreigners. As discussed above, while nationalism posits distinct and discrete spaces for national subjects and foreigners, both already exist in the same space. In this regard, then, our sense of closeness with or distance from others is not a geographical distinction (i.e. who is inside or outside the nation-state per se) but a social and legal distinction.

There are two related ways to understand the character of this shared space. One is that nationals and foreigners exist within the same nationalized space in which they are ideologically and legally positioned as stark opposites. In this sense, foreigners are not alien interlopers into national space; they are an intrinsic part of it. This is borne out historically. Indeed, there has never existed a national state composed only of its citizens. All nation-states have people considered (and often legally categorized as) foreigners living within their borders. Thus, despite the organization of "difference" between the two, people categorized as either nationals or foreigners often live side by side (sometimes in the same household!), work side by side, use the same transportation systems, pay the same taxes, and so on. In short, they live in the same nationalized space.

Another related way of looking at the shared character of space inhabited by nationals and foreigners is that they live together in a society that can only be regarded as global. In other words, in many respects society is neither scaled nor organized as national. Rather, it is more useful to recognize that national states govern and regulate a global capitalist society through the making of differences, and therefore competition, between people within the world. Indeed, historically the organization of humans into nations, and particularly the creation of nation-states, was organized long after the advent of the global capitalist system.

Although dating the global character of **capitalism** is an imprecise task, certainly by the seventeenth century, people, other animals, plants, and ideas were all brought together into a global arena of capitalist relationships of commodification and ex-ploitation. People in what we now know as the Caribbean and the Americas were brought into this "new world" through the force of "blood and fire," as Karl Marx put it. Significantly, no amount of fire and blood was spared for people in places now known as Africa, Asia, and the Pacific, as they too found themselves enclosed within a globalizing system of expropriation and exploitation. And, of course, terror, immiseration, and death were visited upon great numbers of people in Europe as well, even though some of the wealthiest and most powerful people and empires were also based there. What was created, then, was a global system of deep, often violent, sometimes cooperative, but nonetheless always connected human relationships.

As Peter Linebaugh and Marcus Rediker (2000) show, it was in these connections that challenges to the emerging global system of capitalism lay. Indeed, the history of the formative period of capitalism is replete with numerous efforts to overthrow it. That these revolts were led by truly motley crews of people hailing from all parts of the world where capitalist social relationships had been imposed was an important part of why they were considered so dangerous by the newly forming capitalist elite and state officials. For these persons, the dissolution of the closeness of people across the world, intimacies wrought by shared exploitation, was seen as absolutely essential to their power. A major tool in this regard was the making of "difference."

Thus, as Sylvia Federici (2004:63–64) argues, accompanying the process of capital accumulation there was an "accumulation of differences and divisions within the working class, whereby hierarchies built upon gender, as well as 'race' and age, became constitutive of class rule." As nationalism rose, it too came to be a crucial difference, for one of the ways in which people were convinced that they were disconnected was through ideas of separate, competing, and hostile nationalized spaces and identifications. There was, of course, a structural element to the emergence of a nationalist subjectivity: the capitalist revolution (or, more accurately, counterrevolution) relied on the growing power of the state to discipline and order workers. The centralization of state power came to be regarded by ruling groups as the only institutional structure capable of safeguarding capitalist relations. As Federici (2004:49) puts it, "the state became the ultimate manager of class relations, and the supervisor of the reproduction of labor-power." By the late nineteenth century, the national form of the state came to be seen as especially helpful in this regard. National identities served to conceal the global character of power and of the relationship among people. Indeed, the nationalist notion that there are and ought to be differential rights for nationals and foreigners structured the devastating competition existing between people located in increasingly differentiated national labour markets.

In fact, it could be said that the grossly uneven and unequal distribution of rights, security, peace, prosperity, and power within and across the nation-states of the world more or less guarantees that people will move. People's migrations are patterned in ways that are very much connected to these global inequalities. National citizenship and immigration policies are what allow states to continually absorb—and ideologically obscure—these gross inequalities into a "flexible" and legally subordinate workforce within nationalized labour markets. Indeed, immigration policies are the conduits through which the global movement of people is channeled for the benefit of both nation-states and employers hiring within nationalized labour markets. Thus, such policies assist nation-states in organizing the circumstances through which capital can be accumulated within the territories they control. The work that these policies do in the accumulation process helps to explain most immigration policy changes in Canada since the late 1960s and especially the expansion of temporary foreign workers programs in 1973.

While legally organized racism (discrimination against negatively racialized people), **sexism**, or heterosexism has mostly (but certainly not completely) been made illegal in Canada, including in immigration law, nationalism and the distinctions made between citizens and noncitizens continues to provide a legal—and socially legitimate—avenue for discrimination. Such distinctions continue to be made and continue to keep certain people in conditions of legal subordination because of the citizenship and immigration status that they have been accorded in the national community. This is a form of apartheid, a global apartheid that, like all forms of apartheid, exists not only at the level of keeping migrants out, but by "differently including" them as lawfully subordinated persons (Richmond 1994; Deleuze and Guattari 1987).

No Borders!

One very important challenge to the right of nation-states to accord differential citizenship and (im)migration statuses to persons is the emergent No Borders movement. Within this movement, border controls are seen to actively create inequalities, competition, and divisions between people and therefore to stifle our efforts to achieve social justice. A No Borders politics is thus centred on a struggle against the denial of free human mobility within the current international governance system of nation-states. By insisting that every person has the freedom to move and the concomitant freedom to not be forced to move (i.e. the freedom to stay), those within the No Borders movement are challenging—and repoliticizing—the very legitimacy of migration regulations and restrictions. Far from reaffirming citizenship, those in the No Borders movement also call into question the global system of nation-states itself and the related global system of capitalism. Thus, in making their demands, the No Borders movement brings to the fore the centrality of border controls to capitalist social relations, relationships borne of—and still dependent on—practices

Case Example 2: Don't Ask, Don't Tell Campaigns

Don't Ask, Don't Tell campaigns originated in the United States, particularly in response to changes enacted from 1996 onward by Congress that enabled new immigration enforcement and intelligence roles for local police. Don't Ask, Don't Tell campaigns affirm the right to public services for all residents regardless of their (im) migration status. Such campaigns pose an important challenge to the ways that states make some migrants vulnerable by giving them precarious (im)migration statuses (like temporary foreign worker or illegal). In the United States, more than 50 cities have passed legislation that forbids the use of municipal funds, resources, and workers for the enforcement of federal immigration laws. Other cities, such as Los Angeles, Chicago, Seattle, and New York City, specifically bar city workers from inquiring into or disseminating information regarding a person's (im)migration status. Don't Ask, Don't Tell campaigns have also been initiated in cities in Canada, particularly in Toronto, where the Toronto District School Board has been convinced to not ask for, report, or share information about a student's (im)migration status. Such campaigns originate in the work done by (im)migrants, refugees, and persons and groups supporting them.

of displacement, expropriation, and exploitation.

Acting on No Borders politics (sometimes only implicitly) are a wide variety of individuals and groups. They include groups of self-conscious activists directly confronting the state's imposition of barriers on people's mobilities. Those within No Borders movements work to shut down migrant detention camps and to end deportation schemes and other forms of harassment by police. Examples of such groups are the *Sans Papiers* in France and groups inspired by their actions in other parts of Europe, such as the *Sin Papeles* in Spain. In Europe there is also the broader No Border network, a loose affiliation of individuals, sometimes in organizations, who reject any controls on people's migration, and stage actions aimed at preventing deportations and other acts of solidarity with demonized and detained migrants.

Informed by No Borders politics, there also exist campaigns that attempt to eliminate the use of immigration status as a tool of control over migrants. These include Don't Ask, Don't Tell campaigners calling for an end to immigration status distinctions between people in the provision of social services and in the receipt of state protections (e.g. from violence). In Canada, various No One Is Illegal groups in Montreal, Toronto, and Vancouver have been at the forefront of such efforts.

Elsewhere, there exist groups such as Doctors of the World who provide needed medical assistance regardless of one's state-issued status. Such groups often call for legalization (or regularization) of **illegalized migrants** as a means by which to gain rights and entitlements currently restricted to citizens and some permanent residents.

Other groups within the broader No Borders movement include "sanctuary movements" that provide much-needed support in the form of information, shelter, water, and food to travelling migrants; trade unions that purposefully ignore a person's (im)migration status in their organizing drives or even specifically address the vulnerabilities faced by persons because of their illegal or temporary status; and other individuals and groups who argue for the abolition of the multiple borders that national states impose, such as borders created by laws regarding official languages and other banal forms of nationalism (Billig 1995). These include groups such as No More Deaths, which works at the US-Mexico border, and labour unions, such as the United Food and Commercial Workers Union (UFCW) in Canada. Some unions, thus, have crossed the ideological divide between nationals and foreigners in order to secure higher wages, better working conditions, and healthcare for any worker in the occupational sectors they organize.

The rejection of national distinctions is what links disparate campaigns, groups, and individuals together within the No Borders movement. In eschewing nationalist forms of solidarity (and hostility), the No Border movement acknowledges that a key aspect of the ideological work of nationalism is to make the global character of human society and relationships disappear. Many within the No Borders movement, therefore, move from challenging national forms of "belonging" to trying to activate other ways of being in the world and other ways of understanding ourselves, ones that correspond with the global level at which human society is organized and experienced. The No Borders movement, thus, redefines equality by positing it as a relationship among co-members of a global society and not one among citizens. In doing so, the No Borders movement affirms a conception of freedom based on the collective political action of equals. The related rights to move and to stay are seen as necessary to the creation of this equality.

Conclusion

Placing persons in different state categories of membership in national societies is a key way that inequalities are legalized and legitimated. Such categorical distinctions between people are ranked in a hierarchical order with citizens at the top and various groups of noncitizens at the bottom. Such distinctions work to the benefit of nation-states and employers. People in certain state categories, such as temporary foreign worker, are legally prohibited from making claims on the state (e.g. for social services). Moreover, persons within this category are legally tied to a specific employer and in specific occupation, thus giving employers far greater power and control over those made into temporary foreign workers.

Nation-states are given the right to make such distinctions because of their concern over national membership. Nation-states, more so than other kinds of states, such as monarchies or imperial states, assert their "right" to regulate and restrict human mobility. Such a right is currently entrenched within international law. However, this has not always been so. It is a relatively recent development, dating only to the end of the nineteenth century in Canada and the United States. Prior to this, (monarchical or imperial) states were much less concerned with controlling the entry of migrants, if they were at all. Thus, state restrictions on human migration are historically linked to the project of nation-building. Nations were (and continue to be) constructed using ideas of **"race"** and normative ideas of the "proper roles" for persons gendered men or women. In the making of nations, the entry of negatively racialized persons and those deemed by the state (or its officials) to be "immoral" was severely controlled.

Nation-states such as Canada and the United States continue to exercise their power to differently include various groups of migrants to shift the status they give to people. In both Canada and the US, many more persons are now admitted under a state category (foreign worker) that renders people unfree than are admitted under the permanent resident category that comes with legally guaranteed rights and entitlements (although these rights too are being diminished). Thus, we see nation-states using their power over national membership to radically reorganize the availability of rights and entitlements associated with national citizenship. Such state powers shape the kind of labour force that is available to employers within national territories. By using immigration policy to tie workers to specific employers and occupations, the state is able to create a highly vulnerable workforce that is structurally less able to challenge employers' demands.

Such legislated inequalities are not going unchallenged. Far from it. First and foremost, those persons assigned highly subordinated immigration statuses resist such severe encroachments on their freedoms. They have organized in defence of their liberty and in defence of the idea that human beings should have the freedom to move across the space of what is truly a global society. Many people have joined these struggles. Persons acting within No Borders movements have especially challenged the rights of nation-states to limit human mobility by showing how immigration regulations and restrictions—as well as the general exercise of national sovereignty—are used by states against workers and for capitalists. They argue for a different world: a world in which persons across the world are acknowledged as each other's equals, each with the freedom to move or to stay and each living a life free from oppression and exploitation.

Questions for Critical Thought

1. Nationalists tell us that "society" is coterminus with the "nation." Can such views account for the fact that many people are either socially or legally classified as "not-belonging" to the very "society" that they live, work, and sometimes die, in?
2. Thinking *non-ideologically*, what is the actual scale and scope of "society"? Who are we connected to and with and how?
3. What are the social, political, and economic processes that produce the idea that we are disconnected from those said to belong to other "nations," "races," or "cultures"?

Key Readings

Anderson, Bridget (2013) *Us and Them? The Dangerous Politics of Immigration Control.* Oxford: Oxford University Press, 2013.

Sharma, Nandita (2006) *Home Economics: Nationalism and the Making of 'Migrant Workers' in Canada.* Toronto: University of Toronto Press.

Sutcliffe, Bob (2001) Migration and Citizenship: Why Can Birds, Whales, Butterflies and Ants Cross International Frontiers More Easily than Cows, Dogs and Human Beings? In Subrata Ghatak and Anne Showstack Sassoon (eds.) *Migration and Mobility: The European Context.* New York: Palgrave.

Media Links

Migrant Workers in Canada Listserv:
migrantworkers-travailleursmigrants-canada-subscribe@lists.riseup.net
You can subscribe to the Migrant Workers—Travailleurs Migrants—Canada listserv to receive current news and analysis of Canada's temporary foreign workers program.

Migration: The COMPAS Anthology:

compasanthology.co.uk

COMPAS (the Centre on Migration, Policy and Society) at Oxford University has produced a valuable anthology on migration edited by professors Bridget Anderson and Michael Keith. It "is designed both as a teaching and research resource and as a provocation. Contributions range from personal reflections to succinct overviews, and include poetry and images, posing questions and sharing insights on the multifaceted phenomenon that we call 'migration', and linking it to wider patterns of social change."

No Border Network:

www.noborder.org

This website serves as both an archive about the history of No Border agitations, primarily in Europe, as well as a platform to inform readers about No Border–affiliated projects. Articles on migration, as well as the multilingual newsletter *Crossing Borders*, are also available here.

References

Anderson, Benedict (1991) *Imagined Communities: Reflections on the Origin and Spread of Nationalism*. London: Verso.

Arat-Koç, Sedef (1992) Immigration Policies, Migrant Domestic Workers and the Definition of Citizenship in Canada. In Vic Satzewich (ed.) *Deconstructing a Nation: Immigration, Multiculturalism and Racism in 90's Canada*, pp. 229–242. Halifax: Fernwood Publishing.

Billig, Michael (1995) *Banal Nationalism*. London: Sage.

Citizenship and Immigration Canada (CIC) (2012) Canada Facts and Figures: Immigration Overview, Permanent and Temporary Residents, Ci1-8/2012E-PDF, ISSN: 1495-6578. www.cic.gc.ca/english/resources/statistics/menu-fact.asp

Deleuze, Gilles and Félix Guattari (1987) *A Thousand Plateaus: Capitalism and Schizophrenia*. B. Massumi (translator). Minneapolis: University of Minnesota Press.

Federici, Sylvia (2004) *Caliban and the Witch*. Brooklyn, NY: Autonomedia.

Flecker, Karl (2014) "Not Wanted on the Voyage": Migrant Workers' Needs And Rights Continue To Be Ignored." Canadian Centre for Policy Alternatives, www.policyalternatives.ca/publications/monitor/not-wanted-voyage#sthash.MwNoRgnN.pdf (Accessed June 14, 2014)

House of Commons Debates (1971) Official Report. Third Session-Twenty Eighth Parliament, Vol. V 1971 (March 22 to May 5). Ottawa: Queen's Printer for Canada.

House of Commons Debates (1973) Official Report. First Session-Twenty Ninth Parliament, Vol. VI 1973 (July 19 to September 21). Ottawa: Queen's Printer for Canada.

Linebaugh, Peter and Marcus Rediker (2000) *The Many-Headed Hydra: Sailors, Slaves, Commoners, and the Hidden History of the Revolutionary Atlantic.* Boston: Beacon Press.

Preibisch, Kerry (2010) Pick-Your-Own Labor: Migrant Workers and Flexibility in Canadian Agriculture. *International Migration Review* 44(2):404–441.

Richmond, Anthony H. (1994). *Global Apartheid: Refugees, Racism, and the New World Order.* Toronto: Oxford University Press.

Chapter 9

Ethnic Retailing

Zhixi Cecilia Zhuang,
Tony Hernandez, and Shuguang Wang

Introduction

If you take a walk through many major metropolitan markets in North America, it will probably not be too long before you find yourself in an area with a distinctive ethnic character. You may notice the ethnicity in any number of ways: the languages that you hear spoken on the street, the way people dress, or the music being played in the local bars and restaurants. One of the most visual clues, however, will be the type of businesses that you see—from retail (e.g. grocery, fashion, and jewellery stores) to a multitude of business and personal services (e.g. legal services, real estate agents, beauticians, and restaurants) that cater to both ethnic and nonethnic consumers.

There is no universally agreed upon definition of **ethnic retail**. Some researchers use "business ownership" as the defining factor; others use customer orientation as the key criterion. The difficulty of defining ethnic retail results from the facts that not all retail businesses that are owned and operated by ethnic minorities target customers of the same ethnicity, and many mainstream businesses (particularly banks) operate outlets in an exclusively ethnic neighbourhood, with a contingent of staff, from managers to clerks, being members of that ethnicity.

The term ethnic retail used within this chapter refers to a mixture of retail and service businesses that are clustered spatially in the form of a strip or a centre and represent certain ethno-cultural characteristics in 1) the goods and services offered and/or 2) the physical features of their storefronts or streetscapes. What makes ethnic retail distinct from other types of retailing? How has ethnic retailing impacted urban environments across North America? And how is it likely to change in the future? These are some of the questions that will be addressed in this chapter.

The Emergence of Ethnic Retailing

Historically, ethnic retailing was closely associated with **immigration** of minorities. Ethnic retailing occurred when the **concentration** of ethnic households reached a threshold and generated sufficient demand for a range of goods and services. After that, each wave of immigration added new demand for more ethnic retailing and consumer services.

The character of many major North America cities has been shaped by the array of businesses and services that have served their growing **immigrant** populations—from Italians in New York and Chinese in San Francisco to South Asians in Toronto. These cities have all experienced successive waves of immigration over time, which in turn brought about the rapid expansion of retail activities. Immigrants not only constitute a large segment of the consumer market, they include many innovative entrepreneurs who successfully set up new businesses to meet the demand of their co-ethnic consumers. In the past, ethnic retail businesses were small in scale and were relevant only to small groups of minorities with few impacts on mainstream society. Today, in some subsectors of retailing, ethnic businesses are taking significant market shares away from mainstream retailers. Recent developments in ethnic retailing have, however, dramatically changed the urban form and commercial landscape of the host cities. This is especially visible in the change in ethnic retail activities that manifest themselves both along street-fronted retail strips and within shopping centres located in both inner-urban and suburban areas, typically those that have experienced the most significant immigrant **settlement**. These ethnic retail areas act as symbols of urban diversity and beacons of **multiculturalism**.

Based on the increasing awareness of and sensitivity to culture, ethnicity has become commodified. Culture and commerce are no longer seen as separate objects, but as an encompassing commercial culture that leverages ethnic differences (Jackson 2002). As Sharon Zukin (1995:180) argues, cultural production has become the "symbolic economy" of the city. **Cultural pluralism** evokes the revival of ethnic expression in today's ethnic commercial landscapes. In a way, the symbolism expressed in ethnic businesses strengthens and reinforces ethnicity and demonstrates "ethnic revival." Meanwhile, ethnicity also sells as a commodity because of the "ethnic chic" that has become attractive to the mainstream public.

On a *macro-level*, ethnic retail districts generally consist of concentrated co-ethnic (i.e. same ethnicity) businesses, with well-recognized neighourhood labels replicated across North American cities, such as Chinatown, Greektown, Little Italy, and Little India. Ethnic business clusters represent diverse and distinct images of various ethnic groups that physically differentiate them from their mainstream counterparts. These clusters are easily identified through store signage, store merchandise, distinctive exterior and interior decoration, and street furniture.

On a *micro-level*, ethnic retail areas have distinct dynamics. It may take years for them to come to fruition and they function in different ways. For example, ethnic retail areas can serve (often in combination with one another) as ports of entry for new immigrants, with relatively low barriers to start a business or to get a job compared to the mainstream consumer service sector. Ethnic retail areas also serve as neighbourhood centres providing for daily ethnic needs and the functioning of an ethnic community. In addition, there are regional ethnic centres that serve multiple neighbourhoods and contribute to broader community cohesion. A final example of the diverse role of ethnic retail areas is that they function as tourist attractions and in their own right facilitate and promote multiculturalism and intergroup communication. Ethnic retail areas over time may develop into major **ethnic retail hotspots** that are identified by their large concentration of ethnic retail businesses. Often such hotspots will serve both a regional market and tourist function.[1]

Their various spatial and physical manifestations point to diverse stages and processes of development and the possible involvement of different stakeholders in their establishment and evolution. Ethnic retail not only reflects the current wave of new immigrants but also the legacy of prior waves of immigration. That is, ethnic retail areas serve the needs of both new and established immigrants and may act as longstanding symbols of previous generations of immigration. As such, ethnic retail areas often transition in their character over time and go through various stages of evolutionary development. Collectively, these eclectic clusters of ethnic businesses provide the street-front and shopping centre–based ethno-cultural character found within parts of many North America metropolises.

Overall, ethnic retailing generates significant benefits to urban economies, to immigrant settlement, and to the redevelopment of traditional neighbourhoods. First, the presence of ethnic retail areas not only promotes the creation of small businesses and hence employment, but also diversifies the urban retail environment and contributes to the local economy. Ethnic retail areas function as important additions to the mainstream retail and service offering (particularly, ethnic foods and restaurants that have broader appeal). They provide a mechanism for new immigrant business investment and labour force **integration** through the employment opportunities that they provide to their communities. Second, ethnic retailing contributes to the settlement of immigrants, both socially and culturally, as ethnic retail areas serve as "little homelands" or social hubs for immigrants who have strong cultural attachments

Image 9.1
Store Space Dedicated to Ethnic Foods in a Walmart Supercentre in Toronto, ON, Canada

Source: Photograph by Shugang Wang (2013).

within these areas. For the community at large, ethnic retail areas that showcase diverse ethno-cultural heritages are often treated as symbols of *multicultural diversity* in Canada and the *immigrant* **melting pot** in the US. Third, ethnic retailing has the potential to stabilize and sustain the economy of traditional retailing streets by providing local, small-scale, and easily accessible shopping options, helping them face competition from corporate big box stores and thereby contributing to the identity of the neigbourhood.

With ethnic retail areas often selling goods and services that were not available in mainstream retail environments (e.g. distinct styles of clothing or niche grocery items and exotic fresh produce) they were somewhat protected from direct competition with mainstream retailers. However, this situation has been changing over recent years as the size of the ethnic market has registered on the radar screen of corporate North America. Given the scale of ethnic consumer spending, it cannot be ignored by mainstream retailers. More and more mainstream retailers have been attempting to meet the specific needs of ethnic consumers by extending their product ranges and service offerings to cater to the **ethnic niche** as a complement to their core retail offer. In Canada, for example, Walmart sells multiple lines of ethnic goods in its generic supercentres (see Image 9.1). Loblaws, a mainstream grocery retailer, acquired T & T Supermarkets, a regional-scaled Chinese grocery chain, reportedly as a means of reaching into the lucrative Chinese consumer base in Toronto, Vancouver, Calgary, Edmonton, and Ottawa (Strauss 2009, 2011). The acquisition of T & T also allowed Loblaws to use T & T's established supply chain network in China to source products for other Loblaws stores across the country.

The physical and environmental dimensions of ethnic retailing contribute to the vitality of traditional urban spaces and to community-building. There are, however, concerns that ethnic retailing also has divisive impacts on urban landscapes. The characterization of enclave or **ghetto** may be reinforced through the **clustering** of ethnic businesses serving concentrations of ethnic consumers. The enclave setting of many ethnic retail districts and their narrow services to particular groups could be easily construed as cultural exclusivity and insularity. For example, this may be seen from the negative perspective of discriminatory co-ethnic staffing practices to the more general dominance of co-ethnic customers that may act to deter other shoppers. As well, development of ethnic retailing naturally leads to a higher level of **institutional completeness**, which may discourage integration of recent immigrants within the broader society. Therefore, from a community-wide planning perspective, since ethnic retail districts generally provide retail activities targeting specific groups, their relationships with surrounding neighbourhoods are arguably weak. As ethnic retail activities increasingly diversify and as many ethnic entrepreneurs with trans-planted business skills do business in innovative ways, the current planning system in many municipalities is being challenged to cope with these changes. As a result, controversial issues related to land use, traffic flow, and parking allocation have often been reported (Preston and Lo 2000; Qadeer 1997; Wang 1999).

To understand existing and plan for future commercial activities, the need to assess the positive *and* the negative impacts of the ethnic retail phenomenon is becoming ever more important. Ethnic retailing creates an immense and long-lasting physical imprint on our urban landscapes. It is somewhat surprising that there remain major gaps in our understanding of the dynamics and complexity of the ethnic retail phenomenon, especially with regards to its physical dimensions within urban spaces and its interactions with the general urban economy.

Many of the existing studies ignore the spatial and physical dimensions of the **ethnic economy**. The participation of ethnic businesses in the general urban economy can be seen to generate a series of subset economies that operate at different spatial scales: first, the ethnic economy consists of self-employed, employers, and co-ethnic employees (Bonacich and Modell 1980; Light, Sabagh, Mehdi, and Der-Martirosian 1994; Light and Gold 2000); second, the **ethnic enclave economy** is a specific kind of ethnic economy of spatially clustered and interdependent businesses with co-ethnic

Case Example 1: How to Identify Ethnic Retail

The business owners, management, staff, and clientele of an ethnic retail district may or may not be from the same ethnic group, but the three subset ethnic economies (i.e. ethnic, ethnic enclave, and mixed) are represented in the majority of businesses in these districts. Ethnic retail can be identified in a number of different ways, including:

- the physical features and language of the storefront (store fascia), signage, streetscape;
- the retail offer—the mix of goods and services that are provided;
- the ethnicity of the business owner, investor, management, staff; and
- the ethnicity of the customers.

Image 9.2
Scenes of Ethnic Retail in Toronto, ON, Canada

Top row, from left to right: 1) Mississauga Chinese Centre; 2) Pacific Mall in Markham; 3) Splendid China Tower in Toronto.

Bottom row, from left to right: 1) Great Punjab Business Centre in Mississauga; 2) South Asian retail strip in Toronto; 3) Mix of Chinese and South Asian stores in retail plaza in Scarborough, Toronto.

Source: Photographs by Tony Hernandez (2013).

owners and employees primarily serving their co-ethnic community (Light et al. 1994; Light and Gold 2000; Portes and Bach 1985; Portes and Manning 1986; Wilson and Portes 1980); and third, the **mixed economy** reflects both ethnic and nonethnic business components, and "their markets are spatially and ethnically unbounded" (Lo, Preston, Wang, Reil, Havey, and Siu 2000:12).

The most significant difference between an ethnic economy and an ethnic enclave economy is that the latter stresses spatial clustering and co-ethnic clients. As Ivan Light and associates (1994:73) note, "every immigrant group or ethnic minority has an ethnic economy, but only a few have an ethnic enclave economy." **Ethnic enclave** economies are therefore determined by their scale and level of spatial concentration. It is important to explore the spatial dimension of the ethnic economy because space and place are important factors in ethnic entrepreneurship and its related activities. Ethnic business location choices are strongly related to the geographic distribution of ethnic population. Alejandro Portes's theory of the ethnic enclave economy stresses the importance of the physical concentration of co-ethnic entrepreneurs, employees, and clientele in a territorially clustered business core (Light et al. 1994:77). Portes espouses this type of economy as "concentrated networks of ethnic firms that offer economic advancements by creating jobs and opportunities for entrepreneurship" (Portes and Jensen 1992:419). Others redefine ethnic enclaves and argue that they are associated with residences rather than workplaces, despite the conceptual vagueness of their boundaries (Nee and Sanders 1994). Moreover, there are higher returns for **human capital** outside the enclave economy, though gender inequality continues to exist (Sanders and Nee 1987, 1992; Nee and Sanders 1994; Zhou and Logan 1989).

From a geographic perspective, David Kaplan (1998) illustrates four general ways in which spatial concentration can have a positive impact on ethnic businesses: first, incubator effects describe the process by which a protected market is created through the proximity of ethnic businesses to residential concentration. Second, linkage effects result from close proximity among ethnic businesses that facilitates linkages between co-ethnic suppliers and co-ethnic customers. Third, agglomeration effects are related to improvements in accessibility and efficiency related to spatial proximity that facilitate opportunities for new ethnic businesses. Fourth, focus effects refer to a concentrated ethnic economy that can act as a focal point serving a residentially dispersed ethnic community. These various effects illustrate the complex and dynamic nature of ethnic retailing in North America.

Urban Market Dynamics as Drivers of Ethnic Retail Development: A Canadian Example

Immigration has long been a key factor in North American population growth. In Canada, according to the 2011 census more than one-fifth (20.6%) of the total population was foreign born (Statistics Canada 2013). The **immigration policy** launched in the late 1960s was a watershed event for immigration flows to Canada that drew a sharp increase in the number of skilled workers with non-European backgrounds who were selected based on their age, education, work experience, language skills, secured employment, and adaptability. A subcategory of the economic class, the so-called business class, enabled applicants who met different sets of requirements in terms of personal net worth, business operational experience, job creation ability, and potential contribution to the cultural or artistic landscape to enter Canada. In addition to the benefits of population growth and economic vitality, cultural diversity has been a major contribution of immigration over the past several decades (Reitz 1998).

Following the changes in Canadian immigration policy, there has been an increasing influx of non-European immigrants, especially from Asia (Norris and Hernandez 2008). According to the landing records maintained by Citizenship and Immigration Canada, those from Asia, Africa, and Latin America accounted for 80% of the total immigrants to Canada between 2001 and 2010 (see Table 9.1), while immigrants from the traditional source countries of the United Kingdom, the United States, Australia, and other Western European countries accounted for only 20%.

Table 9.1

World Regions of Last Permanent Residence for Canada's Immigrants, 2001–2010

World Region	Number of Immigrants	Percentage of Total
Africa and Middle East	511,648	20.7
Asia	1,225,843	49.7
Latin America	238,748	9.7
Europe (except the UK)	333,653	13.5
US, UK, and Australia	157,067	6.4
US	85,560	3.5
United Kingdom	70,188	2.8
Australia	1,319	<0.1
Unclassified	597	<0.1
Total	**2,467,556**	**100.0**

Source: Citizenship and Immigration Canada (2011).

More than 200 different countries of origin were reported in the landing records. The changes in source countries over time are illustrated in Figure 9.1.

Another notable "new" phenomenon of international migration is the transnational diaspora. Current transnational movements feature multiple, circular, and return migrations rather than the single journeys, from one space to another, characteristic of past migration movements (Foner 1997). Luin Goldring (cited in Hyndman and Walton-Roberts 1999:6) argues that **transnational communities** are "dense social fields consisting of people, money, goods, and information that are constructed and maintained by migrants over time, across space and through circuits which repeatedly cross borders." This new trend of transnational movements raises questions of how **transnationalism** affects immigrants' social and economic ties in countries of origin and settlement, as well as the communities in which they live.

Figure 9.1
New Immigrants to Canada by Place of Birth, Pre-1961 to 2001–2006

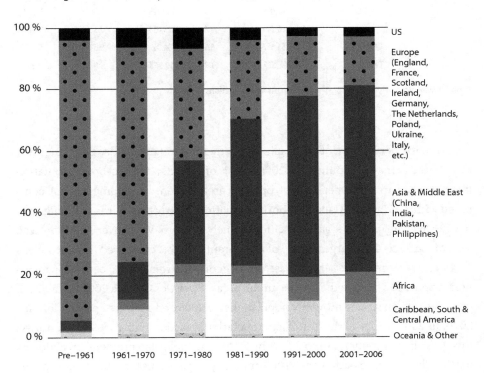

Source: Norris and Hernandez (2008).

Table 9.2

Visible Minority Population in Major Metropolitan Markets in Canada (2005 Estimate with Projection for 2020)

Visible Minority	Metro Area	2005	Percentage in Metro Area	2020	Percentage in Metro Area	Change 2005–2020
All Visible Minorities	Toronto	2,159,507	41.7	3,161,474	50.2	1,001,967
	Montreal	569,347	15.9	981,549	23.2	412,202
	Vancouver	866,555	40.6	1,282,279	48.4	415,724
	Calgary	230,863	21.4	484,577	34.8	253,714
	Canada	**4,961,032**	**15.7**	**8,418,479**	**23.1**	**3,457,447**
Chinese	Toronto	491,057	9.7	557,917	8.9	66,860
	Montreal	68,658	1.9	118,824	2.8	50,166
	Vancouver	384,552	18.0	442,633	16.7	58,081
	Calgary	66,318	6.1	106,825	7.7	40,507
	Canada	**1,211,868**	**3.8**	**1,645,177**	**4.5**	**433,309**
South Asian	Toronto	678,942	13.1	995,302	15.8	316,360
	Montreal	69,059	1.9	106,128	2.5	37,069
	Vancouver	205,744	9.6	325,658	12.3	119,914
	Calgary	55,377	5.1	134,052	9.6	78,675
	Canada	**1,243,527**	**3.9**	**2,119,903**	**5.8**	**876,376**

Source: Environics Analytics, Demographic Estimates and Projections Data 2010.

From the perspective of geographic settlement, immigration has been unevenly distributed across the country. In 2006, 94.9% of Canada's foreign-born population lived in urban areas (i.e. census metropolitan areas or census agglomerations), compared with 77.5% of the Canadian-born population. Nearly two-thirds of immigrants (62.9%) lived in just three "gateway cities," namely Toronto, Vancouver, and Montreal. Toronto attracted the largest share of immigrants, 37.5%, compared to Vancouver's 13.4% and Montreal's 12%. In contrast, just over one-quarter (27.1%) of the Canadian-born population lived in these three urban areas (Statistics Canada 2006a). Table 9.2 provides data on **visible minority** populations for 2005 and projected populations for 2020. In 2005, 15.7% of the Canadian population was identified as visible minority; this is projected to increase to 23.1% by 2020. The table also provides breakdowns for the Chinese and South Asian visible minority populations for four selected major Canadian urban markets. The significant number (i.e. market size) and proportion (i.e. market character) of Chinese and South Asian populations in Toronto and Vancouver can be clearly identified.

The data on contemporary immigration highlights the fact that new immigrants tend to settle in these large urban regions, rather than in smaller urban centres or rural areas. The extreme concentration of recent immigrant settlement has implications for the Canadian urban system, especially in increasing differences between the large metropolitan areas and small- to medium-sized cities. The large metropolitan areas have become more heterogeneous with a growing diversity, while small- and medium-sized cities have remained comparatively homogeneous in terms of their ethno-cultural composition (Bourne and Rose 2001), albeit with a growing immigrant population in second-tier centres such as Kitchener, London, and Kelowna.

It is a difficult task to depict today's immigrants' settlement experiences accurately. Immigrants may follow multiple paths and undergo unpredictable transformations in their social and economic lives. Traditionally, the inner city played an important role in immigrant settlement, as a "port of entry" and reception area for immigrants. Ethnic concentration was viewed as a way of attaining and maintaining mutual support from co-ethnic people and avoiding potential discrimination by the dominant group. Today, the inner city is no longer the typical destination for immigrants, who instead choose to bypass it and settle directly in suburban areas. As Chapter 16 by Sutama Ghosh and Raymond M. Garrison illustrates, varying degrees of concentration or segregation among groups are observed in large North American metropolitan regions as well. Furthermore, empirical studies share the notable conclusion that residential concentration or segregation is not necessarily related to social deprivation or exclusion, as previously assumed. Rather, **settlement patterns** are shaped by local **housing markets**, public policy, the degree of institutional completeness of an ethnic group, their location preference, and economic mobility (Borjas 1997; Qadeer 2003). Aside from the notions of ethnic concentration or segregation, Brian Ray (2009) reveals that ethno-culturally diverse neighbourhoods are widely spread in the metropolitan areas of Toronto, Vancouver, and Montreal.

Ethnic Retail and the Urban Retail System

Maurice Yeates (2000, 2011) refers to ethnic commercial activities as submarkets in the mainstream commercial structure. Figure 9.2 shows the genealogy of the urban retail system (Jones 2000; Jones and Simmons 1993), comprising "two distinct and competing retailing systems—the planned shopping center hierarchy and the remaining unplanned retail areas" (Jones, 2000:404). Within this framework, ethnic retail takes place in unplanned ethnic retail strips in inner cities and planned suburban ethnic shopping centres.

Figure 9.2
The Urban Retail Structure and Ethnic Retail

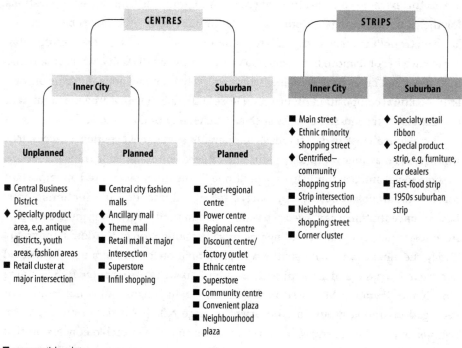

CENTRES

STRIPS

Inner City

Suburban

Inner City

Suburban

- ■ Main street
- ◆ Ethnic minority shopping street
- ◆ Gentrified– community shopping strip
- ■ Strip intersection
- ■ Neighbourhood shopping street
- ■ Corner cluster

- ◆ Specialty retail ribbon
- ◆ Special product strip, e.g. furniture, car dealers
- ■ Fast-food strip
- ■ 1950s suburban strip

Unplanned

Planned

Planned

- ■ Central Business District
- ◆ Specialty product area, e.g. antique districts, youth areas, fashion areas
- ■ Retail cluster at major intersection

- ■ Central city fashion malls
- ◆ Ancillary mall
- ◆ Theme mall
- ■ Retail mall at major intersection
- ■ Superstore
- ■ Infill shopping

- ■ Super-regional centre
- ■ Power centre
- ■ Regional centre
- ■ Discount centre/ factory outlet
- ■ Ethnic centre
- ■ Superstore
- ■ Community centre
- ■ Convenient plaza
- ■ Neighbourhood plaza

■ serves spatial markets
◆ serves specialized markets

Note: In this classification the term *planned* refers to a retail environment that is developed, designed, and managed as a unit and where the tenancy and common areas are under corporate control.

Source: Based on Jones (2000, p. 417).

Ethnic Retail Strips

Early immigrants, who arrived before the suburbanization movement in the 1960s, tended to concentrate with co-ethnic people within the inner-city boundaries. Mixed neighbourhoods, where one ethnic group was adjacent to another, were also very common in the early stages of immigration. These neighbourhoods were normally a place of work, residence, worship, and leisure for co-ethnic people, such as Kensington Market in Toronto, Ontario; the Lower East Side in Manhattan, New York; and Little Havana in Miami, Florida. Later, the suburbanization process in the 1980s and onward began to dominate immigrant settlement patterns. Earlier immigrants tended to move away from the inner city, while recent immigrants landed directly in suburban areas. Some ethnic groups have high degrees of spatial proximity between their businesses and residences, such as Jews and Chinese (Hiebert 1993,

Figure 9.3
Selected South Asian Ethnic Retail Clusters in Toronto, ON, Canada

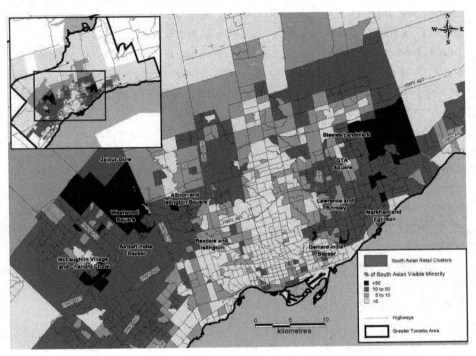

Sources: CSCA Greater Toronto Retail Data 2013; Statistics Canada Census of Population 2006.

2000; Kobayashi 1993; Lo et al. 2000; Marger and Horffman 1992; Thompson 1989). For other groups, the ethnic retail area in the inner city serves a spatially dispersed co-ethnic population, like Little Portugal and Gerrard India Bazaar in Toronto or Little Tokyo in Los Angeles (Teixeira 1998).

The traditional immigrant focal points in the inner city played an important role as ports of entry, reception centres, or little homelands. The ethnic businesses mainly served the neighbourhood's basic needs of daily life (Gale 1972; Jones 2000; Jones and Simmons 1993), such as laundry and groceries. With the growth of the ethnic community and consequent increases in its demands, the functions of these ethnic businesses became more diversified and expanded into various retail and service sectors, such as specialty retailing, food and beverage services, personal and household services, recreational services, manufacturing, and business services. This is exemplified by the new development patterns of ethnic Chinese retailing in Toronto (Wang 1999). Some of the business focal points have become tourist attractions in their own right (Jones 2000; Jones and Simmons 1993), such as Chinatown, Kensington Market, Little Italy, Greektown, and Gerrard India Bazaar (see Figure 9.3) in Toronto (Simmons, Kamikihara, and Hernandez 2010), with these areas having more specialized functions in relation to the tourist industry. Some of the uses and designs of the open space in these areas are consistent with ethnic themes, including street furniture (e.g. map of Italy–shaped street lamps in Little Italy or traditional lantern–shaped lamps in Chinatown), sidewalk stalls, and festival space. Overall, changes in business type and function inevitably impact store facades, window displays, signage, decoration treatments, as well as the atmosphere of the neighbourhood.

In sum, ethnic strips have evolved through the following stages: first serving as entry points for new immigrants, then turning into neighbourhood centres serving daily ethnic needs, and finally, catering to an ethnic population throughout the metropolitan area or even becoming tourist attractions (Jones 2000; Jones and Simmons 1993). A study of retail strips conducted in Metro Toronto (now the City of Toronto) found that among a total of 170 retail strips with 15,400 stores, 19% were reported to be ethnic-oriented, with Chinese being the dominant group, at 5.4% (Sinopoli 1996; see also Hernandez, Helik, and Moore 2006). Considering the diversity of the ethnic population, ethnic retail strips play an increasingly important role in a society that is much more diverse than in the past.

Ethnic Shopping Centres and the Ethnoburbs

Ethnic suburban dispersion is not a homogeneous process as is conceptualized by the classic spatial models of urban form (e.g. the concentric zone, sectoral, multiple nuclei concepts). Such models do not account for the complexities and dynamics of the **adaptation** processes experienced by different ethno-cultural groups. There is no sophisticated model to depict immigrants' settlement patterns or answer the question "Why do some groups concentrate in specific areas of the city while others are widely dispersed?" (Kobayashi 1993:145). In addition, ethnic groups are not internally homogeneous. Ethnic subgroups have internal differences, such as the Chinese from Mainland China, Hong Kong, Taiwan, and the rest of the world. Their heterogeneous regional backgrounds, varying economic classes, and other factors may affect the convergence or divergence of their settlement (Lo and Wang 1997). Wei Li (1998a, 1998b) proposed a new model of ethnic settlement, the ethnoburb, based on her study of the Chinese community in Los Angeles. Wei Li (1998b:504) described the **ethnoburbs** as follows:

> Ethnoburbs can be recognized as suburban clusters of residential areas
> and business districts in large metropolitan areas, especially in those

Figure 9.4
Selected Chinese Retail Clusters in Toronto

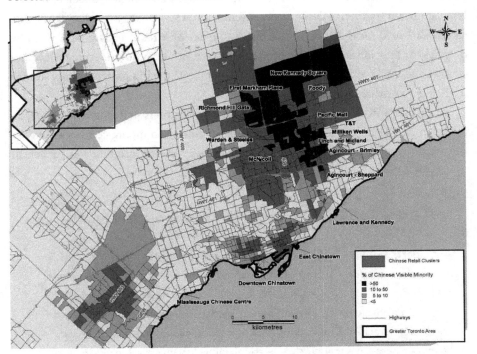

Sources: Greater Toronto Retails Database, Centre for Study of Commercial Activity, Ryerson University, 2013;
Statistics Canada, Census of Population 2006.

"global cities". Ethnoburbs are multi-ethnic communities, in which one ethnic minority group has a significant concentration, but does not necessarily comprise a majority. The establishment of the ethnoburb overlaid an ethnic economy onto a local mainstream economy, which was then transformed into a global economic outpost and direct target for international capital investment, making the ethnoburb a vital area of economic activities and job opportunities.

Although this model may not be generalized to other ethnic groups or metropolitan areas, its potential for understanding how the ethnic economy channels the local or even global economies deserves further exploration, especially with the growing transnational movement of migrants today. In addition, the clustering of settlement patterns points to the heterogeneous nature of the suburban **dispersal** of **ethnic communities** in many of the larger metropolitan areas throughout North America.

Suburban ethnic commercial activities tend to manifest in the form of ethnic shopping centres, both plazas and shopping malls. In terms of their architectural forms, some of them consist of mainly modernist boxy buildings (Qadeer 1998) and lack significant traditional design. These architectural forms are barely distinguishable as ethnic based on the style of the building exterior, except for signage, window displays, or interior decorations. On the contrary, other suburban ethnic shopping centres and malls contain more tangible and symbolic meanings of ethnicity similar to their inner urban counterparts.

In terms of ethnic retail, new suburban development patterns have emerged in North America over the past two decades. Chinese shopping centres are by far the most prominent and rapidly growing examples in Toronto and Vancouver, in

Case Example 2: Ethnic Shopping Centre Development

A number of features distinguish the ethnic Chinese shopping centres from the mainstream shopping malls in metropolitan Toronto (Preston and Lo 2000; Qadeer 1998; Wang 1999). Most of the Chinese shopping centres developed after 1990 are of *condominium ownership* (vs. leasehold), a model of development transplanted from Hong Kong by the new immigrants. In a condominium shopping centre, each unit is purchased and therefore owned by an individual investor. Individual owners then form a condominium corporation and collectively own the building and the shared spaces such as corridors and parking and loading areas. The condominium corporation levies common-area maintenance charges as its annual expenses to operate the entire facility and to develop a reserve fund for future renovations. Three explanations have been put forward for the popularity of condominium retailing among both developers and Chinese retailers (John Winter Associates Limited 1994; Wang 1999). First, condominium ownership spreads financing responsibilities from the developer to small investors. By selling instead of leasing units to investors, developers can get their investment returned faster and make a quicker profit. Besides, once the units are sold, developers need not worry about high vacancy rates during economic downturns. Second, by owning retail spaces, store owners do not have to pay periodic rent increases or percentage rent to developers or mall owners. Third, condominium ownership also provides investment and immigration opportunities.[2] Smart developers have tailored store units in condominium malls from 300 to 1,500 square feet (with some as small as 150 square feet) to suit the needs of various immigrant investors. It should be pointed out that development of condominium shopping centres was not entirely an ethnic enterprise. It was a market-led phenomenon in which opportunities for Chinese investors brought forth a response from both

Chinese and non-Chinese developers (Qadeer and Leung 1994). In fact, most large Chinese shopping centres were developed by non-Chinese developers and capital (Wang, Hii, Zhong, and Du 2013). For example, Pacific Mall was developed by Torgan Group; Market Village was built by Cedarland Properties Limited; First Markham Place was developed by Kerbel Group Inc., and Splendid China Tower was converted from a (mainstream) Canadian Tire hardware store to an ethnic Chinese mall by the Jewish-owned Splendid China Development Inc.

The way new Chinese businesses do business raised interesting questions concerning shopping centre design and marketing. Commonly, conventional shopping centres have three important features: anchor stores, a planned tenant mix, and consistent hours. Yet, each of these features is said to have been lost in the Chinese shopping malls. Anchor stores, usually referring to department stores, are considered to be engines of a shopping centre because anchors advertise and draw customers for the entire facility. Yet Chinese shopping centres have no conventional anchors at all. They comprise clusters of boutique-sized stores, with the largest being either a supermarket or a restaurant. Only recently has a Chinese-owned and operated chain of a junior department store—The Best Shop (大多百)—begun to anchor some Chinese shopping centres.[3] Developers of condominium malls were also criticized for ignoring business efficiencies. Once the units were sold and their capital investment with profit was returned, developers needed not worry about the business success of store owners. As a result, there was ineffective tenant mix control, which makes it difficult for mall management to adapt to market changes for the benefit of the facility as a whole.

The catalytic development strategy was the third important characteristic of Chinese shopping centre development. This refers to a development sequence in which the shopping centre predates residential development and may serve as a community focal point. In the outer suburbs, a number of new Chinese shopping centres were developed in the early 1990s at selected locations as "catalysts" to attract more Chinese immigrants to move into the surrounding areas. This catalyst strategy was not a Chinese invention, though; it was the norm of mainstream shopping centre development in North American cities in the 1970s (Jones and Simmons 1993). Nonetheless, this is in striking contrast with the older patterns of simultaneous growth in the central-city Chinatowns. The South Asian group is following a catalytic development strategy with several shopping centres emerging in selected suburbs in the Toronto area (Bascaramurty 2012).

In the United States, Asian-themed shopping centres are also commonly seen in a number of large metropolitan cities. In addition to new developments, some ethnic shopping centres resulted from the transformation of mainstream centres. A typical example is a Vietnamese shopping centre in the city of Falls Church in northern Virginia, a suburb of Washington, DC (Wood 2006). Ethnic Vietnamese retailing in northern Virginia began in the early 1970s (shortly after the end of the Vietnam War) due to a steady flow of Vietnamese immigrants. The first business locus was Clarendon, a commercial ribbon, and Arlington's downtown in the 1930s and 1940s. In the 1980s, Vietnamese Americans sought out alternative retail settings outside of the inner city, and Plaza Seven—a mainstream shopping centre—was chosen as the venue for new development. To begin with, a former grocery store in the plaza was replaced by a 20,000 square foot Vietnamese supermarket—Eden Center (which was named after a once-thriving shopping arcade in Saigon, to recreate a familiar retail environment). Soon after, more co-ethnic retailers followed suit, triggering the transformation of the mainstream plaza into a community hub to meet the needs of the Vietnamese Americans. Today, more than 100 stores cluster in the centre, where "signs are in Vietnamese, arcade music is Vietnamese, and the clientele is almost exclusively Vietnamese, or at least Asian" (Wood 2006:33). This has also become an example of immigrants altering traditional retail landscapes in contemporary metropolitan areas. Like many large Chinese shopping centres in Toronto that were developed by non-Chinese developers, Plaza Seven is owned by a non-Vietnamese developer—Norman Ebenstein of Boca Raton, Florida (Wood 2006). Seeing business opportunities afforded by thriving ethnic retailing, the owner of Plaza Seven invested to expand the centre by adding new retail and parking spaces, plus an Asian-style pagoda gate at the entrance of the plaza (similar to the gate at Mississauga's Chinese Centre in Toronto).

Canada, and in San Francisco and Los Angeles, in the US. This new type of ethnic retail development is attributed to strong demand, sufficient buying power, as well as market supply. With more than 1 million people, the Chinese are the second-largest group of ethnic minorities in Canada, after the South Asians (Statistics Canada 2006b). Yet there are many more Chinese shopping centres than South Asian–focused malls and plazas in Toronto and Vancouver. For example, there exist more than 60 Chinese shopping centres of various sizes in the Toronto Census Metropolitan Area, compared with fewer than 10 South Asian shopping centres. Having built a strong community with a high degree of institutional completeness, Chinese entrepreneurs and consumers are able to sustain a more self-sufficient economy (Qadeer 1997; Wang 1999; Wang and Lo 2007a, 2007b). In addition, Chinese corporate investment and business class immigrants injected large amounts of surplus capital into the local Canadian market (Li 1993). Over recent years an emergent retail form, the **condominium ethnic mall**, has been developed rapidly in selected suburban areas of fast-growing metropolitan markets. For example, Pacific Mall in Markham, a suburb of Toronto, has more than 300 ethnic retail units within a footprint of just over 270,000 square feet—with an average store size of less than 300 square feet. The South Asian group is following in these footsteps, and several South Asian shopping centres are emerging across the Greater Toronto Area (Bascaramurty 2012).

Conclusion

Ethnic retailing is not only essential to immigrant community life, but also has become a distinct and increasingly important component of the urban retail system by supporting a growing submarket driven by large immigrant populations. However, our knowledge of the nature and dynamics of ethnic retailing is still limited, especially in relation to its spatial and physical dimensions. Questions regarding locations, sizes, retail forms, development patterns, identity construction, and processes and mechanisms underlying visual changes in streetscapes remain largely unanswered. How do you best plan for ethnic retail? Should there be separate policies supporting ethnic business formation to facilitate immigrant integration and societal diversity? Current gaps in research affect our knowledge of the nature of ethnic retail activities and their impact on urban space, as well as the role that public policy and associated stakeholders (such as municipal planners) have in addressing related issues, and the role in their final resolution. To date, the differences between ethnic and mainstream retailing have caused a series of conflicts among planners and the public. Retail planning policies tend to use a hierarchical system to classify shopping centres at the neighbourhood, community, and regional levels based on several criteria, such as floor area, store numbers, market size, and sales (Jones 2000, 2005; Jones and Simmons 1993; Yeates 1998, 2000). However, when planning ethnic malls, this hierarchical system is inadequate in determining parking standards, retail sizes and uses, retail facilities (e.g. anchor stores), and retail forms.

Public policy at the municipal level on issues of economic development, land use, and transportation planning in relation to ethnic retail development has been relatively uninformed. As ethnic retailing evolves from a niche to the mainstream, there is a growing need to explore the processes underlying the spatial and physical changes of ethnic retail so as to better accommodate ethnic businesses, facilitate the expression of ethnic identity in the commercial landscape, and realize the economic potential of immigrant entrepreneurs. Fundamentally, the impacts of ethnic retailing and the ethnic consumer are complex and far-reaching. There is an increasing need for debate between policymakers and the stakeholders involved in ethnic retail development and business formation, so that the land-use planners, developers, and business owners/investors (including retailers) can better understand the dynamics and complexities of ethnic retailing and the communities and consumers that they serve.

Notes

1. The retail geography literature does not classify retail activities as ethnic, except for the notions of the ethnic strip and the ethnic shopping centre in the typology of the urban retail system and structure (Jones 2000). Moreover, the International Council of Shopping Centers (ICSC) makes no distinction between ethnic and nonethnic shopping centres in either their Canadian or US Shopping Centre definitions (see www.icsc.org).

2. According to Canada's business immigrant program, revised in the mid-1980s (Government of Canada 1993), immigrants applying to enter Canada as investors must have accumulated a wealth of $500,000 or more and promise to make a productive investment of at least $250,000 in direct business ventures and create some jobs in Canada, before landed immigrant status can be granted. To investors from Hong Kong, $250,000 is far from an astronomical figure, for it is equivalent only to the price of a modest apartment in Hong Kong and is a relatively low price to buy a residence permit to live in Canada.

3. Four Best Shop department stores now anchor Mississauga's Golden Square Centre, Markham's Pacific Mall and Century Plaza, and Scarborough's Oriental Centre.

Questions for Critical Thought

1. What is the social and economic importance of ethnic retailing in a multicultural society?
2. How has ethnic retail evolved over time?
3. What factors contribute to the successful development of ethnic retailing? Are some ethnic groups more successful than others? If so, why?
4. What is the role of local government planning with regard to ethnic retail places?

Key Readings

Wang, S., R. Hii, J. Zhong, and P. Du (2013) Recent Trends in Ethnic Chinese Retailing
in Metropolitan Toronto. *International Journal of Applied Geospatial Research*
3(4):49–66.

Wang, S. and J. Zhong (2013) *Delineating Ethnoburbs in Metropolitan Toronto*. (CERIS
Working Paper No. 100). Toronto: CERIS—The Ontario Metropolis Centre.
www.ceris.metropolis.net/wp-content/uploads/2013/04/CWP_100_Wang_Zhong.pdf

Zhuang, Z. (2015) Planning for Diversity in a Suburban Retrofit Context: The Case Study of
Ethnic Shopping Malls. In. R. Thomas (ed.) *Planning Canada: A Case Study Approach*.
Toronto: Oxford University Press. Forthcoming in 2015.

Media Links

In-Store Trends: Ethnic Retailing:

www.instoretrends.com/index.php/tag/ethnic-retailing

This website is maintained by RetailNet Group and interprets ethnic retailing as a new
trend in the larger retail industry, with case studies in the United States.

Canadian Ethnic Retailing:

salesisnotsimple.com/ethnic-retailing-in-canada

This website is maintained by the consulting firm SINS and interprets ethnic retailing, with
case studies in Canada.

T & T Supermarket:

www.tnt-supermarket.com/en/cprofile.php

This is the corporate website of T & T Supermarket. Students can read the corporate
profile, mission statement, and news releases.

References

Bascaramurty, D. (2012) The Rise and Fall of the Ethnic Mall. *Globe and Mail*, 15 June.

Bonacich, E. and J. Modell (1980) *The Economic Basis of Ethnic Solidarity: Small Businesses
in the Japanese American Community*. Berkeley, CA: University of California Press.

Borjas, G. (1997) *To Ghetto or Not to Ghetto: Ethnicity and Residential Segregation*.
Cambridge, MA: National Bureau of Economic Research.

Bourne, L.S. and D. Rose (2001) The Changing Face of Canada: The Uneven Geographies of Population and Social Change. *The Canadian Geographer* 45(1):105–119.

Citizenship and Immigration Canada (2011) The Permanent Residents Data. Ottawa: CIC.

Foner, N. (1997) What's New about Transnationalism? New York Immigrants Today and at the Turn of the Century. *Diaspora* 6(3):355–375.

Gale, D. (1972) The Impact of Canadian Italians on Retail Functions and Facades in Vancouver, 1921–1961. In Julian V. Minghi (ed.) *People of the Living Land: Geography of Cultural Diversity in British Columbia*. Vancouver: Tantalus Research.

Government of Canada (1993) Immigration and Doing Business in Canada. Ottawa: Government of Canada.

Hernandez, T., J. Helik, and P. Moore (2006) The Changing Character of Retail Strips in the City of Toronto: 1996–2005. CSCA Research Report 2006–07, Centre for the Study of Commercial Activity, Ryerson University, Toronto.

Hiebert, D. (1993) Integrating Production and Consumption: Industry, Class, Ethnicity, and the Jews of Toronto. In L. Bourne and D. Ley (eds.) *The Changing Social Geography of Canadian Cities*. Montreal: McGill-Queen's University Press.

Hiebert, D. (2000) Immigration and the Changing Canadian City. *The Canadian Geographer* 44(1):25–43.

Hyndman, J. and M. Walton-Roberts (1999) *Transnational Migration and Nation: Burmese Refugees in Vancouver*. Vancouver: Research on Immigration and Integration in the Metropolis.

Jackson, P. (2002) Commercial Cultures: Transcending the Cultural and the Economic. *Progress in Human Geography* 26(1):3–18.

John Winter Associates Limited (1994) Condominium Retailing in Markham: A Consulting Report Prepared for the Planning Department, Town of Markham. Toronto: John Winter Associates.

Jones, K. (2000) Dynamics of the Canadian Retail Environment. In T. Bunting and P. Filion (eds.) *Canadian Cities in Transition*, pp. 404–422. Don Mills, ON: Oxford University Press.

Jones, K. (2005) Retail Sector Planning in the Greater Toronto Area (English Version). In B.M. Massam and S.S. Han (eds.) *Urban Planning Overseas 2005: Special Issues on Urban Planning in Toronto*, pp. 66–75. Toronto: Urban Studies Program, York University.

Jones, K. and J. Simmons (1993) *Location, Location, Location: Analyzing the Retail Environment*. 2nd ed. Scarborough, ON: Nelson Canada.

Kaplan, D. (1998) The Spatial Structure of Urban Ethnic Economies. *Urban Geography* 19(6):489–501.

Kobayashi, A. (1993) Multiculturalism: Representing a Canadian Institution. In J. Duncan and D. Ley (eds.) *Place/Culture/Representation*. New York: Routledge.

Li, P.S. (1993) Chinese Investment and Business in Canada: Ethnic Entrepreneurship Reconsidered. *Pacific Affairs* 66:219–243.

Li, W. (1998a) Anatomy of a New Ethnic Settlement: The Chinese Ethnoburb in Los Angeles. *Urban Studies* 35(3):479–501.

Li, W. (1998b) Los Angeles' Chinese Ethnoburb: From Ethnic Service Center to Global Economy Outpost. *Urban Geography* 19(6):502–517.

Light, I. and S.J. Gold (2000) *Ethnic Economies*. San Diego: Academic Press.

Light, I., G. Sabagh, B. Mehdi, and C. Der-Martirosian (1994) Beyond the Ethnic Enclave Economy. *Social Problems* 41(1):65–80.

Lo, L., V. Preston, S. Wang, L. Reil, E. Havey, and B. Siu (2000) *Immigrants' Economic Status in Toronto: Rethinking Settlement and Integration Strategies*. Toronto: Joint Centre of Excellence for Research on Immigration and Settlement-Toronto (CERIS). Working Paper No. 15.

Lo, L. and S. Wang (1997) Settlement Patterns of Toronto's Chinese Immigrants: Convergence or Divergence? *Canadian Journal of Regional Science* 20:49–72.

Marger, M.N. and C.A. Horffman (1992) Ethnic Enterprises in Ontario: Immigrant Participation in the Small Business Sector. *International Migration Review* 26:969–981.

Nee, V. and J.M. Sanders (1994) Job Transitions in an Immigrant Metropolis: Ethnic Boundaries and the Mixed Economy. *American Sociological Review* 59(6):849–872.

Norris, D. and T. Hernandez (2008) Implications of Demographic Change for Retailers. CSCA Research Report 2008–06, Centre for the Study of Commercial Activity, Ryerson University, Toronto.

Portes, A. and R.L. Bach (1985) *Latin Journey: Cuban and Mexican Immigrants in the United States*. Berkeley, CA: University of California Press.

Portes, A. and L. Jensen (1992) Disproving the Enclave Hypothesis. *American Sociological Review* 57:418–420.

Portes, A. and R. Manning (1986) The Immigrant Enclave Theory and Empirical Examples. In S. Olzak and J. Nagel (eds.) *Competitive Ethnic Relations*, pp. 47–68. New York: Academic Press.

Preston, V. and L. Lo (2000) Asian Theme Malls in Suburban Toronto: Land Use Conflict in Richmond Hill. *Canadian Geographer* 44(2):182–190.

Qadeer, M.A. (1997) Pluralistic Planning for Multicultural Cities. *APA Journal* 63(4):481–494.

Qadeer, M.A. (1998) *Ethnic Malls and Plazas: Chinese Commercial Developments in Scarborough, Ontario*. Working Paper. Toronto: Joint Centre of Excellence for Research on Immigration and Settlement (CERIS).

Qadeer, M.A. (2003) Ethnic Segregation in Toronto and the New Multiculturalism. (Research Bulletin #12). Toronto: Centre for Urban and Community Studies.

Qadeer, M.A. and A. Leung (1994) The Planning System and the Development of Chinese Shopping Malls in Suburban Scarborough, Ontario (unpublished research report).

Ray, B. (2009) So Where Is Ethnocultural Diversity in Canadian Cities? *Plan Canada* Special Edition:83–88.

Reitz, J.G. (1998) Measuring Down: The Economic Performance of New Canadians is Declining; If We Want to Change That, We Need to Rethink Immigration Policy. In C. Davies (ed.) *Post 2000: Business Wisdom for the Next Century*, pp. 157–163. Toronto: Key Porter Books.

Sanders, J.M. and V. Nee (1987) Limits of Ethnic Solidarity in the Enclave Economy. *American Sociological Review* 52:745–773.

Sanders, J.M. and V. Nee (1992) Problem in Resolving the Enclave Economy Debate. *American Sociological Review* 57(3):415–418.

Simmons, J., S. Kamikihara, and T. Hernandez (2010) *Ethnic Markets in the Greater Toronto Area*. Toronto: Centre for the Study of Commercial Activity, Ryerson University.

Sinopoli, T. (1996) *The Diversity of Retail Strips in Metropolitan Toronto*. Toronto: Centre of the Study of Commercial Activity, Ryerson University.

Statistics Canada (2006a) Immigration in Canada: A Portrait of the Foreign-born Population, 2006 Census. Ottawa: Government of Canada.

Statistics Canada (2006b) Canada's Ethnocultural Mosaic, 2006 Census. Ottawa: Government of Canada.

Statistics Canada (2013) 2011 National Household Survey: Immigration, Place of Birth, Citizenship, Ethnic Origin, Visible Minorities, Language and Religion. www.statcan.gc.ca/daily-quotidien/130508/dq130508b-eng.htm

Strauss, M. (2009) Loblaws Buys Asian Grocery Chain. *Globe and Mail*, 24 July.

Strauss, M. (2011) Ethnic Consumer the Goal for New Loblaws President. *Globe and Mail*, 24 February.

Teixeira, C. (1998) Cultural Resources and Ethnic Entrepreneurship: A Case Study of the Portuguese Real Estate Industry in Toronto. *Canadian Geographer* 42:267–281.

Thompson, R.H. (1989) *Toronto's Chinatown: The Changing Social Organization of an Ethnic Community*. New York: AMS Press.

Walton-Roberts, M. and D. Hiebert (1997) Immigration, Entrepreneurship, and the Family: Indo-Canadian Enterprise in the Construction Industry of Greater Vancouver. *Canadian Journal of Regional Science* 21:119–140.

Wang, L. and L. Lo (2007a) Immigrant Grocery-Shopping Behavior: Ethnic Identity versus Accessibility. *Environment and Planning A* 39:684–699.

Wang, L. and L. Lo (2007b) Global Connectivity, Local Consumption, and Chinese Immigrant Experience. *GeoJournal* 68:183–194.

Wang, S. (1999) Chinese Commercial Activity in the Toronto CMA: New Development Patterns and Impacts. *Canadian Geographer* 43(1):19–35.

Wang, S., R. Hii, J. Zhong, and P. Du (2013) Recent Trends in Ethnic Chinese Retailing in Metropolitan Toronto. *International Journal of Applied Geospatial Research* 3(4):49–66.

Wilson, K.L. and A. Portes (1980) Immigrant Enclaves: An Analysis of the Labor Market Experiences of Cubans in Miami. *American Journal of Sociology* 86:295–319.

Wood, J.S. (2006) Making America at Eden Center. In Wei Li (ed.) *From Urban Enclave to Ethnic Suburbs: New Asian Communities in Pacific Rim Countries*. Honolulu, HI: University of Hawai'i Press.

Yeates, M. (1998) *The North American City*. 5th ed. New York: Longman.

Yeates, M. (2000) *The GTA @ Y2K: The Dynamics of Change in the Commercial Structure of the Greater Toronto Area*. Toronto: Centre for the Study of Commercial Activity, Ryerson University.

Yeates, M. (2011) *Charting the GTA*. Toronto: Centre for the Study of Commercial Activity, Ryerson University.

Zhou, M. and J.R. Logan (1989) Returns on Human Capital in Ethnic Enclaves: New York City's Chinatown. *American Sociological Review* 54(5):809–920.

Zukin, S. (1995) *The Cultures of Cities*. Cambridge, MA: Blackwell.

Chapter 10

IMMIGRANT WOMEN IN CANADA AND THE UNITED STATES

LESLIE NICHOLS AND VAPPU TYYSKÄ

Introduction

Canada and the United States are nations with large numbers of immigrants. In Canada, according to 2011 census figures, 20.6% of the population is foreign-born, the largest proportion in the wealthy G8 countries. Most new immigrants are from Asia, with the three leading source countries in 2011 being the Philippines, China, and India (Canada Press 2013). In the total Canadian population, 19.1% are members of **racialized** groups and three-quarters of them are immigrants (Citizenship and Immigration Canada 2012). Comparatively, in the United States close to 13% of the population are immigrants, with Asians being the largest category (Monger and Yankay 2013). In 2010, about 28% of the American population were members of racialized groups, with the largest growth between 2000 and 2010 among the Hispanic population (Ennis, Rios-Vargas, and Albert 2011). European immigrants in both countries are a minority in recent years (Monger and Yankay 2013).

The gender balance is reflective of the general landscape of **immigration**. Over the past two decades women have outnumbered men as migrants (Labadie-Jackson 2008–2009). In fact, over half of the world's 214 million migrants are women (Deen 2013). As of 2011, one in five women in Canada was foreign born (Chui 2011), while in the US, **immigrant women** made up 12% of the female population in 2008 (Batalova 2009). South Asian and Hispanic women are the largest groups of immigrant women in Canada and the United States, respectively.

Against this backdrop, this chapter will show that "immigrant women" is a diverse category with respect to age, education, social class, family status, region, and membership in racialized groups. The chapter will outline the social construction of "immigrant women" as a category, based on the colonial history of Canada and the United States. It will address the issues faced by female migrants at different stages of their lives: as children and youth, adults, and older adults. For adult women, there will be a focus on employment outcomes and family lives including spousal relations, mothering, and interpersonal violence (IPV). The issues of identity and belonging faced by first- and second-generation young women will be taken up, along with the specific needs of senior immigrant women. While the focus will be on permanent residents, we will also provide examples from other migrant categories (refugees, temporary workers, undocumented migrants) where relevant.

Historical Considerations: The Social Construction of "Immigrant Women"

Canada and the United States are clear examples of "settler" nations, in which colonizers came to a "new land" forging a new emphasis of a common destiny for all—an **imagined community** (Anderson 1983). Since the earliest days of the settlement of new world **colonies**, immigrant women have remained marginalized and disadvantaged in the establishment and perpetuation of the imagined communities of Canada and the United States. Gender and **race** are points of social identity that are often used to marginalize and categorize immigrants. The term immigrant woman is customarily used to label many women of colour, whether they are immigrants or not. "Immigrant woman" is a social category that names not only women who have come to live in Canada or United States permanently, but specifically those women who do not fit the national idea of a woman, based on their characteristics or presumed social location (Folson 2004:30, 31).

When Canada and the United States were first colonized, British immigrant women were seen as co-creators of the imagined community, whose main role was to give birth to and raise British subjects. In the early years of **settlement**, women were only considered "immigrants" if they did not conform to a standard white British ideal (Arat-Koç 2006a:200; Roberts 1979:201). Therefore, the creation of the nation-state involved the process of **othering** certain populations within and outside the Canadian and American state (Baines and Sharma 2002:85). For instance, in the history of the United States, the European- and British-based immigration flows (the "old" or "settler" immigrants) only started to diversify in the late 1800s. At that time, industrial and farm workers were arriving also from Asia, Mexico, and French

Canada (the "new" or "labour" migrants), not fitting the old ideals, and being othered (Gabaccia 2003:8–9).

In the case of Canada, the process of constructing an imagined Canadian woman was intimately tied to the larger colonialist and imperialist project of settling the nation and imagining its appropriate community and colour (Folson 2004; Carter 1996; Dua 2004, Arat-Koç 2006a). White women settlers, rather than Indigenous women, were positioned as the "mothers of the nation" (Folson 2004; Arat-Koç 2006a); they would reproduce the nation as appropriate marital partners and mothers who would give birth and raise its citizens. From the beginning of the colonization process, British immigrant women were not seen as outsiders, but rather co-settlers with their male counterparts. As Barbara Roberts (1979:201) notes, "the nation was the home and the home was the women; all were best British."

Along with indigenous women, racialized Immigrant women did not fit into the imagined community. In 1908, the government declared that immigrants needed $200 to enter Canada and must travel to the country in one continuous journey (Dua 2004), effectively prohibiting South Asian women's entry. Conversely, a "bachelor society" of working male immigrants allowed the Canadian state and employers to keep the immigrant males' income artificially low on the grounds that they did not have families to support (Das Gupta 2000:229). At the same time, however, many advocated allowing South Asian women to enter the country out of fear that South Asian men would marry white women and "dilute" Canadian identity (Dua 2000:59, 68). It was not until 1919 that South Asian married women were permitted to enter Canada (Das Gupta 2000: 221). This same logic was at work again in the government's decision to implement a **head tax** on Chinese immigrants in the late nineteenth and early twentieth century (Das Gupta 2000:220). In these two examples we can see how would-be immigrant women were constructed as a liability to the cultural and economic health of Canada's emerging imagined community and as a result were often simply refused entry to the country. And, when they were permitted entry, it was due to a fear that their absence would create a mixed race culture like the Métis (Carter 1996), who are offspring of the French Canadian population and First Nations. It is clear that racist and sexist sentiments have played a central role in guiding Canadian immigration policy.

The same process is echoed in what occurred in the United States; the second migration movement, as noted above, mostly consisted of bachelors. It was not until post-1965 that, as a result of a domestic civil rights legislation, more gender-balanced immigration emerged (Gabaccia 2003:9). In Canada, the improvements in gender ratios are clearly linked to a goal of providing appropriate wives and mothers for the nation; these women were hurried through an immigration process with "selection, protection and supervision procedures" (Roberts 1979:191) that examined their values, morals, and general intellectual and physical health.

That race is a consideration in addition to gender in immigration policy is exemplified in the case of black Caribbean women, who came to Canada as domestic workers, after the first wave of British and Finnish domestic immigrants to Canada (1900–1930) (Das Gupta 2000:222). Unlike the group of white European women, Caribbean domestics were given temporary contracts and were not allowed to change their immigrant status once in Canada. When their contracts were done or not renewed, they were forced to go home, their job and status being entirely tied to their employer. It was not until 1981 that this group of immigrant women domestics (by now also including an increasing number of Filipinas) was finally allowed to apply for immigration to Canada after two years of employment (Das Gupta 2000). This immigrant community of female domestic workers has always been marginalized; originally, they were supposed to be single and only here temporarily and, even though this policy has changed throughout the years, the family reunification of this category of migrant women is still poor (Das Gupta 2000:224; Arat-Koç 2006a). Ironically, the very women who are good enough to raise white Canadian children cannot raise their own children, who are not allowed entry with them (Das Gupta 2000:224).

Concerns over **social reproduction**, labour costs, and the welfare state also inform much recent immigration policy. Grace Chang outlines the panic in California over the presence of undocumented Mexican immigrant women who are seen to be a "burden to the state" and a drain on social welfare budgets (Chang 2000:2). The **sexism** in these assumptions ignores the ways in which immigrant women support working men in the home and therefore contribute to the economy through their unpaid domestic work, including childcare. Instead, the belief that these immigrant women absorb social welfare costs led to legislative changes (Chang 2000) that included a reduction of all kinds of social assistance, particularly to undocumented immigrants. Critics argue that as a result of this treatment, immigrant women are structurally disadvantaged as they are rendered "more receptive to scorned, low-paid service jobs once they arrive" (Chang 2000:16).

There are around 11 million undocumented immigrants in the United States, and the numbers of women among them are on the rise, from less than 20% 2 decades ago to around 34 to 45% currently. Women's share has risen simply because of rising poverty levels south of the border (see Case Example 1), and despite the hardships and dangers of crossing the border, these women share the sentiment "it's worth it" (Alvarez and Broder 2006).

Case Example 1: More and More, Women Risk All to Enter US

TUCSON—It took years for Normaeli Gallardo, a single mother from Acapulco, to drum up the courage to join the growing stream of Mexican women illegally crossing the border on the promise of a job, in her case working in a Kansas meatpacking plant for $5.15 an hour.

First, she had to grapple with the idea of landing in an unfamiliar country, all alone, with no grasp of English and no place to live.

Then she had to imagine crossing the Arizona desert, where immigrants face heat exhaustion by day, frostbite by night and the cunning of the "coyotes"—smugglers who charge as much as $1,500 to guide people into the United States and who make a habit of robbing and sexually assaulting them.

And finally, Ms. Gallardo, 38, who earned $50 a week at an Acapulco hotel, had to contemplate life without her two vivacious daughters, Isabel, 7, and Fernanda, 5. That once unimaginable trade-off—leaving her children behind so they could one day leave poverty behind—had suddenly become her only option.

She simply did not earn enough money, she said. If she paid the electric bill, she fell behind on rent; if she paid the water bill, she could forget about new clothes for the children.

[…]

Undaunted by a backlash against illegal immigrants here, Ms. Gallardo is part of what some experts say is a largely unnoticed phenomenon: the increasing number of women, many without male companions, enduring danger and the risk of capture to come to the United States to work and to settle.

[…]

Source: Alvarez and Broder 2006. Retrieved from www.nytimes.com/2006/01/10/national/10women.html?pagewanted=print&_r=0

Feminist and Intersectional Analysis

Feminism can help us better understand the ways in which women of various social positions and identities have differential access to rights and citizenship (Das Gupta 2000:222). Feminist scholars identify a difference between sex and gender. Sex is biologically determined, while gender consists of the social constructions that are developed around sex and that function "to maintain social hierarchy" (Browne and Misra 2003:489–490). The hierarchy in question is manifested in patriarchal social relations, which privilege the needs and demands of men over those of women. In sum, the main assumption of feminist thought is that gender is a social construct used to support patriarchal forms of oppression. For feminists, patriarchy permeates all aspects of private (family) and public life, including the structures of the state (Randall 2010). Analyzing the experiences of different groups of women brought in under different immigration schemes, through an **intersectionality** lens, can highlight the "complex and sometimes contradictory intersection of gender, class, race and nationality" (Arat-Koç 2006a:199). These intersections are evident in immigrant women's experiences in economy and the family, as will be detailed below.

Adult Immigrant Women

Employment and Economic Experiences

Research on Canadian immigrants indicates that 1) economic difficulties are common for many years following migration to Canada; 2) more recent immigrants are not doing as well as those who immigrated to Canada prior to the 1990s; and 3) compared to Canadian-born degree holders those immigrants who hold degrees do not fare as well, particularly if race is taken into account. To this we can add that 4) the reason for the poorer economic outcomes of more recent immigrants has to be linked to their racialized status. Further, 5) the difficult economic situation that newcomers face leads to difficulties in finding affordable housing and accessing healthcare, education, and training, along with low rates of home ownership (Tyyskä 2007).

Taking gender into account further complicates this picture. Immigrant men in both Canada and the United States are overrepresented as the principal applicant (the person making the immigration application) in the economic class, due to the tendency of men to be primary breadwinners. In fact during 2012 in Canada, 51.5% of men entered as the primary applicant, while 57.6% of women entered through the family class (Citizenship and Immigration Canada 2012). Similarly, in the United States during 2011, 51.6% of male immigrants were primary applicants compared to

Figure 10.1

Primary versus Family Class Applicants to Canada

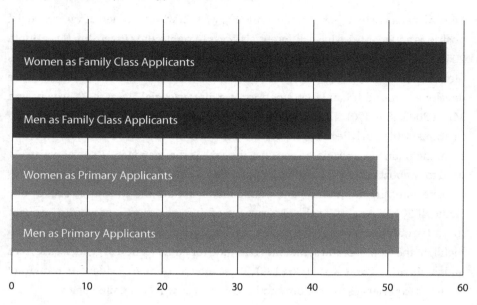

Source: Citizenship and Immigration Canada (2012). Canada Facts and Figures: Immigration Overview Permanent and Temporary Residents. www.cic.gc.ca/english/pdf/research-stats/facts2012.pdf

women's 52.6% in the family class (Homeland Security 2012).

The employment rates of immigrant women are a few percentage points lower than those of native-born women. In 2009, 51.4% of American immigrant women were employed (Batalova 2009), while the rate in Canada in the same year was 47.9 % (Statistics Canada 2011). Comparatively, 53.6% of native-born American women were employed in 2010 (Gibbs 2012) and 50.1% native-born Canadian women were employed in 2009 (Ferrao 2010). In keeping with these statistics, unemployment rates are high for most immigrant women. Women immigrants to Canada in 2009 had an unemployment rate of 7.0%, while in 2012, the unemployment rate in this category was 8.4% in the US (Chui 2012; United States Bureau of Labor 2013).

There is a clear **gender division of labour** between women and men in Canada and the US, whereby women tend to occupy service and caring work while men more commonly occupy manual labour positions in the primary and secondary sectors. This also holds for immigrants. Immigrant women in the US tend to work in office and administration support, nursing and domestic work, sales, and related industries while men work in construction, manufacturing, and extraction (Pearce 2006:1). Powers and Seltzer note that women tend to not advance in their careers as

Figure 10.2
Primary versus Family Class Applicants in the United States

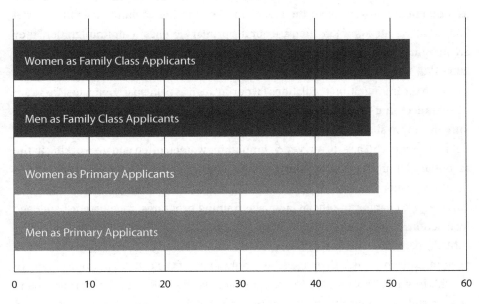

Source: Homeland Security (2012, 2011) Yearbook of Immigration Statistics: Office of Immigration Statistics. Washington, DC: U.S. Department of Homeland Security, Office of Immigration Statistics. www.dhs.gov/sites/default/files/publications/immigration-statistics/yearbook/2011/ois_yb_2011.pdf

much as men, and end up holding fewer managerial and other powerful positions (1998:478). This is in keeping with the general distinction between men as primary breadwinners and women as primary caregivers in families. Meanwhile, there is evidence that many immigrant women in Canada tend to find full-time employment faster than immigrant men because they are willing to accept any survival job (Ali and Kilbride 2004).

This gender-based division of work is reflected in wages. In 2003 in America, 61.7% of immigrant women had a yearly income of less than US$25,000 compared to 54.4% of native-born women and 47.8% of immigrant men (Pearce 2006:2). Furthermore, in 2003 only 5.2% of immigrant women had an annual wage of US$75,000 or more, compared to 4.7% of native-born women and 10.8% of immigrant men (Pearce 2006:2). In Canada, the median income for immigrant women in 2010 was C$15,590 for very recent immigrants who arrived that same year (Statistics Canada 2013).

Immigrant women's economic and cultural **integration** is directly linked to the way women are positioned in immigration policy (Gabriel 2006; Arat-Koç 1999). Current Canadian immigration policies tend to favour those who have money, investments, or significant **human capital** (education, training, occupational skills, experience, and official language facility), as reflected in the **points system** introduced in 1967 (Gabriel 2006:162, 164, 171; Man 2004:135). The immigrant is positioned as a potential contributor to the labour market and the economy overall (Gabriel 2006:164). Because women often are not the primary applicant for immigration, they are marginalized in terms of their perceived lack of economic contributions (Gabriel 2006:172, 164; Arat-Koç 1999:36).

With the immigration regulations favouring men as principal applicants, there are benefits accruing to them. For example, Canadian language training programs were initially only available to men as the main breadwinners (Arat-Koç 1999:39). This is not in keeping with a reality in which immigrant women often end up working in the secondary labour market, supporting a male spouse as they complete their settlement programs, thereby contributing to the Canadian economy (Thobani 2000:39, 40). Despite changes in official language training programs, the current Language Instruction for Newcomers to Canada (LINC) and Labour Market Language Training (LMLT) programs are not gender neutral. They limit eligibility to those who have been in Canada for less than a year and only some of the centres provide childcare for children from six months to six years old. Despite this childcare service, many women still miss language classes due to caring for children who are unable to attend their childcare facilities due to illness or other issues (Pothier 2012).

The suppression of immigrant women's potential economic contributions through legislative means is also evident in the United States, as the previous example of Mexican immigrant women (Chang 2000) illustrates. Another example is the case of immigrant nurses. Between 1965 and 1985, 25,000 nurses from the Philippines migrated to the United States through the Immigration and Nationality Act Amendments (1965), which accepted applications from people in preferred occupations, including nurses (Grammage 2003:84). Ultimately, these nurses ended up as a nursing underclass, also due to the devaluing of their foreign credentials (Choy 2000:123).

In Canada (although this also applies to the US), Sheryl Nestel (2006) notes how this phenomenon of professional **gatekeeping** (Li 2008) operates to exclude many immigrant women. For example, immigrant midwives lack the resources necessary to become registered in Canada, such as social networks or access to organizations and volunteer jobs to get experience. This information is often not shared with them and as a result can be seen as a kind of "white knowledge" (Nestel 2006:14).

Immigrant Women and Families

Spousal Relations

It should be no surprise that transnational living can stress spousal relations; lengthy separations can result in extramarital affairs, couples growing apart, and negative emotions including "jealousy, hostility, depression and indifference" (Tyyskä 2012:107). Yet Guida Man (2003) found that while some Chinese immigrant women living in Vancouver, BC, Canada, dealt with spousal estrangement and extramarital affairs, others noted improvements in their spousal relationships while also reporting reduced domestic burdens because higher incomes allowed for the hiring of household help.

Some research indicates that immigrant women's employment may result in more egalitarian gender and family relations (Jain and Belsky 1997; Anisef, Kilbride, Ochocka, and Janzen 2001). However, research also indicates that women's employment may put pressure on men to perform domestic work, resulting in a loss of the traditional male breadwinner role and a negative impact on men's self-esteem (Ali and Kilbride 2004). Changes in traditional gender arrangements can at times result in tensions that can lead to either the onset or escalation of male violence against women and children (Tyyskä 2005, 2008).

Often within families, whether immigrant or nonmigrant, the husband/father holds more status than the wife/mother (Tyyskä 2002a, 2002b, 2003a). Intimate partner violence (IPV) is traditionally linked to patriarchy, which is present in all cultural groups. Studies of prevalence of IPV in immigrant families compared to nonmigrant families are mostly inconclusive. For example, a study by Janice Du Mont and associates (2012) found that immigrant women who have lived in Canada for more than 20 years and Canadian-born women reported no difference in risk of abuse. The accuracy of family violence rates is also in question, due to reluctance to report. Some American studies indicate that, when socioeconomic factors are taken into account, there is no difference from other social groups in rates of partner violence (Tjaden and Theonnes 2000; González-Guarda, Vasquez, and Mitrani 2000). Therefore, the higher rates in IPV among Hispanics over "whites" (Caetano, Field, Ramisetty-Mikler, and McGarth 2005) may reflect socioeconomic differences, in that the Hispanic population is one of the most economically marginalized in the US.

The issue of economic and other immigrant settlement stressors figures prominently in research on family violence. As stated above, some immigrant women and also adolescents may find employment more readily than immigrant men, challenging traditional hierarchies, which can be manifested in family violence or conflict (Smith 2004; Creese, Dyck, and McLaren 1999). Both Canadian and US research has shown that there is a connection between loss of employment status and an increase in the level of male/father aggression (Tyyskä 2005:127–128; González-Guarda et al.

Case Example 2: Honour a Key Theme in Shafia Trial (Chung 2012)

Honour killings, according to experts, are on the rise in the world. They take place most often in the Middle East, North Africa and parts of South Asia. As many as 5,000 women and girls are murdered every year in these types of killings, according to a 2000 United Nations Population Fund report. In 1999, at least 1,000 women were killed in Pakistan alone.

Sexual chastity and virginity are often at the centre of these cases. Many of the women who are killed have been raped, and the perpetrator is often a member of their own extended family. In some places, the perpetrators of the honour killing are excused or given light sentences since the family's "dishonour" is taken into account.

A recent example of honour killings is that of an Afghani immigrant family in Montreal, Canada. In 2012, Mohammad Shafia, his wife Tooba Mohammad Yahya, and their eldest son, Hamed, were charged and convicted with killing sisters Zainab (19), Sahar (17), and Geeti (13) and Shafia's first wife, Rona Amir Mohammad. During the trial it was revealed that the murders were preceded by abuse reported to the police and school authorities and a suicide attempt by one of the daughters. Shahrzad Mojab, a University of Toronto professor and an expert on honour killings, points out that though it's often associated with Islam, the practice exists among Hindus, Jews, and Christians, and is not specific to Arabs of the Middle East (Chung 2012). She states, "It's really about men's need to control women's sexuality and freedom" (Chung 2012).

2009). Rosa M. González-Guarda and associates (2009), also show violence as more likely within Hispanic couples where the woman makes more money than her male partner. This connection shows up in Canadian interviews with immigrant women who report that abuse either began (Tyyskä 2009a) or intensified (Tyyskä 2005, 2008) upon immigration.

Changes in family composition may make it even more difficult for women to cope with violence. Many current immigrants arrive from countries where they had lived in extended families. As family members separate in migration, this possible source of deterrence to violence is removed (Morrison, Guruge, and Snarr 1999; Tyyskä 2008).

Lewis Okun notes that in the United States, women often take between 2.5 and 5 attempts to leave an unhealthy relationship before they are ultimately successful (1988:107, 113). Leaving a violent situation is made more complex by immigrant and racialized status. Anti-racist feminism takes into consideration the complex intersections between gender and race (Abbott and Wallace 1997). In keeping with this theory, racialized women may view the family as a safe place from the harsh racist realities of the public world, despite the possible presence of violence in their lives. Rather than wanting to escape the traditional family, they will uphold it (Moghissi 1999). This attitude may contribute to keeping family violence a private matter, particularly in racialized immigrant families, in order to avoid the stigma. The cultural sensitivity in the community service–providing sector is not necessarily present to address this (Dinshaw 2005; Tyyskä, Dinshaw, Redmond, and Gomes 2012). The difficulties of addressing the issue are most starkly demonstrated in the case of "honour killings" of female members of the family. This topic is wrought with media sensationalism and misconceptions, as seen in Case Example 2.

Mothering

A key reason for migration is often the desire to improve children's lives. Canadian and American studies show that fear over children's potential economic hardships through their adulthood often leads to pressure exerted on children related to their education and career planning (Tyyskä 2005, 2006; Fuligni 1997).

Immigrant parents also worry about their children's relations and social behaviours with their peers (Wong 1999), spouse selection (Morrison, Guruge, and Snarr 1999; Zaidi and Shuraydi 2002), and maintenance of their culture (James 1999). There are often resultant tensions for immigrant youth, between their parents' expectations and their desire to fit into their social environment (Tyyskä 2003b, 2006). The general issue is captured in the **acculturation thesis**, which addresses the degree to which an immigrant assimilates into the host society. This means that there is an assumed progression toward adopting more of the "behaviours, rules, values, and norms of the host society" with each subsequent immigrant generation (Boyd and Norris 2000:138, in Tyyskä 2001:105–106), with different expectations between generations. The resultant clashes are often referred to as the "generation gap" between parents who connect to their original culture and their children who adjust more readily to mainstream norms and values (Tyyskä 2005, 2006, 2008).

Thus, parenting roles may be strained due to role reversals between parents and their children, due to children learning the official or dominant language and culture at faster rates (Anisef et al. 2001) or acting as "cultural brokers" for the parents in their dealings with mainstream institutions such as schools, hospitals, or social services (Ali and Kilbride 2004; Creese et al. 1999; Tyyskä 2005, 2006).

An added complication is separation from extended family. Many immigrant families are not based on the typical North American nuclear family unit but count more relatives as their closest kin (Creese et al. 1999). While some families are able to arrive as multigenerational units (Noivo 1993), not every family is so lucky. Rather, it is common for one parent to arrive, followed by a spouse, children, and other family members. Therefore, one typical loss is that there are no longer extend family members to help with caring for and raising children, putting more pressure on parents and particularly mothers (Anisef et al. 2001; Tyyskä 2002b, 2003b).

Due to customary parenting roles, mothers spend more time with children and are generally more likely, compared to fathers, to abuse a child. Additionally, a high number of households lead by single mothers (Rosenberg and Wilcox 2006). Research indicates that there are different forms of abuse committed by mothers and fathers, with mothers reporting more use of physical discipline while men's physical violence is likely to result in more serious injuries. As well, men are often the perpetrators of sexual violence toward both female and male victims (Krug, Dahlberg, Mercy, Zwi, and Lozano 2002).

Being a child witness of the harmful effects of domestic violence is also a form of child abuse. Canadian national statistics from 2009 noted that 52% of family violence victims with children "reported that their children heard or saw assaults on them in the previous five years" (Brownbridge 2009:96). The situation is complicated by immigrant status. Sunaina Assanand (2004) noted in a Canadian study that immigrant women who do not have proficiency in English may not be able to make a 911 call and must rely on their children to help. As a result, the children can be further traumatized by being responsible for the injured mother.

Young Immigrant Women

In most immigrant communities, parental expectations for sons and daughters differ (Tyyskä 2003b). Studies note that young men are subjected to less parental control, with more freedom and decision-making power in comparison to their sisters (Anisef et al. 2001; Handa 2003; Tyyskä 2001, 2006, 2007, 2008). Concerns about daughters were related to premarital dating and sexuality, while concerns about sons related to violence and drugs (Anisef et al. 2001; Tyyskä 2006b, 2007, 2008).

Protectiveness of their children, particularly daughters, is heightened in Muslim and Asian families compared to Western cultures (Aapola, Gonick, and Harris 2005:93–94). Concerns about loss of cultural identity, in combination of fear of losing their children, have influenced many parents to push for conservative sexual norms. This most notably impacts girls, as they hold a significant location as "cultural vessels," who are expected to pass on to their children the culture's central norms, beliefs, and ideals (Handa 2003; Tyyskä 2006b). However, this may lead some young immigrant women to live in two worlds, manifested in hiding parts of their lives from their parents as a means of living up to the expectations of both their parents and peers. This often shows up in heightened mother-daughter conflict as mothers are deemed responsible for the socialization of their children, and particularly their daughters, into culturally approved behaviours (Dyck and McLaren 2002:9; Tyyskä 2006b). However, there is a range of parenting practices from traditional (conservative or protective) to modern (liberal or permissive) in some communities (Tyyskä 2003b).

One area of continuing research regards spouse selection in immigrant families. In the case of Hispanics in the United States, both men and women are encouraged by their families to marry their first partner (Fuschel, Murphy, and Dufresne 2012:267). Historically, one form of arranged marriages among Japanese immigrants were "picture brides," who were brought from Japan to North America. Men were introduced to these prospective brides through photos, due to the difficulty and expense of travelling back and forth in search of a suitable wife in an era where single men migrated en masse (Ichioka 1980). Arranged marriages are also presently common among some immigrant communities from Asia and the Middle East, though the practice is gradually waning globally (Ghimire and Axinn 2013). Nevertheless, South Asian families in both the US (Ternikar 2008) and Canada (Netting 2001, 2006) practise this more formal system of family introductions of potential partners to one another, with the aim of bringing together not only the couple but the two families. The usual determinant for the appropriate timing of marriage is the conclusion of a young woman's education and the young man's ability to earn an income (Netting 2001). The notion of arranged marriage shows that "[n]ew immigrant family patterns are shaped by cultural meaning and social practices that immigrants bring with them from their home countries as well as by social, economic and cultural forces" (Foner 2005:157).

With the presence of arranged marriages, there are also renewed concerns about forced marriages in Western countries, including Canada and the United States (Tahirih Justice Center 2011; Anis, Konanur, and Mattoo 2014), though their numbers are not known. The unfamiliar marriage patterns of some non-Western immigrants have resulted in "moral panics" by media and governments, reflecting the same negative and overblown coverage that was discussed above in relation to honour killings.

Older Immigrant Women

While the majority of current immigrants are younger arrivals, older adult immigration is increasing in both Canada and the United States. In Canada during 2012, 50.4% of recent immigrant women were between the ages of 25 and 44 years old, 12.5% were between 45 and 64 years old, and only 4.3% were 65 years of age or older (Citizenship and Immigration Canada 2012). In the United States during 2012, 42.4% of recent immigrant women were between the ages of 25 and 44 years old, 20.6% were between 45 and 64 years old, and only 5.8% were 65 years of age or older (Homeland Security 2012).

Older immigrant women have different needs and vulnerabilities. As Mark A. Leach (2008–2009:35, 36) notes in the American context, nonexistent or limited comprehension of English compounded with lack of familiarity with US society leads to greater reliance on familiar ties, which in turn can create isolation and lack of access to social services such as healthcare, transportation to healthcare, and other social services. Steven Ruggles and associates (2007) noted that 71% of recent older immigrants either spoke no English or did not speak it very well. Another issue that immigrant women tend to face more so than immigrant men is widowhood, as women tend to outlive men within both native-born and foreign-born couples. This results in the widow having to rely more on extended family members (Leach 2008–2009). Atsuko Matsuoka and associates (2012–2013) note a similar situation in the Canadian context: there are various factors leading to the abuse or vulnerability of older immigrant women, including social isolation, language difficulties, financial difficulties and dependency, and poor access to information and appropriate resources. These reflect the "intersection of systemic issues such as sexism, **ageism**, and **racism** in Canadian society" (Matsuoka, Guruge, Koehn, Beaulieu, Ploeg 2012–2013:111).

In the discussion of IPV above, it was noted that extended families can serve as a protection. On the other hand, existing patterns of family violence may continue in the new setting. One phenomenon of family violence noted in the South Asian community is the abuse of daughters-in-law by mothers-in-law. The in-laws may also create a social environment where violence by the male partner can occur, by either ignorance of the situation or by actively encouraging it (Fernandez 1997; Assisi 2006; Tyyskä et al. 2012).

A study conducted by Marilyn Fernandez (1997) indicated that violence by extended family members in India reflects familial gender hierarchies. Within these families, all men rule over women and senior women are expected to supervise younger women, particularly their daughters-in-law. As a result, senior women are accountable to men within their families, while their loyalties to the younger women are conflicted. However, the economic dependence of daughters-in-law creates a complex set of hierarchical relationships, often leading to older women's abuse of their daughters-in-law. Meanwhile, other studies indicate that daughters-in-law may and retaliate by abusing their in-laws, particularly when they are in the category of dependent older people.

Conclusion

Even though Canada and United States are long past their "settler" periods of nation-building and are considered open, tolerant, and liberal societies, colonial, white, and patriarchal interests persist in the immigration policies of these nations. As Chapter 8 by Nandita Sharma shows, the processes of creating a "citizen" through structural mechanisms of inclusion and exclusion are well established. These processes show no signs of disappearing and, as we have demonstrated in this chapter, marginalize immigrant women. This is manifested in multiple ways. In the past, this could be seen in the denial of female immigrants' entry or admitting only married women. Current Canadian evidence of this includes the admission of women mostly within the family or domestic class immigration categories or as incoming spouses to male economic class immigrants, limiting their access to English language classes; and female immigrant youths' difficulties in integration into the new culture, combined with changes in parenting roles within the receiving society. As a result, immigrant women are denied full citizenship rights. Clearly, women have always occupied a marginal and dependent position in relation to the nation-state; they are reduced to their reproductive and nurturing capacities (Gabriel 2006:166) while their economic contributions are downplayed. This gendered role intersects with racial exclusion. As Enakshi Dua notes, the Canadian state (and this can be extended to the United States as well), remains, in the words of John A. Macdonald, a "white man's country" (2000:57).

Questions for Critical Thought

1. Do immigrant women have more freedoms in North America than they do in their countries of origin?
2. Do adult women and men change in their approach to relationships and gender relations upon immigration?
3. Are there grounds for more conflict between young women and their parents in immigrant families than there are in native-born North-American families?

Key Readings

Dlamini, N., U. Anucha, and B. Wolfe (2012) Negotiated Positions: Immigrant Women's Views and Experiences of Employment in Canada. *Affilia: Journal Of Women & Social Work* 27(4):420–434.

Donkor, M. (2005) Marching to the Tune: Colonization, Globalization, Immigration, and the Ghanaian Diaspora. *Africa Today* 52(1):27–44.

Flores-Gonzales, N. and R. Gomberg-Muños (2013) Transnational Labor, Motherhood, and Activism. In N. Flores-Gonzales, A.R. Guevarra, M. Toromorn, and G. Chan (eds.) *Immigrant Women in the Neoliberal Age*, pp. 262–276. Champaign, IL: University of Illinois Press.

Media Links

Marriage Fraud: Stories from Victims (Government of Canada):
www.cic.gc.ca/english/department/media/multimedia/video/marriage-fraud/marriage-fraud.asp
This video is an official Citizenship and Immigration Canada (2013) public service video, identifying marriage fraud as a moral panic, among others identified in this chapter.

Immigration Reform: The Struggle of 'Immigrant Women' in the US:
www.youtube.com/watch?v=yYzouoO7Pew
In this eight-minute YouTube video, commentator Melissa Harris-Perry (MSNBC 2013) and a panel of experts discuss current issues for racialized immigrant women in the United States.

Between Worlds: Immigrant Women and Domestic Violence:
www.youtube.com/watch?v=QEXCbI8N6hU
This 19-minute Penn Law (2013) video, titled "Between Worlds: Immigrant Women and Domestic Violence," presents the issues and barriers that face immigrant women who experience violence and look for help.

References

Aapola, S., M. Gonick, and A. Harris (2005) *Young Femininity: Girlhood, Power and Social Change.* London: Palgrave McMillan.

Abbott, P. and C. Wallace (1997) *An Introduction to Sociology: Feminist Perspectives.* 2nd ed. New York: Routledge.

Ali, M. and K.M. Kilbride (2004) Forging New Ties: Improving Parenting and Family Support Services for New Canadians with Young Children. Ottawa: Human Resources and Skill Development Canada.

Alvarez, L. and J.M. Broder (2006) More and More, Women Risk All to Enter U.S. *New York Times*, 10 January. www.nytimes.com/2006/01/10/national/10women. html?pagewanted=all&_r=0

Anderson, B. (1983) *Imagined Communities: Reflections on the Origin and Spread of Nationalism*. London: Verso.

Anis, M., S. Konanur, and D. Mattoo (2014) *Who / If / When to Marry: The Incidence of Forced Marriage in Ontario*. Toronto: South Asian Legal Clinic.

Anisef, P., K.M. Kilbride, J. Ochocka, and R. Janzen (2001) Parenting Issues of Newcomer Families in Ontario. Kitchener, ON: Centre for Research and Education in Human Services and Centre of Excellence for Research on Immigration and Settlement.

Arat-Koç, S. (1999) Neo-Liberalism, State Restructuring and Immigration: Changes in Canadian Policies in the 1990s. *Journal of Canadian Studies* 34(2):31–56.

Arat-Koç, S. (2006a) From "Mothers of the Nation" to Migrant Workers. In M. Gleason and A. Perry (eds.) *Rethinking Canada: The Promise of Women's History*, pp.195–209. Don Mills, ON: Oxford University Press.

Arat-Koç, S. (2006b) Whose Social Reproduction? Transnational Motherhood and Challenges to Feminist Political Economy. In K. Bezanson and M. Luxton (eds.) *Social Reproduction: Feminist Political Economy Challenges Neo-Liberalism*, pp.72–92. Montreal: McGill-Queen's University Press.

Assanand, S. (2004) Homelessness: Immigrant Women and Domestic Violence. *BC Institute Against Family Violence Newsletter*. www.bcifv.or/resources/newsletter/ 2004/fall/immigrant.shtml

Assisi, F.C. (2006) Study Reveals Desi American Women Abused by In-laws. INDOlink-Indian Diaspora. www.indolink.com/display/ArticleS.php?id=110806080303

Baines, D. and N. Sharma (2002) Migrant Workers as Non-Citizens: The Case Against Citizenship as a Social Policy Concept. *Studies in Political Economy* 69:75–107.

Batalova, J. (2009) Immigrant Women in the United States. Washington, DC: Migration Policy Institute. www.migrationinformation.org/USfocus/print.cfm?ID=763

Boyd, M. and D. Norris (2000) Demographic Change and Young Adults Living with Parents, 1981–1996. *Canadian Studies in Population* 27(2):267–281.

Brownbridge, D.A. (2009) *Violence Against Women: Vulnerable Populations*. London: Taylor & Francis.

Browne, I. and J. Misra (2003) Intersection of Gender and Race in the Labour Market. *Annual Review of Sociology* 29:487–513.

Caetano, R., G.A. Field, S. Ramisetty-Mikler, and C. McGarth (2005) Intimate Partner Violence and Drinking Patterns among White, Black and Hispanic Couples in the U.S. *Journal of Substance Abuse* 11(2):123–138.

Canadian Council on Social Development (2003) Census Shows Growing Polarization of Income in Canada. Ottawa: Canadian Council on Social Development. http://www.homelesshub.ca/resource/census-shows-growing-polarization-income-canada

Canada Press (2013) Canada's Foreign-born Population Soars to 6.8 Million. 8 May.

Carter, S. (1996) Categories and Terrains of Exclusion: Constructing the "Indian Woman" in the Early Settlement Era in Western Canada. In J. Parr and M. Rosenfeld (eds.) *Gender and History in Canada*, pp. 30–49. Toronto: Copp Clark.

Chang, G. (2000) *Disposable Domestics: Immigrant Women Workers in the Global Economy*. Cambridge, MA: South End Press.

Chung, A. (2012) Honour a Key Theme in Shafia Trial: At the Heart of the Trial of Mohammad Shafia, His Wife Tooba Mohammad Yahya and Their Eldest Son Hamed Is the Allegation That They Killed over Honour. *Toronto Star*, 27 January. www.thestar.com/news/canada/2012/01/27/honour_a_key_theme_in_shafia_trial.html

Choy, C.C. (2000) Exported to Care: A Transnational History of Filipino Nurse Migration to the United States. In N. Forner, R. Rumbaut, and S. Gold (eds.) *Immigration Research for a New Century: Multidisciplinary Perspectives*, pp. 113–133. New York: Russell Sage Foundation.

Chui, T. (2011) Immigrant Women. Ottawa: Statistics Canada. www.statcan.gc.ca/pub/89-503-x/2010001/article/11528-eng.pdf

Citizenship and Immigration Canada (CIC) (2007) Facts and Figures. www.cic.gc.ca/english/resources/statistics/menu-fact.asp

Citizenship and Immigration Canada (2012) Canada Facts and Figures: Immigration Overview Permanent and Temporary Residents. www.cic.gc.ca/english/pdf/research-stats/facts2012.pdf

Creese, G., I. Dyck, and A. McLaren (1999) *Reconstituting the Family: Negotiating Immigration and Settlement*. Vancouver: RIIM Working Paper 99–10.

Das Gupta, T. (2000) Families of Native Peoples, Immigrants and People of Colour. In B. Crow and L. Gotell (eds.) *Open Boundaries: A Canadian Women's Studies Reader*, pp. 215–230. Toronto: Prentice Hall Canada.

Deen, T. (2013) Over 100 Million Women Lead Migrant Workers Worldwide. Inter Press Service News Agency. www.ipsnews.net/2013/04/over-100-million-women-lead-migrant-workers-worldwide

Dinshaw, F. (2005) Elder Abuse: South Asian Women Speak Up. Toronto: COSTI Immigrant Services.

Du Mont, J., I. Hyman, K. O'Brien, M. White, F. Odette, and V. Tyyskä (2012) Immigration Status and Abuse by a Former Partner [Research Summary]. Toronto: CERIS—The Ontario Metropolis Centre. www.ceris.metropolis.net/wp-content/uploads/2012/03/Exploring-intimate-partner-abuse.pdf

Dua, E. (2004) "The Hindu Women's Question": Canadian Nation Building and the Social Construction of Gender for South Asian-Canadian Women. In A. Calliste and G.J. Sefa Dei (eds.) *Anti-Racist Feminism: Critical Race and Gender Studies*, pp. 55–72. Halifax: Fernwood Publishing.

Dyck, I. and A.T. McLaren (2002) Becoming Canadian? Girls, Home and School and Renegotiating Feminine Identity. Vancouver: RIIM.

Ennis, S. R., M. Rios-Vargas, and N.G. Albert (2011) The Hispanic Population: 2010. 2010 Census Briefs. Washington, DC: U.S. Census Bureau.

Fernandez, M. (1997) Domestic Violence by Extended Family Members in India: Interplay of Gender and Generation. *Journal of Interpersonal Violence* 12(3):433–455.

Ferrao, V. (2010) Paid Work. Ottawa: Statistics Canada. www.statcan.gc.ca/pub/89-503-x/2010001/article/11387-eng.pdf

Folson, R.B. (2004) Representation of the Immigrant. In R.B. Folson (ed.) *Calculated Kindness: Global Restructuring, Immigration and Settlement in Canada*, pp. 21–32. Halifax: Fernwood Publishing.

Foner, N. (2005) The Immigrant Family: Cultural Legacies and Cultural Changes. *International Migration Review* 31(4):961–974.

Fuligni, A.J. (1997) The Academic Achievement of Adolescents from Immigrant Families: The Roles of Family Background, Attitudes, and Behavior. *Child Development* 68(2):351–363.

Fuligni, A.J. and K. Yoshikawa (2003) Socioeconomic Resources, Parenting, and the Child Development among Immigrant Families. In M. Bornstein and R. Bradley (eds.) *Socioeconomic Status, Parenting, and Child Development*, pp. 107–124. Mahwah, NJ: Lawrence Erlbaum Associates.

Fuschel, C.L.M., S.B. Murphy, and R. Dufresne (2012) Domestic Violence, Culture, and Relationship Dynamics Among Immigrant Mexican Women. *Affilia: Journal of Women and Social Work* 27(3):263–274.

Gabaccia, D.R. (2003) Today's Immigrant Women in Historical Perspective. In P. Strum and D. Tarantolo (eds.) *Women Immigrants in the United States*, pp. 7–22. Washington, DC: Woodrow Wilson International Center for Scholars.

Gabriel, C. (2006) A Question of Skills: Gender, Migration Policy and the Global Political Economy. In K. van der Pijl, L. Assassi, and D. Wigen (eds.) *Global Regulation: Managing Crises After the Imperial Turn*, pp. 163–176. New York: Palgrave Macmillan.

Ghimire, D.J. and W.G. Axinn (2013) Marital Processes, Arranged Marriage, and Contraception to Limit Fertility. *Demography* 50:1663–1686.

Gibbs, L. (2012) Women's Employment Rate, 2010 (FP-12-20). National Center for Family & Marriage Research. ncfmr.bgsu.edu/pdf/family_profiles/file117987.pdf

González-Guarda, R., E.P. Vasquez, and V.B. Mitrani (2009) Intimate Partner Violence, Depression and Resource Availability among a Community Sample of Hispanic Women. *Issues in Mental Health Nursing* 30:227–236.

Grammage, S. (2003) Women Immigrants in the U.S. Labor Market: Second-Rate Jobs in the First World. In P. Strum and D. Tarantolo (eds.) *Women Immigrants in the United States*, pp. 75–94. Washington, DC: Woodrow Wilson International Center for Scholars.

Handa, A. (2003) *Of Silk Saris and Mini-skirts: South Asian Girls Walk the Tightrope of Culture*. Toronto: Women's Press.

Homeland Security (2012) 2011 Yearbook of Immigration Statistics: Office of Immigration Statistics. Washington, DC: U.S. Department of Homeland Security, Office of Immigration Statistics. www.dhs.gov/sites/default/files/publications/immigration-statistics/yearbook/2011/ois_yb_2011.pdf

Hopkins, E. (1986) A Prison House for Prosperity: The Immigrant Experience of the 19th-Century Upper Class British Woman in Canada. In J. Burnet (ed.) *Looking into My Sister's Eyes: An Exploration in Women's History*, pp. 7–19. Toronto: The Multicultural History Society of Ontario.

Ichioka, Y. (1980) Amerika Nadeshiko: Japanese Immigrant Women in the United States, 1900–1924. *Pacific Historical Review* 49(2):339–357.

Jain, A. and J. Belsky (1997) Fathering and Acculturation: Immigrant Indian Families with Young Children. *Journal of Marriage and Family* 59:873–883.

James, C.E. (1999) *Seeing Ourselves: Exploring Race, Ethnicity and Culture*. 2nd ed. Toronto: Thompson Educational Publishing.

Kilbride, K.M., P. Anisef, E. Baichman-Anisef, and R. Khattar (2001) *Between Two Worlds: The Experiences and Concerns of Immigrant Youth in Ontario*. Toronto: Joint Centre of Excellence for Research on Immigration and Settlement.

Krug, E., L.L. Dahlberg, J.A. Mercy, A.B. Zwi, and R. Lozano (2002) *World Report on Violence and Health*. Geneva, Switzerland: World Health Organization.

Labadie-Jackson, G. (2008–2009) Reflections on Domestic Work and the Feminization of Migration. *Campbell Review Law* 31:67–90.

Latimer, J. (1998) The Consequences of Child Maltreatment. Ottawa: National Clearinghouse on Family Violence.

Leach, M.A. (2008–2009) America's Older Immigrants: A Profile. *Generations* 32(4):34–39.

Li, P.S. (2001) The Market Worth of Immigrants' Educational Credentials. *Canadian Public Policy* 27(1):23–38.

Liu, J. and D. Kerr (2003) Family Change and Economic Well-being in Canada: The Case of Recent Immigrant Families with Children. *International Migration* 41(4):113–140.

MacLeod, L. and M. Shin (1993) "Like a Wingless Bird ...": A Tribute to the Survival and Courage of Women Are Abused and Who Speak Neither English nor French. Ottawa: National Clearinghouse on Family Violence.

Maguire, D. (2010) Marxism. In D. Marsh and G. Stoker (eds.) *Theory and Methods in Political Science*, pp. 136–155. London: Palgrave MacMillan.

Man, G. (2003) The Experience of Middle Class Women in Recent Hong Kong Chinese Immigrant Families in Canada. In M. Lynn (ed.) *Voices: Essays on Canadian Families* 2nd ed. Toronto: Thomson Nelson.

Man, G. (2004) Gender, Work and Migration: Deskilling Chinese Immigrant Women in Canada. *Women's Studies International Forum* 27:135–148.

Matsuoka, A., S. Guruge, S. Koehn, M. Beaulieu, and J. Ploeg (2012–2013) Prevention of Abuse of Older Women in the Post-Migration Context in Canada. *Canadian Review of Social Policy* 68/69:107–120.

Moghissi, H. (1999) Away from Home: Iranian Women, Displacement, Cultural Resistance and Change. *Journal of Comparative Family Studies* 30(2):207–218.

Monger, R. and J. Yankay (2013) U.S. Legal Permanent Residents: 2012. Office of Immigration Statistics, Policy Directorate. Washington, DC: U.S. Department of Homeland Security.

Morrison, L., S. Guruge, and K.A. Snarr (1999) Sri Lankan Tamil Immigrants in Toronto: Gender, Marriage Patterns, and Sexuality. In G. Kelson and D. DeLaet (eds.) *Gender and Immigration*, pp. 144–162. New York: NYU Press.

Nestel, S. (2006) *Obstructed Labour: Race and Gender in the Re-Emergence of Midwifery*. Vancouver: UBC Press.

Netting, N.S. (2001) Indo-Canadian Youth: Love and Identity. Paper presented at the Annual Meeting of the Canadian Sociology and Anthropology Association, Laval University, Quebec City, QC, Canada.

Netting, N.S. (2006) Two Lives, One Partner: Indo-Canadian Youth between Love and Arranged Marriage. *Journal of Comparative Family Studies* 37(1):129–146.

Noivo, E. (1993) Ethnic Families and the Social Injuries of Class, Migration, Gender, Generation and Minority Status. *Canadian Ethnic Studies* 23(3):66–76.

Okun, L. (1988) Termination or Resumption of Cohabitation of Women in Battering Relationships: A Statistical Study. In G.T. Hotaling, D. Finkelhar, J.T. Kirkpatrick, and M.A. Straus (eds.) *Coping with Family Violence: Research and Policy Perspectives*. Thousand Oaks, CA: Sage Press.

Orloff, L. (2003) Women Immigrants and Domestic Violence. In P. Strum and D. Tarantolo (eds.) *Women Immigrants in the United States*, pp. 49–58. Washington, DC: Woodrow Wilson International Center for Scholars.

Pearce, S. (2006) *Immigrant Women in the United States: A Demographic Portrait.* Washington, DC: American Immigration Law Foundation.

Pothier, M. (2012) *LINCing Literatices: Literacy Practices among Somali Refugee Women in the LINC Program.* University of Toronto: Unpublished Thesis.

Powers, M.G. and Q. Seltzer (1998) Occupational Status and Mobility among Undocumented Immigrants by Gender. *International Migration Review* 12:21–55.

Randall, V. (2010) Feminism. In D. Marsh and G. Stoker (eds.) *Theory and Methods in Political Science,* pp. 114–135. London: Palgrave MacMillan.

Roberts, B. (1979) "A Work of Empire": Canadian Reformers and British Female Immigration. In L. Kealey (ed.) *A Not Unreasonable Claim: Women and Reform in Canada, 1880s–1920s,* pp. 185–201, 231–233. Toronto: Women's Press.

Rosenberg, J. and W.B.Wilcox (2006) The Importance of Fathers in the Healthy Development of Children. Washington, DC: U.S. Department of Health and Human Services, Children's Bureau.

Ruggles, S., M. Sobek, C.A. Fitch, P.K. Hall and C. Ronnander (2007) Integrated Public Use Microdata Series: Version 2.0. Historical Census Projects, Department of History, University of Minnesota.

Seat, R. (2000) *Factors Affecting the Settlement and Adaptation Process of Canadian Adolescent Newcomers 16–19 Years of Age.* Toronto: Family Service Association of Toronto.

Shields, J. (2004) *No Safe Haven: Markets,Welfare, and Migrants.* CERIS Working Paper 22 (January 2003):1–39. Toronto: A Report of the Joint Centre of Excellence for Research on Immigration and Settlement (CERIS)

Shimoni, E., D. Este, and D. Clark (2003) Paternal Engagement in Immigrant and Refugee Families. *Journal of Comparative Family Studies* 34(4):555–571.

Smith, E. (2004) Nowhere to Turn? Responding to Partner Violence against Immigrant and Visible Minority Women. Ottawa: Department of Justice, Sectoral Involvement in Departmental Policy Development (SIDPD).

Statistics Canada (2005a) Longitudinal Survey of Immigrants to Canada: A Portrait of Early Settlement Experiences. Cat. No. 89-614-XIE. www5.statcan.gc.ca/bsolc/olc-cel/olc-cel?catno=89-614-X&lang=eng

Statistics Canada (2005b) Decline in Homeownership Rates among Immigrant Families. *The Daily,* 3 February. www.statcan.gc.ca/daily-quotidien/050203/dq050203a-eng.htm

Statistics Canada (2006) Canada's Changing Labour Force, 2006 Census: The Provinces and Territories. www12.statcan.ca/english/census06/analysis/labour/ov-cclf-29.cfm

Statistics Canada (2011) Women in Canada: A Gender-based Statistical Report. Catalogue 89-503-XWE. www5.statcan.gc.ca/bsolc/olc-cel/olc-cel?catno=89-503-XWE&lang=eng

Statistics Canada (2013) Table 054-0001—Immigrant Income, by Sex, Landing Age Group, Immigrant Admission Category, Years since Landing and Landing Year, 2010 Constant Dollars, Annual.

Tahirih Justice Center (2011) Forced Marriage in Immigrant Communities in the United States: 2011 National Survey Results. Church, VA: Tahirih Justice Center. www.tahirih. org/site/wp-content/uploads/2011/09/REPORT-Tahirih-Survey-on-Forced-Marriage-in-Immigrant-Communities-in-the-United-States-September-2011.pdf

Ternikar, F. (2008) To Arrange or Not: Marriage Trends in the South Asian American Community. *Ethnic Studies Review* 31:153–181.

The Métis National Council (2013) The Métis Nation. The Métis National Council. www.metisnation.ca/index.php/who-are-the-metis

Thobani, S. (2000) Closing Ranks: Racism and Sexism in Canada's Immigration Policy. *Race and Class* 42(1):35–55.

Tiuriukanova, E. (2005) Female Labor Migration Trends and Human Trafficking: Policy Recommendation. In *Human Traffic and Transnational Crime*. Lanham, MD: Rowman & Littlefield.

Tjaden, P. and N. Theonnes (2000) Full Report of the Prevalence, Incidence, and Consequences of Violence against Women: Finding from the National Violence against Women Survey. Washington, DC: National Institute of Justice.

Tyyskä, V. (2001) *Long and Winding Road: Adolescents and Youth in Canada Today*. Toronto: Canadian Scholars' Press.

Tyyskä, V. (2002a) Report of Key Informant Interviews—Toronto. Improving Parenting and Family Supports for New Canadians with Young Children: Focus on Resources for Service Providers (unpublished).

Tyyskä, V. (2002b) Report of Individual Interviews with Parents—Toronto. Improving Parenting and Family Supports for New Canadians with Young Children: Focus on Resources for Service Providers (unpublished).

Tyyskä, V. (2003a) Report of Focus Groups with Newcomer Parents. Improving Parenting and Family Supports for New Canadians with Young Children: Focus on Resources for Service Providers (unpublished).

Tyyskä, V. (2003b) Solidarity and Conflict: Teen-Parent Relationships in Iranian Immigrant Families in Toronto. In M. Lynn (ed.) *Voices: Essays on Canadian Families*. 2nd ed. pp. 312–331. Toronto: Nelson Canada.

Tyyskä, V. (2005) Immigrant Adjustment and Parenting of Teens: A Study of Newcomer Groups in Toronto, Canada. In V. Puuronen, J. Soilevuo-Grønnerød, and J. Herranen, *Youth-Similarities, Differences, Inequalities*. Joensuu, Finland: Joensuu University, Reports of the Karelian Institute, No. 1/2005.

Tyyskä, V. (ed.) (2006a) *Action and Analysis: Readings in Sociology of Gender*. Toronto: Nelson Thomson.

Tyyskä, V. (2006b) *Teen Perspectives on Family Relations in the Toronto Tamil Community.* CERIS Working Paper No. 45. March 2006. Toronto: CERIS.

Tyyskä, V. (2007) Immigrant Families in Sociology. In J.E. Lansford, K. Deater-Deckard, and M.H. Bornstein (eds.) *Immigrant Families in Contemporary Society*, pp. 83–99. New York: The Guilford Press.

Tyyskä, V. (2008) *Youth and Society: The Long and Winding Road.* 2nd ed. Toronto: Canadian Scholars' Press.

Tyyskä, V. (2009a) *Families and Violence in Punjabi and Tamil Communities in Toronto.* CERIS Working Paper No. 74. Toronto: CERIS. www.ceris.metropolis.net/Virtual%20 Library/WKPP%20List/WKPP2009/CWP7 4.pdf

Tyyskä, V. (2010) Immigrant and Racialized Families. In A. Duffy, and N. Mandell (eds.) *Canadian Families: Diversity, Conflict and Change.* 4th ed., pp. 86–122. Toronto: Nelson.

Tyyskä, V., F. Dinshaw, C. Redmond, and F. Gomes (2012). "Where We Have Come and Are Now Trapped": Views of Victims and Service Providers on Abuse of Older Adults in Tamil and Punjabi Families. *Canadian Ethnic Studies* 44(3):59–78.

United States Bureau of Labour (2013) Foreign-born Workers in the U.S. Labor Force. Washington, DC: United States Department of Labour. www.bls.gov/spotlight/2013/ foreign-born/home.htm

Wiebe, K. (1991) *Violence against Immigrant Women and Children: An Overview of Community Workers.* 2nd ed. Vancouver: Women Against Violence Against Women/ Rape Crisis Centre.

Wolfe, D.A., C.V. Crooks, V. Lee, A. McIntyre-Smith, and P.G. Jaffe (2003) The Effects of Children's Exposure to Domestic Violence: A Meta-analysis and Critique. *Clinical Child and Family Psychology Review* 6(3):171–187.

Wong, S.K. (1999) Acculturation, Peer Relations, and Delinquent Behaviour of Chinese-Canadian Youth. *Adolescence* 34(133):107–119.

Zaidi, A. and M. Shuraydi (2002) Perceptions of Arranged Marriages by Young Pakistani Muslim Women Living in Western Society. *Journal of Comparative Family Studies* 33(4):37–57.

Chapter 11

The Schooling
of Children of Immigrants

Mehrunnisa Ahmad Ali

Introduction

Families who migrate to a new country take a lot of risks. **Immigrant** parents often
claim that they do so for the possibility of a brighter future for their children (Anisef,
Brown, Phythian, Sweet, and Walters 2010). They believe that their children's futures
will be secured by successful **integration** in schools in their new countries, followed
by post-secondary education, well-paid jobs, and socioeconomic prosperity. Almost
all of them have high educational aspirations for their children and see schools as
places where their children will begin to acquire the knowledge and skills they will
need to be successful in the new environment. However, the structures and cultures
of public schools in Canada and the United States are designed to selectively support
or neglect children of immigrants. Children of some immigrant groups adapt readily
to these schools while others do not. Because public schools have been idealized
as "the great equalizer" in these countries, there is often a sense of moral outrage
when they are seen to create or perpetuate inequities based on differences such as
socioeconomic status, language, **race**, religion, and immigration status.

This chapter begins with a brief history of how public schools were first set up
in Canada and the United States. It then examines how children of immigrants have
been supported or neglected in public schools through physical segregation, language
instruction policies and practices, the official curriculum, and parent-teacher relations. The chapter concludes with the identification of children of immigrant groups
who have benefited from or suffered neglect in school systems in the two countries.

Historical Background

Starting in the sixteenth century, immigrants to North America came primarily from Britain and other parts of Europe. They referred to themselves as pioneers or settlers because they established themselves in the land they had "discovered." In the early years of European **immigration**, children of wealthy immigrants attended private schools or were tutored at home. In some places missionaries set up religious schools that admitted children who could otherwise not afford to go to school.

The idea of public schooling gradually gained support in the late nineteenth century, particularly in response to higher levels of immigration and industrialization in North America. Political leaders at that time realized that an educated population was necessarily for economic, political, and social progress. As a result, they began to establish state-funded public schools, known as "common schools," which—at least in theory—were open to all children in specified catchment areas. However, differences in historical and geographic factors shaped schooling opportunities for children of subsequent immigrants in both countries.

School Segregation

European immigrants in the Southern United States had accumulated large agricultural holdings requiring a lot of manual labour. To meet this need slave traders captured black people from Africa and shipped them to the new country, where they were bought and sold as slaves. Children of these **involuntary migrants** were also considered slaves and expected to work for their white masters. These children were not permitted to go to school, or even to learn to read and write, for fear they would get "out of control," challenge their status as slaves, and no longer work for their owners. If their owners discovered that the slaves could read or write, the slaves as well as whoever had taught them were severely punished.

In the northern part of the United States, however, land holdings were smaller and slaves were fewer in number, and there was greater consensus among white political leaders that an educated population was necessary for industrialization and socioeconomic progress in the country. In the early 1900s, they decided to make elementary schooling compulsory in most Northern states, and the Southern states gradually followed suit. At this time both white and black children were legally required to go to school, but racially segregated schools were set up throughout the United States. Schools for black children had much lower levels of funding than those for white children, as well as inadequate facilities and poorly educated teachers. Parents of black children soon realized that the poor schooling of their children would restrict their opportunities for **higher education**, well-paid jobs, and improved socioeconomic status. Over the years they challenged school segregation laws many times, but racial segregation was so widely ingrained in society that even the United States Supreme Court did not overturn the law. Instead, it tried to appease black families by offering them the option of **separate but equal schools**. Having long known that separate schools would never provide their children the same quality of education, parents continued to challenge the laws that would perpetuate their children's status as an **underclass**.

It was not until the landmark ruling known as *Brown v. Board of Education* in 1954 that black parents finally won the right to send their children to public schools attended by white children, if their homes fell within the defined catchment area. The change in the law, however, did not necessarily lead to the desegregation of schools right away. Parents of white children, and in many instances school principals and teachers as well, strongly protested the change. Some of them tried to physically stop black children from entering "their" schools, and the police had to be called upon by local public administrators to intervene. In other cases, whites ostracized black children and parents within the school, which made it very difficult for black families to benefit from the higher quality of education. In some communities white residents drove out black families from entire neighbourhoods by harassing them, boycotting their businesses, or socially isolating them.

Segregated schools in Canada were first set up as a result of black migration from the United States, primarily in the provinces of Nova Scotia, Ontario, and New Brunswick, although they were present in other provinces as well (Joshee and Johnson 2007). Intense pressure from politically important white families to protect their children from the corrupting influence of "Negro children" resulted in legislation to establish separate schools for black children in Nova Scotia in 1836 and in Ontario in 1850. As in the United States, schools for black children were poorly resourced. In Nova Scotia, for example, a policy amendment in 1884 dictated that schools for black children could not hire teachers with higher levels of education than grade four (Winks, cited in Joshee and Johnson 2007). In places where the black population was too small to warrant a separate school, black children were required to use separate benches in the same room. In Nova Scotia separate schools for black children were maintained until the 1960s, while most of them in Ontario closed in the 1950s.

Children of black immigrants were not the only group who suffered racial discrimination at the hands of the white European settlers. Late in the nineteenth century the federal government in Canada also began to establish separate schools for children of its Aboriginal population, including Inuit, Métis, and First Nations peoples. These schools were run by missionaries of the Catholic and other Christian churches, and their purpose was to "civilize" children of the native population by teaching them European languages and curricula. In the beginning, many native families resisted sending their children to school but when a law was passed to make schooling compulsory for all children under the age of 16 years, they were forced to do so. As a result children were forcibly taken from their families and kept in **residential schools**, forbidden to speak their native languages or follow their own cultural practices. Not only did these children lose their language and cultural identity, but many of them also suffered physical, emotional, and sexual abuse at the hands of those who were responsible for educating them. The last residential school for Aboriginal children was closed in 1996. Political leaders in Canada have since publically acknowledged, offered compensation for, and apologized to native communities for the harm done to them by European settlers.

Immigrants from China, Japan, and India began arriving on the West Coast of Canada in the early 1900s to build the railway, grow the fishing industry, and farm the vast tracts of available land. Partial segregation of immigrant, as well as Canadian-born children of Chinese and Japanese descent, was attempted by politically important white families in this area on suspicions of their corrupting influence on white children. Following the 1941 bombing of Pearl Harbor by the Japanese during the Second World War, thousands of Japanese-Canadian children were turned away from schools in Vancouver and sent to makeshift schools with inadequate resources in internment camps.

Religious affiliation has been another historical reason for segregated schooling for immigrants. The earlier Protestant immigrants arriving in the United States had established the public school system. When Catholic immigrants began arriving from Ireland and then other countries such as Germany, Italy, and Poland, they wanted to set up Catholic schools. But state funding for these schools was refused and the Catholic immigrants were pressured to send their children to public schools for promoting a common American national identity. Nevertheless, some of these religious groups set up what became known as "parochial schools" without state funding, where religious traditions and languages from "the old country" were taught. Unlike schooling the United States, schooling in Canada at the time of the country's founding in 1867 was influenced by both Catholic and Protestant churches. Because of the political power of a large Catholic French population, as well as a strong Protestant presence, the duality of religious affiliations was a recognized quite early in Canadian schools.

As religious institutions began to lose ground in Europe and immigrant populations in Canada and the United States became more religiously and culturally diverse, schools became more secular in both countries. Provincial governments were made responsible for schooling in their own jurisdictions, based on their own populations and political climates. Funding for **faith-based schools** in the United States comes primarily from tuition fees or donations raised by the religious community that sponsors the schools. Currently 4 Canadian provinces provide no funding for faith-based schools, and only Ontario provides full funding for about 200 Catholic schools with a population of 93,000 children (www.tcdsb.on.ca). Other religious schools in Ontario do not receive public funds, but a significant number of children of immigrants attend religious schools. For example, there are 35 Muslim schools in Ontario, with an estimated student population of more than 3,500 children (Memon, cited in Zine 2008). According to Jasmine Zine (2008) the number of children enrolled in Islamic schools in Ontario increased rapidly as a result of the backlash Muslim children received in public schools in response to the events of September 11, 2001.

Involuntary segregation of children based on their race or religion is no longer legal in either Canada or the United States, and a vast majority of children of immigrants attend public schools in both countries. However, school segregation of immigrant children from different backgrounds continues, primarily based on the neighbourhood in which their parents choose, or can afford, to live. Immigrants are attracted to neighbourhoods where they can readily find other families with whom they share a culture and a language. Newer immigrants as a whole are also less financially secure than nonmigrants and tend to live in relatively poorer areas. Schools that serve these areas have a high concentration of immigrants in general, and sometimes a very high percentage of a particular ethno-linguistic group. In Thorncliffe Park Public School in Toronto, for example, 96% of the enrolled children do not speak English as their first language and 68% of them live in lower income households (www.edu.gov.on.ca). Similarly, James Banks (2009) claims that Latin American and African American students in the United States attend schools that are more segregated than ever before because they live in low-income neighbourhoods, from which white middle-class populations have fled. Pedro Noguera (2006) points out that Latino children and youth make up the majority of the school population in New York, Los Angeles, and Chicago, but they are disproportionately consigned to poor quality, underfunded, and overcrowded schools. Furthermore, other scholars (e.g. Suárez-Orozco and Gaytán 2010) have found that highly segregated schools, where more than three-quarters of the students are children of colour, are in low-income neighbourhoods where most people do not use English as their first language. These three factors are consistently linked to children's poor performance in schools.

Language Policies and Practices

Carlos Ovando and Terrence Wiley (2007) report that when slaves began arriving in the United States, they brought with them many different African languages.

However, they were forbidden to use their heritage languages and required to only speak English with each other and with their owners. Subsequent groups of immigrants were also expected to abandon their original languages based on the **ideology** of the **melting pot** sustained by enduring myths, such as language diversity has a disuniting effect; multilingualism is an abnormal condition; and programs for bilingual education prevent children's success in schools.

Immigration to the United States from primarily European and Asian countries continued well into the twentieth century. However, toward the end of the century there was unprecedented growth in immigration to the United States from South American countries. It is estimated that Latinos now constitute 15% of the total population, and there are more Spanish-speaking people in the US than in any other country except Mexico. Latino children are the fastest growing population in American schools but also the immigrant group with the highest dropout rate (Fry 2003).

For children of immigrants, the socioeconomic disadvantages of not knowing the dominant language used in the destination country are well documented. Those who were born elsewhere, and even those born in Canada or the United States to families who use a different language at home, have little exposure to the language of instruction used in schools. Unable to engage the curriculum in a different language, these children tend to fall behind their peers in academic performance. Effects of this disadvantage persist for a long time and limit their opportunities for higher education or employment. As a result of their relatively weaker performance on tests designed for native speakers of English (and French in parts of Canada), they are often streamed into nonacademic programs, which lead to an early entry into low-paid, low-status jobs rather than to colleges and universities. Bernhard (2010) has pointed out at the dropout rate for Spanish-speaking high school students in Toronto is twice the average for English-speaking students. Some schools try to mitigate the ill effects of this disadvantage by offering additional support, such as classes in English as a Second Language (ESL) to speakers of other languages. But due to a variety of reasons, including inadequate funding and untrained teachers, children of immigrants often do not get sufficient and timely support for learning the language of instruction used in schools.

Schools in the United States usually take a "sink or swim" approach to language-minority children, and political opposition to bilingual education continues even today. Given the large numbers of Spanish-speaking children of immigrants, as well as children of immigrants from Asia and other parts of the world, some schools have experimented with English immersion programs, bilingual instruction, or transitional programs, but these programs are often discontinued because of funding cuts. Using data from a five-year study, Suarez-Orozco and Gaytán (2010) mapped the academic pathways of 309 immigrant children from China, Central America, the Dominican Republic, Haiti, and Mexico. They found that among school-level factors, proficiency in English was the single most important predictor of children's academic performance in schools. Citing other scholars, they claimed that it takes five to seven years for children to become proficient in using English for academic purposes, but schools simply don't offer this level of support to immigrant children.

In Canada, language policies and practices are somewhat different from those in the United States. When Canada became an independent country in 1867, English and French were declared as its two official languages because of the earlier and politically strong French-speaking settlers in the province of Quebec. In the following years, the demographic features of Canada's population changed a great deal but the official languages remained the same. Perhaps because of the early recognition of two distinct linguistic groups, Canadians have historically accepted linguistic diversity more readily than Americans.

Currently, almost one-fifth of the Canadian population is made up of immigrants, most of whom have settled in its major cities. For example, only 44% of students in the Toronto District School Board (TDSB)—the largest in the country with over two million students—speak English as their first language. Students in the TDSB come from 190 countries, about a third of them have a mother tongue other than English, and 22% learn another language at home in addition to English.

Immigrant children seeking admission to Canadian schools (other than those in Quebec) are first tested for proficiency in English by the local school board and their scores are sent to the schools where they intend to go. Based on the priorities of the school board and available resources, students who are not fluent in English are offered one of three models of support for learning English: 1) learning in a separate class for the whole day, taught by a trained ESL teacher if possible; 2) being "pulled out" from their regular classroom for short periods of time to receive language instruction; or 3) having a teacher translate and interpret for them within the classroom they normally attend. As Jim Cummins (1986) has pointed out, it takes five to eight years to learn a new language to a level that is comparable to native speakers. Children of immigrants therefore need sustained support in learning the language of instruction in schools. Provincial allocations for ESL programs, however, varies from only two to five years, and children born in Canada to immigrant families are not always eligible for these programs. Furthermore, the use of these funds is subject to the discretion of school trustees and principals, and it is widely claimed that the funds are spent on other services and materials rather than ESL, primarily because immigrant families are poorly represented in decision-making processes.

Derwing and Munro (2007) suggests that, typically, older students get priority for funded ESL support in Canada because it is assumed that younger children can learn the "concrete" subject matter at the elementary level despite their lack of fluency in English, and have many more years to "catch up" with their peers. But research suggests that children entering school without English do not catch up with their peers until they are about 13 years old. The many years of difficulty in following instructions or communicating with teachers and classmates are likely to make schooling a painful experience for these children. While children requiring support in learning English are present in many schools in Canadian cities, regular classroom teachers are not able to assist them because their professional training does not include preparation for working with such children.

Curriculum

Immigrant families who migrated to Canada or the United States in the last few decades tend to maintain their social, political, and economic ties to their countries of origin. The ease with which they can now travel and communicate with friends and relatives left behind has also strengthened these ties. Canada's policy of **multiculturalism** has encouraged immigrants to promote their linguistic and cultural heritage and pass it on to their children. Although there is no similar policy in the United States, many ethno-linguistic groups are large and spatially concentrated enough to be able to maintain their cultural heritage.

Children of immigrant families have multiple, flexible, evolving identities and affiliations. They feel they belong to the country in which they or their parents were born, but also to the country in which they now live. They do not see their affiliations in binary terms and do not feel the need to choose between the two (Ali 2009). They are concerned about their local neighbourhoods, countries they left behind as well as those in which they now live, and global issues of poverty, violence, and environmental degradation. Their firsthand knowledge of their country of their origin, which many of them regularly travel to, or information they have garnered from friends and relatives, parents, or co-ethnic immigrant communities usually makes them much more globally connected than their monocultural peers.

Several scholars (e.g. Banks 2009; Davies 2006) have argued that the presence of children of immigrants in our schools opens up possibilities of teaching global citizenship to all our children. The concept of **global citizenship education** has many interpretations, varying from preparation of cosmopolitan citizens who can compete for profits in the global market to ethical stewardship of an increasingly interdependent and fragile world (Richardson 2008). Irrespective of how this concept is defined, it is easy to see that a curriculum designed for this purpose has a global orientation, is inclusive of multiple perspectives, and has a focus on issues that extend beyond national boundaries.

School curricula in Canada and the United States have changed much more slowly than the demographic profile of the children attending school in these countries. The overarching purpose of school curricula in both places seems to be the promotion of national unity. This is evident in the almost exclusive focus on national history and geography, ideology, and perspectives. For example, the Ontario social studies curriculum document for grades 9–10 (Ministry of Education 2005), entitled *Canadian and World Studies* states that

> Students who come to Ontario from other countries will find the study
> of subjects within Canadian and world studies particularly useful.
> Through this study, they can develop an understanding of Canadian
> economics, geography, history, law, and politics that will help them to
> become well-informed Canadian citizens. (23)

A more detailed examination of the course descriptions shows that even when Canada's global connections are specifically mentioned, the guidelines emphasize Canada's humanitarian aid and peacekeeping role in other countries but not its combative role in Afghanistan, which has been a topic of considerable public debate. Individuals who have achieved national or international fame, such as David Suzuki, Oscar Peterson, or Michael Ondaatje, are always identified as Canadian heroes, but not as immigrants or children of immigrants (Ali 2009).

Some may argue that it is even more important for children who come from other places to learn about the positive aspects of their new country so they have a sense of national pride and loyalty. This view is based on the fear that unless the nation-state is explicitly glorified in the school curriculum, children of immigrants may not become sufficiently loyal to it. However, there is no available evidence to justify this fear. In fact, research suggests that children of immigrants know about their parents' reasons for migration and appreciate the opportunities their new countries have provided them. They are able to compare living conditions in both places, and are often grateful for the security and freedom they now have. They particularly appreciate the cultural diversity in their new environment, which allows them to see their differences as "normal" (Sicakkan 2005). They do, however, expect to be treated fairly, and recognize and resent discrimination on the basis of race, ethnicity, accent, or other markers of difference (Ali 2008). For these students, a school curriculum that explains global economic, political, and social relations could be much more helpful in understanding their past and imagining their future. Learning about the struggles of other immigrants with whom they can identify—rather than just the achievements of the early European settlers—as well as the contributions they made to Canada or the United States, could help them conceptualize their own roles as nation builders.

Parent-Teacher Relations

Parent-teacher relationships are widely believed to have a strong influence on students' academic and social success in schools (Englund, Luckner, Whaley, and Egeland 2004). When parents and teachers have a common understanding about the purpose of schooling, as well as each other's roles and strategies in children's schooling, it is easy to work in consonance. Shared values, beliefs, experiences, culture, and language make it easier for them to agree upon what a student needs to learn and how, and they can readily communicate with each other to help ensure the student's success. Immigrant parents and their children's teachers do not have such common understandings.

Schoolteachers in both the United States and Canada are predominantly white middle-class women, while their students come from many different socioeconomic, racial, and ethnic backgrounds. Several recent studies have shown that despite the good intentions of school administrators and teachers, the sociocultural and linguistic distances between them and immigrant parents often leads to mistrust and miscommunication.

Immigrant parents arrive in their new country with images of schooling based on their own and their children's prior experiences. For example, some parents expect teachers to rank their children's academic performance in comparison to other students in the class, or to assign the same amount of homework that they had in their previous schools, or to reprimand students for a disheveled appearance. Meanwhile, teachers do not necessarily know that parents have these different expectations and may not agree with what the parents want even if they were told this. Teachers' images of their own roles and responsibilities are guided by their personal backgrounds, experiences of schooling, and professional training. They may expect immigrant parents to supervise their children's homework, but not realize that parents who do not know the language of instruction will not be able to do so. Immigrant parents who work very long hours may also not have the time to do so. Schools typically do not create opportunities for teachers and immigrant parents to talk about these differences and try to address them. When immigrant parents and their children's teachers remain ignorant about each other's goals for the children and expectations about how to help them reach those goals, tensions arise. Sometimes these tensions can also lead to inner conflicts for the child (Roer-Strier 2001).

A major reason for the lack of effective communication between immigrant parents and their children's teachers is the absence of a common language. Although some schools try to provide translators and interpreters during parent-teacher meetings, the endemic shortage of funding for this service in most jurisdictions makes it difficult for them to communicate frequently, in a timely and effective way.

Another reason for the communication gap is immigrant parents' decreased sense of self-efficacy in their parental role. Many of them experience downward mobility in employment-related socioeconomic status when they move to a new country. They are unfamiliar with the languages and cultures of institutions, such as schools, in the new environment. Their children, in contrast, seem to learn the dominant language and culture much faster than they do. As a result, they lose self-confidence in their ability to meet their role obligations as parents, which includes providing for, mediating on behalf of, and guiding and protecting their children. Some scholars (e.g. Jones and Prinz 2005) have pointed out that parental self-efficacy is linked to parenting competence, and its loss also directly and indirectly affects children's confidence and self-esteem.

Judith Bernhard (2010) claims that Canadian teachers are ill-equipped to interact with immigrant parents. The assumptions they make about the parents, the language barrier, and most importantly, the power differential between the two are reasons for the lack of effective interactions between them. Bernhard (2010) reports on research she conducted with colleagues, which offered a series of interventions to help Latino parents in particular to reclaim their roles in their children's education. Results from the study of these interventions show they were highly successful in helping parents gain the confidence and the skills to participate in their children's schooling. However, the programs were externally funded and their long-term effects are unknown. Furthermore, they were designed to support immigrant parents and did not include teachers who work with them.

My own research (Ali 2012) shows that most recent immigrants have come to Canada from countries that were colonized by European powers. This research suggests that immigrant parents and their children's teachers realize that they have different expectations from each other and from the child, but they are unable to negotiate these differences because of the baggage of their colonial legacies. Immigrants coming to Western countries are widely perceived to have deficits in social, economic, and cultural capital. Teachers want them to learn "Canadian ways" of parenting their children and participating in their schooling. Immigrant parents, in turn, think that teachers are prejudiced against them because of their race, culture, or religion and consider them inferior because of their lower socioeconomic status, parenting style, lack of fluency in English, or inordinate ambition for their children.

To begin addressing this issue, it is important to remember that children of immigrants will make up an increasing percentage of the school population in the foreseeable future. Immigrant-receiving countries cannot afford to have a generation of children who do not thrive in school for lack of mutually supportive relations between their parents and teachers. Both immigrant parents and teachers need to first acknowledge the historical and current imbalance of power, which has led to asymmetrical relations

> **Case Example 1: Teacher and Immigrant Parent Stereotypes**
>
> In focus groups, my colleagues and I interviewed 32 immigrant parents from 6 different language groups and 29 teachers. An analysis of the data showed that both parents and teachers held stereotypical views about each other; they had different role expectations from each other based on prior experiences or assumptions; and communication between them was controlled by the school (Ali 2012). The research showed that stereotypes can be challenged and different expectations can be negotiated through sufficient and appropriate communication. But this is difficult in the contact zone of the school because the relationship is highly asymmetrical. A key reason for this is the legacy of colonialism, which affects both parties. Teachers perceive immigrant parents as having social, economic, and cultural deficits, and try to teach them Canadian ways of parenting. Parents think teachers are patronizing, dismissive, and sometimes racist. Given that good relations between the two is crucial for children's success in school, it would be important for both parties to build this relationship by 1) explicitly acknowledging historical and current socioeconomic and political injustices; 2) learning more about each other's personal and group histories, cultures, and beliefs; and 3) taking an ethical problem-solving approach toward working together for the children in whom both are invested.

between them. They should then take a problem-solving approach to figure out ways to jointly support students, keeping in mind that they are both invested in the children's success.

Differentiated Schooling Experiences

Children of immigrants arrive in Canada and the United States from many different parts of the world. Their personal characteristics, familial and cultural backgrounds, reasons for migrations, and **settlement** processes lead to different kinds of responses from the receiving society in general, and schools in particular. For example, adapting to schools is relatively easy for girls compared to boys, for children of families with high socioeconomic status, and for members of tightly knit **ethnic communities** (Portes and MacLeod 2005). However, children's success in school is mediated by other factors, such as the neighbourhood in which they live and the quality of the school they attend.

In capitalist societies one of the most significant characteristics of families is their socioeconomic status. Immigrant families who had high socioeconomic status in their country of origin may be able to transfer their human, cultural, and **social capital** to their new country. Some of them send their children to private schools, following the practice in their country of origin. Others, who choose to send their children to public schools, first look for the best performing schools in the district where they want to live before selecting their home. Adults in such families are often highly educated and well-travelled, and expect their children to be at the top of the class in school. They actively participate in their children's schooling and often enroll them in supplementary academic programs, as well as programs for sports, music, or other cultural activities (Foner 2010; Portes and MacLeod 2005). Some such families experience a relatively short period of financial insecurity upon their migration. In such cases, they begin by living in a less-expensive neighbourhood when they first arrive and send their children to the local public school, but they move to a more affluent area as soon as they can.

Children of immigrants at the other end of this spectrum end up living in "the projects" in the United States or "social housing" in Canada. These neighbourhoods consist of poor quality housing subsidized by the local or provincial government. Unemployment or **underemployment**, high rates of crime, gang violence, and drug trafficking are often associated with these areas. Schools in such neighbourhoods are focused much more on keeping children in school and off the streets, rather than on high academic achievement. They are more concerned about reducing their high dropout rates than about facilitating their students' access to universities.

Although public schools were initially conceptualized as social institutions to help level the playing field for all children, it is now widely accepted that they simply do not compensate for the different experiences children have growing up in richer or poorer families. A family's socioeconomic status is still the most reliable predictor of children's success in school, unless of course they have physical, intellectual, or emotional disabilities. This applies to children of immigrants as much as to nonmigrants.

Nancy Foner (2010) compared the educational trajectories of Jewish and Italian-origin children living in New York City in the last century to conclude that the cultural heritage of immigrant communities also plays a significant role in their children's schooling. Although both groups started out with low socioeconomic status and experienced discrimination, Jewish children stayed in school longer and performed much better than Italian-descent children because of the long-held Jewish tradition of valuing academic learning. Italian families who came from rural communities were more interested in teaching their children practical skills to help generate an income, rather than having them stay in school. In the contemporary era, the success of Chinese-, Korean-, and Indian-origin children in American schools can be attributed to their families' high expectations regarding work ethic and performance, as well as investment in after-school tutoring or other educational programs. These expectations are reflected in teachers' perceptions about children of "the model minority," which in turn reinforce the children's advantage.

Immigrant families' linguistic backgrounds also have an important impact on their children's experiences of schooling. Schools are institutions that are highly dependent on the use of a common language. Children who arrive with fluency in English (or French in Canada) find it far easier to seamlessly transition to their new schools, because they can understand their teachers and classmates and can read and write more or less at the same level as their peers. Those who do not know the language of the school are unable to demonstrate their academic competence because this is only done in the language used in the school. These children continue to struggle in school, and those who are fortunate enough get some support in learning English (or French) take a long time to catch up with their peers and miss the opportunity to learn essential knowledge and skills that they can build on as they move into higher grades. Furthermore, they get labelled as children with deficits, which lowers teachers' expectations from them, resulting in long-term negative consequences for their academic performance. Other children also begin to see them as incompetent students, which affects their social relations as well as their self-esteem.

Children who are older when their families migrate to Canada or the United States sometimes know the language of the school but speak with a different accent. These children are also at risk of being ostracized at school. Teachers can sometimes not understand them, and other children are quick to make fun of them, which results in silencing. Children who are silenced are also unable to demonstrate their academic competence and can get caught in the downward spiral of low expectations and poor performance in class.

Differentiating children based on their racial profile is no longer sanctioned by law in Canada or the United States, but the practice continues in subtle ways. According to a 2012 report based on a survey of 72,000 schools, released by the United States Department of Education, African American children get suspended or expelled from school much more frequently than their white peers; only 29% of high-minority schools offered calculus, compared to 55% of low-minority schools; and teachers in high-minority schools get paid, on average, $2,250 per year less than their colleagues in low-minority schools in the same district (U.S. Department of Education 2012). Systematic **racism** also exists in Canadian schools. Children of colour are routinely placed into lower academic streams, are expelled or suspended more often than white children for the same transgression, perform poorly in provincial tests, and are overrepresented among children with special needs (Bernhard, Cummins, Campoy, Ada, Winsler, and Bleiker 2006). In general, Canadians tend to

Case Example 2: Discrimination and Muslim Children

Discrimination in schools based on religious identity is also not a new phenomenon but has acquired greater magnitude since the "war on terror" led by the United States. Children who are identified as Muslim are associated with terrorists, harassed, intimidated, and sometimes even attacked in schools. In some instances, even teachers have been implicated in ostracizing these children and the State Departments of Justice or Education have been forced to intervene. Anti-Muslim sentiment is also strong in Canadian schools. Zine (2008) and others have reported that children of Muslim immigrants have been driven out of public schools because they had become targets of bullying. These children end up going to privately funded Muslim schools, which protect them from religious discrimination. However, some scholars argue that in the long run their isolation in separate schools is likely to delay their integration and underscore their disconnection from "mainstream" society.

deny racism in their schools, compare themselves favourably with the United States, and feel complacent in reiterating the rhetoric of **multiculturalism**. Racial incidents in schools are downplayed as unique or unusual events. Some school administrators suggest that all children experience some amount of bullying, or that teachers do not have racist intention but may act in ways that are seen as racist due to ignorance or oversight (see Lund 2006).

Children of immigrants who arrive in Canada or the United States as refugees often encounter several of the above disadvantages, and more. Their families have low incomes, they do not know English (or French in the case of Canada), and are usually from **racialized** groups, and often Muslim. In addition, they are likely to have had very impoverished schooling, if any, and suffered from traumatic experiences. Such children find it very difficult to integrate in schools, especially those that do not offer sufficient support in ESL, appropriate counselling services, or flexible opportunities to complete their school-level education.

Some school-aged children in Canada or the United States do not have a legal status in the country, or may have one or more family members who have been illegalized. Although public schools in both countries are legally required to admit such children, the students' own or their parents' lack of legal status often complicates their experience of schooling. Families without legal status tend to move often because of unstable housing and working conditions (Suarez-Orozco and Yoshikawa 2013). Some children are separated from one or both parents for long periods and others may live in fear of deportation. Such families' access to healthcare is very limited, both in Canada and the United States. Undocumented parents are also less likely to access other public or community resources for children and families for fear of exposure, lack of information, or stress, which could have negative implications for their children's social and cognitive development (Yoshikawa 2011). Older children, who realize that their access to higher education may be in jeopardy because they will not qualify for grants and loans and that they may be charged international fees, are likely to lose the motivation to do well in schools.

Conclusion

Children of immigrants going to school in Canada or the United States clearly encounter a lot of challenges. These challenges include school segregation based on neighbourhoods differentiated by housing prices, the almost exclusive use of English or French for instructional purposes, a curriculum that does not reflect the children's interests and affiliations, and weak parent-teacher relations. However, these challenges affect different groups of immigrants differently, depending on their personal characteristics, socioeconomic status, prior knowledge of the official or dominant language(s), racial or religious identity, the strength of their ethnic or religious community, and their migration history. More research is needed to figure out which factors are more significant in which contexts, and which factors mediate the effects of others. More specifically, research is needed to determine which policies and practices help to mitigate the various disadvantages children of immigrants encounter in schools.

While there is no quick or easy way to address all of the above issues, their persistence over decades indicates a lack of political will to fully support the transition of children of immigrants into public schools. Although the political rhetoric in both countries welcomes immigrant families and celebrates ethno-linguistic diversity, and although differentiation on the basis of socioeconomic status, language, race, or religion is illegal in both Canada and the US, the experiences of children of immigrants speak of a different reality. Policymakers and educators need to realize that insufficient support for children of immigrants in their schools may create an underclass, which in the short-term will preserve the power and privileges of those who currently have them. But in the long run it is not in the interest of either country to have an increasing number of poorly educated citizens.

Questions for Critical Thought

1. Why do you think children of immigrants have historically been discriminated against in public schools in North America?
2. If you could advocate for one single change in school policy and/or practice that would improve the schooling of children of immigrants, what would it be? Why do you think this is the most important change?
3. Do you think schools should still be conceptualized as "the great equalizer"? Why or why not?

Key Readings

Banks, J. and C. McGee Banks (eds.) (2009) *Multicultural Education: Issues and Perspectives*. 7th ed. Hoboken, NJ: John Wiley & Sons.

Ghosh, R. and A.A. Abdi (2004) *Education and the Politics of Difference: Canadian Perspectives*. Toronto: Canadian Scholars' Press.

Salomone, R. (2010) *True American: Language, Identity and the Education of Immigrant Children*. Cambridge, MA: Harvard University Press.

Media Links

The Flat World and Education:
fora.tv/2010/08/02/Linda_Darling-Hammond_The_Flat_World_and_Education
A lecture by Linda Darling-Hammond.

New Immigrants Share Their Stories:
www.youtube.com/watch?v=33OINi3xVbc
This is a short video of immigrant students sharing some clips from their video diaries and discussing their experiences as newcomers.

A World Unknown: Immigrant Parent Experiences with School Systems:
www.youtube.com/watch?v=4CQ61S1OQrM
This video portrays the experiences of immigrant parents who come from countries of war or high poverty in their encounters with the Alberta school system in Canada.

References

Ali, M.A. (2008) Loss of Parenting Self-efficacy among Immigrant Parents. *Contemporary Issues in Early Childhood* 9(2):148–160.

Ali, M.A. (2009) Preparing Citizens for a Globalized World: The Role of the Social Studies Curriculum. *International Journal of Education for Democracy* 2(2):100–118.

Ali, M.A. (2012) The Shadow of Colonialism on Relations between Immigrant Parents and Their Children's Teachers. *Alberta Journal of Educational Research* 58(2):198–215.

Anisef, P., R. Brown, K. Phythian, R. Sweet, and D. Walters (2010) Early School Leaving among Immigrants in Toronto Secondary Schools. *Canadian Review of Sociology* 47(2):103–128.

Banks, J. (ed.) (2009) *The Routledge International Companion to Multicultural Education.* New York: Routledge.

Bernhard, J.K. (2010) From Theory to Practice: Engaging Immigrant Parents in Their Children's Education. *The Alberta Journal of Educational Research* 56(3):319–334.

Bernhard, J.K., J. Cummins, F.I. Campoy, F.A. Ada, A.Winsler, and C. Bleiker (2006) Identity Texts and Literacy Development among Preschool English Language Learners: Enhancing Learning Opportunities for Children at Risk of Learning Disabilities. *Teachers College Press* 108(11):2380–2405.

Cummins, J. (1986) Empowering Minority Students: A Framework for Intervention. *Harvard Educational Review* 56(1):18–36.

Derwing, T. and M.J. Munro (2007) Canadian Policies on Immigrant Language Education. In R. Joshee and L. Johnson (eds.) *Multicultural Education Policies in Canada and the United States.* Vancouver: UBC Press.

Englund, M.M., A.E. Luckner, G. Whaley, and B. Egeland (2004) Children's achievement in Early Elementary School: Longitudinal Effects of Parental Involvement, Expectations and Quality of Assistance. *Journal of Educational Psychology* 96(4):723–730.

Foner, N. (2010) Questions of Success: Lessons from the Last Great Immigration. In G. Sonnert and G. Holton (eds.) *Helping Young Refugees and Immigrants Succeed.* New York: Palgrave Macmillan.

Fry, R. (2003) *Hispanic Youth Dropping out of U.S. Schools: Measuring the Challenge.* Washington, DC: Pew Hispanic Centre.

Davies, L. (2006) Global Citizenship: Abstraction or Framework for Action? *Educational Review* 58(1):5–25.

Jones, T.L. and R.J. Prinz (2005) Potential Roles of Parental Self-efficacy and Child Adjustment: A Review. *Clinical Psychology Review* 25(3):341–363.

Joshee, R. and L. Johnson (2007) *Multicultural Education Policies in Canada and the United States.* Vancouver: UBC Press.

Lund, D. (2006) Rocking the Racism Boat: School-based Activists Speak out on Denial and Avoidance. *Race, Ethnicity and Education* 9(2):203–221.

Ministry of Education (2005) *The Ontario Curriculum: Canadian and World Studies.* Toronto: Queen's Printer for Ontario.

Noguero, P. (2006) Latino Youth: Immigration, Education, and the Future. *Latino Studies.* (Accessed on May 21, 2014)

Ovando, C.J. and T.G. Wiley (2007) A Critical Examination of Language Policies and Practices in Canada and the United States. In R. Joshee and L. Johnson (eds.) *Multicultural Education Policies in Canada and the United States.* Vancouver: UBC Press.

Portes, A. and D. MacLeod (2005) Educational Progress of Children of Immigrants: The Roles of Class, Ethnicity, and School Context. In M. Suarez-Orozco, C. Suarez-Orozco, and D.B. Qin (eds.) *The New Immigration: An Interdisciplinary Reader.* New York: Taylor & Francis.

Roer-Strier, D. (2001) Reducing Risk for Children in Changing Cultural Contexts: Recommendations for Intervention and Training. *Child Abuse and Neglect* 25:231–248.

Richardson, G. (2008) Conflicting Imaginaries: Global Citizenship Education in Canada as a Site of Contestation. In M. O'Sullivan and K. Pashby (eds.) *Citizenship Education in the Era of Globalization*, pp. 53–70. Rotterdam, Netherlands: Sense Publishers.

Suárez-Orozco, C. and F. Gaytán (2010) Schooling Pathways of Newcomer Immigrant Youth. In G. Sonnert and G. Holton (eds.) *Helping Young Refugees and Immigrants Succeed.* New York: Palgrave Macmillan.

Suárez-Orozco, C. and H. Yoshikawa (2013) Undocumented Status: Implications for Child Development, Policy, and Ethical Research. In M.G. Hernándes, J. Nguyen, C.L. Saetermoe, and C. Suárez-Orozco (eds.) *Frameworks and Ethics for Research with Immigrants. New Directions for Child and Adolescent Development* 141:61–78.

Sicakken, H.G. (2005) *How Is a Diverse European Society Possible? An Exploration into New Public Spaces in Six European Countries.* AMID Working paper series. Aalborg, Denmark: AMID.

U.S. Department of Education (2012) New Data from U.S. Department of Education Highlights Educational Inequities Around Teacher Experience, Discipline and High School Rigor. www.ed.gov/news/press-releases/new-data-us-department-education-highlights-educational-inequities-around-teache

Yoshikawa, H. (2011) *Immigrants Raising Citizens: Undocumented Parents and Their Young Children.* New York: Russell Sage.

Zine, J. (2008) *Canadian Islamic Schools: Unravelling the Politics of Faith, Gender, Knowledge, and Identity.* Toronto: University of Toronto Press.

Chapter 12

Newcomer Food Security and Safety

Mustafa Koc, Kristen Soo, and Lichun Willa Liu

Introduction

Food is not only an essential of human health but it also is a crucial component of culture. What we eat, how we eat, and when and with whom we eat is shaped by a wide range of social and cultural arrangements. To maintain their sustenance, humans enter into complex relations with each other and with nature. Food enters into our lives as nutriens, an important part of our culture, a commodity, and an identity badge. Most human interactions involve producing, preparing, and consuming food. From birth to death, almost all human rituals involve food. Food is an important element that unites family members around the table. It denotes ethnic, regional, and national identity. It helps us develop friendships and provide hospitality, and serves as a gift. It is an important part of holidays, celebrations, and special occasions. It carries an important role in many religious rituals and taboos. It can be used as a marker of status (Koc, Sumner, and Winson 2012).

Food also plays an important role in human socialization, developing an awareness of body and self, language acquisition, and personality development. Food is central to our sense of identity. We learn our culture in the unique social, historical, and cultural context in which we live. The socialization process is also a life-long process of enculturation. Through consuming and producing food, we learn our culture, we learn who we are, how we differ from "others," what we like, what we desire.

Cultural identity is expressed in various everyday practices such as language, clothing, music, table manners, leisure activities, religious observations, literature, and music. By observing cultural practices and preferences, such as food choice, we gain valuable insights into the levels of individual or collective behaviour.

Food is thus a central feature of everyday life. When people move to a new physical, social, and cultural environment, depending on the level of difference, they may experience difficulties in **adaptation**. Adaptation refers to whether or to what extent migrants adapt to new patterns of cultural conduct and willingly include different forms of behaviour into their everyday practices (Koc and Welsh 2002). The dominant culture in the country of destination often puts pressures on minorities and immigrants to assimilate. Conversely, **cultural pluralism** implies that there will be less pressure for **assimilation** and diverse cultural practices will find room in the broader social context to remain side by side (see **multiculturalism**) or merge into a new hybrid culture (see **melting pot**).

Immigrant Identity and Food

Moving between the boundaries of cultural and geographical space, the **immigrant** experience provides us with important insights in the retention of culture, identity formation, and change and resistance against these processes. In our understanding, culture is fluid and ever changing. The idea that culture can be authentic—as original, genuine, and unique practice—is only a fiction of our imagination. All cultures change. In the last few centuries these changes have been magnified under the influence of processes of industrialization, modernization, globalization, and the increased mobility of populations. As people, commodities, and cultural products have moved in multiple directions, cultural change has been intensified. This process of cultural change is complex. In some contexts cultural change exhibits tendencies for homogeneity and the expansion of similarities; in other contexts it leads to heterogeneity and differentiation. The results are often **creolized cultures** and **hybrid identities** that include local and global, traditional and modern, and old and new aspects (Hall 1990:31–34).

Cultural meanings attached to food are often based on conflicting notions of physical health, aesthetics, tastes, and social prestige, reflecting the contradictions between the domestic (home) and public (work) spheres. Like our identities, our food is also creolized in complex ways, bringing together diverse influences and traditions. As people who move between different cultural spaces, immigrants, in particular, experience this complex cultural creolization.

As other chapters in this volume illustrate, immigrants often undergo a dramatic cultural transition, and the familiarity or unfamiliarity of cultural experiences and consumption patterns, as well as rights, entitlements, choices, and quality of life have immediate effects on the health and well-being of immigrants and their families. When we talk about food we need to examine not only familiarity with food but also *accessibility* to food as an important issue of cultural adaptation and identity formation.

Food Security and the Immigrant Experience

Food security is defined as access by all people, at all times, to food that is safe, nutritionally adequate, and personally acceptable, and that is obtained in a manner that respects human dignity (Koc 2013). The lack of food security has long been a problem for the most vulnerable segments of the population.

Statistics Canada's Household Food Security Survey Module, which was part of the annual Canadian Community Health Survey, indicated that in 2011, 1.6 million Canadian households, or slightly more than 12%, experienced some level of food insecurity. This amounted to nearly 1 in 8 households, and 3.9 million individuals in Canada, including 1.1 million children. There were 450,000 more Canadians living in households affected by food insecurity in 2011 than in 2008 (Tarasuk, Mitchell, and Dachner 2011). An earlier Population Health Survey in 2007–2008 indicated that the prevalence of household food insecurity was higher among recent immigrant households. Of recent immigrant households—that is, households whose inhabitants have been in Canada for fewer than 5 years—12.6% were food insecure. This is high compared to the 7.5% of nonimmigrant households and the 7.8% of nonrecent immigrant households that reported they were uncertain of having, or unable to acquire, enough food to meet the needs of all their members because they had insufficient money for food (Health Canada 2007).

Food insecurity among recent immigrants is similarly high in the United States. Looking at infants of foreign-born parents, Capps, Horowitz, Fortuny, Bronte-Tinkew, and Zaslow (2009) estimated that 18.8% of infants with foreign-born parents were food insecure, compared to 11.3% of infants in US-born citizen families. The situation was worse for children who had at least one noncitizen parent. Among infant children of noncitizen parents, 22.3% experienced food insecurity, compared with 11% of infants whose parents were naturalized immigrants. Language proficiency was also a factor. Children of immigrants whose parents did not speak English very well were twice as likely as infants with English-proficient parents to live in food insecure households (Capps et al. 2009).

Upon arrival, new immigrants are faced with a myriad of circumstances and experiences that may impact on their food security. Unavailability or high costs of foods used in traditional diets, changes in lifestyle and working conditions, and pressures for **integration** to a new culture result in dietary modifications, often with negative impacts on health. A recent survey of the literature on diet and immigrant health indicates that although recent immigrants to Canada are healthier than Canadian-born (i.e. the **healthy immigrant effect**), as a result of transitions in their dietary habits their health deteriorates in the long term (Sanou, O'Reilly, Ngnie-Teta, Batal, Mondain, Andrew, Newbold, and Bourgeault 2013). Katherine Fennely points out that first-generation immigrants to the United States tend to be healthier than people of similar ethnic backgrounds who were born in the country. However, over time, factors such as poverty, substandard housing, lack of access to medical care, dietary change, smoking, and substance abuse reduce the newcomers' health advantages (2007).

Part of the immigrant experience involves navigating the essentials of everyday life. For newcomers, food is not only a basic for survival but also plays an important role in the settlement process. Food is both physical and symbolic, as its quantity and nutritional quality have an impact on physical health, and at the same time, the type of food and conditions surrounding it convey meaning to ourselves and others about who we are. Food can signal collective identity, allowing us to express our affiliations, and also influences how others perceive us (Kittler and Sucher 2004). Specifically for immigrants and their children, food can be a way to remain connected to the sending or ancestral culture, or to assert an acculturated identity (Vallianatos and Raine 2008; Guendelman, Cheryan, and Monin 2011).

In line with this role of food, food security and the factors that encourage or hinder it are important for feelings of self-worth and belonging in society. This situation is particularly salient in the context of newcomer settlement:

> For immigrants who go through a dramatic cultural and spatial transition, not only the familiarity of cultural experiences and consumption patterns, but also rights, entitlements and quality of life make important points of comparison between past and present, as these will have immediate effects on health and well-being of immigrants and their families. (Koc and Welsh 2002:4)

In this way, food insecurity is not only about lack of food, but about broader economic and social circumstances that lead immigrants to lack access to safe, nutritious, and personally acceptable food.

Ryerson University's Centre for Studies in Food Security (2012) identifies five components of food security:

1. Availability: sufficiency in quantity of food
2. Accessibility: economic and physical aspects of obtaining food
3. Adequacy: nutritional value and safety of food, as well as the production methods
4. Acceptability: cultural preferences in food
5. Agency: policies and processes that enable food security

Below we examine each of these five components in greater detail.

Availability

Food deserts are low-income urban neighbourhoods that are characterized by their lack of access to healthy, nutritious food. The literature points toward the existence of food deserts in the US. Findings as to whether food deserts exist or not in Canada vary depending on the cities being studied as well as the measures being used (Beaulac, Kristjansson, and Cummins 2009).

As the Canadian literature on food deserts does not directly discuss immigrant status or ethnicity in relation to food deserts, literature on **ethnic enclaves** can be drawn on to inform the discussion. The defining characteristics of Canada's ethnic enclaves are that they have an ethnic **concentration** and are institutionally complete, in that they feature ethnic businesses, institutions, associations, and services (Qadeer, Agrawal, and Lovell 2010). This means that immigrants who opt to live among co-ethnics in enclaves will have access to local ethnic businesses, including grocery stores.

The prevalence and nature of both food deserts and ethnic enclaves in the US are markedly different from those in Canada, making it difficult to draw comparisons. However, in both the US and Canada, availability of food is not as simple as geographic proximity. There can be food in the neighbourhoods in which immigrants live, but the choice is often between commuting for long periods of time to access lower priced foods or paying more in stores that are located closer to home. So while scarcity of food and physical access to food stores may not be considered problems by immigrants, the indirectly related issues of high prices of healthy food close to home, limited time for shopping, and arranging transportation and childcare can pose challenges (Dubowitz, Acevedo-Garcia, Salkeld, Lindsay, Subramanian, and Peterson 2007; Kirkpatrick and Tarasuk 2010).

Accessibility

Accessibility, particularly economic accessibility, represents a major challenge to food security for immigrants in North America. Financial ability to obtain food is a necessary condition for food security, and this is a particular issue for immigrants who face difficulty in obtaining gainful employment. Low socioeconomic status is not a barrier to food security unique to immigrants; the same income-related factors that hinder immigrants from attaining food security can also hinder the general population. Immigrants, however, often face challenges above and beyond those experienced by the locally born population in gaining income. Recent immigrants have been described as facing "a particularly complex set of circumstances" with respect to securing employment (Che 2009:37), as Chapter 6 by Michael Samers and Mitchell Snider attests.

The difficulties that immigrants face with securing employment and income lead to financial challenges in accessing food. Studies indicate that recent Latin American immigrants in Canada, despite high levels of education, experienced food insecurity due to income-related factors. Income and length of residence in Canada were reported to be inversely related to food insecurity, and use of social assistance as main source of income, use of food banks, and limited English language proficiency were strong predictors of food insecurity (Vahabi, Damba, Rocha, and Montoya 2011; Rush, Ng, Irwin, Stitt, and He 2007). For undocumented Latin American immigrants in the US, engaging in day labour was found to be a predictor of food insecurity, likely because the low pay and uncertain nature of the work results in large fluxes in income (Hadley, Galea, Nandi, Nandi, Lopez, Strongarone, and Ompad 2007). Among West African asylum seekers and resettled refugees in the US, income and employment status were found to be associated with food insecurity (Hadley, Patil, and Nahayo 2010).

Cost of housing often exacerbates the problem of food insecurity for immigrants. Immigrants, compared to the overall population, are more likely to spend more than 30% of their household income on housing. Housing that costs 30% or less of household income is considered affordable. About 23% of all Canadian households spend more than 30% on housing, but more than 80% of new immigrants spend more than 30% of their income on housing (Canada Mortgage and Housing Corporation 2007; Preston, Murdie, D'Addario, Sibanda, Murnaghan, Logan, and Ahn 2011). For 30% of asylum seekers, housing takes up more than 75% of their household income. The struggles with housing costs persist among immigrants who have been in Canada for 5 to 10 years (Preston et al. 2011). Almost 20 and 25% of low-income immigrant families in New York and Los Angeles, respectively, reported problems paying rent, mortgage, or utilities (Capps, Ku, Fix, Furgiuele, Passel, Ramchand, McNiven, and Perez-Lopez 2002). The problem of affordable housing is directly linked to food security: the cost of rent is fixed and must be paid every month, while food intake can be adjusted by eating less or buying less expensive foods. Often, immigrants must make a choice between eating a meal and paying rent on time. This situation is well expressed in the poignant phrase "pay the rent or feed the kids" (Kirkpatrick and Tarasuk 2007:1465). A similar situation is observed in the US. Looking at the age and condition of the housing stock and availability of rental units in rural areas, an Iowa study found that lack of affordable housing played a significant role in food insecurity among Latino immigrants (Greder, Cook, Garasky, and Ortiz 2007).

Faced with a lack of employment or low income, immigrants may turn to social assistance, but this still may not be adequate for both food and other expenses such as housing or medication. Canada's large food banks have called for improvements to both social assistance and employment insurance, as a large proportion of food bank users rely on these sources of income (Food Banks Canada 2011). In the US, certain legal immigrants can access various welfare or social assistance programs; however, it has been found that eligible immigrant families tend to use these services, including the Supplemental Nutrition Assistance Program (formerly called the Food Stamp Program) at much lower rates than US-born families. Potential rationales for this low participation rate include lack of knowledge of the programs and eligibility criteria, social stigma, onerous program enrollment and compliance requirements, and fear that taking part could jeopardize residential status or eligibility for US citizenship (Skinner 2011).

Adequacy

Adequate food that is nutritious and safe, and that was produced in a manner that meets cultural expectations, is not always available to newcomers. The adjustment to adequate foods available in Canada and the US—which are often less healthy than the foods from immigrants' sending countries—is another contributor to unhealthy eating for newcomers. The change in dietary patterns attributable to the availability of food in the destination country leads to **dietary acculturation**, which can be defined as "the process that occurs when members of a minority group adopt the eating patterns/food choices of the host country" (Satia 2010:220). Dietary acculturation is often associated with the adoption of an inadequate diet.

Dietary acculturation has been shown to have negative effects on immigrants' health, because the styles of food available in high-income countries like Canada and the US tend to be more energy-dense and include processed foods and high levels of animal products. Acculturating to a Western diet also usually means a decreased intake of fruits, vegetables, and whole grains, and an increase in snacking and eating away from home. These dietary changes are often coupled with lower physical activity. The outcome is higher rates of obesity and other chronic diet-related diseases (Satia 2010; also see Chapter 13 by Morton Beiser).

The literature suggests that dietary acculturation is a dynamic, nonlinear process: rather than moving straight along a continuum from traditional to acculturated dietary choices, immigrants will often find new ways to use traditional foods, exclude certain foods, and introduce Western foods into their diets. This can result in bicultural eating patterns, whereby traditional eating habits will be maintained for certain meals and occasions, but the host country's eating patterns will be incorporated as well (Satia 2010).

Not all immigrants will acculturate their diets at the same pace or to the same extent, and the health consequences of the dietary changes will vary. Much of the research on this topic focuses on one specific immigrant ethnic group, or compares changes between groups, and the reasons why and ways in which their diets acculturate. For example, a study of Chinese immigrants in the US found that their consumption of all seven food groups (grains, vegetables, fruits, meat/meat alternatives, dairy products, fats/sweets, and beverages) as well as of Western foods increased, while intake of traditional Chinese foods dropped (Lv and Cason 2004). It is not only the types of foods that change with acculturation, but also the portion sizes and where the food is from: Chinese immigrants who have lived in Canada the longest eat significantly greater portion sizes, dine out more often, and consume convenience foods more frequently (Rosenmöller, Gasevic, Seidell, and Lear 2011). Younger, **highly educated immigrants** who have lived longer in the US, and especially women with jobs outside the home, have the most acculturated diets in that country (Satia, Patterson, Kristal, Hislop, Yasui, and Taylor 2001; Oster and Yung 2010).

A study compared Hmong adults who had been in the US for less than five years, more than five years, and who had been born in the US. The authors found that dietary acculturation was influenced by age at **immigration**, length of residency in the US, and use of food assistance programs. Some families prepare two different evening meals: one of Hmong food for the parents, and one of American food for the children (Franzen and Smith 2009). In this vein, a study with Liberian and Bantu refugees in the US showed that children are often a strong influence over the dietary acculturation of their caretakers. Children attending daycare or school will have the opportunity to learn English and interact with children of the receiving culture. Their caretakers, however, will often be working in jobs that do not allow for as many opportunities to interact with peers and learn English. English-language advertising then has a greater effect on the children, and as the children now have more advanced English language skills, the caretakers may trust them more with providing information about foods (Patil, Hadley, and Nahayo 2009).

Case Example 1: Immigrant Nutrition Education Programs

Communities are recognizing that food is an important part of immigrant integration and are beginning to offer nutrition education programs specifically tailored for newcomers. Below are three examples.

Toronto's Regent Park Community Health Centre provides nutrition and health education services to newcomers. A community health worker and dietician facilitate the program in multiple languages. The goals are to increase awareness of certain health conditions as well as to prevent or care for chronic diseases by encouraging healthy lifestyles (Regent Park Community Health Centre 2012).

Winnipeg's Immigrant Centre provides free cooking and nutrition classes and presentations for newcomers of all English levels. Newcomers can learn about healthy eating and new recipes, and can go grocery shopping with a teacher to learn about saving money and reading food labels (Immigrant Centre 2013).

The Heartland Alliance, an anti-poverty organization based in Chicago, runs a nutrition program for refugees who have recently been resettled. Working with five resettlement agencies, two health clinics, and other community partners, the program provides individual nutrition screening and medical nutrition therapy, monthly cooking groups, a community gardening project, and culturally and linguistically appropriate nutrition education materials (Heartland Alliance 2014).

Acceptability

While immigrants may choose to incorporate more Western foods into their diets, acceptability of food is still a consideration. Cultural acceptability, in terms of food choices and the way the foods are sourced and prepared, is an important aspect of food security for immigrants. Food plays a central role in the formation and expression of identity. Therefore, if it is difficult to access food that suits immigrants' tastes or dietary requirements (for example, for kosher or halal ingredients), it can be frustrating and alienating. A study conducted by Jennifer Welsh and colleagues (1998) indicated that most of the participants, who were immigrants and people who serve immigrants, reported that finding familiar, culturally acceptable, and fresh foods was important.

Most aspects surrounding the acceptability of food are profoundly connected to identity, and for immigrants who are undergoing a process of uprooting and putting down new roots in a destination country, this is particularly salient. Iara Lessa and Cecilia Rocha's (2009) interviews with **immigrant women** demonstrated that food can be used to give concrete form to the nostalgic longing for home and offers what they call "diasporic healing." Food is used as a reminder of home, missing a certain food is a way to talk about missing home, and cooking and eating a certain food creates a sense of comfort and erases time and distance. Food can also lead to **othering** and exclusion, as is the case when food is prohibitively expensive. The inability to afford certain food items can be deeply marginalizing, and as a result, many of the women interviewed managed costs by substituting ingredients, travelling for long times to find better prices, and spending time studying ads. In addition, marginalization takes place when husbands and children who bring food to work and school, respectively, become the subject of jokes, shaming, discrimination, and segregation. The authors note that ethnic foods are often not welcomed into mainstream society. At the same time, food can create positive interactions with the receiving country. An example would be when an immigrant discovers a new ingredient and creates an integrated recipe, thus creating a hybrid space in the home that helps mitigate against the hostility faced outside: "offering favourite traditional foods, unique hybrid dishes and surprising new foods can transform the home into a distinctive space that exists in the present but also in the re-lived experiences evoked by the tastes of the homeland" (Lessa and Rocha 2009:153). Preparing food in the home is also often chosen over eating in restaurants due to concern over ingesting prohibited foods. "I have to cook everything at home because of the Halal factor," noted one interviewee in a study of South Asian and Arabic women in Canada (Vallianatos and Raine 2008).

Agency

The policies and processes that enable food security can be considered through the lenses of two approaches: the anti-poverty approach (also called the social justice approach) and the sustainable food systems approach (Power 1999). The anti-poverty approach is rooted in the notion that North America has enough available food to feed the population and that the problem lies in lack of access to that food. As Canada and the US are industrialized nations with market economies, and most residents buy almost all of their food, this approach focuses on the lack of money to buy food. Problems related to food security in terms of economic accessibility, the difficulty immigrants face in securing employment, and the insufficiency of social

Case Example 2: Changes in Diet and Food Safety Practices

In the Greater Toronto Area, we conducted a small-scale survey with 22 recent Chinese immigrant participants, two focus groups, as well as three individual interviews with a community worker and two public health professionals. In this survey, 20 out of 22 immigrant respondents reported adopting new food items into their diet, such as bread, dairy products, pasta, and salads. Many of the respondents also reported increased consumption of meat, frozen food, desserts, and organic food. More than two-thirds of the respondents reported maintaining a traditional diet, with rice and noodles as their staple foods, but with slightly reduced consumption of steamed bread, another traditional Chinese staple food. However, in contrast with literature on Chinese immigrant dietary acculturation (Lv and Cason 2004; Satia 1999; Wang 2007), half of the respondents consumed less processed or ready-to-eat food than before. This difference is probably because of their reduced income after immigration, as the majority of them did not have a full-time job. More than half of the respondents reported eating out less often since they immigrated to Canada.

All the participants reported that they were concerned about food safety when they went grocery shopping. Many of them said that they would take the following factors into consideration when grocery shopping: expiry date, freshness, location of stores, personal/family preferences, food prices, and nutrition. A relatively small number of the respondents said they cared about local food or brand-name food, which were likely to be more expensive and thus less affordable for the new immigrants. The majority of respondents were concerned about nutrition, food preferences, and food safety when they cooked or prepared food for themselves and their family.

Overall, nearly all the recent immigrants in the focus group felt that the foods they ate were safer in Canada than in their home country, with reduced or strictly controlled use of pesticides, additives, and hormones. With the exception of two who said that they had always been concerned about food safety, before and after immigration, the majority of the participants in the focus group said that they became more aware of food safety, nutrition, and health since coming to Canada. Many also reported learning new practices in purchasing, preparing, cooking, and storing food. These include checking food labels for the expiry date, using separate chopping boards for cutting raw meats and cooked food, and avoiding heating food in Styrofoam boxes.

The research on Chinese immigrants' food safety practices reveals several gaps in their food safety knowledge and practices. Despite showing great concern for food safety, most of the participants lacked adequate knowledge of Canadian food safety guidelines and recommended food handling practices. Most of the Chinese immigrants, especially newcomers and older adults, mentioned their difficulty in communicating in English as the biggest challenge in accessing information on food safety (Koc, Liu, and Guclu-Ustundag 2010).

assistance, are all problems of poverty. Under this approach, the government would bear the main responsibility for addressing the root causes of poverty and thereby food insecurity.

The second approach to promoting food security is the sustainable food systems approach, which sees "corporate control of the food system and the commodification of food [as] the predominant threats to food security" (Power 1999:33). The environmental movement has added that this capitalistic food system is unsustainable, as it disregards threats to human living standards and well-being as well as environmental degradation. Initiatives such as community gardens and collective kitchens would fall under this approach; these initiatives are mainly the domain of community organizations, though they can be strengthened by the support of various levels of government.

Food Safety and Immigrant Experience

Food safety, which is the proper ways of handing, preparing, and storing food to prevent food-borne diseases, is of crucial importance to our health and economy (Jevšnik, Hlebec, and Raspor 2008). Food safety refers to the absence of hazards, whether chronic or acute, that may make food injurious to the health of the consumer (Food and Agriculture Organization/World Health Organization 2003).

Food contamination creates an enormous social and economic burden on communities and their health systems. It is estimated that in the last 20 years these economic losses amounted to nearly 1.0 to 1.2 billion dollars globally (Jevsnik et al. 2008). Study shows that between 50 and 87% of reported food-borne disease outbreaks have occurred within the home (Redmond and Griffith 2003). Contaminated raw foods, inadequate cooking, and consumption of food from an unsafe source were the factors most commonly associated with reported outbreaks of food-borne illness in homes (Medeiros et al., 2001).

Analysis of longitudinal data from the US Food Safety Survey (1988 to 2010) found that there was a substantial improvement in food handling and consumption practices and an increase in perceived risk from food-borne illness, and that changes in safety of practices over the survey years are consistent with the change in the number of media stories about food safety in the periods between surveys. These findings suggest that increased media attention to food safety issues may raise awareness of food safety hazards and increase vigilance in food handling by consumers. However, the researchers also found differences by gender, age, and level of education. Women had safer food handling and consumption practices than men. The oldest and youngest respondents and those with the highest education had the least-safe food handling behaviours (Fein, Lando, Levy, Teisl, and Noblet 2011). Food safety has been the top priority of the Canadian and US public health agencies. However, there are wide knowledge gaps in the area of traditional foods and food safety, such as information on traditional foods, food handling and preparation practices, and the educational needs of public health officials and newcomers (Papadopoulos, Isaacs, and Marshall 2009). While public health agencies have particularly been concerned about traditional ways of food handling as a safety risk, newcomers often face challenges in dealing with food safety practice in an industrial food system. Newcomers' often unwarranted trust in the industrial food system tends to increase their vulnerability to food-borne illnesses. For example, what might be considered as safe practice when handling fresh meat in the country of origin may be a safety hazard when it is applied to handling frozen poultry raised in industrial farms contaminated with dangerous bacteria (Ying 2000).

Conclusion

As a culturally and spatially transitional stage, the immigration process introduces possibilities of change and resistance to new cultural experiences. Especially in the case of new immigrants who deal with tensions of adaptation or resistance to changes in lifestyle, consumption patterns and forms of cultural expression can have consequences on their physical and mental health, their perceptions of self and relations with the others, and their potential for successful settlement and integration.

In its broadest definition, food security includes not only availability of food at all times but also accessibility to all. Equality of access, notions of entitlements, and the basic rights of citizenship create public obligations for food security. This makes both the politics of equality and the politics of recognition relevant to the food security concerns of new immigrants.

Food security for new immigrants implies, first of all, access to sufficient, nutritious, and quality food at all times. Food security is part of "feeling at home"—a comfort that is not only limited to or defined by access to food, but also access to the basic essentials of life offered to citizens in a modern state, such as an equitable and accessible work environment, housing, healthcare, public education, and social services. The feeling of belonging, or identification with the host society, requires a subjective interpretation of inclusion and entitlement.

Immigration experience is fraught with various opportunities as well as risks for the newcomer as well as the host society when it comes to culinary practices. Potentials for cultural exchange create opportunities for learning from diverse traditions. Culinary creolization, for example, provides potentials for fusion and cross-cultural interchange. However, dietary acculturation may also lead to a decline in health as a result of immigrants adapting to the unhealthy eating habits of the host society, in what is known as the healthy immigrant effect. Food safety practices also carry similar public health risks in the forms of food poisoning or other food-borne illnesses. Traditional food safety practices or unfamiliarity with food safety rules in the host country may carry risks both for the host society and the newcomer,

"Feeling at home" is not simply limited to having access to nutritionally sufficient foods, but also to culturally appropriate diets. Availability and accessibility to culturally appropriate foods brings a sense of comfort, a sense of "home feeling." The rich multicultural diversity of the food markets or restaurants available in global cities, such as Toronto, provide cultural comfort zones for the global citizens. Dismissing the importance of culinary diversity as a form of folkloric multiculturalism underestimates the significance of cosmopolitan diets in effective settlement. Furthermore, the collective experience of sharing seemingly mundane everyday acts such as eating, dressing, and listening to music make cultural boundaries of membership permeable.

For many newcomers, talking about food insecurity or lack of food preparation and food safety skills is an embarrassing admission (Koyama 2014). Many would choose to fill their stomachs with starches and other staples instead of going to a food bank to avoid the stigma attached with that act. Governments, on the others hand, see poverty and food insecurity more as a transitional phenomenon among newcomers and do not collect long-term data to gain insights on the impacts of food insecurity and food safety on the health of immigrants and their families. Longitudinal studies by social scientists, nutritionists, and public health experts are needed to find out the extent and impacts of nutrition transition, food insecurity, and food safety on the health and well-being of immigrants.

Questions for Critical Thought

1. What challenges do recent immigrants encounter in their food safety practices?
2. What can be done to raise and improve food safety awareness among recent immigrants?
3. In what ways could food insecurity affect immigrants' perception of the receiving society?
4. Think of your favourite food. What does it convey about your identity?

Key Readings

Lessa, I. and C. Rocha (2009) Nourishing Belonging: Food in the Lives of New Immigrants in T.O. In C. Palassio and A. Wilcox (eds.) *The Edible City: Toronto's Food from Farm to Fork*, pp. 148–153. Toronto: Coach House Books.

Koç, M. and J. Welsh (2002) Food, Foodways and Immigrant Experience. Paper written for the Multiculturalism Program, Department of Canadian Heritage. www.canada. metropolis.net/events/ethnocultural/publications /aliments_e.pdf (Accessed December 13, 2013)

Media Links

Meal Exchange—An Introduction to Food Security
www.youtube.com/watch?v=PE1-RYPJNdg
This five-minute video provides an introduction to food security, focusing on the components of accessibility, availability, adequacy, and acceptability discussed in this chapter.

How to: Be Food Safe Canada:
www.youtube.com/watch?v=sf7ic4Lhnv8
A short educational video by the Canadian Partnership for Consumer Food Safety Education that demonstrates safe food-handling practices for the home cook.

Voices of Disposable People:
A 52-minute documentary about farm workers in the Dominican Republic and the US. Director: R. Cornellier (2003). Montreal: Macumba International. Distributed by Ciné Fête.

Fast Food Nation:

A drama loosely based on Eric Schlosser's book *Fast Food Nation*, a journalistic exposé of the dark side of the fast food economy. It sheds light on the difficult lives of illegal migrant Mexican workers at meat processing plants. Director: R. Linklater (2006). Distributed by Fox Searchlight Pictures.

Food, Inc.:

A documentary film that examines the problems with the corporate farming's impact on farmers, farm workers, human health, and animals in the US. Director: R. Kenner (2009). Magnolia Pictures. Montreal: Alliance Vivafilm.

References

Beaulac, J., E. Kristjansson, and S. Cummins (2009) A Systematic Review of Food Deserts, 1966–2007. *Preventing Chronic Disease* 6(3):A105.

Canada Mortgage and Housing Corporation (2007) *Canadian Housing Observer 2007*. Ottawa: Canada Mortgage and Housing Corporation.

Capps, R., L. Ku, M.E. Fix, C. Furgiuele, J.S. Passel, R. Ramchand, S. McNiven, and D. Perez-Lopez (2002) How Are Immigrants Faring After Welfare Reform? Preliminary Evidence from Los Angeles and New York City—Final Report. Report for Office of the Assistant Secretary for Planning and Evaluation. Washington, DC: U.S. Department of Health and Human Services. www.urban.org/UploadedPDF/410426_final_report.pdf (Accessed January 11, 2014)

Capps, R., A. Horowitz, K. Fortuny, J. Bronte-Tinkew, and M. Zaslow (2009) Young Children in Immigrant Families Face Higher Risk of Food Insecurity. *Child Trends* 2009:07.

Centre for Studies in Food Security (2012) Food Security Defined. www.ryerson.ca/foodsecurity/definition/index.html (Accessed December 13, 2013)

Che, C. (2009) Immigrant Settlement and the Use of Food Banks. *Esurio: Journal of Hunger and Poverty* 1(2):34–45.

Dubowitz, T., D. Acevedo-Garcia, J. Salkeld, A.C. Lindsay, S.V. Subramanian, and K.E. Peterson (2007) Lifecourse, Immigrant Status and Acculturation in Food Purchasing and Preparation among Low-income Mothers. *Public Health Nutrition* 10(4):396–404.

Fein, S.B., A.M. Lando, A.S. Levy, M.F. Teisl, and C. Noblet (2011) Trends in US Consumers' Safe Handling and Consumption of Food and Their Risk Perceptions, 1988 through 2010. *Journal of Food Protection* 74(9):1513–1523.

Fennely, K. (2007) The "Healthy Migrant" Effect. *Minnesota Medicine.*
www.minnesotamedicine.com/PastIssues/PastIssues2007/March2007/
FennellyClinicalMarch2007.aspx (Accessed January 14, 2014)

Food and Agriculture Organization (FAO)/World Health Organization (WHO) (2003)
Assuring Food Safety and Quality: Guidelines for Strengthening National Food
Control Systems.

Food Banks Canada (2011) *Hunger Count: A Comprehensive Report on Hunger and Food
Bank Use in Canada, and Recommendations for Change.* www.foodbankscanada.ca/
getmedia/3f717aba-27f7-4ea0-9b78-36da94dcfe4e/HungerCount_2011_EN-REV.pdf.
aspx?ext=.pdf (Accessed December 13, 2013)

Franzen, L. and C. Smith (2009) Acculturation and Environmental Change Impacts Dietary
Habits among Adult Hmong. *Appetite* 52(1):173–183.

Greder, K., C. Cook, S. Garasky, and L. Ortiz (2007) Latino Immigrants: Food and
Housing Insecurity Fastest-Growing Minority. Des Moines, IA: Iowa State University,
University Extension. www.extension.iastate.edu/publications/sp305.pdf (Accessed
January 14, 2014)

Guendelman, M.D., S. Cheryan, and B. Monin (2011) Fitting in but Getting Fat: Identity
Threat and Dietary Choices among U.S. Immigrant Groups. *Psychological Science*
22(7):959–967.

Hadley, C., S. Galea, V. Nandi, A. Nandi, G. Lopez, S. Strongarone, and D. Ompad (2007)
Hunger and Health among Undocumented Mexican Migrants in a US Urban Area.
Public Health Nutrition 11(2):151–158.

Hadley, C., C.L. Patil, and D. Nahayo (2010) Difficulty in the Food Environment and the
Experience of Food Insecurity among Refugees Resettled in the United States. *Ecology
of Food and Nutrition* 49(5):390–407.

Hall, S. (1990) Cultural Identity and Diaspora. In J. Rutherford (ed.) *Identity: Community,
Culture, Difference.* London: Lawrence and Wishart.

Health Canada (2007) Canadian Community Health Survey, Cycle 2.2, Nutrition (2004):
Income-related Household Food Security in Canada (H164-42/2007E-PDF).
www.hc-sc.gc.ca/fn-an/surveill/nutrition/commun/income_food_sec-sec_alim-eng.
php (Accessed December 13, 2013)

Heartland Alliance (2014) Refugee Nutrition. www.heartlandalliance.org/whatwedo/our-
programs/directory/refugee-nutrition.html (Accessed January 11, 2014)

Immigrant Centre (2013) Nutrition Services. www.icmanitoba.com/services/nutrition-
services (Accessed December 13, 2013)

Jevšnik, M., V. Hlebec, and P. Raspor (2008) Consumers' Awareness of Food Safety from
Shopping to Eating. *Food Control* 19(8):737–745.

Kirkpatrick, S.I. and V. Tarasuk (2007) Adequacy of Food Spending Is Related to Housing Expenditures among Lower-income Canadian Households. *Public Health Nutrition* 10(12):1464–1473.

Kirkpatrick, S.I. and V. Tarasuk (2010) Assessing the Relevance of Neighbourhood Characteristics to the Household Food Security of Low-income Toronto Families. *Public Health Nutrition* 13(7):1139–1148.

Kittler, P.G. and K.P. Sucher (2004) *Food and Culture*. 4th ed. Belmont, CA: Wadsworth.

Koc, M. (2013) Discourses of Food Security. In B. Karaagac (ed.) *Accumulations, Crises, Struggles: Capital and Labour in Contemporary Capitalism*. Berlin: LIT Verlag.

Koc, M., J. Summer, and T. Winson (eds.) (2012) *Critical Perspectives in Food Studies*. Toronto: Oxford University Press.

Koc, M., L.W. Liu, and O. Guclu-Ustundag (2010) Food Safety and Diversity: Knowledge Transfer/Translation and Chinese Newcomers in Toronto. Report prepared for the Public Health Agency of Canada.

Koc, M. and J. Welsh (2002) Food, Foodways and Immigrant Experience. Paper written for the Multiculturalism Program, Department of Canadian Heritage at the Canadian Ethnic Studies Association Conference, Halifax. www.canada.metropolis.net/ events/ ethnocultural/publications/aliments_e.pdf (Accessed December 13, 2013)

Koyama, J. (2014) Why So Many Children of Immigrants Are Going Hungry. *Pacific Standard Magazine*, 17 April. www.psmag.com/navigation/health-and-behavior/ many-immigrant-kids-going-hungry-79344 (Accessed May 18, 2014)

Lessa, I. and C. Rocha (2009) Nourishing Belonging: Food in the Lives of New Immigrants in T.O. In C. Palassio and A. Wilcox (eds.) *The Edible City: Toronto's Food from Farm to Fork*, pp. 148–153. Toronto: Coach House Books.

Lv, N. and K.L. Cason (2004) Dietary Pattern Change and Acculturation of Chinese Americans in Pennsylvania. *Journal of the American Dietetic Association* 104(5):771–778.

Medeiros, L., V. Hillers, P. Kendall, and A. Mason (2001) Evaluation of Food Safety Education for Consumers. *Journal of Nutrition Education* 33:S27–S34.

Oster, A. and J. Yung (2010) Dietary Acculturation, Obesity, and Diabetes among Chinese Immigrants in New York City. *Diabetes Care* 33(8):e109.

Papadopoulos, A., S. Isaacs, and B. Marshall (2009) *Cultural Diversity in Food Safety Issues: Identifying Challenges, Knowledge Gaps and Opportunities for the Future*. Guelph, ON: University of Guelph.

Patil, C.L., C. Hadley, and P.D. Nahayo (2009) Unpacking Dietary Acculturation among New Americans: Results from Formative Research with African Refugees. *Journal of Immigrant and Minority Health* 11:342–358.

Power, E. (1999) Combining Social Justice and Sustainability for Food Security. In M. Koç, R. MacRae, L.J.A. Mougeot, and J. Welsh (eds.) *For Hunger-Proof Cities: Sustainable Urban Food Systems*, pp. 30–27. Ottawa: International Development Research Centre.

Preston, V., R. Murdie, S. D'Addario, P. Sibanda, A.M. Murnaghan, J. Logan, and M.H. Ahn (2011) *Precarious Housing and Hidden Homelessness among Refugees, Asylum Seekers, and Immigrants in the Toronto Metropolitan Area*. CERIS Working Paper No. 87. Toronto: CERIS. www.mbc.metropolis.net/assets/uploads/files/Precarious_Housing_Toronto_study.pdf (Accessed December 13, 2013)

Qadeer, M., S. Agrawal, and A. Lovell (2010) Evolution of Ethnic Enclaves in the Toronto Metropolitan Area, 2001–2006. *Journal of International Migration and Integration* 11(3):315–339.

Redmond, E.C. and C.J. Griffith (2003) Consumer Food Handling in the Home: A Review of Food Safety Studies. *Journal of Food Protection* 66(1):130–161.

Regent Park Community Health Centre (2012) Nutrition and Health Education Services for Immgirants/Refugees. www.regentparkchc.org/immigrant-refugee-programs/nutrition-and-health-education-services-immigrants-refugees (Accessed December 13, 2013)

Rosenmöller, D.J., D. Gasevic, J. Seidell, and S.A. Lear (2011) Determinants of Changes in Dietary Patterns among Chinese Immigrants: A Cross-sectional Analysis. *International Journal of Behavioral Nutrition and Physical Activity* 8:42.

Rush, T.J., V. Ng, J.D. Irwin, L.W. Stitt, and M. He (2007) Food Insecurity and Dietary Intake of Immigrant Food Bank Users. *Canadian Journal of Dietetic Practice and Research* 68(2):73–8.

Sanou, D., E. O'Reilly, I. Ngnie-Teta, M. Batal, N. Mondain, C. Andrew, B.K. Newbold, and I.L. Bourgeault (2013) Acculturation and Nutritional Health of Immigrants in Canada: A Scoping Review. *Journal of Immigrant Minority Health*. www.ncbi.nlm.nih.gov/pubmed/23595263 (Accessed December 13, 2013)

Satia, J.A. (1999) Diet, Acculturation, and Health in Chinese-American Women. PhD dissertation, University of Washington.

Satia, J.A. (2010) Dietary Acculturation and the Nutrition Transition: An Overview. *Applied Physiology, Nutrition and Metabolism* 35:219–223.

Satia, J.A., R.E. Patterson, A.R. Kristal, T.G. Hislop, Y. Yasui, and V.M. Taylor (2001) Development of Scales to Measure Dietary Acculturation among Chinese-Americans and Chinese-Canadians. *Journal of the American Dietetic Association* 101(7):548–553.

Skinner, C. (2011) SNAP Take-up among Immigrant Families with Children. Report for the National Center for Children in Poverty, Mailman School of Public Health, Columbia University. academiccommons.columbia.edu/catalog/ac:135847 (Accessed January 11, 2014)

Soo, K. (2012) *Newcomers and Food Insecurity: A Critical Literature Review on Immigration Food Security*. Unpublished Master's Major Research Paper, Ryerson University, Toronto.

Tarasuk, V., A. Mitchell, and N. Dachner (2011) Household Food Insecurity in Canada, 2011. nutritionalsciences.lamp.utoronto.ca

Vahabi, M., C. Damba, C. Rocha, and E.C. Montoya (2011) Food Insecurity among Latin American Recent Immigrants in Toronto. *Journal of Immigrant and Minority Health* 13(5):929–939.

Vallianatos, H. and K. Raine (2008) Consuming Food and Constructing Identities among Arabic and South Asian Immigrant Women. *Food, Culture and Society: An International Journal of Multidisciplinary Research* 11(3):355–373.

Wang, C. (2007) From China to the US: Nutrition, Diet and Acculturation of Chinese Employed in High-tech Industries—Results from a Web-based Survey. Doctoral dissertation, University of Maryland, College Park.

Welsh, J., S. Anstice, M. Koc, A. Murray, F. Paris, A. Premat, P. Van Esterik, and P.W.L. Wong (1998) *Food Security, Health and the Immigrant Experience*. Toronto: Centre of Excellence for Research on Immigration and Settlement. www.ryerson.ca/content/dam/foodsecurity/projects/immigrationsettlement/ Welsh1998.pdf (Accessed December 13, 2013)

Ying, J. (2000) Chinese-style Barbecue Meats: A Public Health Challenge. *Canadian Journal of Public Health* 91(5):386–389.

Chapter 13

THE HEALTH OF IMMIGRANTS AND REFUGEES

MORTON BEISER

Introduction

Immigrant-receiving countries tend to consider health an important factor in selecting immigrants, but to forget about it when it comes to resettling them. Canada,
for example, is very explicit about how health concerns affect selection: applicants
can be denied **immigrant** status if they have a condition or conditions that could
jeopardize the public health of resident Canadians, create a threat to public safety,
or result in excessive demand for scarce health or social services. On the whole, the
health of immigrants coming to both Canada and the US is better than the health
of the native-born. Ensuring that immigrants are healthy at the point of arrival is,
however, no guarantee that they will stay that way. Safeguarding health is imperative,
and neither country has been remarkably successful in, nor sufficiently concerned
about, addressing it.

The issue is both moral and pragmatic. Good health is increasingly viewed as a
human right regardless of place of birth or length of residence in a particular country.
Furthermore, poor health jeopardizes individual productivity and creates a financial
burden for the state. There is yet another, less obvious, reason to be concerned about
immigrant health: its use as metaphor. Although health may be the ostensible focus
of discussion, disease can function as a metaphor for foreignness. Discussions that
would not be possible about the stranger are legitimized when the stranger becomes
the sick.

This chapter addresses the importance of health in immigration discourse by means of three sets of questions: 1) Does immigrant health jeopardize the health of the native-born and end up costing the state a great deal of money? To what extent can sickness as metaphor pervert this discourse? 2) What happens to immigrants' health over time: does it improve, stay the same, or get worse? 3) Are some illnesses and health conditions more characteristic of immigrant than of other populations? If so, what are the public health and economic implications?

Question 1: Does Immigrant Health Jeopardize the Health of the Native-born and End Up Costing the State a Great Deal of Money? Is Sickness Sometimes a Metaphor?

Rather than setting up health guidelines for selecting immigrants, Canada and the US have evolved policies and practices designed to exclude people who might constitute a risk to public health or to public safety, or become a drain on an already overextended healthcare system. The proposition seems reasonable, but its very reasonableness can provide a cover for darker ideologies (see Case Example 1).

The SS *Massilia* is a particular case of the **sick immigrant**, an **ideology** that figured very prominently in late nineteenth-century and early twentieth-century North American thought (Shah 2001; Mawani 2003). The idea that immigrants were sick—that they harboured physical and mental illnesses that threatened the health of the native-born and the integrity of the emerging Canadian and US nations—was very widely held.

The not-unreasonable premise that immigration should not be allowed to create threats to national health and well-being was contaminated by a political goal—keeping the populations of Canada and the US "pure" (which meant white and preferably Anglo-Saxon). By the late nineteenth century, the Aboriginal populations of the two countries had been almost wiped out by the measles, smallpox, and syphilis that European settlers had brought with them, and it was felt that those who were left could be handled by confinement on reserves and through absorption. As long as old stock immigrants from northern Europe continued to outnumber immigrants from elsewhere, the status quo would be safe. However, as the nineteenth century turned into the twentieth, the balance began to shift from the "right kind" of immigrant to the "wrong" (Markel and Stern 2002).

Immigration policymakers turned an eye toward public health as a form of crowd control. About 75% of all immigrants to the US during the close of the nineteenth century and the opening years of the twentieth had to pass health inspections at

Case Example 1: The Case of the SS *Massilia*

A ship called the SS *Massilia* arrived in New York Harbor in 1892. A few days after the passengers disembarked, a physician reported four cases of typhoid among former passengers who were now living on the Lower East Side. The Department of Infectious Diseases responded by creating a dragnet to round up all recently arrived immigrants. About 1,200 immigrants, most of them healthy, were quarantined in Riverside Hospital. Since no precautions were taken to protect them, about 15% developed typhus and 18 died. Interestingly, the only immigrants to be quarantined were Jews: although there were also a lot of Italian passengers in steerage, they were never rounded up for quarantine (Markel 1997). Germs had become conflated with "foreignness" (Markel and Stern 2002) and health had become a tool for the politics of immigrant selection.

New York Harbor. First- and second-class steamship passengers received either no medical exams or only cursory appraisals onboard ship. **Steerage** passengers were taken by barge to Ellis Island. Despite rough, often humiliating exams, the immigrants proved to be remarkably healthy. Only about 1% were turned back each year for medical reasons (Kraut 1994).

As the Ellis Island experience illustrates, using health to limit the entry of less than desirable immigrants did not always work. However, health could still be used as a justification for confining or removing at least some of them (see Case Example 2). Expulsion on health grounds was another effective tool to help keep the country pure (see Case Example 3).

Although vestiges of the conflation of racial impurity and illness still haunt contemporary thought, a more recent construct—the healthy immigrant— is increasingly widely promulgated. Health research has demonstrated an "epidemiological paradox," or a counterintuitive finding. On the whole, newly arrived immigrants are in better health than the native-born populations of upper-income countries like Canada and the US and, at least during the early years of resettlement, immigrants retain that advantage. This has become known as the **healthy immigrant effect** (HIE), a concept derived from investigations of physical health (Akresh and Frank 2008; McDonald and Kennedy 2004; Newbold and Danforth 2003; Gushulak 2007). The HIE also applies to the mental health of adults (Beiser 1999; Ali 2002; Bergeron, Auger, and Hamel 2009; Wu and Schimmele 2005) and of children (Beiser, Hou, Hyman, and Tousignant 2002).

Case Example 2: Confining the Problem: Leprosy in Canada

Although the number of cases was never large, a great deal was made of the fact that almost all cases of leprosy on Canada's west coast occurred among Chinese, and this was used to justify forcing Chinese into quarantine. They were confined to **ghettos** that eventually came to be called Chinatown. Even though medical authorities of the early twentieth century did not feel that leprosy was very contagious, a leper colony was built offshore and Chinese lepers forced to live there for more than 20 years. In contrast, all cases of leprosy on Canada's east coast occurred among Scandinavians. The east coast never developed urban quarantine areas or leper **colonies** for affected Scandinavians (Mawani 2003). Confining "undesirables" on health grounds was one method of crowd control.

Case Example 3: Expulsion: Immigrants as Mentally Ill

Between the beginning of the twentieth century and the end of World War II, Canada expelled roughly 10,000 people per year. Of these expulsions, 10%—nearly 1,000 per year—were for psychiatric reasons. People from Eastern Europe who developed severe psychiatric problems were five to ten times more likely to be sent back than similarly afflicted immigrants from the UK (Menzies 1998). It is difficult to gauge the extent to which this imbalance was due to discriminatory attitudes or to lack of understanding based on linguistic and cultural barriers. It is, however, important to keep past injustices in mind because, according to some authorities, culturally based difficulties in assessing mental health problems may still be resulting in unjustified deportations (Moran 2010).

The most serious shortcoming in the research on the healthy immigrant effect is the almost exclusive reliance on two measures, both of which are self-reports. The most popular method relies on a single question, "How is your health in general?" that may or may not have the same meaning in all cultures (Jurges 2007). On the other hand, research shows that this simple question is a powerful predictor of morbidity and mortality (DeSalvo, Bloser, Reynolds, He, and Muntner 2006). The second method is also a self-report, but this one is phrased as "Has a health professional ever told you that you had …?" This stem question, or a similar variant, is followed by a list of chronic physical illnesses such as asthma, arthritis, back problems, and high blood pressure. A second question, beginning with "Did a medical professional ever tell you that you had …?" is followed by a list of mental disorders including depression, bipolar disorder, and panic disorder.

Immigrant-receiving countries practise some form of selection but Canada's **points system**, largely based on **human capital** characteristics such as good education, facility in English or French, and employment history, is probably the most highly standardized. Immigrants with diseases that are deemed a threat to public health or conditions deemed a threat to public safety are denied entrance. According to some authorities, the result of all this careful selection is that people accepted as immigrants tend to be exceptionally healthy. Self-selection is another possible explanation: people who choose to emigrate are a self-selected group, and they may be people in exceptionally good health.

Do we want immigrants or don't we? Just as the sick immigrant model fit with yesterday's policies of excluding immigrants, the healthy immigrant effect discourse fits comfortably with contemporary immigration policies aimed at attracting new settlers and convincing the native-born that immigration will be of benefit. To be fair, there is one big difference between then and now: we now have a better base of scientific knowledge to inform policy and to constrain and correct conjecture.

Question 2: What Happens to Immigrants' Health over Time: Does It Improve, Stay the Same, or Get Worse?

The healthy immigrant picture has an unfortunate sequel. According to a considerable amount of research (Chen, Ng, and Wilkins 1996b; DeMaio and Kemp 2010; Newbold 2009), the longer immigrants remain in resettlement countries, the greater the likelihood of losing their initial health advantage. In some cases, immigrant health deteriorates to the level of the native-born, while in others, it deteriorates but still remains better than the health of age-matched native-born counterparts. Before accepting the inference that resettlement makes people sick, it is important to keep other explanations in mind, including the possible effects of out-migration and of research methods.

People who choose to emigrate are obviously a self-selected group, and they may be people in exceptionally good health. Those who choose to leave after immigrating are also a self-selected group. Immigrants do not always stay in first-destination countries. If it were the case that the healthiest immigrants were also the group most likely to leave a first-destination country in order to migrate elsewhere, this could help explain the healthy immigrant effect. According to a Canadian study (Dryburgh and Humel 2004), the most highly skilled immigrants are the ones most likely to emigrate from Canada, and Australian data (Kliewer and Jones 1997) suggest that the most highly skilled immigrants are also the healthiest.

Some interpretations of the healthy immigrant effect have a ring of fatalism that is antithetical to health planning or prevention. The concept of "convergence" is an example (Kliewer and Smith 1995a; Kliewer and Ward 1988; Dunn and Dyck 2000). The idea is that exposure to the physical, social, cultural, and environmental influences in a destination country sets in motion a process in which migrant patterns of morbidity and mortality shift so that they come to resemble the (usually worse) health norms of the resettlement country. By definition, the **convergence model** proposes that immigrant health declines to a point where it equals that found among the members of the receiving society. Convergence, however, is neither inevitable nor universal. Whether immigrants stay as healthy as they are on arrival or whether their health deteriorates depends on an interaction among individual characteristics, **social capital**, socioenvironmental challenge, and opportunity.

At the level of the individual, conditions of entry play an important role. Compared with economic- and family-class immigrants, refugees have experienced repression, persecution, and other traumas that have long-term health implications over and above the adjustments required of all immigrant classes (Beiser and Edwards 1994; Lindert, Ehrenstein, Priebe, Mielick, and Brahler 2009). Bilingualism—proficiency in both the heritage language and the language of the receiving society—protects against health decline among immigrants (Schachter, Kimbro, and Gorman 2012) for women even more than for men (Beiser and Hou 2001; Setia, Lynch, Abrahamowicz, Tousignant, and Quesnel-Vallee 2011). Source country also has an effect on health outcome. Coming from a country with a low human development index (HDI) or high infant mortality rate increases the risk of developing poor health: immigrants apparently carry with them some of the health risks that exist in their home countries (Setia et al. 2011). Marriage, one dimension of social capital, is protective for male immigrants, but not for female immigrants (Setia et al. 2011). Additionally, men who continue to identify with their home culture tend to retain a health advantage (Setia et al. 2011), perhaps because ethnic retention is a form of social capital that helps immigrants adjust to **settlement** stressors (Lieber, Chin, Nihira, and Mink 2001; Beiser and Hou 2006). Retaining home culture may be easier for immigrants living in or near a like-ethnic community of significant size than for others in more isolated circumstances, which may help to explain the apparent health protection effect of the like-ethnic community (Beiser 1988, 1999).

Most immigrants come to resettlement countries in search of opportunity; when that goal is frustrated, deteriorating health may be a consequence. Unemployment jeopardizes health, particularly for men (Beiser, Johnson, and Turner 1993; Beiser

1999; Setia et al. 2011). Aside from frustration, resettlement may expose immigrants to new stressors such as prejudice and discrimination, both of which may negatively affect health (Beiser 1988, 1999; Noh, Beiser, Kaspar, Hou, and Rummens 1999; Setia et al. 2011). Further, region of resettlement affects mental health. According to a Canadian study, children in immigrant families in Toronto and Montreal had worse mental health than similar children in Winnipeg, Calgary, Edmonton, and Vancouver. Family income did not make a difference, but differing levels of environmental demand, neighbourhood quality, and prejudice accounted in large part for these regional discrepancies (Beiser, Simich, Pandalangat, Nowakowski, and Tian 2011).

In sum, migration and resettlement do not, in and of themselves, explain why some immigrants who are healthy at arrival retain this advantage while others lose it. Instead, the answer lies in an interaction between personal characteristics, human and social capital, and the social and environmental contingencies surrounding the resettlement experience, and—very importantly—the type of illness under consideration.

Question 3: Are Some Illnesses or Health Conditions More Characteristic of Immigrants Than of Other Populations? If So, What Are the Public Health and Economic Implications?

Immigrant- and refugee-based research focused on specific illnesses falls into three large categories: 1) infectious illnesses; 2) noninfectious physical illnesses and health conditions; and 3) mental health and substance use.

1. Infectious Illnesses

Tuberculosis (TB, see Appendix)
Contrary to the convergence hypothesis, rates for TB among immigrants do not converge to general population rates. They radically overshoot. Furthermore, the changes in health do not occur gradually. Most immigrants who are going to develop TB get sick within the first five years after coming to Canada.

TB is an air-borne infectious disease transmitted from person to person. If a noninfected person is exposed to the TB Mycobacteria, one of three outcomes is possible: 1) The immune system disposes of the bacteria; 2) The bacteria remain alive but the immune system isolates them. The disease remains inactive and noninfectious unless a physiological challenge overwhelms the immune response; 3) The TB bacteria become active.

Although the foreign-born make up less than 20% of the population of Canada, they account for 65% of all cases of TB. Immigrant-receiving countries in Europe, Australia, and North America report consistent findings: immigrants and refugees have a 4- to 10-time greater risk of developing tuberculosis than do non-Aboriginal native-born people (Weis, Moonan, Pogoda, Turk, King, Freeman-Thompson, and Burgess 2001; McKenna, McCray, and Onorato 1995; Raviglione, Sudre, Rieder, Spinacis, and Kochi 1995).

The increased risk of TB among immigrants and refugees is attributable, at least in large part, to the fact that many of the major source countries for contemporary immigration are burdened with high rates of the disease. For example, in the Philippines and China—the two major sources of Canadian immigration during the first decade of the twenty-first century—the rates are 316 per 100,000 and 88 per 100,000, respectively.

The fact that most, if not all, countries routinely screen prospective immigrants and refugees for tuberculosis argues against the interpretation that immigrants and refugees bring TB with them. Both Canada and the US require a negative sputum culture and a normal chest X-ray as prerequisites for admission. Immigrant applicants with active TB are not allowed to enter Canada until they have completed a course of treatment and a Canadian medical examiner confirms that they are disease-free. After arriving in Canada, these immigrants are placed under medical surveillance and required to report to provincial or territorial public health authorities for five years. Canada does not routinely test for latent TB except in the case of immigrants who will work in healthcare or childcare settings (Reitmanova and Gustafson 2012). Anecdotes about immigrants submitting false medical examinations and false X-rays arouse interest but, even if this were true in a small number of cases, it could hardly account for the tremendous overrepresentation of TB among immigrants. Most experts attribute tuberculosis among immigrants to reactivation of previous illness or to the activation of latent TB. Most of the reactivation seems to occur within the first five to seven years after arrival (McKenna et al. 1995; Kerbel, 1997; Orr, Manfreda, and Hershfield 1990; Greenaway, Sandoe, Vissandjee, Kitai, Gruner, Wobeser, Pottie, Ueffing, Menzies, and Schwartzman 2011). Two approaches have been suggested to address the burden of tuberculosis in immigrants: one within the medical tradition, the other within a tradition that emphasizes **social determinants of health**. The medical perspective emphasizes identifying and treating people with latent TB. Medical authorities point out that pre-migration screening and post-landing surveillance programs have little impact on controlling tuberculosis. Fewer than 1% of immigrants screened prior to entering Canada have active TB and 3 to 5% have the inactive disease (Greenaway et al. 2011). The emphasis should, therefore, be on identifying and treating the 10% of immigrants with latent TB most likely to proceed to develop the active disease.

The social determinants of health perspective focuses on socioenvironmental factors that might contribute to activating or reactivating disease. Proponents of this approach point out that alleviating poverty and improving social conditions played a significant role in reducing the burden of TB among the Canadian-born white population between the middle and the end of the twentieth century (Reitmanova and Gustafson 2012). Why should the same approach not work for Canada's newest residents?

2. Noninfectious Physical Illnesses and Health Conditions

Although the trend toward deterioration in immigrant health over time seems to apply to chronic conditions in the aggregate, the true picture is murkier than it first seems. For example, the longer male immigrants stay in resettlement countries, the greater the risk of heart disease, and the longer female immigrants stay in resettlement countries, the greater the risk of cancer. However, there is no demonstrable association between length of residence and increased risk of heart disease among women, or cancer among men, or of diabetes or high blood pressure among either sex (Perez 2002). These diseases are all important causes of disability and each demands separate attention.

Cardiovascular Diseases (see Appendix)
Heart conditions, stroke, and related diseases make up one-third of the annual toll of global deaths (World Health Organization 2003). According to the World Health Organization, high blood pressure, high blood cholesterol, type 2 diabetes, and obesity are major *biological* risk factors, and unhealthy diets—high in saturated facts, salt, and refined carbohydrates, and low in fruits and vegetables—are major *contributing* factors.

Minority and low-income populations experience a disproportionate burden of death and disability from cardiovascular disease, as well as rates of risk-inducing conditions such as being overweight, hypertension, and elevated cholesterol levels higher than those found among members of majority culture, middle and upper-income groups (Brenfleck 2001). Studies (Marmot, Smith, Stansfeld, Patel, North, Head, While, Brunner, and Feeney 1991) have suggested an association between social marginalization—a common experience of minority and immigrant groups—and compromised cardiovascular health. Acculturation, the process through which immigrants incorporate the attitudes, beliefs, and behaviours of the receiving society (Berry 1995, 1997), can be a health stressor. In a well-known study (Marmot and Syme 1976), two investigators compared heart disease among Japanese male migrants to California and Hawaii with Japanese in their home country, and found a higher prevalence of disease among the migrants. The authors also found what could be viewed as a dose-response relationship between acculturation and health risk: coronary heart disease was three to five times more common among the most-acculturated, as compared to the least-acculturated immigrants. First-generation Japanese immigrants in Hawaii had less cardiovascular disease than the second generation, whose health profiles approximated those found among native-born Hawaiians. Research such as Marmot and Syme's, suggests that immigrants adopt the receiving society's bad habits and, along with the habits, the associated health risks.

According to Canadian studies, immigrants have better cardiovascular health than the native-born. A study (Nair, Nargundkar, Johansen, and Stachan 1990) comparing foreign- and native-born residents of Canada found that standardized mortality rates (SMR) for both immigrants and the Canadian-born declined between the time period from 1969 to 1973 and 1984 to 1988 but, at each time, immigrants had lower SMRs than native-born Canadians.

Immigrants are not all alike. Gender, for example, makes an important difference (Perez 2002). Male immigrants' cardiovascular health declines with increased length of residence, but women's does not. Ethnicity also affects cardiovascular health. Regardless of where they resettle, South Asians have high rates of cardiovascular disease, and Chinese low rates. Constitutional predisposition may be part of the explanation (McKeigue, Miller, and Marmot 1989). Some researchers (Jolly, Pais, and Rihal 1996; McKeigue, Ferrie, and Pierpoint 1993) feel this predisposition involves resistance to insulin, a hormone necessary for metabolizing carbohydrates.

Cancer (see Appendix)

Worldwide, approximately 20 million people suffer from cancer, a figure projected to rise to 30 million by 2020. In Canada, cancer is the second leading cause of death, and is responsible for at least a third of potential years of life lost (Federal, Provincial, and Territorial Advisory Committee on Population Health 1999a, 1999b). Cancers of the lung, prostate, colon, and rectum are the most common forms of cancer among men. For women, breast cancer is by far the most common, with cancer of the cervix a fairly distant second.

Research has identified risk factors for cancer with potential relevance for immigrant populations. Marginal socioeconomic status, an unfortunate fact of life for many immigrants during the early years of resettlement, not only increases the likelihood of exposure to risk factors, but compromises cancer survival rates (United Nations 2002). Nonparticipation in screening programs due to limited language proficiency and lack of awareness among immigrant groups is an important part of the problem (Kliewer and Jones 1997, 1998; United Nations 2002).

Dietary change may contribute to the development of certain forms of cancer among immigrants. Compared to US-born Caucasians, Chinese and Filipino immigrants have lower rates of colorectal cancer. However, Chinese and Filipinos born in the US have higher rates than either immigrants living in the US who were born abroad or Chinese and Filipinos living in their home countries. It is tempting to speculate that as Asians adopt Western diets, which are typically high in meat, sugar, and alcohol—foods associated with increased risk for cancer (Potter, Slattery, Bostick, and Gapstur 1993)—the risk of developing the disease rises accordingly. An interaction between predisposition and environment seems the most likely explanation (Kampman, Slattery, Bigler, Leppert, Samowitz, Caan, and Potter 1999; Maskarinec 2000). Certain Asian groups may be genetically predisposed to developing colorectal cancer, but their traditional diets mitigate against the development of the disease. Migration to North America increases the likelihood that traditional, protective diets will be abandoned in favour of higher-risk foods. Although the risk of cancer seems to increase with time spent in the resettlement country for all immigrants, this change is more marked for men than for women. One possible explanation is that, during resettlement, women change their diets more slowly than men (Balzi, Geddes, Brancker, and Parkin 1995).

The research on cancer also highlights the importance of accurate information. Evidence contradicts the popular view that Asians tend to be free of cancer, a view that can foster a false sense of security among healthcare providers and immigrants themselves (Saphir 1997).

Obesity and Diabetes (see Appendix)

More than 1 billion of the world's adults are overweight, and at least 300 million among them are clinically obese. In Canada, the prevalence of obesity rose from 5.6% in 1985 to 14.8% in 1998 (Katzmarzyk 2002). US data implicate obesity as a significant causative agent in 280,000 deaths annually (Anderson 2000). There are striking parallels between worldwide patterns of obesity and type 2, or noninsulin-dependent, diabetes. Type 2 diabetes accounts for 90% of all cases of diabetes, a condition that, according to year 2000 estimates, affects 177 million people around the world. Approximately 4 million deaths per year are attributable to the complications of diabetes. Inappropriate diet and increasingly sedentary lifestyles are major factors accounting for what has been called the epidemic of obesity (World Health Organization 1990, 2003a, 2003b).

On the whole, immigrants are less likely to be obese than native-born Canadians, but the likelihood of being overweight (body mass index, or BMI, greater than 25) increases with increasing length of stay in Canada (Cairney and Ostbye 1999). Although there is a tendency to attribute weight changes to acculturation-related convergence—that is, the more immigrants take on receiving-country culture, the more likely they are to substitute junk foods for their more nutritious ethnic diets and become sedentary—the reality is not quite so simple. For example, there are important ethnic differences in the trajectory of obesity. When they first arrive in Canada, Chinese, Southeast Asian, Filipina, and Arab female immigrants are less likely than native-born women to be overweight. Regardless of length of residence in Canada, women in these **ethnic communities** remain less likely than the native-born to become overweight. On the other hand, the longer they remain in Canada, the more likely South Asian, Hispanic, European, and Afro-Caribbean **immigrant women** are to lose their comparative weight advantage. With the exception of Arab-origin immigrants, male patterns are similar to female (McDonald and Kennedy 2005).

Both recent and long-term immigrants have higher rates of diabetes than the native-born, and length of residence increases the risk for developing diabetes (Chiu, Austin, Manuel, and Tu 2012; Creatore 2010). Like TB, diabetes in immigrants follows a pattern of illness overshoot, not convergence. In addition, it has been shown that all minorities living in the US (for whom the data exist) suffer a higher prevalence of diabetes than residents of their respective countries of origin (Carter, Pugh, and Monterrosa 1996). South Asian immigrants in Canada and in the UK have particularly high rates of type 2 diabetes (Greenhalgh 1997; Sheth, Nair, Nargundkar, Anand, and Yusuf 1999). These findings suggest that certain ethnic groups, such as South Asians, have a predisposition for obesity and/or diabetes (McKeigue et al. 1993; Greenhalgh 1997; Carter et al. 1996) or are particularly likely to be exposed to risk-inducing conditions, or a combination of the two. From the perspective of exposure to risk in resettlement countries, many studies focus on "Westernization": adopting diets higher in total calories and fat but lower in fibre, and becoming increasingly sedentary (Flaskerud and Kim 1999; Helman 1990). The social environment, particularly the like-ethnic community, also plays an important role in determining immigrant risk for obesity. If an individual immigrant lives in a neighbourhood with a relatively large ethnic community in which individuals are less likely to be overweight than the average Canadian, then the individual immigrant is less likely to be overweight. Conversely, if an immigrant lives in a community of individuals who tend to have a higher prevalence of excess weight than the average Canadian, the chance for the individual migrant to become overweight is higher than for a native-born individual (McDonald and Kennedy 2005). From an acculturation perspective, it seems reasonable to posit that living in an ethnically homogeneous neighbourhood makes it more likely that an individual immigrant will retain traditional health-promoting diet and exercise patterns. A more pragmatic explanation is also possible. High ethnic-group **concentration** within neighbourhoods creates a market for traditional goods large enough to support merchants who can supply those goods (Chiswick and Miller 2004, quoted in McDonald and Kennedy 2005).

A predispositional-environmental interaction—a combination of physiological predisposition among certain ethno-cultural or country-of-origin groups, lack of exercise, and the adoption of unhealthy diets—seems a more likely explanation for obesity and diabetes among immigrants than any of these variables in isolation (Chiu et al. 2012; Creatore 2010; Ozra-Frank and Narayan 2010).

3. Mental Health and Substance Abuse

One in four persons suffers a mental or neurological disorder at some point in their lives (WHO 2001). During the early years of the twentieth century, the paradigm of the *mentally and morally weak immigrant* dominated popular discourse in Canada. Pre–World War II science portrayed immigrants as mentally fragile individuals who chose to leave home because they were the least well-integrated and perhaps the least competent people in their respective societies (see Salvendy 1983; Goldlust and Richmond 1974).

Theories characterizing immigrants and refugees as mentally fragile propelled a host of studies comparing migrant rates of disorder with people from their home communities, as well as between immigrants and native-born members of the receiving society. Approximately half the studies produced results consistent with the prediction that immigrant mental health would be worse. The other half demonstrated no differences in the mental health of migrants and indigenes or between migrants and their counterparts in the country of origin (Canadian Task Force on Mental Health Issues Affecting Immigrants and Refugees 1988). Methodological problems help account for these inconsistencies. Many of the results showing a mental health advantage for indigenes over migrants were based on group comparisons of the rates of hospitalization for mental disorder (Carpenter and Brockington,1980; Cheung and Dobkin de Rios 1982; Dean, Walsh, Downing, and Shelley 1981). However, hospital admission statistics confuse the amount of mental disorder a group suffers with the resources they can call upon to deal with problems. When mental illness strikes a member of a small, isolated, or fragmented social group, he or she may experience different treatment than someone suffering the same type of disorder but who belongs to a well-established community. Hospitalization—usually the last resort in an episode of illness—may take place quickly in the first case. In the second case, traditional healers, supportive family, and healthcare professionals who understand the language and share a patient's ethno-cultural background constitute important resources than can obviate the need for institutional care.

In the 1950s, community surveys began to replace analyses of hospital statistics as the way to measure population mental health. Studies using this methodological advance to compare rates of disorder between immigrants and indigenes yielded results at odds with the research based on treatment data. Some (Cochrane and Stopes-Roe 1981; Munroe-Blum, Boyle, Offord, and Kates 1989) found no difference in rates of psychological disturbance between immigrants and natives of the receiving society, and some (Ali 2002; Halldin 1985; Roskies 1978; Beiser 1999) even suggested that immigrants, and indeed refugees, have fewer emotional problems than native-born persons.

Scientific attention has shifted to the resettlement experience itself as the possible source of disorder. Data from the Canadian Community Health Survey, a study of 131,000 Canadians aged 12 or older, showed that all immigrants, with the exception of those who had been in the country 30 years or more, had lower rates of depression and alcohol dependence than the Canadian-born population (Ali 2002). The risk of mental disorder among long-stay immigrants was, however, higher than that for the age-matched segment of the general Canadian population.

Like the convergence model underlying Ali's work, the disillusionment paradigm addresses process-based or environmental factors that jeopardize immigrant mental health. Although based on a limited number of observations, primarily of refugee patients coming for treatment in the immediate post–World War II era, the **disillusionment model** has become very popular. According to this model, the psychological process of adapting to a new country follows predictable phases (Tyhurst 1977; Grinberg 1984; Rumbaut 1985; Bagheri 1992). During an initial phase—sometimes called the euphoria of arrival—the mental health of immigrants is equal to, or even better than, that of the host country population. The second phase, inevitably overtaking the first, is a phase of disillusionment and nostalgia for the past that had to be abandoned in order to move to a new country. During this phase, people are at high risk for developing psychiatric disorders. Eventually, **adaptation** to the new environment takes place; new settlers begin to act more and more like people in the majority population and their mental health improves.

Community-based studies (Rumbaut 1985, 1988; Beiser 1988; Bagheri 1992) confirm the idea that the period between 10 and 24 months after arrival is a time of high risk for the development of depressive disorder. The question remains: is this an inevitable process, or a consequence of particular contingencies surrounding the resettlement process? The fact that a small proportion of, but not all, immigrants and refugees become psychiatric casualties supports the latter view. Furthermore, research suggests that specific stressors contribute to mental health risk, and that certain psychological and social resources protect against its development (Beiser 1988, 1999).

Case Example 4: Refugees and Mental Health

It was 1981 and Canada had just finished admitting 60,000 refugees from Southeast Asia.

"I'm so nervous, I can't talk English with you." Corpulent, sweaty, and flushed, Chan Min Ran sat in her kitchen mopping her forehead while she talked to the interviewer who had contacted her to take part in a community mental health survey. She apologized for everything from her reliance on an interpreter to the dilapidated state of her crowded East Vancouver apartment. The piles of garbage on the floor, the stove covered with layers of brown grease, the empty egg cartons taking up every available inch of counter space seemed to reflect the internal jumble of her mind. In Min Ran's opinion, she lost her mind during the years before she left Cambodia. She expected to feel better once she got to Canada. She doesn't: she feels worse.

Min Ran and her two sons are survivors of Pol Pot. The wife of a teacher and the daughter of the owner of a food processing plant, Min is well-educated and speaks three languages not counting her native tongue, Cantonese. As they did for all ethnic Chinese in Cambodia beginning in 1975, the Khmer Rouge put an end to Min's comfortable upper middle-class life. Soldiers rounded up her husband and herself, their six children, and a half dozen other members of their extended family, confiscated their valuables, and marched them at gunpoint into the forest. During the march, Min's breastmilk dried up and her four-month-old baby died. Once in the forest, the family had to build their own shelters from whatever they could find and work at back-breaking, essentially useless, projects. People died from the hard labour, from drinking contaminated water, from starvation, from disease, and from physical abuse. The guards came one day and took Min's husband away. No one ever saw him again.

Four years after Min and her family arrived in the forest, the Vietnamese invaded Cambodia and, in the ensuing confusion, people finally found an opportunity to escape. Of Min's 14-member family, she and 2 sons were the only ones left. Attesting to her resourcefulness and intelligence, Min managed to avoid border guards, protect herself and her two young boys, find a way to get to a refugee camp in Thailand, and convince Canadian immigration officers that she and her sons would make good future citizens.

She changed a lot after arriving in Vancouver. Min's sons work long hours washing dishes in Chinese restaurants while their mother stays by herself trying to dam up the memories that have begun to flood back. When the memories become too insistent, she cries. She has nightmares. She loves her children but finds that she is becomingly increasingly cold towards them. She is afraid she will lose them just as she lost everybody else. She has no incentive and no hope.

Source: Personal interviews conducted by the author who was also the Principal Investigator for the Refguee Resettlement Project, a study of 1,300 Southeast Asian refugees in Canada from 1981 through 1991. To protect confidentiality, the case is a composite of several similar histories rather than the history of a particular individual. For more details see Beiser 1999, 2009.

Lists of potential mental health stressors usually include pre-migration experience (Beiser, Turner, and Ganesan 1989; Hollifield, Warner, Lian, Krakow, Jenkins, Kessler, Stevenson, and Westermeyer 2002), intolerable memories (Baskaukos 1981; Hogman 1985; Beiser 1987; Beiser and Hyman 1997), acculturation (Berry 1995, 1997), un-employment (Beiser, Johnson, and Turner, 1993), and structural characteristics of the new society that block opportunity or oppress newcomers (Beiser, Noh, Hou, Kaspar, and Rummens 2001; Beiser, Zilber, Simich, Youngmann, Zohar, Taa, and Hou 2011).

Pre-migration trauma, such as internment in refugee camps, jeopardize mental health after arrival in a country of permanent resettlement. Research suggests that the effect tends to be evanescent, and no longer demonstrable six months or so after arriving in a country of permanent resettlement (Beiser et al. 1989). It is, however, possible that memories of traumatic experience do not go away, but instead bubble like lava beneath an apparently calm surface, and occasionally erupt into symptomatic states such as post-traumatic stress disorder (PTSD, see Appendix), depression, and somatization (Levav 1998; Breslau 2002; Mollica, Poole, and Tor 1998; Boehnlein and Kinzie 1995; Sack, McSharry, Clarke, Kinney, Seeley, and Lewinsohn 1994; see Case Example 4).

Like many refugees, Min Ran suffers from a mixture of PTSD and depression. According to the world literature (Fazel, Wheeler, and Danesh 2005), about 1 in 10 refugees in resettlement countries has PTSD. A Canadian study of Tamil refugees from Sri Lanka (Beiser et al. 2011) reported a prevalence rate of 12%.

Torture, a heinous practice used to terrorize people in many refugee-producing countries, is a unique stressor. During the Min Ran family's four years in the forests of Cambodia, the Pol Pot regime separated children from their parents. One of Min Ran's children was so lonesome that he couldn't resist trying to escape the children's camp to find his parents. He was caught. As punishment, the guards hung him upside down for 24 hours and beat him during their spare time.

Torture betrays core beliefs about, and trust in, human nature, thereby creating a profound existential dilemma among survivors (Turner and Grost-Unsworth, 1990). In addition, physical abuse may cause brain damage, which can contribute to high rates of depression and post-traumatic stress disorder in its aftermath (Mollica et al. 1998).

Aside from pre-migration history, the mental health of immigrants and refugees depends on the challenges and opportunities of resettlement and on the coping strategies new settlers mobilize to adapt to them.

Research (Beiser 1987, 1999; Beiser and Hyman 1997; Beiser and Wickrama 2004) suggests that many refugees cope with traumatic events by repressing memories of them. Over time, however, recovery of the past, with its attendant mental health risk, becomes increasingly pressing. Occupational success and an enduring relationship— none of which Min Ran enjoys—each buffer the mental health risk associated with recovering a repressed past (Beiser and Wickrama 2004).

Acculturation, a process of taking on the habits, attitudes, beliefs, and behaviours of the receiving society, is intrinsic to the process of resettlement. In a well-known model, John W. Berry (1995, 1997) proposes four types of reaction to acculturative forces—**assimilation**, defined as abandoning the culture of origin in favour of the new; integration, a creative blending of the two; rejection, in which the new culture is rejected in favour of the heritage culture; and marginalization, in which neither the old nor the new is accepted. According to Berry, marginalization is accompanied by the highest degree of mental health risk, integration by the least.

When acculturation changes aspirations, but the means for achieving ambitions are slight, mental disorder is a highly likely result. New settlers are interested in employment and in economic success for themselves and their families. However, it can take as long as 10 years for new settlers to achieve their economic potential (deVoretz 1995; Beiser 1999). Unemployment not only frustrates ambition but jeopardizes mental health (Beiser, Johnson, and Turner 1993). Despite the expectation that immigrants will contribute to the gross national product of countries of resettlement, many immigrants find themselves living in poverty. In Canada, for example, more than 30% of immigrant families live below the officially defined poverty line during their first 10 years in Canada (Beiser, Hou, Hyman, and Tousignant 2002).

Studies of immigrant poverty reveal another epidemiological paradox. Although poverty is one of the major risk factors for the mental health of children, and although immigrant children are almost three times as likely as their nonmigrant counterparts to live in poverty, immigrant children enjoy better mental health and evidence fewer behavioural disturbances. The strength of immigrant family life provides one of the explanations for the paradox. Poverty among immigrant families appears to be a phenomenon quite different from poverty among nonmigrants. Being poor is, for example, far less likely to be associated with broken homes and family violence in immigrant, as compared with nonmigrant, households (Beiser et al. 2002). Results such as these point out the need for research to address not only the challenges of resettlement, but the strengths that individuals and families bring to the task.

Selective admission policies help ensure that immigrants are, on the whole, highly educated and well-trained. The fact that it takes so long for them to establish themselves suggests that the shortcomings are in the policies regarding resettlement rather than in selection. Lack of recognition of foreign credentials by potential employers is a long-recognized problem that continues to elude solution (Canadian Task Force, 1988). Discrimination in the labour market as well as in other social settings is probably another part of the explanation for unemployment and poverty. Research reveals that as many as one in four **visible minority** immigrants reports experiencing some form of discrimination during the early years of resettlement. The research also suggests that perceived discrimination induces depression (Beiser 1999; Beiser et al. 2001; Noh et al. 1999).

With some exceptions (Simich and Andermann 2014), immigrant **resilience** has received insufficient research attention. A longstanding intimate relationship has a protective effect on mental health, regardless of the level of satisfaction with the relationship (Beiser and Wickrama 2004; Beiser 1988). Early studies of community-based resilience were based on critical mass theory, whose premise is that immigrants who settle in areas where there is an established like-ethnic community have a mental health advantage over immigrants deprived of such community (Murphy 1955, 1973, 1977). According to one well-known Canadian study by H.B.M. Murphy (1973), mental-illness hospitalization rates for immigrant groups in Canada increased as the size of the like-ethnic community decreased. Community-based studies (Beiser 1988, 1999) support the idea that a like-ethnic community of significant size confers a mental health advantage.

Theoreticians have suggested that receiving countries offer different "levels of hospitality" to newcomers (Aylesworth and Ossorio 1983). Although the proposition that the more hospitable the reception, the better the chances of maintaining good mental health (Starr and Roberts 1982) makes intuitive sense, testing the proposition is difficult because it is hard to know how to measure hospitality. A study of Southeast Asian refugees in Canada (Beiser 1999) compared the mental health and adaptation of government-sponsored and privately sponsored refugees. Reasoning that refugees sponsored by private groups would receive more individualized attention than others left to the care of government bureaucracies, the study predicted a mental health advantage for the privately sponsored group. Results failed to confirm the prediction. Further investigation revealed that undue pressure by sponsoring groups could have the reverse effect, that is that the dependence of refugees on their sponsors made them vulnerable to exploitation, insensitivity, and compromised mental health (Beiser

1999; Beiser et al. 1989; Woon, 1987). A follow-up study, however, revealed that, at the end of 10 years, privately sponsored refugees were better integrated than their government-sponsored counterparts (Beiser and Johnson 2003).

Conclusion

Selection can do only so much to ensure the health of newly admitted immigrants. In fact, all immigrant-receiving countries like Canada and the US are facing human rights challenges to their ableism-directed policies (Iyioha 2008). The increasing challenge to health-directed constraints on admission calls for a re-examination of assumptions and policies. From the point of view of the receiving society, the fact that immigrants with chronic health conditions are nevertheless more likely to be in the labour force than native-born Canadians (Beiser and Hou 2014) is good news. The fact that immigrants with chronic illnesses use fewer healthcare resources than the native-born—good news from a cost-benefit perspective—is more disquieting. There is evidence that neglecting health, and particularly mental health, needs during the early years has deleterious long-term consequences (Beiser and Hou 2014). Neglecting the health of newcomers is never a good idea.

The time has come to shift the balance from a too-exclusive preoccupation with selecting the right immigrants to developing policies that will safeguard health and promote resilience (Beiser 2009). Healthcare policies and institutions have been slow to adapt to the challenges of changing populations but this has not deterred clinicians and providers from beginning to evolve a professional response to the care of immigrants and refugees. Important examples of this include the development of evidence-based healthcare guidelines for immigrants in general in Canada (see Canadian Medical Association Journal under Media Links) and in the US (Walker and Barnett 2007), and the Canadian Paediatrics Society's leadership in focusing on the health of immigrant and refugee children (see Caring for Kids New to Canada under Media Links).

Selection policies and practices have helped ensure that the people who come to Canada and the US to settle are healthy, and for the most part, endowed with a lot of human capital. However, the relative neglect of what happens to immigrants after entry violates the moral imperative to safeguard health, causes needless suffering, and robs the country of the full measure of economic and social benefit that could result from immigration.

Questions for Critical Thought

1. People are always interested in comparisons. One frequent question is, are immigrants in worse health than the native-born? The answer is not straightforward. When reflecting on it, consider factors such as the phase of resettlement, how various studies measure health and illness, and the heterogeneity of immigrants and refugees.

2. Do immigrants have the same access to preventive or curative health services as everybody else? If not, why not?

3. The concept of "social determinants of health" posits that conditions such as poverty, deprivation, and social support play a role as important as, or perhaps even more important than, pathogens in determining sickness or health. For example, one of the best-established relationships in health research is that poverty increases the risk of mental illness. What are some social determinants specific to immigration and resettlement that could affect the health and well-being of newcomers?

Key Readings

Beiser, M. (2009) Resettling Refugees and Safeguarding Their Mental Health: Lessons Learned from the Refugee Resettlement Project. *Transcultural Psychiatry* 46:539–583.

Beiser, M., F. Hou, I. Hyman, and M. Tousignant (2002) Poverty and Mental Health among Immigrant and Non-immigrant Children. *American Journal of Public Health* 92(2):220–227.

Gushulak, B. (2007) Healthier on Arrival? Further Insight into the "Healthy Immigrant Effect." *Canadian Medical Association Journal* 176:1439–1440.

Iyioha, I. (2008) A Different Picture through the Looking-Glass: Equality, Liberalism and the Question of Fairness in Canadian Immigration Health Policy. *Georgetown Immigration Law Journal* 22(4):621–662.

Markel, H. and A.M. Stern (2002) The Foreignness of Germs: The Persistent Association of Immigrants and Disease in American Society. *Milbank Quarterly* 80(4):757–788.

Media Links

New Canadian Children and Youth Study (NCCYS):
www.nccys.com
A Canada-wide investigation of health, mental health, and achievement, providing a
wealth of information about social determinants of health based on a study of more than
4,000 immigrant children, youth, and their families, as well as from cross-cultural studies.
The website also contains discussion papers and videos regarding policy and practice
implications arising from research.

Caring for Kids New to Canada:
www.kidsnewtocanada.ca
In the 1990s, the Canadian Paediatrics Society pioneered the development of practice
guidelines for healthcare professionals dealing with immigrant children and families. The
society has now developed an online, constantly revised and updated, and vastly expanded
version of this pioneering work.

Canadian Medical Association Journal (CMAJ):
www.cmaj.ca/cgi/collection/canadian_guidelines_for_immigrant_health
Nine articles by teams of experts dealing with immigrant health and the delivery of
healthcare make up this invaluable online publication by the Canadian Medical Association
Journal.

Immigrant Medicine:
www.sciencedirect.com/science/book/9780323034548
The online version (available through ScienceDirect) of Walker and Barnett's
groundbreaking text, largely focused on the US experience.

References

Akresh, I.R. and R. Frank (2008) Health Selection among New Immigrants. *American
    Journal of Public Health* 98:2058–2064.

Ali, J. (2002) Mental Health of Canada's Immigrants. Statistics Canada, catalogue 82-003.
    Supplement to Health Reports 13:101–113.

Anderson, R.E. (2000) The Spread of the Childhood Obesity Epidemic, Commentary.
    Canadian Medical Association 163(11).

Aylesworth, L.S. and P.G. Ossorio (1983) Refugees: Cultural Displacement and Its Effects.
    Advances in Descriptive Psychology 3:45–93.

Bagheri, A. (1992) Psychiatric Problems among Iranian Immigrants in Canada. *Canadian Journal of Psychiatry* 37(1):7–11.

Balzi, D., M. Geddes, A. Brancker, and D.M. Parkin (1995) Cancer Mortality in Italian Immigrants and Their Offspring in Canada. *Cancer Causes and Control* 6(1):68–74.

Baskaukos, L. (1981) The Lithuanian Refugee Experience and Grief. *International Migration Review* 15:276–291.

Beiser, M. (1987) Changing Time Perspective and Mental Health among Southeast Asian Refugees' Culture. *Medicine and Psychiatry* 11:437–464.

Beiser, M. (1988) Influences of Time, Ethnicity, and Attachment on Depression in Southeast Asian Refugees. *American Journal of Psychiatry* 145(1):46–51.

Beiser, M. (1999) *Strangers at the Gate: The "Boat People's" First Ten Years in Canada.* Toronto: University of Toronto Press.

Beiser, M. and R.G. Edwards (1994) Mental Health of Immigrants and Refugees. In L.L. Bachrach, P. Goering, and D. Wasylenki (eds.) *Mental Health Care in Canada*, pp. 73–86. San Francisco: Jossey-Bass.

Beiser, M. and F. Hou (2001) Language Acquisition, Unemployment and Depressive Disorder among Southeast Asian Refugees: A 10-year Study. *Social Science & Medicine* 53:1321–1334.

Beiser, M. and F. Hou (2006) Ethnic Identity, Resettlement Stress and Depressive Affect among Southeast Asian Refugees in Canada. *Social Science and Medicine* 63:137–150.

Beiser, M. and F. Hou (2014) Effects of Chronic Physical and Mental Conditions on Economic Performance and Resource Consumption among Immigrants in Canada. *International Journal of Public Health* 59(3):541–547.

Beiser, M., F. Hou, I. Hyman, and M. Tousignant (2002) Poverty and Mental Health among Immigrant and Non-immigrant Children. *American Journal of Public Health* 92(2):220–227.

Beiser, M. and I. Hyman (1997) Refugees' Time Perspective and Mental Health. *American Journal of Psychiatry* 154:996–1002.

Beiser, M. and P.J. Johnson (2003) Sponsorship and Resettlement Success. *Journal of International Migration and Integration* 4(2):203–216.

Beiser, M., P.J. Johnson, and R.J. Turner (1993) Unemployment, Underemployment and Depressive Affect among Southeast Asian Refugees. *Psychological Medicine* 23:731–743.

Beiser, M., S. Noh, F. Hou, V. Kaspar, and J. Rummens (2001) Southeast Asian Refugees' Perceptions of Racial Discrimination in Canada. *Canadian Ethnic Studies* 23(1).

Beiser, M., L. Simich, N. Pandalangat, M. Nowakowski, and F. Tian (2011) Stresses of Passage, Balms of Resettlement and PTSD among Sri Lankan Tamils in Canada. *Canadian Journal of Psychiatry* 56(6):333–340.

Beiser, M., R.J. Turner, and S. Ganesan (1989) Catastrophic Stress and Factors Affecting Its Consequences among Southeast Asian Refugees. *Social Science & Medicine* 28:183–195.

Beiser, M. and K.A.S. Wickrama (2004) Trauma, Time and Mental Health: A Study of Temporal Reintegration and Depressive Disorder among Southeast Asian Refugees. *Psychological Medicine* 34(5):899–910.

Beiser, M., N. Zilber, L. Simich, R. Youngmann, A. Zohar, B. Taa, and F. Hou (2011) Regional Effects on the Mental Health of Immigrant Children: Results from the New Canadian Children and Youth Study (NCCYS). *Health and Place* 17:822–829.

Bergeron, P., N. Auger, and D. Hamel (2009) Weight, General Health and Mental Health: Status of Diverse Subgroups of Immigrants in Canada. *Canadian Journal of Public Health* 100(3):215–220.

Berry, J.W. (1995) Psychology of Acculturation. In N.R. Goldberg and J.B. Veroff (eds.) *The Culture and Psychology Reader*, pp. 457–488. New York: NYU Press.

Berry, J.W. (1997) Immigration, Acculturation and Adaptation. *Applied Psychology: An International Review* 46(1):5–34.

Boehnein, J.K. and J.D. Kinzie (1995) Refugee Trauma. *Transcultural Psychiatric Research Review* 32:223–252.

Brennfleck, J.S. (2001) *Ethnic Diseases: Sourcebook*. Health Reference Series. Detroit: Omnigraphics.

Breslau, N. (2002) Epidemiologic Studies of Trauma, Postraumatic Stress Disorder and Other Psychiatric Disorders. *Canadian Journal of Psychiatry* 44(10):923–929.

Cairney, J. and T. Ostbye (1999) Time since Immigration and Excess Body Weight. *Canadian Journal of Public Health* 90(2):120–124.

Canadian Task Force on Mental Health Issues Affecting Immigrants and Refugees (1988) *After the Door Has Been Opened: Mental Health Issues Affecting Immigrants and Refugees in Canada*. No. Ci96-38/1988E. Ottawa: Ministry of Supply and Services Canada.

Carpenter, L. and I.F. Brockington (1980) A Study of Mental Illness in Asians, West Indians, and Africans Living in Manchester. *British Journal of Psychiatry* 137:201–205.

Carter, J.S., J.A. Pugh, and A. Monterrosa (1996) Non-insulin Dependent Diabetes Mellitus in Minorities in the United States. *Annals of Internal Medicine* 125(3):221–232.

Chen, J., E. Ng, and R. Wilkins (1996a) The Health of Canada's Immigrants in 1994–95. *Health Reports* 7(4):33–45.

Chen, J., E. Ng, and R. Wilkins (1996b) Health Expectancy by Immigrant Status. *Health Reports* 8(3):29–37.

Cheung, F. and M.F. Dobkin de Rios (1982) Recent Trends in the Study of the Mental Health of Chinese Immigrants to the United States. *Research in Race and Ethnic Relations* 3:145–163.

Chiu M., P.C. Austin, D.G. Manuel, and J.V. Tu (2012) Cardiovascular Risk Factor Profiles of Recent Immigrants vs. Long-term Residents of Ontario: A Multi-ethnic Study. *The Canadian Journal of Cardiology* 28(1):20–26.

Cochrane, R. and M. Stopes-Roe (1981) Psychological Symptom Levels in Indian Immigrants to England: A Comparison with Native English. *Psychological Medicine* 11:319–327.

Creatore, M.I. (2010) Age- and Sex-related Prevalence of Diabetes Mellitus among Immigrants to Ontario, Canada. *Canadian Medical Association Journal* 182(8):781–789.

Dean, G., D. Walsh, H. Downing, and E. Shelley (1981) First Admission of Native-born and Immigrants to Psychiatric Hospitals in South-East England 1976. *British Journal of Psychiatry* 139:506–512.

DeMaio, F.G. and E. Kemp (2010) The Deterioration of Health Status among Immigrants to Canada. *Global Public Health* 5(5):462–478.

DeSalvo, K.B., N. Bloser, K. Reynolds, J. He, and P. Muntner (2006) Mortality Prediction with a Single General Self-rated Health Question: A Meta-analysis. *Journal of General Internal Medicine* 21(3):267–275.

DeVoretz, D. (1995) *Diminishing Returns: The Economics of Immigration Policy.* Toronto: University of Toronto Press.

Dryburgh, H.B. and J. Humel (2004) Immigrants in Demand: Staying or Leaving? *Canadian Social Trends* 74(12).

Dunn, J.R. and I. Dyck (2000) Social Determinants of Health in Canada's Immigrant Population: Results from the National Population Health Survey. *Social Science and Medicine* 51:1573–1593.

Fazel, M., J. Wheeler, and J. Danesh (2005) Prevalence of Serious Mental Disorder in 7000 Refugees Resettled in Western Countries: A Systematic Review. *Lancet* 365:1309–1314.

Federal, Provincial, and Territorial Advisory Committee on Population Health (1999a) Statistical Report on the Health of Canadians. Ottawa: Minister of Public Works and Government Services Canada.

Federal, Provincial, and Territorial Advisory Committee on Population Health (1999b) Toward a Healthy Future: Second Report on the Health of Canadians. Ottawa: Minister of Public Works and Government Services Canada.

Flaskerud, J.H. and S. Kim (1999) Health Problems of Asian and Latino Immigrants. *Nursing Clinics of North America* 34(20):359–380.

Goldlust, J. and A.H. Richmond (1974) A Multivariate Model of Immigrant Adaptation. *International Migration Review* 8(2):193–225.

Greenaway, C., A. Sandoe, B. Vissandjee, I. Kitai, D. Gruner, W. Wobeser, K. Pottie, E. Ueffing, D. Menzies, and K. Schwartzman (2011) Tuberculosis: Evidence Review for Newly Arriving Immigrants and Refugees. *Canadian Medical Association Journal* 183(12):939–951.

Greenhalgh, P.M. (1997) Diabetes in British South Asians: Nature, Nurture, and Culture. *Diabetic Medicine* 14:10–18.

Grinberg, L. (1984) A Psychoanalytic Study of Migration: Its Normal and Pathological Aspects. *Journal American Psychoanalytic Association* 32:13–38.

Gushulak, B. (2007) Healthier on Arrival? Further Insight into the "Healthy Immigrant Effect." *Canadian Medical Association Journal* 176:1439–1440.

Halldin, J. (1985) Prevalence of Mental Disorder in an Urban Population in Central Sweden in Relation to Social Class, Marital Status and Immigration. *Acta Psychiatrica Scandinavica* 71:117–127.

Helman, C. (1990) *Culture, Health and Illness*. London, ON: Butterworth Heinemann.

Hogman, P. (1985) Role of Memories in Lives of World War II Orphans. *Journal of the American Academy of Child Psychology* 2:390–396.

Hollifield, M., T.D. Warner, N. Lian, B. Krakow, J.H. Jenkins, J. Kessler, J. Stevenson, and J. Westermeyer (2002) Measuring Trauma and Health Status in Refugees: A Critical Review. *Journal of the American Medical Association* 288(5):611–621.

Iyioha, I. (2008) A Different Picture through the Looking-glass: Equality, Liberalism and the Question of Fairness in Canadian Immigration Health Policy. *Georgetown Immigration Law Journal* 22(4):621–662.

Jolly, K.S., P. Pais, and C.S. Rihal (1996) Coronary Artery Disease among South Asians: Identification of a High Risk Population. *Canadian Journal of Cardiology* 12(6):569–571.

Jurges, H. (2007) True Health vs. Response Styles: Exploring Cross-country Differences in Self-reported Health. *Health Economics* 16(2):163–178.

Kampman, E., M.L. Slattery, J. Bigler, M. Leppert, W. Samowitz, B.J. Caan, and J.D. Potter (1999) Meat Consumption, Genetic Susceptibility, and Colon Cancer Risk: A United States Multicenter Case-control Study. *Cancer and Epidemiological Biomarkers in Prevention* 8:69–75.

Katzmarzyk, P.T. (2002) The Canadian Obesity Epidemic 1985–1998, Commentary. *Canadian Medical Association*.

Kerbel, D. (1997) Epidemiology of Tuberculosis in Ontario 1995. *PHERO* 8(4):81–93.

Kliewer, E.V. and R. Jones (1997) *Immigrant Health and the Use of Medical Services: Results from the Longitudinal Survey of Immigrants to Australia*. Canberra, Australia: Department of Immigration and Multicultural Affairs.

Kliewer, E.V. and R. Jones (1998) *Changing Patterns of Immigrant Health and Use of Medical Services. Results from the Longitudinal Survey of Immigrant to Australia (LSIA).* Canberra, Australia: Department of Immigration and Multicultural Affairs.

Kliewer, E.V. and K.R. Smith (1995) Breast Cancer Mortality among Immigrants in Australia and Canada. *Journal of the National Cancer Institute* 87(15):1154–1161.

Kliewer, E.V. and D. Ward (1988) Convergence of Immigrant Suicide Rates to Those in the Destination Country. *American Journal of Epidemiology* 127(3):640–653.

Kraut, A.M. (1994) *Silent Travelers: Germs, Genes, and the "Immigrant Menace."* New York: Basic Books.

Levav, I. (1998) Individuals under Conditions of Maximum Adversity: The Holocaust. In B.P. Dohrenwend (ed.) *Adversity, Stress and Psychopathology.* New York: Oxford University Press.

Lieber, E., D. Chin, K. Nihira, and L.T. Mink (2001) Holding on and Letting Go: Identity and Acculturation among Chinese Immigrants. *Cultural Diversity and Ethnic Minority Psychology* 7(3):247–261.

Lindert, J., O.S. Ehrenstein, S. Priebe, A. Mielick, and E. Brahler (2009) Depression and Anxiety in Labor Migrants and Refugees—A Systematic Review and Meta-analysis. *Social Science & Medicine* 69(2):246–257.

Markel, H. (1997) *Quarantine!: East European Jewish Immigrants and the New York City Epidemics of 1892.* Baltimore, MD: Johns Hopkins University Press.

Markel, H. and A.M. Stern (2002) The Foreignness of Germs: The Persistent Association of Immigrants and Disease in American Society. *Milbank Quarterly* 80(4):757–788.

Marmot, M.G, and S.L. Syme (1976) Acculturation and Coronary Heart Disease in Japanese Americans. *American Journal of Epidemiology* 104(3):225–247.

Marmot, M.G., G.D. Smith, S. Stansfeld, C. Patel, F. North, J. Head, I. While, E. Brunner, and A. Feeney (1991) Health Inequality among British Civil Servants: The Whitehall II Study. *Lancet* 337:1387–1393.

Maskarinec, G. (2000) Breast Cancer—Interaction between Ethnicity and Environment. *Vivo* 14: 115–124.

Mawani, R. (2003) The "Island of the Unclean": Race, Colonialism and "Chinese Leprosy" in British Columbia, 1891–1924. *Law, Social Justice & Global Development Journal (LGD)* 1.

McDonald, J.T. and S. Kennedy (2004) Insights into the "Healthy Immigrant Effect." Health Status and Health Service Use of Immigrants to Canada. *Social Science and Medicine* 59:1613–1627.

McDonald, J.T. and S. Kennedy (2005) Is Migration to Canada Associated with Unhealthy Weight Gain? Overweight and Obesity among Canada's Immigrants. *Social Science & Medicine* 61:2469–2481.

McKeigue, P.M., G.J. Miller, and M.G. Marmot (1989) Coronary Heart Disease in South Asian Overseas: A Review. *Journal of Clinical Epidemiology* 41(7):597–609.

McKeigue, P.M., J.E. Ferrie, and T. Pierpoint (1993) Association of Early Onset Coronary Heart Disease in South Asian Men with Glucose Intolerance and Hyperinsulinemia. *Circulation* 87:142–161.

McKenna, M.T., E. McCray, and I. Onorato (1995) The Epidemiology of Tuberculosis among Foreign-born Persons in the United States, 1986 to 1995. *New England Journal of Medicine* 332:1071–1076.

Menzies, R. (1998) Governing Mentalities: The Deportation of "Insane" and "Feebleminded" Immigrants out of British Columbia from Confederation to World War II. *Canadian Journal of Law and Society* 13(2):135.

Mollica, R.F., C. Poole, and S. Tor (1998) Symptoms, Functioning and Health Problems in a Massively Traumatized Population: The Legacy of the Cambodian Tragedy. In B.P. Dohrenwend (ed.) *Adversity, Stress and Psychopathology*. New York: Oxford University Press.

Moran, M. (2010) Deportation Process Penalizes Mentally Ill Immigrants. *Psychiatric News* 45(17):1–1, 26.

Munroe-Blum, H., M.G. Boyle, D.R. Offord, and N. Kates (1989) Immigrant Children: Psychiatric Disorder, School Performance, and Service Utilization. *American Journal of Orthopsychiatry* 59:510–519.

Murphy, H.B.M. (1955) *Flight and Resettlement*. Paris: UNESCO.

Murphy, H.B.M. (1973) Migration and the Major Mental Disorders: A Reappraisal. In C. Zwingmann and M. Pfister-Ammende (eds.) *Uprooting and After*, pp. 204–220. New York: Springer-Verlag.

Murphy, H.B.M. (1977) Migration, Culture and Mental Health. *Psychological Medicine* 7(4):677–684.

Nair, C., H. Nargundkar, H. Johansen, and J. Stachan (1990) Canadian Cardiovascular Disease Mortality: First Generation Immigrants versus Canadian Born. *Health Reports* 293:203–228.

Newbold, K.B. (2009) The Short-term Health of Canada's New Immigrant Arrivals: Evidence from the LSIC. *Ethnicity & Health* 14(3):315–336.

Newbold, K.B. and J. Danforth (2003) Health Status and Canada's Immigrant Population. *Social Science and Medicine* 57:1981–1995.

Noh, S., M. Beiser, V. Kaspar, F. Hou, and J. Rummens (1999) Perceived Racial Discrimination, Depression, and Coping: A Study of Southeast Asian Refugees in Canada. *The Journal of Health and Social Behavior* 40:193–207.

Orr, P.H., J. Manfreda, and E.S. Hershfield (1990) Tuberculosis Surveillance in Immigrants to Manitoba. *Canadian Medical Association Journal* 142(5):453–458.

Ozra-Frank, R. and K.M.V. Narayan (2010) Overweight and Diabetes Prevalence among US Immigrants. *American Journal of Public Health* 100(4):661–668.

Perez, C.F. (2002) Health Status and Health Behaviour among Immigrants. Statistics Canada, Catalogue 82-003. *Supplement for Health Reports* 13:89–100.

Potter, J.D., M.L. Slattery, R.M. Bostick, and S.M. Gapstur (1993) Colon Cancer: A Review of the Epidemiology. *Epidemiology Review* 15:499–545.

Raviglione, M.G., P. Sudre, H.I. Rieder, S. Spinacis, and A. Kochi (1995) Secular Trends of Tuberculosis in Western Europe. *WHO Bulletin* 71:291–306.

Reitmanova, S. and D. Gustafson (2012) Rethinking Immigrant Tuberculosis Control in Canada: From Medical Surveillance to Tackling Social Determinants of Health. *Journal of Immigrant and Minority Health* 14:6–13.

Roskies, E. (1978) Sex, Culture and Illness: An Overview. *Social Science and Medicine* 12:139–141.

Rumbaut, R.G. (1985) Mental Health and the Refugee Experience: A Comparative Study of Southeast Asian Refugees. In T. Owan, B. Bliatout, and K.M. Lin (eds.) *Southeast Asian Mental Health: Treatment, Prevention, Services, and Research*. DHHS Publication ADM–1399. Rockville, MD: National Institute of Mental Health.

Rumbaut, R.G. (1988) Portraits, Patterns and Predictors of the Refugee Adaptation Process: A Comparative Study of Southeast Asian Refugees. In D.W. Haines (ed.) *Refugees and Immigrants: Cambodians, Laotians, and Vietnamese in America*. Totowa, NJ: Rowman & Littlefield.

Sack, W.H., S. McSharry, G.N. Clarke R. Kinney, J. Seeley, and P. Lewinsohn (1994) The Khmer Adolescent Project, I: Epidemiologic Findings in Two Generations of Cambodian Refugees. *Journal of Nervous and Mental Disease* 182(7):387–395.

Salvendy, J.T. (1983) The Mental Health of Immigrants: A Reassessment of Concepts. *Canada's Mental Health* 31:9–12.

Saphir, A. (1997) Asian Americans and Cancer: Discarding the Myth of the "Model Minority." *Journal of the National Cancer Institute* 89(310):1572–1574.

Setia, M.S., J. Lynch, M. Abrahamowicz, P. Tousignant, and A. Quesnel-Vallee (2011) Self-rated Health in Canadian Immigrants: Analysis of the Longitudinal Survey of Immigrants to Canada. *Health and Place* 17:658–670.

Shah, N. (2001) *Contagious Divides: Epidemics and Race in San Francisco's Chinatown*. Berkeley, CA: University of California Press.

Sheth, T., C. Nair, M. Nargundkar, S. Anand, and S. Yusuf (1999) Cardiovascular and Cancer Mortality among Canadians of European, South Asian and Chinese Origin from 1979 to 1993: An Analysis of 1.2 Million Deaths. *Canadian Medical Association Journal* 161(20):131–138.

Simich, L. and L. Andermann (2014) *Refugee Resettlement and Mental Health*. New York: Springer.

Starr, P.D. and A.E. Roberts (1982) Community Structure and Vietnamese Refugee Adaptation: The Significance of Context. *International Migration Review* 16:595–618.

Turner, S.W. and C. Grost-Unsworth (1990) Psychological Sequelae of Torture: A Descriptive Model. *British Journal of Psychiatry* 157:475–480.

Tyhurst, L. (1977) Psychological First Aid for Refugees. *Mental Health and Society* 4:319–343.

United Nations (2002) Press Release: Number of World's Migrants Reaches 175 Million Mark: Migrant Population Has Doubled in Twenty-five Years.

Walker, P.F. and E.D. Barnett (eds.) (2007) *Immigrant Medicine.* Philadelphia: Saunders Elsevier.

Weis, S.E., P.K. Moonan, J.M. Pogoda, L. Turk, B. King, S. Freeman-Thompson, and G. Burgess (2001) Tuberculosis in the Foreign-born Population of Tarrant County, Texas, by Immigration Status. *American Journal of Respiratory Critical Care Medicine* 164:953–957.

Woon, Y. (1987) The Mode of Refugee Sponsorship and the Socio-economic Adaptation of Vietnamese in Victoria: A Three-year Perspective. In K.B. Chan and D.M. Indra (eds.) *Uprooting, Loss and Adaptation: The Resettlement of Indochinese in Canada* pp. 132–146. Ottawa: Canadian Public Health Association.

World Health Organization (WHO) (1990) Multinational Project for Childhood Diabetes. WHO Diamond Project Group, Diabetes Care.

World Health Organization (WHO) (2001) Mental and Neurological Disorders, Fact Sheet No. 265. www.who.int/whr/2001/media_centre/en/whr01_fact_sheet1_en.pdf

World Health Organization (WHO) (2003a) Cardiovascular Disease (CVD) Fact Sheet. www.who.int/mediacentre/factsheets/fs317/en

World Health Organization (WHO) (2003b) Obesity and Overweight, Fact Sheet. www.who.int/mediacentre/factsheets/fs311/en

Wu, Z. and C. Schimmele (2005) The Healthy Migrant Effect on Depression: Variations over Time? *Canadian Studies in Population* 32(2):271–298.

Appendix

Tuberculosis (TB): An air-borne infectious disease transmitted from person to person. If a noninfected person is exposed to the TB Mycobacteria, one of three outcomes is possible: 1) The immune system disposes of the bacteria; 2) The bacteria remain alive but the immune system isolates them. The disease remains inactive and noninfectious unless a physiological challenge overwhelms the immune response; 3) The TB bacteria become active.

Cardiovascular disease: A group of disorders of the heart and blood vessels that includes the following:

- coronary heart disease: disease of the blood vessels supplying the heart muscle;
- cerebrovascular disease: disease of the blood vessels supplying the brain;
- peripheral arterial disease: disease of blood vessels supplying the arms and legs;
- rheumatic heart disease: damage to the heart muscle and heart valves from rheumatic fever, caused by streptococcal bacteria;
- congenital heart disease: malformations of heart structure existing at birth; and
- deep vein thrombosis and pulmonary embolism: blood clots in the leg veins, which can dislodge and move to the heart and lungs.

Heart attacks and strokes are usually acute events and are mainly caused by a blockage that prevents blood from flowing to the heart or brain. The most common reason is a buildup of fatty deposits on the inner walls of the blood vessels. Strokes can be caused by bleeding from a blood vessel in the brain or by blood clots.

Diabetes: Diabetes refers to a group of metabolic diseases in which a person has high blood sugar, either because the pancreas does not produce enough insulin, or because cells do not respond to the insulin that is produced. Elevated blood sugar produces the classical symptoms of polyuria (frequent urination), polydipsia (increased thirst), and polyphagia (increased hunger). There are three recognized types of diabetes:

- Type 1: A chronic disease in which the pancreas fails to produce insulin, a hormone that helps the body control the level of glucose (sugar) in the blood. Without insulin, glucose builds up in the blood instead of being used for energy. Uncontrolled diabetes leads to serious damage to many of the body's systems, especially the nerves and blood vessels. About 10% of all cases of diabetes are type 1.
- Type 2. Occurs as a result of insulin resistance within the body. The pancreas attempts to make extra insulin to compensate, but eventually is unable to keep up. Obesity is very commonly associated with type 2 diabetes.
- Type 3 or gestational diabetes: Occurs when pregnant women without a previous diagnosis of diabetes develop a high blood glucose level. It may precede development of type 2 diabetes.

Cancer: *Cancer* is a term used for diseases in which abnormal cells divide without control and are able to invade other tissues. Cancer cells can spread to other parts of the body through the blood and lymph systems. There are more than 100 different types of cancer. Most cancers are named for the organ or type of cell in which they start—for example, cancer that begins in the colon is called colon cancer; cancer that begins in the melanocytes of the skin is called melanoma.

Overweight and Obesity: For adults, overweight and obesity ranges are determined by using weight and height to calculate a number called the body mass index (BMI). BMI is used because, for most people, it correlates with their amount of body fat. An adult who has a BMI between 25 and 29.9 is considered overweight. An adult who has a BMI of 30 or higher is considered obese.

A child's weight status is determined using an age- and sex-specific percentile for BMI rather than the BMI categories used for adults because children's body composition varies as they age and varies between boys and girls. US Center for Disease Control and Prevention (CDC) growth charts are used to determine the corresponding BMI for age and sex percentile. For children and adolescents (aged 2 to 19 years), being overweight is defined as having a BMI at or above the 85th percentile and below the 95th percentile for children of the same age and sex. Obesity is defined as a BMI at or above the 95th percentile for children of the same age and sex.

Post-traumatic Stress Disorder (PTSD): A severe condition that may develop after a person is exposed to one or more traumatic events, such as sexual assault, serious injury, or the threat of death. Not everyone exposed to severe trauma develops PTSD. Traumas of human design, such as persecution and torture, are more likely than natural traumas, such as earthquakes, to give rise to PTSD. Symptoms include recurrent and distressing reexperiencing of the event or events in the form of flashbacks, repeated nightmares, or acting as if one were back in the distressing situation; avoidance of thoughts, feelings, or stimuli associated with the event; sleep disturbance often because of nightmares; avoidance of memories of the event; emotional numbing and withdrawal from others; loss of ambition; and hyperarousal.

Chapter 14

Immigrant Health Services and Healthcare

Lu Wang

Introduction

Health and well-being are critical indicators of quality of life (Somarriba and Pena 2009). People who have good health and easy access to quality healthcare can have not only better lives but also better life expectancy than those who have poor health and limited access to healthcare. Good health and healthcare, however, are not always shared equally within a population that is heterogeneous in socioeconomic and cultural composition. Immigrants typically face numerous challenges settling in the host society. Apart from the difficulties in finding employment and housing and in securing language training and other important resources, many immigrants find themselves experiencing fast-declining health and facing barriers in accessing primary healthcare and other essential health services. For example, uninsured immigrants of low socioeconomic status are at a distinct disadvantage in accessing healthcare, an expensive service to consume. Immigrants lacking proficiency in English (or French, in Canada) are also challenged in their encounters with care providers, their health beliefs, and health practices often being misunderstood or discounted. Underutilization of healthcare can lead to poor health and, in turn, poor outcomes for both the individual and the system, as the cost of care is much higher if one's health is not monitored on a regular basis.

The next section of this chapter discusses the differences in the Canadian and US healthcare systems, thus providing a backdrop for understanding many of the challenges immigrants face in accessing care. The **healthy immigrant effect** (see Chapter 13) is revisited, as health status and access to healthcare are closely related. An important concept discussed is the so-called **ethnic density effect**, which describes the relationship between ethnic homogeneity in a neighbourhood and health outcomes. An empirical case example is provided to illustrate the relationship between ethnic density and low birth-weight for infants of Bangladeshi women in New York City.

Following this, the chapter focuses on the experience of immigrants in accessing health services in two highly contrasting Canadian and US healthcare systems. Three types of barriers in accessing care are examined: economic barriers related to insurance and financial ability to consume health services; geographical barriers resulting from a **spatial mismatch** between distribution of care providers and location of patients; and sociocultural barriers related to language, health beliefs, and health practices. Another empirical case example is used to highlight the sociocultural and geographical barriers facing Chinese immigrants in Toronto in accessing primary care physicians.

Immigrant Health and Healthcare

Meeting the health needs of immigrants is critically important to their **adaptation** and integration. This section first introduces the main characteristics of the Canadian and American healthcare systems, which play an important role in **immigrant** health by shaping access to care. It then focuses on the healthy immigrant effect and the ethnic density effect, two useful theoretical perspectives for understanding why health and healthcare access are experienced unequally among groups who differ in ethnicity, culture, class, neighbourhood, and other characteristics.

Healthcare System

Canada and the United States have fundamentally different healthcare systems. The Canadian system is predominantly publicly funded and administered. Under the Constitution Act, 1867, the provinces are responsible for establishing, maintaining, and managing most health resources. The main role of the federal government in healthcare is developing and implementing national principles for the system under the 1984 Canada Health Act (CHA) and financially supporting the provinces and territories. Public health in Canada is delivered through an interlocking set of 10 provincial and 3 territorial health insurance plans that cover medically necessary hospital and physician services provided on a prepaid basis, without charge at the point of service. Provinces may charge their residents a healthcare premium to help pay for publicly funded health services. The CHA established five criteria and conditions that provincial and territorial health insurance plans must meet: public administration (i.e. insurance plans are administered on a nonprofit basis by a public authority); comprehensiveness (all medically necessary services are covered); universality (all eligible residents are entitled to the insured services); portability (residents moving within Canada are covered for insured services); and accessibility (all insured persons have reasonable access to insured services) (Health Canada 2012). Although immigrants in Canada are covered under universal health insurance, research has found that they use health services less than the native-born population, face many barriers in accessing primary care, and experience deteriorating health status (Leduc and Proulx 2004; Newbold 2005). These aspects will be discussed in detail below.

In contrast, the US healthcare system is highly privatized—in fact the United States is the only wealthy, industrialized nation that does not have universal healthcare (Kumar, Ghildayal, and Shah 2011). Both governments and markets play a significant role in providing healthcare for US citizens and immigrants. Private healthcare is largely provided by employers or purchased by individuals, and public healthcare is delivered through government programs such as Medicare, Medicaid, and programs for children, military personnel, and Native Americans (Kovner and Knickman 2008). Medicare is a federally funded program for people aged 65 and over. Medicaid is a state-administered program for people in financial need, particularly the aged, the disabled, and families with dependent children. David Squires (2011) reports that healthcare spending in the United States ranks at the top, both per capita and as a percentage of gross domestic product, among the 12 OECD countries based on 2008 health data. In particular, private healthcare spending per capita in terms of US dollars is substantially higher in the United States ($3,119) than in other OECD countries (Canada being second at $616 and France third at $548); also, out-of-pocket spending is higher per capita in the United States ($912) than in all other countries except Switzerland ($1,424) ($600 for Canada). US per capita public healthcare spending ($3,507), primarily on Medicare and Medicaid, outstrips public spending in all other countries except Norway ($4,213) ($2,863 for Canada) (Squires 2011).

In the United States, health insurance has become the dominant means of paying for medical services. However, nearly 47 million people in the country are uninsured (Smith 2008); they have limited or no access to essential health services, leading to very poor health outcomes. Immigrants in the United States are more likely to be uninsured, and for longer periods, than their US-born counterparts, and their medical expenditures are approximately one-half to two-thirds higher than those of the US-born population (Ku 2009). In March 2010, the Patient Protection and

Affordable Care Act (ACA), commonly referred to as Obamacare, was passed into law by US President Barack Obama. As an epic policy breakthrough built upon continued effort in the country's health reform over the last century, the ACA aims to expand access to affordable and quality healthcare services to more Americans through consumer protections, regulations, subsidies, taxation, insurance exchanges, and means without replacing private insurance, Medicare, or Medicaid (Orient 2010; Thompson 2013). The health reforms specified in the ACA roll out year by year until 2022, with numerous policy and administration challenges facing the implementation of the act. It is hard to assess the full impact of the ACA on immigrant health and healthcare. However, the expansion of health coverage for the vast majority of the currently uninsured population will likely benefit the growing **immigration** population in the US. For example, Medicaid coverage will be extended to those whose income does not exceed 133% of the poverty line in order to provide coverage for 15 million uninsured low-income Americans, and this could possibly give health insurance to immigrants in poverty who would not have been eligible for Medicaid under the current system (Orient 2012; Wilensky 2013).

In Canada, while "medically necessary" services are covered under provincial health insurance programs, there remains a range of uninsured medical services. Medicines may be unaffordable for those without an extended health plan, which is usually tied to employment. Immigrants, especially recent arrivals, often have difficulty integrating into the Canadian labour market due to the absence of mechanisms and regulations for recognizing foreign credentials and other barriers. In both Canada and the United States, lack of employment-related health coverage is not unusual among immigrants; this can affect health outcomes negatively. Immigrants in Canada are also affected by the general shortage of physicians, with many being unable to secure a primary care physician even years after immigrating (Dean and Wilson 2010). The long wait times for diagnosis and treatment typical of the Canadian healthcare system can lead to underutilization of care, self-diagnosis, and self-treatment among immigrants (Wang, Rosenberg, and Lo 2008). Newcomers to Canada may also be subject to a waiting period imposed by a province or territory before they are entitled to insured healthcare (in Ontario, the current waiting period is three months after arrival in Canada). In both Canada and the United States, the healthcare system plays a large role in how immigrants use health services (Wang, Chacko, and Withers 2011).

Ethnic Inequality in Health and Healthcare

The "population health" or "**social determinants of health**" perspective is a well-established framework for understanding health disparities or the social patterning of disease within a population (Willson 2009). This perspective suggests that the socioeconomic status of individuals and populations is more important than medical factors or lifestyle (e.g. tobacco use, physical activity, diet) in terms of health outcomes (Dunn and Dyck 2000; Pathak, Low, Franzini, and Swint 2012). Income, social status, employment, culture, and ethnicity are some of the individual-level social determinants of health identified in the health literature and by government agencies such as the Public Health Agency of Canada. Social determinants of health often intertwine and work in complex ways to affect human health.

Research based on large national population health surveys has found health inequalities between immigrant and nonmigrant populations in countries such as Australia, Canada, and the United States (Chen, Ng, and Wilkins 1996; Dunn and Dyck 2000; Son 2013). The health gap between foreign-born and native-born populations is worrisome. Recent immigrants are often found to have better health status than the native-born population, even among those from countries with poor health indicators. However, immigrants tend to lose this advantage over time, as evidenced by self-reported health and functional health measures (Gee, Kobayashi, and Prus 2004; McDonald and Kennedy 2005). This phenomenon, called the healthy immigrant effect (HIE) (see also Chapter 13), has been found in Australia, Canada, the United Kingdom, and the United States and is more evident for immigrants from developing countries than for those from developed countries (Kennedy, McDonald, and Biddle 2006). The health advantage of newly arrived immigrants results largely from the immigration screening process (including medical examination) and immigrant self-selection in the emigration process (Ng, Wilkins, Gendron, and Berthelot 2005). The subsequent deterioration in health in the receiving country may be due to a number of intertwining factors, such as declining socioeconomic status, adoption of an unhealthy lifestyle and behavioural norms, cultural and language barriers to health-service access, aging, and stress related to migration and resettlement.

Specific findings on the HIE vary across contexts. An important study by Jiajian Chen and associates (1996), based on the National Population Health Survey, was one of the earliest to point to a HIE in Canada by revealing that the health advantage of recent non-European immigrants, in terms of chronic conditions and disability, disappeared after about 10 years of residency. Bruce Newbold (2011), using the results of the Longitudinal Survey of Immigrants to Canada (LSIC), found significant decline in immigrants' health in as little as two years post-arrival. According to James McDonald and Steven Kennedy (2004), the HIE in Canada shows stronger evidence on chronic conditions than self-assessed status. There is clear evidence of a HIE in the United States, with more studies than those in Canada focusing on specific ethnic groups rather than on the overall foreign-born population. A study by Juyeon Son (2013), based on the National Health Interview Survey (NHIS), reveals that immigrants in the United States from Central America and the former Soviet Union exhibit significant health disadvantages (self-reported health and functional difficulties) compared to those from East and Southeast Asia. Among immigrants in Canada, unhealthy weight meets or exceeds native-born levels after 20 to 30 years of residency, whereas the prevalence of obesity among immigrants in the United States approaches that among US-born adults after just 15 years (McDonald and Kennedy 2005; Goel, McCarthy, Phillips, and Wee 2004).

The factors that contribute to the HIE have been of persistent interest to scholars. Many "predictors" (determinants, or risk factors) have been identified using the population perspective discussed earlier. Aging and duration of residency in the host country are closely associated with declining health among immigrants. Lower socioeconomic status (e.g. education) in general results in declining health. Among socioeconomic factors, income has been identified as particularly important, accounting for health variation even after controlling for other socioeconomic status variables (Zsembik and Fennell 2005; Pickett and Wilkinson 2008). Healthcare utilization among immigrants generally increases with length of residency. Yet both recent and long-term immigrants can face strong barriers to accessing linguistically and culturally appropriate care. Acculturation, adoption of an unhealthy Western lifestyle and diet, and settlement stress in the post-migration period can also lead to a decline in mental and physical health (Gordon-Larsen, Harris, Ward, and Popkin 2003; Noh and Kaspar 2003).

The foreign-born population in Canada and the United States is extremely diverse in terms of country of origin, socioeconomic status, and **settlement patterns**. Partly due to data limitation, scholars have paid more attention to the health of the overall immigrant population or broad ethnic categories (e.g. Hispanic, South Asian) than to the health of country-specific immigrant groups. However, we can still see much variability in health outcomes across immigrant groups. For example, administrative health data show a high prevalence of diabetes among South Asian immigrants in Canada (Creatore, Moineddin, Booth, Glazier, and Manuel 2012). Using a random sampling method, Sonia Anand and associates (2000) found that, in the province of Ontario, the prevalence of heart disease was higher among people of South Asian origin (11%) than among Europeans (5%) and Chinese (2%). Maninder Setia and associates (2011) analyzed the LSIC data and found that South Asian and Chinese women in Canada are more likely to rate their health as poor compared to white **immigrant women**. A study based on a different data set—the Canadian Community Health

Survey (CCHS)—found that age and gender have the greatest effect on self-assessed health among Chinese immigrants, followed by immigrants overall and nonmigrants (who are on average younger than immigrants), and that older female Chinese immigrants are particularly disadvantaged in maintaining their health (Wang and Hu 2013). Hispanics in the United States, despite their relatively low socioeconomic status and the barriers they face in accessing healthcare, have lower levels of infant and adult mortality, a phenomenon often called the **Hispanic paradox** (Zsembik and Fennell 2005; Shaw and Pickett 2013). The Hispanic paradox has been largely attributed to favourable health behaviour related to Latino culture. Hispanics are less likely than members of other groups to drink and smoke and more likely to follow a high-fibre, high-protein diet (Abraído-Lanza, Chao, and Flórez 2005). However, there is evidence that, as a result of acculturation, the healthy behaviour of Hispanic immigrants in the United States tends to decline over time; in fact Hispanics show poorer self-rated health status than non-Hispanic whites and members of other ethnic groups (Bzostek, Goldman, and Pebley 2007). Also, the effect of the Hispanic paradox is not observed equally among Hispanic subgroups from different source countries or regions and of different socioeconomic status (Borrell and Lancet 2012). Low self-reported health is associated with higher socioeconomic status among Mexican Hispanics but with lower socioeconomic status among immigrants from the Caribbean Islands (Barbara 2005).

Neighbourhood, Health, and Healthcare

Where people live can affect their health and degree of healthcare access. At the most basic level, living in an area where there is a good supply of healthcare providers and within close proximity to healthcare facilities can lead to reasonably good physical accessibility (see the section titled "Sociocultural and Geographical Barriers"). One's neighbourhood can affect health and healthcare in complex ways. Geographical variation in health can be explained by both individual differences in socioeconomic status and contextual effects due to differences between places or neighbourhoods (Diez Roux and Mair 2010; Macintyre and Ellaway 2003). Contextual effects can be measured by physical and social neighbourhood traits. The poor social environment of some minority neighbourhoods, including poverty, violence, inferior schooling, and lack of social support and **social capital**, can have adverse mental health outcomes for immigrants (Hanks 2008). Poor minority neighbourhoods in some US cities are also exposed to high levels of environmental pollution due to traffic density and proximity to polluting facilities, causing a structural disparity in health (Houston, Wu, Ong, and Winer 2006). In New York City, for example, a strong relationship

Case Example 1: Ethnic Density and Maternal and Infant Health Inequalities

Sara McLafferty and her colleagues (2012) studied the association between low infant birth weight and ethnic density among Bangladeshi immigrant mothers in New York City from 1990 to 2000. Ethnic **concentration** in a neighbourhood can result in social and material support for immigrant women during pregnancy. In this study, the relationship between ethnic density and low birth weight was not linear but changed over time. Logistic regression models indicated no statistically significant association between ethnic density and low birth weight in 1990, 1993, or 1996, when the Bangladeshi population had not yet reached a sufficient size to cluster in neighbourhoods. However, in 2000 this population reached a larger size and a statistically significant U-shaped association between low birth weight and density could be observed. Women living in ethnically isolated settings and in high-density enclaves were more vulnerable to poor infant health outcomes than women living in neighbourhoods of medium ethnic density. Women living in residential areas with few Bangladeshi neighbours may experience a social and spatial isolation from their own ethnic group, whereas those living in areas of high Bangladeshi density may experience a different form of isolation due to decreased social interaction with other ethnic groups. Women in medium-density neighbourhoods were able to maximize social capital from within- and inter-group interactions that provided a protective effect on health.

has been found between rates of hospitalization for asthma, low median household income, and neighbourhoods that are high-percentage minority (black and Hispanic), and many disadvantaged neighbourhoods that have high percentages of dilapidated and deteriorating housing as well as polluting facilities (Corburn et al. 2006).

A concentration of people sharing the same ethnic background in a neighbourhood is socially important for immigrants (Cummins, Curtis, Diez-Roux, and Macintyre 2007). Living in an area that is ethnically homogeneous has been found to have a protective effect on health, even in materially deprived neighbourhoods; this phenomenon is called the ethnic density effect (Karlsen, Nazroo, and Stephenson 2002; Pickett and Wilkinson 2008; Menezes, Georgiades, and Boyle 2011). Ethnic concentration, especially voluntary segregation, may promote a sense of community, reduce exposure to **racism** and discrimination, foster neighbourhood cohesion, and provide appropriate social support, thus reducing social disparities in health (Stafford,

Becares, and Nazroo 2009). However, the relationship between ethnic density and health outcome is not always linear and can vary by context. In New York City, ethnic density has been found to be negatively associated with the preterm birth rates for non-Hispanic blacks (Mason, Kaufman, Daniels, Emch, Hogan, and Savitz 2011). Also, a U-shaped association between ethnic density and low birth weight for the infants of Bangladeshi immigrant women has been found, with those living in areas of very low and very high density being the most vulnerable (McLafferty, Widener, Chakrabarti, and Grady 2012) (see Case Example 1). In Canada, ethnic concentration is associated with poor self-rated health for the overall foreign-born population but has a slight protective health effect for Chinese immigrants (Wang and Hu 2013).

Ethnicity and Access to Care

Above, we have seen examples of ethnic variation in health in Canada and the United States. This section now focuses on the ways in which different ethnic and immigrant groups access health services and the barriers they face in doing so. Among the many risk factors discussed earlier, access to healthcare is regarded as an increasingly important social determinant of health. Poor access likely results in low utilization of services and negatively affects one's health outcome. In reality, access to care is never equal within a population. For example, senior citizens may not be able to visit a physician as frequently as needed due to low mobility, and impoverished people may not be able to afford healthcare due to a lack of insurance. Also, different neighbourhoods are often associated with different levels of accessibility. This is not hard to understand, as the further away one is from a hospital or community clinic, the more effort one must expend to get there. Immigrant and ethnic minority populations face numerous barriers (economic, geographical, and sociocultural) in accessing health services. Some of the barriers are unique to immigrants due to their newcomer status, while others affect both foreign-born and native-born populations. Different barriers often work simultaneously to affect immigrant health and healthcare.

Economic Barriers

Wide income inequality between immigrants and nonmigrants and within the overall foreign-born population exists in both Canada and the United States, as well as in other countries. This inequality is reflected in the consumption of health services, as well as in health outcomes (as discussed in the section titled "Ethnic Inequality in Health and Healthcare"), as healthcare is a type of service that is expensive to consume without insurance. Unlike in Canada, which has a longstanding policy of universal healthcare, in the United States health insurance acts as a gatekeeper to healthcare access (Kim and Keefe 2010). Availability of health insurance is largely tied to income and employment. In 2012 about 32% of the US foreign-born population (12.8 million), 43% of noncitizens (9.5 million), and 13% of citizens (35.1 million) had no private or government health insurance. This represents an increase over the 1999 noncoverage rates, which were 31%, 40%, and 11.5% for the foreign-born, noncitizen, and citizen populations (US Census Bureau 2012). People who are not insured are at a disadvantage in accessing needed care, receive a lower quality of care, and experience worse health outcomes than those who are insured (McWilliams 2009).

Data from the Joint Canada/United States Survey of Health indicate that health insurance is a major cause of differences between immigrants and nonmigrants in the two countries in terms of access to primary care. Insured immigrants in the United States do not differ significantly from immigrants in Canada (who are all insured under the universal healthcare system) in terms of unmet health needs and care by a regular doctor, whereas noninsured immigrants in the United States demonstrate a high rate of unmet health needs and lack of a regular doctor (Siddiqi, Zuberi, and Nguyen 2009). Different levels of health insurance also affect decisions and outcomes with regard to healthcare utilization. Kim and Keefe (2010) found that uninsured or inadequately insured Asian immigrants may resort to less-costly alternative medicines and approaches, some of which are underregulated and of questionable quality. As discussed earlier, once implemented fully, the Affordable Care Act (Obamacare) would likely change the picture. The main goal of the ACA is to provide health coverage to approximately 30 million previously uninsured people through Medicaid expansion and with subsidized private coverage purchased in state insurance exchanges (Wilensky 2012). For previously uninsured immigrants, change of health insurance status would have great long-term impact on health outcome.

In Canada, despite its publicly financed healthcare system, immigrants still face economic barriers to care. Uninsured foreign-born people include newly arrived permanent residents (who, in Ontario, are subject to a three-month waiting period for provincial coverage), successful refugee claimants not covered by the Interim Federal Health Program (IFHP), asylum seekers who have filed a refugee claim, those whose refugee claim has been denied, and undocumented or partially documented migrants whose visitor's visa or work permit has expired (Wilson-Mitchell and Rummens 2013). The IFHP, a federal program in Canada that provides basic temporary health coverage to accepted refugees and refugee claimants, has undergone sweeping changes in the last few years, resulting in drastically reduced coverage for many refugees (Sheikh, Rashid, Berger, and Hume 2013). This can have a long-term adverse effect on refugee health and healthcare. Compared to immigrants in the

United States, immigrants with legal status in Canada face a less significant economic barrier to care, as they are insured under provincial systems for medically necessary hospital and physician services. However, without extended health insurance normally provided by employers or purchased, those in economic hardship cannot access needed pharmaceuticals, eye care, dental care, and other essential services, including mental healthcare. Compared to other OECD countries, Canada has longer wait times for both emergency and nonurgent care. This is a much-lamented issue in Canada, part of the ongoing public debate about the viability of single-tier publicly funded healthcare (Siciliani, Borowitz, and Moran 2013). Long wait times for care can lead to underutilization of primary care physicians and negatively affect immigrant health (Wang et al. 2008).

Sociocultural and Geographical Barriers

Immigrants in Canada and the United States experience sociocultural barriers in accessing health care. Cultural differences between care providers and immigrants affect communication and treatment through misinterpretation of patients' symptoms and difficulty transmitting mainstream Western medical knowledge to patients from traditional **ethnic communities**. Joseph Betancourt and associates (2005) identify the types of sociocultural barrier that contribute to ethnic disparities in health and health care. These include organizational barriers (e.g. under-representation of minorities in medical institutions and the healthcare workforce), structural barriers (e.g. lack of interpreter services), and clinical barriers (e.g. different socioculturally based health beliefs and practices between patient and physician). These barriers can lead to a lack of **cultural competency** in healthcare delivery.

Cultural competency has been recognized as important in addressing culturally specific health needs, improving quality of care, and eliminating ethnic disparities in health and healthcare (Eshleman and Davidhizar, 2006). In Canada and the United States, linguistic and cultural barriers are still commonly experienced by immigrants, who are highly diverse in mother tongue, language proficiency, ethnic origin, religion, health beliefs, and health behaviours. Proficiency in English (or French, in Canada) is regarded as a key measurement of acculturation (the process of change in culture and value system that occurs when immigrants are exposed to their host country's mainstream culture). Limited proficiency can be a significant barrier to obtaining health information and healthcare and is found to relate to poor health status (e.g. self-reported health, breast and colon cancer) for immigrant groups such as Chinese Canadians and Asian, Latino, and African Americans (Schachter, Kimbro, and Gorman 2012; Todd, Harvey, and Hoffman-Goetz 2012; Okafor, Carter-Porkras,

Picot, and Zhan 2013). One way to enhance cultural competency in primary care delivery is to encourage more qualified foreign-trained physicians with appropriate linguistic skills to practise in communities where there is poor access to same-language physicians (Wang et al. 2008).

In a comparative study of immigrant healthcare in Canada and the United States based on representative national health survey data, Lydie Lebrun (2012) found that immigrants with limited English (or French, in Canada) language proficiency and shorter length of residency in the host country (less than 10 years) generally had lower rates of access to and use of healthcare compared to those with language proficiency and longer length of residency. Furthermore, the persistent disparities among immigrants in Canada in using primary and preventive care, based on language proficiency and length of residency suggest that the universal healthcare system may not be providing equal access to the country's diverse immigrant population. For immigrants with mental health challenges, lack of information on available resources, language difficulties, resettlement stress, lack of familiarity with the healthcare system, and stigma associated with mental illness significantly impact access to mental healthcare and special mental health programs (Reitmanova and Gustafson 2009; Crooks, Hynie, Killian, Giesbrecht, and Gastleden 2011). In this regard, cultural competency refers not only to providing care in ethnic languages through multilingual health practitioners or the use of interpreters, but also being culturally sensitive and open-minded to different health beliefs and traditions, and actively promoting health, including mental health, to minority groups. In Canada, official language minority communities (for example, French-speaking communities living outside Quebec and English-speaking communities living in Quebec) also experience language barriers in receiving timely diagnosis and treatment. Access to health services in one's preferred language (English or French) is a critical health issue for official language minority groups in Canada (CIHR 2009).

Spatial mismatch in the context of healthcare refers to the discordance between where healthcare providers are located and where immigrants reside. Spatial mismatch represents a geographical barrier in access to care, as travel is needed in most cases of healthcare utilization. Therefore, distance plays an important role in **healthcare accessibility**, which refers to the relative ease with which individuals from one location can reach other locations. At a regional scale, the concentration of physicians and healthcare facilities in cities leaves immigrants in rural communities with poor access to linguistically and culturally competent physicians or interpretation services. For instance, Latinos, who are increasingly settling in rural areas in the Midwest US, are found to face communication barriers in seeking and accessing healthcare due to a lack of local trained medical interpreters (Cristancho, Garces, Peters, and Mueller 2008). At an urban scale, the distribution of primary care providers and healthcare facilities does not always match the settlement pattern of immigrant populations, resulting in underserved areas. Case Example 2 illustrates the geographical barrier experienced by Chinese immigrants in Toronto when accessing and utilizing Chinese-speaking family physicians and how geographical and linguistic barriers work together to influence access to care.

Coping Strategies

Immigrants in Canada and the United States have developed various strategies for addressing the health challenges they face. In the United States, a lack of health insurance and high costs have driven many Mexican immigrants, especially those residing near the border, to travel back to Mexico for low-cost hospital and physician services, a phenomenon called medical return. Medical return is a good example of uninsured immigrants confronting the American healthcare system, which is costly for immigrants who are impoverished or who lack employment-related health coverage (Portes, Fernandez-Kelly, and Light 2012). In studies by Michael Seid and his colleagues (2003) and Dejun Su and Daphne Wang (2012), close to 50% and 40% of the Latinos surveyed in San Diego County and in 32 Texas counties close to the US-Mexico border are medical returnees, due to a lack of insurance in the United States and limited proficiency in English. In other countries, there is also evidence on migrants' use of homeland health services due to a combination of cultural-linguistic factors and long wait times for care in the host country (e.g. Korean immigrants in Canada and New Zealand, South Africans in the United Kingdom) (Lee, Kearns, and Friesen 2010; Thomas 2010; Wang and Kwak 2013). For example, many Korean immigrants in Canada have been found to travel regularly to South Korea for health services. Those services include comprehensive medical examinations, which are not insured under the Canadian universal healthcare system, and medical procedures that typically have long wait times in Canada (Wang and Kwak 2013).

Some immigrants resort to alternative and complementary medicines outside the formal healthcare system as a way of coping with barriers to access. South Asian immigrants in Greater Vancouver use Desi remedies for minor ailments (Dyck 2004). Asian immigrants in both Canada and the United States have been found to use traditional Chinese medicine (Ma 1999; Zhang and Verhoef 2002). Traditional Chinese medicine is widely practised in China and some other Asian countries. While traditional Chinese medicine may be less costly than primary care for uninsured migrants in the United States if paid out of pocket (Kim and Keefe 2010), in Canada it is expensive when considered in light of universally insured medical services. Despite its high cost, traditional Chinese medicine is popular

Case Example 2: Access to Linguistically Matched Family Physicians by Immigrants in Toronto, ON, Canada

The Toronto Census Metropolitan Area (CMA) receives about 43% of all recent arrivals in Canada, compared to 16% for Vancouver and 14% for Montreal (CIC 2001). According to the 2006 Canadian Census, approximately 46% of the CMA's population is foreign-born. Despite the availability of universal healthcare, immigrants of various origins experience significant barriers in accessing quality primary care provided by family physicians, who act as gatekeepers to other specialist physicians. For immigrants arriving from non-English-speaking countries, language can be a strong barrier to healthcare access due to difficulty understanding English medical terminology and poor distribution of same-language physicians.

A recent study (Wang 2011) examined the geographical distribution of eight selected recent and longstanding immigrant groups in Toronto in relation to the location patterns of linguistically matched family physicians. Physician-to-population ratio in Table 14.1 is a broad indicator of the relative abundance of same-language family physicians (SLFPs). The two Chinese subgroups have the largest number of SLFPs. Low physician-to-population ratios are observed for Iranian, Portuguese, and Sri Lankan immigrants. Among recent arrivals, Iranians, Mainland Chinese, Pakistanis, and Sri Lankans have lower physician-to-population ratios than the CMA average. However, the ratios do not consider where the physicians and immigrants are located. A high ratio does not necessarily ensure adequate geographical access to physicians if the physicians are poorly distributed. For example, in the case of Hong Kong Chinese, census tracts associated with a high level of SLFP accessibility do not necessarily have large co-ethnic populations—suggesting a clear spatial discordance between SLPF location and population settlement (see Figure 14.1). Hong Kong Chinese cluster in Markham and north of Scarborough and North York, whereas census tracts in the city core are generally associated with good SLFP accessibility, largely due to the concentration of physicians and hospitals in the area. Accessibility is calculated by using the two-step floating catchment area model, implemented in a Geographic Information System.

Table 14.1
Immigrant Population and Same-Language Family Physician (SLFP) in Toronto CMA

Source Country	Count	%	SLFPs Count	%	SLFPs/1,000 immigrants	Recent arrivals (in past 5 years) Count	%	SLFPs accepting new patients Count	%	SLFPs accepting new patients/1,000 recent arrivals
Iran	45,205	0.9	37	0.6	0.82	13,965	0.03	8	1.0	0.57
Hong Kong	102,675	2.0	404*	6.6	3.93	3,060	0.01	104	12.5	33.99**
Mainland China	190,515	3.8	360*	5.9	1.89	63,370	0.14	88	10.5	1.39
Pakistan	85,195	1.7	212	3.5	2.49	36,975	0.08	61	7.3	1.65
Russia	29,875	0.6	63	1.0	2.11	9,895	0.02	23	2.8	2.32
Sri Lanka	83,835	1.7	42	0.7	0.52	17,135	0.04	18	2.2	1.05
Italy	130,325	2.6	144	2.4	1.12	N/A	N/A	43	5.1	N/A
Portugal	76,025	1.5	58	0.9	0.75	N/A	N/A	13	1.6	N/A

* Some physicians self-reported speaking both Mandarin and Cantonese, the two Chinese languages most commonly spoken by Mainland and Hong Kong Chinese, respectively.
** The high ratio results from the much-reduced number of immigrants from Hong Kong after 1997, when Hong Kong, until then a British colony, was returned to China and when immigration from Hong Kong to Canada tailed off.

Source: Wang (2011).

Figure 14.1
Spatial Access of Hong Kong Chinese Immigrants to Same-Language Family Physicians

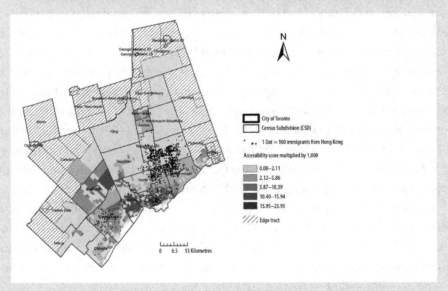

Source: Extracted from Wang et al. (2008) and Wang (2011).

among Chinese immigrants in Canada, as it is generally believed to treat the cause of the disease, leading to a permanent cure, whereas Western medicines act quickly to ease the symptom but may not cure the disease completely. One study showed that Chinese immigrants used traditional Chinese medicine as well as food remedies by combining foods and medicinal herbs for healing or preventive purposes (Wang et al. 2008). Due to cultural-linguistic and geographical barriers to accessing family physicians in Canada, immigrants also practised self-diagnosis and self-treatment using medicines brought from their country of origin, including both antibiotics and traditional herb-based Chinese medicines. Importing medicines and health products from the country of origin could be viewed as a form of cross-border care seeking, as evidenced not only in the Chinese group but in other groups, such as South Asian immigrants in Canada, Brazilians in the United States, and South African migrants in the United Kingdom (Ahmad, Shik, Vanza, Cheung, George, and Stewart 2004; Messias 2002; Thomas 2010).

Conclusion

This chapter provides an introduction to the ethnic disparities in health and healthcare in Canada and the United States. In order to understand the contributors to the observed health utilization and outcome patterns for immigrants, it is important to look at the characteristics of the healthcare system, which plays a different role in each country in shaping immigrants' health and healthcare experiences. An important phenomenon is the healthy immigrant effect, which describes the superior health status of new arrivals relative to the native-born population but declining health with increased length of residency in the host country. The extent of the HIE varies across contexts for different groups and areas. For example, the HIE can be observed in the overall foreign-born population but may not be the same for all small, country-specific immigrant groups. Contributing factors for the HIE, and more generally for health outcomes among immigrants, can be identified using the social determinants of health framework and could include socioeconomic status, acculturation, and other individual or contextual variables. Neighbourhood contextual factors reflect socioeconomic conditions in the community where immigrants reside. Ethnic density (concentration of people sharing the same ethnicity) and level of material deprivation in a neighbourhood influence immigrant health.

In both Canada and the United States, immigrants face multiple barriers in accessing primary healthcare. These can be grouped into economic barriers (related to insurance and ability to pay for services), sociocultural barriers (related to language, health beliefs, etc.), and geographical barriers (related to distance and distribution).

These are not distinct categories but often overlap and work together in shaping immigrant access to care. In responding to the challenges they face in accessing healthcare, immigrants employ different coping strategies, including transnational care-seeking, self-treatment, and use of alternative medicines and food remedies.

Immigrant health and healthcare should be understood not only on the basis of health statistics but as a multifaceted phenomenon situated in intertwining social, cultural, and (healthcare system) policy contexts of the specific country of destination. As highlighted in the chapter, both commonalities and differences exist between the immigrant populations in Canada and the United States in health outcomes and healthcare-seeking behaviour. In both countries, the pattern of change in health status among the foreign-born population can be similarly characterized by the so-called healthy immigrant effect and the significant barriers in access to care have that been observed for immigrants. The differences between immigrant health and healthcare in the two countries are, however, largely attributed to the differences in the healthcare systems, immigration patterns, and ethnic and socioeconomic composition of the populations. While ethnic disparities in health have been observed in both countries, uninsured immigrants in the US are particularly disadvantaged with a high rate of unmet health needs and lack of a regular doctor compared to native-born counterparts (Siddiqi et al. 2009). The healthcare reform that is enacted by the Affordable Care Act (or Obamacare) and has been slowly rolling out since 2012 will likely provide insurance to many previously uninsured immigrants and thus change the landscape of immigration and healthcare in the US. Immigrants in Canada under a universal healthcare system are still found to experience various types of barriers (sociocultural, geographical, economic) in access to health services. Availability of primary care physicians who are able to provide culturally competent healthcare is a critically beneficial factor of immigrant health. Specific immigrant and ethnic groups also demonstrate unique patterns in health and healthcare use, as evidenced by the **Hispanic Paradox** and various effects of ethnic density on health across different groups in different settings. Ethnicity and healthcare is an important issue in immigration and settlement studies. Good health improves quality of life. Maintaining a satisfactory health status in the post-migration period and enjoying reasonably good access to essential healthcare are critically important aspects of the successful integration of immigrants.

Questions for Critical Thought

1. How do the health insurance systems in Canada and the US differ from each other in providing care to their immigrant and foreign-born populations?
2. What are the major barriers for immigrants in accessing needed healthcare in the two countries?
3. You learned in this chapter about the healthy immigrant effect (HIE). What can governments and society do to ensure that immigrants maintain their health advantage?

Key Readings

Chen, J., E. Ng, and R. Wilkins (1996) The Health of Canada's Immigrants in 1994–1995. *Health Reports* 7(4).

Gatrell, A.C. (2002) *Geographies of Health: An Introduction*. Malden, MA: Blackwell.

Newbold, B. (2011) The Short-term Health of Canada's New Immigrant Arrivals: Evidence from LSIC. *Ethnicity and Health* 14(3):315–336.

Noh, S. and V. Kaspar (2003) Diversity and Immigrant Health. In P. Anisef and M. Lanphier (eds.) *The World in a City*, pp. 316–351. Toronto: University of Toronto Press.

Wang, L., E. Chacko, and L. Withers (2011) Immigration, Health and Health Care. In C. Teixeira, W. Li, and A. Kobayashi (eds.) *Immigrant Geographies of North American Cities*, pp. 158–178. Don Mills, ON: Oxford University Press.

Media Links

Sicko:
www.michaelmoore.com/movies
Sicko, a documentary produced by Michael Moore in 2007, discusses the highly privatized US healthcare system compared to the system in other countries, such as Canada and Cuba.

Access Alliance:
accessalliance.ca
Numerous useful materials (publications and reports) can be accessed from the website of Access Alliance Multicultural Health and Community Services, a successful NGO that provides primary healthcare (in various non-official languages) to Toronto's immigrant and refugee communities.

Immigration to Canada for Doctors:

Part 1: www.youtube.com/watch?v=iJ-dVa0GJ_k

Part 2: www.youtube.com/watch?v=OZ4b8Dl5STo

Part 3: www.youtube.com/watch?v=_FewZR89FQE

Part 4: www.youtube.com/watch?v=_Dr4XRs889I

Health Care 911: The Plight of Immigrant Medical Doctors:
This documentary shows how challenging it is for foreign-trained medical graduates to practise in Canada, despite a doctor shortage in the country. Directed by J. Gol. Produced by Artizan Productions, E. Mussolum and M. Welygan.

References

Abraído-Lanza, A.F., M.T. Chao, and K.R. Flórez (2005) Do Healthy Behaviors Decline with Greater Acculturation? Implications for the Latino Mortality Paradox. *Social Science and Medicine* 61:1243–1255.

Ahmad, F., A. Shik, R. Vanza, A.M. Cheung, U. George, and D.E. Stewart (2004) Voices of South Asian Women: Immigration and Mental Health. *Women and Health* 40(4):113–129.

Anand S.S., S. Yusuf, V. Vuksan, S. Devanessen, K.K. Teo, P.A. Montague, L. Kelemen, C. Yi, E. Lonn, H. Gerstein, and R.A. Hegele (2000) Differences in Risk Factors, Atherosclerosis, and Cardiovascular Disease between Ethnic Groups in Canada: The Study of Health Assessment and Risk in Ethnic Groups (SHARE). *Lancet* 356:279–284.

Barbara, A.Z. (2005) Ethnic Variation in Health and the Determinants of Health among Latinos. *Social Science and Medicine* 61:53–63.

Betancourt, J.R., A.R. Green, J.E. Carrillo, and E.R. Park (2005) Cultural Competence and Health Care Disparities: Key Perspectives and Trends. *Health Affairs* 24(2):499–505.

Borrell, L.N. and E.A. Lancet (2012) Race/Ethnicity and All-Cause Mortality in US Adults: Revisiting the Hispanic Paradox. *American Journal of Public Health* 102(5):836–843.

Bzostek, S., N. Goldman, and A. Pebley (2007) Why Do Hispanics in the USA Report Poor Health? *Social Science and Medicine* 65:990–1003.

Chen, J., E. Ng, and R. Wilkins (1996) The Health of Canada's Immigrants in 1994–95. *Health Reports* 7(4).

Citizenship and Immigration Canada (CIC) (2001) Recent Immigrants in Metropolitan Areas. www.cic.gc.ca/english/pdf/research-stats/2001-toronto.pdf. Ottawa: CIC. (Accessed September 13, 2011)

Canadian Institute of Health Research (CIHR) (2009) Official Language Minority Communities Initiative: Past, Present, Future—Status Report 2009. www.cihr-irsc.gc.ca/e/41538.html (Accessed November 25, 2013)

Corburn, J., J. Osleeb, and M. Porter (2006) Urban Asthma and the Neighbourhood Environment in New York City. *Health and Place* 12:167–179.

Creatore, M.I., R. Moineddin, G. Booth, R.H. Glazier, and D.H. Manuel (2012) Diabetes Screening among Immigrants: A Population-based Urban Cohort Study. *Diabetes Care* 35(4):754–761.

Cristancho, S., D.M. Garces, K.E. Peters, and B.C. Mueller (2008) Listening to Rural Hispanic Immigrants in the Midwest: A Community-based Participatory Assessment of Major Barriers to Health Care Access and Use. *Qualitative Health Research* 18(5):633–646.

Crooks, V.A., M. Hynie, K. Killian, M. Giesbrecht, and H. Gastleden (2011) Female Newcomers' Adjustment to Life in Toronto, Canada: Sources of Mental Stress and Their Implications for Delivering Primary Mental Health Care. *Geojournal* 76:139–149.

Cummins, S., S. Curtis, A.V. Diez-Roux, and S. Macintyre (2007) Understanding and Representing "Place" in Health Research: A Relational Approach. *Social Science and Medicine* 65:1825–1838.

Dean, J. and K. Wilson (2010) "My Health Has Improved Because I Always Have Everything I Need Here ...": A Qualitative Exploration of Health Improvement and Decline among Immigrants. *Social Science and Medicine* 70(8):1219–1228.

Diez Roux, A.V. and C. Mair (2010) Neighborhoods and Health. *Annals of the New York Academy of Science* 1186(1):125–145.

Dunn, J. and I. Dyck (2000) Social Determinants of Health in Canada's Immigrant Population: Results from the National Population Health Survey. *Social Science and Medicine* 51(11):1573–1593.

Dyck, I. (2004) *Immigration, Place and Health: South Asian Women's Accounts of Health, Illness and Everyday Life.* Vancouver: RIIM Working Paper Series.

Eshleman, J. and R.E. Davidhizar (2006) Strategies for Developing Cultural Competency in an RN-BSN Program. *Journal of Transcultural Nursing* 17:179–183.

Gee, E.M., K.M. Kobayashi, and S.G. Prus (2004) Examining the Healthy Immigrant Effect in Mid- to Later Life: Findings from the Canadian Community Health Survey. *Canadian Journal on Aging* 23:S61–69.

Goel, M.S., E.P. McCarthy, R.S. Phillips, and C.C. Wee (2004) Obesity among US Immigrant Subgroups by Duration of Residence. *Journal of the American Medical Association* 292(23):2860–2867.

Gordon-Larsen, P., K.M. Harris, D.S. Ward, and B.M. Popkin (2003) Acculturation and Overweight-related Behaviors among Hispanic Immigrants to the US: The National Longitudinal Study of Adolescent Health. *Social Science and Medicine* 57(11):2023–2034.

Hanks, C.A. (2008) Social Capital in an Impoverished Minority Neighborhood: Emergence and Effects on Children's Mental Health. *Journal of Child and Adolescent Psychiatric Nursing* 21:126–136.

Health Canada (2012) *Canada Health Act Annual Report 2011–2012*. Ottawa: Health Canada. www.hc-sc.gc.ca/hcs-sss/pubs/cha-lcs/2012-cha-lcs-ar-ra/index-eng.php#a3 (Accessed October 15, 2013)

Houston, D., J. Wu, P. Ong, and A. Winer (2006) Structural Disparities of Urban Traffic in Southern California: Implications for Vehicle-related Air Pollution Exposure in Minority and High-poverty Neighborhoods. *Journal of Urban Affairs* 26(5):565–592.

Karlsen, S., J. Nazroo, and P. Stephenson (2002) Ethnicity, Environment and Health: Putting Ethnic Inequalities in Health in Their Place. *Social Science and Medicine* 55:1647–1661.

Kennedy, S., J.T. McDonald, and N. Biddle (2006) *The Healthy Immigrant Effect and Immigrant Selection: Evidence from Four Countries*. Unpublished manuscript. www5.carleton.ca/sppa/ccms/wp-content/ccms-files/chesg-mcdonald.pdf (Accessed May 1, 2012)

Kim, W. and R.H. Keefe (2010) Barriers to Healthcare among Asian Americans. *Social Work in Public Health* 25:286–295.

Kovner, A.R. and J.R. Knickman (eds.) (2008) *Jonas and Kovner's Health Care Delivery in the United States*. New York: Springer.

Ku, L. (2009) Health Insurance Coverage and Medical Expenditures of Immigrants and Native-born Citizens in the United States. *American Journal of Public Health* 99(7):1322–1328.

Kumar S., N.S. Ghildayal, and R.N. Shah (2011) Examining Quality and Efficiency of the US Healthcare System. *International Journal of Health Care* 24(5):366–388.

Lebrun, L.A. (2012) Effects of Length of Stay and Language Proficiency on Health Care Experiences among Immigrants in Canada and the United States. *Social Science and Medicine* 74:1062–1072.

Leduc, N. and M. Proulx (2004) Patterns of Health Services Utilization by Recent Immigrants. *Journal of Immigrant Health* 6(1):15–27.

Lee, J.Y., R.A. Kearns, and W. Friesen (2010) Seeking Affective Health Care: Korean Immigrants' Use of Homeland Medical Services. *Health and Place* 16:108–115.

Ma, G.X. (1999) *The Culture of Health: Asian Communities in the United States*. Westport, CT: Bergin & Garvey.

Macintyre, S. and A. Ellaway (2003) Neighborhoods and Health: An Overview. In U. Kawachi and L. Berkman (eds.) *Neighborhoods and Health*, pp. 20–42. New York: Oxford University Press.

Mason, S.M., J.S. Kaufman, U. Daniels, M.E. Emch, V.K. Hogan, and D. Savitz (2011) Neighborhood Ethnic Density and Preterm Birth across Seven Ethnic Groups in New York City. *Health and Place* 17:280–288.

McDonald, J.T. and S. Kennedy (2005) Is Migration to Canada Associated with Unhealthy Weight Gain? Overweight and Obesity among Canada's Immigrants. *Social Science and Medicine* 61(12):2469–2481.

McLafferty, S., M. Widener, R. Chakrabarti, and S. Grady (2012) Ethnic Density and Maternal and Infant Health Inequalities: Bangladeshi Immigrant Women in New York City in the 1990s. *Annals of the Association of American Geographers* 102(5):893–903.

McWilliams, J.M. (2009) Health Consequences of Uninsurance among Adults in the United States: Recent Evidence and Implications. *Milbank Quarterly* 87(2):443–494.

Menezes, N., K. Georgiades, and M. Boyle (2011) The Influence of Immigrant Status and Concentration on Psychiatric Disorder in Canada: A Multi-level Analysis. *Psychological Medicine* 41:2221–2231.

Messias, D.K.H. (2002) Transnational Health Resources, Practices, and Perspectives: Brazilian Immigrant Women's Narratives. *Journal of Immigrant Health* 4(4):183–200.

Newbold, B. (2011) The Short-term Health of Canada's New Immigrant Arrivals: Evidence from LSIC. *Ethnicity and Health* 14(3):315–336.

Newbold, K.B. (2005) Self-rated Health within the Canadian Immigrant Population: Risk and the Healthy Immigrant Effect. *Social Science and Medicine* 60(6):1359–1370.

Ng, E., R. Wilkins, F. Gendron, and J.-M. Berthelot (2005) *Dynamics of Immigrants' Health in Canada: Evidence from the National Population Health Survey.* Catalogue 82–618. Ottawa: Statistics Canada.

Noh, S. and V. Kaspar (2003) Diversity and Immigrant Health. In P. Anisef and M. Lanphier (eds.) *The World in a City*, pp. 316–351. Toronto: University of Toronto Press.

Okafor, M.T., O.D. Carter-Porkras, S.J. Picot, and M. Zhan (2013) The Relationship of Language Acculturation (English Proficiency) to Current Self-rated Health among African Immigrant Adults. *Journal of Immigrant Minority Health* 15:499–509.

Orient J.M. (2012) "ObamaCare": What Is in It. *Journal of American Physicians and Surgeons* 15(3):87–93.

Pathak, S., M.D. Low, L. Franzini, and J.M. Swint (2012) A Review of Canadian Policy on Social Determinants of Health. *Review of European Studies* 4(4):8–22.

Pickett, K. and R. Wilkinson (2008) People Like Us: Ethnic Group Density Effects on Health. *Ethnicity and Health* 13:321–334.

Portes, A., P. Fernandez-Kelly, and D. Light (2012) Life on the Edge: Immigrants Confront the American Health System. *Ethnic and Racial Studies* 35(1):3–22.

Reitmanova, S. and D.L. Gustafson (2009) Primary Mental Health Care Information and Services for St. John's Visible Minority Immigrants: Gaps and Opportunities. *Issues in Mental Health Nursing* 30(6):615–623.

Schachter, A., R. Kimbro, and B. Gorman (2012) Language Proficiency and Health Status: Are Bilingual Immigrants Healthier? *Journal of Health and Social Behavior* 53(1):124–145.

Seid, M., D. Castaneda, R. Mize, M. Zivkovic, and J.W. Varni (2003) Crossing the Border for Health Care: Access and Primary Care Characteristics for Young Children of Latino Farm Workers along the US–Mexico Border. *Ambulatory Pediatrics* 3(3):121–130.

Setia, M.S., J. Lynch, M. Abrahamowicz, P. Tousignant, and A. Quesnel-Vallee (2011) Self-rated Health in Canadian Immigrants: Analysis of the Longitudinal Survey of Immigrants to Canada. *Health and Place* 17(2):658–670.

Shaw, R.J. and K.E. Pickett (2013) The Health Benefits of Hispanic Communities for Non-Hispanic Mothers and Infants: Another Hispanic Paradox. *American Journal of Public Health* 103(6):1052–1057.

Sheikh, H., R. Rashid, P. Berger, and J. Hume (2013) Refugee Health: Providing the Best Possible Care in the Face of Crippling Cuts. *Canadian Family Physician* 59:605–606

Siciliani, L., M. Borowitz, and V. Moran (2013) *Waiting Time Policies in the Health Sector: What Works?* OECD Health Policy Studies. Paris, France: Organization for Economic Cooperation and Development.

Siddiqi, A., D. Zuberi, and A.C. Nguyen (2009) The Role of Health Insurance in Explaining Immigrant versus Non–immigrant Disparities in Access to Health Care: Comparing the United States to Canada. *Social Science and Medicine* 69:1452–1459.

Smith, D.G. (2008) The Uninsured in the US Healthcare System. *Journal of Healthcare Management* 53(2):79–81.

Somarriba, N. and B. Pena (2009) Synthetic Indicators of Quality of Life in Europe. *Social Indicators Research* 94:115–133.

Son, J. (2013) Are Immigrants from Asia Healthier Than Immigrants from Other Regions? Self-Reported Health Status and Functional Difficulties of Immigrants in the USA. *Journal of International Migration and Integration* 14(1):19–38.

Squires, D.A. (2011) The U.S. Health System in Perspective: A Comparison of Twelve Industrialized Nations. *Commonwealth Fund* 1532(16):1–13.

Stafford, M., L. Becares, and J. Nazroo (2009) Objective and Perceived Ethnic Density and Health: Findings from a United Kingdom General Population Survey. *American Journal of Epidemiology* 170(4):484–493.

Su, D. and D. Wang (2013) Acculturation and Cross-Border Utilization of Health Services. *Journal of Immigrant Minority Health* 14:563–569.

Thomas, F. (2010) Transnational Health and Treatment Networks: Meaning, Value and Place in Health Seeking amongst Southern African Migrants in London. *Health and Place* 16:606–612.

Thompson, F.J. (2013) Health Reform, Polarization, and Public Administration. *Public Administration Review* 73(51):s3–s12.

Todd, L., E. Harvey, and L. Hoffman-Goetz (2012) Predicting Breast and Colon Cancer Screening among English-as-a-Second-Language Older Chinese Immigrant Women to Canada. *Journal of Cancer Education* 26:161–169.

US Census Bureau (2012) HIB-7. *Health Insurance Coverage Status and Type of Coverage by Nativity: 1999 to 2012.* Washington, DC: US Bureau of the Census. www.census.gov/hhes/www/hlthins/data/historical/HIB_tables.html (Accessed October 28, 2013)

Wang, L. (2011) Analyzing Spatial Accessibility to Health Care: A Case Study of Access by Different Immigrant Groups to Primary Care Physicians in Toronto. *Annals of GIS* 17(4):237–251.

Wang, L. and W. Hu (2013) Immigrant Health, Place Effect and Regional Disparities in Canada. *Social Science and Medicine* 98:8–17.

Wang, L. and M.J. Kwak (2013) *Immigration, Health and Transnational Ties.* Paper presented at 15th International Symposium in Medical/Health Geography, July 7–12, Michigan State University, East Lansing.

Wang, L., E. Chacko, and L. Withers (2011) Immigration, Health and Health Care. In C. Teixeira, W. Li, and A. Kobayashi (eds.) *Immigrant Geographies of North American Cities*, pp. 158–178. Don Mills, ON: Oxford University Press.

Wang, L., M. Rosenberg, and L. Lo (2008) Ethnicity, Accessibility, and Utilization of Family Physicians: A Case Study of Mainland Chinese Immigrants in Toronto, Canada. *Social Science and Medicine* 67(9):1410–1422.

Wilensky G.R. (2013) The Shortfalls of "Obamacare." *New England Journal of Medicine* 367(16):1479–1481.

Willson, A.E. (2009) "Fundamental Causes" of Health Disparities: A Comparative Analysis of Canada and the United States. *International Sociology* 14(1):93–113.

Wilson-Mitchell, K. and J.A. Rummens (2013) Perinatal Outcomes of Uninsured Immigrant, Refugee and Migrant Mothers and Newborns Living in Toronto, Canada. *International Journal of Environmental Research and Public Health* 10:2198–2213.

Zhang, J. and M.J. Verhoef (2002) Illness Management Strategies among Chinese Immigrants Living with Arthritis. *Social Science and Medicine* 55(10):1795–1802.

Zsembik, B.A. and D. Fennell (2005) Ethnic Variation in Health and the Determinants of Health among Latinos. *Social Science and Medicine* 61:53–63.

Chapter 15

Ethnic Media: On the Margins No More

April Lindgren

Introduction

Ethnic news organizations and the journalists who work for them are coming into their own after years of being overshadowed by mainstream media (Matsaganis, Katz, and Ball-Rokeach 2011). During the summer of 2013, the American Hispanic television network Univision, for the first time ever, beat the English-language networks FOX, NBC, CBS, and ABC for viewership among coveted 18- to 49-year-olds. In cities like New York, Los Angeles, and Houston, where there are large Spanish-speaking populations, the network now also has the most-watched local news shows (Lopez 2013).

When Hurricane Sandy ravaged the east coast of the United States in 2012, putting 60 million people at risk, ethnic news organizations acted as conduits between their communities and emergency services. Media outlets serving Chinese, Bangladeshi, and other residents translated advisories released by local authorities in English and posted the information on their websites, making instructions about preparedness, safety, and shelters available to thousands of potentially vulnerable people (Advincula 2012).

In Canada, Prime Minister Stephen Harper and his Conservative Party of Canada courted journalists working for **ethnic media** in the run-up to the 2011 federal election, and during the race itself offered them exclusive interviews and briefings (Taber 2012). The Conservatives "had a system in place, they had the grassroots networks to be able to connect to small papers like ours ... we were kept in the loop,"

Case Example 1: Ethnic Media on the Political Radar

Journalists working for ethnic media have long complained of being marginalized and ignored by the political establishment (Matsaganis et al. 2011) so it was hailed as a breakthrough for ethnic news organizations when President Barack Obama's first interviews following his 2009 inauguration went to a business magazine targeting African Americans, a Los Angeles–based Latino talk-show host, and the Washington bureau chief of the Dubai-based Arab-language network Al Arabiya.

Political calculation, however, played a big part in Obama's choices: he owed much of his electoral success in 2008 and again in 2012 to immigrant and minority community voters. Ethnic media are a means of communicating with these electors, particularly when they are concentrated in a single geographic space. During the last presidential election, for instance, Latinos, who make up 23% of California's voters, backed Obama over Republication candidate Mitt Romney at a rate of 3 to 1 (Challet 2012).

In Canada, a growing number of electoral districts in major cities are also home to large groups of ethnic voters, many of whom are immigrants. The foreign-born population, for instance, makes up more than 40% of the population in 28 of the 47 electoral districts in the Greater Toronto Area (Statistics Canada 2008). In a document obtained by the news media during Canada's 2011 national election, the governing Conservative Party of Canada identified 10 potentially winnable "very ethnic" electoral districts nationwide and highlighted the need to "positively brand" the party in those areas with a television advertising strategy aimed at the South Asian, Mandarin, and Cantonese-speaking communities in particular (Kenney 2011).

Sunil Rao, editor of the Brampton, Ontario–based *South Asian Focus* newspaper, observed following the election (Monk School of Global Affairs 2011). Canada's federal government now buys ethnic media monitoring services and Harper has described ethnic news outlets as "the new mainstream media" (Cheadle and Levitz 2012).

Recognition of ethnic print, broadcast, and digital news media as important institutions coincides with the emergence of diverse societies where immigrants and cultural, linguistic, and racial minority groups are a growing demographic force. Members of these groups are eager consumers of news tailored to their needs. One-third of immigrant Hispanics in America say they get their news in Spanish only (Lopez and Gonzalez-Barrera 2013). During the 2012 presidential election in the United States, 48% of Asian Americans surveyed in exit polls cited ethnic media (television in particular) as their main source of news (Agence France-Press 2013). In Canada, a survey of Chinese immigrants in the Toronto and Vancouver areas found that 52% of respondents read Chinese newspapers and magazines exclusively (Ipsos Reid 2007). Politicians, advertisers, governments, and others who are eager to reach these audiences are taking notice.

Scholars, for their part, have long been interested in ethnic media. Key areas of research include examining their role in helping newcomers adapt, the information they convey to audiences, and the news outlets' journalism values and practices (Park 1922). Defining the term ethnic media is an important starting point for all such investigations (Johnson 2010). In this chapter, the focus is on news produced by and for immigrants rather than media that serve established minority groups such as African Americans or Aboriginal communities. The chapter begins with an overview of ethnic media and then discusses the role of these institutions in immigrant communities.

Ethnic Media in North America

The vibrant ethnic media scene in North America owes much to the steady stream of newcomers to Canada and the United States. Immigrants are a ready-made, constantly replenished audience for news in myriad languages and formats. News outlets that target immigrants play a variety of community roles. During the first half of the twentieth century, many Chinese-language newspapers were established primarily to seek support from overseas Chinese for various political factions in their country of origin (Yang 2008). Over the years, ethnic media have also been platforms for protest against discriminatory laws and other injustices, a role they continue to play today. Journalists working for ethnic news outlets have won awards for everything from investigations of how the American military treats Chinese-American recruits (Chuang 2009) to a Vietnamese reporter's account of being stopped by police because officers associated the bandana he was wearing with gang membership (New America Media Advisory 2013). In Canada, where the Philippines is a major immigration source country (Friesen 2011), Filipino newspapers have chronicled problems with the country's live-in caregiver program and championed efforts by Filipino caregivers to secure changes that make them less vulnerable to abuse by employers (Kronfli 2013).

The ethnic mediascape, however, is in a constant state of flux. Researchers who set out to create a directory of ethnic media in the Canadian province of British Columbia, for instance, identified 20 publications that had failed and 9 that were launched during the 6 months they worked to compile a list of 144 news outlets (Murray, Yu, and Ahadi 2007). One reason for the flux is that it is relatively easy to start an ethnic news website, newspaper, or magazine—there are no regulatory barriers to get in the way. Government licensing and other requirements for radio and television stations in Canada and, to a lesser extent, in the United States make it more challenging to launch a broadcast service. New digital and satellite technologies, however, increasingly allow entrepreneurs to bypass these restrictions.

In the United States, New America Media lists approximately 3,000 ethnic news organizations in a directory that is regularly updated (New America Media 2013a). In New York alone there are 9 daily newspapers published in languages other than English and a total of 270 community and ethnic media outlets that produce news in 36 languages (Bartlett 2013).

Canada has an estimated 650 ethnic newspapers and magazines across the country (National Ethnic Press and Media Council of Canada 2012). At last count, the tally included 10 daily ethnic newspapers in the Toronto area (Diversity Institute 2010), which is also served by more than 200 other ethnic publications that appear less frequently (DiversiPro 2007). Canada's broadcast regulator, meanwhile, lists 36 radio and 162 television services aired in languages other than English or French, the country's 2 official languages (Canadian Radio-television and Telecommunications Commission 2012).

Ethnic news outlets vary dramatically in size, focus, and ownership structure. The majority are small businesses that operate on a shoestring budget. A survey of 223 ethnic print media in Canada found that 37% had just 1 or 2 employees and 43% reported no earnings. More than 70% of publishers said they had employment outside of their journalism endeavours (Huston 2012).

At the other end of the spectrum are companies like US-based Univision: its Spanish-language television and radio stations reported net revenues of $676.5 million in the second quarter of 2013, up 10.4% from a year earlier (de la Feunte 2013). Mainstream newspaper companies in the United States and Canada have started or acquired newspapers that publish in languages other than English. Foreign-owned corporations, meanwhile, are also players in the ethnic media marketplace. The Toronto and Vancouver editions of the Chinese-language newspaper *Ming Pao*, for instance, are part of Media Chinese International, a profitable Hong Kong–based multinational corporation (Russell 2013).

Technological innovation also plays a role in making news increasingly accessible to immigrants in their mother tongue. NEXTV, for instance, streams video, audio, and television services from a variety of countries to North American subscribers' televisions and other devices. The joint venture between EURO World Network and the Toronto-based Ethnic Channels Group provides the Arabic, Hispanic, German,

Russian, Ukrainian, Albanian, Bosnian, Croatian, Serbian, Macedonian, Greek, Israeli, Filipino, and Vietnamese communities with access to programming from their homelands (NEXTV 2013).

Why Ethnic Media Matter

A variety of theoretical perspectives have been used to investigate the role of ethnic media in immigrant communities. German sociologist Jürgen Habermas's (1989) idea of the **public sphere** has been used to explain the place of ethnic news outlets in diverse democratic societies. In his analysis of the link between communication and the emergence of civil society in eighteenth-century Europe, Habermas envisioned the public sphere as a place where free and open public discourse about matters of public concern occurred among citizens and in the newspapers of the time. Habermas's formulation of the public sphere came under fire, however, by critics who pointed out that women, minorities, the poor, and other groups are often shut out of debate and may have concerns and interests that diverge from those who tend to dominate public discussion (Fraser 1993). This led to refinements of the public sphere concept so that, in the context of ethnic media, it embraces the idea of multiple discourses taking place in distinct "sphericules" that overlap with the dominant public sphere to "produce distinct civic discourses not often heard in hegemonic spaces like the mass media" (Karim 2002:231). This conceptual framework prompts a series of questions: What types of conversations occur in these sphericules? How does the conversation compare to debates in the dominant public sphere? What role does the civic discourse in ethnic media play in **ethnic communities**? What challenges arise for journalists working in these news media?

Researchers have made various attempts to answer these questions. Scholars in the early twentieth century saw immigrant **assimilation**—a process whereby people set aside their own culture and embrace the culture of the receiving nation—as desirable and examined the role of ethnic news outlets in this context (Johnson 2000). Over time, however, the idea that ethnic media help newcomers adapt to their adopted country while simultaneously reinforcing their cultural identity has gained currency. Canadian sociologist Augie Fleras, for instance, argues that ethnic news outlets play a bridging, integrative role by championing community interests in public debate and fostering intercultural dialogue with the host society. At the same time, he says, they also strengthen the bonds or ties within groups. In this way, ethnic media promote both "cultural preservation and societal incorporation" (2011:247) and help build confident ethnic communities equipped to go forth and flourish on the broader societal stage.

The bridging capacity of ethnic news outlets is evident in the role they play in communicating immigrants' concerns to governments. In early 2013, for instance, more than 50 ethnic media outlets in the United States worked together to publish the same editorial, drawing attention to the urgent need for immigration reform (New America Media 2013b). In cases where newcomers struggle with English, ethnic newspapers, broadcast media, and websites also build bridges to newcomers' adopted place by providing them with the information they need to settle.

At the same time, ethnic media strengthen bonds among members of immigrant communities by helping them preserve their mother tongue, reporting on home country news, and creating a safe, comfortable cultural space where people of the same background can share experiences (Zhou and Cai 2002). Indeed, one investigation of Korean immigrants in the United States found that ethnic media use was highest among newcomers who experienced the most stress from having to use English, living in a different culture, and being treated differently (Seo and Moon 2013).

Ethnic media also reinforce community bonds by producing narratives about immigrants that differ markedly from the stories commonly found in mainstream news coverage (Husband 2005). **Visible minorities**, many of whom are immigrants, remain underrepresented on television news and in English-language newspapers serving the general market. When members of these communities do make an appearance, they are often demonized, stereotyped, and portrayed as problems (Houssein 2012; Mahtani 2001). Reporting about Toronto's Vietnamese and Jamaican communities in the city's major daily newspapers, for instance, has tended to focus on stories related to crime, justice, and social problems (Henry 1999). Ethnic news outlets counteract this narrative by telling stories that are ignored by mainstream media and by highlighting community success stories: during Canada's 2011 federal election, for instance, Chinese and Punjabi-language newspapers in Toronto provided much more comprehensive coverage of races involving Chinese and Punjabi candidates than the *Toronto Star*, the area's largest English-language daily newspaper (Lindgren, forthcoming).

Indeed, some critics have suggested ethnic media are so effective at bringing community members together that they actually promote insularity and a reluctance to engage with broader society. When he was the Republican governor of California, Arnold Schwarzenegger made headlines when he urged Latino immigrants who want to improve their English to avoid Spanish-language news media (Associated Press 2007). Schwarzenegger was drawing upon his own experience as a German-speaking immigrant from Austria, but scholars have voiced similar concerns about the potential for ethnic media to hinder immigrant **integration**. In their study of Chinese news media in major American cities, Zhou and Cai concluded that, while the media outlets they examined provide Chinese immigrants with a "roadmap" for navigating the unknowns of American society, they also reinforce "immigrants' sense of 'we-ness'... [This] lowers their incentive to expand their social and personal networks to include members of other racial and ethnic groups" (2002:438). In cases where immigrants lived in enclaves that were rich in Chinese businesses, Chinese-language news media, and other Chinese institutions, they found there was little need to speak English or meet people who were not members of the Chinese community (Zhou and Cai 2002). Other researchers, meanwhile, worry that the potential for ethnic media to foster insularity is even greater now that the Internet and satellite technologies give immigrants access to news from their countries of origin in real time, as if they had never left (Howe 2007).

A growing body of research suggests that concern about the insular nature of ethnic media is most justified where an abundance of home country news overshadows useful, culturally relevant stories about the local immigrant community (Chen, Ognyanova, Zhao, Liu, Gerson, Ball-Rokeach, and Parks 2013). In some cases, local news is well represented: one analysis of newspapers and television programming serving Mandarin, Cantonese, Korean, and Punjabi speakers in Vancouver found that a respectable 40% of news content dealt with local city and ethnic community news (Murray, Yu, and Ahadi 2007). In other cases, however, researchers have found that local reporting by ethnic media is either limited or nonexistent. When researchers examined 51 ethnic newspapers in Asian and Latino neighbourhoods in Los Angeles, for instance, they found that almost half of their content focused on news from immigrants' countries of origin, while just 16% dealt with local neighbourhood, county, or regional news (Lin and Song 2006). A study of news content in the Toronto edition of the Chinese-language daily newspaper *Ming Pao* found that only 8% of stories were local, while more than half reported on China (Lindgren 2011).

Scholars have offered a variety of explanations for why local coverage matters in terms of the bridging and bonding potential of ethnic media. One explanation is that news media that provide local news relevant to their target audiences function as "cultural interpreters" for immigrants (Ojo 2006:358). Simply placing a local story on the front page of a newspaper or at the start of a news broadcast, for instance, signals that the topic merits attention.

Local news outlets that tell stories about immigrant communities and their place in the host society also help newcomers adapt by forging what American scholar Benedict Anderson calls an **imagined community**. Anderson's original theory addressed the role of newspapers in the formation of nations. He argued that they help build "an imagined political community ... imagined because the members of even the smallest nation will never know most of their fellow-members, meet them, or even hear of them, yet in the minds of each lives the image of their communion" (1991:6).

Others have suggested that this notion of imagined community also applies at the regional or city level in that people come to understand community norms, issues, people, places, and events through "the simultaneous consumption or 'imagining' of the stories" that appear in local media (Paek, So-Hyang, and Shah 2005:590).

Scholars at the Metamorphosis Project at the University of Southern California, meanwhile, have linked the amount of local news in ethnic media to **civic engagement**. They found that when ethnic media in immigrant neighbourhoods in Los Angeles covered news about community organizations, people discussed the news and shared it with each other as part of a "neighbourhood storytelling network" (Matsaganis et al. 2011:215). These storytelling activities encourage residents' "involvement in local activities that develop their sense of belonging to the local community, their sense of collective efficacy, and encourage their participation in political processes at the local or larger levels" (Matsaganis et al. 2011:216). An earlier study by the Metamorphosis Project team involved measuring residents' sense of belonging in Los Angeles neighbourhoods with a high proportion of recently arrived Chinese and Korean immigrants and local ethnic media outlets that emphasize home country news in their coverage. They found that members of these Asian communities expressed lower levels of belonging than residents of more established African American and Latino neighbourhoods, where community-focused ethnic media nurtured local storytelling networks (Ball-Rokeach, Yong-Chan, and Matei 2001).

While local news about immigrant groups and the issues that affect them helps newcomers build a sense of community and integrate with the host society, news from their country of origin is also important because it is comfortably familiar and has implications for the friends, family, and businesses they have left behind. The balance between local and home country news is relevant for scholars who have been exploring the extent to which ethnic media nurture a sense of **transnational identity** among immigrants. Nowadays, digital and satellite technological innovations mean news from home is available to immigrants in a way that is "more sustained and simultaneous in nature" than ever before (Shumow 2012:817). When this hyper-connectivity is combined with local "hybrid" stories that meld news from "here" with news from "there" (Matsaganis et al. 2011:64), it heightens immigrants' sense of belonging to both their country of origin *and* their adopted place. *Ming Pao*'s role in cultivating a transnational identity among Toronto residents of Chinese origin was evident, for example, in the newspaper's extensive coverage of local fundraising and relief efforts for victims of the 2008 earthquake in Sichuan province (Lindgren 2011). Some scholars have suggested that broad acceptance of the idea that immigrants can embrace "multiple homelands and multiple attachments" may help put an end to persistent questions about newcomers' allegiances (Cheng 2005:156).

Challenges

Ethnic media, in many cases, are managing better than their mainstream counterparts when it comes to weathering the perfect storm that has hit the news industry (New America Media 2009). In the United States, for instance, advertising spending in ethnic magazines has been increasing, the mortality rate and circulation declines for Hispanic newspapers have been less pronounced than for the English-language press, viewership for Spanish-language television continues to grow, and more radio stations have committed to having outside firms formally measure their audience size so they have reliable data available for potential advertisers (Guskin and Mitchell 2011). In Canada, the proliferation of South Asian media in and around the suburban city of Brampton, just northwest of Toronto, is such that the city recently hired a Punjabi-speaking communications officer to monitor stories covered by the 75 newspapers and more than 55 radio and television productions serving the local Punjabi-speaking community (Bascaramurty 2013).

Nevertheless, running an ethnic news organization is not for the faint of heart. The vast majority rely almost exclusively upon businesses owned by community members for advertising (Bartlett 2013; Huston 2012) and are therefore vulnerable to pressure from local merchants who might want to influence news coverage. While corporations are starting to recognize local ethnic media as a way to reach an important group of consumers (Fleras 2011), many still hesitate to make advertising purchases because accurate data on newspaper readership and broadcast ratings remain scarce (Matsaganis et al. 2011). Competition from online news sites that provide up-to-date home country news, the inability of *any* news organization to earn real money from online advertising, and anxieties about dwindling interest in ethnic media among the children and grandchildren of immigrants add to the financial headaches of many of these news organizations (Lopez and Gonzalez-Barrera 2013; Huston 2012; Zlotkowski 2011).

Preoccupation with the bottom line, in turn, is linked in many cases to problems of journalism quality. Poor pay for journalists who work for ethnic media makes attracting and retaining well-qualified staff difficult (Connectus Consulting Inc. 2013; Husband 2005; Zhou and Cai 2002). Low wages, for instance, were a key issue during an 11-week strike by the 140 journalists, press, and sales staff responsible for producing *Ming Pao*'s Toronto edition. At one point, the newspaper's striking employees demonstrated outside the multinational company's headquarters in Hong Kong. The Toronto workers, the majority of whom earned between $10 and $14 per hour, eventually won a first contract with reduced work hours and improvements to vacation time and pay, but only after company bulletins compared union supporters to communists and drug addicts (Russell 2013).

Lack of resources, combined with poorly trained journalists, are at the root of other difficulties for ethnic media. Local news often gets short shrift because it is more expensive to gather compared to home country news that is available from the Internet, wire services, or, in the case of a multinational subsidiary, the main newsroom in the country of origin (Lin, Song, and Ball-Rokeach 2010). Ethnic media outlets have been criticized for publishing government and business press releases verbatim, cribbing stories by other news organizations without acknowledging their source (Bascaramurty 2013), and making deals with local businesses to run stories that are thinly disguised advertisements (Zhou and Cai 2002). Research by the Local News Research Project at Ryerson University, for instance, found that 14% of local stories in one Toronto-area Russian-language weekly promoted a business or product featured in a nearby advertisement in the same issue of the newspaper (Lindgren 2013).

Members of the Chinese Canadian community have complained about the quality of journalism aired on Canada's Chinese-language television stations (Yip 2010) and accused the local Chinese-language daily *Sing Tao* of toadying to the Chinese government by injecting anti-Tibet propaganda into stories the newspaper obtains (and translates) from its mainstream *Toronto Star* parent company. Although many Chinese-language media are locally owned, critics say journalists working for these news outlets remain vulnerable to pressure from the Chinese government and that, in many cases, publications use copy taken straight from Beijing-controlled media (Hune-Brown 2008).

Punjabi-language media have come under fire for taking sides, often against women, when reporting on cases of alleged marriage fraud (Aulakh 2011). The prominent editor of a Punjabi newspaper, meanwhile, has warned that editors in the ethnic press often choose not to cover sensitive homeland-related issues for fear of retaliation by extremists (Fatima 2012).

Journalists who work for ethnic media are also torn between dual obligations. On the one hand, they are often under pressure to act as community advocates; on the other hand, they feel an obligation to adhere to the widely held professional norm of journalistic impartiality or **objectivity**. This is generally defined as reporting that distinguishes between fact and opinion, is a fair and balanced account of what is going on, and involves the verification of information (Franklin, Hamer, Hanna, Kinsey, and Richardson 2005). Though much disparaged by critics who argue that there is no such thing as unbiased reporting, objectivity remains a cornerstone of journalistic practice. The conflict between journalism norms and community expectations was evident among journalists of Venezuelan origin in the United States who have pointed to the angst arising from their commitment to acting professionally and their desire to take a stand against the Chavez government (Shumow 2012). In another instance, a journalist working for a Somali community news program in Toronto told

Case Example 2: Risky Business

While attacks on journalists employed by mainstream news media are relatively rare in North America, journalists working for ethnic media have been beaten, murdered, and threatened with disturbing regularity, including in the following cases:

- The editor of the Toronto-based Tamil newspaper *Uthayan* received threatening telephone calls at home on February 20, 2010, and hours later the newspaper's office was vandalized. The threats came after editor Kula Sellathurai met with Sri Lanka's president to deliver funds raised by Tamil businesses in Canada for children orphaned and displaced in Sri Lanka.

- Jagdish Grewal, publisher of the *Canadian Punjabi Post*, was attacked on October 23, 2009, by masked men in the parking lot of his Brampton, Ontario newsroom. The attackers, who pointed a gun at his head, smashed his car windows, and attempted to drag him toward a waiting van, were scared off by one of Grewal's employees. He says the attack may have occurred because of his criticism of the violence used by Sikh separatists.

- Tara Sigh Hayer, publisher of the *Indo-Canadian Times*, became the only journalist ever assassinated in Canada when he was shot in Surrey, British Columbia, on November 18, 1998. Hayer, an outspoken critic of Sikh extremists, survived an earlier assassination attempt in 1988 that left him partially paralyzed.

- Dona St. Plite, a Haitian-born reporter and radio commentator, was murdered on October 24, 1993, in Miami while attending a benefit for the family of a colleague killed two years earlier. The third Haitian-born journalist killed in Miami in as many years, his name was on a hit list of supporters of ousted president Jean-Bertrand Aristide.

- Cuban-American Manuel de Dios Unanue, the editor of *El Diario/La Prensa*, was shot in the head in a New York City restaurant on March 11, 1992. Police believe that drug traffickers plotted the murder in retaliation for hard-hitting stories he had written about their drug and money-laundering operations.

- Five Vietnamese journalists were killed in California, Texas, and Virginia between 1980 and 1991. Police suspect an anti-Communist group with ties to the former South Vietnamese Army was responsible for the murders.

Case Example 3: Ethnic News Media and Diversity Coverage

The role of the news in shaping our perceptions of others has been well established. When whole groups of people are invisible on nightly television newscasts and in newspapers, online stories, and other news media, it sends a message that members of these communities are irrelevant or do not exist. Meanwhile, coverage that repeatedly links ethnic and/or racialized groups to criminal activities "leads to the erroneous impression that every member that shares any kind of resemblance to this group has a proclivity to crime" (Jiwani 2006:47).

While representations of diversity in the mainstream news media have been studied extensively, much less is known about how ethnic news organizations cover groups beyond their own target audience. In Canada forecasters predict that **visible minority** residents in the Greater Toronto Area will be the majority by 2031 (Statistics Canada 2008) and this has prompted calls for research "on the particular stereotypes and beliefs racialized groups hold about others and how they are communicated in the ethnic press" (Mahtani 2008:247).

In a bid to fill some of the gaps in knowledge, one study undertook to examine the extent to which the Toronto edition of the Chinese-language daily newspaper *Ming Pao* introduced its audience members to people unlike themselves. Did the newspaper play a role in building bridges between communities, fostering intercultural understanding, and helping readers understand the diversity that is a defining characteristic of the Greater Toronto Area (Lindgren, 2011–2012)? The study concluded that members of the white community were referenced in the newspaper more frequently than any other group except members of the Chinese community and that coverage of both these groups was generally positive. Other ethno-cultural groups appeared much less frequently, and members of the Vietnamese and, to a lesser extent, the black community, were often cast in an unflattering light in crime-related stories and photos.

researchers that he encourages mosque officials to talk to reporters from mainstream news organizations. At the same time, he said, when those reporters contact him for information about mosque activities, he makes a point of warning mosque managers so they can prepare for the subsequent follow-up questions (Houssein 2012). Such practices fuel concerns about the credibility of ethnic news outlets in some quarters

(Matsaganis et al. 2011). Others have argued, however, that advocacy is a completely legitimate role for journalists employed in the sector (Husband 2005).

Finally, scholars have questioned the role of ethnic media in promoting interethnic understanding and reporting on intergroup tensions (Lindgren 2011; Murray, Yu, and Ahadi 2007). In 2007, this issue attracted widespread attention when San Francisco–based *AsianWeek* published an inflammatory article entitled "Why I Hate Blacks" (Citizens Against Racism and Discrimination 2007). Nine major ethnic newspapers and New America Media responded by commissioning a poll that found the majority of African Americans and a significant percentage of Hispanics and Asian Americans viewed news coverage of race-related problems in the ethnic media as irresponsible. The majority of those surveyed also said, however, that ethnic media have an important responsibility when it comes to improving race relations (New America Media 2007).

Conclusion

Ethnic newspapers, websites, and broadcast outlets are no longer confined to the margins of the news industry as politicians, advertisers, and others recognize they are an efficient conduit to minority communities, a demographic that includes many immigrants. Scholars who study ethnic media and their role as institutions find themselves exploring issues central to the immigrant experience, including questions related to transnational identity, how newcomers forge a sense of belonging to their adopted place, and whether an immigrant's strong identification with an ethnic community helps or hinders the process of integration.

Among immigrants, ethnic media function on one level as a practical source of information on everything from the weather to job prospects and housing options. Many newcomers, however, also arrive with only a basic understanding of the prevailing values, norms, and customs of their adopted land. Journalists who work for ethnic media help fill in the blanks by telling stories that introduce immigrants to the locales, people, events, and ideas that define the place they now call home. A story about recognition awards for outstanding volunteers, for instance, sends a message about how voluntarism is valued in North American society. A story about dog owners who let their pets run amok in parks sends a message about responsible pet ownership. Crime and court stories are morality tales about what society will and won't tolerate and what punishments are deemed to fit the crime. Taken together, these types of narratives help immigrants navigate their adopted community and nourish their evolving sense of the place.

The growing recognition of ethnic news organizations as important community institutions means, however, that they are also subject to closer scrutiny. As problems in the sector are being identified and more openly acknowledged, efforts are under-way to address them. The National Ethnic Press and Media Council of Canada (2013) is running training seminars for its members. The City University of New York's School of Journalism, meanwhile, is just one example of a post-secondary institution that has stepped up to the plate. Drawing upon its diverse student population, it has established a directory of local ethnic news outlets, set up a journalism awards competition for ethnic media, and launched a website that publishes translations of the best stories from 90 ethnic publications. The school also runs dozens of journalism training sessions (Bartlett 2013).

The reality, however, is that some ethnic media will always do a better job on behalf of their readers and viewers than others, just as there are good and not-so-good mainstream news organizations. The weakest news outlets will be little more than advertising vehicles offering outdated information about a community's country of origin. At their best, however, ethnic news outlets counter mainstream media stereotypes, challenge injustices, build a sense of community, cover local news and events that fuel civic engagement, provide audiences with news they can use, and help newcomers understand their new society while keeping them abreast of events in their country of origin. They are, in other words, institutions that make a difference in the lives of immigrants.

Questions for Critical Thought

1.   You are a recent immigrant. Why would you turn to ethnic media for news and information?
2.   Ethnic media have been criticized for promoting insularity within ethnic communities. Do you think this criticism is justified?
3.   Do you think it's possible for newcomers to feel a transnational sense of identity, that is, simultaneously feel a sense of belonging to both their country of origin and their adopted home? Do ethnic media help or hinder the development of these attachments?
4.   Some scholars have argued that if there is broad acceptance of the idea that immigrants can feel attachment to both their country of origin and to their host country, this could minimize concerns that sometimes surface about newcomers' fundamental allegiances. Do you accept this argument?

Key Readings

Bartlett, S. (2013) Ethnic Media Is More than a Niche: It's Worth Your Attention. *Nieman Journalism Lab*. www.niemanlab.org/2013/07/ethnic-media-is-more-than-a-niche-its-worth-your-attention (Accessed September 29, 2013)

Fleras, A. (2011) Ethnic Media: Empowering the People. In *The Media Gaze: Representations of Diversities in Canada*, pp. 229–250. Vancouver: UBC Press.

Houssein, C. (2012) Diaspora, Memory, and Ethnic Media: Media Use by Somalis Living in Canada. *Bildhaan: An International Journal of Somali Studies* 12(1):87–105. digitalcommons.macalester.edu/bildhaan/vol12/iss1/11 (Accessed September 29, 2013)

Karim, K.H. (2002) Public Sphere and Public Sphericules: Civic Discourse in Ethnic Media. In S. Devereaux Ferguson and L. Regan Shade (eds.) *Civic Discourse and Cultural Politics in Canada*, pp. 230–242. Westport, CT: Ablex.

Zhou, M. and G. Cai (2002) Chinese Language Media in the United States: Immigration and Assimilation in American Life. *Qualitative Sociology* 25(3):419–441.

Media Links

New Canadian Media:

newcanadianmedia.ca

A Canadian website that aggregates content in English from ethnic media publishers and also publishes original journalism dealing with immigrant issues.

New America Media:

newamericamedia.org

This site produces, aggregates, and disseminates multimedia content and services from ethnic media sectors in the United States.

Metamorphosis:

www.metamorph.org

A project based out of the University of Southern California's Annenberg School of Communication, which studies the role of communication in urban transformation. Los Angeles, with its many ethnic communities and geo-ethnic media, is the focus of the project's research.

References

Advincula, A. (2012) In Hurricane's Wake, Ethnic Media Are a Lifeline to Immigrants. *New America Media*, 31 October. newamericamedia.org/2012/10/in-hurricanes-wake-ethnic-media-are-a-lifeline-to-immigrants.php (Accessed September 29, 2013)

Agence France-Press. Half of Asian Americans Rely on Ethnic Media—Poll, 18 January. globalnation.inquirer.net/61833/half-of-asian-americans-rely-on-ethnic-media-poll (Accessed September 19, 2013)

Anderson, B. (1991) *Imagined Communities: Reflections on the Origins and Spread of Nationalism*. London: Verso.

Aulakh, R. (2011) Powerful Punjabi Press Has Its Fans and Foes. *Toronto Star*, 6 November 2011. www.thestar.com/news/article/1082245—powerful-punjabi-press-has-its-fans-and-foes (Accessed September 29, 2013)

Ball-Rokeach, S.J., K. Yong-Chan, and S. Matei (2001) Storytelling Neighborhood: Paths to Belonging in Diverse Urban Environments. *Communication Research* 28(4):392–428.

Bartlett, S. (2013) Ethnic Media Is More than a Niche: It's Worth Your Attention. *Nieman Journalism Lab*, 25 July. www.niemanlab.org/2013/07/ethnic-media-is-more-than-a-niche-its-worth-your-attention (Accessed September 29, 2013)

Bascaramurty, D. (2013) How the Punjabi Post Is Joining the GTA's Mainstream Media. *Globe and Mail*, 27 July. www.theglobeandmail.com/news/toronto/how-the-punjabi-post-is-joining-the-gtas-mainstream-media/article13464039/ (Accessed September 29, 2013)

Kenney, Jason (2011) Breaking through Building the Conservative Brand: Conservative Ethnic Paid Media Strategy, 3 March [Leaked Conservative Party document]. *Maclean's*. www2.macleans.ca/wp-content/uploads/2011/03/2011-03-03-breaking-through-building-the-conservative-brand-in-cultural-communities11.pdf (Accessed September 29, 2013)

Canadian Radio-television and Telecommunications Commission (2012) *CRTC Communications Monitoring Report*. www.crtc.gc.ca/eng/publications/reports/PolicyMonitoring/2012/cmr4.htm (Accessed September 29, 2013)

Challet, A. (2012) Field Poll: Ethnic Voters to Determine California's Political Course. *New America Media*, 3 November. newamericamedia.org/2012/11/field-poll-ethnic-voters-to-determine-californias-political-course.php (Accessed September 29, 2013)

Cheadle, B. and S. Levitz (2012) Privy Council Office Spending Thousands to Keep Tabs on Ethnic Press. *Canadian Press*, 14 November. www.thestar.com/news/canada/article/1287988--privy-council-office-spending-thousands-to-keep-tabs-on-ethnic-press (Accessed September 29, 2013)

Chen, N.-T.N., K. Ognyanova, N. Zhao, W. Liu, D. Gerson, S. Ball-Rokeach, and M. Parks (2013) Communication and Socio-demographic Forces Shaping Civic Engagement Patterns in a Multiethnic City. In P. Moy (ed.) *Communication and Community*. New York: Hampton Press.

Cheng, H.L. (2005) Constructing a Transnational, Multilocal Sense of Belonging: An Analysis of *Ming Pao. Journal of Communication Inquiry* 29(2):141–159.

Chuang, A. (2009) New Data Show Ethnic Media Is Growing, but Challenges Remain. *Poynter Institute*, 8 June. www.poynter.org/how-tos/newsgathering-storytelling/diversity-at-work/96189/new-data-show-ethnic-media-is-growing-but-challenges-remain/ (Accessed September 29, 2013)

Citizens Against Racism and Discrimination (2007) Racist Article in AsianWeek "Why I Hate Blacks." card.wordpress.com/2007/02/28/racist-article-in-asianweek-why-i-hate-blacks (Accessed September 29, 2013)

de la Fuente, A.M. (2013) Spanish-lingo Giant Riding Momentum of Historic Primetime Win. *Variety*, 25 July. variety.com/2013/tv/news/ratings-growth-drives-univision-q2-profit-revenue-gains-1200568336 (Accessed September 29, 2013)

Diversity Institute (2010) *DiverseCity Counts 2: A Snapshot of Diverse Leadership in the GTA*. Toronto: Ryerson University.

DiversiPro (2007) *Research on Settlement Programming Through the Media*. Ottawa: Citizenship and Immigration Canada. www.settlement.org/downloads/atwork/Research_on_Settlement_Programming_Through_the_Media.pdf (Accessed September 29, 2013)

Fatima, S. (2012) "There Is Nothing Called Freedom" for Journalists Working in Ethnic Media. *J-Source*, 14 March. j-source.ca/article/there-nothing-called-freedom-journalists-working-ethnic-media (Accessed September 29, 2013)

Fleras, A. (2011) *The Media Gaze: Representations of Diversities in Canada*. Vancouver: UBC Press.

Franklin, B., Hamer, M. Hanna, M. Kinsey, and J.E. Richardson. (2005) *Key Concepts in Journalism Studies*. London: Sage.

Fraser, N. (1993) Rethinking the Public Sphere: A Contribution to the Critique of Actually Existing Democracy. In B. Robbins (ed.) *The Phantom Public Sphere*, pp. 1–32. Minneapolis: University of Minnesota Press.

Friesen, J. (2011) The Philippines Is Now Canada's Top Source of Immigrants. *Globe and Mail*, 18 March. license.icopyright.net/user/viewFreeUse.act?fuid=MTc0MzM5OTY%3D (Accessed September 29, 2013)

Guskin, E. and A. Mitchell (2011) Hispanic Media: Fairing Better than the Mainstream Media. *The State of the News Media 2011*. Pew Research Centre's Project for Excellence in Journalism. stateofthemedia.org/2011/hispanic-media-fairing-better-than-the-mainstream-media (Accessed September 29, 2013)

Habermas, J. (1989) *The Structural Transformation of the Public Sphere: An Inquiry into a Category of Bourgeois Society*. Cambridge, MA: MIT Press.

Henry, F. (1999) *The Racialization of Crime in Toronto's Print Media: A Research Project*. Toronto: School of Journalism, Ryerson University.

Connectus Consulting Inc. (2013) *Study of Ethnocultural Publishing in Canada*. Ottawa: Department of Canadian Heritage.

Houssein, C. (2012) Diaspora, Memory, and Ethnic Media: Media Use by Somalis Living in Canada. *Bildhaan: An International Journal of Somali Studies* 12(1):87–105. digitalcommons.macalester.edu/bildhaan/vol12/iss1/11 (Accessed September 29, 2013)

Howe, P. (2007) The Political Engagement of New Canadians: A Comparative Perspective. In K. Banting, T.J. Courchene, and F.L. Seidle (eds.) *Belonging: Diversity, Recognition and Shared Citizenship in Canada*, pp. 611–646. Montreal: Institute for Research on Public Policy.

Hune-Brown, N. (2008) Lost in Translation. *Toronto Life*, August, 29–35.

Husband, C. (2005) Minority Ethnic Media as Communities of Practice: Professionalism and Identity Politics in Interaction. *Journal of Ethnic and Migration Studies* 31(3):461–479.

Huston, G.A. (2012) Canada's Ethnic Press and Media: A National Socio-Economic Report on Canada's Community-Based Ethnic Press and Media. *National Ethnic Press and Media Council of Canada*. nationalethnicpress.com/wp-content/uploads/2012/02/ NEPMCC-Report-TD-Final2012.pdf (Accessed September 29, 2013)

Ipsos Reid (2007) Ipsos Reid 2007 Canadian Chinese Media Monitor. www.fairchildtv.com/ english/ppt/ipsos_reid_2007_tor.pdf (Accessed September 29, 2013)

Jiwani, Y. (2006) *Discourses of Denial: Mediations of Race, Gender and Violence*. Vancouver: UBC Press.

Johnson, M.A. (2000) How Ethnic Are U.S. Ethnic Media: The Case Study of Latina Magazines. *Mass Communication and Society* 3(2/3):229–248.

Johnson, M.A. (2010) Incorporating Self-Categorization Concepts into Ethnic Media Research. *Communication Theory* 20(1):106–125.

Karim, K.H. (2002) Public Sphere and Public Sphericules: Civic Discourse in Ethnic Media. In S. Devereaux Ferguson and L. Regan Shade (eds.) *Civic Discourse and Cultural Politics in Canada*, pp. 230–242. Westport, CT: Ablex.

Kronfli, C. (2013) *Nannies Strike Back: The Representation of Live-in Caregivers and the Live-In Caregiver Program in the Mainstream and Ethnic Press*. Unpublished Master's Major Research Paper. Toronto: Ryerson University.

Lin, W.-Y. and H. Song (2006) Geo-ethnic Storytelling. *Journalism* 7(3):362–388.

Lin, W., H. Song, and S. Ball-Rokeach (2010) Localizing the Global: Exploring the Transnational Ties That Bind in New Immigrant Communities. *Journal of Communication* 60(2):205–229.

Lindgren, A. (2013) [Local News Research Project]. Unpublished raw data.

Lindgren, A. (2011–2012) Missing and Misrepresented: Portrayals of Other Ethnic and Racialized Groups in a Greater Toronto Area Ethnocultural Newspaper. *Canadian Ethnic Studies* 43–44(3–1):99–121.

Lindgren, A. (2011) Interpreting the City: Portrayals of Place in a Toronto-area Ethnic Newspaper. *Aether: The Journal of Media Geography* 8a:68–88. geogdata.csun. edu/~aether/pdf/volume_08a/lindgren.pdf (Accessed September 29, 2013)

Lindgren, A. (2014) Toronto-area Ethnic Newspapers and Canada's 2011 Federal Election: An Investigation of Content, Focus and Partisanship. *Canadian Journal of Political Science* 47(4).

Lopez, M.H. (2013) What Univision's Milestone Says about U.S. Demographics. Pew Research Center, 29 July. www.pewresearch.org/fact-tank/2013/07/29/what-univisions-milestone-says-about-u-s-demographics (Accessed September 29, 2013)

Lopez, M.H. and A. Gonzalez-Barrera (2013) A Growing Share of Latinos Get Their News in English. Pew Research Hispanic Trends Project, 23 July. www.pewhispanic. org/2013/07/23/a-growing-share-of-latinos-get-their-news-in-english (Accessed September 29, 2013)

Mahtani, M. (2008) How Are Immigrants Seen—and What Do They Want to See? Contemporary Research on the Presentation of Immigrants in the Canadian English-language Media. In J. Biles, M. Burstein, and J. Frideres (eds.) *Immigration and Integration in Canada in the Twenty-first Century*, pp. 231–251. Kingston, ON: Queen's University.

Mahtani, M. (2001) Representing Minorities: Canadian Media and Minority Identities. *Canadian Ethnic Studies* 33(3):99–131.

Matsaganis, M.D., V.S. Katz, and S.J. Ball-Rokeach (2011) *Understanding Ethnic Media: Producers, Consumers and Societies*. Thousand Oaks, CA: Sage.

Monk School of Global Affairs. (2011) Elections and the Ethnic Vote: Numbers Lottery or Political Representation? [Video file]. hosting.epresence.tv/MUNK/1/watch/269. aspx?q=election (Accessed September 29, 2013)

Murray, C., S. Yu, and D. Ahadi (2007) *Cultural Diversity and Ethnic Media in BC. A Report to Department of Canadian Heritage, Western Region (Study No. 451933670)*. Simon Fraser University: Center for Policy Studies on Culture and Communities. www.bcethnicmedia.ca/research.html (Accessed September 29, 2013)

New America Media Advisory (2013) NAM Honours Best in Ethnic Media at 2013 Southern California Awards Gala, 14 March. newamericamedia.org/2013-new-america-media-ethnic-media-awards-southern-california.php (Accessed September 29, 2013)

National Ethnic Press and Media Council of Canada (2013) National Ethnic Press and Media Council of Canada Professional Development and Training Seminar December 6–9, 2013. nationalethnicpress.com/educational-seminar/topics-presenters/ (Accessed May 13, 2014)

National Ethnic Press and Media Council of Canada (2012) Message from the President. nationalethnicpress.com/aboutus/our-contributions (Accessed September 29, 2013)

New America Media (2007) Deep Divisions, Shared Destiny: A Poll of African Americans, Hispanics and Asian Americans on Race Relations Sponsored by New America Media and Nine Founding Ethnic Media Partners, 12 December. news.newamericamedia. org/news/view_article.html?article_id=28501933d0e5c5344b21f9640dc13754 (Accessed September 29, 2013)

New America Media (2009) Ethnic Media Here to Stay and Growing—A National Study on the Penetration of Ethnic Media in America, 9 June. news.newamericamedia.org/ news/view_article.html?article_id=cef90deffc1b85bfb7253499cd65040b (Accessed September 29, 2013)

New America Media (2013a) About New America Media. newamericamedia.org/about (Accessed September 29, 2013)

New America Media (2013b) Ethnic Media's Collective Message to the White House: Do It Now, 28 January. newamericamedia.org/2013/01/ethnic-medias-collective-message-to-the-white-house-do-it-now.php (Accessed September 29, 2013)

NEXTV (2013) What Is NEXTV? www.nextv-canada.com/what_is_nextv.html (Accessed September 29, 2013)

Ojo, T. (2006) Ethnic Print Media in the Multicultural Nation of Canada. *Journalism* 7(3):343–361.

Paek, H.-J., Y. So-Hyang, and D.V. Shah (2005) Local News, Social Integration, and Community Participation: Hierarchical Linear Modeling of Contextual and Cross-level Effects. *Journalism and Mass Communication Quarterly* 82(3):587–606.

Park, R.E. (1922) *The Immigrant Press and Its Control*. New York: Harper and Brothers Publishers.

Russell, R. (2013) *Ming Pao*: Unionized at Last. *Ryerson Review of Journalism*, 6 March. www.rrj.ca/b26969/ (Accessed September 29, 2013)

Associated Press (2007) Schwarzenegger to Immigrants: Avoid Spanish-language News, 15 June. www.foxnews.com/story/2007/06/15/schwarzenegger-to-immigrants-avoid-spanish-language-media (Accessed September 29, 2013)

Seo, M. and S. Moon (2013) Ethnic Identity, Acculturative Stress, News Uses, and Two Domains of Civic Engagement: A Case of Korean Immigrants in the United States. *Mass Communication and Society* 16(2):245–267.

Shumow, M. (2012) Immigrant Journalism, Ideology and the Production of Transnational Media Spaces. *Media, Culture and Society* 34(7):815–831.

Statistics Canada (2008) Federal Electoral District (FED) Profile, 2006 Census (Catalogue no. 92-595-XWE). www12.statcan.ca/census-recensement/2006/dp-pd/prof/92-595/ p2c.cfm?TPL=INDX&LANG=E (Accessed September 29, 2013)

Taber, J. (2012) Harper Hires "Eminence Grise" of Ethnic Media as Communciations Chief. *Globe and Mail*, 10 September. http://www.theglobeandmail.com/news/politics/ottawa-notebook/harper-hires-eminence-grise-of-ethnic-media-as-communications-chief/article617060/ (Accessed September 29, 2013)

Yang, T. (2008) *Press, Community and Library: A Study of the Chinese-language Newspapers Published in North America.* eprints.rclis.org/13145/1/cl27yang.pdf (Accessed September 29, 2013)

Yip, J. (2010) State of Disarray. *Ryerson Review of Journalism* Summer, 67–70.

Zhou, M. and G. Cai (2002) Chinese Language Media in the United States: Immigration and Assimilation in American Life. *Qualitative Sociology* 25(3):419–441.

Zlotkowski, E. (2011) Poles Apart. *Ryerson Review of Journalism* (Winter), 29–31.

Chapter 16

Changing Immigrant Settlement Patterns in North America's Gateway Cities

Sutama Ghosh
and Raymond M. Garrison

Introduction

International migration to North America has been far from uniform either by volume or by nature. At different time periods, people have arrived from diverse places of birth and source countries, embodying distinct socioeconomic and political backgrounds. Upon their arrival in the United States and Canada, immigrants not only gravitate toward certain cities—especially large metropolitan areas—they also settle in specific neighbourhoods within those cities. As a result, where immigrants settle varies by inter- (between) and intra- (within) urban contexts.

Sometimes the decisions regarding *where to settle* are influenced by external factors, that is issues beyond the control of the **immigrant** group or the household. These external factors may include the attitudes of the **charter groups** toward the newly arrived groups, as well as the availability of employment (both in terms of source of employment and earnings) and housing opportunities (cost and quality of dwellings and neighbourhoods) in that city. The term *charter group* is generally used to identify the first settlers. The charter group in the US comprises the "whites"— mainly of European ancestry (British, German, Dutch, French). In the Canadian

Image 16.1

Toronto's Annual South Asian Festival on Gerrard Street, Also Known as Gerrard India Bazaar

Source: Photograph by Sutama Ghosh and Raymond M. Garrison (2009).

context there are two European-based charter groups: the British and the French, with the French concentrated in the province of Quebec. For newcomer groups, the question is often of where they *can* settle as opposed to where they *want to* settle. However, to some extent immigrants may also choose to live in certain cities and within specific neighbourhoods based on their own group- and household-level needs and preferences. Often these decisions regarding where they *want to* settle are influenced by their own social, cultural, economic, and political identities, as well as their ties and networks. Thus, immigrant **settlement patterns** are the outcome of a complex web of social processes, often leading to diverse urban forms and associated urbanisms.

In this chapter, the main objective is to explore two interrelated questions: What are some of the similarities and differences in immigrant settlement patterns in North American cities? What are their spatial outcomes? In answering the first question, comparisons will be drawn between North American cities; however, the main focus will be on Toronto, Montreal, and Vancouver—Canada's three largest immigrant-receiving cities.[1] In answering the second question (i.e. spatial outcomes of immigrant settlement patterns) Toronto will be studied in greater detail because it is one of the most diverse of all North American cities (Statistics Canada 2011; Walks 2010), and therefore most likely to portray an array of urban forms and associated urbanisms.

Settlement Patterns

In the early 1920s, the Chicago school sociologists pioneered the study of immigrant settlement patterns in urban settings. Seeing the city as an organism, they suggested that immigrants from poor economic backgrounds would "naturally" concentrate in impoverished inner city areas when they first arrived. Once they got better jobs and attained upward economic mobility, they were likely to leave the inner city and disperse in the suburbs. When they left, the space would be occupied by another newly arrived immigrant group, in the form of an "invasion and succession" process. Despite their various accomplishments, the Chicago school failed to theorize why people of certain ethnicities tend to concentrate residentially.

Examining the settlement patterns of immigrant groups who entered the United States in the late nineteenth century, Douglas Massey (1985) extended the work of the Chicago school by developing a spatial **assimilation** model of immigrant residential location. According to this model, immigrants achieve spatial assimilation after they attain cultural and economic assimilation. Providing similar explanations as the Chicago school, Massey argued that when immigrant groups first entered the United States, it was only "natural" for them to live near people of similar ethnic and economic backgrounds, primarily for practical reasons. Over time, by learning the language and the norms of the host society, they attained cultural assimilation. Next, by obtaining new skills they improved their existing economic position. Once both culturally and economically assimilated, they moved out of the ethnic clusters and sought residence in the suburbs. In Massey's view, ethnic clusters are thus "transitory sites" providing newly arrived immigrants with temporary shelters and familiar environments in an otherwise alien society (Bauder and Sharpe 2002:207; Logan, Zhang, and Alba 2002:299; Pamuk 2004).

Motivated by the intellectual agenda of immigrant integration, the main focus of the settlement pattern literature in North America and Western Europe has been on mapping, explaining, and theorizing the uneven distribution of immigrant groups across various geographical scales (e.g. national, and inter- and intra-urban). In all three spatial contexts, when most members of an immigrant group live in one or more specific areas of the city, the result is called **clustering**. The opposite of this situation is **dispersal**. In this case, people are distributed uniformly throughout urban space, and there is no readily identifiable spatial **concentration** (Boal 1996). Although dispersal generally has been regarded as a sign of the integration of immigrant groups with the host society and clustering as the lack thereof, new studies have argued that spatial dispersal may not always mean integration, and in the same vein spatial concentration may not always mean a lack of integration (Murdie and Ghosh 2010). The underlying premise is that immigrant settlement patterns mirror numerous complex social processes, one of which is the extent of their exclusion from the host society.

The literature on immigrant **settlement** patterns includes two main subthemes: **residential segregation** and **ethnic enclave** formation, focusing on the *what* and *where* of immigrant settlement. Residential segregation is the degree to which immigrant groups are spatially, and by extension socially, separated from each other. Although segregation and concentration are sometimes used interchangeably to describe immigrant clustering, they have slightly different connotations (Smith 1998:3). Immigrant groups are spatially segregated when they are unevenly distributed compared to the broader population (Van Kempen and Özüekeren 1998:1632). Although concentration loosely means segregation, it occurs when a particular group overwhelmingly resides within a single area or a few neighbourhoods of the city. Arguably, concentration is a form of acute segregation. Ethnic enclave, on the other hand, refers to the development of well-defined immigrant concentrations with identifiable institutional and business structures serving the needs of the community.

Measures of Residential Segregation

The extent of residential segregation can be measured using numerous statistical methods. Of these methods, the segregation index (SI) and index of dissimilarity (ID) are the most popular. Conceptually, the SI indicates the percentage of a particular group that would have to move in order to yield an even distribution. A value of 100 indicates complete segregation, and a value of 0 indicates no segregation. While the segregation index is calculated between one group and all other groups (e.g. between Bengalis and the rest of the population), the index of dissimilarity measures the residential segregation between two groups (e.g. Indians and Pakistanis). Often ID is measured between an immigrant group and the charter group. The basic calculation of the indices of segregation is the same in both cases. For example:

- SI: The extent to which the Greeks are segregated from the rest of the population in a North American city like Toronto or Miami.
- ID: The extent to which Greeks are segregated from each of the non-Greek "ethnic" groups in Toronto or Miami.

Figure 16.1
Degrees of Residential Segregation

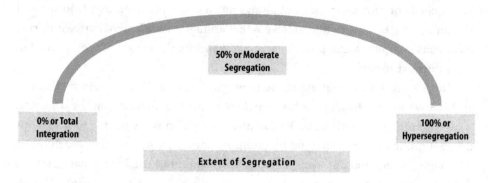

As shown in Figure 16.1 above, the index ranges in value from 0% to 100%, where 0% denotes total spatial assimilation and 100% indicates total or hypersegregation (Massey and Denton 1993:10). Hypothetically, if the segregation index of Asians in New Jersey is 49%, this would mean that Asians are moderately segregated from non-Asians in New Jersey. And, in order to achieve an equal distribution of Asians in every census tract[2] of New Jersey, 49% of them would have to move residences. With respect to interpreting the index of dissimilarity, if the ID between Asians and the charter group in New Jersey is found to be 64%, this would mean that the segregation level between these two groups is relatively high because a majority of all Asians would have to move residences in order to achieve an equal spatial distribution with the group.

Causes of Immigrant Residential Segregation

For decades, geographers and sociologists have debated why segregation exists and have provided numerous explanations. Juliet Saltman (1991:5) classifies these explanations into five perspectives: ecological, economic, inter-group, social-psychological, and institutional. Unlike the ecological perspective (e.g. Park and Burgess 1925), in which segregation is considered to be an inevitable result of impersonal forces such as social **stratification**, and Marxist economic theory (e.g. Harvey 1973) that suggests that income differences cause segregation, other theories take a more behavioural approach (e.g. Wolpert 1965; Brown and Moore 1970). Inter-group theories relate segregation to power differentials (e.g. Massey and Denton 1988, 1993), sociopsychological theory suggests that human preferences play an important role in residential segregation (e.g. Dahya 1974), and institutional theory points at the discriminatory factors that initiate segregation processes (e.g. Sarre, Philips, and Skellington 1989).

Depending on their perspective, scholars have identified the following factors as the causes of residential segregation of immigrant groups: increase in **immigration**, changes in economic structure and labour market conditions, access to and availability of housing stock, household structure, gender, cultural and religious preferences, and the phenomenon of "white flight" (e.g. Massey and Denton 1993; Pacione 2001). It is also argued that whereas some of these factors—such as household structure, gender, and cultural preferences—may direct immigrant groups to segregate voluntarily (i.e. by choice), others—such as changes in labour market conditions, and access to and availability of housing stock—may force them to segregate.

Spatial Manifestations of Residential Segregation

Scholars have identified four ways in which residential segregation is spatially manifested: **colonies, ethnic enclaves, ethnic communities**, and **ghettos**. Although these are not mutually exclusive and should be thought of more as a continuum, each of these spatial manifestations has some distinct characteristics. Colonies are spaces where an immigrant group first settles upon their arrival in a city. This settlement is mostly by choice. At this location they may develop several institutions, such as grocery stores, churches, and cultural centres. Over time, the group may leave this space and assimilate. An example of such a colony is in Roncesvalles in Toronto (see Image 16.2). This was one of the earliest settlements of the Polish community in Toronto. Although the Poles have now assimilated, some of their institutions remain in the area and attract many tourists.

Ethnic enclaves are formed when people of particular racial, ethnic, or religious backgrounds congregate voluntarily to enhance their economic, social, political, and cultural development (Marcuse 1997). These enclaves are variously denoted in the literature as "spaces of cultural identity," "community of choice," and "ethnic economy" (Logan et al. 2002). They are also associated with various degrees of **institutional completeness**. This refers to an area where "the ethnic community [can] perform all the services required by its members" (Breton 1964:194). An ethnic community would achieve institutional completeness when the "members would never have to make use of native institutions for the satisfaction of any of their needs, such as education, work, food and clothing, medical care, or social assistance" (Breton 1964:194). Latino enclaves in Miami, Indian enclaves in San Jose, Tamil enclaves in downtown Toronto and Markham, and Punjabi enclaves in the Sunset neighbourhood of South Vancouver are good examples of institutional completeness.

Image 16.2
Polish Institutions in the Roncesvalles Neighbourhood

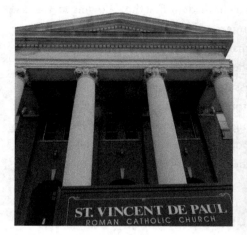

The church on the left (St. Vincent de Paul Roman Catholic Church) has served the Polish community for several decades, since Poles first settled here in the 1950s. A large mural on one of the buildings (above right) captures the vibrancy of the neighbourhood. Once full of Polish bakeries, cafes, restaurants, and grocery stores, many of these social and cultural spaces have now been replaced by well-known North American restaurant and supermarket chains, altering the character of the neighbourhood.

Source: Photographs by Sutama Ghosh and Raymond M. Garrison (2014).

Not all immigrant groups build enclaves. In the US, for instance, Alejandro Portes and Rubén Rumabut (1996) found that compared to labour migrants, professional immigrants seldom live in clusters. In other words, clustered settlement patterns are more common among immigrants of lower socioeconomic status. In Canada's gateway cities, while some groups have developed distinct enclaves (e.g. Italians, Greeks, Vietnamese, Koreans, Filipinos, Punjabi Sikhs, and Bangladeshis), others have not done so (e.g. Germans, Dutch, Colombians, Sinhalese, Indian Bengalis, and Laotians). There may be several reasons for this. Often the small size of the group and their recency of arrival may slow down the processes of enclave formation. Research has also shown that events preceding emigration, the attitude of the host society toward the group upon their arrival, their desires of return, physical distance between the country of origin and settlement, and distinct cross-border engagements or transnationalisms (explained below) may also play a decisive role in this regard.

Image 16.3
A Sri Lankan Tamil Temple in St. James Town (Cabbagetown) in Downtown Toronto

Source: Photograph by Sutama Ghosh and Raymond M. Garrison (2009).

Sometimes struggles with social chaos, violence, and poverty in the home country compounded with the negative attitude of the government and the host society create strong communal bonds among immigrants and refugees, which also trigger the development of enclaves. In the US, for example, Salvadorian refugees have been discriminated against by the government and the host society, and as a consequence have formed well-established communities (Landolt et al. 1999). Corroborating these findings in the US, recent Canadian research has found that Sri Lankan Tamils, who are arriving predominantly as refugees from war-torn Sri Lanka (where they faced serious human rights violations), are often labelled by government and the media as a group that regularly engages in cross-border terrorism. Despite these issues, and regardless of arriving with little financial and educational resources, over time this group has developed several institutionally complete enclaves in Toronto. Conversely, other refugee groups have shown little propensity to engage in similar activities. A recent case study of Colombians in Toronto, for example, contends that due to their ongoing violent political struggles in the home country, the group prefers to remain invisible (Restrepo 2012).

In the US, Portes (2003) argues, immigrant groups who wish to return to their country of origin often develop loose (economic and social) ties in the country of migration and do not build enclaves. In Canada this was particularly found to be the case among Ghanaians who possess similar desires of return and seldom invest in businesses or purchase homes in the migrant city (Owusu 1999). Ludger Pries (2004) further suggests that the geographical proximity of immigrants who share some sort of a collective identity may facilitate the creation of communities. In this regard, Sri Lankan Tamil and Caribbean youths who may have little in common culturally seem to have developed bonds of solidarity because they reside in the same neighbourhoods. On the other hand, groups with more dispersed residential locations find it more difficult to develop strong communities (Portes 2003). In Toronto, for instance, the Indian Bengali community lives dispersedly. Even though it has established several spaces where members may congregate occasionally, it has not developed an institutionally complete community (Ghosh 2006, 2007).

While immigrant **transnationalism** may lead to residential clusters, clustered living may also affect their transnationalisms. **Transnational communities** are a dense system of social networks that transcend international borders. Through actions and practices of reciprocity and solidarity such networks tie individuals and groups to both country of origin and country of destination, enabling immigrants to create new social spaces that not only shape their economic and political behaviours but also their individual and group identities in the destination country (Faist 1999; Glick-Schiller, Basch, and Szanton-Blanc 1995; Vertovec 2009). As a side effect, the social structures of the original community are sometimes replicated in the new country.

Ethnic communities have been defined by John Logan and associates (2002) as residential concentrations of affluent immigrant groups in the suburbs. They argue that in the current context of international migration, diverse immigrant groups enter the city with disparate human and financial capital. Contingent upon their capital, some immigrant groups may live temporarily in impoverished ethnic enclaves, while others may concentrate permanently in affluent suburban "ethnic communities." When choosing to live in ethnic communities, immigrants are often driven by motivations "associated more with taste and preference than with economic necessity, or even with the ambition to create neighbourhoods that will symbolise and sustain ethnic identity" (Logan et al. 2002:300). Thus, ethnic communities are more likely to retain group members for longer periods of time than ethnic enclaves, which often lose population when group members gain economic mobility.

Building upon the idea of an ethnic community, Wei Li (1998) coined the term **ethnoburb** in reference to Asian immigrants in suburban Los Angeles. Li defines ethnoburbs as residential concentrations of immigrant groups and their businesses in the suburbs. Shuguang Wang and Jason Jhong (2013) argue that there is a need

Case Example 1: Ethnoburbs in Toronto

In their attempt to study ethnoburbs systematically, Wang and Jhong (2013) divided Toronto into four zones: first, the inner city, consisting of three municipalities the former city of Toronto, East York and York; second, the inner suburbs comprising Etobicoke, North York, and Scarborough; third, the fringe or the "edge cities" comprising Mississauga, Brampton, Vaughan, Richmond Hill, Markham, Pickering, and Ajax; and fourth, the outer suburbs, consisting of the rest of the Greater Toronto Area (GTA). The authors argue that one way to delineate ethnoburbs is to 1) measure the critical mass of the ethno-racial group in specific geographical units; 2) examine their commercial activities (e.g. grocery stores) in the area; 3) consider the presence of their cultural institutions in those localities (e.g. temples), 4) account for political participation; and 5) include a measure for income. The study concludes that given the rapidly changing sociodemographic profile of cities like Toronto, it is quite likely that not only the suburbs but also the edge cities and the outer suburbs will soon transform into ethnoburbs or rather, ethno-cities. This conclusion supports a continuing dispersal of immigrant settlement patterns.

for defining these areas more systematically using specific variables. Based on the example of Toronto, they conclude that ethnoburbs are rapidly growing in congruence with sociodemographic changes as a result of immigration, and that ethnoburbs seem to exist not only in the inner suburbs of Toronto (comprising Etobicoke, North York, and Scarborough), but also in the fringe (Mississauga, Brampton, Vaughan, Richmond Hill, Markham, Pickering, and Ajax) and the outer suburbs. In some of these ethnoburbs, often a particular **visible minority** group (e.g. Chinese or South Asian) dominates. In Toronto, for instance, Chinese ethnoburbs seem to dominate Scarborough and Markham (see Image 16.4), while South Asian ethnoburbs are more common in Brampton and Mississauga.

In the post–World War II period, African Americans in US cities became segregated on many dimensions. They were not only unevenly distributed in space, but also isolated, concentrated, clustered, and centralized—that is, they were hypersegregated. The spatial outcome of hypersegregation is a ghetto. After the Second World War, ghettos in US cities increased in both area and number of inhabitants, and experienced greater racial isolation (Kaplan and Holloway 1998:53). In a ghetto, people are forced to segregate by a number of external forces, and there is little opportunity for upward economic mobility, and therefore minimal chances

Image 16.4
Residential and Retail Characteristics of the Times Square Area in Richmond Hill

One of the most recent housing developments in this area has been the construction of luxury high-rise ownership condominiums (somewhat replicating Hong Kong–style living). Many of the businesses are also owned by immigrants from Hong Kong. Several Chinese owned, and operated restaurants, bakeries, grocery stores, banks, financial institutions, and educational and cultural centres are located here. The clientele is also primarily Chinese.

Source: Photographs by Sutama Ghosh and Raymond M. Garrison (2014).

of "absorption, adaptation, and adjustment" (Massey and Denton 1993:33) into the larger society. External coercion often occurs in the form of systemic discrimination. Although it is generally believed that immigrant groups build ethnic enclaves voluntarily and form ghettos as a result of external pressures, in reality, there is an ethnic enclave/ghetto continuum (Boal 1976).

Scholars distinguish between two types of ghettos—reputational ghetto and real ghetto (Knox and McCarthy 2005). A reputational ghetto occurs when only a small portion of an ethno-racial minority group lives in an area. A real ghetto forms "when a large portion of ethnic minorities live in an area and forms the majority" (Knox and McCarthy 2005:299). In the US context, a good example of a reputational ghetto would be the Irish and the Polish settlements in Chicago. In the Canadian

Image 16.5
Residential and Retail Characteristics of Jane and Finch, an Impoverished Neighbourhood in Toronto's Inner Suburb of North York

Strewn with numerous rental high-rises built primarily in the 1970s, Jane and Finch serves as a major immigrant reception area. Although racialized minorities are a majority in the area, it is by no means dominated by a single ethnic group. Besides some well-known North American chain grocery stores, banks, and restaurants, there are also several Italian-, Caribbean-, Chinese-, Vietnamese-, Guyanese-, Indian-, and Sri Lankan–owned and operated grocery stores, restaurants, hair salons, and jewellery stores.

Source: Photographs by Sutama Ghosh and Raymond M. Garrison (2014).

context, although the Jane and Finch neighbourhood of Toronto (see Image 16.5) is often popularly regarded as a Caribbean ghetto, Caribbean immigrants do not form a majority in this area. Often African American neighbourhoods in Chicago, Philadelphia, Detroit, and Los Angeles, are considered to be real ghettos. In the Canadian context, there is an ongoing debate in the literature about whether or not there are any ghettos or near-ghettos in Canadian cities (see Murdie 1994; Walks and Bourne 2006).

Consequences of Immigrant Residential Segregation

Numerous scholars have speculated on the positive and negative consequences of ethnic residential segregation and arrived at diverse conclusions depending on the geographic context, the groups studied, and the research design. Scholars have pointed out that there could be several advantages and disadvantages to spatial segregation. Gideon Bolt and colleagues (1998), for instance, argue that spatial segregation may have a "favourable impact on the economic progress of immigrant groups who reside in them." Echoing Bolt, several other scholars have also suggested that segregation may be a "good thing" from the perspective of minority groups because segregation allows them to perform four functions: defence, avoidance, cultural preservation, and attack (Bolt, Ozuekren, and Phillips 2010). Highlighting the interactive relationship between class and ethnicity in the segregation process, Bolt states that that segregation serves as a "base for class formation and maintenance, for defence against threatening intrusions, for avoidance of undesired contact and for the generation of community organisation in the political and perhaps physically, rebellious spheres" (Bolt, Burgers, and van Kempen1998:108). Reviewing these reasons for and functions of residential segregation, Peach (1996:228) summarizes them as "positive and negative, dominant and recessive factors" that act as choices or constraints in immigrant groups' access to housing.

In the US context, in the late 1990s George Galster and associates (1999) argued that exposure to people of similar ethnic backgrounds hinders the social and economic mobility of immigrant groups. Many Canadian scholars, particularly A. Germain and J. Gagnon (1999), have countered Galster's suggestion by asserting that since neighbourhoods are multidimensional (functional, social, and symbolic) and their boundaries are fluid (not necessarily confined within census tract borders), they are differentially experienced by immigrants in various ways. Therefore, it cannot be generalized that the socioeconomic mobility of immigrant groups is blocked when they live in ethnic clusters. In fact, ethnic clusters often play a positive role in assisting newly arrived immigrant groups with their social and economic adjustments in the migrant city (Ley and Smith 1997). On this subject, Bob Murdie and Sutama Ghosh (2010) state that "the presence of central city ethnic enclaves and new forms of suburban enclaves raises the question of whether these ethnic concentrations inhibit integration." By drawing on the example of Jewish immigrants in Toronto it is argued that although the underlying premise of immigrant clustering is their exclusion from the receiving society, this may *not* always be true. For example, although the Jewish population in Toronto is highly clustered, it is not economically disadvantaged.

Understanding Immigrant Residential Segregation in Gateway Cities

The level of residential segregation has been much higher among immigrant groups in the US compared to Canada (Walks and Bourne 2006). In both countries, however, levels of immigrant residential segregation vary by group and by city. In Canada, Toronto, Montreal, and Vancouver—Canada's three largest gateway cities—have been the most segregated. Relatively smaller immigrant cities like Calgary, Ottawa, Abbotsford, Saskatoon, Edmonton, and Windsor seem to be more spatially integrated. In the three Canadian gateway cities, among all immigrant groups the South Asians and the Chinese—the two largest visible minorities—and relatively newer arrivals are also the most segregated groups. Compared to "blacks" and "Latinos" in the US, though, their levels of segregation seldom exceed 60%, thus indicating high levels of segregation but not hypersegregation (Walks and Bourne 2006; Walks 2010). Although important, these findings (in both US and Canada) may not capture the entire picture. Analyses of residential segregation of immigrant groups often accept census driven categories uncritically. Whereas in most US studies analytical groups often follow racial lines (e.g. whites, blacks, and Asians) in Canada the groups are arbitrarily defined, often based on erroneous assumptions of cultural commonalities (e.g. Chinese, blacks, South Asians). This has led to unrealistic and generalized understandings of immigrant residential segregation and associated immigrant experiences (e.g. Hiebert 2010).

Recognizing the problems associated with overgeneralizing immigrant experiences in the US, Kim and White (2010) used the concept of **panethnicity** as a way of delineating groups and measuring the extent of their racial segregation from all others and each other. For instance, they measured the extent to which Asians are residentially segregated from all non-Asians, as well to what extent various ethnic groups (e.g. whites, blacks, Asians, and Latinos) are segregated from each other. As a concept, panethnicity recognises that internal diversities exist within various racial groups and argues that, even though the boundaries of ethnicity may be more expansive than national borders and encompass a range of groups who share some common structural and cultural traits, these do not necessarily cross ethno-national lines. In other words, "ethnic boundaries persist despite interactions between groups and as a result of it" (Kim and White 2010:1559). In that sense, although migrants from India and Pakistan may interact with each other, in certain spheres of life, boundaries are maintained (e.g. political beliefs and religious norms). The study concluded that in the US, groups who share a panethnic boundary (e.g. blacks and Latinos) often exhibit more residential proximity than those who do not share such similar traits (e.g. Asians). Also, residential segregation levels are higher among Asian immigrants compared to those born in the United States. Finally, even when living in close proximity, ethno-national boundaries between people were seldom reduced. In Canada, recent studies have also shown that differences in levels of residential segregation exist within large immigrant categories (Murdie and Ghosh 2010). This issue will be discussed in detail below.

Segregation levels of immigrant groups also change over time. In the US, for instance, using data sets from the census, Edward Glaser and Jacob Vigdor (2012) recently claimed that segregation between African Americans and Caucasians in particular had reached its lowest level in 2010. In explaining the reasons for such decline, a recent study argued that reforms to the **housing market** (e.g. the Fair Housing Act) have expanded the residential choices of African Americans, thereby reducing hypersegregation. Housing markets are defined as specific types of housing that are located in a city (e.g. rental, ownership, and public or social housing). Often due to various types of overt and covert discriminatory practices of institutions and agencies, ethnic minorities get trapped in poor-quality, unaffordable housing. In their report, Glaser and Vigdor (2012) also claimed that the movement of non-white groups from the inner cities to the suburbs, as well as their interregional migration from the Rust Belt (i.e. the rapidly declining manufacturing belt in the North and Northeastern Central United States) to the Sun Belt (Southern and Southwestern United States) since the 1960s, may have resulted in more Caucasian and African American families moving away from more segregated to less segregated states. These claims have been severely criticized by both the general public as well as social scientists at large. Using New York City as a case study for instance, Richard Alba and Steven Romalewski (2012) not only questioned Glaser and Vigdor's findings, they also presented a nuanced understanding of the current state of segregation in the US. They argue that not only has the pace of residential integration become "modest," but segregation also remains substantial particularly in "ghetto-like contexts, where many poor blacks and poor Hispanics live side by side in underserved neighborhoods." Therefore, just because these two communities live side by side does not mean that they have achieved integration.

Arguably, changes in immigrant segregation levels were noted in Canada's gateway cities as well. For instance, segregation levels of European groups have been traditionally lower than that of the visible minorities. Also, compared to those who arrived before the 1990s, those who came after that time generally experienced more segregation (Murdie and Ghosh 2010). In Toronto, European immigrants (e.g. Italians, Greeks, Portuguese, and Polish) who arrived between the 1950s and the 1980s demonstrate higher levels of spatial assimilation compared to other visible minority groups who also came during the same period. This is primarily because compared to the Italians, the Greeks, and the Portuguese these immigrant groups (e.g. Jamaicans) were unable to achieve similar degrees of economic prosperity and

Figure 16.2

Concentrations of Ethnic South Asians (Left) and British (Right) in the Vancouver CMA

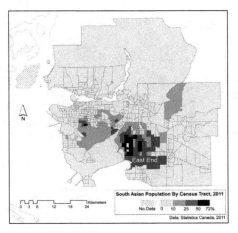 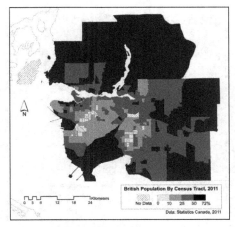

The largest areas of South Asian concentration contain barely any British-origin residents.

Source: Statistics Canada, Census of Population 2011.

consequently spatial mobility (Murdie, Chambon, Hulchanski, and Teixeira 1997).

As mentioned earlier, in Canada some studies have revealed differences in levels of residential segregation between and within large immigrant categories (e.g. Ghosh 2006). To further demonstrate such inter- and intra-immigrant group differences in levels of segregation, we will now present our research on the "Chinese" and "South Asian" immigrant groups in Toronto, Montreal, and Vancouver using publicly available data from the 2011 Canadian census. We have calculated both segregation index (SI) and indices of dissimilarities (ID) both between and within these two large immigrant categories (i.e. the Chinese and the South Asian). The results reveal that, overall, both groups seem more segregated in Montreal than in Toronto and Vancouver. More importantly however, their level of segregation from the charter group (i.e. the French) was also the highest for Montreal. Compared to the Chinese, South Asians were more segregated from the French. The Chinese and South Asians were most segregated from each other in Vancouver compared to the other two cities. One reason why the ID values between the Chinese and the South Asians were found to be the lowest for Montreal could be that in Montreal they share similar anglophone (i.e. English-speaking people living in Quebec) neighbourhoods. For Toronto, the segregation levels of the Chinese and the South Asians from people of British origin remained unchanged between 2006 and 2011. Whereas in 2006, South Asians were 49% segregated from the rest of the population in Toronto, in 2011 they were segregated by 50%. Similarly, the segregation level of the Chinese group had

Figure 16.3

Concentrations of Punjabis (left) and Tamils (Right) in the Toronto CMA

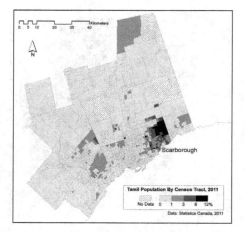
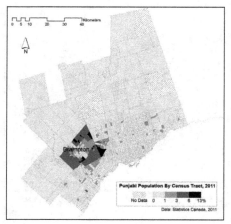

While most Punjabis live in Brampton, most Tamils are in Scarborough.

Source: Statistics Canada, Census of Population, 2011.

also increased minimally (from 52% in 2006 to 53% in 2011). These numbers suggest that the length of residence in Toronto may have had little impact on these groups with respect to their residential location.

A further analysis of the publicly available 2011 language and religion data from the National Household Survey demonstrates complex residential geographies of immigrants in Toronto, Montreal, and Vancouver. To illustrate some of these complexities, first, the two largest linguistic subgroups were chosen *within* the Chinese (Mandarin and Cantonese) and South Asian (Punjabi and Tamil) immigrant groups for comparative purposes. The results show some interesting variations:

- The South Asian subgroups (Punjabis and Tamils) were more residentially segregated from each other than the Chinese (Mandarin and Cantonese) subgroups.
- The levels of segregation between the two South Asian subgroups were particularly high in Toronto and Montreal.
- Among South Asians, the level of segregation of the Punjabis from the charter groups (the British in Vancouver and Toronto and the French in Montreal) were consistently higher than those of the Tamils.
- Among the Chinese, the segregation levels of the Cantonese speakers from the charter groups were found to be slightly higher than the Mandarin speakers in all three cities.

Figure 16.4

Concentration of Mulisms (Left) and Catholics (Right) in the Montreal CMA

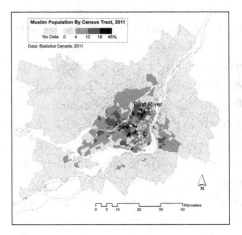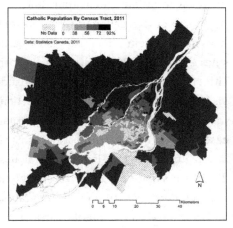

Source: Statistics Canada, Census of Population, 2011.

Using religion as an additional analytical category permitted further investigation of differences at the subgroup level.

- In Montreal, Muslims seem to experience very high levels of segregation (90%), particularly from Catholics (most of whom are French Canadians).
- Muslims also experience very high levels of segregation from the Punjabi Sikhs (80%) in all three cities, further corroborating the panethnicity thesis, that is, even though Sikhs and Muslims may share certain structural traits, ethno-racial boundaries are often maintained.

Why is it that the Punjabis and the Cantonese are more segregated from the charter group despite their long history and settlements? Perhaps the answers to these questions lie in their history—how did they function with each other both in their country of origin and when they first arrived in Canada centuries ago? As is well documented in the literature, both Punjabis and Cantonese were once colonized by the British and when they came to Canada both groups faced severe discrimination during the initial settlement phase. Unfortunately—as has been highlighted by David Ley (1997) in his work on the debate surrounding "Monster Homes" in Vancouver and Margaret Walton-Roberts (1998) in her work on the "Three readings of the Sikh Turban"—discrimination against these groups continues to exist in various overt and covert ways in Canada. Perhaps for these reasons, the Punjabis and the Cantonese tend to distance themselves from the charter group.

Unequal access to labour and housing markets may also explain some of these inter- and intra-immigrant group differences in residential location and, consequently, their levels of segregation in Toronto, Montreal, and Vancouver. Several recent studies have shown that in comparison to the earlier arrivals, those who have entered Canada since the mid-1990s have been particularly vulnerable in the labour markets of large cities (Chen, Myles, and Picot 2012; Bauder 2003). Despite high levels of education, visible minorities and refugees in particular are earning less and remaining longer in the most disadvantaged housing situations (Hiebert 2010; Murdie 2010). In the case of housing, for the most part this situation may be directly attributed to the lack of affordable housing in general and social housing in particular (Hulchanski 2004). The situation is aggravated in the current context where, despite arriving with more credentials than previous migrants, many newcomers to Toronto, Montreal, and Vancouver find themselves in a precarious economic position: earning less, yet spending more than half of their total household income on housing. Clearly then, compared to the earlier migrants, not only do the recently arrived groups remain segregated in Canada's gateway cities, their housing is more diverse. As more new immigrants gravitated toward enclaves, ethnic clusters enlarged and, in many cases, institutional completeness increased. The more disturbing part of this scenario, however, is that, over time, the connections between "**race**," poverty, and high-rises also strengthened, particularly in the inner suburbs (United Way of Toronto 2004, 2011). Currently, more than half a million people reside in aging high-rise buildings, 43% of whom are low-income families, and a majority of these families are visible minorities (United Way of Toronto 2011).

A pertinent question arises from the above discussion of immigrant residential segregation and their poor economic and housing conditions. Does Canada have ghettos? Most scholars in Canada have argued that Canadian cities do not have ghettos (Qadeer and Kumar 2006; Walks and Bourne 2006). Nevertheless, the evidence cited supporting this claim is based on the examination of broadly defined visible minority groups such as "blacks" and "South Asians," which are internally diverse. Furthermore, it is important to recognize that our reference points for "ghettos" tend to be US cities like Chicago, Detroit, and Philadelphia. Compared to US cities it is quite possible that trends of ghettoization in the Canadian context may be different both quantitatively and qualitatively (Murdie and Ghosh 2010).

Case Example 2: Immigrants and Neighbourhood Research

Although social scientists have remained fascinated with neighbourhoods since the early 1900s, the relevance of neighbourhoods and the need for neighbourhood research was increasingly scrutinized since the early 1990s, particularly with the advent of digitization and web-based networks. Recent geopolitical events, especially the debates around "home grown terrorism," however, brought ethnic minority/ immigrant neighbourhoods back to the centre stage of public interest and academic research. In view of the current context it seems rather important for scholars to realize that it is not *whether* neighbourhoods matter, but rather *how* neighbourhoods matter that needs more attention (Ellen and Turner 1997). It is in this line of inquiry (i.e. how neighbourhoods matter), that scholars have made significant contributions by studying the relative influence of neighbourhoods on the lives of their residents, differentiated along the axes of "race," ethnicity, and gender (e.g. Bauder 2002; Hulchanski et al. 2010). In the United States, some neighbourhood-based research projects are being undertaken, such as the Justice, Infrastructure and Environment Project, which is privately sponsored by a nonprofit organization called the RAND corporation (www.rand.org/jie/projects/safeneighborhoods.html). Another such project is the Make Home Affordable (MHA) project. It is a federal government project that aims to assist low-income families in accessing affordable housing in US cities (www.makinghomeaffordable.gov/about-mha/Pages/what-is-mha.aspx). In Canada, research on neighbourhoods is currently progressing in a cooperative way involving university professors, various levels of government (municipal and provincial), several nongovernmental social service organizations (e.g. the United Way, St. Christopher House), and community organizations.

Conclusion

In this chapter we have explored the processes underlying the changing immigrant settlement patterns in North American cities, highlighting Toronto as an example. The evolving literature on settlement pattern development in the North American context has been summarized, highlighting the two main subthemes of residential segregation and ethnic enclave formation. It has been demonstrated that settlement patterns vary widely depending on cultural, socioeconomic, and structural (i.e. built form) aspects of local contexts. The development and function of colonies, ethnic enclaves, and ethnic communities throughout North America has been examined and exemplified, highlighting a complex interplay of both ethnicity and class that, over time, makes these areas highly dynamic in nature. Immigrant settlement experiences vary widely, particularly at the subgroup level, contributing to the dynamism. The controversy surrounding the nature of reputational or real "ghettos" in Canada versus those in the United States has been raised as well. Researchers need to avoid overgeneralization in their studies of immigrant settlement patterns and processes, focusing more on the immigrant subgroup level and avoiding broad units of analyses, such as "black" and "Asian."

Notes

1. Of all immigrants who arrived between 2001 and 2006, almost 70% settled in these 3 cities (Toronto 40%, Montreal 15%, and Vancouver 14%) (Statistics Canada 2009).
2. Census tracts are geographical units of analysis.

Questions for Critical Thought

1. Thinking of residential segregation in migrant cities, how might residential segregation be advantageous for newcomers? Conversely, how might ethnic enclaves impede social and economic integration?
2. Do you know of any neighbourhoods close to your home that seem like segregated communities? What are the characteristics of one of these neighbourhoods?
3. Take a walking tour of a neighbourhood that has a reputation of being an ethnic enclave. Look for clues in the built form, symbols (e.g. flags and artifacts), businesses and their clientele, places of worship (churches, mosques, temples), and languages you hear spoken.

Key Readings

Bolt, G.A., S. Ozuekren, and D. Phillips (2010) Linking Integration and Residential Segregation. *Journal of Ethnic and Migration Studies* 36(2):169–186.

Marcuse, P. (1997) The Enclave, the Citadel, and the Ghetto: What Has Changed in the Post-Fordist U.S. City. *Urban Affairs Review* 33(2):233–243.

Walks, R.A. and L. Bourne (2006) Ghettos in Canada's Cities? Racial Segregation, Ethnic Enclaves and Poverty Concentration in Canadian Urban Areas. *Canadian Geographer* 50(3):273–297.

Media Links

Ethnic Enclaves of Toronto:

www.youtube.com/watch?v=5IayzgdvAeM

This is a short YouTube video that showcases the sights and sounds of some of Toronto's well-known ethnic enclaves. Although the majority of a particular ethnic group may no longer be living in these enclaves, many ethnic businesses remain, attracting a large number of tourists.

Only The Strong Survive:

www.youtube.com/watch?v=WzRSYwG5T_U

A 10-minute documentary on Roseland, a predominantly black neighbourhood located on the south side of Chicago. Although the neighbourhood has a controversial reputation, the documentary depicts people's sense of place and attachment to it.

How New York Reacts to Muslims:

www.youtube.com/watch?v=GEvojpq-1HE

A 15-minute video created by a young Arab Muslim man, Karim, who lives in New York City and wanted to know for himself how people (not just Americans) think of Muslims in their everyday lives. The video demonstrates a wide range of human emotions, ignorance, knowledge, fear, and sense of security and insecurity.

References

Alba, R. and S. Romalewski (2012) *The End of Segregation? Hardly*. New York: New York City Institute of Graduate Research.

Bauder, H. (2002) Neighbourhood Effects and Cultural Exclusion. *Urban Studies* 39(1):85–93.

Bauder, H. (2003) "Brain Abuse," or the Devaluation of Immigrant Labour in Canada. *Antipode* 35(4):699–717.

Bauder, H. and B. Sharpe (2002) Residential Segregation of Visible Minorities in Canada's Gateway Cities. *Canadian Geographer* 46:204–222.

Boal, F. (1976) Ethnic Residential Segregation. In D.T. Herbert and R.J. Johnston (eds.) *Social Areas in the Cities: Spatial Processes and Form*, pp. 41–79. New York: Wiley.

Boal, F. (1996) Immigration and Ethnicity in the Urban Milieu. In C.H. Roseman, D. Laux, and G. Thieme (eds.) *EthniCity: Geographic Perspective*, pp. 283–304. London: Littlefield Publishers.

Bolt, G., J. Burgers, and R. van Kempen (1998) On the Social Significance of Spatial Location: Spatial Segregation and Social Exclusion. *Netherlands Journal of Housing and the Built Environment* 13(1):83–95.

Bolt, G.A., S. Ozuekren, and D. Phillips (2010) Linking Integration and Residential Segregation. *Journal of Ethnic and Migration Studies* 36(2):169–186.

Breton, R. (1964) Institutional Completeness of Ethnic Communities and the Personal Relations of Immigrants. *American Journal of Sociology* 70(2):193–205.

Brown, L. and E. Moore (1970) The Intra-urban Migration Process: A Perspective. *Geografiska Annaler*, Series B, 52B(1):1–13.

Chen, W., J. Myles, and G. Picot (2012) Why Have Poorer Neighbourhoods Stagnated Economically while the Richer Have Flourished? Neighbourhood Income Inequality in Canadian Cities. *Urban Studies* 49(4):877–896.

Dahya, B. (1974) The Nature of Pakistani Ethnicity in Industrial Cities in Britain. In A. Cohen (ed.) *Urban Ethnicity*, pp. 77–118. London, ON: Tavistock.

Ellen, I.G. and M.A. Turner (1997) Does Neighborhood Matter? Assessing Recent Evidence. *Housing Policy Debate* 8(4):833–866.

Faist, T. (1999) *Transnationalization in International Migration: Implications for the Study of Citizenship and Culture*. Working Paper. Institute for International Studies, University of Bremen.

Galster, G., K. Metzger, and R. Waite (1999) Neighbourhood Opportunity Structures and Immigrants Socio-economic Advancement. *Journal of Housing Research* 10(1):95–127.

Germain, A. and J. Gagnon (1999) Is Neighbourhood a Black Box? A Reply to Galster, Metzer and Waite. *Canadian Journal of Urban Research* 8(2):172–184.

Ghosh, S. (2006) *We Are Not All the Same: The Differential Migration, Settlement Patterns, and Housing Trajectories of Indian Bengalis and Bangladeshis in Toronto*. Toronto, Unpublished PhD Dissertation, York University.

Ghosh, S. (2007) Transnational Ties and Intra-immigrant Group Settlement Experiences: A Case Study of Indian Bengalis and Bangladeshis in Toronto. *GeoJournal* 68(2–3):223–242.

Glaser, E. and J. Vigdor (2012) *The End of the Segregated Century: Racial Separation in America's Neighbourhoods, 1890–2010*. New York: Manhattan Institute Report.

Glick-Schiller, N., L. Basch, and C. Szanton-Blanc (1995) From Immigrant to Transmigrant: Theorising Transnational Migration. *Anthropological Quarterly* 68:48–63.

Harvey, D. (1973) *Social Justice and the City*. Baltimore, MD: Johns Hopkins University Press.

Hiebert, D. (2010) Newcomers in the Canadian Housing Market. *Canadian Issues/ Thèmes Canadiens: Newcomer's Experiences of Housing and Homelessness in Canada*. Association for Canadian Studies, Fall:8–15.

Hulchanski, J.D. (2004) How Did We Get Here? The Evolution of Canada's Exclusionary Housing System. In J.D. Hulchanski and M. Shapcott (eds.) *Finding Room: Policy Options for a Canadian Rental Housing Strategy*, pp. 179–194. Toronto: University of Toronto Press.

Hulchanski, J.D. (2010) *The Three Cities within Toronto: Income Polarization in Toronto's Neighbourhoods, 1975–2005.* Toronto: University of Toronto.

Itzigsohn, J., C. Cabral, E. Medina, and O. Vazquez (1999) Mapping Dominican Transnationalism: Narrow and Broad Transnational Spaces. *Ethnic and Racial Studies* 22(2):316–339.

Kaplan, D. and Holloway, S.R. (1998) *Segregation in Cities.* Washington, DC: Association of American Geographers.

Kim, A.H. and M.J. White (2010) Panethnicity, Ethnic Diversity and Residential Segregation. *American Journal of Sociology* 115(5):1558–1596.

Knowles, V. (1997) *Strangers at Our Gates: Canadian Immigration and Immigration Policy, 1540–1997.* Toronto: Dundurn Press.

Knox., P. and L. McCarthy (2005) *Urbanization: An Introduction to Urban Geography.* Upper Saddle River, NJ: Prentice Hall.

Landolt, P., L. Autler, and S. Baires (1999) From Hermano Lejano to Hermano Mayor: The Dialectics of Salvadoran Transnationalism. *Ethnic and Racial Studies* 22(2):290–315.

Ley, D. (1997) The Rhetoric of Racism and the Politics of Explanation in the Vancouver Housing Market. In E. Laquian, A. Laquian, and T. McGee (eds.) *The Silent Debate: Asian Immigration and Racism in Canada,* pp. 331–348. Vancouver: UBC Press.

Ley, D. and H. Smith (1997) *Is There an Immigrant "Underclass" in Canadian Cities?* Vancouver: RIIM. Working Paper 97–08, 73 pp.

Li, W. (1998) Anatomy of a New Ethnic Settlement: The Chinese Ethnoburb in Los Angeles. *Urban Studies* 35(3):479–501.

Logan, J.R., W. Zhang, and R.D. Alba (2002) Immigrant Enclaves and Ethnic Communities in New York and Los Angeles. *American Sociological Review* 67:299–322.

Marcuse, P. (1997) The Enclave, the Citadel, and the Ghetto: What Has Changed in the Post-Fordist U.S. City. *Urban Affairs Review* 33(2):233–243.

Massey, D. (1985) The Settlement Process among Mexican Migrants to the United States: New Methods and Findings. In D. Levine, K. Hill, and R. Warren (eds.) *Immigration Statistics: A Story of Neglect,* pp. 255–292. Washington, DC: National Academy Press.

Massey, D. and N.A. Denton (1988) The Dimensions of Residential Segregation. *Social Forces* 67:281–315.

Massey, D. and N.A. Denton (1993) *American Apartheid: Segregation and the Making of the Underclass.* Cambridge, MA: Harvard University Press.

Massey, D., J. Arango, G. Hugo, A. Kouaouci, A. Pellegrino, and J.E. Taylor (1998) *Worlds in Motion: Understanding International Migration at the End of the Millennium.* Oxford: Clarendon Press.

Murdie, R.A. (1994) Blacks in Near Ghettos? Black Visible Minority Population in Metropolitan Toronto Housing Authority Public Housing Units. *Housing Studies* 9:42–62.

Murdie, R.A. (2010) Precarious Beginnings: The Housing Situation of Canada's Refugees. *Canadian Issues/Thèmes Canadiens: Newcomer's Experiences of Housing and Homelessness in Canada.* Fall:47–53.

Murdie, R.A. and S. Ghosh (2010) Does Spatial Concentration Always Mean a Lack of Integration? Exploring Ethnic Concentration and Integration in Toronto. *Journal of Ethnic and Migration Studies* 36(2):293–311.

Murdie, R.A., A.S. Chambon, J.D. Hulchanski, and C. Teixeira (1997) *Differential Incorporation and Housing Trajectories of Recent Immigrant Households: Towards a Conceptual Framework.* Paper presented at Housing in the 21st Century: Looking Forward, An International Conference, Alexandria, Virginia.

Owusu, T. (1999) Residential Patterns and Housing Choices of Ghanaian Immigrants in Toronto, Canada. *Housing Studies* 14(1):40–52.

Pacione, M. (2001) *Urban Geography: A Global Perspective.* London: Routledge.

Pamuk, A. (2004) Geography of Immigrant Clusters in Global Cities: A Case Study of San Francisco, 2000. *International Journal of Urban and Regional Research* 28(2):287–307.

Park, R.E. and E.W. Burgess (eds.) (1925) *The City.* Chicago: University of Chicago Press.

Peach, C. (1996) Does Britain Have Ghettos? *Transactions* 21:216–235.

Portes, A. (2003) Conclusion: Theoretical Convergences and Empirical Evidence in the Study of Immigrant Transnationalism. *International Migration Review* 37(3):874–892.

Portes, A. and R. Rumbaut (1996) *Immigrant America: A Portrait.* Los Angeles, CA: University of California Press.

Pries, L. (2004) Determining the Causes and Durability of Transnational Labour Migration between Mexico and the United States: Some Empirical Findings. *International Migration* 42(2):3–40.

Pries, L. (1999) *Migration and Transnational Social Spaces.* Brookfield, VT: Ashgate.

Qadeer, M. and S. Kumar (2006) Ethnic Enclaves and Social Cohesion. *Canadian Journal of Urban Research* 15(2) Supplement:1–17.

Restrepo, S. (2012) *Transnational Habitus and the Formation of a Colombian Community in Toronto.* Major Research Paper, Immigration and Settlement, Ryerson University.

Saltman, J. (1991) Theoretical Orientation: Residential Segregation. In E. Huttman (ed.) *Urban Housing Segregation of Minorities in Western Europe and the United States,* pp. 1–17. Durham, NC: Duke University Press.

Sarre, P., D. Philips, and R. Skellington (1989) *Ethnic Minority Housing: Explanations and Policies.* Brookfield, VT: Gower.

Smith, H. (1998) *Spatial Concentration: Residential Patterns and Marginalisation.* Research Bulletin 1. Vancouver: RIIM.

Statistics Canada (2006) Cumulative Profile—Large Urban Centres in Canada (table), 2006 Census of Population (48 Census Metropolitan Areas/Census Agglomerations and Census Tracts) (database), Using E-STAT (distributor).

Statistics Canada (2009) Immigration in Canada: A Portrait of the Foreign-born Population, 2006 Census: Portraits of Major Metropolitan Centres. Ottawa: Supply and Services Canada. www12.statcan.ca/census-recensement/2006/as-sa/97-557/p22-eng.cfm

Statistics Canada (2011) Immigration and Citizenship: 2011 Census of Canada. Ottawa: Supply and Services Canada.

United Way of Toronto (2004) Poverty by Postal Code Executive Summary. www.unitedwaytoronto.com/document.doc?id=60

United Way of Toronto (2011) Vertical Poverty Poverty by Postal Code 2. www.unitedwaytoronto.com/document.doc?id=64

Van Kempen, R. and S. Özüekren (1998) Ethnic Segregation in Cities: New Forms and Explanations in a Dynamic World. *Urban Studies* 35(10):1631–1656.

Vertovec, S. (2009) *Transnationalism*. New York: Routledge.

Vigdor, J. (2013) Weighing and Measuring the Decline in Residential Segregation. *City and Community* 12(2):169–177.

Walks, R.A. and L. Bourne (2006) Ghettos in Canada's Cities? Racial Segregation, Ethnic Enclaves and Poverty Concentration in Canadian Urban Areas. *Canadian Geographer* 50(3):273–297.

Walks, A. (2010) New Divisions: Social Polarization and Neighbourhood Inequality in the Canadian City. In T.E. Bunting, P. Filion, and R. Walker (eds.) *Canadian Cities in Transition: New Directions in the Twenty-first Century*, pp. 170–190. Oxford: Oxford University Press.

Walton-Roberts, M. (1998) Three Readings of the Turban: Sikh Identity in Greater Vancouver. *Urban Geography* 19(4):311–331.

Wang, S. and J. Jhong (2013) *Delineating Ethnoburbs in Metroploitan Toronto*. CERIS Working Paper Series No. 100.

Wolpert, J. (1965) Behavioural Aspects of the Decision to Migrate. *Papers and Readings of Regional Science Association* 15:159–169.

Glossary of Key Concepts

1986 Immigration Reform and Control Act (IRCA): The first attempt of the US government to implement a comprehensive strategy for reforming the immigration system and controlling unauthorized migration. IRCA is well known for its "amnesty" program that allowed for the legalization of several million "unauthorized" migrants.

1996 Immigration Reform Act: US legislation, also known as the Illegal Immigration Reform and Immigrant Responsibility Act (IIRIRA), that is widely credited with laying the legal and policy groundwork for the get-tough immigration enforcement practices of the current era.

1996 Welfare Reform Act: US legislation also known as the Personal Responsibility, Opportunity and Work Reconciliation Act (PROWRA). In addition to reducing federal welfare benefits for all US residents, the PROWRA introduced unprecedented restrictions on immigrant welfare access.

Absorptive capacity: With respect to immigration, this refers to the number of immigrants that a country can admit without harming the economy, the rate of unemployment, or the standard of living of the existing residents of the country. This is a concept that is easier to state than determine.

Acculturation thesis: The proposition that each immigrant generation adopts more of the receiving society's values and behaviours than the previous generation did.

Adaptation: Whether or to what extent migrants adapt to new patterns of cultural conduct and willingly include different forms of behaviour in their everyday practices.

Adjustee population: Noncitizens who adjusted to legal permanent resident status after living in the US for a period of years on a temporary legal status, compared to those who received legal permanent residence on entry.

Agriculturalists: A term that was used in Canada to define desirable immigrants. The term embraced farmers, farm workers, and others assessed by immigration officers as willing and able to work on a farm.

Anchor baby discourse: A body of public and media discourse that has asserted that undocumented migrant women deliberately have children on US soil so that at least one member of their household will be a US citizen. In this way the newborn acts as a legal-political "anchor" for the household.

Assimilation: The process whereby immigrants leave behind the culture of their country of origin and embrace the culture of their newly adopted country.

Assimilation theory: A conceptualization of the process through which cultural, value, ideational, and socioeconomic differences between migrants and native-born populations blur over time, which usually entails the incorporation of migrants into a "mainstream" culture.

Border enforcement: Actions and strategies, typically carried out by the national border control authorities, that are focused on apprehending unauthorized border crossers at or near the border.

Brain drain: The large-scale emigration of individuals with technical skills or knowledge, producing a flight of human capital often from developing to developed countries. In this case, developing societies lose their "investments" in educating and training the migrants.

Brain gain: The phenomenon of large-scale migration of individuals with technical skills or knowledge to receiving countries. Typically, this migration results in an increase of the stock of human capital in the developed countries.

Brain waste: A situation in which immigrants cannot apply the skills and education they acquired abroad after they immigrate to and settle in their new country.

Capitalism: A system in which the private ownership of capital (materials of production, physical machinery, money, credit, and so on) is in the hands of one class (capitalists) to the exclusion of the rest of humanity, who are consequently turned into a working class (proletariat). In such a system, the processes of commodification (including of labour) and exploitation of the labour of workers is central. The social relations of such a system are based on competition, individualism, and conflict.

Charter groups: A term generally used to identify the first settlers. The charter group in the US comprises the "whites"—mainly of European ancestry (British, German, Dutch, French). In the Canadian context the charter group for Quebec is French and for the rest of Canada it is the British.

Civic engagement: Citizen involvement in debates and activities that shape the course of events in their communities. Indicators of civic engagement range from whether people vote, donate to charities, or follow local news, to their involvement in political or civic organizations, and feelings of attachment to their community.

Clustering: Most members of an immigrant group live in one or more specific areas of the city.

Colonies: Spaces where an immigrant group first settles upon their arrival in a country or city. This location of settlement is mostly by choice.

Concentration: When a particular group overwhelmingly resides within a single area or a few neighbourhoods of the city. (See also **residential segregation**.)

Condominium ethnic malls: A type of shopping centre with individual retail units sold to business investors. They also features other characteristics that distinguish them from conventional shopping malls, such as smaller store sizes, variable store hours, restaurants or grocery stores acting as retail anchors, and catalyst development strategies.

Convergence model: The effect of health decline to the more mediocre receiving country average because immigrants are exposed to the health risks encountered by residents of the receiving society and because they tend to adopt the (usually worse) health behaviours of the majority culture. While convergence has been used to explain immigrants' health decline, the evidence for this decline is not firm. (See **healthy immigrant effect**.)

Coolie labour: A racist term, used in the late nineteenth and early twentieth centuries to describe unskilled workers who came to Canada and the US from China.

Creolized cultures/hybrid identities: The merging of diverse cultural traditions to create new identities and practices by incorporating local and global, traditional and modern, and old and new aspects.

Cultural competency: The ability to effectively engage and navigate different cultures. It has been recognized as an important skill among professionals in addressing culturally specific needs, including improving quality of healthcare and eliminating ethnic disparities in health and healthcare.

Cultural pluralism: A condition in which diverse cultural practices will find room in the broader social context to remain side by side (see **multiculturalism**) or merge into a new hybrid culture (see **melting pot**). It implies that there will be less pressure on minority groups for assimilation. (See also **ethnic pluralist theory**.)

Deflection of immigrants: A shift of settlement location away from traditional gateway cities toward settlement in mid-size and smaller cities and towns, where labour markets are less saturated and living costs are lower.

Devaluation of immigrant labour: The effects of the decisions by governments, employers, and other labour market actors on relegating workers to lower positions in the labour market than they would normally encounter given their education, skills, qualifications, and aspirations.

Dietary acculturation: The process of newcomers adopting the eating patterns and food choices of the country of destination.

Differential inclusion: A concept developed by Gilles Deleuze and Félix Guattari to understand how racism is globally managed. They argue that negatively racialized persons are not merely excluded from national societies but are often included in a subordinated manner.

Disillusionment model: A theory that suggests that adapting to a new country follows a series of predictable phases: 1) the euphoria of arrival lasts for two years or less, when the mental health of new settlers is equal to, or better than, mental health among the native-born; 2) disillusionment and nostalgia, when people are at high risk for developing psychiatric disorders, particularly depression; 3) gradual adaptation to the new environment with concomitant improvement in mental health. Despite methodological problems, the model gained enormous popularity to the point that it was accepted as the inevitable process through which immigrants and refugees adapted to life in new countries.

Dispersal: Settlement patterns without readily identifiable spatial concentration. It is the opposite of **clustering**.

Employment (or ethnic) niches: An economic sector or set of occupations numerically dominated by immigrants or co-nationals that may or may not be citizens.

Ethnic communities: In a geographical sense, residential concentrations of immigration groups. Often they consist of relatively affluent immigrants who settle in suburbs.

Ethnic density effect: The phenomenon that living in an ethnically homogeneous area has a protective effect on minority health, even in materially deprived neighbourhoods.

Ethnic economy: The self-employed, employers, and their co-ethnic employees.

Ethnic enclave economy: A specific kind of ethnic economy, having spatially clustered and interdependent businesses with co-ethnic owners and employees primarily serving their co-ethnic community.

Ethnic enclaves: When people of particular racial, ethnic, or religious backgrounds congregate voluntarily to enhance their economic, social, political, and cultural development.

Ethnic media: News media produced by and for immigrants as well as cultural, racial, ethnic, linguistic, and religious minorities.

Ethnic pluralist theory: A theory that conceptualizes the retention of inherited culture among the immigrant population and that has typically shown how cultural retention can occur in tandem with socioeconomic integration. (See **cultural pluralism**.)

Ethnic retail hotspots: Large concentrations of ethnic retail businesses. Often such hotspots serve both a regional market and a tourist function.

Ethnic retail: A mixture of retail and service businesses that are clustered spatially in the form of a retail strip or a centre, and represent certain ethno-cultural characteristics in the goods and services offered and/or the physical features of their storefronts or streetscapes.

Ethnoburbs: Suburban clusters of residential areas and business districts in large metropolitan areas, especially in "global cities." Ethnoburbs feature multi-ethnic communities, overlaying an ethnic economy onto a local mainstream economy.

Faith-based schools: Established by religious communities to teach their children religious beliefs and practices in addition to the regular curriculum mandated by the state.

Feminism: A theory and practice aimed at criticizing and overcoming patriarchy (male domination of women and children). There are multiple theoretical schools of feminism that address the roots of and solutions for gender inequality in different ways.

Feminization of migration: A gender-shift in migration, with women becoming increasingly numerous as migrants and assuming increasingly important economic roles in destination countries.

Food deserts: Geographic areas in which residents have poor access to healthy and affordable food.

Food safety: The absence of hazards, whether chronic or acute, that may make food injurious to the health of the consumer.

Food security: A situation that exists when all people, at all times, have physical, social, and economic access to sufficient, safe, and nutritious food that meets their dietary needs and food preferences for an active and healthy life.

Gatekeeping: The exclusionary practices used by professional accreditation associations to undervalue and restrict foreign-trained workers' entry into and advancement within a profession.

Gender division of labour: The measurable tendency for women and men to perform different economic tasks. It is based on the socially created understanding that there are different work areas for women and men, measured in their performance of different waged and nonwaged tasks.

Ghettos: Historically the forced segration of Jews in Europe to confined residential areas. In a North American migration and settlement context, it refers to the hypersegregation of particular ethnic groups due to discrimination and lack of residential choice.

Global citizenship education: A worldview that recognizes the social, political, economic, and environmental interconnectedness among all people of the world.

Globalization as ideology: A worldview that pushes for the supremacy of the free market in order to have unbridled mobility of financial and industrial capital around the globe. The almost exclusive reliance on the free market achieves the most favourable economic outcomes for business while restricting government intervention in economic and social affairs.

Head tax: Originally, a uniform tax imposed upon an individual person, unrelated to income or property value or ethnic origin. In the immigration context, small head taxes were levied, in the 18th and 19th century, first by Canadian provinces and American states and later by the respective federal governments, on arriving immigrants in order to create funds to care for sick or indigent immigrants. However, from 1885 to 1923, Canada levied a punitive Head Tax solely on newcomers from China, intended to discourage Chinese immigration to Canada. This is now regarded as a prime example of discriminatory, racist immigration policy in Canada's early history. In 2006, the Canadian government issued an apology for both the earlier imposition of the head tax, and from 1923 to 1947, complete exclusion of immigration from China.

Healthcare accessibility: The relative ease with which individuals can reach health service locations from other locations.

Healthy immigrant effect: When immigrants first arrive and shortly thereafter, they have better health status than the native-born population, but they tend to lose their health advantage with length of residency. Methodological problems and inconsistencies in results suggest caution in accepting that immigrants' health advantage does not last and that the longer immigrants remain in a resettlement country, the more their health comes to resemble that of the native-born.

Higher education: Instruction that occurs after the completion of secondary education. Higher education institutions include universities, colleges, institutes of technology, as well as college-level institutions such as vocational and trade schools.

Highly educated immigrants (high-skilled immigrants, knowledge immigrants): Individuals who obtained university degrees in their country of origin prior to migrating to a new country.

Hispanic paradox: See **Latino (or Hispanic) paradox**.

Housing markets: Different types of housing that are located in a city (e.g. rental, ownership, public, or social housing). Due to various forms of overt and covert discrimination, ethnic minorities often get trapped in poor quality and unaffordable housing.

Human capital: The attributes that workers bring to the labour market in terms of their level of formal education, skills, and work experience. Human capital is utilized to perform labour and to produce economic value. Employers use human capital to assess the fit between workers and jobs and to legitimate the wages workers earn. The Canadian points system is based on human capital considerations (**see points system**).

Ideology: A set of beliefs that privileges distinctive economic, political, and social ideas and values to influence outcomes.

Illegalized migrant: A migrant who does not have the right to work or reside in the country in which he or she lives because state policies have rendered him or her "illegal."

Imagined community: A term coined by American scholar Benedict Anderson to describe how information about national events, people, and places is used to convey to citizens that they possess a shared identity. This national community is "imagined" because it is too large for people to know each other personally. (See **nationalism**.)

Immigrant: A person who comes from a different country. In the US, an immigrant is officially defined as an "alien" granted permission to live permanently and work without restrictions in the country. In Canada, an immigrant is officially defined as a foreign-born person who has been granted the right to live permanently in Canada and will be eligible for Canadian citizenship after three years of residency.

Immigrant entrepreneurship: This term refers to all economic activities in which an immigrant establishes or owns a business that serves not only her/his own co-nationals or co-ethnics (in other words, an "ethnic business") but mainly other immigrants. Immigrant entrereneurship typically refers to small businesses.

Immigrant women: A diverse category with respect to age, education, social class, family status, region, and membership in racialized groups, in contrast to the popular image of this category as a group of racialized, uneducated women with large numbers of children.

Immigration: The arrival of migrants from another country, who intend and are given the opportunity to settle permanently in the country of destination. Immigration can be driven by various factors including economic and quality of life motivations, and family reunification. Formally speaking, immigrants, in contrast to refugees, are engaged in a "voluntary" migration.

Immigration policy: Government decisions, services, and programs related to the transit of persons across national borders, the selection of who qualifies to be an immigrant, and matters of integration of foreign-born persons in a country as permanent or temporary residents. In North America, immigration policy focuses particularly on migrants permitted to work or stay permanently in the country.

Immigration statuses: Categories accorded to persons by nation-states, usually, but not always, applied to persons born outside of the territory claimed by any given nation-state.

Informal employment: This term generally refers to employment that remains unregistered or hidden from various governmental authorities in terms of violations of labour law, social insurance/security contributions, or taxes.

Institutional completeness: An area in which the ethnic community can offer all the services required by its members. (See **ethnic communities**.)

Integration: The process of incorporation into the social fabric of the destination country. It is often measured by a general convergence between native-born and immigrant labour market outcomes and life chances. It can also entail that immigrants identify with the receiving country, participate with the institutions of broader society, learn the official or dominant language(s), and build friendships and networks that extend beyond their ethno-specific group. The concept is contested. For example, critics argue that it incorrectly implies that there is a cohesive national body into which an immigrant is supposed to integrate, and that immigrants have a democratic right to participate in society, independent of others identifying them as integrated or not.

Interior enforcement: Enforcement strategies that apprehend immigration violators who typically have been living in the US for many years, including unauthorized border crossers and legal entrants who jeopardized their legal status after entry. (See **illegalized migrant**.)

Intersectionality: The understanding that aspects of identity, such as gender, intersect with other inequalities. (See **immigrant women**.)

Involuntary migrants: Individuals or groups who do not migrate by choice but are forced to leave their homelands for various reasons, including persecution based on race, religion, or ethnicity. Examples include slaves who were brought to the United States or refugees fleeing war.

***Jus domicile* (law of residence)**: A principle according to which persons are granted citizenship based on where they reside. This principle differs from *jus soli* (law of soil, i.e. based on the country where a person is born) and *jus sanguinis* (law of blood, i.e. based on the nationality of the parent).

Labour market incorporation: The process by which migrants or immigrants find paid employment and the outcomes of these searches in terms of specific sectors, occupations, wages, incomes, working conditions, and promotion possibilities.

Labour market outcomes: Various economic indicators that measure the successful integration of an individual or group into the labour force (e.g. employment status, earnings, type of employment, occupational status, job satisfaction).

Latino (or Hispanic) paradox: Refers to the apparent contradiction between the disproportionately low socioeconomic status of most Latino migrants and the physical and mental health of recent Latino migrants, which is superior to most US native-born populations.

Liberal paradox: Refers to the apparent contradiction between the historic openness of Western liberal democracies to international migrant flows and the intensification of immigration enforcement and homeland security policies in these same nations.

Melting pot: A metaphor used to describe the melting together of different cultural groups into a single entity. The term often refers to the assimilation of immigrants in the United States.

Methodological nationalism: The assumption that nation-states are the natural framework for understanding global migration and other phenomena.

Migration-security nexus: The linking of international migration to security and terrorism, which forces a convergence of politics, policy, and scholarship on securitization for the creation of a nexus between security and migration.

Mixed economy: Both ethnic and non-ethnic components in the mix, ownership, and operation of the businesses, with their market spatially and ethnically unbounded.

Model minorities: Immigrant minorities who have been favourably compared with native-born minorities because of their apparent success integrating into the mainstream society. In the US, the model minority discourse has typically been used to contrast the experiences of Asian and African American minorities.

Multiculturalism: The coexistence of people with different cultural identities and practices in a common space, community, society, or state. The ideology of multiculturalism is to preserve this cultural diversity.

Nationalism: An ideology which specifies an ideal political organization of the world into nation-states and which assumes that the persons said to belong to any given "nation" form a unified community. (See **imagined community**.)

Naturalization: The acquisition by foreign-born persons of citizenship of the country to which they have migrated.

Neoclassical labour market theory: A paradigm that suggests that the labour market is regulated through the interaction between the number of persons available for work (supply) and the number of jobs available (demand), and that supply and demand determine wage rates.

Neoliberalism: A phenomenon of market liberalization, privatization, and deregulation, that claims that a "free market" and a broadly unregulated capitalist system is best positioned to achieve optimal economic performance and efficient economic growth, technical progress, and fair distribution of resources. As a political outlook, neoliberalism promotes reducing the size and role of government, favouring business and markets as decision-makers.

Net immigration: The balance of the number of immigrants who arrive in a particular country and the number of emigrants leaving that same country.

Nonimmigrants: Migrants who enter a country with a temporary legal status, under the expectation that they will return to their home country before this legal status expires.

Nontraditional students: A term that describes a category of students who do not follow traditional pathways to higher education. They are usually adults, attend school part-time, work full-time, have family obligations, or have other characteristics that hinder the pursuit of higher education after finishing high school.

Objectivity: Journalistic reporting that is unbiased, based on verifiable information, and provides a fair and balanced account of events. The term is often used interchangeably with *impartiality*. It is much criticized by those who say all accounts are biased in some way.

Occupational churning: The phenomenon in which workers change jobs often, but do not necessarily receive promotions or climb the occupational hierarchy while doing so.

Occupational mismatch: The situation in which individuals work in an occupation that is highly unrelated to the occupation for which they are qualified or in which they gained previous work experience.

Open borders: An approach to migration policy that insists that the free flow of goods and trade should also be accompanied by the free flow of labour. Open borders arguments typically oppose immigration restrictions on economic, humanitarian, or philosophical grounds.

Order in Council: In the Canadian Constitution of 1867 (sections 12 and 13), an Order in Council is a direction from the Governor General "by and with the consent of the Queen's Privy Council for Canada." This is known as the "Governor-in-Council." In practice, it is the form in which, pursuant to the regulation-making authority in a specific law, such as the Immigration Act, regulations to implement the law and subsequent amendments to the regulations are promulgated. Orders in Council are developed within government departments and the minister responsible for that department presents the draft order to Cabinet for approval. Once approved by Cabinet, the Order in Council is submitted to the Governor General for signature. Orders in Council are referred to with the prefix PC for Privy Council, the year and the number of the order. Hence, the eighty-second Order in Council approved in 1962 is referred to as PC 1962-0082. (See **Presidential Instruction** for the US case.)

Other: A culturally and phenotypically different individual or group considered to be separate and apart from the dominant mainstream Western community, culture, or religion.

Othering: Considering and treating a category of people as unlike oneself; a process of emphasizing differences, with the intent of categorizing and excluding. (See **other**.)

Panethnicity: An aggregated identity that groups together different national and/or ethnic origins.

Paper sons: A term that describes Chinese immigrants who created false papers during the mid-twentieth century. The papers stated that they belonged to a Chinese family that resided in Canada or the US legally. These papers enabled them to cross the borders into Canada and the US.

Points system: An immigrant-selection system, first established in Canada in 1967, assessing applicants based on human capital criteria of education, language, occupation, work experience, employment prospects, and age. (see **human capital**.)

Presidential Instruction: Also known as an Executive Order, a Presidential Instruction is a directive from the president to an agency of government interpreting how a law should be enforced. Presidential Instructions are usually developed within an agency and proposed to the president by the agency head. While there is no specific authority in the American Constitution, successive presidents have relied on Article 2 of the Constitution, which states that "the executive power shall be vested in a President of the United States." (See **Order in Council** for the Canadian case.)

Public policy paradigm: An intellectual framework—the key ideas especially related to the "proper" role of the state within society and economy—through which policymakers and other key opinion-makers in society make sense of their world, and which are used to guide their policy actions.

Public sphere: German sociologist Jürgen Habermas conceived of the public sphere as a space where citizens confer freely in conversation and in the news media about matters of general interest. These discussions lead to the formation of public opinion that ultimately influences governments.

Race: The *idea* that there exist distinct biological types of humans. *Race* as a category is not real; it is a social construct. However, the assertion that there exist "racial" differences amongst human beings continues to be powerful and is the base assumption of racist ideologies and practices. Real or imagined physical and/or cultural markers, such as skin colour, religion, or nationality, become associated with "racial" difference and form the basis for the creation of hierarchical differences between persons in dominant privileged groups and those in subordinate marginalized groups.

Racialization: The Social and historical *process* of creating "racial" groups by the exercise of power, and by ascribing physical and/or cultural difference to the "other," to the benefit of those in the dominant group. Through this process, "race," which is not real, acquires social meaning. (See **race** and **other**.)

Racialized: Individuals or groups living in a society in which ideas of "race" and processes of racialization inform people's subjectivities. In racist societies, people in dominant groups are positively racialized while members of subordinated groups are negatively racialized.

Racism: An *ideology* that attributes the dominant group with certain desirable attributes while simultaneously characterizing the subordinate individuals/groups in society as inferior on the basis of real or imagined physical and cultural markers. The ideological manifestation of racism underlies the assertion of power and is meant to inflict pain, harm, and/or loss on subordinate individuals and groups in society. (See **race** and **racialized**.)

Residential segregation: The degree to which immigrant groups are spatially, and by extension socially, separated from each other and the nonmigrant population.

Resilience: In the context of migration and settlement research, the ability to adapt, despite risk and hardship, using personal resources such as self-efficacy, hopefulness, and ethnic identity as well as social and community resources including societal cohesion, moral order, access to material goods, and opportunities for meaningful relationships.

Securitization: A process whereby those who fit a certain identity-based profile—of the "terrorist" other or someone viewed as liable to indulge in criminal activity to harm state and society—are targeted, treated suspiciously, and/or subjected to racism from ordinary members of mainstream Western society, media, and security forces. (See **other** and **racism**.)

Segmented assimilation theory: A variant of assimilation theory that posits that there are at least two distinct pathways to assimilation: one that tracks migrants into the mainstream society and another that leads migrants to be incorporated into a racialized "underclass" population. (See **assimilation theory** and **underclass**.)

Segmented labour market theory: A framework that suggests that the labour market is divided into a primary segment with jobs that provide high wages, good working conditions, employment stability, and equity, and a secondary segment with jobs that offer low wages, few benefits, poor working conditions, and inequity.

Separate but equal schools: Institutions designed to segregate school children based on their race. Schools for black children were almost always poorer in quality, but the separation was justified by the constitutional law of the United States.

Settlement: The period after newcomers arrive and adapt to their new environment.

Settlement patterns: The geographical distributions of residence, which are the outcome of complex social processes.

Settler societies: Nations that were founded by large-scale immigration and permanent settlement in a new territory. In the North American historical context, the settlers were mostly Europeans who conquered, displaced, and often brutally murdered Indigenous populations.

Sexism: The ideology that assumes that real or alleged biological differences in sex ("male" or "female") determine a person's capacities, interests, behaviour, and social worth. Sexism employs a binary in which persons gendered as "men" (and "boys") or "women" (and "girls") are seen to be opposites, where those gendered men are generally seen to embody superior characteristics while those gendered women are relegated to an inferior rank. Sexism works to legitimize the oppression and exploitation of women as well as the violence directed at them.

Sick immigrant: A prominent mode of thinking about immigrants in Canada and the US, particularly in the late nineteenth and early twentieth century, suggesting that the physically and mentally weak who were misfits in their home societies were the most likely to emigrate and, in so doing, to threaten the health and the economic well-being of others in the countries in which they resettled. The sick immigrant concept provided convenient support for nativist sentiment.

Social capital: In the context of immigration, the resources generated by networks or contacts with other immigrants or citizens in the country of destination.

Social determinants of health: A framework for addressing inequalities in health both within and between nation states. This perspective suggests that the socio-economic status of individuals and populations is more important than genetics or lifestyle in terms of health outcomes. The World Health Organization has identified two broad areas of social determinants of health: (1) daily living conditions, including the physical environment, fair employment, social protection, and access to health care; and (2) distribution of power, money, and resources, including equity in health programs, economic equality, resources depletion, gender equity, political empowerment, and prosperity among nations.

Social reproduction: The processes and conditions necessary for individuals to live and to work in society, such as those related to housing, food, clothing, health, and education. In a capitalist society, the social reproduction of labour power through child rearing, education, health services, and so on, enables the production of goods, services, and information.

Spatial mismatch: In the context of healthcare, refers to the discordance between where healthcare providers are located and where immigrants reside.

Steerage: The lowest class available on a passenger vessel. This was the only class most immigrants could afford. It was named *steerage* because the accommodation was on the lowest deck at the stern, near to the steerage (steering) equipment, the least desirable place to be on a ship.

Stratification: The enduring socioeconomic inequalities between immigrant and native-born populations that have been shaped by laissez-faire labour market recruitment practices, restricted access to permanent legal status, and the intensification of immigration enforcement, among other factors.

Tap-on, tap-off: A term used to describe matching immigrant admissions to immediate economic conditions, with many admitted in times of economic growth and few admitted during economic stagnation.

Temporary foreign worker (TFW): A person who has been given permission to temporarily work in a country for a specific period of time. In Canada and the US, unskilled TFWs must typically return to the country of their citizenship when their work permit exprires, while high-skilled TFWs are allowed to apply for permanent residency.

Transnational communities: A dense system of social networks that transcend international borders (see **transnationalism**).

Transnational identity: Immigrants' dual sense of belonging to their home country and their adopted country. This idea that both places can be "home" has overtaken earlier notions that immigrants must choose between the two locations (see **transnationalism**).

Transnationalism: The process by which immigrants forge and sustain simultaneous economic, social, cultural, and political ties in their countries of origin and settlement.

Underclass: A term used to refer to (often racialized) groups who are believed to have relatively low levels of economic, educational, cultural, and social resources, and to be associated with violence and crime.

Underemployment: The situation in which individuals work in jobs which require a lower level of education than they possess.

Unfree labour: A person who is deprived of the liberty (freedom) to choose whom to work for, what occupation to do, where to work, or even whether to work or not. Most closely associated with slavery, the more common form since the early nineteenth century is a system of "contract labour" in which workers sign contracts to work for a specific period of time and, sometimes, for a specified employer and occupation. Such contracts—which assume that both parties to the contract are under no duress—often does the ideological work of obscuring unfree employment relationships and conditions.

Visa over-stayer: A migrant who loses status and becomes illegalized or "undocumented" because his or her temporary legal status has either expired or was jeopardized by a civil or criminal violation. The visa over-stayer can be contrasted against the unauthorized border crosser, who entered a country without the national government's permission (see **illegalized migrants**).

Visible minority: Canada's official terminology to identify nonwhite persons, referring to "persons, other than Aboriginal persons, who are non-Caucasian in race or non-white in colour."

Wage theft: Illegal, informalized practices that lead workers to be deprived of wages, break time, sick days, and other legal entitlements, and which are especially prevalent in low-wage employment sectors with large concentrations of foreign-born workers.

Index

Copyright Acknowledgements

Figure 9.2: Jones, Ken, in Bunting/Fillion (eds.), *Canadian Cities in Transition* 2/e © Oxford University Press Canada 2000. Reprinted by permission of the publisher.